S0-FCW-037

STATE GOVERNMENT
IN THE UNITED STATES

THE MACMILLAN COMPANY
NEW YORK · BOSTON · CHICAGO · DALLAS
ATLANTA · SAN FRANCISCO

MACMILLAN & CO., LIMITED
LONDON · BOMBAY · CALCUTTA
MELBOURNE

THE MACMILLAN CO. OF CANADA, LTD.
TORONTO

STATE GOVERNMENT
IN THE
UNITED STATES

BY

ARTHUR N. HOLCOMBE

PROFESSOR OF GOVERNMENT IN HARVARD UNIVERSITY

SECOND EDITION, REVISED AND ENLARGED
WITH THE COLLABORATION OF

ROGER H. WELLS

ASSISTANT PROFESSOR OF POLITICS IN BRYN MAWR COLLEGE.

New York

THE MACMILLAN COMPANY

1926

Set up and electrotyped.
Published, December, 1916.
Revised Edition, September, 1926.

Printed in the United States of America by
J. J. LITTLE AND IVES COMPANY, NEW YORK

TO

MY WIFE

"No government can now expect to be permanent unless it guarantees progress as well as order; nor can it continue really to secure order unless it promotes progress."

J. S. Mill: The French Revolution and its Assailants.

PREFACE TO THE REVISED EDITION

The ten years which have passed since the first edition of this book was completed have witnessed many changes in state government in the United States. They have been such changes as will vindicate the judgment of those who maintain that, by taking thought, the governments of the states can be improved. At the same time they can not fail to strengthen the faith that the foundations of American government are sound. The most striking change doubtless is the extension of the suffrage to women throughout the Union. In several states also the electoral process has been notably purified by improvements in ballot laws and in methods of conducting campaigns, and the legislative process by improvements in the organization and procedure of the legislatures. But the most significant changes in the structure and operation of the state governments have taken place in the executive branch. State administration has been reorganized in many states, and administrative, especially fiscal, procedure has been improved in almost all.

Time was when the state legislatures were deemed the weakest factors in state government. At that time the attention of the people was directed particularly to the political aspects of state government. They were concerned with the limitation of legislative powers, the control of the legislative product through direct action by the voters, and the control of the political leaders and bosses through the regulation of the processes of nomination and election. During the last decade, however, attention has shifted more and more to problems of administration. Primarily it has been the executive department of state government which has been most subject to criticism. But since the World War the people have begun to take a new interest also in the administration of justice. Executive organization and procedure already give promise of higher standards of performance in that department of government. Judicial organization and procedure seem to be next in line for improvement. Those who are most familiar with the experience of the past will have the most confidence that, by taking further thought, the further improvement of state government will gradually be accomplished.

In bringing the record of development down to the present time I have profited greatly by the friendly criticism of numerous students of state government. Among them I ought particularly to mention my colleague, Professor A. C. Hanford, also Professor J. A. Fairlie of the University of Illinois, Professor Victor J. West of Leland Stanford University, Professor Morris B. Lambie of the University of Minnesota, and above all Professor R. H. Wells of Bryn Mawr College. Professor Wells has carefully scrutinized the entire text, and verified all the data relating to changes during the past decade. His assistance has been especially helpful in Part III, most of the additions to which are by his hand. While I can not alienate my responsibility for the conclusions which are set forth in this volume, I wish to acknowledge my obligation to Professor Wells for well-informed and thoughtful counsel during the reconsideration of opinions originally formed ten or more years ago. The spirit of government is more difficult to grasp than the form, and must vary to some extent in different parts of a widely-extended and diversified Union like the American. A book like this, which deals with no one government in particular, but in a more general manner with forty-eight separate governments for forty-eight more or less independent peoples, must be read with that qualification in mind.

A. N. H.

CAMBRIDGE, MASSACHUSETTS,
August, 1926.

PREFACE TO THE FIRST EDITION

State Government in the United States is a subject on which many books might be written. This book is designed to furnish a critical analysis of the principles of state government in the United States. Beginning with a statement of the principles upon which the governments of the original states were established, it explains how the original forms of government have developed in response to changing conditions, how the present state governments are meeting present needs, and concludes with a brief consideration of some of the contemporary plans for further reform. Why should we change our form of government? Has the time come for discarding the eighteenth century doctrine of the separation of powers? These are some of the more fundamental questions to which the book attempts to give an answer. But the book is not solely concerned with the political philosophy of American state government. It also treats of the more practical problems arising out of the growth of the functions of the modern state and the increase of its administrative activities.

For the convenience of those readers who may wish to pursue further the study of contemporary state government, I have prepared a bibliographical appendix, containing a selected list of the most useful titles. References cited in the text or in the footnotes are, for the most part, omitted from this list. It has not seemed necessary to include either in the text or elsewhere much statistical matter relating to the forms of government, such as tables of the numbers and tenure of members of state legislatures, or to the conduct of administration, such as tables of enlistments in the state militia or of salient features in industrial or labor legislation. Such information is readily obtainable in various well-known publications, notably in the *American Year Book,* published annually since 1910.

I have many personal debts to acknowledge. To secretaries of state and other officials in all the states I am deeply indebted for prompt and courteous responses to many requests for official publications. To certain officers of the Associated Harvard Clubs, and to secretaries and members of Harvard Clubs in all parts of the country, I am indebted for painstaking coöperation in procuring information concerning the working of state government, especially of election laws, corrupt practices acts, and rules of procedure in legislative bodies, and for the supply of publications by local civic organizations. To President Lowell of Harvard, to my colleagues in the Department of Government, Professors Hart, Munro, and McIlwain, to Professor Felix Frankfurter of the Harvard Law School, to Professor Lewis J. Johnson of the Harvard Graduate School of Applied Science, to former Lieutenant-Governor Robert Luce of Massachusetts, and to Mr. Hector M. Holmes of the Massachusetts Bar, each of whom has kindly read a portion of the proofs and made many helpful suggestions, I am under the greatest obligations. I am also greatly indebted to Mr. G. W. Robinson, Secretary of the Harvard Graduate School of Arts and Sciences, for vigilant help in the preparation of my manuscript for the press. It may be needless to add that none of these gentlemen is responsible for the imperfections of my book.

A. N. HOLCOMBE.

CAMBRIDGE, MASSACHUSETTS,
November 3, 1916.

CONTENTS

PART I.

INTRODUCTION

PART II.

THE ORIGIN AND DEVELOPMENT OF THE STATE GOVERNMENTS

PART III.

THE WORKING OF THE STATE GOVERNMENTS

PART IV.

CONCLUSION

APPENDICES

STATE GOVERNMENT IN THE UNITED STATES

PART I

INTRODUCTION

STATE GOVERNMENT IN THE UNITED STATES

CHAPTER I

THE UNION AND THE STATES

A state is usually defined as a political body or body politic.[1] A body politic differs from other bodies of people by the purposes of its organization and the powers with which it is endowed. The purposes of its organization are well put in the preamble to the Constitution of the United States. They are: to form a more perfect union of the people concerned, establish justice, insure domestic tranquillity, provide for the common defense, promote the general welfare, and secure the blessings of liberty to the people of the body politic and their posterity. The powers which may be vested in a body politic extend to a complete control over the lives, liberty, and property of the people thereof. No body of people except a body politic may possess such unlimited authority, although unlimited authority is not necessarily possessed by every body politic. When unlimited or absolute political authority is possessed by a state, it is a sovereign state or sovereignty.

THE NATURE OF THE UNION

The states of the American Union are not states in the sense of being sovereign states or sovereignties. This proposition was long disputed. The most eminent statesmen and political scientists were to be found on each side of the discussion. The issue was finally decided only after an appeal to arms. It was thus settled that the people of a particular state do not possess sov-

[1] For a definition of the term, "body politic," as understood at the Revolution, see the Preamble to the Constitution of the Commonwealth of Massachusetts, 1780, in Thorpe, *Federal and State Constitutions*, iii, pp. 1888-9. This Preamble is reprinted also in Appendix A.

ereign powers. As Abraham Lincoln has said: "Our states have neither more nor less power than that reserved to them in the Union by the Constitution, none of them ever having been a state out of the Union."[1] Their place in the Union is a subordinate one, for, as Lincoln pointed out, "The Union is older than any of the states, and in fact it created them as states." Whatever may have been the case when Lincoln wrote these words, there is now no doubt of the soundness of his views. The people of the whole United States are the only people possessing sovereignty in the United States.[2]

The Problem of States Rights.

The principle of the sovereignty of the people of the United States has been misunderstood on account of the peculiar division of power between the federal government and the governments of the several states. The federal government possesses those powers which have been granted to it by the people of the United States, either expressly in the Federal Constitution or by a reasonable implication therefrom. Of the remaining powers of government, the Federal Constitution attempts to make a summary disposition in the following terms: "The powers not delegated to the United States by the Constitution, nor prohibited by it to the states, are reserved to the states, respectively, or to the people."[3]

The ambiguity of this statement long served to cloak with a garment of legality the most contradictory doctrines concerning the respective powers of the federal and state governments. For example, has a state the right to secede from the Union? The Constitution does not expressly say. If the Constitution neither delegates to the federal government the power to compel a

[1] See A. Lincoln, *Special Message to Congress, July 4, 1861.* This statement is not literally true, though true in substance, for North Carolina, Rhode Island, Vermont, and Texas have been temporarily states outside of the Union. The first two were out of the Union because they delayed the ratification of the Constitution of 1787 until after the "more perfect union" had been established in 1789. The last two were out of the Union because Congress could not agree sooner to their admission. Each was admitted, however, not by means of a treaty between the government of the Union and that of an independent state, but by means of an ordinary act or resolution of Congress. None of the thirteen original states was ever an independent state before the formation of the Union, and all other states upon admission acquired the same constitutional status.

[2] Texas v. White, 7 Wall. 700.

[3] See Constitution of the United States, art. x of the Amendments.

state to remain in the Union, nor prohibits to the states the power to withdraw from the Union, the right of secession, that is to say, the power to terminate the Union, must be reserved either to the states, respectively, or to the people. But to which? The Constitution does not say. When secession was actually attempted, the persons seeking to withdraw from the Union, upon forming a constitution for their confederacy, revised this distributory clause for the purpose of giving clearer expression to their peculiar view of the relation that should obtain between the states and the Union. Their rendering was as follows: "The powers not delegated to the Confederate States by the Constitution, nor prohibited by it to the States, are reserved to the States, respectively, or to the people thereof." Thus, by the addition of the one word "thereof," they reserved all powers not delegated to the confederacy to the people of the states respectively.[1] Certainly the tenth amendment to the Constitution of the United States was not intended thus to transfer to the people of the several states all powers not delegated by the people of the United States to the federal government. On the contrary, the framers of that amendment must have intended to reserve a portion of the powers not delegated either to the federal government or to the governments of the several states for future use, in case of need, by the people of the United States themselves. If that had not been their intention, the closing words of the distributory clause, "or to the people," would have been superfluous. But what was the extent of these reservations? The Constitution does not say.

In most cases this question may not be of much practical importance. In a few, however, it might become of great practical importance. Thus Congress must call a convention to revise the Federal Constitution upon demand of two-thirds of the states. But the Constitution does not say whether Congress, in calling a constitutional convention, shall be bound by the rules governing the organization and procedure of the Convention of 1787, or shall have power to determine for itself how a fresh convention shall be organized and what rules of procedure it shall adopt. If any state should claim a right to be represented therein by a delegation consisting of any number of members it should please, and to have the vote of its delegation counted as a unit equal

[1] See Confederate Constitution, art. vi, par. 6.

in importance to that of the delegation of any other state, the Constitution could not be cited either in express affirmation or in denial of that claim. This question could not be settled by means of a constitutional amendment, if a majority of the smaller states were to insist upon maintaining equality of representation in federal constitutional conventions, and a majority of the larger states were to insist upon representation according to the method employed in the electoral college. It manifestly could not be settled by means of a constitutional convention. This question might seem, therefore, to be as great a constitutional puzzle as was the question of secession.

The Sovereignty of the People.

The preamble to the Constitution of the United States declares one of the purposes of the people to be to establish a more perfect union. This must mean a union more perfect than that formed under the Articles of Confederation and Perpetual Union, framed in 1777 and finally adopted in 1781. The perpetual union of 1781, however, was terminated on April 30, 1789, when George Washington took the oath of office as president of the United States under the Constitution of 1787. This second constitution provided for the establishment of the "more perfect union" on the ruins of the old, if nine of the thirteen states should agree thereto. In fact eleven agreed in season to participate in the inauguration of President Washington. The other two were temporarily left to continue under the Articles of Confederation or shift for themselves. Now if the "perpetual union" of 1781 could thus be broken up by nine or eleven states, how much more perfect must the union of 1789 be in order that no majority of states, however large, may have power to exclude a minority, and in order that any majority, however small, may have power to coerce a minority from secession? The Constitution gives no answer. This question could not be settled by the regular methods of constitutional interpretation, nor by public opinion without an appeal to arms. The result of that appeal to arms was to settle, not only the disputed doctrine of secession, but the whole problem of the relation between the federal government and the governments of the states. It was thereby settled that the people of the United States, and not those of the individual states, are the final judges of the extent of their own powers;

that the federal union is a union of people, and not merely a union of states. In short, the United States is itself a state.[1]

The ambiguous tenth amendment may now be restated as follows: The powers not delegated to the federal government by the people of the United States, nor prohibited by them to the people of the states, are reserved to the people of the states, respectively, or to the sovereign people of the United States. Of the powers so reserved, those exercised by the people of the several states before the formation of the more perfect union of 1789 are presumably still reserved to them, if not necessary and proper for the maintenance of the sovereignty of the people of the United States. All other powers, including those prohibited both to the federal government and to the governments of the states, are reserved to the people of the United States. Whenever doubt arises concerning the application of this principle to particular cases, the true rule of interpretation is that stated by Lincoln: "This relative matter of national power and states' rights, as a principle, is no other than the principle of *generality* and *locality*. Whatever concerns the whole should be confided to the whole, to the general government, while what concerns *only* the state should be left exclusively to the state." The duty of interpretation rests primarily with the officers of the federal government, that is, with Congress, the President, or the Supreme Court, according to the nature of the case; but ultimately the decision must depend for its validity upon the consent of the people of the United States. The power of public opinion, the opinion of the nation, must finally determine the status and functions of the organs of local government, including therewith the governments of the states and the people thereof.

The sovereignty of the people of the United States is, therefore, unimpaired by the peculiar distribution of powers between the federal and state governments by the Constitution of 1787. The states are a species of local government with limited, though not always accurately defined, powers. The limits between the powers of the states and those of the United States are constantly being more accurately defined, as cases of actual doubt arise, by the proper organs of the federal government, generally

[1] For a recent statement of the contrary view concerning the nature of the Union, see James B. Scott, *James Madison's Notes of Debates in the Federal Convention of 1787 . . .* (Washington, 1918), pp. 46-50.

by the Supreme Court, and may ultimately be determined in cases of persistent doubt by the people of the United States through the process of amendment to the Federal Constitution. It is this power of interpreting the Federal Constitution, vested in the first instance in the federal government and ultimately in the people of the Union, which is the final proof of national sovereignty.[1] The states, therefore, must recognize the Federal Constitution, and the laws of the United States which may be made in pursuance thereof, and all treaties made under the authority of the United States, as the supreme law of the land; and the judges in every state are bound thereby, anything in the constitution or laws of any state to the contrary notwithstanding.[2] Indeed not only the judges but also the members of the several state legislatures and all executive officers of the states are required to take oath or make affirmation to support the Constitution of the United States.[3]

Federal and State Relations.

The people of the several states are subject to the sovereignty of the people of the Union, but the people of each state are equal to the people of any other state before the law of the Federal Constitution. Congress has power to admit new states to the Union, and there is no limit to the number or character of the new states that may be admitted, provided that their governments are republican in form, except that no new state may be formed within the jurisdiction of any other state, and no state may be formed by the junction of two or more states or parts of states, without the consent of the legislatures of the states concerned.[4] Congress may also impose conditions upon the admission of new states, in addition to those imposed upon the existing states by the Federal Constitution, but, unless these conditions are imposed in the form of constitutional amendments and are accepted by the people of the United States, thus applying to all states alike, there is no practical means by which they may be enforced.[5] For example, Congress required New Mexico

[1] Cf. J. C. Calhoun, *Disquisition on Government and Discourses on the Constitution and Government of the United States, passim.*

[2] Constitution of the United States, vi, 2.

[3] *Ibid.*, vi, 3.

[4] *Ibid.*, iv, 3, 1.

[5] However, contractual obligations involving property rights may be enforced. Stearns v. Minnesota, 179 U. S. 223 (1900).

and Arizona to amend the constitutions under which they sought admission to the Union in 1911, but the latter state, once admitted, promptly reinserted in its constitution the forbidden clause providing for the recall of judges by the people. Likewise in 1907 Congress required Oklahoma as a condition of admission to leave the location of the capital undisturbed for a period of years, but presently the people of Oklahoma adopted a constitutional amendment removing the capital to another location, and the Supreme Court held them to be within their rights in so doing.[1] In 1895 Congress required Utah, as a condition of admission, to abolish the institution of polygamy, but since the admission of Utah, Congress has possessed no more power to prevent the reëstablishment of polygamy in that state than to prevent its establishment in any other state of the Union. The people of a state may be subjected to any humiliation in order to gain admission to the Union, but once within the sacred edifice, they become endowed with all the rights and privileges possessed by the people of any of their fellow states. The states of the Union are not equal in influence upon the government of the Union, but within the sphere reserved to the states, respectively, each state is the peer of any of the others.

For the exercise of the powers falling within their sphere, the governments of the states are responsible to the people thereof, subject to the limitations hereafter to be enumerated. The people of the United States have their own government, the government of the Union, and in the main are not dependent upon the state governments for the execution of their general will. The spheres of the federal government and of the governments of the states are separate and distinct. For certain special purposes, however, the people of the states and the state governments are required to act as agents of the people of the Union.[2] Thus the members of the Congress of the United States must be chosen by the people of the several states at the times and places and in the manner prescribed by Congress, and in the absence of federal legislation concerning such elections, the state legislatures must make the necessary regulations for themselves. The states must also appoint, in such manner as their legislatures

[1] Coyle v. Smith, 221 U. S. 559 (1911).

[2] See A. N. Holcombe, "The States as Agents of the Nation," *Southwestern Political Science Quarterly*, i, pp. 307-327 (1921).

may direct, their respective numbers of presidential electors. If, however, states neglect to make such appointments, there seems to be no way by which Congress may compel them to do so. Finally amendments to the Federal Constitution may be initiated by the legislatures of two-thirds of the states, and must be referred to the legislatures or special state conventions, whichever Congress may determine, and be ratified by three-fourths of them, in order to become a part of the supreme law of the land. The states are also entrusted with the authority to appoint the officers of the militia and supervise their training according to the discipline prescribed by Congress, but Congress may of course establish a federal army of its own wholly independent of the state militia.

Moreover, the use of the states as agents of the people of the United States is not necessarily limited to those cases which are specifically mentioned in the Federal Constitution. Recently, the question of federal subsidies to the states has become of great importance. In form, these grants are purely voluntary and no state need accept them, but, if accepted, their acceptance necessitates compliance with the conditions laid down by Congress. Federal appropriations of this character are made for specific purposes such as highways, vocational education, and maternity and infant welfare, and usually require equal contributions from the recipient states. The federal government prescribes standards of performance and exercises a close supervision over the expenditure of funds on federal-aided projects, even though it has little or no power to deal directly with these matters. The effect of this subvention system is to render less distinct the respective spheres of the federal and state governments.[1] With these exceptions, the governments of the states are the agencies solely of the people of the states, respectively, and the people of the Union are not dependent upon them for the exercise of their sovereign powers.

The governments of the several states, though responsible primarily and mainly to the people thereof respectively, are also placed under obligations towards one another. The people of

[1] On federal subsidies, see Austin F. Macdonald, *Federal Subsidies to the States* (Philadelphia, 1923), and an article by the same author in the *National Municipal Review*, xiv, pp. 692-701 (1925). The constitutionality of federal subsidies was upheld in Massachusetts v. Mellon, 262 U. S. 447 (1923).

the Union insist that each state must give full faith and credit to the public acts, records, and judicial proceedings of every other state; [1] must extend the same privileges and immunities to citizens of the other states as to its own; [2] and must deliver up a fugitive from justice, upon demand of the executive authority of the state from which he fled, to be removed to the state having jurisdiction of the crime.[3] Finally, controversies between two or more states, not settled by mutual agreement, must be submitted to the arbitrament of the Supreme Court of the United States.[4] Thus the federal government is ultimately responsible for enforcement of the mutual obligations of the states, and the maintenance of the supremacy of the rights of the nation is thereby assured.

The Right to a Republican Form of Government.

The Federal Constitution also imposes on the government of the Union certain obligations towards the people of the states respectively. It provides that the United States shall guarantee to every state the republican form of government; and shall protect each of them against invasion, and, on application of the legislature, or of the executive when the legislature cannot be convened, against domestic violence.[5] The duty of keeping the peace against both external and internal enemies falls therefore ultimately upon the federal government, and the responsibility of the states is limited to ordinary occasions of internal policing. The most significant limitation, however, upon the responsibility of the states is contained in the former portion of the above provision. Thus the people of the United States, when creating their more perfect union in the form of a republic, determined also that the states should be restricted to the same form of government. Their liberty to adopt any other form of government was taken away forever.

No act of the Federal Convention of 1787, except the construction of the more perfect union itself, was felt to be more important than this guarantee to the states of the republican form of government. Yet nowhere in the Federal Constitution is there any definition of the term republican. No particular government is

[1] Constitution of the United States, iv, 1.
[2] *Ibid.*, iv, 2.
[3] *Ibid.*, iv, 2.
[4] *Ibid.*, iii, 2.
[5] *Ibid.*, iv, 4.

designated as republican, nor is the exact form to be guaranteed in any manner especially described. Nevertheless, by providing that the United States shall guarantee to every state the republican form, the people of the Union necessarily entrusted to the federal government the task of determining in cases of doubt what is a republican form of government, and several cases of doubt have in fact arisen. What the Fathers of the republic understood by the term, "a republican form of government," will be discussed in the next chapter. It is sufficient to point out here that the federal government, not the states, has the final authority to determine cases of doubt as they shall arise, and may enforce its determinations by the exclusion from Congress of senators and representatives chosen by a state not possessing a republican form of government, or, if necessary, by the use of force. Doubtless the supreme power in the several states resides in the people thereof, but their power is supreme only within the limits prescribed by the people of the Union, and these limits may be altered only with the consent of the whole people obtained in the manner appointed for the amendment of the Constitution of the United States. The most conclusive evidence of the ultimate sovereignty of the people of the Union and of the dependent status of the people of any particular state is afforded by this provision that the United States shall guarantee to every state a republican form of government, whether the people of every state wish such a government or not.

THE POWERS OF THE STATES

The nature and extent of the sphere reserved to the states may be shown most clearly by describing the distribution of powers between the governments of the states, respectively, and of the Union, as expressed in the Federal Constitution.

Effect of Delegation of Powers to Federal Government.

The first limitation upon the powers of the states consists in the delegation of certain powers by the Federal Constitution to the government of the Union.[1] Not all the powers delegated to the federal government, however, operate to limit directly those of the states. For example, the powers to lay and collect taxes, to borrow money on the credit of the United States, and to govern

[1] Constitution of the United States, i, 8.

the District of Columbia and the territories, do not directly affect the powers of the states. Indirectly, nevertheless, these powers may be used by the federal government to influence or control the action of the states. Thus the power to govern the District of Columbia may be used to establish a model child labor law or form of municipal government for the states to copy, and the power to levy taxes has been used to put an end to the circulation of bank notes issued by state banks and to the manufacture of oleomargarine in imitation of butter and of matches containing a dangerous admixture of poisonous phosphorus.[1] Other powers delegated to the federal government, such as the powers to coin money, declare war, grant letters of marque and reprisal, raise and support armies, and provide and maintain a navy, are reënforced by express prohibitions upon the states to exercise similar powers. The power to provide for organizing, arming, and disciplining the militia, and for governing such parts thereof as may be employed in the service of the United States, imposes corresponding limitations upon the power of the states to control the militia. In effect the Constitution reserves to the latter only the appointment of the officers and the supervision of training according to the discipline prescribed by Congress.

A number of federal powers remain which also operate to limit the powers of the states, but in a manner not altogether clear and precise. Thus the power to establish a uniform rule of naturalization and uniform bankruptcy laws leaves the states free to regulate those subjects in the absence of federal legislation; and the power to fix the standards of weights and measures also leaves the states free to regulate such standards in the absence of regulation by Congress. In some cases, however, it might be understood that the absence of regulation by Congress indicated a purpose, not to leave the matter to the states but to leave the matter unregulated by any political authority. For example, the power of the states to regulate commerce within their respective boundaries is limited by the federal power to regulate interstate and foreign commerce, but the absence of complete federal regulation of interstate commerce leaves an indefinite field of regulation to the states. The powers delegated

[1] But Congress may not prohibit child labor in the states through the use of the taxing power. Bailey v. Drexel Furniture Co., 259 U. S. 20 (1922).

to the federal government with respect to post offices and post roads, patents and copyrights, also leave a rather indefinite field for state action. The more accurate delimitation of these "twilight regions" between the more clearly defined regions of state and federal authority, respectively, is the task of federal constitutional law, and is to be sought in a treatise on the law of the Federal Constitution rather than in a description of the government of the states.[1] In connection with the subsequent discussion of the state judiciary, however, the general trend of the interpretation of the Federal Constitution with respect to the powers of the states, and its effects upon the government of the states, will be considered.

The most important power delegated to the government of the Union and serving to limit the powers of the states is the treaty-making power. The exclusive power to make treaties was vested in the government of the Union both under the Articles of Confederation and under the Constitution of 1787. Certain reservations to the states, which operated as restrictions upon the federal treaty-making power, were expressed in the Articles of Confederation, but no reservations were made in the Constitution of 1787 except such as may be implied in the statement that all treaties made "under the authority of the United States" shall be the supreme law of the land. There can be little doubt, for example, that the federal government may, by treaty, define the status of foreign subjects within the states, regulate their personal and property rights, prescribe their privileges and immunities, and provide for their welfare in general, the constitutions and laws of the states to the contrary notwithstanding.[2] In cases involving a conflict between the authority of a state and the supremacy of a treaty of the Union, the power of the federal courts may always be invoked to enforce the latter. As Mr. Root puts it: "The treaty-making power is not distributed; it is all vested in the national government; no part of it is vested in or reserved to the states. . . . It is, of course, conceivable that, under pretense of exercising the treaty-making power, the

[1] The existence of concurrent power over the same subject gives rise to special difficulties. This has become most evident since the adoption of the eighteenth amendment with its explicit grant of concurrent powers to enforce the prohibition of the liquor traffic.

[2] Even migratory wild birds may be protected by the federal government under the treaty power. Missouri v. Holland, 252 U. S. 416 (1920).

President and Senate might attempt to make provisions regarding matters which are not proper subjects of international agreement, and which would be only a colorable — not a real — exercise of the treaty-making power; but so far as the real exercise of the power goes, there can be no question of state rights, because the Constitution itself, in the most explicit terms, has precluded the existence of any such question."[1]

The delegation to Congress of power to make all laws which may be necessary and proper for carrying into execution the powers vested by the Federal Constitution in the government of the United States, or in any department or officer thereof, also serves to limit the powers of the states.[2] It follows from this general delegation of law-making power that any power necessary and proper for the maintenance of the national sovereignty may be employed by the federal government, for example, to aid in executing a treaty duly made under the authority of the United States, and that in the first instance the President and Congress are the judges of the necessity and propriety thereof. Thus, although the federal government is not expressly authorized to regulate the common school system of any state, it may establish a common school system of its own in any state for the purpose of fulfilling a treaty obligation to afford the children of alien parents school facilities equivalent to those enjoyed by the children of citizens. Hence in effect no state may deny equal school facilities to alien children within its borders, if such denial is contrary to the policy of the people of the United States, although the power to provide for the education of the people is one of those exercised exclusively by the states before 1789 and is presumably still reserved to them, so far as not inconsistent with the sovereignty of the people of the Union.

Powers Denied to the States.

The second limitation upon the powers of the states consists in certain prohibitions expressly imposed upon the states in the Federal Constitution. No state may enter into any treaty, alliance, or confederation; grant letters of marque or reprisal; coin money; emit bills of credit; make anything but gold and silver coin a tender in payment of debts; pass any bill of at-

[1] Elihu Root, *Addresses on International Subjects* (1916), p. 14.
[2] Constitution of the United States, i, 8, 18.

tainder, *ex post facto* law, or law impairing the obligation of contracts, or grant any title of nobility.[1] No state may, without the consent of Congress, lay any impost or duties on imports or exports, except what may be absolutely necessary for executing its inspection laws; and the net produce of all duties and imposts, laid by any state on imports or exports, must be for the use of the treasury of the United States; and all such laws must be subject to the revision and control of Congress.[2] No state may, without the consent of Congress, lay any duty of tonnage, keep troops or ships of war in time of peace, enter into any agreement or compact with another state or with a foreign power, or engage in war, unless actually invaded or in such imminent danger as will not admit of delay.[3] No state may establish slavery or involuntary servitude, except as a punishment for crime whereof the party must be duly convicted; no state may make or enforce any law which shall abridge the privileges or immunities of citizens of the United States; nor may any state deprive any person of life, liberty, or property, without due process of law, nor deny to any person within its jurisdiction the equal protection of the laws; nor may any state deny or abridge the right of an American citizen to vote on account of race, color, previous condition of servitude, or sex.[4] The effects of most of these prohibitions upon the power of the states are apparent, but the effects of a few, especially of those contained in the fourteenth amendment, are not apparent, though profound and far-reaching. The effects will be discussed subsequently in connection with the discussion of the powers of the several organs of state government.

Operation of the Unwritten Constitution.

The third limitation upon the powers of the states consists in the reservation to the people of the United States of all powers

[1] Constitution of the United States, i, 10, 1.

[2] *Ibid.*, i, 10, 2.

[3] *Ibid.*, i, 10, 3.

[4] *Ibid.*, Amendments, arts. xiii-xv, xix. In addition, the fourteenth amendment of the Federal Constitution imposes a penalty upon any state which denies the right to vote to any of its adult male citizens except for participation in rebellion or other crimes. The penalty, which consists in a proportionate reduction of representation in the federal house of representatives and in the electoral college, has never been imposed, and, for practical purposes, that portion of the amendment may now be regarded as obsolete.

necessary and proper for the maintenance of their sovereignty. Powers reserved to the people of the several states before the formation of the more perfect union of 1789, but necessary and proper for the maintenance of the sovereignty of the people of the United States, are generally, but not always, specified in the Federal Constitution. Thus the power to define and punish piracies and felonies committed on the high seas, and to make rules concerning captures on land and sea, was vested in the government of the Union by the Articles of Confederation, but there was no general and comprehensive grant of the power to define and punish offenses against the law of nations. This power, necessary for the maintenance of the sovereignty of the nation, was expressly delegated by the Constitution of 1787 to the government of the more perfect union.[1] The most important instance of the reservation of a power necessary and proper for the maintenance of the national sovereignty is that already referred to, namely, the power to determine the organization and procedure of a federal constitutional convention. This power is neither delegated to Congress nor prohibited to the states, but it cannot be vested in the people of the states, respectively, without seriously impairing the sovereignty of the people of the United States. It must be vested in the Union. Though not expressly delegated to the federal government, it may be implied in the specific grant of the power to make all laws necessary and proper for carrying into execution the power to call a constitutional convention,[2] or it may be comprehended in the general charge placed upon the federal government as the agency of the people to accomplish the purposes expressed in the preamble of the Federal Constitution.[3]

The special limitation imposed upon the exercise of the reserved sovereign powers is that contained in the unwritten constitution of the United States, namely, that such powers be derived from the consent of the people of the Union, that is, that they be exercised only with the approval of public opinion throughout the United States. There are many acts of assumed power by officers of the United States which cannot be justified except upon this theory. For example, the powers to emit bills

[1] Constitution of the United States, i, 8, 10.
[2] *Ibid.*, i, 8, 18.
[3] Fong Yue Ting v. the United States, 149 U. S. 698 (1893).

of credit and make anything but gold and silver coin a tender in payment of debts are not expressly delegated to the federal government, although expressly prohibited to the states. These powers may be implied in the power to borrow money on the credit of the United States, or to coin money and regulate the value thereof, but it seems more candid to justify the emission of bills of credit by the federal government and the forced circulation of such paper as a legal tender in payment of private debts upon the theory that Congress may resort to a reserved sovereign power in case of need with the consent of the people of the Union.[1] So too, the suspension by President Lincoln of the privilege of the writ of habeas corpus in the spring of 1861 without previous authority from Congress was either a lawless usurpation of arbitrary power or a necessary and proper exercise of a reserved sovereign power, sanctioned by the consent of the people of the United States and hence not in conflict with the unwritten law of the Constitution. It must be recognized, however, that such an exercise of power is dangerous, and not to be resorted to without a clear mandate from the people, for the written constitution is intended to be the supreme law of the land, subject to the maxim, *salus populi suprema lex.*

The Importance of State Government.

The powers which are reserved to the states, though limited, are nevertheless very extensive and highly important. They include among others the following: (1) the power to establish and maintain organized governments, including governments for the subdivisions of the states, counties, towns, villages, and cities, subject to the single condition that they be republican in form; (2) the power to regulate the suffrage, subject to the condition that no citizen may be denied the right to vote on account of race, color, previous condition of servitude, or sex; (3) the power to levy and collect taxes, except upon interstate and foreign commerce, and upon instruments of the federal government; (4) the police power, including the whole field of legislation to preserve the peace within the state, to protect the public health and morals, and to promote the common welfare, when threatened by the unrestrained activity of persons within the

[1] See the Legal Tender cases, 8 Wall, 603; 12 Wall, 457; 110 U. S. 421.

borders of the respective states, subject to the condition that no person be deprived of life, liberty, or property without due process of law, nor be denied the equal protection of the laws; (5) hitherto unfathomed powers to deal with the vast subjects of religion, education, and the supply of public utilities, with the exception of the comparatively few public services, such as the post office, delegated to the federal government; (6) the power to create corporations and trusts; and (7) to deal with the whole subject of private law, including the power to regulate the vital institutions of modern civilization, such as the family and the institution of private property. The bare enumeration of these vast powers shows the transcendent importance in the American federal system of the governments of the states.

PART II

THE ORIGIN AND DEVELOPMENT OF THE STATE GOVERNMENTS

CHAPTER II

THE ORIGINAL PRINCIPLES OF STATE GOVERNMENT

The principles upon which the original state governments were established cannot be traced to any single source. In part they were founded upon the experience of the American people under the colonial governments provided for the several royal and proprietary provinces and chartered plantations. In part they were derived from the colonists' knowledge of the structure and operation of the British government, as set forth in the writings of Blackstone and Montesquieu. In part also they were deduced from the general principles of political science, as understood by the Whig party in England and expounded in the writings of Milton, Harrington, and Sidney, and above all John Locke. In the Puritan and Quaker colonies, the people's ideas of civil government were much influenced by the success of democracy in the government of the church.[1] Rousseau and other contemporary European writers of the social-compact school of political philosophy became known to the Americans during the progress of their struggle for independence, too late, however, to exert much influence upon the substance of their political principles. As the need for political reconstruction grew urgent, the Revolutionary leaders acquainted themselves with the whole literature of political science. Plato and Aristotle, Polybius and Cicero, were studied with the same care as the modern writers. The constitutional history of the ancient commonwealths of Greece and Rome became as familiar as that of the more modern Swiss confederacy and Dutch republic. As Burke in his speech on Conciliation with America candidly avowed, there probably was never a time or place at which interest in the science of government was deeper or more widespread than among the American people during the Revolution.

[1] See John Wise, *Vindication of the Government of New England Churches, 1715* (2d ed., 1772), Demonstration II. Cf. Oscar S. Straus, *Origin of the Republican Form of Government in the United States.*

THE DOCTRINE OF NATURAL RIGHTS

The first of the original principles of state government was expressed in the doctrine of natural rights. This doctrine has been stated in imperishable language in the opening sentences of the Declaration of Independence, and forms the most cherished element of the political creed of the American people. "We hold these truths to be self-evident, that all men are created equal; that they are endowed by their Creator with certain unalienable rights; that among these are life, liberty and the pursuit of happiness." The foundation of this belief in the natural equality of mankind was explained by Thomas Paine as follows: [1] "Every child born into the world must be considered as deriving its existence from God. The world is as new to him as it was to the first man that existed, and his natural right in it is of the same kind. The Mosaic account of the creation [2] . . . shows that the equality of man, so far from being a modern doctrine, is the oldest upon record." Such was the contemporary explanation of the American principle of equal rights.

The Natural Equality of Men.

The language of this declaration of faith in the rights of man has given rise to much fruitless discussion. It is so obvious that all men are not born equal, and that their natural inequality is enhanced by the operation of many of the laws of society, that there has been some difficulty in understanding just what the Revolutionary Fathers meant by their doctrine of natural rights. Nor were the Revolutionary leaders themselves blind to this fact. Thus John Adams wrote: "But what are we to understand by equality? Are the citizens all to be of the same age, sex, size, strength, stature, activity, courage, hardiness, industry, patience, ingenuity, wealth, knowledge, fame, wit, temperance, constancy, and wisdom? Was there, or will there ever be, a nation whose individuals were all equal in natural and acquired qualities, in virtues, talents, and riches? The answer of all mankind must

[1] *The Rights of Man* (ed. of 1792), pt. i, p. 37.

[2] "And God said, 'Let us make man in our own image,' . . . in the image of God created he him; male and female created he them." The distinction of sexes is pointed out, Paine observes, but no other distinction is even implied.

be in the negative."[1] Certainly in a land which legalized negro slavery all men could not be said actually to be born equal. Later, when the struggle over slavery was at its height, Senator Douglas declared: "No man can vindicate the character, motives, and conduct of the signers of the Declaration of Independence, except upon the hypothesis that they referred to the white race alone, and not to the African, when they declared all men have been created equal; that they were speaking of British subjects on this continent being equal to British subjects born and residing in Great Britain."[2] Another United States senator of the same period tersely condemned the "self-evident truths" of the Declaration as "self-evident lies."

In fact it is only in a qualified sense of the terms that all men can be said to be created equal, but the qualifications are not those set forth by Douglas. The true interpretation of the doctrine of natural rights is that so patiently and convincingly expounded by Abraham Lincoln. "I think the authors of that notable instrument [the Declaration of Independence] intended to include all men, but that they did not intend to declare all men equal in all respects. They did not mean to say that all were equal in color, size, intellect, moral development, or social capacity. They defined with tolerable distinctness in what respects they did consider all men created equal — equal in certain inalienable rights, among which are life, liberty, and the pursuit of happiness. This they said and this they meant. They did not mean to assert the obvious untruth, that all men were then actually enjoying that equality, nor yet that they were about to confer it upon them. In fact, they had no power to confer such a boon. They meant simply to declare the right, so that the enforcement of it might follow as fast as circumstances should permit. They meant to set up a standard maxim for free society which should be familiar to all and revered by all — constantly looked to, constantly labored for, and even, though never perfectly attained, constantly approximated; and thereby constantly spreading and deepening its influence and augmenting the

[1] For a further discussion of the inequality of man see John Adams, *Defence of the Constitutions of the United States*, pp. 108-120. For a contemporary, and very judicious, discussion of the vexed question of racial inequality, see Thomas Jefferson, *Notes on Virginia* (ch. 14), pp. 143-151.

[2] Stephen A. Douglas, *Speech at Springfield, June 12, 1857.*

happiness and value of life to all people, of all colors, everywhere."[1]

The doctrine of natural rights itself was never more than a mode of expressing a profound belief in the American people.[2] As a mode of expression it never gained universal acceptance, and has since been generally discarded by political philosophers in favor of more scientific modes of expression. The underlying belief did not, however, derive its validity from the form of expression, but from the very nature of the people who began and carried through to final success the struggle for liberty and union. The men and women of the American Revolution held a deep conviction of the worthiness of the lives and purposes of common men and women. These "common people" believed in themselves; and so believing, believed also that the world owed them an opportunity to live, and not only to live, but to make the most and best of their lives, each after his own fashion, so far as was consistent with like opportunities for the others. The doctrine of the natural rights of man really meant to the people of the Revolution the belief in the natural nobility of mankind,[3] a belief aptly summed up in Jefferson's familiar phrase: "equal opportunities to all, special privileges to none."

The Idea of Liberty.

The Massachusetts declaration of rights declares not simply that all men are created equal, but that they are created "free and equal."[4] Without doubt the idea of freedom was as essential as that of equality to the Revolutionary belief in the natural nobility of man. Also the idea of freedom has proved as difficult of definition as that of equality. "There is no word that admits of more various significations, and has made more different impressions on the human mind, than that of Liberty," said Montesquieu.[5] Many of the Fathers were brought up under the influence of the Puritan ways of thinking. They would have held with Milton that "real and substantial liberty is rather to be sought from within than from without; its existence depends,

[1] Lincoln, *Speech at Springfield, June 26, 1857.*

[2] See Nathaniel Chipman, *Sketches of the Principles of Government* (Rutland, Vermont, 1793), sketch iv, sect. 1, and sketch v, sect. 1.

[3] Cf. Francis Lieber, *Miscellaneous Writings*, ii, p. 84.

[4] Art i. See Appendix A.

[5] *L'Esprit des Lois*, bk. xi, ch. iv. See also Francis Lieber, *Civil Liberty and Self-Government*, ch. ii.

not so much on the terror of the sword, as in sobriety of conduct and integrity of life." [1] The political philosophy of the times, however, called for a definition of liberty in accordance with the doctrine of natural rights. Natural liberty was the liberty enjoyed by men living in a state of nature. "Men living together according to reason without a common superior on earth with authority to judge between them is properly the state of Nature," declared Locke.[2] To found, however, such a state of anarchy, "imbecile anarchy," John Quincy Adams called it,[3] was not the object of the Revolutionary Fathers, but rather a state of civilized government in which civil liberty should be substituted for natural liberty.[4]

The speculative consideration of what constituted civil liberty in the abstract seems to have had little interest for the men of the Revolution. Both in the American Revolution and in the English Revolution of the preceding century men were concerned chiefly in establishing certain specific rights in particular, rather than civil rights in general. The great constitutional documents of the English race, Magna Charta, the Petition of Right, the Bill of Rights, the Act of Settlement, the Declaration of Independence, all deal with the redress of notorious grievances rather than the definition of political abstractions. Many of the elements of freedom are specified in the various Revolutionary declarations of rights, but for a complete description of the idea of freedom entertained by the Fathers we must look to their deeds as well as to their words.

Personal Liberty.

The Revolutionary idea of civil liberty certainly extended as far as to comprise complete liberty of the person. Outside of the two southernmost states, the leaders of the people in the revolution all professed their dislike of slavery. None did so more decidedly than the leaders in Virginia, where slavery was nevertheless permitted to endure.[5] In the northern states, where the

[1] See Milton's *Second Defence of the People of England.* This whole *Defence* is a powerful plea that men who would govern one another must first be fit to govern themselves.

[2] John Locke, *Second Treatise of Government*, ch. iii.

[3] See his *Letters of Publicola*, attacking Paine's *Rights of Man* (1792).

[4] See Thomas Paine, *Rights of Man*, pt. i, pp. 38-40. See also John Locke, *Second Treatise of Government*, ch. ix.

[5] Scc, for a statement of some of the obstacles to emancipation, Jefferson, *Notes on Virginia*, p. 151.

practical difficulties in the way of a thorough application of the idea of personal freedom were less serious, negro slavery was abolished under the influence of the Revolutionary spirit. In Pennsylvania the article of the declaration of rights establishing the principle of natural equality was held to require the speedy enactment of laws to free the slaves. In Vermont the same article was followed by another in the declaration of rights itself proclaiming expressly the personal freedom of the negroes. In Massachusetts a similar article was interpreted by the supreme court to have emancipated the slaves of its own force without further legislation. Throughout the North the effect of the Declaration of Independence was to free the slaves at once or to inaugurate a movement which resulted in their eventual peaceful emancipation by state action. Under the influence of the same ideal of personal liberty, the Congress of the Confederation provided for the exclusion of slavery from the Northwest Territories. The fact that the slaves were not immediately emancipated throughout the entire extent of the Union does not indicate that the Fathers were insincere in their professions of belief in civil liberty, but rather that they were the victims of adverse circumstances.

How much farther than mere personal freedom from physical restraint the Revolutionary idea of liberty extended is difficult to ascertain. Other elements of freedom, such as freedom of speech and of the press, are enumerated in all the revolutionary declarations of rights. It is certain, however, that the idea of freedom entertained by the Fathers did not extend so far as to include what we now call freedom of contract.[1]

Liberty of Conscience.

The Revolutionary idea of liberty logically required the acknowledgment of the principle of liberty of conscience, that is, the liberty of the individual publicly to profess his religious faith and to worship according to the dictates of his own conscience. It cannot be said that religious liberty was a doctrine to which the American people were naturally inclined. In several of the

[1] Lieber, for example, in his work on *Civil Liberty and Self-Government* (1st ed., 1853), makes no mention of freedom of contract. A proposition to amend the declaration of rights, by adding an express declaration of the right to freedom of contract, was made in the Massachusetts constitutional convention of 1853, but was not adopted.

colonies it had been vigorously denied, and only Rhode Island and Pennsylvania expressly tolerated all Christian sects. The Puritan idea of liberty, as has been stated, laid less stress on legal rights than on moral attitudes, but the formation of the Union and the growth of a national spirit rendered sectarian intolerance archaic, thus enabling Puritanism at last to rid itself of its worst defect. To the Revolutionary leaders freedom of thought was as vital as freedom of conduct, and to their lasting renown they established liberty of the conscience on the same basis as liberty of the person among the "natural, essential, and unalienable" rights of man.[1]

The Revolutionary idea of religious toleration did not require that the public offices should be thrown open indiscriminately to all persons without regard to religious faith. In Massachusetts all state officers chosen by popular election were expressly required to declare their belief in the Christian religion, and in New Hampshire they had to be Protestants. Virginia set a better example by the abolition of religious tests for office-holding when the first state constitution was adopted in 1776, but a majority of the states which adopted constitutions during the Revolutionary period required some sort of a religious qualification from the holders of the principal public offices. The opposition to religious tests was, however, strong and growing, and in 1787 the Federal Convention provided that no religious test should ever be required as a qualification for any office or public trust under the United States. Public opinion by that time had clearly turned against it, and most of the states got rid of their religious tests for office-holding at the first revision of their constitutions.

The doctrine of the complete separation of Church and State was more difficult to establish. Several of the colonies had been founded for the express purpose of providing a haven for particular sects, and in most of them the care of religion was generally felt to be a sacred duty of government. At the beginning of the Revolution the Church of England was established by law and the clergy of that church were maintained out of the public treasury in Virginia, Maryland, and the Carolinas. The same church was specially favored by the colonial governments of New York and New Jersey. In New England, outside of Rhode Island, the Independent or Congregational Churches were

[1] See Massachusetts Declaration of Rights, art. ii.

strongly favored, and the Massachusetts declaration of rights emphatically proclaimed the necessity of making suitable provision at public expense "for the institution of the public worship of God."[1] With the lapse of time, however, the established and favored churches had become less suited to the needs of the people, and with the growth of the Revolutionary spirit the idea of a privileged church came into conflict with the principle of freedom of conscience. One of Jefferson's most cherished enterprises was the disestablishment of the Church of England in Virginia. This was accomplished immediately after the close of the Revolution.[2] The assessment of the citizens for the support of religion by public authority was finally abandoned in Massachusetts a half century later.[3] With the fall of the privileged churches came the rise of the doctrine of the complete separation of Church and State, a doctrine which followed logically, even if slowly, from the Revolutionary belief in the natural nobility of man.

The Principle of Popular Sovereignty.

The most important consequence of the Fathers' belief in the natural nobility of man was the establishment of the principle of the sovereignty of the people. This principle was expressed in the Massachusetts declaration of rights as follows: "The people of this commonwealth have the sole and exclusive right of governing themselves, as a free, sovereign, and independent state; and do, and forever hereafter shall, exercise and enjoy every power, jurisdiction, and right, which is not, or may not hereafter be, by them expressly delegated to the United States of America, in Congress assembled."[4] It is not necessary to inquire again into the question of the nature of the American Union. The relation between the several states and the United States has already been sufficiently discussed. The people of the several states were made free and independent of all foreign states by the Declaration of Independence and the force of arms; but they were never free and independent of one another. Their union in subjection to Great Britain was succeeded without any break by their union in association with one another. The several states are sovereign states within the Union only in the

[1] Art. iii.
[2] See Jefferson's *Notes on Virginia*, Appendix iii.
[3] See Constitution of 1780, article xi of the Amendments, adopted in 1833.
[4] Art. iv.

sense that they are mutually equal before the law of the Federal Constitution, and that they are independent of one another within the sphere reserved to the states. Strictly speaking, the people of a single state are in no sense sovereign, for there is no power reserved to them of which they may not be stripped without their consent, provided that the people of three-fourths of the states of the Union so will it. The time-honored phrase, a sovereign state, is a flattering fiction to which the people of the states are still pleased to adhere; but in truth it means no more than a paraphrase of the guarantee contained in the Federal Constitution that each state shall enjoy a republican form of government.

The essence of the principle of the sovereignty of the people, as applied to the government of the states, does not lie in the extent of the powers conferred upon the state governments under the federal system, but in the fact that those powers in the last analysis reside in the people themselves. The Declaration of Independence was published "in the name and by the authority of the good people of these colonies." The Revolutionary state constitutions and declarations of rights were all likewise published in the name of the "good people" of the several states. The Massachusetts declaration of rights is very explicit on this point. "All power residing originally in the people, and being derived from them, the several magistrates and officers of government, vested with authority, whether legislative, executive, or judicial, are their substitutes and agents, and are at all times accountable to them."[1] The term, sovereignty of the people, therefore, as applied to the government of the states, does not mean state sovereignty. It means popular sovereignty. It does not even mean popular sovereignty in the technical language of the political scientist. It has a more general meaning, which Lincoln has so well expressed in the phrase, "government of the people, by the people, and for the people." The chief significance of the doctrine of natural rights, as understood by those who were instrumental in framing the original state constitutions, is that it helped to establish the principle that the governments of the American states should be governments of, by, and for the people.

[1] Art. v.

THE DOCTRINE OF THE SOCIAL COMPACT

The second of the original principles of state government was expressed in the doctrine of the social compact. This doctrine, like that of natural rights, has been stated in imperishable language in the Declaration of Independence, and also forms one of the most cherished elements of the political creed of the American people. To secure the rights with which men are endowed by their Creator, "governments are instituted among men, deriving their just powers from the consent of the governed." This doctrine has been set forth with greater elaboration and precision in the preamble to the Massachusetts declaration of rights. "The body politic is formed by a voluntary association of individuals: it is a social compact, by which the whole people covenants with each citizen, and each citizen with the whole people, that all shall be governed by certain laws for the common good."[1] The reason for this was acceptably furnished by Locke. "God, having made man such a creature, that, in His own judgment, it was not good for him to be alone, put him under strong obligations of necessity, convenience, and inclination, to drive him into society, as well as fitted him with understanding and language to continue and enjoy it"; but, "men being, as has been said, by nature all free, equal, and independent, no one can be put out of this estate and subjected to the political power of another without his own consent, which is done by agreeing with other men to join and unite into a community for their comfortable, safe, and peaceable living one amongst another."

The doctrine of the social compact therefore really meant to the Fathers of the Revolution the belief that established governments of some sort were necessary for the protection of the rights of the people and were proper institutions for the control of the people if founded upon their consent. But who were these "people"?

The first authoritative answer to this question was that of the

[1] For the then currently accepted explanation of the doctrine of the social compact, see John Locke, *Second Treatise of Government*, chs. vii, viii. See also, Thomas Paine, *Rights of Man* (Am. ed. of 1792), pp. 38-40. For a contemporary criticism of the theory of the origin of government in a social compact, see Chipman's discussion of Paine's treatment of this subject, in his *Sketches of the Principles of Government* (1793), pp. 108-110. See also David Hume, *Essays*, no. 34, "Of the Original Contract," Edmund Burke's *Reflections on the Revolution in France*, and Reeves's *History of English Law*, cited by Dicey, *Introduction to the Study of the Law of the Constitution*, 7th ed., pp. 420-421.

United States Supreme Court in the famous case of Dred Scott. The people, said the court in substance, are the citizens of the states; the two expressions have the same meaning. Unfortunately the Dred Scott decision left a persistent doubt as to who were citizens. This doubt was finally cleared up by the fourteenth amendment to the Federal Constitution. "All persons born or naturalized in the United States, and subject to the jurisdiction thereof, are citizens of the United States and of the state wherein they reside." They are also the people, in the constitutional sense of the term, of the United States and of the state wherein they reside. The people of a state are the men, women, and children who make up the body of American citizens in that state. Certainly these men, women, and children, as a body, play no active part in the working of the political institutions of the state. Is their authority limited to a passive acquiescence in the acts of those who assume to speak in their name? If so, popular sovereignty is but a sham, a convenient fiction with which the powers that be may cloak with a garb of legality the most arbitrary and tyrannical designs.

The Right of Revolution.

Popular sovereignty, as understood by the Fathers, was no sham, but a stern reality. The Declaration of Independence asserts that "whenever any form of government becomes destructive of these ends" (that is, the ends to which "governments are instituted among men"), "it is the right of the people to alter or abolish it, and to institute a new government, laying its foundation on such principles, and organizing its powers in such form as shall seem most likely to effect their safety and happiness." This is the "sacred right of revolution" to which the members of the Continental Congress appealed "in the name and by the authority of the good people" of the United Colonies. It is asserted in a more philosophical manner in the Massachusetts declaration of rights of 1780. "Government is instituted for the common good; for the protection, safety, prosperity, and happiness of the people; and not for the profit, honor, or private interest of any one man, family, or class of men: Therefore the people alone have an incontestable, inalienable, and indefeasible right to institute government; and to reform, alter, or totally change the same, when their protection, safety, prosperity, and happiness require it."[1] Furthermore, lest this right of revolution be rendered worthless by powerful and lawless usurpers, the Massachusetts declaration of rights also declared that "the people have a right to keep and to bear arms for the common defence."[2] The right of the people to keep and bear arms was guaranteed in the same manner and for the same purpose in the constitutions of the original states generally as well as in that of the United States.[3]

There was nothing revolutionary in the doctrine of the right of revolution. "Common sense teaches us," wrote Hume, who will hardly be classed among revolutionary writers, "that, as government binds us to obedience only on account of its tendency to public utility, that duty must always in extraordinary cases, when public ruin would evidently attend obedience, yield to the primary and original obligation [*i.e.* the obligation to pursue the interests of society]. . . . Resistance, therefore, being admitted to extraordinary emergencies, the question can only be among good reasoners, with regard to the degree of necessity which can justify resistance and render it lawful or commendable."[4] The majority of the American people at the time of the Revolution certainly believed that the instances of oppression cited in the Declaration of Independence justified resistance. How much less would have been regarded as due cause for violent revolt we have no means of determining. Certainly not much less, or the Revolution would have begun sooner. Opinion among the Revolutionary leaders varied greatly. Jefferson has recorded the sentiment that "a little rebellion now and then is a good thing. . . . It is a medicine necessary for the sound health of government."[5] Adams, we know by his own confession, was possessed of more misgiving with reference to the value of a resort to violence.[6] That there can be no wrong without a remedy is the very essence of the spirit of American government. If the remedy cannot be found within the law, it must be sought with-

[1] Art. vii.

[2] Art. xvii.

[3] Cf. Constitution of the United States, art. ii of the Amendments. But this right does not extend to aliens, nor does it operate to prevent a state legislature from enacting reasonable regulations concerning the manner in which arms shall be kept or borne, as regulations prohibiting the carrying of concealed weapons.

[4] David Hume, *Essays*, no. 35, "Of Passive Obedience."

[5] See his letter to James Madison (1787). *Works* (Ford's ed.), iv, p. 362.

[6] See his Inaugural Address to Congress, March 4, 1797.

out the law. The final test of right and wrong exists in the individual conscience, and the individual must assume the responsibility for deciding when his duty requires him to raise his hand against the law.

By the Federal Constitution of 1787, the right of revolution was definitely taken away from the people of the separate states and reserved exclusively to the people of the United States as a whole. Under the more perfect union the whole power of the United States stands ready to protect the established government of any state against domestic violence.[1] There can be no state revolution, therefore, which is not at the same time a national revolution. The constitutions of most of the states still declare that the people have at all times the right to "reform, alter, or totally change" their state governments, but in several of these it is expressly stipulated that this right may be exercised only "by lawful and constitutional methods." This is clearly meant to exclude a resort to arms. In three states, however, New Hampshire, Maryland, and Tennessee, the doctrine of non-resistance is still declared to be wrong,[2] which seems like an attempt to preserve the original right of state revolution. This attempt is certainly beyond the power of the people of a single state, since the right of revolution was denied to the people of a single state by the people of the United States at the time of the adoption of the Federal Constitution. The right of revolution still exists, but may now be exercised, consistently with the principles of American government, only by the sovereign people of the United States.[3]

The Power of Public Opinion.

The power that remains to the people of the several states is the power of public opinion. The nature of this power need

[1] Cf. art. iv, sect. 4.

[2] "The doctrine of non-resistance against arbitrary power and oppression is absurd, slavish, and destructive of the good and happiness of mankind," is the language of the New Hampshire bill of rights.

[3] See Luther *v.* Borden, 7 How. 1. Some writers contend that the right of state revolution still exists. See R. S. Hoar, *Constitutional Conventions: Their Nature, Powers, and Limitations* (Boston, 1917), pp. 15, 168, 169. Certainly there are instances where changes in state constitutions have been made without due process of law. See *post.*, pp. 99-100, 129. But it seems to the present writer clear that the federal government might constitutionally have intervened in these cases to maintain the due process of law, had it desired to do so, since the guarantee of a republican form of government includes the guarantee of a reign of law.

not be discussed here, but it should be pointed out that the principle of the sovereignty of the people, as understood at the time of the Revolution, was broad enough to include all those rights which were felt to be necessary and proper for a free and effective expression of the opinion of the people. Thus the Massachusetts declaration of rights provides for the liberty of the press, freedom of speech and of public meeting, and the right of petition for the redress of grievances, and for freedom of debate in the legislature.[1] Similar provisions to protect and cherish the power of public opinion were inserted in the constitutions of all the states and of the United States. The Massachusetts declaration of rights also contains an express exhortation of the people to make good use of their power.[2] Opinions differed as to the practical effect of such provisions in the state declarations of rights. It was clearly the intention of the founders of the original state governments, however, that the will of the people should prevail.

The Reign of Law.

Since the people can ordinarily exercise no direct power except that of public opinion, the only sure way in which the will of the people can be made to prevail is through the reign of law,[3] depending for its force upon the consent of the governed. This was what the framers of the Massachusetts constitution meant when they declared the object of the social compact to be a covenant of the people with one another, "that all shall be governed by certain laws for the common good."[4] Hence their declaration of rights asserts that "each individual of the society has a right to be protected by it in the enjoyment of his life, liberty, and property, according to standing laws."[5] The same principle was established in all the states. For every wrong there is intended to be a remedy at law. Not even the public officer may set himself above the law, substituting his will for that of the people. He must submit like the rest of the people to the rule of the people's law, "to the end it may be a government of laws

[1] Arts. xvi, xix, and xxi.

[2] Art. xviii.

[3] For a discussion of the meaning of "the reign of law," see A. N. Holcombe, *The Foundations of the Modern Commonwealth* (New York, 1923), ch. xi.

[4] See Preamble to the Constitution of Massachusetts.

[5] Art. x. See also arts. xi and xxx.

and not of men." The chief significance of the doctrine of the social compact, as understood by the Fathers, is that it helped to establish the principle that the government of the American states should be a government of laws, deriving their force from the consent of the governed.

The principle of the reign of law has never been directly attacked in America except by those who are opposed to the maintenance of established governments of any sort, but it has often been indirectly attacked by means of strained interpretations of the meaning of the term, law. By some it has been said that a law is a rule of conduct that will be enforced in the courts.[1] Such an interpretation converts the reign of law into an arbitrary personal government by judges. Others have said that law is the executive's notion of the will of the people.[2] This interpretation converts the reign of law into an arbitrary personal government by governors, mayors, and other persons temporarily entrusted by the people with executive authority. The state governments were not orginally intended to be either judicial oligarchies or executive tyrannies. Law, as the founders of the state governments used the term, meant the will of the people as understood and formulated in the shape of constitutions and statutes, ordinances and by-laws, and other proper acts of authority by the people themselves or those to whom the power of law-making should be duly delegated.[3] Difficulties may, and in fact do, arise in connection with the interpretation and enforcement of law, when made, but the law of the land is to be sought in the intent of the people or their representatives, as indicated by their formal enactment of rules for the good conduct of society.

The purpose to establish as firmly as possible the reign of law is revealed particularly in the declaration that "no subject shall be arrested, imprisoned, despoiled, or deprived of his property, immunities, or privileges, put out of the protection of the law, exiled, or deprived of his life, liberty or estate, but by the judgment of his peers, or the law of the land."[4] This purpose is further revealed in the declarations against taxation without representation[5] and in the articles defining the relations between

[1] J. C. Gray, *The Nature and Sources of the Law*, pp. 97-98, 101.
[2] Brand Whitlock, *On the Enforcement of Law in Cities.*
[3] Francis Lieber, *Principles of Political and Legal Hermeneutics.*
[4] Massachusetts declaration of rights, art. xii.
[5] *Ibid.*, arts. xxiii and x.

the civil and military authorities.[1] Finally it is expressly declared that "the power of suspending the laws, or the execution of the laws, ought never to be exercised but by the legislature, or by authority derived from it, to be exercised in such particular cases only as the legislature shall expressly provide for." [2] This last declaration covers not only the suspension of the habeas corpus act,[3] but also of all acts whatsoever. Thus the sovereignty of the people was to be established through the reign of law.

The principle of the reign of law, unlike that of the sovereignty of the people, is one of the ancient principles of the English race, and was inherited by the American people along with their language.[4] It received, however, a new and broader meaning in America through its connection with the principle of the sovereignty of the people. Ours is a government of, by, and for the people, but the people govern by maintaining the supremacy of laws, sanctioned by public opinion.

THE REPUBLICAN FORM OF GOVERNMENT

We are now in a position to answer the question, What is a republican form of government? The question is important, since several cases of doubt have already arisen and others are likely to arise.

The obligation imposed upon the United States to guarantee to the states a republican form of government implies a duty on the part of the states themselves to provide governments republican in form. All the states had governments when the Federal Constitution was adopted, and all these state governments were left by the Constitution unchanged. They were accepted precisely as they were, and therefore it is to be presumed that they were such as it was the duty of the states to provide. Hence, when some eighty years later it was contended that a state which denied the suffrage to women was not republican in form, the reply was conclusive that, although one of the original states granted votes to women at the time of the adoption of the Constitution, the others did not, and therefore equal suffrage for men

[1] Massachusetts declaration of rights, arts. xxvii, xxviii, and xvii.
[2] *Ibid.*, art. xx.
[3] Cf. Constitution of the United States, i, 9.
[4] See A. V. Dicey, *Introduction to the Study of the Law of the Constitution*, pt. ii.

and women could not be essential to the republican form of government in the United States.[1]

Early Definitions of "Republican."

The original state governments were certainly republican in form, but were they the only republican forms permitted by the Federal Constitution? James Madison, a leading member of the Federal Convention of 1787, observed that "whenever the states may choose to substitute other republican forms, they have a right to do so and to claim the federal guaranty for the latter."[2] Just how different the various other forms may be and still be republican within the meaning of the Constitution, neither Madison nor any other member of the Federal Convention ventured to say. Recently the system of direct legislation or, as it is often designated, the initiative and referendum, has been assailed on the ground that its adoption by a state is a violation of the republican form, and hence forbidden by the Federal Constitution. Congress, however, has not refused to admit the senators and representatives chosen by the states which have adopted the initiative and referendum, and that form of government must therefore be regarded as duly republican.[3] What other innovations in state government may be adopted without exceeding the limits of the republican form can be likewise determined by experiment. The states are free to establish such political institutions for the expression and execution of the will of the people thereof as they see fit, but the United States is the final judge of the fitness of the institutions so established.

The constitutionality of procedure for direct legislation by the people was attacked upon the theory that the republican form of government is bound up with so-called representative government, that is, a form of government in which the will of the people is expressed only through the instrumentality of their representatives. Some evidence in support of this view is to be found in the writings of the Fathers. Madison, whose opinion is inferior to none, wrote in one place that he meant by the term, *republic*, "a government in which the scheme of representation

[1] Cf. Minor v. Happersett, 21 Wall. 162 (1874).

[2] *The Federalist*, no. 43.

[3] Cf. Pacific States Telephone and Telegraph Co. *v.* Oregon, 223 U. S. 118 (1912).

takes place."[1] Jefferson also has used language which seems to imply that he deemed representative government the chief characteristic of republicanism.[2] In another place, however, Madison seems to hold a different opinion.[3] "What then," he inquires, "are the distinctive characters of the republican form? Were an answer to this question to be sought, not by recurring to principles, but in the application of the term by political writers to the constitutions of different states, no satisfactory one would ever be found. Holland, in which no particle of the supreme authority is derived from the people, has passed almost universally under the denomination of a republic. The same title has been bestowed on Venice, where absolute power over the great body of the people is exercised in the most absolute manner by a small body of hereditary nobles. Poland, which is a mixture of aristocracy and of monarchy in their worst forms, has been dignified with the same appellation. The government of England, which has one republican branch only,[4] combined with an hereditary aristocracy and monarchy, has with equal impropriety been frequently placed on the list of republics. These examples, which are nearly as dissimilar to each other as to a genuine republic, show the extreme inaccuracy with which the term has been used in political disquisitions."

Madison's own definition follows. "If we resort for a criterion to the different principles on which different forms of government are established, we may define a republic to be, or at least may bestow that name on, a government which derives all its powers directly or indirectly from the great body of the people, and is administered by persons holding their offices during pleasure, for a limited period, or during good behavior. It is *essential* to such a government that it be derived from the great body of the society, not from an inconsiderable proportion, or a favored class of it; otherwise a handful of tyrannical nobles, exercising their oppressions by a delegation of their powers, might aspire to the rank of republicans and claim for their government the honorable title of republic. It is *sufficient* for such a government that the

[1] See *The Federalist*, no. 10. See also *ibid.*, no. 14.

[2] See his First Inaugural. See also his letters to Dupont de Nemours and Samuel Kercheval (1816); *Works* (Ford's ed.), x, pp. 24, 28.

[3] *The Federalist*, no. 39.

[4] Madison means the House of Commons. John Adams sometimes described the government of England as a "monarchical republic." See C. M. Walsh, *The Political Science of John Adams*, ch. xviii.

persons administering it be appointed, either directly or indirectly, by the people; and that they hold their appointment by either of the tenures just specified; otherwise every government in the United States, as well as every other popular government that has been or can be well organized or well executed, would be degraded from the republican character."

An entirely different view is set forth by Paine.[1] "The only forms of government are the democratical, the aristocratical, the monarchical, and what is now called the representative. What is called a *republic,* is not any *particular form* of government. . . . Republican government is no other than government established and conducted for the interest of the public. . . . It is not necessarily connected with any particular form, but it most naturally associates with the representative form, as being best calculated to secure the end for which a nation is at the expense of supporting it." Thus Paine solves the perplexing problem concerning the nature of the republican form of government by denying the existence of such a form.

Final Definition.

There is a better solution of the problem. The first act of the convention which framed the Massachusetts constitution of 1780 was to vote that the new government to be established be a "free republic." The second act was to define that term as follows: "It is the essence of a free republic that the people be governed by fixed laws of their own making."[2] This definition is nothing more nor less than a straightforward statement of the two fundamental principles upon which all the original state governments were established, namely, the principles of the sovereignty of the people and of the reign of law. A republican form of government, therefore, is one in which the will of the people is the highest source of authority and looks for its interpretation and execution to responsible agents acting under the forms of law.[3]

[1] Thomas Paine, *The Rights of Man* (Am. ed. of 1792), pt. ii, pp. 18-19.

[2] *Journal of the Massachusetts Constitutional Convention, 1779–1780,* p. 24.

[3] See the opinion of Justice James Wilson in Chisholm *v.* Georgia, 2 Dall., 419 (1793). Cf. *Wilson's Works,* I, 366.

CHAPTER III

THE ORIGINAL FORMS OF STATE GOVERNMENT

The republican form of government obviously admits a wide latitude in the adoption of institutions by which the fundamental principles of republicanism may be reduced to practice. Although no standard or uniform type of republican government was adopted by the states during the revolutionary period, there was substantial agreement concerning the main features of such a government.

ADOPTION OF ORIGINAL CONSTITUTIONS

Revolutionary Conventions.

In the beginning the fundamental laws for the government of the states were systematically and authoritatively set forth in special written documents or constitutions. These constitutions were prepared in various ways. In Virginia the first constitution was drafted by a revolutionary convention in the spring of 1776 without express authority from the people. It was put into effect by the body which drafted it, and which continued to exist as an ordinary legislature exercising authority by virtue of the constitution promulgated by itself. Jefferson criticized this mode of preparing a constitution as grossly irregular, since the convention had in effect usurped the "natural right" of the people to determine for themselves the conditions of the "social compact."[1] This constitution endured, however, for more than half a century, and, though never formally submitted to the people for their approval, received the sanction of public opinion. The same mode of proceeding was adopted in several of the original states.[2] In Pennsylvania a less objectionable mode of pro-

[1] *Notes on Virginia* (ed. of 1829), pp. 125-130.

[2] Notably in South Carolina (1776) and New Jersey (1777). In form the original constitutions of these three states were in no wise different from ordinary statutes. In four other states, New Hampshire (1776), Delaware (1776), New York (1777), and Georgia (1777), the original constitutions were framed by legislative bodies which had express authority therefor from the people, but did not provide for the submission thereof in any manner to the people. See W. F. Dodd, *The Revision and Amendment of State Constitutions*, ch. i, esp. at p. 24.

ceeding was pursued.[1] In Connecticut and Rhode Island the governments established under the royal charters of 1662 and 1663 were continued in force by the legislatures of 1776 without special action by the people.[2]

Development of Constitutional Convention.

In Massachusetts the provisional government established in 1775 continued on a purely revolutionary basis until 1780. The legislature of 1778 attempted to substitute a constitutional basis, but the draft of a new constitution, when submitted to the people for their approval at a special election, was rejected by an overwhelming majority, chiefly on the ground that no ordinary legislature had the power to draft a new constitution, even for the purpose of submission to the people. The legislature of 1779 therefore submitted to the people the proposition whether or not they would elect delegates to a special constitutional convention. The people accepted the proposition, whereupon the legislature called a special election of delegates, who framed a new draft of a constitution, submitted it to the people for their approval, and adjourned until the election should have been held. This constitution met with the popular approval, and was duly proclaimed on their authority by the convention, which thereupon adjourned *sine die*. Such was the latest of the various methods by which the people of the original states exchanged their "natural rights" for civil rights upon the secure basis of a "social compact." [3]

Thus was developed the characteristic American practice with respect to the adoption of written constitutions. This practice, though not at first uniform, tended towards the recognition of three main principles: (1) the distinction between constitutional and statutory law; (2) the distinction between the constitutional convention and the ordinary legislative body of the state; and

[1] See Thomas Paine, *The Rights of Man* (ed. of 1792), pt. ii, pp. 24-25.
The Pennsylvania plan of special authorization by the people and informal submission to the people was followed in Maryland (1776), North Carolina (1776), and South Carolina (1778). In Massachusetts (1778) there was a formal submission to the people in their town-meetings, but the document so submitted was rejected by them.

[2] See Thayer's *Cases on Constitutional Law*, i, p. 433.

[3] This method was pursued in New Hampshire in 1781 and 1782, but the documents so submitted were rejected by the people; and again, this time successfully, in 1783.

(3) the submission of proposed constitutions to a direct vote of the people.

RESERVATION OF CIVIL RIGHTS TO PEOPLE

The prime object of the adoption of written constitutions was to set forth the fundamental laws for the government of the states, that is, the laws governing the frame of government and the distribution of powers between the various depositaries of political authority, and thereby securely to establish the sovereignty of the people through the reign of law. At the same time, conscious of the sovereignty of the people and relying on the reign of law, the framers of the original constitutions seized the opportunity to write into them, and thus put beyond the power of temporary custodians of public authority to impair or destroy, certain ancient privileges of freeborn Englishmen, now at last placed for Americans on the secure footing of popular rights. These rights must be distinguished from principles of government, strictly speaking, although the two were often thrown together in the state papers of the American Revolution. They may be traced through the great constitutional documents of the English race, Magna Charta, the Petition of Right, the Bill of Rights, and various notable acts of Parliament, to the Declaration of Independence and the other declarations of rights contained in American Revolutionary state papers. No two of these declarations of rights are precisely the same. Since, however, unusual care was devoted to the preparation of the declaration of rights contained in the Massachusetts constitution of 1780, this document may be regarded as the standard American declaration of rights.[1] Some of these rights have already been enumerated. The rest in the main were intended to establish on the firmest possible basis the forms and procedure of the English common law as the basis of the American legal system. Thus trial by jury was to be "held sacred." In addition the issue of general search warrants, the enactment of *ex post facto* laws and bills of attainder, the exaction of excessive bail, and the imposition of excessive fines or of cruel and unusual punishments were prohibited.[2] Most of the guarantees of rights of this character were afterwards repeated in the Federal Constitution.[3]

[1] See Appendix A.
[2] See Declaration of Rights, arts. xii, xiii, xiv, xv, xxiv, xxv, and xxvi.
[3] Art. i, sect. 9; art. iii, sect. 2; and arts. i to viii of the amendments.

These declarations of rights were in substance constitutional limitations upon the powers of the state and federal governments, and this practice of limiting the powers of the established governments in state and nation by the reservation of rights to the people has been universally followed in the United States. It constitutes one of the most important of the contributions of the Fathers to the science of government.

Rights of Men and of Citizens.

It should be observed that the Massachusetts declaration of rights makes no distinction between the rights of men in general and those of citizens in particular. Apparently it was assumed that there would be no considerable class of persons within the Commonwealth who would not also be citizens. In most of the original states, however, there were such classes of persons in considerable numbers, namely, immigrant indentured servants and negro slaves. The former consisted of persons "held to service" only temporarily and destined eventually to enjoy the civil and political rights of citizenship on the same terms as native citizens. The latter in several of the states were not admitted to full citizenship, even if manumitted. Outside of the southernmost states, however, the leaders of public opinion seem to have expected, or at any rate desired, the ultimate abolition of racial discriminations in American law.[1] Ultimately indeed this came to pass, and the negro was admitted to full civil and political equality with the white citizen.[2] At the same time the growth of a very considerable class of persons was recognized, who were not citizens, namely, alien and unnaturalized immigrants. Accordingly when the fourteenth amendment to the Federal Constitution was framed, an important distinction was made between citizens and other persons subject to the jurisdiction of the states. No state may abridge the privileges or immunities of citizens of the United States, and in addition no state may deprive any person of life, liberty, or property without due process of law, nor deny to any person the equal protection of the laws. Hence aliens may not claim as of right the special privileges and immunities of citizens,[3] but they

[1] A. Lincoln, *Address at Cooper Union, Feb. 27, 1860.*

[2] Constitution of the United States, amendments, arts. xiv and xv.

[3] For example, the "right" to own land or the "right" to vote. But as will appear, aliens have often been granted special privileges of citizenship in advance of naturalization.

are entitled to all the benefits of the reign of law and to the same protection against arbitrary and tyrannical oppression as native citizens.[1]

THE RIGHT TO VOTE AND HOLD OFFICE

There is nothing in the original declarations of rights to indicate that the electoral franchise or so-called "right" to vote was regarded as one of the "natural, essential and unalienable" rights of man or even of citizens. Indeed the language of the Massachusetts declaration of rights seems to imply that the suffrage was a privilege to be conferred only upon those whose claims thereto could be proven by some general test of fitness; but what that test of fitness should be is not indicated.[2] The language of the Virginia declaration of rights is more explicit. "All men, having sufficient evidence of permanent common interest with, and attachment to, the community, have the right of suffrage."[3] This rule, or the similar rule laid down in the Pennsylvania declaration of rights,[4] clearly recognizes a right to vote, but also clearly implies that that right extends only to those who have something at stake in the maintenance of the sovereignty of the people and the reign of law, or, as it is commonly called, in the maintenance of law and order. What should be the requisite "sufficient evidence," however, is not specified in any declaration of rights.

Original Suffrage Qualifications.

In the first constitutions of most of the original states, the suffrage qualifications actually established were in fact substantially the same as those that had existed under the colonial governments before the Revolution. Indeed this is expressly provided in the Virginia constitution, and consequently the right to vote in that state was restricted to the owners of fifty acres of uninhabited land or of twenty-five acres with a house, or in towns to the owners of a house and lot. In Massachusetts the suffrage was restricted to "male inhabitants of twenty-one years of age and upwards, having a freehold estate within the Commonwealth of the annual income of three pounds, or any estate of the value of sixty pounds." In the states generally the

[1] See an act of Connecticut, 1776, par. 4, cited by J. B. Thayer, *Cases on Constitutional Law*, i, p. 433.

[2] Art. ix. [3] Art. vi. [4] Art. vii.

suffrage was restricted to the owners of fifty acres of land, more or less, or an equivalent amount of property in some other tangible form. In Pennsylvania, however, the suffrage was extended to all taxpayers, in Georgia, to all tax payers possessing property valued at ten pounds and also to "mechanics," and in Vermont, which copied the article of the Pennsylvania declaration of rights relating to the suffrage, the vote was granted to "every man . . . who is of a quiet and peaceable behavior and will take the following oath (or affirmation)," called the freeman's oath: "I solemnly swear, by the ever living God (or affirm, in the presence of Almighty God), that whenever I am called to give my vote or suffrage, touching any matter that concerns the State of Vermont, I will do it so, as in my conscience, I shall judge will most conduce to the best good of the same, as established by the constitution, without fear or favor of any man."

Distrust of Manhood Suffrage.

This is the closest approach to manhood suffrage to be found in any state under the original state constitutions. In Virginia, Jefferson tells us, "the majority of the men in the state, who pay and fight for its support, are unrepresented in the legislature; the roll of freeholders entitled to vote not including generally the half of those on the roll of the militia, or of the taxgatherers."[1] In Massachusetts, it has been estimated, approximately sixteen or seventeen per cent of the population were entitled to vote, that is, about three-fourths of the adult males.[2] In Pennsylvania and Vermont the proportion of the adult males entitled to vote must have been larger, but in the other northern states the franchise was restricted to nearly the same extent as in Massachusetts, and Virginia was fairly typical of conditions in the South.[3] Jefferson, in his plan of a constitution for Virginia, drafted in 1783, when it was supposed by him that a constitutional convention would be shortly summoned, advocated that the franchise be conferred on all free male citizens of full age and sound mind, who should reside in any county of the state

[1] *Notes on Virginia*, ch. xiii.

[2] J. F. Jameson, "Did the Fathers vote?" in the *New England Magazine*, Jan. 1890.

[3] In Georgia, however, there was a comparatively low property qualification, and in North Carolina there was only a tax-paying qualification for electors of members of the lower house of the legislature.

for one year preceding an election or who should possess real property therein, or be enrolled in the militia. This would have been substantially the same as manhood suffrage with apparently the possibility of plural votes for land-owners, unless the elections in all counties should be held on the same day. This plan, however, came to nothing. The franchise provided for the Northwest Territory under the Ordinance of 1787, which also represented Jefferson's ideas of sound public policy, was restricted to the owners of fifty acres of land. Under the conditions, especially the land policy, then prevailing in the old Northwest, this franchise confined the use of the ballot to settlers of some substance, and without doubt accurately expressed the public opinion of the time with respect to the composition of the electorate.

In short, the principle of manhood suffrage was not among the original principles of state government. It was not inconsistent with them, however, nor was the admission of women to the electoral franchise inconsistent with the principles upon which the original state electorates were constructed. Indeed, in New Jersey properly qualified women were specifically authorized to vote from 1790 to 1807.[1] But in general, the franchise was limited to men possessing at least homesteads of their own, or equivalent amounts of stock in trade, and thereby gaining independent livelihoods. The wage-earning classes were for the most part excluded from the electorate. This exclusion did not affect so large a proportion of the people as it would to-day. But it restricted the use of the ballot in the main to the independent farmers and proprietors of plantations and to the commercial and professional classes. In other words, the people placed their governments in the hands of the propertied classes, preferring in practice a somewhat aristocratic government to that government of the masses which their theory of the natural nobility of man would seem to have demanded.

Property Qualifications for Office-Holding.

The same rules were acted upon in the construction of all the organs of state government. The members of the several state legislatures, the governors and other high executive officers, and the judiciary were necessarily required to possess at least the

[1] Edward R. Turner, "Women's Suffrage in New Jersey, 1790-1807," *Smith College Studies in History*, vol. i, no. 4 (1916).

same qualifications as ordinary voters, and in many cases the property qualifications were considerably greater. Thus in Massachusetts members of the lower branch of the legislature were required to possess real estate of the value of at least one hundred pounds, or other property of at least twice that value. Senators were required to possess not less than three times as much property as representatives, and the governor was required to possess not less than one thousand pounds in real estate. Similar real estate qualifications were required in New Hampshire and North Carolina. In Maryland the qualification imposed upon the governor was that he should possess five thousand pounds in lawful money, and in South Carolina the sum was fixed at ten thousand pounds. In the remaining states the theory of government by a governing class was not pushed so far. In all, nevertheless, the fundamental principle obtained that government is a delegated and limited trust, that all authority not conferred is reserved, and that in fact there are grave questions, lying deeper than the ordinary problems of government, and over which government in none of its branches has just control. Indeed, unless this principle had been recognized, some of the original state governments would not have been people's governments at all, but oligarchies based upon wealth and masquerading under republican forms.

THE SEPARATION OF POWERS

The principle of the separation of powers was set forth in the Massachusetts declaration of rights as follows: "In the government of this commonwealth the legislative department shall never exercise the executive and judicial powers or either of them; the executive shall never exercise the legislative and judicial powers or either of them; the judicial shall never exercise the legislative and executive powers or either of them: to the end it may be a government of laws and not of men."[1] The constitution of New Hampshire, adopted in 1783, declared that "the legislative, executive, and judicial [powers] ought to be kept as separate from, and independent of, each other as the nature of a free government will admit, or as is consistent with that chain of connection that binds the whole fabric of the con-

[1] Art. xxx.

stitution in one indissoluble bond of union and amity." Maryland adopted the maxim in the most unqualified terms, declaring that "the legislative, executive and judicial powers of government ought to be forever separate and distinct from each other." Six of the twelve states which adopted new constitutions during the Revolutionary period, that is, all the states which adopted declarations of rights with the exception of Pennsylvania and Vermont, explicitly affirmed the doctrine of the separation of powers.

Original Obscurity of the Doctrine.

There was no attempt, however, at a philosophical definition of these three kinds of powers. The fact is, that the Fathers did not know themselves exactly what they meant by these terms. Locke, one of the first writers to speak of three powers, specifies the legislative or law-making power, the executive or law-enforcing power, and the federative power or power of treating on behalf of a state with other states. Clearly this is not the definition of powers in the minds of the framers of the original state constitutions. Jefferson appreciated the difficulty when he attempted to draft a model constitution for the state of Virginia.[1] "By executive powers," he observed, "we mean no reference to those powers exercised under our former government by the crown as its prerogative, nor that these shall be the standard of what may or may not be deemed the rightful powers of the governor. We give him those powers only, which are necessary to execute the laws (and administer the government) and which are not in their nature either legislative or judiciary. The application of this idea must be left to reason." Jefferson did not attempt to elaborate further the idea which he declared should be left to reason, although he did expressly deny to the governor a number of royal prerogative powers, such as erecting courts, offices, boroughs, corporations, fairs, markets, ports, etc. Paine subsequently made the attempt and reached the conclusion that notwithstanding "it has been customary to consider government under three distinct heads, the legislative, the executive, and the judicial, if we permit our judgment to act unincumbered by the habit of multiplied terms, we can perceive no more than two divisions of power . . . that

[1] See *Notes on Virginia*, Appendix ii.

of legislating or enacting laws, and that of executing or administering them. . . . That which is called the judicial power, is strictly and properly the executive power. . . ."[1]

Although no successful attempt at a philosophical definition of the three kinds of powers seems to have been made by the framers of the original state constitutions, there is no doubt that such a definition is possible.[2] The two main functions of government distinguished by Paine may be described respectively as the functions of politics and of administration. The former has to do with policies or expressions of the state-will. The latter has to do with the execution of these policies. Officers entrusted with the execution of the state-will, however, may be further distinguished as judicial officers and administrative officers proper. The former have merely to decide what is the law applicable to the facts brought before them in specific cases, involving controversies between private individuals or between private individuals and government officers concerning their rights under the law. The latter must determine, of course, what is the law, but also they must decide whether, in cases where their legal powers are sufficient, it is wise to act. The former consider justice only, the latter justice and expediency. Now it is likely that this is what the Fathers had in mind when they declared their belief in the existence of three kinds of governmental powers.

Its Practical Significance.

The important matter, however, is their further belief that tyranny became possible only when these three kinds of powers were joined in the same hands. "The accumulation of all powers, legislative, executive and judiciary, in the same hands, whether of one, a few, or many, and whether hereditary, self-appointed, or elective," wrote Madison, "may justly be pronounced the very definition of tyranny."[3] This belief is clearly set forth in Jefferson's criticism of the first state government established in Virginia. That government, as has been shown, was established

[1] Thomas Paine, *The Rights of Man*, pt. ii, p. 33. See, for a recent and conclusive statement of the same thesis, F. J. Goodnow, *Politics and Administration*.

[2] F. J. Goodnow, *Principles of the Administrative Law of the United States*, bk. i, ch. i.

[3] See *The Federalist*, no. 47 (Ford's ed).

by the legislature of the state, and was put into operation without reference to the people of the state. The constitution not only emanated from the legislature, but committed to the legislature the election of both executive and judiciary. It could be repealed at any time by the legislature, at least many persons then so supposed, and any alterations could be made at the will thereof, even to putting all power into the hands of a single dictator. As Jefferson remarked, "one hundred and seventy-three despots" (the number of members of the legislature) "would surely be as oppressive as one." [1] If, however, the three kinds of powers were distributed among three separate and distinct departments of government, and if the constitution itself were made by a special organ of government and were dependent for its validity upon the express approval of the electorate, the danger of tyranny through the consolidation of all powers in the hands of a single person or body of persons would be destroyed.

The doctrine of the separation of powers originated with Montesquieu, or at least was first brought by him to the notice of eighteenth-century political philosophers. Montesquieu, however, as Madison has clearly pointed out, did not mean that the three departments of government should have no partial agency in, or control over, the acts of each other. Neither the government of England nor that of any of the original American states was established upon such a principle. Montesquieu's meaning simply was, "that where the *whole* power of one department is exercised by the same hands which possess the *whole* power of another department, the fundamental principles of a free constitution are subverted." [2] Hence the doctrine of the separation of powers, as a maxim of government, "does not require that the legislative, executive, and judiciary departments should be wholly unconnected with each other." On the contrary, "unless these departments be so far connected and blended as to give to each a constitutional control over the others, the degree of separation which the maxim requires, as essential to a free government, can never in practice be duly maintained." [3] The principle of the separation of powers among three departments of government was first logically worked out in the constitution of New

[1] See Jefferson's *Notes on Virginia*, ch. xiii.

[2] See *The Federalist*, no. 47.

[3] See *The Federalist*, no. 48.

York, adopted by a revolutionary convention in 1777. The principle of the separation of powers, and the practice of framing a constitution by a special convention subject to the express approval of the electorate, were first combined by the people of Massachusetts in 1779–1780. This combination forms the corner stone of constitutional government in the United States.

Effective Distributions of Power.

The New York constitution of 1777 merits further examination. The legislative power was vested in the first instance in a legislature composed of two houses. The legislature, however, exercised several important non-legislative powers. For example, it elected the treasurer of the state, and the lower house also elected four members of the upper house to act under the presidency of the governor as a council of appointment. The chancellor and judges of the supreme court and all executive officers, except the governor and lieutenant-governor, who were elected by the people, and the treasurer, were appointed by the governor subject to the consent of this council. The lower branch of the legislature also possessed the power to impeach any executive or judicial officer, and the upper house together with the chancellor and judges of the supreme court were constituted the court for the trial of impeachments. The governor was commander-in-chief of the state militia and navy, and possessed the prerogative powers of convening and proroguing the legislature, provided such prorogations should not exceed sixty days in the space of any one year, and of granting reprieves and pardons to persons convicted of crimes other than treason and murder. In the latter cases he was empowered to suspend execution of sentence until it should be reported to the legislature at the next session, when the latter might either pardon, or direct the execution of the criminal, or grant a further reprieve. The governor was further bound to take care that the laws be faithfully executed, to expedite all such measures as should be resolved upon by the legislature, and to inform the latter at every session of the condition of the state and to recommend such matters to their consideration as should appear to him to concern its good government, welfare, and prosperity. The governor, together with the chancellor and judges of the supreme court, was made a council of revision, to which was committed the duty of examining and, if necessary, revising all acts of the legislature, and returning to the legislature, with its objections in writing, all acts which it deemed improper to become laws of the state in the form in which they were passed by the legislature. The legislature, however, might reënact such laws in their original form by two-thirds majorities in each branch. The chancellor and judges of the supreme court, once appointed, should hold office during good behavior or until they should attain the age of sixty years. Military officers should be commissioned by the governor and hold office during his pleasure. Other officers should enjoy such tenure of office as should be provided by statute.

Obviously here was not a separation, but a confusion, of the three kinds of governmental powers. The powers of each department of government were defined clearly enough, but they were not all of one kind. The powers of each of the three kinds were granted clearly enough, but they were not granted to the three departments respectively. There was a distribution of powers which gave powers of each kind to each of the three departments and duties of all three kinds to all of the departments.

The Massachusetts constitution of 1780 was framed upon similar principles. The two houses of the legislature in joint session were empowered to elect the secretary of the commonwealth, the treasurer, the commissary-general, notaries public, and naval officers. All other executive officers and all judicial officers were to be appointed by the governor "by and with the advice and consent of the council," a body of nine, chosen from the senate by the two houses of the legislature in joint session, and the lieutenant-governor. The governor presided at meetings. The governor was granted the power of pardoning offenses, with the consent of the council, and of withholding his approval from acts of the legislature regardless of the advice of the council. Acts not approved by the governor should be returned to the legislature, and, as in New York, might be reënacted by the latter by two-thirds majorities in both branches. All judicial officers were authorized to hold their offices during good behavior, provided nevertheless that the governor, with the consent of the council, might remove them upon the address of both houses of the legislature. Each branch of the legislature, as well as the governor and council, was granted authority to require the opinions of the judges of the supreme court "upon important questions of law and upon solemn occasions." The power to bring impeachments was vested in the lower house of the legislature, and the upper house was constituted the court for the trial thereof. All causes of marriage, divorce, and alimony, and all appeals from the judges of probate were to be heard by the governor and council, until the legislature should make other provision therefor by law. Thus the legislature exercised executive and judicial powers, the governor exercised legislative and judicial powers, and the judiciary exercised legislative and executive powers. Each department, however, exercised only those powers granted to it by the constitution.

The New Hampshire constitution of 1783 was very similar in form to that of Massachusetts, and, except for the omission of the gubernatorial veto power, embodied the principle of the separation of powers in the same way.

Ineffective Distributions of Power.

The constitutions of Rhode Island and Connecticut were never intended to embody the principle of the separation of powers. They were indeed precisely the same as the royal charters under which those two colonies had been governed for more than a century. These charters were nothing more nor less than the charters of business corporations, and provided a form of government such as any trading company of the seventeenth century, enjoying special privileges granted by the crown, might have possessed. The important difference between the governments of Rhode Island and Connecticut and that of the English East India Company, for example, lay in the fact that the former admitted to the privileges of the charter (admitted as freemen of the company, they said; we should say, stockholders) all actual settlers of good reputation and independent means, whereas the latter restricted the benefits of the chartered privileges to the original investors (merchant adventurers, they called themselves) and their successors. In Rhode Island and Connecticut, the governor, deputy-governor, council (board of directors or senate), and house of representatives (stockholders' meeting by deputy instead of by person) were elected by the people (freemen of the company, or voters of the commonwealth). The judiciary and the remaining executive officers were elected by the legislature, and held office for terms of only one year. The judiciary exercised judicial functions only, and the executive none but executive functions. The principle of the separation of powers, however, as expounded by Madison, was hardly recognizable, for there was no effective check to the authority of the legislature. The charter or constitution was, to be sure, the supreme law of the state, but the legislature was without an important rival as the interpreter thereof, and could rule practically uncontrolled except by public opinion. In short, the governments of these two states were representative democracies characterized by the legal supremacy of their legislatures.[1]

In the remaining states where the framers of the original constitutions professed a belief in the doctrine of the separation of powers, New Jersey, Delaware, Maryland, Virginia, North Carolina, South Carolina, and Georgia, the application of the doctrine left even more to be desired than in Rhode Island and Connecticut. The governor was universally elected by the legislature, and, except in South Carolina and Delaware, his term of office was restricted to one year. In addition, in the six southern states, restrictions were placed upon his eligibility for reëlection. In every state there was an executive council, chosen except in New Jersey by the legislature, which the governor was required to consult on all important matters, and which in most cases incidentally served to restrict such powers of appointment and pardon as he might possess. In New Jersey the upper branch of the legislature, the legislative council as it was called, served as an executive council. The power possessed by the colonial governors to dissolve the legislature was everywhere abolished. The judges were elected by the state legislature in all these states except Maryland, where they were appointed by the governor with the consent of the council. This mode of selection really amounted to indirect legislative appointment, since the governor and council were elected annually by the legislature. In all these states except Georgia, where the legislature consisted of only a single house, the executives and judiciary could be impeached by the lower branch of the legislature and removed from office upon conviction by the upper. In Delaware, Mary-

[1] See W. C. Morey, "The Genesis of a Written Constitution," *Ann. Am. Acad. Pol. Soc. Sci.*, i, 4 (April, 1891), and also, "The First State Constitutions," *ibid.*, iv, 2 (Sept., 1893).

land, and South Carolina they could be removed from office by the governor upon address by both branches of the legislature. The judges were usually entitled to hold office, nominally at least, during good behavior, but in New Jersey the judges were chosen for terms of seven years, and in Georgia they were chosen annually. Thus, whether executive and judicial officers were appointed by the governor or elected by the legislature, the effect was the same, namely, to concentrate all powers ultimately in the legislature. In South Carolina, indeed, by the constitution of 1776 a power of absolute veto over legislation was granted to the governor, but this was withdrawn when the first constitution was revised by the legislature two years later. In none of the other states was there any power of executive veto.[1] In short, the legislatures, under the original constitutions of these states, were not seriously limited either by the executives or by the courts.[2] They had all the law-making power in their hands and they made the very constitutions themselves. Unchecked by either executive or judicial branches of the government, they practically ruled supreme. Well might Jefferson exclaim that this was "an elective despotism" and "not the government we fought for."[3]

The doctrine of the separation of powers, as we have seen, meant no more than that no one of the three departments of government should exercise the constitutional powers of another department. In this sense of the term, the government of Virginia was a government of separated powers, since the declaration of rights explicitly stated that "the legislative and executive powers of the state should be kept separate and distinct from the judiciary."[4] "But no barrier was provided between these several powers. The judiciary and executive members were left dependent on the legislative, for their subsistence in office, and some of them for their continuance in it. If, therefore, the legislative assumes executive and judiciary powers, no opposition is likely to be made; nor, if made, can it be effectual; because in that case they may put their proceedings into the form of an act

[1] Jefferson, however, in his plan of a government for Virginia (1783) proposed a council of revision with an organization and powers much like that of New York. This plan is reprinted in appendix B.

[2] Cf. J. Allen Smith, *The Spirit of American Government*, ch. ii.

[3] See his *Notes on Virginia*, ch. xiii.

[4] Virginia Bill of Rights, sec. 5.

of assembly, which will render them obligatory on the other branches. They have accordingly, in many instances, decided rights which should have been left to judiciary controversy; and the direction of the executive, during the whole time of their session, is becoming habitual and familiar."[1] It thus becomes clear that, as Madison observed, "a mere demarcation on parchment of the constitutional limits of the several departments is not a sufficient guard against those encroachments which lead to a tyrannical concentration of all the powers of government in the same hands."[2]

The Censorial System.

In Pennsylvania the framers of the original constitution of 1776 did not expressly affirm their belief in the doctrine of the separation of powers, but they practically affirmed it, at least in part, by providing that the supreme legislative power should be vested in a house of representatives and the supreme executive power in a president and council. The former was granted all the powers "necessary for the legislature of a free state or commonwealth: But they shall have no power to add to, alter, abolish, or infringe any part of this constitution." The supreme executive council consisted of twelve persons elected by the freemen of the city of Philadelphia and of the counties, one from the city and one from each of the counties, for terms of three years, one third retiring annually. The governor was chosen annually from among the members of the council by the house of representatives and council in joint session, but had no greater powers than any other councillor. The council possessed the ordinary executive powers, including that of granting pardons, subject to certain exceptions, and also the power to lay embargoes during recesses of the house of representatives for periods not exceeding thirty days. The councillors were furthermore charged with the duties of preparing such business as they should judge necessary to lay before the house of representatives, and of sitting as judges to hear cases of impeachment, taking to their assistance for advice only the justices of the supreme court. The framers of this Pennsylvania constitution, however, did not trust solely to "a mere demarcation on parchment of the constitutional limits of

[1] Jefferson, *Notes on Virginia*, ch. xiii.
[2] *The Federalist*, no. 48.

the several departments" to protect the people against oppression and tyranny. They introduced a special organ of government for this purpose, called the council of censors.

The Pennsylvania council of censors was composed of twenty-four censors, two being elected by the people of each of the eleven counties and the city of Philadelphia. The censors were to be chosen every seventh year, and were charged with the duties of inquiring whether the constitution had been preserved inviolate, and whether the legislative and executive branches of government had performed their duties properly without assuming unconstitutional powers. They were also to inquire whether the public taxes had been justly levied and collected, in what manner they had been spent, and whether the laws had been duly executed. They were empowered to send for persons, papers, and records, to pass public censures, to order impeachments, and to recommend to the legislature the repeal of such laws as should appear to them to have been enacted contrary to the principles of the constitution.[1] Furthermore, they were empowered to call by a two-thirds vote a constitutional convention to amend any article of the constitution which might be defective, explain such as might be thought not clearly expressed, and add such as might be necessary for the preservation of the rights and happiness of the people. "But the articles to be amended, and the amendments to be proposed, and such articles as are proposed to be added or abolished, shall be promulgated at least six months before the day appointed for the election of such convention, for the previous consideration of the people, that they may have an opportunity of instructing their delegates on the subject." The state of Vermont, which in its constitution of 1777 followed in most respects the model of the government of Connecticut, also adopted this institution of a council of censors.[2]

Appeals to the People.

In lieu of such periodical appeals to the people to correct infractions of the constitution, several other states provided for appeals to be taken as occasion should require. Thus the Massachusetts constitution of 1780 ordered the legislature to submit to

[1] Pennsylvania Constitution of 1776, Art. 47.

[2] The Vermont council was composed of thirteen censors, elected at large by the people of the whole state, not by districts as in Pennsylvania. The history of these councils of censors will be discussed later. See ch. iv.

a vote of the people in the year 1795 the question whether they desired a fresh constitutional convention to be called, "in order the more effectually to adhere to the principles of the constitution, and to correct those violations which by any means may be made therein, as well as to form such alterations as from experience shall be found necessary."[1] By implication, this article recognizes a power in the legislature to submit the question of a call for a constitutional convention at any time. In New Hampshire the practice was established of taking the sense of the voters every seven years as to the need for a constitutional convention.[2] In Georgia it was provided that the legislature should call a constitutional convention upon the receipt of petitions from a majority of the counties of the state signed by a majority of voters in each county, specifying the alterations to be made.[3] This cumbersome form of the constitutional initiative, however, proved unworkable, and was omitted from the constitution of 1789. In New York, where the doctrine of the separation of powers was first worked out in a logical way, the responsibility for the prevention of the violation of the constitution by the enactment of laws "inconsistent with the spirit" thereof was expressly vested in the council of revision,[4] but for the further protection of the people a court for the correction of errors was created, consisting of the lieutenant-governor, the members of the senate, the chancellor, and the judges of the supreme court.[5] No special arrangements for protection against violations of the constitution, either by appeals to the people or otherwise, were made in any other of the original state constitutions. Apparently the people generally put their trust in the power of public opinion and the good faith of their representatives. Thus in Connecticut it was expressly declared that "free and annual elections" were "the best security for the preservation of civil and religious rights and liberties."[6]

Jefferson's plan for the preservation of state constitutions inviolate was to provide for an appeal to the people, in the form of a call for a constitutional convention, whenever two-thirds of the members of each of any two of the departments of government

[1] Ch. vi, art. x.
[2] See Constitution of 1783 and of 1792, art. 99 (100).
[3] See Constitution of 1777, art. 63.
[4] Art. iii.
[5] Art. xxxii.
[6] See 1 Poore's *Constitutions*, 257.

should deem it necessary.[1] Madison, however, had little confidence in the value of appeals to the people, no matter how provided. Writing in 1788, after more than a decade of experience with the governments of the original states, he declared that the chief danger of violations of the constitutions was to be apprehended from the legislatures, and that whether the appeals to the people were taken periodically or occasionally, they did not promise adequate relief. A constitutional convention, he argued, would be composed of the same elements as a legislature, and would be inclined to take the same view of constitutional questions. Even if the precaution were taken of excluding from the convention all persons connected with the government whose acts were to be reviewed, the result, he believed, would be substantially the same.[2] "To what expedient, then, shall we finally resort, for maintaining in practice the necessary partition of power among the several departments, as laid down in the constitution?" "The only answer that can be given is, that as all these exterior provisions are found to be inadequate, the defect must be supplied, by so contriving the interior structure of the government as that its several parts may, by their mutual relations, be the means of keeping each other in their proper places . . . the great security against a gradual concentration of the several powers in the same department consists in giving to those who administer each department the necessary constitutional means and personal motives to resist encroachments of the others."[3]

CHECKS AND BALANCES

Thus the principle of the separation of powers becomes the doctrine of checks and balances. As Jefferson himself had said: "The powers of government should be so divided and balanced among several bodies of magistracy, as that no one could transcend their legal limits without being effectually checked and restrained by the others."[4] But during the half dozen years intervening between the time when Jefferson wrote his *Notes on*

[1] See his *Notes on Virginia*, app. ii, reprinted as Appendix B.

[2] *The Federalist*, nos. 49, 50.

[3] *The Federalist*, no. 51.

[4] *Notes on Virginia*, ch. xiii. Cf. J. Q. Adams, in the "Letters of Publicola," no. vii. "Divide your power so that every part of it may at all times be used for your advantage, but in such a manner that your rights may never depend upon the will of one man or body of men. . . ." *Writings of J. Q. Adams* (Ford's ed.), i, p. 93.

Virginia and that when Madison contributed to *The Federalist*, a change was taking place in the significance of the doctrine of checks and balances. As we have seen, not only Jefferson but also those who framed several of the original state constitutions looked to the people, or, strictly speaking, the electorates, as the special guardians of the constitutions. Madison, however, had discovered something in the doctrine itself which rendered superfluous the practice of appealing to the people to correct infractions of the constitutions. That something was the power of judicial review of unconstitutional acts of legislatures and executives.

Original Practice of Legislative Supremacy.

There is no evidence, as we have seen, in the constitution or bill of rights of any one of the original states, that the judiciary were originally looked to by the Fathers as the special guardians of the constitutions. On the contrary, the implication is decidedly the other way. In New York, for instance, the judiciary were certainly expected to accept the construction of the constitution adopted by the council of revision, or in the last instance by the court of errors, a court in which the judicial element was in a minority. In most of the states, moreover, the principle of the separation of powers was either not logically worked out, as it was in New York, or not recognized at all. Thus, in Rhode Island, the supreme court, in the celebrated case of Trevett *v.* Weeden, decided in 1786, refused to enforce a legal tender law devised to compel the circulation of paper money.[1] The legislature, however, being determined to have its will executed, declined to reëlect those judges the following year, and filled their places with others more subservient. Doubtless there were not a few instances of cases decided during the first years of the original state governments in which courts held acts of legislatures unconstitutional.[2] The governments of the original states, however, were for the most part governments characterized by the supremacy of the legislature, and if judicial interference with legislative acts was sometimes tolerated, the operation of the governmental system was not consciously altered thereby. In

[1] See *Cambridge Modern History*, vii, p. 313.

[2] Brinton Coxe, *Judicial Power and Unconstitutional Legislation*. See also C. G. Haines, *The American Doctrine of Judicial Supremacy*, ch. iv.

Massachusetts the declaration of rights laid unusual stress on the importance of the independence of the judiciary.[1] The constitution further provided for the independence of judges by declaring that they should receive fixed and honorable salaries, which should not be diminished during the term of the individual judge. Yet the governor, with the consent of his council, if supported by a bare majority of the legislature, could remove any judge without trial.[2] Moreover, the executive and the legislative branches were authorized to "require the opinions of the justices of the supreme judicial court upon important questions of law and upon solemn occasions."[3] In cases of doubt concerning the true meaning of the constitution, the judiciary could thus be required to express their views before the other branches acted. Doubtless it was intended that the law-making authorities, the legislature and governor, should give due consideration to the opinions of the judges in matters concerning the construction and interpretation of the constitution. But their decision, when made, was expected to be final. It was not intended to leave the last word in constitutional interpretation to the courts. The main reliance of the framers of the Massachusetts constitution for the protection of the rights of the people was placed in the legislature.[4] This was also the case in the beginning throughout the United States.

Development of Doctrine of Judicial Review.

The speedy transfer of this reliance from the legislatures to the courts was, however, inevitable from the very nature of the American political system. Any logical interpretation of the principle of the separation of powers required that each department of government be recognized as the judge of the nature and extent of its own duties and powers. If the legislature, for example, might not only judge of the extent of its own powers, but bind the other departments to accept its opinions on all questions involving a conflict of authority between different departments, the supremacy of the legislature would be absolutely unchecked. In order to maintain even the semblance of a proper balance, no department could be allowed to define the constitutional rights of any other department without giving

[1] Art. xxix.

[2] Ch. iii, art. i.

[3] Ch. iii, art. ii.

[4] See declaration of rights, art. xxii.

that other department an opportunity to be heard. Where departments, however, are theoretically coördinate and equal, that which acts last has a clear advantage over the others. Now, in the ordinary course of government through law, the department which acts last upon questions involving the interpretation of the constitution is the judiciary. The legislature, to be sure, may appeal from a decision of the courts by setting in motion the machinery of constitutional amendment, but if this machinery is hard to move, or if public opinion is opposed to its frequent use, the opinions of the legislature on constitutional questions, though theoretically of equal validity, will actually become subordinate to those of the courts. Unless, therefore, the early state legislatures kept a tight hold on the machinery for the amendment and revision of the constitutions, the judiciary, acting last on disputed questions of constitutional law, would be likely to make their views most effective. That the judiciary would not hesitate to express their views, when at variance with those of the legislature, was quickly made manifest.[1]

The courts were clearly destined to become the special guardians of the constitutions, because the power of judicial review was inherent in the American governmental system. Moreover the Fathers quickly perceived that the principle of the separation of powers was broad enough to include the electorate among the organs of government between which the powers of government were to be shared. It was the *people* who were to be protected against oppression and tyranny, and the tyranny of a majority of the electorate was felt to be as undesirable as any other kind of tyranny. Not the least important of the checks and balances therefore were those which were designed to prevent a casual majority of the voters from changing the established forms of government or principles of legislation without the approval of public opinion. The voters were checked by the necessity of accomplishing their purposes through the other organs of government, and the power of the electorate was balanced by the powers vested in constitutional conventions, legislatures, executives, and judiciary. These powers, as for example in many states the powers of the constitutional convention, were not necessarily contained in the written constitution, but were im-

[1] See C. G. Haines, *The American Doctrine of Judicial Supremacy*, Table of early cases, pp. 74-77.

plied by the nature of the principles, that is, in the very spirit, of American government. Since the sovereignty of the people was to be maintained through the reign of law, it inevitably followed that the judiciary, if made even slightly independent of the other departments of government, would assume the task of preserving inviolate the fundamental principles of American government, as understood by them. In practice this meant that the courts of law would intervene with a judicial veto to protect the rights of minorities against encroachments of the majority acting through the organs of government most directly controlled by the electorate.[1] Thus the function of judicial review came to be associated with the protection of the rights of the people.[2]

This power of review, however, was not final. It was in its turn subject to the sovereign power of the people.[3] Writing in 1820 Jefferson found it necessary to say: [4] "You seem . . . to consider the judges as the ultimate arbiters of all constitutional questions — a very dangerous doctrine indeed, and one which would place us under the despotism of an oligarchy. Our judges are as honest as other men, and not more so. They have, with others, the same passions for party, for power and for the privi-

[1] G. C. Tiedeman, *The Unwritten Constitution of the United States*, ch. xii.

[2] J. B. Thayer, "The Origin and Scope of the American Doctrine of Constitutional Law," in his *Legal Essays*, pp. 1-41. Cf. the same author's *Life of John Marshall*, chs. iii-v. There has been much controversy concerning the exact time when the doctrine of judicial review was recognized by the American people. See A. C. McLaughlin, *The Courts, the Constitution, and Parties*, and the review thereof by C. A. Beard in the *American Historical Review*, January, 1913, pp. 378 f.; see also C. A. Beard, *The Supreme Court and the Constitution*, and J. H. Dougherty, *Power of Federal Judiciary over Legislation*, and the reviews thereof by W. F. Dodd in the same, pp. 380 f. See also Max Farrand, *The Framing of the Constitution of the United States*. But cf. H. A. Davis, "Amendment of Legislation by the Supreme Court" in the *Am. Pol. Sci. Rev.*, vii, pp. 541-587. Cf. also, *ibid.*, "The Judicial Veto." It seems clear that the doctrine grew rapidly in favor among leading Federalist politicians, and although it was not expressly endorsed in the federal Constitutional Convention of 1787, it probably would not have been opposed by the majority of the members. The doctrine was set upon its feet, as a national principle of government, by the federal Supreme Court under John Marshall, and thereupon seems to have been accepted almost unquestioned, not only by the state courts but by the legislatures and people generally. Yet as late as 1808 two judges of the supreme court of Ohio were impeached for declaring an act of the legislature unconstitutional, and were removed from office. See T. M. Cooley, *Constitutional Limitations*, 7th ed., p. 229, note. See also C. G. Haines, *The American Doctrine of Judicial Supremacy*.

[3] See J. Q. Adams, "Letter of Menander" (1792), in *Writings of J. Q. Adams* (Ford's ed.), i, p. 127.

[4] Jefferson's *Writings* (Ford's ed.), vii, p. 177.

lege of their corps. Their maxim is, *Boni judicis est amplicare jurisdictionem:* and their power is the more dangerous as they are in office for life, and not responsible, as the other functionaries, to the elective control. The Constitution has created no such single tribunal, knowing that, to whatever hands confided, with the corruptions of time and party, its members would become despots. It has more wisely made all the departments co-equal and co-sovereign within themselves." There can be no doubt that Jefferson set forth the true doctrine of the case. The judges in ten of the original states (that is, in all except Rhode Island, Connecticut, and Pennsylvania) were arbiters of all constitutional questions, as has been shown, in the sense that they had the same right as the other departments of government to construe the constitution. They possessed the important advantage, moreover, of acting upon constitutional questions as a rule after the other departments of government had acted. But the ultimate arbiters were the people. The real question at stake was that concerning the mode in which the opinion of the people should be ascertained and made effective. As we have seen, several different modes were tried, but, as the event proved, none was satisfactory, and in default of a better solution of the problem, the task of interpreting the constitution was finally permitted to rest with the judiciary during the intervals between constitutional conventions.[1]

Thus the principle of the separation of powers was perfected by the invention, or better the discovery, of the doctrine of judicial review, and the system of checks and balances was made a workable substitute for that of legislative supremacy. The fact remains, however, that in the beginning the latter system rather than the former chiefly prevailed in practice.

Principle of Concurrent Majorities.

There was another aspect of the system of checks and balances, which was not mentioned in any of the original declarations of rights. This was embodied in the principle of concurrent majorities. "Most of the political writers of modern times, who have had any idea of a free government, have contended for a

[1] For a discussion of the original position of the judiciary in Vermont, where the same principles of legislative supremacy prevailed as in Rhode Island, Connecticut, and Pennsylvania, see Chipman's *Sketches of the Principles of Government* (1793), pp. 119-127.

division of the legislative power. They would have, in the legislature, one body of men, representing the commonalty; a senate, representing the wealthy and more honorable part of the community; and the head of the executive, whether king, president, or governor, representing the individuality or sovereignty of the state. These bodies, for the purpose of maintaining an exact balance of the several interests in the state, are to have a mutual negative in passing all laws. The balance is to be supported, and the happiness of the people secured, by a mutual opposition of rights, interests, and powers."[1]

The most outspoken advocate of the principle of concurrent majorities was John Adams.[2] Nor was he alone in favoring the division of the state legislatures into two branches in order that, while the members of the lower house might represent the poorer voters, the control of the upper house should rest with the rich. In the original state constitutions, the balance of the rights of property against the rights of mere man was the general rule. The most extreme instance was in South Carolina, where by the constitution of 1778 senators were required to possess two thousand pounds in land, representatives, fifty acres of land or their equivalent. In North Carolina the constitution of 1776 granted the franchise for electors of members of the lower house to all tax-payers,[3] and restricted the right to vote for members of the senate to owners of not less than fifty acres.[4] In New York the electorate for the upper house was restricted by a much higher property qualification than that of ordinary electors, the senatorial and gubernatorial electors being less than one-fourth as numerous as the latter. In Massachusetts the arrangement in the rejected constitution of 1778 was much like that in North Carolina. In the constitution of 1780 the same effect was sought through a different system of apportionment. The franchise was the same for electors of senators and representatives, but the members of the upper house were apportioned according to taxable property, those of the lower according to population. The same plan was adopted and is still used in New Hampshire. In

[1] See Chipman's *Sketches of the Principles of Government*, sketch iv. sec. iii.

[2] See the Preface to his *Defence of the Constitutions of Government of the United States of America*, especially at p. xiii. See also C. M. Walsh, *The Political Science of John Adams*.

[3] Arts. viii, ix.

[4] Art. vii.

Virginia and several other states, qualifications of electors and methods of apportionment of members were the same for both houses, the chief difference being the smaller size of the upper house and in some cases the longer term of its members. Jefferson criticized this arrangement on the ground that the maintenance of two houses, both representing the same electorate, served no useful purpose, and declared that if the electorate for the lower house could not be made more popular than that for the upper, one of the houses would be superfluous and should be dispensed with altogether.[1] In Pennsylvania, Georgia, and Vermont the latter view prevailed, and the legislatures of the original state governments consisted of only one house. Man alone was represented.

The principle of concurrent majorities and the corresponding system of checks and balances within the state legislatures were, indeed, far from obtaining universal acceptance. The framers of the Pennsylvania constitution of 1776, of whom Franklin was the chief, certainly did not accept it.[2] Jefferson also must be classed among its opponents. It is true that in his plan of a constitution for Virginia, drafted in 1783, he proposed a senate consisting of one-sixth as many members as the lower house and serving for two years instead of one, and to be chosen by colleges of electors representing the voters of the several senatorial districts, as was actually the practice at that time in Maryland. Jefferson's purpose, however, in creating a senate was not to give separate representation to different economic interests and social classes, but to provide for greater deliberation in the enactment of laws. As Paine pointed out: "The objection against a single house is, that it is always in a condition of committing itself too soon." [3] On the other hand, democrats like Paine saw even more serious objections to two houses, and on the whole were inclined to reject the principle of a bicameral legislature. Paine himself advocated a legislature of a single chamber, and the adoption of a system of legislative procedure, designed to encourage the development of responsible legislative committees, as a substitute for a second house.[4] Other early democrats, like Chipman, favored the retention of the bicameral system, but expressly

[1] *Notes on Virginia*, ch. xii.
[2] Adams, *Defence* (London ed. of 1787), letter xxv, pp. 105-120.
[3] *The Rights of Man*, pt. ii, p. 34.
[4] *Ibid.*, p. 35.

repudiated Adams's doctrine of the separate representation of class interests.[1] Adams's theory of class representation, a theory which savors of Polybius and of Machiavelli[2] as much as of Montesquieu, eventually gained for him the distrust of the Jeffersonian republicans and the nickname of "monocrat." Though it was probably held by most of those who later formed the Federalist party, it was never accepted by the American people to the same extent as the more democratic version of the separation of powers held by Jefferson and Madison. Though the practice of a separate representation of different social and economic interests survived into the nineteenth century in several states, it was not further extended in any state except South Carolina,[3] and it was not systematically defended by any prominent statesman except Calhoun.[4] In short, beyond the recognition of the principle that political authority should be delegated to a responsible portion of the people to be exercised on behalf of the whole, the attempt to introduce class distinctions into the American political system was out of harmony with the spirit of American life.

[1] See his *Sketches of the Principles of Government*, pp. 140-142.

[2] Adams quotes with great approval the following passage from Machiavelli's *Discourse upon the Proper Ways and Means of Reforming the Government of Florence.* "There are three orders of men in every state, and for that reason there should be also three ranks or degrees in a republic, and no more; nor can that be said to be a true and durable commonwealth, where certain humors and inclinations are not gratified, which otherwise must naturally end in its ruin. Those who model a commonwealth must take such provisions as may gratify three sorts of men, of which all states are composed; that is, the high, the middle sort, and the low."

Adams's comment is as follows: "Machiavel by these observations demonstrates that he was fully convinced of this great truth, this eternal principle, without the knowledge of which every speculation upon government must be imperfect, and every scheme of a commonwealth essentially defective."—John Adams, *Defence of the Constitutions of Government of the United States*, ii, ch. iv, "Machiavel's Plan of a Perfect Commonwealth."

In accordance with this principle, Adams in Massachusetts, as also Jay in New York, devised the governorship to represent the higher sort of men, the senate to represent the middle sort, and the house of representatives to represent the lower. Hamilton would have been content to have followed the precepts of Montesquieu literally, and established a government of kings, lords, and commons, but Adams certainly would not have gone so far as that. Needless to say that the opinion of the people of the Revolution was against both Adams and Hamilton and with Jefferson, who repudiated altogether the doctrine of Montesquieu with reference to the separate representation of different social classes. Cf. C. M. Walsh, *The Political Science of John Adams*, chs. 6, 7, and 21.

[3] Constitution of 1790, amendments adopted in 1808.

[4] See John C. Calhoun, *Disquisition on Government and Discourse on the Constitution and Government of the United States*, pp. 396-406.

GENERAL CHARACTER OF ORIGINAL STATE GOVERNMENTS

The true character of the original institutions of state government is revealed by a comparison with the institutions of colonial government which had gone before. At the close of the colonial period, each colony had its legislative body, elected by the voters, but, except in Rhode Island and Connecticut, possessing practically no independent powers. The representatives of the people could choose a speaker, adopt rules of procedure, and adjourn, but there their autonomous powers ended. In all the colonies except Pennsylvania and Georgia there was also an upper house or council, whose consent was necessary before laws could be enacted or any positive action accomplished. The members of this branch of the legislature were appointed by the governor, except in Massachusetts, where they were elected by the lower house subject to the approval of the governor, and in Rhode Island and Connecticut, where they were chosen by the electorate. In all the colonies except the last two, the governor was appointed from England, and possessed many important powers. He was commander-in-chief of the armed forces of the colony, appointed the judges and all other civil and military officers, appointed and could suspend the council, convened and could dissolve the legislature, could exercise an unqualified veto on all legislative acts, and had an unrestricted power to pardon offenders.

The possession of these unlimited powers gave to the royal or proprietary governor complete independence of local control except in the single matter of finance.[1] The use of the judicial veto to maintain imperial sovereignty was unnecessary except in Rhode Island and Connecticut. In those two colonies, appeals to the judicial committee of the privy council could be taken for the purpose of maintaining the supremacy of the laws of England, in case of a conflict with colonial laws, but not for the purpose of enforcing the arbitrary will of the British sovereign. Elsewhere the power of the lower house to withhold its consent to taxation was the sole political power for the defense of the rights of the colonists.

Thus the legislatures came to be the people's bulwarks against royal and proprietary tyranny, and after the Revolution naturally

[1] See E. B. Greene, *The Provincial Governor.*

retained an undue share of the people's confidence. The result was, that except in Massachusetts, New Hampshire, and New York the doctrine of the separation of powers was not followed to the extent of making the three departments of government actually independent and coördinate. On the contrary, the executive was either deprived altogether of its powers of appointment, revision, pardon, and legislative control, or greatly limited in their exercise, and the independence of the judiciary was also compromised by the pretensions of the legislatures. The reconstruction of the political institutions of the original states was in the main the achievement of a tidal wave of insurgency, which sought expression through the state legislatures. The effect was to establish in practice the supremacy of the legislature, except in Pennsylvania and Vermont, where an attempt was made to work out the theory of popular sovereignty through the invention of a special organ of the popular will, the council of censors. But the legal supremacy of the legislatures was always subordinate to the political sovereignty of the people, and, as we have seen, it was necessarily expressed through the enactment of law depending for its ultimate force upon the power of public opinion.

The original state governments were representative democracies. They were founded upon written constitutions, setting forth both the rights of the people and the duties of those entrusted by them with political authority. These constitutions were not intended, however, to be narrowly construed like ordinary legal documents. They were political documents to be construed broadly, and to reflect the lives and purposes of all the people at all times. The main features of the governments established in the original states were three in number: (1) the reservation of civil rights to the people; (2) the delegation of political authority to the electorate; and (3) the distribution of powers between the legislative, the executive, and the judiciary. The rights reserved to the people fell into three main classes: (1) the right of revolution; (2) the rights essential to the free expression of public opinion; and (3) the right to law. The delegation of political authority to the electorate implied the existence of a fourth right, the right to vote, vested in those duly qualified for the exercise thereof. The distribution of powers between coördinate departments of government was designed to make possible the establishment of governments which should be strong enough effectively to foster the common welfare without being so independent of popular control as to menace the liberties of the people. The acceptance of the principle of the separation of powers compelled the recognition of the power of judicial review of all legislative and executive acts involving the interpretation of a constitution. The judiciary thereby became the special guardians of the fundamental law, subject like other departments of government to the sanction of public opinion.

The Unwritten Constitution.

It is commonly supposed that all the leading principles of the fundamental law of the land were expressed in written constitutions. An examination of the original constitutions shows that this supposition is not correct. The most important of the fundamental principles of American constitutional law relate to the organization and powers of the constitutional convention. The procedure of the original states, however, with regard to the preparation and adoption of the first state constitutions was far from uniform. The best procedure was not developed until the adoption of the Massachusetts constitution of 1780, the last of the original state constitutions. Only five of the original states, including Vermont, made any provision for constitutional revision by special conventions. Three others made provision for amendment by special legislative action. Six states made no express formal distinction between the process of ordinary statute-making and that of constitution-making. In short, there was nothing in the constitutions or laws of most of the states to prevent a revolutionary legislature or convention from usurping unto itself all the powers of government, like the French Convention of 1792–95. Yet we are safe in asserting that such a usurpation could not have been effected. The unwritten law of the constitution forbade the establishment on American soil of any such tyrannical body as the French Convention.

But what, it is proper to ask, is the sanction by which obedience to the unwritten constitution is ultimately enforced? It is not enough to answer that usurpation would not have been tolerated by an indignant people, and that, if the force of public opinion proved insufficient, it would have been opposed by force of arms. The true answer is, that obedience to the unwritten as well as to the written constitution is enforced by the power of the law itself, for the breach of the fundamental principles of American government, the principles of popular sovereignty and the reign of law, will inevitably bring the offender into conflict with the law of the land.[1] The declaration that "no subject shall be arrested . . . or deprived of his life, liberty, or estate, but by the judgment of his peers or the law of the land" was not intended to be an empty phrase.[2] For protection against all but the most violent attacks upon their liberties, the people would look to the law courts. If the judges failed them, there remained the juries, composed of men from their own midst, to interpose a popular veto to schemes of oppression. Any man who had been indicted for a crime might submit his cause to the judgment of the petty jury with confidence that his fate would be decided by those who were his peers and who would be responsible only to their own consciences.

De Tocqueville, who well understood the spirit of the original judicial system, justly observed that the jury was preëminently a political institution and should be regarded as one form of the sovereignty of the people.[3] "The institution of the jury . . .," he wrote, "places the real direction of society in the hands of the governed, . . . and not in that of the government. Force is never more than a transient element of success, and after force

[1] See Kamper *v.* Hawkins, 1 Virginia Cases, 20 (1793). This was a case involving the validity of a statute designed to confer upon certain inferior courts of justice certain judicial powers in equity granted by the constitution of 1776 exclusively to the court of chancery. Contrary to the views of those who, like Jefferson, believed that the constitution of 1776 had no more force than an ordinary statute and hence could be freely altered at any time by the legislature, the supreme court held that ordinary statutes in conflict with the constitution were of no effect. See also G. C. Tiedeman, *The Unwritten Constitution of the United States*, ch. xii, and A. V. Dicey, *Introduction to the Study of the Law of the Constitution*, ch. xv. There are of course many political customs in the American states of much consequence in practical politics which cannot be ranked among the principles of the unwritten constitution. Thus the practice of rotation in office or of restricting the choice of representatives to inhabitants of the district to be represented is more or less strongly established by custom in different localities, but neither is essential to the maintenance of the sovereignty of the people or of the reign of law. Only those practices which are essential to the maintenance of these two fundamental principles are a part of the unwritten constitution. Other legal principles may not become a part of the supreme law of the land except by incorporation in a written constitution, and, until so incorporated, have no greater force than that infused into them by public opinion.

[2] See Massachusetts Declaration of Rights, art. xii.

[3] A. de Tocqueville, *Democracy in America*, i, ch. xvi.

comes the notion of right. A government which should be able to reach its enemies only upon a field of battle would soon be destroyed. The true sanction of political laws is to be found in penal legislation; and if that sanction be wanting, the law will sooner or later lose its cogency. He who punishes the criminal is therefore the real master of society. Now the institution of the jury raises the people itself . . . to the bench of judges. The institution of the jury consequently invests the people . . . with the direction of society."[1] Thus was republican government founded by the Fathers on the firm basis of a combination of the sovereignty of the people and the reign of law.[2]

[1] De Tocqueville, *ibid.* (Bowen's ed.), i, p. 361.
[2] St. George Tucker, *Commentaries on Blackstone,* i, pp. 87-92.

CHAPTER IV

THE REFORMATION OF STATE GOVERNMENT

The foundations of state government were laid upon principles that have endured. The twin principles of popular sovereignty and constitutional government furnished a base broad and solid enough to support a stable and progressive political system. The superstructure, however, has undergone important modifications.

In the beginning, as has been shown, there were three distinct types of state government. These types are best represented by the governments originally established in the three leading states, Virginia, Pennsylvania, and Massachusetts. The government of Virginia, to which the governments of the greater number of states more or less closely conformed, was characterized by the restriction of the electoral franchise to those deemed "fit," and by the supremacy of the legislature in the actual conduct of affairs of state. The government of Pennsylvania differed from that of Virginia in various respects, two of which were particularly important. The electorate was much broader than that of Virginia, and the authority of the legislature was limited by the creation of a special organ of the popular will, the council of censors. The government of Vermont resembled that of Pennsylvania in these respects. The government of Georgia was characterized by the supremacy of the legislature, as in Virginia, but the legislature was a unicameral body and there was a comparatively broad electorate, as in Pennsylvania. The government of Massachusetts, like that of Pennsylvania, differed from that of Virginia in two important respects. The executive and judiciary were much more independent of the legislature than in Virginia, and the authority of the legislature was limited by the grant of special powers to the executive and judiciary. The government of New Hampshire closely resembled that of Massachusetts; that of New York was based on similar principles, but resembled it less closely. In Rhode Island and Connecticut the governor was chosen by the people, as in Massachusetts, but the legislature was practically supreme, as in Virginia. Such was the diversity in the forms of government in the original states.

THE BEGINNING OF REFORM

It was impossible that such wide variations in the political institutions of the states should long endure. In practice it would happen that some of them would work better than others, and those that seemed to work best would naturally become models for general imitation. Moreover, theoretically, if the political theory of the Revolution be taken as a guide, some of these forms of government were certainly much less perfect than others. Jefferson, the most popular interpreter of Revolutionary political theory, was not altogether satisfied with any of them. In 1783, when he thought there was to be a constitutional convention in Virginia for the purpose of revising the original form of government, he drafted a model constitution in which his ideas are clearly set forth.[1] Although Jefferson's plan was never adopted in any state, it is now of greater interest than any of the original plans of government which were actually put into operation, for it is the most perfect expression of the Revolutionary theories of state government. It is evident that he was greatly dissatisfied with the existing constitution of his own state. The changes which he proposed are numerous. They all, however, fall under one or the other of two heads. First, there are those which were intended to broaden the electorate and strengthen its control over the other organs of government and over the constitution itself. Secondly, there are those which were intended to bring about a more effective distribution of powers. The constitutional history of the states since Jefferson's time is a history of the triumph of Jeffersonian principles and of the consequences of that triumph.

The constitutions of Georgia and Pennsylvania were the first to be reformed. Doubtless the adoption of an effective system of checks and balances in the Federal Constitution of 1787 accelerated the process in all states where the original distribution of powers was defective. But in those two states the change was brought about earlier than elsewhere by the manifestly un-

[1] See Appendix B.

satisfactory working of their original institutions. In Georgia the only check upon the supremacy of the single-chambered legislature under the constitution of 1777 was that afforded by the direct action of the people through the juries and through the system of constitutional amendment. The juries were the judges both of the law and of the facts, and no alterations could be made in the constitution except by a constitutional convention, which the legislature was to call together upon receipt of a petition setting forth the desired amendments and signed by a majority of the voters in a majority of the counties. The latter provision proved to be unworkable and the former inadequate. In 1789 the original constitution was abandoned, and a new one adopted without regard to the prescribed method of constitutional amendment. A bicameral legislature was created, the executive council was abolished and its duties for the most part transferred to the newly created senate, and the governor, though still dependent on the legislature for his election, was armed with the veto power. The influence of the Federal Constitution is apparent. Thus the original system of legislative supremacy gave way to a form of government somewhat more consistent with Jeffersonian principles.

Reform of the Censorial System.

The most original feature of the Pennsylvania constitution of 1776 was the council of censors. The purpose of this institution was to preserve the constitution against infraction. This was to be accomplished, as has already been pointed out, partly by protecting the several departments from encroachments upon one another's powers, but especially by protecting the people from encroachments upon their reserved rights by any of the departments. To accomplish these purposes, the council of censors was authorized to suggest to the legislature the repeal of unconstitutional legislation, or the enactment of legislation required for the proper performance of constitutional duties, and to censure public officers deemed guilty of misbehavior. It could order impeachments, and, in case of need, call a convention to consider the amendment of the constitution. The council of censors was free to exercise any or all of those various powers at discretion, and there was no means of holding it responsible for a discreet exercise thereof. The operations of the first council, elected in 1783, demonstrated the unwisdom of such a combination of legislative, executive, and judicial functions in a single irresponsible body. Madison has faithfully recorded the results of that experience.[1] The members of the council were for the most part persons who had been active in the affairs of the government the conduct of which they were authorized to review. As might be expected, they brought to their new duties a thoroughly partisan spirit. "Throughout the continuance of the council, it was split into two fixed and violent parties." This was the first cause of the failure of the censorial system. Secondly, the council itself was quite as liable to err in its interpretation of the constitution as the avowedly partisan bodies upon which it professed to sit in judgment. Finally, says Madison, "I have never understood that the decisions of the council on constitutional questions, whether rightly or erroneously formed, have had any effect" in varying the practices which it undertook to censure.

In 1790, when the election of the second council of censors was in order, the legislature, with the approval of public opinion, but without any express constitutional authority, called a constitutional convention instead. This convention adopted a new constitution, providing for the abolition of the council of censors and of the original executive council. It substituted therefor a state senate to serve as a check on the house of representatives, a single chief executive elected directly by the people, armed with the veto power and unhampered by special executive councillors, and an independent judiciary. Indeed most of the principal features of the Massachusetts constitution were adopted, with the exception that the senate, instead of a special executive council, was associated with the governor in the making of executive appointments. At the same time the electorate remained more democratic than in Massachusetts. Probably Jefferson would have pronounced the Pennsylvania constitution of 1790 the most satisfactory then in force in the states.

The censorial system endured for a much longer period in Vermont. In that state censors were elected from the state at large, and not by districts as in Pennsylvania, and members of the government were ineligible. The system seems to have worked much better in Vermont than in Pennsylvania, partly

[1] *The Federalist* (Ford's ed.), no. 50.

no doubt because party lines were less closely drawn in the former state than in the latter, and partly because the system of election made the council a more homogeneous and responsible body. The Vermont council of censors met altogether thirteen times. Thrice it adjourned without proposing any changes in the constitution of the state. Ten times it proposed amendments and called a convention to consider their adoption. Twice the proposed amendments were adopted in part, four times they were adopted in their entirety, and four times they were rejected. In 1836 the transformation of the executive council into a state senate terminated the unicameral legislative system, and in 1870 the adoption of the censors' proposal that no more councils of censors be elected put an end to the censorial system. With the abolition of the Vermont council of censors there disappeared the last vestiges of the peculiar Pennsylvania form of state government.[1]

The failure of the censorial system did not mean that there was no need of any special arrangement to preserve the constitution inviolate. In Pennsylvania, according to Madison's report, the constitution had been violated many times before the election of the first council of censors.[2] Laws had been passed without the due public notice required by the constitution. Legislative powers had been exercised by the legislature which were not granted to it by the constitution. Executive powers also had been usurped. Salaries of judges had been reduced in order to render them more subservient, and lawsuits which should have been decided by the judiciary had frequently been decided by the legislature. It is true that many of these violations had occurred during the period of active military operations, but it is equally true that the record of the Pennsylvania government was besmirched with much unconstitutional conduct that was inexcusable.

The censorial system, and with it the Pennsylvania form of government as a whole, failed because it did not satisfy the requirements of American democracy. The Pennsylvania form was intended to be democratic. Actually the procedure for the revision of the constitution under the censorial system was less

[1] L. H. Meader, "The Council of Censors," in *Papers from Historical Seminary of Brown University* (1899).

[2] *The Federalist* (Ford's ed.), no. 48.

democratic than that originally adopted in Massachusetts, since the council of censors stood between the people and the constitutional convention. The council of censors was intended to safeguard the constitutional distribution of powers. Actually it violated the principle of the separation of powers by concentrating in its own hands arbitrary and yet ineffective powers of all kinds. Regarded as a legislative body, it was impotent except to call a constitutional convention. As an instrument of economy and efficiency in the executive department, it was useless. In the exercise of its judicial powers, it was partisan and pernicious. In short, down to 1790 the censorial system in Pennsylvania had been in practice a system of unchecked legislative supremacy.

General Character of Constitutional Reform.

The revision of the original Georgia and Pennsylvania constitutions marked the beginning of a general process of constitutional development, characterized by the gradual democratization of the forms of government and the redistribution of powers along the lines demanded by the Jeffersonian political theory. The new states, as they came into the Union, quickly showed the influence of Jeffersonian ideas. The older states in some cases were slower to abandon their original aristocratic prejudices and to discard the system of legislative supremacy. The extraordinary success of the "more perfect union" certainly had much to do with the general adoption of more effective arrangements for the distribution of powers, but, as will be shown more clearly in the next chapter, the logic of events favored the system of checks and balances. The explanation of the progress of democracy in the government of the states must be sought in the economic and social conditions of American life. The dominant fact in the life of the American people during the century following the Revolution was the subjugation of the wilderness. The tone of American society was derived from the tone of society on the frontier. But the winning of the west not only opened up vast stores of material wealth for the American people, it also enriched their moral fiber. It stimulated above all the virtues of self-reliance and personal initiative. Every man who was able and willing to toil could be the master of his destiny. The resulting popular self-confidence was the dominant fact in the development of the political institutions of the states. The political fruit, so to speak, of the frontier was manhood suffrage and the general democratization of the forms of state government.

REFORM OF THE ELECTORAL FRANCHISE

The right of suffrage is conferred by the state and is usually prescribed and defined in the state constitution, subject to the provisions of the Federal Constitution that the right of citizens to vote shall not be denied or abridged on account of race, color, previous condition of servitude, or sex. These clauses of the Federal Constitution seems to imply that the suffrage is one of the normal rights of citizenship, but the states have not generally recognized it as such. In the beginning, as has been shown, the original states conferred the suffrage on grounds of political expediency, jealously withholding it from those deemed incapable of exercising the franchise to the common advantage. This attitude was quaintly expressed in the constitution of Vermont (1777), which stipulated that every freeman might vote "who has a sufficient interest in the community." The evidence of sufficient interest chiefly required in the original states was the possession of a certain amount of property. Jefferson, writing shortly after the Revolution, declared that these requirements were too severe, pointing out that in Virginia they disfranchised the majority of the able-bodied men in the state. Thus dissatisfaction with the qualifications for the suffrage existed at the very beginning of the constitutional history of the states, and dissatisfaction of one sort or another has persisted until the present.

Manhood Suffrage.

There have been two conflicting tendencies in the development of the qualifications for the suffrage. On the one hand, the belief in the natural nobility of man, or in equal rights, as the phrase ran, leads easily to the conviction that the right to vote should be included among those to which men are by nature entitled. If all men are "equal," particularly if they have an equal right to the pursuit of happiness, and if the electoral franchise is an important means of engaging in such a pursuit, then all men should have an equal right to vote. The theory of natural rights was supported by more practical considerations, such as the injustice of withholding the vote from landless and even moneyless artisans and craftsmen who nevertheless help support the government by the payment of taxes, directly or indirectly, and defend it by bearing arms. These considerations were reënforced by the conditions of life in most parts of the Union, especially upon the Western frontier. Social democracy on the frontier inevitably gave rise to political democracy, and the same result was facilitated in the older parts of the Union by the competition of parties for popular support. Before the close of the eighteenth century Vermont, Kentucky, and Tennessee came into the Union with the principle of manhood suffrage practically established, if not explicitly recognized, in their constitutions. The states of the old Northwest and Southwest, entering the Union early in the nineteenth century, often included in their electorates not only all adult white male citizens, native and naturalized, but also aliens, even those who had not declared their intention to become naturalized. The original states were slower to adopt the principle of manhood suffrage, and less inclined to grant the franchise to foreign-born males who had not been admitted to citizenship. However, as early as 1809, Maryland abolished all tax and property qualifications and established manhood suffrage for white male citizens. But in New York and Virginia, for example, a similar broadening of the franchise was not fully realized until 1826 and 1850, respectively. Rhode Island was the only state in which resistance to the extension of the suffrage led to violence. There, after the suppression of Dorr's rebellion, the new constitution of 1842 put an end to property qualifications in the election of state officers. With the triumph of the advocates of equal suffrage for adult male citizens of the white race the principle of manhood suffrage, so-called, was regarded as established in the American states.

The Enfranchisement of the Negro.

The negro was not brought within the scope of the principle of manhood suffrage without a more serious struggle. Originally, duly qualified negroes were permitted to vote in seven of the thirteen states, Connecticut, Massachusetts, New Hampshire, New York, New Jersey, North Carolina, and Rhode Island. Subsequently New York, when abolishing the property qualifications for the franchise, provided that the new qualifications should apply to the white race only, leaving the property qualifications in effect for negroes, while Connecticut (1814), North

Carolina (1835), and New Jersey (1844) deprived free negroes of their votes altogether. Rhode Island disfranchised the negroes in 1822 but, after Dorr's rebellion, restored the suffrage to them in 1842.[1] The only new states which granted the franchise in any form to negroes were Vermont, Kentucky, Tennessee, and Maine, and two of these presently took the vote away again.[2] None of the old states except Rhode Island extended the vote to the negro until after the close of the Civil War. Indeed there was no demand for negro suffrage, and manhood suffrage became universally restricted to whites, outside of New England. In 1867, after the issue of negro suffrage had been raised in connection with the reconstruction of the southern states, the people of Minnesota refused by a close vote to strike the word "white" from the article of the constitution relating to the suffrage, and in the following year the people of New York refused to remove the property qualifications from colored voters. The word "white" still remains in the constitutions of three states, Kansas, Maryland, and Oregon, a relic of the ante-bellum discrimination against the negro with respect to the suffrage. In 1870, however, equal suffrage for negroes was established throughout the United States by the adoption of the fifteenth amendment to the Federal Constitution.

Reaction Against Manhood Suffrage.

Despite the extension of the franchise to negroes, the principle of manhood suffrage has never completely triumphed in the United States. It did not triumph in 1870, as is shown not only by the debate in Congress at the time of the submission of the fifteenth amendment to the states, but also by the wording of the amendment itself. There has always been another principle tending to produce the exclusion of certain classes from the franchise. This is the principle of fitness. It is argued that the electoral franchise is not one of the natural rights asserted by the Fathers, but that on the contrary, as has been shown, it was originally conceived as a privilege to be conferred only on those capable of putting it to good use. The vote was intended to be used, not primarily or mainly to foster the interests of the

[1] J. T. Adams, "Disfranchisement of Negroes in New England," *American Historical Review*, xxx, pp. 543-547 (1925).

[2] Kentucky in 1799, Tennessee in 1834.

particular class entrusted therewith, but to protect the rights and promote the welfare of the whole people. No person therefore may claim a "right" to vote, unless he can show that his claim is founded upon considerations pertaining to the general welfare rather than to his own private advantage. The test of fitness for the suffrage, it is urged, is the ability of the individual to voice public opinion, or some shade of opinion needful to bring the opinion of the electorate into harmony with public opinion, rather than a merely personal or private opinion. In the practice of the American states, to be sure, the adult male came to be generally deemed the fittest person to represent the interests of other classes of the people and to voice the opinion of the people as a whole, but this rule of policy, it is contended by the opponents of the doctrine of the natural right to vote, should not be twisted into a principle of universal and indiscriminate application, regardless of the different degrees of fitness possessed by the different classes of adult males.

The Disfranchisement of the Negro.

The chief cause of difficulty in the application of the doctrine of manhood suffrage has been the negro, and the purpose of the white man, particularly in the South, to exclude the colored man from a voice in government has been expressed in the doctrine of the superior fitness of the white race. Negro suffrage was imposed upon eleven states of the South by the reconstruction act of March 3, 1867, and was maintained there with ever-diminishing effectiveness by force of arms. By the time of the final withdrawal of the federal troops from the southern states in 1877, negro suffrage, where it threatened the political supremacy of the white race, had geen generally suppressed by moral suasion, fraud, intimidation, or violence. These methods, however, were unsatisfactory. Beginning in Mississippi in 1890, the white people of the South have adopted the policy of disfranchising the negroes by means of constitutional restrictions upon the suffrage, nominally applying to all citizens alike, but actually discriminating against the negro.

In Mississippi the method was as follows. The requirement of residence was raised to two years in the state and one in the election district; disqualification for crime was extended to the following offenses,—bribery, burglary, theft, arson, obtaining money or goods under false pretenses, perjury, forgery, embezzlement, and bigamy; the payment of all taxes was made a prerequisite to the vote, and a uniform poll-tax of two dollars was established, with the proviso that the board of supervisors of any county might increase it to three dollars and that no criminal proceedings to enforce payment should be allowed.[1] In addition the prospective voter is required to be able to read any section of the constitution or give a reasonable explanation of the same when read to him, and in general to possess a satisfactory understanding of the duties of citizenship. Since the judges of the reasonableness of the required explanations and of the satisfactoriness of the understanding are the white election officers, even the negro who fulfills all the other requirements for the suffrage cannot hope to qualify against the wishes of the whites.

The chief difficulty in the elimination of the negro vote has been to disfranchise the negro without at the same time either disfranchising whites or violating the provision of the fifteenth amendment of the Federal Constitution forbidding racial discrimination. In Mississippi this is evidently intended to be accomplished by avoiding discrimination in the letter of the law and seeking it in the enforcement. Other southern states have sought to escape the dangers of that policy by the use of "old soldier" and "grandfather" clauses. Thus, in Alabama by the constitution of 1901 it was provided that after January 1, 1903,

[1] This policy is frankly explained in the following passage from a recent opinion of the Attorney-General of Mississippi:—"The ostensible purpose in framing this section of the constitution (*i.e.*, sect. 241, relating to the suffrage) was to disfranchise as many negroes as possible, and the injunctions delivered by the section, when well unravelled, make it apparent that the negro as a race would come more clearly within its requirements than any other. In the first place the negro is known in our midst as a nomadic tribe, and as a rule on account of their shiftlessness none of them will hardly reside in an election precinct more than a year, but drift from plantation to plantation and landlord to landlord; and in that way very few, if any, on account of residence as required by this section are qualified voters. Very few, if any, in Mississippi have any taxes except a poll, and with no thought of government and in many instances with no disposition as well as inability to pay this tax, they are as a rule delinquents and are for that reason disqualified. The crimes of burglary, bribery, theft, arson, obtaining money or goods under false pretences, perjury, forgery, embezzlement, or bigamy, I might say are indigenous to the negro's nature . . . and in that way thus so many more are deprived of exercising the right of franchise." (Opinion of Attorney-General S. S. Hudson on what constitutes qualified elector, published by the State Board of Election Commissioners, Jackson, Miss., n. d.)

only those persons may register as voters who can either (1) read and write any article of the Constitution of the United States in English, and who are physically unable to work or who have worked or been regularly engaged in some lawful employment for the greater part of the twelve months next preceding; or else (2) prove title to forty acres of land upon which they reside, or to real estate or personal property assessed at a valuation of not less than $300, upon which all taxes have been paid. But up to December 20, 1902, persons who served in the United States army in the Mexican, Indian, or Spanish wars, or in either the Union or Confederate army in the Civil War, the lawful descendants of such persons, and "all persons of good character who understand the duties and obligations of citizenship under a republican form of government," were entitled to register as voters and to remain on the list of registered voters to the end of their lives, whether able or not to qualify under the educational or property tests. Another example of the so-called "grandfather" clause is contained in the constitution of North Carolina, which provides, by an amendment adopted in 1900, that no person who on January 1, 1867,[1] or prior thereto, was entitled to vote under the laws of any state of the Union wherein he then resided, and no lineal descendant of such person, shall be denied the right to register and vote by reason of failure to possess the required educational qualification, provided that he register prior to December 1, 1908. In Oklahoma, by an amendment of 1910, the "grandfather" clause was adopted in the most extreme form. No person may vote unless able to read and write any section of the state constitution, "but no person who was on January 1, 1866, or any time prior thereto, entitled to vote under any form of government, or who at that time resided in some foreign nation, and no lineal descendant of such person, shall be denied the right to vote because of his inability to so read and write." With the exception of Oklahoma, the various "old soldier" and "grandfather" clauses were temporary and were designed to be enforced only for a limited time,—long enough, however, to allow the otherwise ineligible whites to be enrolled as life voters. The Oklahoma clause was intended to

[1] The congressional reconstruction acts, conferring the franchise upon the negroes, were not adopted until March 3, 1867. See, for fuller information on the development of the electoral franchise, Kirk H. Porter, *A History of Suffrage in the United States* (Chicago, 1919).

be permanent and would have extended its protection for all time to illiterates of every description except negroes, but on the other hand would not have discriminated against literate negroes. However, in 1915, it was declared unconstitutional by the Supreme Court of the United States because in conflict with the fifteenth amendment of the Federal Constitution.[1]

Discrimination Against the Alien.

Another cause of difficulty in the application of the doctrine of manhood suffrage has been the immigrant. When in the late forties the Irish and Germans first began coming in large numbers, the native Americans were prone to regard them as of inferior fitness for the work of operating American political institutions. The short-lived American party was founded upon this assumption, and had for its object the discouragement of immigration by means of legal restrictions against aliens. This party succeeded in Massachusetts in securing the adoption in 1857 of an educational qualification for the suffrage intended to exclude the illiterate immigrants from the electorate. Similar restrictions upon the "right to vote" have since been adopted for the same purpose in other states. Including the southern states where negro disfranchisement is the chief object, about one-half of the states now authorize a literacy test, either as an absolute or as an alternate qualification.[2] On the other hand, many of the newer states in the West and South originally encouraged alien immigrants to settle within their borders by offering them the franchise as soon as they should declare their intention of becoming naturalized. In 1894, fifteen states thus permitted unnaturalized aliens to vote but to-day, as a result of the passing of the "melting pot" idea, the World War, and the recrudescence of Native Americanism in the form of the

[1] Guinn v. United States, 238 U. S. 347; see also Myers v. Anderson, 238 U. S. 368. The question still remained unsettled, whether negroes who were entitled to vote at public elections under the federal and state constitutions could be excluded by law from primary elections. In Texas, for example, where a nomination in the Democratic primaries is ordinarily equivalent to election, a law passed in 1923 restricts the Democratic primaries to white voters only. The constitutionality of this law has been challenged in a case now pending before the Supreme Court of the United States.

[2] The list of such states is given in F. G. Crawford, ""The New York State Literacy Test," *American Political Science Review*, xvii, pp. 260-263 (1923). Oregon is the latest state to adopt a literacy qualification for the suffrage (1924).

Ku Klux Klan and in other ways, Arkansas is the only state where non-citizens may vote.[1] On the Pacific coast the antipathy against immigrants of the yellow race caused their complete exclusion from citizenship. The native-born members of the yellow race, however, may obtain the vote on the same terms as other Americans.

Woman Suffrage.

The modern demand for equal suffrage for women is founded both on the principle of natural rights and on that of fitness. The natural right of women to the ballot is deduced from the fundamental principles of American government. The doctrine of the natural nobility of man is construed to be broad enough to include women. Equal rights for all, it is argued, means for all women as well as for all men. The American states have gone far in giving to women the same civil rights as men, and the demand for political equality is but the logical conclusion of the movement towards full civil equality. As in the case of the demand for manhood suffrage a century ago, the doctrine of equal rights is supported by some more practical considerations, such as the injustice of withholding the franchise from women, who nevertheless help support the government by paying taxes, some directly, others indirectly, and defend it by bearing their share of the burdens of war. These considerations are reënforced by the development of women's work outside the home and the growth of a class of wage-earning women whose interests are felt to need the protection afforded in the case of wage-earning men by the possession of the ballot. The principle of fitness as the test of eligibility to the suffrage may be appealed to with equal justification by the advocates of votes for women. The general education of women on the whole is as good as that of men, and the experience of life enjoyed by women under modern American conditions of civil, industrial, and social equality with men adequately qualifies women for the exercise of the suffrage. Moreover, women's special functions in the home give her special qualifications for dealing with matters relating particularly to the home, and make it imperative that the opinion of woman-

[1] In 1920, Arkansas voted upon a constitutional amendment which required all voters to be citizens. This amendment, though approved by a majority of those voting thereon, was lost because it did not receive the affirmative vote of a majority of all voting at the election.

kind receive that due weight in politics which can be established only by the ballot.

The extension of the franchise to women on the same terms as to men was begun by the grant of equal suffrage in the territory of Wyoming in 1869. In the states the extension of the franchise to women had already been begun by the grant of school suffrage. In the first instance—Kentucky in 1838—the grant was made only to widows with children in the schools, but in general the right to vote in school elections, when granted at all, was granted to all women on the same terms as to men.[1] School suffrage, however, was undoubtedly granted mainly upon the theory that, whatever the natural right of women to full political equality with men, they had a special interest in the conduct of public schools and a special fitness for the determination of questions relating to the education of children. Several states also conferred upon tax-paying women the right to vote in local elections upon questions concerning taxation and indebtedness. One state, Kansas, conferred full municipal suffrage upon women in 1887, but no state ventured to admit women to the electorate on the same terms as men until the admission to statehood in 1890 of the territory of Wyoming. Since then the principle of equal suffrage for women has steadily advanced from state to state until the culmination was reached in 1920 in the adoption of the nineteenth amendment of the Federal Constitution. This provides that "the right of citizens of the United States to vote shall not be denied or abridged by the United States or by any State on account of sex."[2]

Present Suffrage Qualifications.

Notwithstanding the triumph of woman suffrage, the voting qualifications in the several states are still far from uniform. In all states, persons below the age of twenty-one years are excluded from the electorate and in every state except Arkansas, citizenship is a prerequisite for voting. Moreover, idiots and lunatics are generally expressly disqualified, also paupers or other persons constituting a public charge, as well as felons,

[1] Beginning with Kansas in 1861, about one-half of the states conferred separate school suffrage upon women.

[2] For an intimate account of the struggle for the adoption of the nineteenth amendment, see C. C. Catt and N. R. Shuler, *Woman Suffrage and Politics* (New York, 1923).

especially persons guilty of bribery, and, in a few states, duelists. All states require a definite period of legal residence within the state together with shorter periods of residence within the county, city or town, and precinct or ward. For example, to vote in Illinois, a citizen must have resided in the state one year, in the county ninety days, and in the election district thirty days next preceding the election. Such provisions disfranchise permanently all persons without settled abodes and, temporarily, all persons who change their legal residence immediately prior to an election. Formerly, those who were unable to be present in the locality of their legal residence on the day of election were deprived of any means of voting but this difficulty has been removed to a considerable extent through the widespread adoption of absent-voting laws.[1] Finally, most states provide that all qualified voters shall be registered, or at least that all qualified voters residing in towns and cities exceeding a certain minimum size, shall be registered. Registration may be accomplished once for all time, but may be, and in large cities usually is, required periodically, and generally must be performed by the voter in person. Thus a duly qualified voter may be temporarily disfranchised by failure to register in compliance with law.

REFORM OF THE REPRESENTATIVE SYSTEM

One of the early results of the progress of democracy in the states was the abolition of the provisions for the special representation of property in the state legislatures. In New York and North Carolina the establishment of manhood suffrage marked the end of the distinction that had existed between the senatorial electorate and that of the lower branch of the state legislature. All white voters were thereafter permitted to participate in the election of both senators and representatives on equal terms. In Massachusetts and South Carolina the systems

[1] During the Civil War, a number of states authorized their soldiers to "vote in the field." The first civilian absent-voting law was passed in Vermont in 1896. Since that time, absent-voting legislation of one sort or another has been enacted in almost every state. At the present time, only Connecticut, Rhode Island, and Kentucky are without such statutes. The Kentucky law of 1918 was declared unconstitutional by the state supreme court in 1921 and the Pennsylvania civilian absent-voting law of 1923 met a similar fate in 1925. See P. O. Ray, "Absent-voting Laws," *American Political Science Review*, xviii, pp. 321-325 (1924), and "Absent-voting Legislation, 1924-1925," *ibid.*, xx, pp. 347-349 (1926).

of legislative apportionment designed to give special representation to property in the state senates were abandoned in 1840 and 1868, respectively.

Acceptance of Bicameral Legislative System.

The abandonment of the purpose to make one branch of the state legislature the special guardian of the interests of property by means of distinctions between the senatorial electorate and that of the popular house, or between the systems of apportionment, did not lead, however, to the abandonment of the bicameral system. The people still retained their faith in the utility of a second chamber as a means of checking hasty and ill-considered legislation. Moreover the abolition of the original executive councils in most states, which took place at about the same time, and the transfer of their powers of advising and consenting to executive appointments to the state senates, placed new duties upon the latter which could not readily be provided for in any other way without doing violence to the prevailing theories of government. Finally, the special functions of the senate in the trial of impeachments seemed to require the retention of the bicameral system. If the senates had exercised legislative powers only, the question of their abolition might have been debatable; but since they also possessed important executive and judicial powers the question was hardly raised and never seriously considered. The adoption of the bicameral system in the Federal Constitution was followed by the abandonment of the unicameral system in Georgia (1789), Pennsylvania (1790), and Vermont (1836). That action was understood to have settled the matter in favor of the division of the legislatures into two houses.

The early nineteenth-century democracy attempted to preserve the special character of the upper house of the state legislatures by the use of devices less repugnant to the spirit of the people than that of special and exclusive electorates. The senate was generally distinguished from the more popular house by a higher age qualification, a longer term of office, a system of partial renewals, after the fashion of the federal senate, and a less numerous membership. Thus senators were expected to be older and more experiencd men when first elected, and the senates themselves were expected to contain at any given time a smaller proportion of new members than the more popular houses. The less numerous membership usually meant the election of senators in larger districts than members of the lower branch, a circumstance which was expected to attract abler or wealthier candidates. Since the newer states adopted the practice of biennial elections instead of the annual elections which universally prevailed in the beginning, the result was generally to establish quadrennial terms for senators as against biennial terms for members of the lower branch. In New York and New Jersey, however, the practice of annual elections was retained for members of the popular house, and in Massachusetts it was retained for members of both houses until 1920.

Popular Election of Executives and Judges.

Another consequence of the progress of democracy was the strengthening of popular control over executive and judicial officers. In the beginning the only state officers, exclusive of officers of local government, to be elected directly by the people in all the states were their representatives in the lower branch of the state legislatures. The general acceptance of the policy of direct election of the state governor began, however, immediately after the close of the Revolutionary period. Pennsylvania in 1790 and Delaware in 1792 provided for the direct election of the chief executive by the people of the whole state. Kentucky [1] and Tennessee, entering the Union before the end of the century, did likewise, and since then no new state has been admitted to the Union in which provision has not been made for the direct election of the chief executive by the same electorate which is authorized to choose representatives in the legislature. Some of the older states, however, were slow in adopting the direct election of governor by the people.[2] Virginia did not make the change until 1850, and South Carolina, the last to abandon the old system of legislative election, did not yield until 1866.[3]

[1] Kentucky in its first constitution of 1792 provided for the election of governor by electoral colleges created after the Maryland model for the election of senators. In 1799, however, the state went over to the direct election of the governor by the people.

[2] Georgia (1824), North Carolina (1835), Maryland (1837), New Jersey (1844).

[3] Because of the racial question, the present constitution of Mississippi provides for indirect popular election of the governor. See art. v, secs. 140, 141.

The change from legislative to popular election of the governor in the original states was generally accompanied by the abolition of the executive council and the transfer of the powers of the council, at least in relation to appointments, to the senate.[1] Except in the original states, separate executive councils had not been created. Doubtless the example of the federal government was decisive in this respect.

The same arguments that produced the general acceptance of direct election of governors tended also to produce the acceptance of the principle that all executive officers should be elected directly by the people. This principle was applied not only to local officers exercising a portion of the state administrative authority, such as sheriffs, justices of the peace, and the various county officers, but also to all officers serving the state at large, such as, in the beginning, state secretaries, treasurers, and attorneys-general. The application of the principle to judicial officers met with more opposition. There were those who felt that the independence of the judiciary, concerning the importance of maintaining which there was no disagreement, would be jeopardized by their subjection to the authority of the electorate. To this the reply was made that republican government could not be maintained unless the judiciary were to be held accountable to some authority, and that under the original system they were in fact dependent in most states upon the legislature. This was indeed clearly the case in those states in which the judiciary were elected by the legislature for short terms, or subject to impeachment and removal by a majority vote in each house of the legislature. It was less clearly so in such states as Massachusetts, where they were appointed during good behavior, subject to impeachment and removal by a two-thirds vote in the upper house, or to removal by the executive upon address of both branches of the legislature. In the beginning, however, the Massachusetts practice was the exception rather than the rule, and in the majority of the states, therefore, it was a fair argument that the election of judges by the people would increase rather than diminish their independence, especially if they were

[1] For the history of the council of appointment in New York, see C. Z. Lincoln, *Constitutional History of New York*, i, pp. 596-607. See also Gitterman, "The Council of Appointment in New York," in the *Pol. Sci. Q.*, vii, pp. 80 ff.

chosen for comparatively long terms and assured a fixed and liberal compensation.[1]

The general adoption of the direct election of governors was therefore eventually followed by the general acceptance of the principle that all state officers, executive and judicial alike, should be elected directly by the people. Beginning in Mississippi in 1832, the extension of the system of popular election to all executive and judicial offices was rapid throughout the West, and by the middle of the century had become the universal practice outside of the original states. The popular election of minor executive officers was also generally introduced in the original states, and even the popular election of judges was introduced in the most important of the latter, notably in New York in 1846 and in Pennsylvania and Virginia in 1850. In New England these democratic tendencies encountered more stubborn opposition, and in 1853 the refusal of Massachusetts to adopt the popular election of judges, though the state later accepted the popular election of minor executive officers, checked the democratic tide in that part of the Union. New Jersey, which adopted the popular election of governor in 1844, declined to introduce the direct election of other state executive or judicial officers; but South Carolina was the only state to retain intact its original system of legislative election of the executive and judiciary until after the Civil War.

The adoption of the direct popular election of executive and judicial officers was generally accompanied by changes in the terms and tenure of executive and judicial office. The terms of executive officers were lengthened, and their tenure was made more secure by requiring more than bare majorities in each branch of the legislature for removal by process of impeachment. Restrictions originally imposed in many of the states upon eligibility for reëlection to executive office were removed or diminished, and in general, when the people took the business of electing the chief executive directly into their own hands, his position was strengthened. The direct election of other executive officers, however, had the effect of relieving them from responsibility to the governor. Thus at the same time that the political authority of the governor was increased, his administrative

[1] See T. M. Cooley, *Michigan*, in the American Commonwealth series, pp. 303, 304.

authority was diminished. State politics tended to become more responsive to executive leadership; for the governor came to be regarded as peculiarly the representative of the whole people of the state. State administration tended to become less amenable to control by the governor; for actual administrative power was distributed among a group of officers, each of whom was constitutionally as much the representative of the people as the governor himself. The terms of the judicial officers were usually, though not always, lengthened when they were made elective by the people, and the tenure of judicial office was greatly strengthened by the increase of the legislative majorities required for removal by impeachment. Moreover the popular prestige of the judges was greatly enhanced when they became the creatures of popular rather than of legislative favor. The result of the change from legislative to popular election of executive and judicial officers was to deprive the legislatures not only of much political and administrative power, but also of some of the popular prestige which they had originally enjoyed as the special bulwarks of the liberties of the people.

REFORM OF PROCESS OF CONSTITUTION-MAKING

A further consequence of the progress of democracy was the strengthening of popular control over the process of constitutional amendment and revision. In the beginning the standard practice with respect to the framing of state constitutions was not inaugurated by Massachusetts until after the other states had mostly succeeded in transforming their provisional Revolutionary governments into permanent constitutional governments. The first states, however, to revise their original governments,—New Hampshire in 1783, Georgia in 1789, and Pennsylvania in 1790,—adhered more or less closely to the precedent established by Massachusetts. Georgia and Pennsylvania, indeed, in order to do so, were compelled to violate their existing constitutions, which had made other provision for constitutional revision. Since then it has been generally accepted that the only proper mode of making any extensive revision of a state constitution is by a constitutional convention especially elected for that purpose. It was not at once generally accepted, however, that the electorate should be consulted before such a convention should be convoked, and that it should be consulted again before the revised constitution should be put into operation. New Hampshire followed the Massachusetts practice exactly. In Pennsylvania a popular vote was taken before the convention was called, but afterwards the people were consulted only indirectly, and the revised constitution was put into effect without any direct expression of popular approval. In Georgia, the people were not expressly consulted in advance, but the revised constitution was considered by two other special conventions in succession before being declared the supreme law of the state.

The Problem of the Constitutional Convention.

At the present time, the constitutions of thirty-six states make express provision for their revision by constitutional conventions. In the other twelve states the constitutions now in force contain no provisions for the calling of conventions. The question therefore arises, what is the status of the constitutional convention in those states where its existence is not expressly recognized in the written constitution?

Such states might logically be divided into two classes, those in which no express provision for amendment is contained in the written constitution, and those in which some provision is made for amendment through the agency of the ordinary legislature. In the beginning there were half a dozen states in the former class. To deny the right of the legislature of such a state to take the necessary steps for the calling of a convention, would have the effect either of denying the existence of any distinction between constitutional and ordinary statute law, or denying to the people of the state the power of procuring by any legal mode of action a revision of their own constitution. Such a denial is clearly inconsistent with the fundamental principles of state government, as understood at the time of the Revolution. If the right be not affirmed, there is no security in such states either for the maintenance of the sovereignty of the people or of the reign of law. In fact in all those states where no express provision for constitutional revision was contained in the written constitution, the legislatures acted on the assumption that they were duly authorized by the unwritten law of the constitution to start the machinery of constitutional revision by means of special conventions. Subsequently all these states adopted some express provision for constitutional amendment, either by special conventions, or by special legislative action. Hence there is now no state in which there is not some provision for the revision or amendment of the constitution. Our question therefore now takes the form, may not the express provision of another mode of amendment, in states where no mention of the constitutional convention is made in the written constitution, indicate a purpose on the part of the people to dispense with the mode of revision by special convention?

There is some authority for an affirmative answer to this question. In 1883 the question of calling a constitutional convention was under discussion in Rhode Island, and it was argued that the adoption in 1842 of the method of amendment by legislative action implied the abandonment by the people of the mode of revision through special conventions. The mode of amendment adopted by the people in 1842 was itself recommended by a constitutional convention, which at the same time made no proposals for the regulation in the written constitution of the process of revision by special conventions. There was no provision expressly relating thereto either in the original charter of 1663 or in the acts of the legislature which declared that charter the supreme law of the state in 1776. Though the legislature had since then taken the initiative in calling the convention of 1842, the failure of the latter convention to take any action to determine the status of future constitutional conventions indicated, it was urged, an intention to eliminate the constitutional convention from the constitutional structure of state government. This opinion was adopted by the Rhole Island supreme court.[1] It was contended that there was precedent for this opinion in an earlier opinion of the supreme court of Massachusetts.[2] A careful study of the opinion of the Massachusetts court, however, shows that its opinion related to another matter.[3] In no state has the opinion of the Rhole Island court been followed. On the contrary, the practice of the other eleven states has been based on the recognition of the right of the people through their representatives to provide by law for the calling of a convention. This right is construed from the fact that the people undoubtedly possessed the right in the beginning, and

[1] See *In re* The Constitutional Convention, 14 R. I. 649 (1883).
[2] 6 Cush. 573 (1833).
[3] See *post*, ch. v.

have not parted with it by expressly confining amendment to some other method.[1]

Participation of Electorate in Process of Revision.

The practice with regard to the consultation of the people before the calling of a constitutional convention has not yet become uniform. In the greater number of states previous consultation of the people is now required before an election of delegates may be ordered. In most of these states the legislature may use its discretion as to the time of consulting the people.[2] In several states, however, the matter is not left to the discretion of the legislature. The constitution requires the executive officers of the state to submit to the people at stated periods the question whether a constitutional convention shall be called.[3] The theory upon which the arrangements have been adopted for a periodical consideration by the people of the question of calling a convention is this, that the people of each generation should have an equal opportunity to determine for themselves the forms of government under which they shall live. Jefferson was an ardent supporter of this theory, and calculated that, in order that the majority of the voters might, if they wished, always live under a constitution of their own making, the question of calling a convention should be submitted to them once in twenty years. This accordingly is the period most commonly adopted by those states in which provision is made for the periodical submission of the question to the people.[4] Although required by the constitution in only thirty-four of the states, such a popular vote has been taken in most cases in recent years. Thus the practice of obtaining the popular approval for the calling of a convention has become the general rule.

In many of the states which require submission to the people of the question of calling a convention, the assembling of conventions is still largely dependent upon legislative action, even after the people have voted that a convention be held. The

[1] See W. F. Dodd, *The Revision and Amendment of State Constitutions*, pp. 42-46.

[2] In twenty-seven states.

[3] See W. F. Dodd, *op. cit.*, p. 51. Seven states, but in most of these states the legislature is expressly authorized to submit the question of calling a convention at other times than that specified in the constitution. In Oklahoma it may submit the question when it pleases, but must do so at least once in every twenty years.

[4] Four states.

number and apportionment of delegates, the time, place, and manner of election, the organization, and even the rules of procedure, if not determined in the constitution itself, may be determined by legislative enactment. In such cases the failure of the legislature to act will frustrate the will of the people, as happened in New York after a favorable popular vote in 1886. Only three states, New York, Michigan, and Missouri, now make complete provision in their constitutions for the election and assembling of constitutional conventions, but only ten states leave these details altogether to the discretion of the legislatures.[1] In all the states, however, which possess the direct popular initiative, now comprising more than a third of the total number, the electorates are entirely independent of the legislatures with respect to the calling and organization of constitutional conventions, regardless of the lack of express regulations in the constitution itself.

The practice with regard to the consultation of the people after the election of a convention but before the putting into effect of a revised constitution has also not yet become uniform. In New England the Massachusetts precedent has been followed ever since it was established. Outside of New England New York in 1821 was the first state to submit a revised constitution directly to the people for their approval. Virginia did likewise in 1830. Thereafter the practice rapidly became general. Yet at present the constitutions of only nineteen states expressly require the submission of revised constitutions to the people for their approval. In the others apparently either the legislature in issuing the call for a convention may provide that there be no popular submission of its revision or the convention itself may declare its revision in effect without the express approval of the people.[2] In fact, in recent years there have been several conspicuous departures from the practice which had previously been established. In five states conventions have been held, which, among other changes, made provision for the elimination of the negro vote, and then declared the revised constitutions operative without submission to the people.[3] Thus the embarrassing question

[1] W. F. Dodd, *op. cit.*, pp. 55-57.

[2] This matter will be discussed more fully in the following chapter.

[3] Mississippi (1890), South Carolina (1895), Delaware (1897), Louisiana (1898, 1913, 1921), and Virginia (1902). See Dodd, *op. cit.*, pp. 67-71.

was avoided, to which electorate, the old or the new, should the revised constitution be submitted.

The result of the diversity in the practice of the several states with respect to the revision of their constitutions by special conventions is confusing. It is not at once altogether clear precisely what is the status of the constitutional convention in the political system of the states. At present the states must be classified into four groups on the basis of the structural relations between the convention and the other organs of state government. The first group comprises all states in which the electorate exercise a complete control over the call, organization, and proceedings of constitutional conventions. This control may be continuous, as in the states which possess the direct popular initiative, or it may be discontinuous, as in states such as New York, where the structure of the convention is completely regulated by the constitution itself. The second group comprises all states in which control of the constitutional convention is divided between the electorate and the legislature. The third group comprises all states in which the legislature alone exercises such legal control as is recognized to exist. The states of this group, however, differ widely in their actual practice. On the one hand, the Massachusetts legislature would doubtless feel bound by precedent neither to call a convention, nor to authorize a convention, once called, to put its proposed revision into effect, without the express approval of the people. On the other hand, the Mississippi legislature might consistently feel free to call a convention at will and to authorize it at its discretion to dispense with any direct expression of popular approval. The extent to which constitutional conventions in these three groups of states are subject to control by the courts is a question that concerns the distribution of powers between the different departments of government and will subsequently be discussed in that connection. The fourth group comprises the single state of Rhode Island, where the constitutional convention has been held to be unconstitutional.

Distinction between Revision and Amendment.

In the beginning there seems to have been no clear recognition of the necessity for a distinction between the revision and the amendment of state constitutions.[1] In the original states the practice varied. Only three of the original state constitutions contained any special provisions for their amendment by legislative action.[2] Delaware provided that certain parts of the constitution should not be subject to amendment at all, and that "no other part should be altered except with the consent of five out of the seven members of the legislative assembly and seven out of the nine members of the legislative council." South Carolina also established a distinction between the process of ordinary legislation and that of constitutional amendment by requiring an exceptional majority for the adoption of a measure of the latter character. Maryland made a sharper distinction between constitutional amendments and ordinary statutes by requiring that the former, having been adopted by the legislature, should be published at least three months before the election of the next legislature, and then readopted by the latter, in order to become effective. The Maryland plan of action by two successive legislatures was accepted by South Carolina in 1790 and by Delaware in 1792 and grafted upon their own original devices. This arrangement was generally considered at the time to give adequate popular control over the process of amendment, and was adopted in several other states; but the only state which still clings to-day to a process of amendment making no provision for a special popular vote upon each proposed amendment is Delaware.

A somewhat more democratic practice was adopted in Alabama in 1819. This consisted in the provision that an amendment proposed by the legislature should be voted on directly by the people, instead of being merely published for their information, but the power to take final action was still vested in the next succeeding legislature. This plan was never widely copied, and exists to-day in only two states, South Carolina and Mississippi. A still more democratic practice was inaugurated in Connecticut in 1818. Instead of placing the popular vote between the two successive legislative actions the popular vote was placed after

[1] Doubtless the adoption in the Federal Constitution of 1787 of different modes of procedure for extensive revision and minor amendments brought the matter more clearly to the attention of the people of the states. For a complete discussion of this whole subject, see W. F. Dodd, *op. cit.*, pp. 118-132.

[2] Delaware (1776), Maryland (1776), and South Carolina (1778).

the second legislative action, thus giving to the electorate the final decision, and making its action definitive instead of merely advisory. The Connecticut plan was adopted in Maine in 1819 and simplified by the omission of the requirement that a second legislature endorse proposed amendments, thus enabling any legislature to submit its proposals directly to the people. The Connecticut and Maine plans have since been widely copied, and popular control over the process of amendment through legislative initiative has been almost completely established. The final stage in the evolution of the amending process has been the adoption of the direct popular initiative, thus dispensing altogether with legislative intervention. This stage was first entered upon in Oregon in 1902, and is now established in eleven states.[1]

REFORM OF THE PARTY SYSTEM

Nothing could have been more remote from the minds of the Fathers than the legal recognition of the political party. The deliberate organization of a party, or faction, as they preferred to call it, represented to their minds a stage of political depravity but one degree short of treason, and the growth of party spirit presaged the ultimate advent either of foreign invasion or domestic anarchy. Washington devotes the most impressive portions of his Farewell Address to a solemn warning against the evils of faction. The distinguished authors of *The Federalist* devote several numbers[2] to an earnest appeal for the adoption of the constitution of 1787, on the ground that it will mitigate the violence of faction and thus promote the public peace and security. De Tocqueville, in his fascinating description of American politics, written after the first generation of American statesmen had passed from the stage, still reiterates the same pessimistic opinions concerning parties. "Parties," he concedes, "are a necessary evil in free governments"; and he goes on to show why. "Ambitious men will succeed in creating parties, since it is difficult to eject a person from authority upon the mere ground that his place is coveted by others. All the skill of the

[1] Two other states, Nevada and Massachusetts have the indirect initiative for constitutional amendments. See W. F. Dodd, *State Government*, pp. 506-508, for a table of initiative and referendum provisions. The Mississippi initiative and referendum amendment of 1914 was declared void by the state supreme court in Power v. Robertson, 93 So. 769 (1922).

[2] See nos. 9 and 68 by Hamilton, and nos. 10, 14, and 47 by Madison.

actors in the political world lies in the art of creating parties. A political aspirant in the United States begins by discerning his own interest, and discovering those other interests which may be collected around and amalgamated with it. He then contrives to find out some doctrine or principle which may suit the purpose of this new association, and which he adopts in order to bring forward his party and secure his popularity; . . . This being done, the new party is ushered into the political world."[1]

The American people themselves seem to have taken a less gloomy view of the consequences of party spirit. Francis Lieber, a political refugee from Germany, who in many ways understood the American spirit more correctly than his brilliant French contemporary, was certainly more happy in his interpretation of the spirit of party. As he was careful to point out, no free country ever had existed without parties; it seemed to him unlikely that any free country ever would exist without parties; and he did not hesitate to conclude that no free country ought to exist without parties. "It is impossible," he declared, "for civil liberty to exist without parties." He held with Burke that a party is a "body of men united for promoting by their joint endeavor the national interest upon some particular principle in which they are all agreed." He believed it the duty of the citizen to join a party and act with it, so far as his intelligence and conscience would permit, declaring with Fox that "an independent man is a man you can never depend upon."[2] This, the view that came to prevail in the American states, has been most eloquently expressed by Senator G. F. Hoar: "Your party is but the instrument by which freemen execute their will. But it differs from other instruments in this. It is an indispensable instrument made up of the men, and practically of all the men, who wish to accomplish the things you wish to accomplish and deem it vital to the prosperity, honor, and glory of your country. It is an instrument itself possessing intelligence, judgment, conscience, purpose, will."[3]

At all events, for better or for worse, organized political parties sprang into being before the state governments were established,

[1] A. de Tocqueville, *Democracy in America*, i, ch. x.
[2] F. Lieber, *Manual of Political Ethics*, pt. ii, bk. v, ch. 2.
[3] George Frisbie Hoar, *Good Advice to Young Voters*, Speech at Worcester, Mass., Aug. 21, 1884.

and, with the extension of democracy, grew ever stronger and more active. By the time when De Tocqueville and Lieber were forming their impressions of American government, the habit of party regularity had become firmly established, and the forms of party organization were already well developed. These consequences of the democratization of the electorates are commonly associated, therefore, with the advent of the Jacksonian democracy. In fact, however, they were the cause rather than the result of the advent of the Jacksonian democracy. Party spirit began to flourish on a national scale when the American colonists were first divided into Whigs and Tories, and party organization began to develop with the creation of the Revolutionary committees of correspondence. A political party is any two or more persons acting together for the purpose of influencing the result of an election. The organization of parties is inevitable wherever an electoral system exists which awards the election to the person receiving the plurality of votes, for voters will inevitably unite for the purpose of casting the greatest possible number of votes for a mutually acceptable candidate.

Development of Delegate Convention.

Originally nominations for offices to be filled by popular election were made by town and village caucuses or county mass-meetings. In the New England states and New York, where the governors were elected by the state at large, the problem of party organization was more difficult. Gubernatorial candidates were commonly nominated by legislative caucuses, assisted in some cases by special representatives from districts not represented in the legislature by members of the party concerned, or by mass meetings at the seat of the state government. The delegate convention, or representative form of party organization, originated in the middle states, where county conventions were held at the county seats in order to make more representative nominations than were possible at casual mass-meetings.[1] In New England most county officers were not then elected directly by the people, and in the South the aristocratic character of local government rendered formal party organization unnecessary.

[1] See G. D. Luetscher, *Early Political Machinery in the United States;* also F. W. Dallinger, *Nominations to Elective Office*, ch. i.

The demand for more effective party organization in the states arose partly because of the increasing adoption of the direct election of governors and partly because of the then common practice of electing congressmen from the state at large. The response to the demand came first in the middle states, partly because in those states the delegate convention developed first in the county, and partly because the democratic middle states county formed a more convenient basis for the state delegate convention than the democratic New England town or the aristocratic southern county. Delaware seems to have been the first state in which the state delegate convention was permanently established. In New Jersey, and even more in Pennsylvania and New York, the greater distances made more difficult the substitution of the state delegate convention for the legislative caucus. In Delaware the state convention was established during the presidency of Jefferson, and in the middle states generally the legislative caucus had yielded to the delegate convention by the end of Monroe's administration. In New England the development of the state convention was slower, and was not completed in Massachusetts until the time of Jackson. The representative form of party organization was established in the west during the same period, and by the time when the first national conventions were held (1830-32), the delegate convention had become the accepted form of party organization everywhere except in the South. The extension of popular control over the executive and judicial branches of state government increased the demand for efficient nominating machinery in the states, and strengthened both the habit of party regularity and the representative form of party organization.

Introduction of Direct Primary.

The delegate convention system ultimately fell under the suspicion of lending itself too easily to manipulation by persons who could not command the confidence of a majority of the rank and file of the parties. The chief criticisms brought against the system may be summarized as follows: (1) the creation of irresponsible party leadership; (2) the exclusion of the rank and file from effective participation in the management of party affairs; (3) the recognition by candidates of responsibility not to their constituents, nor even to the voters belonging to their party, but to the "bosses" to whom they realized that they owed their nominations; and (4) the possibility of political domination by private "interests" through the connivance of "bosses" in control of party organizations.[1] These criticisms eventually led to the reformation of party organization in the western and northern states by the enactment of laws requiring that political parties should make their nominations in primary elections at which the party members should vote directly for the candidates of their choice. The first state-wide direct primary laws were enacted in Wisconsin (1903) and Oregon (1904). Thereafter the system spread rapidly among the western and northern states.[2] In the southern states, the direct primary was meanwhile being established, first by voluntary party rule, later by statute, primarily for the purpose of facilitating the elimination of the negro vote.[3] At present, there are mandatory direct primary laws in thirty-nine states, and optional laws in six states.[4] In the case of the former, some or all of the candidates for state or local elective offices must be nominated as the direct primary act provides; while in the case of the latter, each political party, through its appropriate committees, may decide whether or not the direct primary law shall be adopted and used by the party in nominating its candidates. Connecticut, New Mexico, and Rhode Island are the only states in which nominations are made exclusively by methods other than the direct primary.

The legal recognition of the political party as an independent organ of government preceded the establishment by law of the direct primary as a mode of making party nominations. There were several stages in the evolution of the party into an organ of government. First, there was the gradual recognition by public

[1] See J. Bryce, *The American Commonwealth*, pt. iii. See also Gov. Charles E. Hughes, *Message to N. Y. Legislature*, 1910.

[2] See C. E. Merriam, *Primary Elections* (1909), and *American Year Book*, 1910-1919, 1925.

[3] See *post*, ch. vii.

[4] See Charles Kettleborough, "Direct Primaries" and "Digest of Primary Election Laws," *Annals American Academy Political and Social Science*, cvi, pp. 11-17 and 181-273 (1923). During the last few years, the direct primary has been subjected to severe attacks. In general, these were unsuccessful except in Idaho (1919) and New York (1921) where delegate conventions were restored for the nomination of candidates for state offices. See Ralph S. Boots, "The Trend of the Direct Primary," *American Political Science Review*, xvi, pp. 412-431 (1922).

opinion of the growing importance of party organizations with respect to the conduct of the elections. This stage in the evolution of the party was well advanced by 1840. Next came the demand that partisan primary elections be surrounded by the same legal safeguards against bribery, intimidation, and other corrupt practices as had been established for the protection of voters at public general elections. This stage was formally initiated by the adoption of the first laws regulating the conduct of primary elections in New York and California in 1866. The recognition of the importance of preventing corrupt practices in primary elections held for the choice of party officers and candidates or of delegates to nominating conventions gradually led to the recognition of the importance of regulating the management of party affairs in other respects, until eventually the whole structure of party organization was brought under public control. The transition to this stage was precipitated by the introduction of the official ballot at general elections, beginning in Massachusetts in 1888.

The final stage in the evolution of the party into an organ of government coincides with the extension to the primary of the whole machinery of electoral regulation and the assimilation of the primary to an ordinary public election, conducted by public officers. This stage was inaugurated by the establishment of the state-wide direct primary and has been characterized by the gradual development of corrupt practices legislation, applying to primary and general elections alike, and the gradual assumption by the state of an increasing share of the cost not only of elections but of electioneering in general. The arrival of this stage is clearly indicated by the adoption of laws in Colorado in 1909 (later declared unconstitutional) and in Oregon in 1910 appropriating public money to the personal use of candidates for office or delegates to political conventions, and of other laws in Oregon and Wisconsin at about the same time making provision for the publication of official campaign bulletins, partly at public expense, for the use of candidates for nomination and of political parties as such. Under present conditions, the political party in most states is as much a part of the legal machinery of government as is the election district or any other formal subdivision of the electorate.

SUMMARY

At the present time there is a remarkable degree of uniformity in the general structure of state government.[1] All the states possess bicameral legislatures, and almost all possess plural executives, an independent judiciary, comparatively broad electorates (except for the elimination of the negro vote in the South), well-developed systems of constitutional amendment and revision, and political parties elaborately organized by authority of law. With respect, however, to the organization and procedure of the legislative, executive, and judicial departments, no two states pursue a precisely identical practice. In many instances the variations are wide, and exercise a profound effect on the actual conduct of state affairs. The most important differences among the existing governments of the states, however, result less from differences in the forms of their governments than from those in the distribution of powers.

[1] For an excellent detailed summary of the development of the forms of state government, see J. Q. Dealey, *The Growth of American State Constitutions* (Boston, 1915), chs. 4-8.

CHAPTER V

THE REDISTRIBUTION OF POWERS

The original distribution of powers between the three departments of government was based upon the theory that a concentration of powers in any one department would lead to tyranny and oppression. In New York, Massachusetts, and New Hampshire this theory was acted upon in a logical manner. The powers of the legislative, executive, and judicial branches of these three state governments were so adjusted that each should serve as a check upon the others and a balance be thereby established between them. In the other states the doctrine of checks and balances was either not properly understood or unintelligently applied, and, except in Pennsylvania and Vermont, there was no apparent check to the supremacy of the legislatures. In Pennsylvania and Vermont the censorial system failed to operate as an effective substitute for the system of checks and balances, and hence in all but three of the original states the original distribution of powers was defective. It became necessary either to redistribute the powers or to abandon the theory upon which the Fathers professed to establish the original state governments.

DECLINE OF SYSTEM OF LEGISLATIVE SUPREMACY

The logic of events favored the redistribution of powers. As Jefferson pointed out, one hundred and seventy-three or any other number of despots were as objectionable as one, and an elective tyranny was not the government for which the people had fought. In fact, the state legislatures began to lose prestige from the beginning. In Pennsylvania the unreliability of the early legislatures was revealed by the first council of censors. In the other states where the system of legislative supremacy originally prevailed there was no equally effective means of revealing legislative usurpation and incapacity, and the confidence of the people in the ability and integrity of their representatives was too strongly entrenched to be easily destroyed. During the Revolutionary

War the legislative system was under an exceptional strain, and the people were prone to believe that with the return of peace there would be a return on the part of their representatives to constitutional modes of government. In Virginia members of one early legislature in a moment of panic caused by a British invasion went so far as to suggest the appointment of a dictator after the fashion of the ancient Romans. Jefferson was then governor, and later enemies of his have ascribed the suggestion of a dictator to consciousness of executive rather than of legislative weakness. Certainly the system of government which then existed in Virginia was characterized by executive weakness, but the failure of the particular government over which Jefferson presided to deal effectively with foreign invasion reflected more discredit upon an omnipotent but incapable legislature than upon the unfortunate holder of a shadowy executive authority. After the close of the war the conduct of the legislatures failed to restore a somewhat shaken confidence. During the trying period between the achievement of independence and the establishment of the "more perfect union" under the constitution of 1787, appropriately described by John Fiske as the critical period of American history, the state legislatures showed themselves clearly unequal to the tasks which they had assumed.

Causes of Decline of Original System.

The primary reason for their failure to justify the public confidence they had originally enjoyed was their inability to take a national view of national problems. The Continental Congress could neither raise money, enforce its treaties with foreign powers, nor regulate commerce between the states and other matters of common concern, without the coöperation of the separate states, and the legislatures of the separate states proved to be under the control of local interests. It became necessary to deprive the state legislatures of their original responsibility for the management of national affairs, and this was effectually done in the Federal Constitution of 1787.

A second reason for the failure of the state legislatures to preserve the public confidence they had originally enjoyed was their inability to deal with state problems in the interest of the whole people of their respective states. The individual legislator, instead of representing the people of the whole state, was prone to regard himself as the representative of his district, or of some other local or private interest, and strove mainly to protect his own special interest, or at best to promote the prosperity of his own particular district. During the colonial period, when the responsibility for the conduct of government rested mainly on the executive, the predominance of local interests in the legislative branch served as a salutary check upon the executive tendency to prefer imperial to local interests of any sort. But when sovereignty passed from the crown to the people, the legislature became the chief representative of the new sovereign, and the predominance of local and private interests signified the subversion of the general public interest. The failure of the state legislatures properly to manage the internal affairs of the separate states was less menacing to the independence and prosperity of the nation than their failure in the conduct of national affairs, but it was sufficiently disastrous to the common welfare to produce a general reaction against the original system of unchecked legislative supremacy.

The enactment of special laws for the benefit of private individuals, without due regard for the interests of the public, was one of the earliest and most serious abuses. Such laws were frequently enacted in the interest of persons desiring to speculate in public lands, or to secure the improvement of local roads and bridges in the furtherance of land speculations. The power to change names and to grant divorces by special act was another source of frequent abuse. Later, the growth of the practice of doing business under corporate forms led to an inordinate demand for the grant by special legislation of charters of incorporation and exclusive or, at least, extraordinary privileges therewith. Land companies, banking companies, turnpike and canal and later railroad companies, finally public utility companies and manufacturing and trading companies of all sorts, resorted to the legislatures for all manner of special privileges. Legislators were tempted to use their power for partisan and personal ends, and all too often there was open and shameless barter of valuable special privileges for private gain, without regard for the interests of the public. Sometimes this abuse of power was the result of ignorance of the public interest, sometimes of indifference to the public welfare, sometimes of negligence or incompetence, sometimes of downright corruption.

Similarly unfortunate conditions resulted from the abuse of legislative power to pass local acts. Public money was freely appropriated for local improvements, not in order to carry out a general plan for the general improvement of the state, but primarily in order to promote purely local interests or even merely personal interests not shared by any locality. Legislative majorities for such appropriations were secured by the practice of log-rolling. The separate local or personal projects of a majority of the legislature were combined into one general measure which would be supported by those interested in the combination for the sake of what each would severally get out of it, or the same result was secured by means of promises of mutual aid for one another's projects. The public interest was lost to view. Much legislation relating to the organization and administration of local government was also enacted in furtherance of private ends. Thus the establishment of county boundaries and the location of county seats, the incorporation of cities and the regulation of municipal powers, and above all, the demarcation of congressional and state legislative districts, were frequently prompted by personal or partisan considerations. Taxes were sometimes levied less for the sake of the revenue they would bring than for the purpose of favoring some special interest, and tax exemptions were granted, not because the legislatures were convinced that they were for the public interest, but because private interests were able to extort them from subservient legislators. States borrowed money to finance enterprises that no prudent citizen would have ventured to undertake at his private risk, and the public credit was extended to suave speculators whose only assets were their cheerful readiness to promote undertakings on the credit of the public when private credit was withheld from them. Such operations may be justified by success, but unfortunately success was too often denied.

IMPROVEMENT OF SYSTEM OF CHECKS AND BALANCES

The reaction against the system of legislative supremacy took the form primarily of a demand for the restriction of the powers of the legislatures. In practice this meant, in the first instance, a demand for the establishment of a system of checks and balances modeled upon that of Massachusetts or New York. The imposition of restrictions upon the authority of the legislatures, however, could not be stopped at the point where it had been begun in the constitutions drafted by Adams and Jay. Direct constitutional limitations upon legislative powers were imposed with ever growing frequency and effect.

The reaction against the system of legislative supremacy took the form secondarily of a demand for the extension of the powers of the electorates. In practice this meant in the first instance a demand for the democratization of the forms of government. The extension of the powers of the electorates, however, could not be stopped when executive and judicial officers had been made elective by the people, and thus rendered comparatively independent of legislative control. Ultimately constitutional reformers began to demand that the electorates have power to veto legislative enactments on their own motion, and, if necessary, to enact their own measures independently of the legislatures. Neither the restriction of the powers of the legislatures nor the extension of those of the electorates could be accomplished without profoundly affecting the position of the constitutional convention, and, indirectly, of the judiciary. Finally, the division of legislative authority and the extension of the work of the electorates has stimulated an unprecedented growth of political parties and the development of a thoroughly partisan system of government. The result has been an extensive and in part unpremeditated redistribution of powers between the several departments of government.

Development of the Executive Veto.

The most conspicuous feature of the system of checks and balances originally established in Massachusetts was the executive veto.[1] The veto upon legislative enactments was exercised by the governor at discretion, subject to the power of the legislature to reënact a vetoed measure by a two-thirds vote. In New York the veto was originally exercised subject to the same qualification by the council of revision, in which the judicial element was preponderant.

The growing distrust of unchecked legislative supremacy was reflected first in the Federal Convention of 1787. The conservative leaders who controlled that body preferred the pure form of

[1] See John A. Fairlie, "The Veto Power of the State Governor." *American Political Science Review*, xi, pp. 473-493 (1917).

executive veto established in Massachusetts to the mixed form established in New York, and the action of the Federal Convention greatly influenced the subsequent action of the states. The first states to revise their original constitutions after the adoption of the Federal Constitution were Georgia in 1789 and Pennsylvania in 1790. Both adopted the Massachusetts form of the veto. New Hampshire, which had imitated the original Massachusetts constitution in most respects but had not conferred the veto power upon the governor, did so in 1792. In the same year Kentucky, the first western state to enter the union, armed its governor with the executive veto. The Massachusetts form of the veto for a time seemed likely to win universal acceptance. The New York form was not introduced in any other state except Illinois, which inserted a provision for the mixed executive and judicial veto in its original constitution of 1818.[1] The New York form was abandoned in that state in 1821 and the Massachusetts form substituted. By that time the existence of the pure judicial veto, derived from the power of judicial review of legislative and executive decisions involving the interpretation of the constitution, had become generally recognized, and the continuance of a special council of revision was seen to be unnecessary. The action of New York in 1821 marks the complete development of the separate executive and judicial veto powers.[2]

The general adoption of the Massachusetts form of executive veto was obstructed by the rising tide of democracy in the states. The feeling grew strong that the governor might well be empowered to delay legislative action and compel reconsideration of measures of doubtful constitutionality or expediency, but ought not to be entrusted with the power to defeat the matured purposes of the people's representatives. In 1792 Delaware, while providing for the popular election of the governor, declined to entrust him with the veto power. Tennessee, upon entering the Union in 1796, and Ohio, six years later, did likewise. In 1799 Kentucky revised her original constitution and incidentally revised the power of executive veto. The new arrangement pro-

[1] However, in Vermont from 1793 to 1836, the veto power was vested in the governor and his executive council. Illinois retained the New York form of veto until 1848. See N. H. Debel, "The Veto Power of the Governor of Illinois," *University of Illinois Studies in the Social Sciences*, vi, nos. 1, 2 (1917).

[2] See C. Z. Lincoln, *Constitutional History of New York*, i, pp. 743-749.

vided that the governor might veto any legislative enactment at discretion, but that the legislature might reënact any vetoed measure, if the measure was approved by a majority of all the members elected to the legislature. Thus the governor could prevent the enactment of legislation by less than a clear majority of the whole legislature, but he could not defeat the will of a constitutional majority. During the succeeding half century the executive veto was established in fifteen states, in a majority of which the Kentucky form of veto was adopted. By 1850 only six of the original states were still without any form of executive veto, and all the new states admitted after Ohio possessed it in some form.

Meanwhile, the position of the governor as the special representative of the whole people of his state had been clearly established, and public opinion was more generally disposed to sanction a vigorous use of his authority. Since 1850 the executive veto has been established in all the states but one, North Carolina, and with only one exception, West Virginia, these states adopted the Massachusetts form. During the same period the Kentucky form has been abandoned in three states and the Massachusetts form substituted. The final victory of the Massachusetts form of executive veto was won when the people recognized that such power was not inconsistent with the progress of democracy, but on the contrary was essential to it.

Since the Civil War the executive veto has been further strengthened by an increase of the legislative majorities required to pass measures over the veto. It had been discovered that the vote upon measures was frequently so small that the two-thirds required to overrule a veto might actually be much less than a majority of the whole legislature. In Pennsylvania in 1873, and in New York in 1874, the requirement was therefore changed from two-thirds of those present and voting on a measure to two-thirds of all the members elected to the legislature. Similar changes have since been made in more than a third of the states, and the position of the governor as the special representative of the state as a whole has been correspondingly strengthened.

A new stage in the development of the executive veto was inaugurated during the Civil War. It had been discovered that the veto in its original form was not suited for dealing effectively with appropriation bills. Bills containing proper appropriations for necessary expenditures might also contain objectionable items, and the president or governor would be forced to approve the objectionable with the rest or veto the whole bill. Legislatures with improper designs upon the public treasury could place all appropriations in a single bill and thus force the hand of the executive, and could even use an important appropriation bill as a vehicle for carrying objectionable measures relating to entirely different subjects. This defect was first corrected in the constitution of the southern Confederacy (1861). This constitution conferred upon the president the item veto, by means of which he might disapprove not only any act as a whole, but also any item of an appropriation act.[1] After the Civil War, the item veto was not lost from view. It was first copied by Georgia (1865) and Texas (1866). It has since spread rapidly throughout the Union so that it now exists in thirty-eight states. A further extension of the same principle was adopted in Washington in 1889 whereby the governor is authorized to negative any bill or any section of any bill, whether it relates to appropriations or not.[2] The latest step in the development of the veto power was taken by Alabama (1901), Virginia (1902), and Massachusetts (1918). The constitutions of these states now formally empower the governor to propose amendments to bills in lieu of disapproving them. Should the legislature fail to accept the amendments, the governor may then exercise his veto prerogative. Thus, the executive power has been extended and fortified.[3]

[1] A second reason for the adoption of the item veto by the Confederate States was that it was introduced as a part of a deliberate plan to adapt English budget principles to American conditions with a view to securing greater harmony between the executive and the legislature. See R. H. Wells, "The Item Veto and State Budget Reform," *American Political Science Review*, xviii, pp. 782-791 (1924). See also New York Constitutional Convention of 1867, *Record of Debates*, ii, pp. 1109-1131.

[2] A similar provision was adopted in Ohio in 1903 but was restricted to appropriation items in 1912. The statement that the South Carolina constitution of 1895 authorizes a partial veto like that of Washington is probably erroneous. See *South Carolina House Journal*, 1914, pp. 1386 ff. In 1921, a constitutional amendment was adopted in Oregon, authorizing the governor to veto emergency clauses in bills. This provision enables the governor to prevent the legislature from nullifying the right of popular referendum.

[3] The development of the executive veto is well illustrated by the case of Illinois. Beginning in 1818 with the original New York plan of mixed executive and judicial veto, the people adopted the Kentucky plan in 1848; in 1870 the requirement of a two-thirds vote of all elected members to override a veto was introduced, and in 1884 the veto was extended to items of appropriation bills. See Debel, *op. cit.*

Further Strengthening of the Executive.

The power of the executive has been further fortified by the adoption of restrictions upon the eligibility of members of the legislature for appointment to office. A number of states have provided that no member of the legislature shall be appointed to any office which has been created, or the emoluments of which have been increased, during his term of service in the legislature. This restriction is nominally a restriction upon the executive power of appointment, but actually it operates to protect the chief executive against the demands of legislators who would trade support for executive measures in exchange for promises of appointment to office.

The strengthening of the executive veto and power of appointment, together with the abolition of the original executive councils and the establishment of independence of tenure for the chief executive through direct popular election, sufficed to create a continuous check upon legislative authority. This check, however, is not yet as effective in most states as that originally established in Massachusetts, because of the existence of the senatorial power of blocking appointments. In Massachusetts, especially since the council was made elective by the people, the governor has been independent of the legislature in the making of appointments. The original Massachusetts system still exists in Maine. Elsewhere the governor's appointments are dependent on the approval of the upper branch of the legislature. The power of the executive to check the enactment of legislation is limited by the power of the legislature to check the distribution of patronage. Everywhere the influence of the executive upon legislation is checked by legislative control of the appropriations necessary for the maintenance of executive authority. The power of the purse still remains, as it was in colonial times, the great bulwark of legislative authority.

Development of the Judicial Veto.

A less conspicuous feature of the system of checks and balances originally established in Massachusetts was the judicial veto. The power of judicial review of the constitutionality of legislative enactments springs from the obligation of deciding what law applies in a case where there is a conflict of laws. Since the courts must apply the higher law, the duty is plain to declare the legislative enactment unconstitutional when constitutions and statutes conflict.

This duty of the judiciary was implied in the original theory of American government, but the original forms of government in most of the states were not such as to facilitate its effective performance. Indeed, it is probable that the people generally were unconscious of the existence of any such judicial duty. Even in the few states which originally made express provision for the exercise of the power of judicial review, the power was by no means so potent as it has since become. In New York the judicial element controlled the council of revision, but the council of revision was compelled to act before final action by the legislature and could be overruled by two-thirds majorities of the latter. The final court of appeal in New York was controlled by the senate, which was not primarily a judicial body at all. In Massachusetts and New Hampshire the power of judicial review was qualified by the provision that the legislature or governor could ask the judges of the supreme judicial court for their opinion of the constitutionality of a proposed measure in advance of its enactment. Clearly the veto of unconstitutional legislation by the courts was intended to be an exception rather than a regular use of judicial power.

The possibilities of the power of judicial review were clearly grasped by the leaders in the Federal Convention of 1787, and the people of the country were made familiar with its vigorous exercise by John Marshall. The adoption of the Massachusetts type of executive veto in New York in 1821 involved the recognition in that state of a separate power of judicial veto, and that date may be accepted as marking the period of its general recognition by the people of the states. The most effective use of the power of judicial veto, however, was dependent upon the establishment of judicial independence of the state legislatures, a process which was not completed in most of the states until the adoption of the popular election of judges towards the middle of the century. When De Tocqueville paid his memorable visit to the United States during the presidency of Andrew Jackson, the practice had, nevertheless, already become well established.

De Tocqueville's judgment has been endorsed with the approval of history. "I am inclined to believe," said he, "that this practice of the American courts is at once most favorable to liberty and to public order. If the judge could only attack the legislator openly and directly, he would sometimes be afraid to oppose him; and at other times, party spirit might encourage him to brave it at every turn. The laws would consequently be attacked when the power from which they emanated was weak, and obeyed when it was strong;—that is to say, when it would be useful to respect them, they would often be contested; and when it would be easy to convert them into an instrument of oppression, they would be respected. But the American judge is brought into the political arena independently of his own will. He only judges the law because he is obliged to judge a case. The political question which he is called upon to resolve is connected with the interests of the parties, and he cannot refuse to decide it without a denial of justice. He performs his functions as a citizen, by fulfilling the precise duties which belong to his profession as a magistrate. It is true that, upon this system, the judicial censorship of the courts of justice over the legislature cannot extend to all laws indiscriminately, inasmuch as some of them can never give rise to the precise species of contest which is termed a lawsuit; and even when such a contest is possible, it may happen that no one cares to bring it before a court of justice. The Americans have often felt this inconvenience; but they have left the remedy incomplete, lest they should give it an efficacy which might in some cases prove dangerous. Within these limits, the power vested in the American courts of justice, of pronouncing a statute to be unconstitutional, forms one of the most powerful barriers which has ever been devised against the tyranny of political assemblies."[1]

The power of judicial review may be exercised in a law court of any grade, and by either judge or jury. It was not uncommon, indeed, in the original states to provide that the jury should determine the law applicable to certain classes of causes as well as the facts thereof. The interests of litigants were safeguarded by granting to the losing party a right to a new trial before another jury. Thus in Georgia, under the original constitution of 1777, the jury were expressly declared to be judges of law as well as of fact, but if any of the jury should have any doubts concerning points of law they were authorized to apply to the judges, "who shall each of them in rotation give their opinion." Dis-

[1] A. de Tocqueville, *Democracy in America* (Bowen's ed.), i, pp. 129-130.

satisfied litigants in civil causes were entitled to appeal from the verdict and demand a new trial in the same court before a special jury. The ordinary jury were to be sworn to bring in a verdict "according to law, and the opinion they entertain of the evidence; provided it be not repugnant to the rules and regulations contained in this constitution." The special jury were to be sworn to bring in a similar verdict, "provided it be not repugnant to justice, equity, and conscience, and the rules and regulations contained in this constitution, of which they shall judge." There could be no clearer expression than this, both of the power of judicial review, and of the duty of the jury to exercise that power. In this instance the power was vested exclusively in the jury, but it is clear that the opinions of the judges were intended to exert such influence as the character of the judges should warrant.

In practice the enforcement of the law of the written constitution, in cases of conflict with legislative enactments, has fallen almost exclusively to the lot of the judges. It was inevitable that judges, and not juries, should in the long run prove the most effective guardians of the popular rights, so far as these rights were expressly guaranteed in written constitutions. The judges were, comparatively at least, learned in the law; the juries were not. The judges were selected, professedly at least, by a test of fitness; the juries were selected casually. The judges were organized into a centralized hierarchy; the juries were unsystematically organized. The judges were employed in the public service for relatively long periods; the juries were employed only temporarily. The judges were free to weigh the force of precedent; the juries were dominated by local interests and ideas. The judges concentrated their attention on the law; the jury, on the facts. Thus, although in criminal cases juries were able to refuse to convict on the ground that the statute on which the prosecution was based was unconstitutional, they tended to rely upon the charge of the judge, and the latter tended to assume the sole function of reviewing the constitutionality of such legislative enactments. Finally, contrary to what must have been the original popular impression, questions concerning the constitutionality of legislative enactments tended to arise in connection with civil rather than criminal cases. In such cases the importance of jury trials is less. Moreover, as De Tocqueville pointed out long ago, it is especially in civil cases that "the judge appears as a disinterested arbiter between the conflicting passions of the parties. The jurors look up to him with confidence, and listen to him with respect, for in this instance his intellect entirely governs theirs. . . . His influence over them is almost unlimited." Thus, "the American judge is constantly surrounded by men who are accustomed to regard his intelligence as superior to their own; and after having exercised his power in the decision of causes, he continues to influence the habits of thought, and even the characters, of those who acted with him in his official capacity. The jury, then, which seems to restrict the rights of the judiciary, does in reality consolidate its power. . . ." [1] In short, the exercise of the power of judicial review was preëmpted by the judges, so far as was necessary for the enforcement of the formal law of the state constitutions, and the juries were confined to the exercise of the power only in cases involving the unwritten law.

Advisory Judicial Opinions.

Whilst the power of judicial veto has been universally recognized, the Massachusetts provision for advisory judicial opinions has been adopted in comparatively few states.[2] Five other states,[3] one of which later abandoned the practice, have provided for obtaining opinions from the judges of the highest court upon application by the executive or legislature. Two states [4] have provided for obtaining such opinions upon application by the executive alone. In Massachusetts the judges are to give their opinions "on important questions of law and upon solemn occasions." In some of the other states the obligation to give advisory opinions is more restricted, and even in Massachusetts the judges are free to withhold their opinions if they do not consider the question of law important or the occasion solemn. Nor are they bound to adhere to their opinion, when once given, if the same question of law should later arise in the course of litigation, and

[1] De Tocqueville, *Democracy in America* (Bowen's ed.), pp. 366-367.

[2] For a study of the advisory opinion, see Albert R. Ellingwood, *Departmental Co-operation in State Government* (New York, 1918). For a recent and unusual decision of the supreme court of Alabama with reference to advisory opinions, see *In re* Opinions of the Justices, 96 So. 487 (1923). This case is reviewed in the *American Political Science Review*, xix, pp. 565-567 (1925).

[3] New Hampshire (1784), Maine (1820), Rhode Island (1842), Missouri (1865-1875), and Colorado (1886).

[4] Florida (1868) and South Dakota (1889).

further reflection, aided by the arguments of counsel, should prompt a different decision. In short, the giving of such opinions by judges is generally not regarded as an exercise of a judicial function, and the opinions therefore have much the same legal status as opinions of the attorney-general in states where that officer is the official legal adviser of the administration. If they are usually received with greater respect, it is because the judges usually enjoy a greater reputation for legal learning, and not because of their official position. The power to require such advisory opinions may be useful to perplexed legislatures and executives, but it does not deprive the courts of the power of judicial veto or impair the exercise thereof.[1]

Growth of Constitutional Limitations on Legislative Powers.

The scope of the judicial veto is determined by the extent of the constitutional limitations upon the powers of the state legislatures. In the beginning it was confined to a comparatively narrow range of subjects, since the powers of the state legislatures were limited only by the general reservations of rights to the people in the original declarations of rights. With the gradual decline, however, in the prestige of the state legislatures the constitutional limitations upon their powers were steadily increased. In other words, the record of legislative folly and corruption in the American states is spread upon their constitutions in the form of a stream of amendments designed to check the abuse of legislative powers. The power to pass special and local acts, the power to tax and to grant tax-exemptions, the power to invest the public money, loan the public credit, and dispose of the public resources in general, all were subjected to a series of restrictions ever increasing in number and stringency.

The limitation of the powers of the legislatures, though never interrupted, has proceeded with conspicuous vigor at three clearly defined periods, each inaugurated by especially impressive examples of legislative incapacity and turpitude. The first period began with the notorious Yazoo land scandal in Georgia, followed by scandalous practices in connection with the grant of banking charters in several of the states, especially in New York. The revision of the constitution of Georgia in 1798 was undertaken mainly for the purpose of preventing the repetition of the land

[1] J. B. Thayer, *Legal Essays*, no. 2.

scandal, and the experience of Georgia was not forgotten when the constitutions of the new states of the old Northwest and Southwest were formed early in the nineteenth century. The period culminated in the reform of the New York constitution in 1821. The second period began with the panic of 1837, followed by the failure of the systems of internal improvements undertaken by many of the states, and the repudiation of several state debts. The constitutions of Pennsylvania in 1838 and New Jersey in 1844 were revised with a view to profiting by these unpleasant experiences, and by the middle of the century the constitutions of most of the states had been revised or were in process of revision. The third period began with the outburst of speculation in special privileges at the close of the Civil War, and is sufficiently characterized by the *Credit Mobilier* scandal in Congress. Beginning in 1870, the constitutions of most of the leading states in the North outside of New England were revised, the culmination of the movement being reached in New York in 1894. At the same time, in the South, the period following the overthrow of negro domination was likewise characterized by the thorough overhauling of the constitutions of the states, with a view to the further limitation of legislative misconduct.

The great extension of the power of judicial veto during the nineteenth century is revealed by a comparison of the constitutional limitations originally imposed on the Massachusetts legislature with those imposed on the legislature of New York in the constitution of 1894. For example, the power to tax in Massachusetts was limited only by the provisions that personal and property taxes should be "proportional and reasonable," that duties and excises should be "reasonable," and that for the purpose of levying poll and property taxes there should be a revaluation of property at least once every ten years. The power to appropriate the proceeds of taxation was limited only by the provision that appropriations should be for a public purpose.[1]

Finally, the legislature was forbidden to suspend the writ of *habeas corpus*, except upon the most urgent and pressing occasions and for not more than twelve months at a time.[2] Except for the limitations set forth in the declaration of rights, there were no other limitations upon the powers of the legislature in the

[1] Ch. i, sect. i, art. iv; ch. ii, sect. i, art. ii.
[2] Ch. vi, art. vii.

Massachusetts constitution of 1780. The power to dispose of the public domain, to incur debt, to charter corporations and confer special privileges upon them, to pass private and local acts, to engage in public enterprises, and to pass public acts of every description, all were conferred in one general grant of legislative power.[1]

In New York, on the other hand, by the constitution of 1894 the powers of the legislature were subjected to important limitations, and legislative procedure was subjected to stringent regulation. No private or local bill might embrace more than one subject, and no private or local bill might be passed at all in any one of a long list of specified cases. Among these were the following: changing the names of persons, laying out roads, locating county seats, providing for changes of venue in civil or criminal cases, incorporating villages, selecting grand or petty jurors, regulating the rate of interest on money, creating allowances for public officers during their terms of office, granting the right to lay down railroad tracks, granting to any private corporation, association, or person any exclusive privilege, or granting to any person or corporation an exemption from taxation on real or personal property. The assent of two-thirds of all the members elected to each branch of the legislature was required for any appropriation of public money or property for private or local purposes; and the assent of a majority of a special quorum consisting of three-fifths of all the members on a special roll-call to be recorded in the official journal was required for the adoption of any act imposing a tax, creating a debt, or making an appropriation. The legislature was forbidden to loan the credit of the state to any person or corporation, or to contract debts in excess of one million dollars for the purpose of meeting deficits in the revenues except in case of insurrection or invasion, or to contract any debts for any other purpose except with the express approval of the people. The legislature was forbidden to dispose of the state forests, or of the canals, or to charge tolls thereon. The legislature was forbidden to authorize any local governing body to loan its credit or incur indebtedness except for its own purposes, and local debts were limited to ten per cent of the assessed valuation of local real estate. The constitution also provided for the classification of cities in three classes according to their population and

[1] Ch. i, sect. i, art. iv.

prescribed a special procedure for the passage of special laws relating to a single city or to any number of cities less than the whole number in a class. Such a law, before being submitted to the governor for his approval, was required first to be transmitted to the mayor or mayors or the city or cities concerned and, if not approved by him or them, to be repassed by the legislature with a statement in the title for the information of the governor that thc bill is passed without the acceptance of the city or cities concerned. The apportionment of the state for the election of members of the legislature was provided for in the constitution itself, and the power of the legislature to redistrict the state was carefully defined. The manner of passing bills was regulated in order to secure due deliberation and adequate publicity at each stage of the procedure, and the legislature was expressly forbidden to audit any private claim against the state, or to authorize the payment of any account not previously allowed according to law. It is apparent that the New York constitution of 1894 afforded far broader scope for the exercise of the power of judicial review than the Massachusetts constitution of 1780.

Present Importance of Constitutional Limitations.

At the present time, the states fall into three groups with respect to the extent to which legislative powers have been restricted by the insertion of express limitations in the state constitutions. The first group consists mainly of states in New England, of which Massachusetts is the most conspicuous representative, and is characterized by a comparatively slight imposition of constitutional limitations upon legislative powers. The second group comprises a somewhat larger group of states, mostly in the East and Middle West, of which New York is the most conspicuous representative, and is characterized by a more extensive limitation of legislative powers, but especially by a more thorough regulation of legislative procedure. The third group comprises the greater number of states, including almost all the states of the South and Far West, of which the most conspicuous representatives are California, Louisiana, and Missouri, and is characterized not only by the extensive limitation of legislative powers, but also by the regulation of the freqnency and duration of the legislative sessions. In most cases, the legislature is permitted to meet only every other year, unless called in special session by the governor, but in Alabama it is permitted to meet only every fourth year. In most cases, the sessions are limited to sixty or ninety days. In a few the limit is lower. In Oregon and Wyoming it is placed as low as forty days. Apparently the people of those states despaired of securing any effective check on the misconduct of their legislatures, and, accepting the view that legislatures are a necessary evil, sought relief by confining the evil within the shortest possible limits of time.[1]

DEVELOPMENT OF THE CONSTITUTIONAL CONVENTION

The widespread adoption of constitutional limitations upon legislative powers, apart from its effect upon the exercise of the power of judicial review, has had important consequences on the general operation of state government.

Growth of Legislative Powers of Conventions.

In the first place, it has greatly altered the position of the constitutional convention in the governmental system. In the beginning the constitutional convention was an extraordinary legislative body, meeting only for the purpose of devising or revising the fundamental organization of the government. As the prestige of the ordinary state legislature declined, however, that of the constitutional convention rose, and its work broadened in scope. From the moment that the convention came to be regarded as the instrument for repairing the mistakes or misdeeds of the ordinary legislature its future became full of promise. At first it generally confined its correctional activities to the single task of imposing upon the legislatures constitutional limitations designed to prevent the abuse of their powers. Then it began to issue orders to the legislatures, enjoining upon them the performance of their duties. Thus, the Georgia constitutional convention of 1798 commanded the Georgia legislature to repeal certain acts relating to the disposal of the public lands, and to enact certain other measures in their stead. It was quickly perceived, however, that this mode of procedure was ineffective, since there was no means of compelling a refractory legislature to comply with the

[1] For an illuminating interpretation of the constitutional history of the state legislatures, see Herbert Croly, *Progressive Democracy*, chs. xi, xii. See also P. S. Reinsch, *American Legislatures and Legislative Methods*, ch. iv.

orders of a convention. The difficulty was the same as that which had frustrated the efforts of the council of censors in Pennsylvania. The constitutional conventions, therefore, quickly adopted the practice of executing their own commands by the simple device of inserting them in the fundamental law, and thus taking the matters to which they referred out of the hands of the legislatures. In other words, the conventions utilized the forms of fundamental law-making for the purpose of enacting ordinary statutory law, and thereby acquired for themselves the powers of an ordinary legislative body, subject in their exercise to the approval of the electorate in those states where the approval of the electorate was required for the revision or amendment of the constitution. In short, the constitutional convention became transformed into an ordinary legislative body, meeting more or less periodically for the purpose of reviewing the conduct of the regular legislature and of enacting, with the approval of the people, such legislation as the occasion should appear to demand.

One indication of the legislative activity of the constitutional conventions is the increase in the length of the state constitutions. The original constitution of Virginia occupies six and one-half printed pages in Thorpe's edition of the state constitutions. The Massachusetts constitution of 1780, the longest of the original constitutions, occupies twenty-three printed pages. The proposed constitution and other acts of the Oklahoma constitutional convention of 1907 occupy seventy-four pages in the same compilation. The original Virginia constitution contains no ordinary legislation. The original Massachusetts constitution contains none, unless articles confirming the privileges of Harvard College and fixing the value of money be deemed such. The constitution of Oklahoma contains eleven pages of legislation relating to the subject of corporations alone, besides much more ordinary legislative matter relating to homesteads and exemptions, banks and banking, insurance, the employment of children, and education. It forbids plural marriages, fixes the maximum rate of interest, abolishes the so-called fellow-servant doctrine and regulates the use of the contributory-negligence and assumption-of-risk doctrines as defenses in certain suits for damages, establishes the eight-hour day on public works and in coal mines, and determines the test for the purity of kerosene oil. The convention also provided for the separate submission to the electorate of a proposal to prohibit the sale of intoxicating liquors. The acts of the Oklahoma convention of 1907 are merely the most striking evidence of the growing tendency throughout the states, especially in the South and West, to transform the constitutional convention into an ordinary legislative body. The fundamentals of state government are predetermined outside of the conventions by public opinion, and the responsibility for alterations in the actual frames of government has been in the main shifted to the electorates.

Relations Between Conventions and State Legislatures.

The result of these developments was to precipitate a struggle for supremacy in some states between the legislature and the constitutional convention. In the course of this struggle three different theories concerning the constitutional position of the constitutional convention have been developed. According to the first, the constitutional convention is a subordinate legislative body, subject to control by the regular legislature of the state. According to the second, it is a sovereign body, possessing for the time being all the powers of the sovereign people. According to the third, it is a coördinate legislative body, subject like the regular legislature to the constitution of the state, but not subject to the authority of any other legislative body.

The conflicting nature of these three theories may be illustrated as follows. The people, let us say, by a majority of the votes of those voting thereon approve an act of the legislature providing for the election of a constitutional convention. Whether the legislature is expressly authorized by the constitution to submit such an act to the people is, as has already been shown, immaterial, except in Rhode Island. The legislature then provides for the election of the delegates to the convention, and in the same act imposes certain limitations upon the powers of the convention, when it shall meet. For example, it may enact that the convention shall not propose amendments to certain sections of the existing constitution, or shall submit amendments to certain sections, if at all, separately to the people, or shall submit them at a certain time and in the manner provided by the law of the state governing elections. The advocate of the supremacy of the ordinary legislature would assert that the convention would have no right to disobey any of these injunctions. The advocate of the supremacy of the convention would assert that it might disobey any or all of them. The advocate of the coördinate authority of legislature and convention would assert that the convention might disobey some of these injunctions but must obey others.

Very few of the state constitutions define the status of the constitutional convention. In all the states, until comparatively recently, and at the present time in almost all, the powers of the constitutional convention are to be discovered only by examination of the unwritten law of the constitution. The two fundamental principles of the unwritten law are the sovereignty of the people and the reign of law. Whatever powers a constitutional convention may possess, therefore, if not defined in the written constitution, must be obtained by a delegation of authority by the people, and the delegation of this authority must be accomplished by due process of law.

There are two distinct cases: first, where the call for the convention is not submitted to the people for an expression of their consent; secondly, where it is so submitted. In the former case, such power as the convention may possess is apparently delegated to it by the legislature on its own authority. It is an accepted principle of the unwritten constitution, however, that legislative power may not be delegated by the body on which the people have conferred it. The calling of a convention, therefore, without a vote of the people must be regarded as an abdication of power by the regular legislature in favor of an extra constitutional body. Such a body is a revolutionary rather than a constitutional convention, and the extent of its powers would apparently be determined by itself, subject only to the limits which the people in their capacity of ultimate sovereign may be able to impose. It cannot be denied that many of the conventions which have been held in the states have been of this character, and the propriety of such a convention has been sustained by the supreme court of Mississippi in a case involving the power of the convention of that state held in 1890 practically to disfranchise the negro voters without their consent.[1]

The more general case at the present time is that in which the call of the convention has been expressly sanctioned by a vote of

[1] See Sproule *v.* Fredericks, 69 Miss. 898 (1892). See also R. S. Hoar, *Constitutional Conventions*, pp. 65-68.

the people. In such a case, the powers of the convention must be derived from the terms of the vote adopted by the people, and the terms of that vote must be formulated in the first instance by the legislature. So far, there can hardly be any disagreement between the advocates of the several theories set forth above. The advocates of legislative supremacy, however, proceed further. They argue that, since the voice of the people is expressed through the legislature, the adoption of a vote by the people authorizing the legislature to call a convention serves also to authorize the legislature to regulate the powers and procedure of the convention in any manner that the legislature may deem necessary and proper. Hence, although whatever powers the convention possesses must be derived from the people, the extent of these powers may be defined by the legislature without any further express approval on the part of the people than that indicated by their sanction of the call. The advocates of the supremacy of the convention, on the other hand, argue that if the vote of the people sanctions the call of a convention, it is a constitutional convention that must be called, a body possessing for the time all the sovereign powers of the people themselves, and not some inferior body subject to the control of the ordinary legislature of the state. The legislature is not authorized to use its discretion with respect to the extent of power that shall be conferred on the people, assembled by their representatives in convention, but simply to issue the call for the election of these representatives.

The advocate of the coördinate authority of convention and legislature reasons in a different manner. Proceeding from the accepted rule that whatever powers the convention may possess must be derived from the people, he argues that the terms of the vote actually adopted by the people are the evidence of the extent of these powers, and that any restrictions which the legislature may seek to impose without the express approval of the people are unauthorized and hence invalid. The legislature may propose to the people whatever limitations it pleases, but these limitations must be accepted by the people in order to take effect upon the convention. The convention should be free to disregard any special limitations which the legislature may seek to impose subsequently to the vote by the people sanctioning the call of the convention, but it should not be free to disregard the general law of the state, whether expressed in the constitution or in the acts of the legislature. A convention, for example, may disregard a legislative act, not submitted to the people for their approval, which seeks to limit the duration of the deliberations of the convention, but it may not disregard a legislative act providing that appropriations for the support of the convention shall lapse after a limited period. In other words, the executive or judiciary of the state would not be justified in turning a convention out of doors after the period set by the legislature for the termination of its deliberations had expired, but they would be justified in withholding further funds. The convention might continue in session, but it would have to look to the people for indemnification for any further expenses that might be incurred.

Present Status of the Constitutional Convention.

No one of these theories with respect to the position of the constitutional convention has been universally accepted in the states. In several of the states no one has even been uniformly followed. The theory of legislative supremacy has been vigorously asserted by the supreme court of Pennsylvania, for example, but it was not accepted by the last convention of that state. The people adopted the constitution which the convention proposed to them, thus exculpating the members of the convention for their disregard of the restrictions which the legislature sought with the approval of the court to impose upon them.[1] The theory of the supremacy of the convention seems to have become the established rule in Virginia. On three occasions, in 1830, 1850, and 1869, the convention extended the right to vote to classes of the population which had not previously possessed it, and then submitted their work to the new electorate for approval. On a fourth occasion, in 1902, the convention deprived an important class of the population of their right to vote and then declined to submit their work to the judgment of the electorate, either old or new.[2] When a convention in Illinois, however, tried in 1862 to usurp ordinary legislative powers, the political situation rendered it inexpedient to attempt to dispense with the formal approval of the electorate, and the work of the convention was repudiated by the people of

[1] See Wells *v.* Bain, 75 Pa. St. 39 (1874), and Wood's Appeal, 75 Pa. St. 59 (1874).

[2] F. A. Magruder, *Recent Administration in Virginia* (Johns Hopkins University Studies, xxx, 1, pp. 78-94), p. 89.

the state.[1] Whilst no one theory can be said to have become generally accepted, the view seems to be tending to prevail, at least in those states where popular approval is required before a convention may be called, that the convention and legislature should be coördinate legislative bodies, each independent of the other in its proper sphere and both alike subject to the supremacy of the constitution.[2]

GROWTH OF POWERS OF THE ELECTORATE

The widespread adoption of constitutional limitations upon legislative powers has greatly altered the position of the electorate in the governmental system. The least conspicuous feature of the system of checks and balances originally established in Massachusetts was the direct popular veto of legislative measures. Since in most states the work of constitutional conventions may become effective only with the express consent of the people, the process of imposing restrictions on the legislatures involved an increase in the activities of the electorate. The feeling that the people were directly participating in the making of laws was intensified when constitutional conventions began to insert substantive law of an ordinary statutory nature in the constitutions. Many conventions still further intensified this feeling by providing for separate submission of measures of an ordinary statutory character, thus making the electors conscious of the distinction between the statutory law and constitutional law in the strict sense of the term. Finally many legislatures themselves have been compelled to enact much legislation in the guise of constitutional amendments, which, but for the restrictions imposed upon them by the conventions, would have been disposed of without reference to the people. The result has been greatly to increase the importance of the state electorates as legislative bodies.

The decline in the powers of the legislatures was the result of the decline of legislative prestige. As the people's respect for the ability and integrity of their representative bodies dwindled, their reliance upon themselves was necessarily bound to grow,

[1] O. M. Dickerson, *The Illinois Constitutional Convention of 1862* (University of Illinois Studies).

[2] See Report of Committee on Judiciary, Elihu Root, chairman, New York Constitutional Convention, 1894, *Documents and Reports*, pp. 79-100.

unless they were to confess popular government a failure. Thus direct action by the electorate came to the support of a declining system of representative government.

The rise of the electorate as an instrument for direct legislative action has been marked by the development of two distinct forms of activity. One has culminated in what is called municipal home rule; the other, in direct legislation by the people. The former has rendered the electorates of the municipalities in those states where it has been adopted independent of the authority of the legislature in local concerns; the latter has rendered the electorates of certain states as a whole independent of the state legislatures. Both systems alike operate as limitations upon legislative power. The referendum alone, whether local or state-wide, makes possible the popular veto of legislative enactments. Municipal home rule and the procedure for direct legislation by the people, when complete, enable the electorate not only to veto legislation that is not desired, but also to take the initiative in the enactment of legislation without awaiting the pleasure of the ordinary legislature of the state. The referendum is negative in its operation; it facilitates the correction of legislative errors of commission. The initiative is positive; it facilitates the correction of errors of omission.

Development of Municipal Home Rule.

The development of home rule has been a gradual process.[1] In the form of the local popular veto it seems to have been introduced first in New England. There the traditional system of local government was characterized by the assemblage of all the voters at least once a year in town meeting for the election of local officers and the ordering of town affairs. When in 1820 the Massachusetts constitutional convention proposed an amendment to define the legislature's power to incorporate cities, it readily provided that the legislature should not grant a municipal charter to any town unless a majority of the townsmen voting in town meeting should approve the change from town to city. Thus the power of the legislature to incorporate cities was limited by the obligation to obtain the consent of the people of the proposed city. Thereafter the local referendum was gradually introduced in all

[1] The standard work on this topic is H. L. McBain, *The Law and the Practice of Municipal Home Rule* (New York, 1916).

parts of the country in connection with legislation affecting the forms, organization, powers and procedures of local government. To-day, by the constitutions of many states, the legislatures are forbidden to enact measures to incorporate villages and cities, to define the boundaries of counties or divide them into townships, to locate county seats or change county names or to alter the forms of local government without the consent of the people of the localities affected.

Once the local referendum had been established by constitutional conventions as an instrument for checking the operations of the legislatures, it was an easy step for the legislatures themselves to extend the use of the local referendum as an instrument for checking the operations of the local governments. Thus statutes were enacted in many states forbidding local governing authorities to lend the public credit for the promotion of private enterprises of a commercial or industrial nature, or forbidding the expenditure of public money directly by the local government itself for local improvements without the express consent of the people. A further step was taken when the legislatures adopted the practice of submitting to the decision of the voters certain questions which the legislatures could not ignore and could not themselves decide without embarrassment. Thus, the question of the control of the traffic in intoxicating liquors was disposed of in many states by the enactment of laws, providing for the decision between a policy of license or no-license directly by the voters in each locality. Local option, as this procedure was called, meant in New England annual referenda in each city and town, in other parts of the country referenda in the county or in subdivisions of the county. Similar procedure has been established in some states for the decision of questions such as the establishment of municipal public services, especially waterworks and lighting plants, and the granting of franchises to public service corporations.

The most important development of the local referendum has been in connection with the adoption and revision of municipal charters. In Massachusetts the legislature early established the practice of submitting to the people of the towns and cities for their acceptance or rejection all proposals for the adoption or revision of charters. In other states this practice was made mandatory upon the legislature by the constitution. The final step in the development of municipal autonomy was taken in Missouri in 1875. The constitution adopted in that year provided that on petition of a certain number of citizens in any city an election should be held for the choice of a board of freeholders whose duty it should be to prepare a charter and submit it to the people. If approved by them, it should go into effect without any special action on the part of the state legislature, nor should the state legislature be able to alter it in any manner except by general law applying to the whole state. Thus an effective power of local popular initiative was added to the local referendum. This or similar procedure for the establishment of municipal home rule has now been adopted in sixteen states.[1] In some states home rule charters must be submitted to the governor of the state for his approval in order to ensure the elimination of provisions in conflict with the general laws of the state, but in most states the adjustment of cases of conflict between home rule charters and the general laws of the state is left to the courts. A further step in the development of local home rule was taken in California (1911) and Maryland (1915), where the application of the procedure for the adoption of home rule charters has been extended to the county.

Development of Legislative Referendum.

The state-wide, like the local, referendum was first employed in Massachusetts, and was subsequently copied and extended by other states. At the present time it may be employed in five different cases: (1) in connection with the revision and amendment of state constitutions, as has already been described; (2) in connection with ordinary legislation, which is submitted by a state legislature to the electorate for approval or disapproval either by reason of a constitutional limitation or directly upon its own motion; (3) in connection with ordinary legislation duly enacted by the legislature and referred to the electorate upon petition by a certain fraction thereof; (4) in connection with proposals for ordinary legislation which the legislature has

[1] In addition to the sixteen states having constitutional provisions on the subject of municipal home rule, a number of states have granted or have attempted to grant home rule by mere legislative enactment. See H. L. McBain, "Home Rule by Legislative Grant," in his *American City Progress and the Law* (New York, 1918); see also "Municipal Home Rule," *Illinois Constitutional Convention Bulletins*, no. 6 (1919).

neglected to enact, submitted to the electorate upon petition of a certain fraction thereof; and (5) in connection with proposed constitutional amendments which may be submitted to the electorate upon petition of a certain fraction thereof without the intervention of the legislature. The third case is that which is often described as the direct popular referendum. The fourth is often described as the popular or statutory initiative, and the fifth as the constitutional initiative. The statutory and constitutional initiatives may be either direct or indirect. If direct, there is a popular vote upon the proposed bill or amendment without any opportunity for action by the regular legislative body. If indirect, the regular legislature must first have an opportunity to act upon the measure presented by popular petition before such measure is voted upon by the electorate. The third and fourth together or the third, fourth, and fifth together constitute the procedure often collectively described as direct legislation by the people. The second case, which may for convenience be described as the legislative referendum, is that which developed next after the development of the referendum upon proposed constitutional revisions and amendments.

Legislative referenda are of two kinds: those expressly authorized by the constitution, and those not expressly authorized. One of the earliest instances of the legislative referendum expressly authorized by the constitution is found in connection with choice of a site for a state capital. Texas was the first state to make provision for the submission by the legislature to the people of a measure to indicate their preference respecting the location of the permanent seat of government. Oregon, Kansas, and Colorado, and several other states more recently, did the same when they were admitted to the Union. The constitutions of at least a dozen states now provide that the legislature shall enact no law providing for the relocation of the capital without the approval of the people. A still earlier instance of the legislative referendum was its use in order to control more effectively the legislative power to raise and expend the public revenues. In 1842 a provision was inserted in the new constitution of Rhode Island forbidding the legislature to contract any indebtedness beyond $50,000, except in time of war or in case of invasion or domestic insurrection, without the approval of the people. Similar limitations upon the power of the legislatures to contract debts have since been adopted, subject to various exceptions respecting the amount of debt in most of the states. The amount of indebtedness for ordinary public purposes which may be contracted without the necessity of ratification by the people varies from $50,000 in Rhode Island to $2,000,000 in Idaho, but the principle is the same. The legislature must keep the state expenditures within its revenues, or secure authority for the contraction of debt directly from the people. This limitation serves also as a limitation upon the power of the legislatures to engage in expensive works of public improvement without the express approval of the people, although in a few states the legislature may not even adopt a project of public improvement, much less finance it, without the express approval of the people. In a few states the legislatures are forbidden to dispose of certain public properties without the express approval of the people, and in a few others they are forbidden even to increase the rate of taxation upon property beyond a maximum fixed in the constitution without the express approval of the people. The state-wide legislative referendum has also been employed in several states to prevent the abuse of the power to create banking corporations. Beginning in Iowa in 1846, the constitutions of seven states, all located in the Middle West, prohibited the legislature from enacting without the express consent of the people any law for the chartering of banks. Thus, through the operation of the legislative referendum in certain classes of cases expressly authorized by the state constitution, both the legislatures and the people have been familiarized with the use of the popular veto in connection with the adoption of ordinary statutes as well as of constitutional amendments and revisions.

It was an easy step for state legislatures to resort to the state-wide referendum upon statutes in cases where they were not authorized to do so by the state constitution. The first instance seems to have occurred in New York in 1849. The legislature was convinced that the people wished to establish a compulsory system of public education, but was uncertain as to the willingness of the people to pay the cost. The legislators therefore sought to evade their responsibility for action in the matter by passing a measure for free compulsory education with the proviso that it should not take effect unless approved by a majority of the voters. The law, however, was declared unconstitutional by the supreme court of the state.[1] The court took the view that legislative power conferred upon the legislature by the constitution was to be used, if at all, by the legislature itself, and might not be delegated by the legislature to others, not even to the state electorate. Had the people wished to reserve to themselves the power to legislate, presumably they would have done so. Since they had not done so, the only reasonable inference, the court believed, was that they had commanded their servant, the legislature, to exercise that power for them. To attempt to shift responsibility back upon the people for the adoption of legislation was therefore a breach of trust on the part of the legislature.

Shortly afterwards the policy of prohibiting the sale of intoxicating liquors, or so-called Maine idea, swept the northern and western states, to the great embarrassment of the state legislatures. In several states they would have preferred to refer the whole matter to the people, but the decision in the New York case stood in the way of such evasion of their responsibility. In Michigan an ingenious device was adopted to gain the same end. A state-wide prohibitory law was enacted in 1853 to go into effect either on December 1, 1853, or on March 1, 1870, and the decision between the two dates was referred to the electorate. In either event the law was to go into effect, unless sooner repealed, and hence there was no delegation of legislative power by the legislature, but simply a direction to the executive to enforce the act from a certain date in the event of a certain contingency, namely a vote in favor of that date by the electorate. This law was declared constitutional by a divided court, but in general legislative attempts to shift the responsibility for legislation to the electorate, except in those cases where such shifting is expressly authorized by the constitution, have found little favor in the courts.[2]

The use of the referendum on proposed legislation of any sort at the discretion of the legislature has been expressly authorized by constitutional amendment in eleven states, beginning with Oregon in 1902. In a larger number of states, where the process of constitutional amendment is short and direct, the legislature can virtually refer any proposed legislation to the electorate

[1] Barto *vs.* Himrod, 4 Seld. (N. Y.), 483. See also State *vs.* Hayes, 61 N. H., 264.

[2] E. P. Oberholtzer, *The Referendum in America*, ch. viii.

by referring it under the guise of a proposed amendment to the constitution. Occasionally a referendum has been ordered by a state legislature for advisory purposes only. In such cases the vote has no legal force and serves simply as an expression of public opinion. In one state, Illinois, the legislature provided in 1901 that an advisory vote may be had on any question submitted by popular petition. This advisory initiative, however, does not actually increase the constitutional power of the electorate. It merely serves as an additional means for the expression of public opinion.

Direct Legislation by the People.

The foundation for the direct popular referendum and initiative may be found in the political institutions and ideas of the people of the American states. The thing itself, however, is a foreign importation. Doubtless the growing use of the constitutional and legislative referendum and of the popular initiative in connection with local home rule would sooner or later have suggested to Americans the adoption of some procedure for direct legislation by the people of a state as a whole. The system that has actually been adopted, however, was suggested by the example of Switzerland.[1] The first state to adopt the statutory initiative and referendum was South Dakota, which took that action in 1898. The statutory initiative and referendum now exist in eighteen states. In addition two states have adopted the direct popular referendum alone. The first state to adopt the constitutional as well as the statutory initiative was Oregon, which took that action in 1902. The constitutional initiative now exists in thirteen states.[2]

The Recall.

The last step in the extension of the powers of the state electorates has been the adoption of the popular recall. The original Massachusetts declaration of rights contained a statement to the effect that "in order to prevent those who are vested with author-

[1] W. E. Rappard, "The Initiative, Referendum, and Recall in Switzerland," in *Annals of the American Academy of Political and Social Science*, Sept., 1912, pp. 114-127.

[2] See "The Initiative, Referendum, and Recall," *Illinois Constitutional Convention Bulletins*, no 2 (1919).

ity from becoming oppressors, the people have a right at such periods and in such manner as they shall establish by their frames of government, to cause their public officers to return to private life." In the beginning frequent elections and short fixed terms of office were deemed an adequate mode of preventing those vested with authority from becoming oppressors. In no state, however, are elections now as frequent as in the beginning, and a need has long been felt in some states for a more direct mode of removing elected officials than that by impeachment. In 1903 the recall was first introduced in Los Angeles for the removal of municipal officers before the expiration of the terms for which they might be elected. Like the procedure for direct legislation by the people, that for the recall of a public officer is set in motion by a petition of a certain fraction of the electorate. Unlike the popular initiative and referendum, the recall was not a conscious imitation of any foreign institution, although it had previously existed in Switzerland.[1] Under the Swiss practice, however, the procedure may be employed not only for the recall of a specified officer but also for that of an entire legislature. Such a practice in effect gives to legislatures an indefinite tenure of office subject to a maximum limit, and the Swiss consistently so fix that limit as to assure their legislators a normal expectation of longer official life than is the case in the American states. The state-wide recall was first introduced in Oregon in 1908 and has since been established in ten other states. In Kansas in 1914 a further stage in this development was reached by extending the application of the recall to appointive as well as to elective officers.[2]

The executive, judicial, and popular vetoes in their modern forms may all be traced back to their beginning in the original distribution of powers adopted in Massachusetts. The modern direct popular initiative is a more radical innovation, for which there seems to be no precedent in the original state constitutions, although the procedure for constitutional amendment adopted in Georgia in 1777, but found to be impracticable, was closely akin to it. There remains another feature of the modern distribution of powers for which there is no precedent whatsoever in the original state constitutions, namely, the endowment of the

[1] W. E. Rappard, *op. cit.*, p. 127.
[2] *The American Year Book* for 1915, p. 82.

political party by law with special powers and duties, like any other recognized organ of government.

GROWTH OF POWERS OF THE POLITICAL PARTY

For many years after the establishment of the party system in American politics the political party remained a private association. It was first endowed by law with a public function when the Australian ballot was introduced into the electoral system. The important power which was then conferred upon the political party was the power of designating official party candidates for all elective offices. The state undertook to print the party designation upon the official ballot, together with the candidate's name, so that the least educated voter could vote the party ticket as easily as under the former system of unofficial ballots. Important powers have also been conferred upon political parties in connection with appointments to non-elective offices. Various appointive bodies, especially election boards, are required to be composed of partisans, and consequently the administration of the affairs of such bodies is a partisan as well as a public function. A more radical step in the extension of the powers of the political party was taken in Kansas. By the terms of the amendment for the recall of public officers, adopted in 1914, it is provided that a petition for the recall of an officer shall be signed by a certain proportion, not of the electorate, but of the members of the particular party to which the officer belongs. Thus the institution of proceedings for the recall in Kansas, like the nomination of public officers in all states, is made a partisan rather than a popular function.[1]

Proportional Representation.

In the transfer of power to the political party, the most radical step which has yet been proposed is the adoption of the repre-

[1] The "party recall," established in South Dakota under the Richards primary law, is somewhat similar to the Kansas experiment. The chief features of the South Dakota party recall are that it is applicable to all public officials who have been elected or appointed as party candidates, and apparently not to those who may have secured their positions independent of any party; it may be invoked and is operated by the party through which the official secured his office, and not by the general electorate; and it is conducted as a quasi-judicial proceeding, with the party committee acting as a sort of jury. See C. A. Berdahl, "The Operation of the Richards Primary," *Annals American Academy Political and Social Science*, cvi, pp. 158-171 (1923).

sentative system called proportional representation. The principle of the proposed reform is that each political party shall be entitled in all representative bodies to a number of representatives proportionate to the number of its voting members. Thus a party casting forty per cent of the total vote in a state election would be entitled to four-tenths of the seats in the state legislature. This proposal is advocated on the ground that a truly representative body should represent as nearly as possible the whole electorate and not merely the greatest number voting for any one candidate in each of the several representative districts, as is the case under the established system of plurality representation.

Proportional representation has not yet been established in any American state,[1] but a somewhat similar system was established in Illinois in 1870. [2] It was provided that the electors in each state senatorial district should be entitled to choose three representatives to the lower branch of the state legislature, and that each elector might cast his three votes for three separate candidates, or cumulate them upon one or two candidates. This system should be described as cumulative voting or minority representation rather than proportional representation, since it would not allow for more than a rough adjustment of representation to party strength. Such as it was, it marked the first recognition in a state constitution of the right of parties as well as of localities to special representation in a legislative body. Recent proposals to extend the application of this principle will be discussed in a later chapter. Suffice it to point out that not only has the political party been recognized as a regular organ of government in the states, but it has also been endowed with powers of considerable and hitherto increasing importance.

SUMMARY

There is nothing inconsistent with the original principles of American government in the various developments which have taken place in the political institutions of the states. The forms

[1] However, proportional representation has been adopted in a number of American cities, usually in connection with the city-manager plan of municipal government. Cleveland and Cincinnati are the most noteworthy examples.

[2] For a full discussion of the Illinois system, see B. F. Moore, "The History of Cumulative Voting and Minority Representation in Illinois, 1870-1919," *University of Illinois Studies in the Social Sciences*, viii, no. 2 (2nd ed., 1919).

of government have undergone some remarkable changes, but they are still republican. The distribution of powers between the different branches of the state governments has been affected by the changes of more than a century even more than the forms, but the people have less occasion than ever before to fear anybody but themselves. The evolution of the state governments has been characterized by the operation of two main tendencies: first, the decrease of legislative authority, and secondly, the increase of that of the electorates. The decline of legislative authority has been marked by the transfer of power from the legislative branch of the original normal type of government to the coördinate branches, the executive and the judiciary. The rise of the authority of the electorates has been marked by the increase of popular control over all three of the coördinate branches. These changes have not been the results of blind chance or the caprice of fate. They have been produced by the continuous adaptation of the political institutions of the states to the needs of the people, as determined by the operation of the fundamental forces in American life, the biological, economic, and social forces that have made the American people what they are.

The forces that have produced such great changes in the past will continue to bring about changes of the same general nature in the future, if they continue to operate. If they do not continue to operate, their place will be taken by other forces which will produce changes of a different sort. Changes of some sort will take place in American political institutions, hereafter as heretofore. The task of the political scientist is to discover the nature of the forces that are at work, and to point out the manner in which existing political institutions may best be adapted to meet the changing needs of a new age.

PART III

THE WORKING OF THE STATE GOVERNMENTS

CHAPTER VI

THE STATE ELECTORATE

The electorate may be defined as the instrument by means of which the people of a state authoritatively declare their will with respect to the matters constitutionally reserved to them. The will of the people may be expressed through public opinion, but it gains its legal force through the electorate. The primary object of political institutions in a democratic state is to facilitate the faithful interpretation and efficient execution of the will of the people, and of these institutions the electorate is the most important. In other words, the electorate is the fundamental organ of state government and is endowed with the function of exercising the powers and performing the duties of government theoretically vested in the people themselves.

WORKING OF SUFFRAGE QUALIFICATIONS

The operation of the laws governing the structure of the various state electorates is often illustrated by a comparison of the votes cast in the several states at general elections. Although the number of votes cast at general elections in different localities is subject to fluctuations produced by purely local causes and tending to impair the value of any general comparison of such votes, yet the public interest in general elections in presidential years is as nearly uniform as public interest in anything connected with politics, and the evidence afforded by a comparison of votes cast at presidential elections throws some light upon the operation of the suffrage laws of the several states. The following table exhibits the ratios between the number of votes cast for presidential electors in 1920 and 1924 and the number of adult citizens in the several states in those years.

Percentage of Votes Cast to Adult Citizens in Presidential Elections of 1920 and 1924, by States [1]

Rank	State	1920	1924	Average
1	West Virginia	71.7	74.8	73.2
2	Indiana	73.1	71.7	72.4
3	Delaware	75.4	69.4	72.4
4	Utah	70.5	71.0	70.7
5	New Hampshire	67.6	69.6	68.6
6	North Dakota	70.3	65.0	67.6
7	Iowa	65.4	69.4	67.4
8	Kentucky	71.9	62.4	67.1
9	Nevada	67.0	67.0	67.0
10	New Mexico	65.9	67.7	66.8
11	Missouri	67.2	65.6	66.4
12	Rhode Island	58.1	71.7	64.9
13	Illinois	60.5	67.9	64.2
14	New Jersey	59.4	66.1	62.7
15	Wyoming	54.7	69.7	62.2
16	Kansas	57.9	66.2	62.0
17	Idaho	61.8	60.9	61.3
18	Minnesota	59.4	63.1	61.2
19	Ohio	62.6	58.4	60.5
20	Colorado	56.1	61.8	58.9
21	Nebraska	52.1	65.6	58.8
22	New York	56.7	60.9	58.8
23	South Dakota	56.5	60.8	58.6
24	Connecticut	58.0	58.9	58.4
25	Montana	61.7	53.3	57.5
26	Wisconsin	52.6	59.9	56.2
27	Oregon	53.2	58.5	55.8
28	Michigan	55.6	56.1	55.8
29	Massachusetts	53.3	57.3	55.3
30	California	48.9	61.7	55.3
31	Washington	52.8	53.1	52.9
32	Arizona	52.9	49.7	51.3
33	Oklahoma	49.5	50.3	49.9
34	Vermont	45.2	51.7	48.4
35	Maryland	52.3	42.1	47.2
36	Maine	47.0	44.9	45.9
37	Pennsylvania	42.7	47.2	44.9
38	North Carolina	44.6	37.9	41.2
39	Tennessee	35.5	24.2	29.8
40	Texas	21.8	27.7	24.7
41	Florida	28.4	19.3	23.8
42	Virginia	19.3	17.9	18.6
43	Arkansas	21.3	15.5	18.4
44	Alabama	21.2	13.8	17.5
45	Georgia	21.7	11.3	16.5
46	Mississippi	18.8	12.8	15.8
47	Louisiana	14.0	13.2	13.6
48	South Carolina	8.6	6.3	7.4
	United States	49.1	51.2	50.1

[1] This table was computed from the census statistics for 1920 and from the election returns of 1920 and 1924. The number of adult citizens in each state in 1920 was found by subtracting from the total number of

Popular Participation in Elections.

From the table, it will be noted that the average ratio of votes cast to adult citizens ranged from a maximum of 73.2 per cent in West Virginia to a minimum of 7.4 per cent in South Carolina. How are such variations to be explained? To what extent are they due to the varying restrictions upon the electoral franchise in the several states? Disregarding the Southern states for the moment where the problem is complicated by the presence of the negro, a few comparisons may be made. Delaware, with an educational qualification and with an average vote of 72.4 per cent, ranks above its neighbor, New Jersey, where neither educational nor property tests are imposed, and yet where the average participation of the electorate is only 62.7 per cent. The ratio for New Hampshire is 68.6 and for Vermont is 48.4; the former has both literacy and tax-paying requirements, the latter has neither. Among the Western states, Wyoming, with an educational restriction upon the suffrage and with a voting record of 62.2 per cent, surpasses Montana where illiterate and propertyless citizens may vote and where the voting average is 57.5 per

adult persons, the Indians, the Chinese, Japanese, and other Asiatics ineligible to citizenship, and the foreign born whites who were not listed as fully naturalized. No account was taken of Indians who had received full citizenship, nor of Chinese and Japanese born in this country. In the spring of 1924, Congress conferred full citizenship upon all Indians born within the territory of the United States and thereby brought them within the protection of the fifteenth amendment. How much effect this legislation had upon the number of citizens in such states as Arizona, New Mexico, and Oklahoma could not be determined with accuracy and, hence, was disregarded in constructing the 1924 percentages. In Arizona, particularly, the number of adult citizens in 1924 may thus have been increased by as much as 10 or 12 per cent. The method of calculating the number of adult citizens in 1924 was as follows. Having the census estimates of total population for each state in 1924, it was possible to ascertain the percentage of increase, if any, over 1920. Assuming that the number of adult citizens changed in the same ratios, these percentages and the statistics for 1920 were used in finding the number of adult citizens in 1924.

No allowance is made in the table for the disfranchisement of criminal, pauper, and insane citizens. In any case, these classes probably amounted to less than 1 per cent of the whole number of adult citizens. Male aliens, who had declared their intention of becoming American citizens, were, in 1920, permitted to vote in five states (Arkansas, Indiana, Missouri, Nebraska, and Texas) and, in 1924, in one state (Arkansas). Under such circumstances, male aliens were counted as citizens in the percentage calculations. As a result of the adoption of the nineteenth amendment, women voted in every state in 1924 and in every state but Georgia and Mississippi in 1920 where they were temporarily prevented by the state registration laws. Accordingly, the 1920 ratios for these two states were based upon the number of adult male citizens only.

cent. It must frankly be admitted that a comparison of the votes cast in the several states at presidential elections, though interesting in itself, throws little light on the effect of the constitutional provisions and statutes governing the structure of the state electorates. In doubtful states much greater efforts are made to bring out a full vote than in states in which the issue is not doubtful. New York and Indiana are bound to be the scene of more hard-fought contests in presidential years than Pennsylvania or Vermont, and, other things being equal, the vote cast will be greater. In the South particularly the size of the vote at presidential elections is a poor measure of the effect of the laws relating to the suffrage. The vote in the states of the so-called solid South at such elections is abnormally light, because the results of the vote are a foregone conclusion. In fact, the southern electorates are much larger than would appear from the comparatively small participation of the adult citizens in presidential elections, and any estimate of the size of those electorates based upon the presidential vote is very misleading.

The Number of Registered Voters.

A better test of the effect of suffrage restrictions in the several states upon the size of the state electorates is afforded by a comparison between the number of registered voters and the number of adult citizens as is shown by the following statistics.

PERCENTAGE OF REGISTERED VOTERS TO ADULT CITIZENS[1]

	1920	1922	1924
Arizona	71.6	67.7	...
California	66.6	70.8	70.8
Connecticut	66.3	67.2	71.1
Indiana	85.7	81.1	...
Louisiana	...	20.9	...
Massachusetts	...	66.5	...
New Hampshire	81.3	...	...
New Jersey	75.4	71.9	81.8
New York	69.1	62.3	72.5
Oregon	81.4	71.7	...
Vermont	...	76.1	...

[1] The above table is compiled from the official statistics contained in the reports of secretaries of state and in the various state manuals, registers, and blue books. The omissions in the table are due to the fact that complete data were not available. Since 1922 was not a presidential year, the registration ratios tended to be less at that time.

Here again, it will be observed that there is considerable variation in the registration ratios. In Indiana in 1922, 81 per cent of the adult citizens were registered while in the same year in Louisiana, the registration amounted only to 21 per cent. This difference is partially explained by the fact that the former is a doubtful state and the latter is solidly Democratic. Nevertheless, a more important explanation lies in the wholesale disfranchisement of the negro in Louisiana. Such disfranchisement is characteristic of the South, although exact figures are difficult to obtain.[1] In the case of Louisiana, however, official registration statistics are available, and they throw a flood of light upon the operation of the constitutional restrictions upon the suffrage in that state.

Registration of Negroes in South.

To vote in Louisiana, the citizen must satisfy a residence requirement and be duly registered. But in order to register, "he shall be of good character and shall understand the duties and obligations of citizenship under a republican form of government." Moreover, he must be able to read and write and must demonstrate that fact by presenting an application "entirely written, dated, and signed by him," and by being able to "read any section of this constitution or the Constitution of the United States, and give a reasonable interpretation thereof." If the applicant is illiterate, he may still register provided he is "of good character," "well disposed to the good order and happiness of the State of Louisiana and of the United States," and "able to understand and give a reasonable interpretation of any section of either constitution when read to him by the Registrar." Finally, the would-be voter, if under sixty years of age, must have paid a poll tax of one dollar per annum for the two years preceding the election and must exhibit his poll tax receipts to the election commissioners before being allowed to vote.[2] Such are the present suffrage qualifications in Louisiana.

[1] In some parts of the South, where the Democratic party is strong enough to ensure the election of its candidates, the exclusion of negroes from the Democratic primaries accomplishes the same result as discrimination against negroes in connection with registration in such states as Louisiana.

[2] Louisiana Constitution of 1921, art. viii.

Formidable as these requirements sound, they are capable of judicious administration as the following statistics indicate.

Louisiana Registration Statistics, 1922[1]

Total number of registered voters	191,789
" " " white poll taxes paid, 1920	222,144
" " " " " " " 1921	227,456
" " " colored poll taxes paid, 1920	12,243
" " " " " " " 1921	13,234
" " " white registered voters	191,191
" " " colored registered voters	598
" " " white voters who write their names	179,808
" " " " " " make their mark	11,396
" " " colored voters who write their names	591
" " " " " " make their mark	3

The estimated number[2] of adult citizens in Louisiana in 1922 was 915,809, of whom 449,373 were white persons and 366,436 were negroes. Poll taxes were paid by approximately one-half of the whites and by less than 5 per cent of the negroes. Of the negroes who did pay poll taxes, only about 5 per cent survived the literacy test and further demonstrated that they had enough "character" and could give a "reasonable interpretation" of the constitution. Illiterate white voters had less difficulty with these latter requirements as is evidenced by the fact that 11,396 white illiterates qualified as against three colored illiterates. It is evident that the Louisiana suffrage tests are effective in eliminating the colored vote and the same may be said of other states in the South.

Effect of Tax Qualifications.

Turning again to the table of registered voters, the next problem is to ascertain the effect of tax-paying qualifications upon the size of the electorates in the various states which possess such requirements. In the case of Louisiana in 1922, only about one-half of all the white citizens had paid their poll taxes. The other half, on account of the non-payment of poll taxes, were debarred not only from general elections but also from the all-important Democratic primaries.[3] It would be absurd to conclude that two

[1] *Report of Secretary of State*, 1923, pp. 306-309.

[2] Author's estimates computed from census estimates.

[3] The constitution provides that none but registered voters "who have such other and additional qualifications as may be prescribed by the party" may vote in the primaries of that party. (Constitution of 1921, art. viii, sec. 4.) Thus are the Democratic primaries safeguarded against the negro.

hundred thousand citizens were prevented from voting because of a one dollar tax and yet it is probable that the white electorate would have been considerably larger if no tax had been imposed. In ten other states of the South where a similar qualification prevails, no definite data are available and the effect of the test is even more obscure. Of the four northern states which maintain a tax-paying prerequisite, Massachusetts simply requires assessment for poll taxes rather than actual payment, in consequence of which few are excluded from voting. In Pennsylvania, a local assessor informed one of the writers that no voter was ever challenged in that state on the ground that he had not paid a state or county tax within two years. This, of course, is an exaggeration; however, if one is challenged, it is possible to make affidavit that the tax receipt has been lost.[1] Moreover, for the Pennsylvania voter who is willing to "vote right," there is always the possibility that his tax bill may be "taken care of" by the party workers. Professor Brooks has estimated that possibly two hundred thousand persons are kept from voting by tax requirements in the four northern states of Massachusetts, Nevada, New Hampshire, and Pennsylvania.[2] This number amounts to only 3 per cent of all the adult citizens in those states. One may conclude, therefore, that tax qualifications have little bearing upon the size of the electorate except in some of the southern states where they are instrumental in excluding the negro, and, to a certain extent, white persons as well.

Effect of Educational Tests.

The evidence with respect to the effect of educational tests upon the size of the electorate is somewhat clearer. Using the illiteracy statistics of the federal census as a basis, the following comparison may be made.[3]

[1] Philadelphia Registration Commission, *Nineteenth Annual Report* (1925), p. 5.

[2] Robert C. Brooks, *Political Parties and Electoral Problems*, p. 409.

[3] According to the census, an illiterate is one who is unable to write any language, which, in general, means a person with no schooling whatever. The census enumerators require no proof of an individual's ability to write and hence fail to count illiterates who refuse to admit that they are such. Moreover, in the above nine states, the educational tests, if fairly enforced, are more severe than the census tests. Arizona requires the reading of the constitution in the English language in such a way as to show that the applicant is neither prompted nor reciting from memory. In order to vote in Washington, one must be able to read and speak the English language. In the other seven states, a

STATE	PERCENTAGE OF ADULT CITIZENS REGISTERED IN 1920	PERCENTAGE OF ADULT CITIZENS ILLITERATE IN 1920	PERCENTAGE OF ADULT CITIZENS LITERATE AND NOT REGISTERED IN 1920
Arizona	71.6	4.5	23.9
California	66.6	2.1	31.3
Connecticut	66.3	4.5	29.2
Delaware	...	6.5	...
Maine	...	2.8	...
Massachusetts	66.5(1922)	3.6	29.9
New Hampshire	81.3	3.3	15.4
Washington	...	1.2	...
Wyoming	...	1.4	...

It will be noted that for every citizen prevented from registering because of his illiteracy, there are from five to fifteen literate citizens who fail to register for other reasons. Even if it be assumed that the Literacy Commission of the National Educational Association is correct in saying that there are twice as many real illiterates in the United States as are shown by the census,[1] nevertheless, the number of non-registered literates still predominates. The failure or inability of the latter class to register and hence to vote must be explained upon other grounds. Sometimes it is the result of indifference and neglect. Sometimes it is caused by temporary absence from the place of residence at the time of registration or by other casual circumstances beyond the control of the person. Sometimes it is the result of permanent removal from the district or state and inability to comply with the residence requirements established in the new place of residence. This is a factor which may account for the temporary disfranchisement of from 1 to 3 per cent of all adult citizens.[2]

citizen may vote if he can read the constitution and write his own name. In view of the fact that the illiteracy statistics of the census are too low, the effect of such educational restrictions is probably greater than the above table indicates.

[1] Literacy Commission, *Report*, p. 13 (1924).

[2] It has been estimated that, in presidential elections, 1 per cent of the adult citizens are unable to vote because of insufficient legal residence in the state and locality. (Robert C. Brooks, *Political Parties and Electoral Problems*, p. 409.) This percentage is too low, at least for the larger cities with their more mobile populations. At the Chicago mayoralty election of April, 1923, between 2 and 3 per cent of the adult citizens of Chicago were probably excluded from voting because of lack of residence qualifications. (Authors' estimate based upon statistics given in C. E. Merriam and H. F. Gosnell, *Non-Voting, passim.*) At that election, the two main classes thus disfranchised were negroes, who, migrating from the South, had lived in the state for less than the year prescribed, and renters of all classes who, while continuing to dwell in the city, had moved and had not resided in their voting precincts for thirty days preceding the election. (*Ibid.*, p. 82.)

Finally, failure to register is sometimes the result of an onerous registration procedure calculated to deter the ignorant or shiftless voter from making good his claim to the ballot.

One may conclude, therefore, that tax-paying, educational and residence qualifications have less effect upon the size of the electorates than do the other factors which now remain to be analyzed. Only with respect to the negro in the southern states will the above statement have to be qualified, for, in those states, suffrage tests are one of the principal means by which the colored citizen is disfranchised.

The Problem of Non-Voting.

In the presidential elections of 1920 and 1924, approximately one-half of the adult citizens of the United States failed to vote. The statistics of these elections brought squarely before the American people for the first time that there was a problem of non-voting. The problem itself, however, is not new for the ratio of votes cast to eligible voters in the United States has been growing smaller and smaller for forty or fifty years.[1] Various explanations have been advanced for this failure of the American electorate to function, but too often these have been "arm-chair generalizations" not founded upon careful statistical inquiry. Recently, the problem has been attacked more methodically by students of politics. Of special importance in this connection is the monograph by Professors Merriam and Gosnell dealing with non-voting in the city of Chicago.[2] The methods and conclusions of that study are summarized here, not because they are universally applicable, but because they illuminate the nature of the whole problem.

The investigation upon which the monograph was based dealt

[1] There is an excellent discussion of this point in A. M. Schlesinger and E. M. Eriksson, "The Vanishing Voter," *New Republic*, xl, pp. 162-167 (1924). The situation in the United States is in striking contrast to that in the more advanced European countries. At the English parliamentary elections of December, 1923, and October, 1924, between 75 and 80 per cent of the electorate voted. The French and German parliamentary elections of May, 1924, brought out between 80 and 85 per cent of the eligible voters. In none of these three countries is compulsory voting employed.

[2] C. E. Merriam and H. F. Gosnell, *Non-Voting: Causes and Methods of Control* (Chicago, 1924). See also Ben A. Arneson, "Non-Voting in a Typical Ohio Community," *American Political Science Review*, vol. xix, pp. 816-825.

solely with the Chicago mayoralty election of April, 1923. At that time, there were approximately 1,400,000 eligible electors in Chicago, of whom 900,000 were registered. Of these 900,000, 723,000 actually voted in the election.[1] Of course, it was not possible to interview personally 700,000 non-voters but a canvass was made of over 5000 citizens who failed to vote. These 5000 included both non-registered and registered citizens and were selected in such a way as to afford a representative sample of the entire body of non-voters. A great variety of reasons were given for non-voting, but these were all reduced to four main categories by the investigators. It was found that 44.3 per cent of the non-voting was due to "inertia," a term which comprised such things as indifference, neglect, ignorance or timidity regarding elections, and failure of the party workers to get out the vote. Next in importance came "physical difficulties" which included illness, absence from the city, and detention at home by one or more helpless members of the family. Physical difficulties explained the non-participation of 25.4 per cent of the persons questioned. "Legal and administrative obstacles" formed the third group of reasons and accounted for 12.6 per cent. Here were found insufficient residence, unwillingness to leave one's work or business because participation in Chicago's many elections would require much time and would involve substantial loss of trade or wages, crowded and poorly located polling booths, and dislike of disclosure of age to the election officials. Finally, disgust with politics and with party politicians, disbelief in woman suffrage, and various other kinds of disbelief in voting claimed 8.9 per cent of the non-voters.[2] In short, assuming the correctness of the reasons offered, a majority of the non-voters were wanting in interest or faith in politics. In fact, because of the tendency of people to "put their best foot forward," the proportions of indifference and hostility to politics were probably greater than the figures indicate.

The Woman Voter.

One interesting point brought out by the study was that women furnished a larger proportion of the non-voters than men. This fact is generally admitted, but in most states official records

[1] *Ibid.*, Preface, pp. viii-x.
[2] *Ibid.*, p. 34 and *passim.*

demonstrating it mathematically are lacking.[1] However, in a few instances, exact statistics can be adduced supporting this proposition. In Illinois, in the presidential election of 1920, 74.1 per cent of the adult male citizens voted compared with 46.5 per cent of the adult female citizens. In the New York state elections of 1923, with figures available from about thirty counties, the number of women voting in each county ranged from 39 to 95 for every 100 men voting.[2] Registration records tell the same story, as the following table indicates.

State or City	Year	Registered Male Voters	Registered Female Voters
Indiana	1920	718,753	599,303
Louisiana	1922	153,667	38,122
Oregon	1922	204,495	128,560
Vermont	1922	89,066	62,088
Chicago	1920	550,060	334,060
Philadelphia	1924	336,957	141,819

It is frequently stated that women in the South are especially negligent about going to the polls and the statistics from Louisiana would seem to bear out this belief. As to the proportion of women who will vote in future elections throughout the United States, one may predict that, as women become more and more accustomed to the suffrage, the disparity between the electoral efficiency of the two sexes will decrease.

One other aspect of non-voting remains to be mentioned. The problem has to do, not only with those who fail to register or, if registered, fail to vote, but also with those who go to the polls and then do not vote for all the offices to be filled and upon all the questions submitted. It is not unusual for 50 per cent of those voting for president or governor to fail to vote upon constitutional amendments submitted at the same election. This is a matter which will be considered in detail in a later chapter and hence requires no further discussion at present. The same situation is found, though to a less degree, in connection with

[1] Professor Hugh L. Keenleyside etsimates that 35 per cent of all eligible women voted in the presidential elections of 1920 and 1924. (*Current History*, xxi, p. 838 (1924-25.) Professors Rice and Willey estimate that between 34.7 and 46.5 per cent of the eligible women voters participated in the presidential election of 1920. (*Ibid.*, xx, p. 643.)

[2] Sarah Schuyler Butler, "Women Who Do Not Vote," *Scribner's*, lxxvi, pp. 529-533 (1924).

the less important elective offices.[1] In Arizona in 1920, 36 per cent of those who voted for president neglected to vote for judge of the state supreme court. In the California election of 1922, there was a difference of 17 per cent between the gubernatorial vote and the vote for state controller. In the same year in Massachusetts, the vote for state auditor was 9 per cent less than that for governor.

Remedies for Non-Voting.

How and to what extent may the problem of non-voting be solved? Three points are of particular importance: first, the tasks placed upon the electorate are too numerous and too burdensome to be performed effectively; second, so long as the present system of elections continues, a large amount of non-voting is inevitable in states where one party is in complete domination;[2] and, finally, politics seems to be less able to hold its own amid the competing interests of American life than was formerly the case.[3] In attempting to solve the first difficulty, the short ballot, less frequent elections, simplified registration procedure, effective absent-voting laws, more convenient polling places and hours, together with many other things, have been suggested. These reforms will merit further consideration in the later pages of this book. For the second difficulty, two alternative remedies have been proposed. Either a bipartisan or multipartisan system should be established in state elections under the stimulus of proportional representation, or state politics should be conducted upon a non-partisan basis. These proposals cannot be appraised until the actual operation of the state governments has been described. For the last difficulty, the question has been raised as to whether civic education alone will be enough or whether that education must be supplemented by a scheme of compulsory voting.

[1] On this point, see R. C. Spencer, "Activities of the Colorado Electorate," *American Political Science Review*, xvii, pp. 101-108 (1923).

[2] Of course, in one-party states, the primary of the dominant party may show a high ratio of voting-participation. For a discussion and classification of "safe" and "doubtful" states, see A. N. Holcombe, *The Political Parties of To-Day: A Study in Republican and Democratic Politics* (2nd ed., New York, 1925), ch. iv, *passim*.

[3] Schlesinger and Eriksson, *op. cit.*, p. 166.

Effect of Suffrage Qualifications on Character of Government.

The influence of the various electoral qualifications upon the character of the electorates, and hence upon the character of government in general, has always been an engrossing topic of speculation.[1] There have been few systematic attempts, however, to check the results of such speculation by inquiry into the known or knowable facts.[2] The principal qualifications designed to improve the character of the electorate are those relating to age,[3] property, education, and, until recently, sex. Those writers who have discussed the exclusion from the electoral franchise of the young, the poor, the ignorant, and the women have usually been much more interested in making out a case for or against the exclusion of such persons than in making known the truth for its own sake. Those voters who have sanctioned the establishment or maintenance of a restrictive franchise have usually been confronted with a condition, not a theory, and have made their decision with a view to its effect on immediate practical problems. In the South, for example, property and educational qualifications have been established by the white voters because such qualifications were known to be more burdensome to negroes than to whites, not because they were desired for their own sake. In certain northern and western states literacy tests have been adopted because they were known to be more burdensome to naturalized aliens than to native-born citizens. The effect of such qualifications upon the character of government reflects the results of the disfranchisement of negroes

[1] See J. S. Mill, *Representative Government*, and Sir H. S. Maine, *Popular Government*, for specimens of the speculation in England in the nineteenth century. For similar speculative discussions of the suffrage by American writers, see Francis Lieber, *Manual of Political Ethics*, and Theodore Woolsey, *Political Science*. See also the Record of Debates in the following state constitutional conventions: Massachusetts, 1820; New York, 1821; and Virginia, 1829-30. See also the *Congressional Record*, 1869, with reference to the proposed submission to the states of the fifteenth amendment.

[2] See Graham Wallas, *Human Nature in Politics*, Introduction.

[3] The exclusion of persons under some prescribed age limit has always been the practice in the United States and the fixing of the limit at twenty-one years of age now awakens no controversy. In some foreign countries, the limit has been placed higher, frequently at twenty-five years, thus increasing the minimum experience of life, so far as age may be regarded as a measure of experience, required of the voter. There is no country where the franchise is conferred upon those below the age of eighteen.

and of aliens, but in most cases throws little light on the probable results of the disfranchisement of the poor and the ignorant, regardless of race, color, or previous condition.

In the states where the effect of property or educational tests is least complicated by extraneous considerations the results of the establishment of such tests are scarcely less obscure. In Pennsylvania and Massachusetts, for example, there are property and educational tests, respectively, and in New Jersey and Ohio there is universal suffrage. But it is exceedingly difficult to discover that, if the two former states are better or worse governed than the two latter, as the case may be, the differences in the character of the government are due to the differences in the character of the electorates. Any Pennsylvanian who can afford to own a dog and pay a tax thereon can qualify under the property test, and in practice such a property qualification cannot be expected to illustrate the effects theoretically claimed for a franchise based on property. Any Massachusetts adult citizen who can read a line of the constitution in English and write his name can qualify under the literacy test, and in practice, at least in a state where a common school education is free and compulsory, such a test cannot be expected to illustrate the effects theoretically claimed for a franchise based on intelligence. In fact the number of Pennsylvania and Massachusetts citizens who are disqualified by the property and educational tests, respectively, is so small compared with the number who are otherwise prevented from voting, and the differences between the governments of New Jersey and Ohio, on the one hand, and those of Massachusetts and Pennsylvania, on the other, are so much greater in other respects than in respect to the franchise, that no clear relation between the suffrage and the general character of government in these states is discernible. In short, it may be candidly confessed that it is not possible to prove that the governments of Massachusetts and Pennsylvania are either better or worse because of the exclusion of a number of impecunious and illiterate citizens from the electorate.

Effect of Woman Suffrage.

Moreover, it is almost equally difficult to discover the effects of the recent enfranchisement of women upon the character of the state governments. Woman suffrage has not perceptibly changed the fortunes of the existing political parties, although it has caused them to accord at least a formal representation to women in the party committees and conventions.[1] On the other hand, equal suffrage has made the party organizations and the state governments somewhat more attentive in dealing with "moral" and "civic" questions to which women are often more responsive than men. The advent of woman's right to vote brought with it in most states a legally equal opportunity to hold public office. Thus far, while individual women have rendered noteworthy service as public officials, the number of such women is almost too small to have any fundamental effect upon the quality of the state governments.[2]

It is upon the character of women themselves, however, that the effects of equal suffrage have been and are most clear. On this point, the conclusion of Miss Helen L. Sumner with respect to the operation of woman suffrage in Colorado sixteen years ago seems to be more or less applicable to all the states at the present time. "The effect of equal suffrage upon the women themselves, their outlook upon life, and their relationship to the home, is, in the opinion of many, the crux of the problem. Over the majority of women, indeed, it is already evident that equal suffrage has exercised a good influence, and one which inevitably reacts to a certain extent upon political life. . . . Equal suffrage has brought, then, practically no loss, and some decided gain, the latter mainly evident in the effect of the possession of the ballot upon the women of Colorado. It has enlarged their interests, quickened their civic consciousness, and developed in many cases ability of a high order which has been of service to the city, the county, and the state. . . . The Colorado experiment certainly indicates that equal suffrage is a step in the direction of a better citizenship, a more effective use of the ability of women as an integral part of the race, and a closer under-

[1] R. C. Brooks, *op. cit.*, pp. 159-164.

[2] In 1924, a total of 126 women were elected to the higher state offices in the forty-eight states. The list includes two governors (Mrs. Ross of Wyoming, elected to succeed her husband, the late Governor Ross, and "Ma" Ferguson of Texas, elected to vindicate the honor of her impeached ex-governor husband), 1 secretary of state, 9 state senators, and 114 state representatives. (Keenleyside, *op. cit.*, p. 839; see also Stuart A. Rice and Malcolm M. Willey, "American Women's Ineffective Use of the Vote," *Current History*, xx, pp. 641-647 (1924).

standing between men and women."[1] Hence, with the passing of time, as women become more accustomed to their new obligations, their electoral activities should result in gradual improvement of the state governments.

The Theory of the Franchise.

The widespread public discussion of the question of votes for women, which preceded the adoption of the nineteenth amendment, served a useful purpose in causing a reëxamination of the general grounds for the exclusion of any class of persons from the electoral franchise. The doctrine of natural rights has been generally understood by Americans to mean equal rights, but when the idea of equal rights is explained as it was explained by Lincoln, and no other explanation is possible if the sincerity of the American people is to be successfully vindicated, it becomes clear that no person can assert a claim to the franchise regardless of his fitness. The doctrine of natural rights, therefore, like the doctrine that the franchise is a privilege to be conferred only upon those who are fit for its exercise, implies the recognition of some suitable standard of fitness. The standards may not be the same, but in either case they would include at least the following: (1) loyalty to the fundamental principles of American government, that is, to the principles of popular sovereignty and the reign of law, and to the constitution of the United States; (2) willingness to use the vote, according to one's conscience, for the best good of the commonwealth without fear or favor; and (3) a reasonable degree of political intelligence. Now neither the ownership of property nor literacy in themselves afford any evidence of the attainment of such a standard of fitness. Property can be acquired by the exploitation of society as well as by the service of society. Mere money-making, even if the money-maker keeps within the law, is not the best training for statesmanship. The accumulation of information, like money-making, is not identical with growth in wisdom. Education may make a clever rogue as well as an intelligent voter. Success does not make a good citizen of a thief, and much book learning is to be found within the walls of our prisons. In short, political intelligence is not discoverable either

[1] Helen L. Sumner, *Equal Suffrage, the Results of an Investigation in Colorado* (New York, 1909), pp. 258-260.

by the tax collector or by the school examiner. Public spirit and loyalty are evidenced by the whole conduct of life, and cannot be tested on life's threshold. Mechanical tests of fitness may facilitate the elimination from the electorates of the feeble-minded and the criminally vicious. More than that is impossible.

The exclusion of women from the electorates, like the exclusion of men with little property or education, cannot be justified in modern times upon either of the theories which have hitherto influenced the mind of the American people. The doctrine of natural rights may not justify the thrusting of the ballot upon a reluctant womanhood, but neither can it justify the withholding of the ballot from women who declare their wish to participate actively in the making of the laws under which they are governed. The demand of women for political equality with men cannot be consistently denied by those who believe in natural rights without denying the humanity of women. The doctrine that the franchise is a privilege to be conferred upon those who are fit is as repugnant to political discriminations against women solely on account of their sex as is the doctrine of natural rights. Women, like men, may be loyal to the principles of our government, public-spirited, and politically intelligent. To the extent that they are so, their "right" to vote, if they wish, like men, must be recognized, whether the theory of the franchise be founded upon the doctrine of natural rights or upon that of fitness. If tests of fitness are to be exacted of applicants for admission to the franchise, they should be applied without distinction of sex. The doctrine that only those should vote who are able, in case of need, to fight is without foundation in the political philosophy of the American people. Neither ability nor inability to fight was originally recognized as pertinent to the question of the suffrage. What is expected by the state from its citizens is not uniform service from all alike, but service from each according to his ability. Young men for war, old men for counsel, is an ancient maxim, which may still serve to show the part to be played by men in the conduct of military operations. In modern warfare many young men, too, must keep out of the fight in order to keep up the supply of the munitions of war. Under the division of labor which characterizes modern industry, whether constructive or destructive, woman's part is no less essential than man's. But the whole discussion of the part of woman in war is beside the point, for service in the army and service in the electorate are two different propositions.

It is coming to be recognized that the electoral franchise is neither a right nor a privilege. It is a public office. The arrangements for selecting the members of the electorate, like those for selecting the holders of any public office, must be justified by the end that the office is intended to fulfill. The electorate is intended to voice the will of the people, and those should be charged with the duty of voting whose experience in life is such as enables them to speak with authority for any class whose welfare is essential to the welfare of the whole people. So long as women's experience of life was gained mainly within the household, the practice of treating the household as a political unit and polling the men only was satisfactory. But when the household ceased to be an industrial unit, because of the development of the factory system of industry and the employment of women in large numbers in capitalistic establishments, the experience of women became something more than the experience of the housewife, and though the household remains a social unit, the opinion of men alone fails to reflect the whole experience of the people. Moreover, the progress of modern civilization has been marked by a gradual expansion of the functions of the state. Many services are now rendered through the instrumentality of governmental officials, which in former times were rendered directly by the members of the household. The supply of water, milk, and food, and of the family necessaries in general is now controlled or regulated to some degree by the state. When these services were chiefly matters of purely domestic concern, woman's experience of life was adequately reflected by her voice in the management of the household. But now that the state is for certain purposes like a great household, women, if they are to continue to exert as heretofore their proper influence in household affairs, must participate in the government of the state. If the state is to perform satisfactorily the household duties which it has assumed, it must be inspired by a spirit that is not only paternal but also maternal. Public officials must feel their responsibility to women as well as to men, and this feeling can be created most effectively by putting the ballot in the hands of women. In short, the modern state needs women voters as well as men voters, because the will of the state should reflect the experience of women as well as the experience of men.

It would be well to exclude from the franchise those who are unfit for the duties of the office, if it were practicable. Unfortunately, it does not seem practicable to do more than exclude a small number of the most conspicuously unfit. This is accomplished more effectually by the requirements of residence and registration than by more specialized tests of fitness such as literacy or the payment of taxes. The principal effect of such a test as that of literacy is indirect rather than direct, for the requirement that every voter be able to read and write enables the state to adopt more efficient registration and election laws than is practicable if provision must be made for illiterate voters. If the states where literacy is required of all voters are better governed than other states, the evidence thereof must be found in a study of the methods of organizing the electorate and managing elections. The legislation regulating the form of the ballot and the conduct of campaigns, the provisions designed to facilitate the expression of a sound and deliberate public opinion at the polls, are more important to a democratic state than specialized tests of fitness for the franchise. The state which would profit most by the wisdom and experience of its members must so organize the electorate and regulate the conduct of elections as to secure the freest and fullest possible expression of honest and enlightened opinion at the polls. Where the electorate is rightly organized and elections are properly conducted, it is more important that all those whose experience of life is socially useful should be enfranchised than that a few more or less of the unfit should be disfranchised.

ORGANIZATION OF THE ELECTORATE

The first step in the organization of the electorate is the division of the state into districts suitable for the choice of the several sorts of public officers. In the beginning the formation of electoral districts was comparatively simple. For most elections the original divisions of the states for purposes of local government were equally suitable. In New England, the town, in the South, the county, was the unit of representation in the lower branch of the legislature. For the election of members of the upper branch more extensive districts were necessary. In

Massachusetts the county originally served as the senatorial district. In New York and elsewhere outside of New England the senatorial district generally consisted of a union of counties. No other districts were required. After the adoption of the Federal Constitution and the inauguration of the practice of choosing members of Congress, and for a time in some states presidential electors, by districts, the necessity arose for the formation of additional districts. In the formation of these districts approximate equality of population was generally considered essential, and it was consequently necessary to form new combinations of the local governmental units, the towns and counties, regardless of the existence of the old. Then the democratization of the state governments through the direct popular election of executive and judicial officers, the creation of new administrative agencies, and the redistribution of population between city and country caused a further multiplication and complication of districts. At present, therefore, in addition to the original division of the states into counties, towns, villages, and cities, there is also a redivision into numerous overlapping legislative, administrative, and judicial electoral districts of various sizes and degrees of importance.

Complexity of Electoral District System.

The result of the formation of all these various electoral districts is the subdivision of the electorate into a corresponding number of special groups for the purpose of choosing the several sorts of public officers elected by the people. The complexity of these groups is well illustrated by the present situation in Philadelphia.[1] For example, a voter residing in the first division or precinct of the first ward of that city is one of 180 registered voters who elect one tax assessor, one judge of elections, and two election inspectors every second year. He is one of 8823 registered voters in the first ward, who elect seven school visitors for four-year terms and two constables for six-year terms. He

[1] Written in 1925. Not all of the officials mentioned are elected at the same time nor even in the same year. For instance, although city councilmen and state senators are elected from the same districts and for the same terms, they are chosen in different years. Moreover, overlapping terms prevent judges and some other officials from being elected all at the same time. Finally, limited voting prevails in connection with judicial offices. These three facts lessen the burden of the individual voter.

is one of 25,341 registered voters in the first state representative district, who elect two members of the lower house of the legislature every other year. He is one of 60,817 registered voters in the first state senatorial district, who elect one city councilman and one state senator for four-year periods. He is one of 78,693 registered voters in the first congressional district, who elect a member of Congress each second year. He is one of 478,776 registered voters in the City and County of Philadelphia, who elect seventy-one city, county, and judicial officers with terms ranging from four to ten years. He is one of several million voters in the state, who elect nineteen executive and judicial officials with terms ranging from four to twenty-one years, thirty-eight presidential electors every fourth year, and two United States senators in the course of each six years. Altogether the voter in question is associated with seven different groups of voters, ranging in number from a few hundreds to a few millions, for the purpose of filling by election between thirty and forty different offices, with different terms, different tenures, different duties, and different requirements on the part of the officeholders.[1]

The first characteristic of these various electoral districts is their artificiality. Where the attempt to divide a state into equal electoral districts is made in good faith, it is found to be difficult, generally indeed impossible, to make them compact in form and at the same time homogeneous in substance. The various local governmental units composing the several districts must be combined without much regard to their respective economic or social conditions or previous habits of political association with one another. The resulting combinations often lack the unity and coherence needful in a group of voters who are to coöperate with one another for the purpose of choosing public officers. Without the consciousness of common interest and common purpose, the group can be nothing more than a mere mass of voters, incapable of organic action, and dependent on external forces for the performance of its proper function.

The second characteristic of the various electoral districts is their instability. Not only is the relationship between the

[1] The above statistics deal only with final elections. As a partisan, the voter is called upon to associate himself with various groups of party voters in the making of party nominations and in the election of party officials and convention delegates.

component parts of a district a casual one, but it is also not infrequently of short duration. Most electoral districts are created for a limited period only, generally for ten years, after which there must be a reapportionment based on the latest census. In order to make the adjustments required by the disproportionate growth of population in different localities, the existing districts must be dissolved, and the local governmental units reassorted in new combinations. Thus as soon as habits of political association between the members of an electoral group begin to form, the group is broken up and the process must be begun over again.[1]

The third characteristic of the various electoral districts is their unwieldiness. Sometimes, to be sure, the voter acts as one of a group of electors numbering only a few hundreds, who can easily meet in a single hall to consider together the qualifications of the candidates for public office and the merits of the issues. More frequently, however, he is compelled to act as one of several thousand or several hundreds of thousands of electors who can never either come into one another's presence in order to take common counsel together or even think of the same thing at the same time. Under such circumstances only the most important offices will receive the general attention of the voters. Only the most conspicuous candidates will awaken a general interest. Only a comparatively few choices will be made deliberately at any one time.[2] Actually, in most states, because of the number and variety of electoral groups with which each voter is associated, his attention is distracted and his interest in the functions of any particular group diminished. The number and variety of offices to be filled by election in some of the districts still

[1] For example, in Ohio, the county is generally the unit in the formation of the higher legislative, administrative, and judicial electoral electoral districts, but there is no apparent attempt to maintain the same combination of counties for different electoral purposes. Thus, Licking County is one of four counties comprising the fifteenth and sixteenth state senatorial districts. It is combined with five other counties to form the seventeenth congressional district, four of which are not in the previous combination. It is one of fourteen counties in the fifth court of appeals district, six of which are not associated with Licking County in either the senatorial or the congressional districts. Formerly, before each county was given a separate court of common pleas, Licking County was one of nine counties constituting the sixth common pleas judicial district. Ten years ago the above combinations were different and ten years hence they will be different again.

[2] See R. S. Childs, *Short Ballot Principles.*

further increases the distraction and diminishes the efficiency of the voter. The practice of holding many elections on the same day, regardless of the dissimilarity in the character of the offices to be filled and of the lack of connection between the issues involved in the various elections, adds to the general confusion. In short, the task imposed upon the contemporary American voter, acting through the various subdivisions of the electorate, is unreasonably heavy and unreasonably complex.

Majority *v.* Plurality Elections.

Originally in several states the burden of the electorate was made even heavier by the practice of majority elections. That is, a majority of all the votes cast for the several candidates for an elective office was required for election. If no candidate received a majority of the votes, there would be no election, and a second election would be called. At this election the voter would have the same freedom of choice as at the first, and if there were still no choice by a majority of the voters, the process would be repeated until some candidate should have received a majority of all the votes. Sometimes irreconcilable differences among the voters would prevent any choice whatever, as formerly happened not infrequently in connection with the choice of United States senators by the state legislatures. More commonly, however, a choice was made at the first ballot. Second and third ballots were the exception rather than the rule in normal times. Such, for example, was the original practice in Massachusetts, provided that in case of no election of governor or other officer chosen in the state at large, the second choice was made by the legislature between the two candidates receiving the greatest numbers of popular votes.[1] Under such an electoral system the voters were protected against the possibility of the choice of a candidate objectionable to a majority of the voters by a mere plurality of votes through the dispersion of the votes of the majority among a number of candidates. This protection, however, was secured at the cost of two or more trips to the polls in case there was no choice at the first ballot, a procedure which was sometimes felt to be excessively burdensome, and for this and other reasons the practice of majority elections was aban-

[1] This system still obtains in gubernatorial elections in New Hampshire.

doned in Massachusetts shortly after the middle of the nineteenth century.[1]

The prevailing system of plurality elections, however, despite its appearance of greater simplicity as compared with the system of majority elections, tends to increase the complexity of the electoral system. In order to diminish the risk that a plurality election will be a minority election, objectionable to a majority of the voters in the district, like-minded voters must make some preliminary arrangements for concentrating their votes upon mutually acceptable candidates, thereby securing for them at the first and only ballot as nearly as possible a majority of the whole number of votes. Voters do not wish to throw away their votes, as they say, by casting them for candidates who cannot win. They wish their choice so far as possible to be effective. This purpose can be accomplished only by organization in advance of the election. Voluntary associations of voters will be formed under any electoral system for the purpose of influencing by their joint action the results of the elections, but the incentive to the formation of such associations is necessarily greater under a plurality than under a majority system, because the danger of the defeat of the will of an unorganized majority of the voters is greater under such a system. The selection of the candidate who will be supported by the greater number of voters is equivalent to his election, and the art of politics has come to consist fundamentally in the establishment and maintenance of electoral associations by means of which such candidates may be selected. The voter who wishes to exert his proper share of political power must participate in these preliminary selections, or as they are commonly called, primary elections. If there be only one efficient political association in a district, the voters' task need be no more complicated than under a system of majority elections. If there be two or more such associations, as must normally be the case, their task is correspondingly complicated, because each voter must choose his association before he can share in the selection of candidates.

Importance of Party Organization.

The establishment of voluntary electoral associations other than those provided by the division of the electorate into elec-

[1] Proceedings of Massachusetts Constitutional Convention of 1853, *Record of Debates.*

toral districts is therefore the second step in the organization of the electorate. Under the contemporary system of plurality elections the organization of such associations, or political parties as they are termed, must be more elaborate than under a system of majority elections. The burden placed upon the electorate by the necessity for their organization and maintenance is further enhanced by the number, artificiality, instability, and unwieldiness of the electoral districts into which the electorate is officially organized. It is not without reason, therefore, that the organization and activity of political parties fills an extremely important place in the government of the states.

CHAPTER VII

THE POLITICAL PARTY

The political party has already been defined as an association of voters united primarily for the purpose of influencing elections to public office. Such a definition, however, does not meet the needs of the situation, if the political party is to be formally recognized by law. Legal recognition of the political party implies the existence for a group of voters not only of a common purpose, but also of an organization, that is, of a constitution and rules of procedure, officers, and some practicable test of party affiliation. Moreover, the party should be important enough to deserve legal recognition. There should be a point somewhere below which an association of voters cannot fall without becoming merely a faction or a propagandist organization. The legal definition of the political party therefore must turn on the record rather than on the purposes of an electoral association.

PARTY ORGANIZATION

Its Legal Basis.

As a matter of fact, the political party, though recognized by law in almost all the states, is not everywhere legally defined. In some states it is merely a group of voters who name a candidate or ticket of candidates for public office in compliance with the procedure provided by law for the printing of the official ballots. The regulation of the conditions upon which the names of the candidates may be printed on the official ballot thus serves practically as the definition of the political party. In all states having an official ballot the names of candidates for election may be placed upon the ballot by petition of a certain number of voters, who thereby become at least temporarily a party. In order to become permanently a party, it is necessary for the same group of voters, though not necessarily the same individuals, to name candidates at subsequent elections. In order that the group may preserve its identity, it may assume a name, and in states where illiterates are permitted to vote, a party emblem. The desirability of protecting the proprietors of a party name and emblem against infringement by other groups of voters has led most states to define the term "party" more carefully.

In these states, though a party may come into existence by placing the names of candidates for office upon the official ballots, it can preserve its existence only by casting not less than a certain number of votes at the election. A nominating group whose candidates fail to secure the required number of votes fails to establish its status as a party and likewise its claims to the exclusive use of a name and emblem. A group which succeeds in polling not less than the required vote thereby becomes entitled to the exclusive use of its name and emblem at subsequent elections so long as it continues to satisfy the requirements. In the states which have established the direct primary system of making nominations, there is sometimes a further distinction between parties which are required to make their nominations in the official primary and those which are free to select their candidates in other ways. The former, which may be described as political parties proper, comprise those parties which poll not less than a certain number of votes. This is always a greater number than that required merely for recognition as a permanent party. Thus in Massachusetts any group of one thousand voters may place a ticket of candidates for offices filled by election in the state at large on the official ballot by signing petitions, called nomination papers. If such a group at three successive biennial elections polls not less than one thousand votes, it thereby becomes a "party" and is thereafter entitled to designate its candidates without the formality of filing special petitions. Certificates of nomination, signed by the proper party officers, are accepted in lieu of nomination papers. If such a party polls not less than three per cent of the total number of votes cast, however, it becomes a "political party" and must thereafter make its nominations in the official primaries. Either a "party" or a "political party" may lose its official recognition by failure to poll at any election the required number or per cent of votes. The technical distinction between a "party" and a "political party," established in Massachusetts, is not generally observed; but the legal recognition of the party because of its ability to poll not less than a certain vote is the general rule. In most states the size of the vote required for recognition ranges from two to ten per cent of the total.

A party therefore must be defined for practical purposes as an electoral association whose record entitles it to put the names of its candidates upon the official ballot without the formality of filing nomination papers. Such associations may be further distinguished as major and minor parties according to their political importance. At the present time in most of the states the major parties may be most conveniently defined as those which make their nominations at direct primary elections; the minor parties, those which nominate by the old convention system.

Delegate Conventions.

The organization of parties is by no means uniform throughout the country. The principal organ of the party, however, is generally the state convention. The functions of the convention so far as they relate to state politics, are (1) the adoption of a constitution for the party and rules of procedure so far as not provided by law, (2) the adoption of a declaration of party principles or platform, (3) the nomination of candidates for offices to be filled by the voters of the state at large, if not nominated at the primaries, and in some cases, (4) the election of permanent party officers. The basis of representation in the convention is generally either the county (in some states the town) or the legislative district (where it does not coincide with the county or town). Delegates may be apportioned among the counties or districts either according to population or according to their respective numbers of partisans as indicated by the votes cast at the last preceding election. As a rule the delegates to conventions are specially chosen for the occasion and for the most part are not themselves candidates for election to public office. A number of states, however, have tried to simplify party organization by providing that the members of certain permanent party committees shall compose the state convention *ex officio*. Other states have provided that the convention shall be composed of the candidates for governor and the state legislature together with hold-over members of the legislature, if any, and sometimes other public officeholders and candidates. Still other states have tried different combinations of these various plans. In most states the state convention is a comparatively numerous body, comprising several times as many delegates as there are members of the state legislature. In some, however, the membership is small. In a few states the convention does not exist under that name, and its place is taken by a so-called party council, consisting of regularly nominated candidates for public office, permanent party committeemen, or both, meeting chiefly for the purpose of adopting a platform. The state conventions generally meet in the even years directly after the primary elections and remain in session only one or two days.

Before the establishment of the direct primary, conventions were also held by the major parties, and they may still be held by minor parties, in each electoral district within the state for the purpose of making nominations for all offices to be filled by election in such district. These district conventions were as various in character as the electoral districts themselves, and the district convention system was as complicated and unwieldy as the electoral district system. Delegates to the most important of the local district conventions, generally the county convention, were elected directly by the members of the several parties in the party primaries or caucuses. Delegates to the less important district conventions were generally chosen indirectly. Delegates to a congressional district convention, for example, might be specially chosen by the several county conventions within the congressional district, or the delegates to the state convention from the counties within the same congressional district might serve *ex officio* as the congressional district convention. Instead, therefore, of coming fresh from the primaries, the delegates to many of the district conventions and even to the state conventions might be, and frequently were, the delegates of delegates, and thus removed two and in some cases even three degrees from the rank and file of the party. At each remove the voice of the rank and file necessarily becomes less distinct, until at last it may become so faint as to be inaudible. Under the direct primary system district conventions were unnecessary and were generally abolished.

Party Committees.

The permanent organs of the party are the standing committees. The functions of the committees are the conduct of campaigns and the management of partisan affairs between campaigns. There must consequently be a special committee for each electoral district within the state. The complication of electoral districts in most states produces a corresponding complication of party committees. The committeemen may all be chosen directly by the members of the party at the primary, or more generally some committeemen may be chosen directly and the others indirectly, either by the local committeemen or by the state convention or otherwise. A number of states have tried to simplify the election of committees by providing that the committees for the more artificial electoral districts shall be composed *ex officio* of members of the committees for the more natural districts. Thus a state senatorial district committee may be composed of the members of the state representative district or county committees lying within the senatorial district. The committee for a congressional district comprising a considerable number of counties may be composed of the chairmen of the several county committees, or it may be composed of the members of the state committee representing the counties or other districts lying within the congressional district. The practice varies greatly in different states, depending partly upon the organization of local government, and partly upon the practice that prevailed before the establishment of the direct primary. Small committees organize by choosing a chairman, a secretary, a treasurer, and such other officers as may be thought necessary, although in a few states the chairmen of committees are specially elected at the primary. Large committees, including the state central committees in most states, also choose an executive committee, or authorize their chairman to appoint an executive committee to which they delegate most of their powers. In a few states, however, the delegation of power by one committee to another is prohibited by law.

The permanent officers of the party organizations, that is, the members of the various party committees, are technically the officers of voluntary associations.[1] They receive no regular compensation for the performance of their important duties, nor is any regular revenue provided by means of which they may defray the expense of maintaining the organization and conducting campaigns. They are generally chosen for fixed terms of two

[1] F. J. Goodnow, *Administrative Law of the United States*, pp. 243-253.

or four years, though local party officers in a few states are chosen annually, and, when elected in official primaries, may receive their credentials from the public election officers. Yet they are not themselves public officers, and cannot be removed from office either by impeachment or by other direct legislative or administrative action. Since they are chosen for fixed terms, they cannot be removed by any partisan body unless the primary law or the party constitution expressly so provides. Frequently there is no provision for the removal of party committeemen before the expiration of their terms. Where there is such provision, it makes the tenure of the local committeemen dependent upon the good will of the majority of the central committee, thus causing a degree of centralization in the party organization incompatible with the maintenance of local autonomy in party government. In the absence of any effective provision for the removal of party committeemen the control of the party organization between campaigns lies entirely in their hands. Whether or not it also lies entirely in their hands at all times depends upon the nature of the test of party affiliation, the method of nominating candidates, and the manner of conducting primaries and conventions.

Party organization in such states as Connecticut, New Mexico, and Rhode Island, which still retain the traditional convention system, is generally highly centralized. The supreme legislative authority is the state convention, and the supreme executive is the state central, or executive, committee. The former makes the rules for the conduct of primaries and the procedure of local conventions and committees, so far as it chooses, and the state committee supervises their enforcement. Any dispute as to the regularity of the proceedings in any primary or convention or party committee may therefore be appealed to the state committee and finally to the state convention. But if the state committee prepares the temporary roll of delegates to the state convention and designates its temporary officers, the balance of power is likely to repose in its hands. In short, under the traditional convention system, that caucus or primary or convention, and hence that nomination of candidates and choice of party committeemen, is regular which is recognized by the next higher committee in the organization of the party. In case of a legal controversy over a nomination and the use of the party name on the ballot, the decisions of the highest committee, that is, of the state central or executive committee, will generally be recognized by the courts as final.[1]

Organization of Socialist Party.

The organization of the minor parties, with one exception, is less formal and less elaborate than that of the major parties and requires no special consideration. The exception is the Socialist party.[2]

The Socialist party organization is substantially the same in all the states and differs in several important respects from that of the other parties. In the first place, the state convention has no final power to adopt a constitution and rules of procedure, but may only propose a constitution and rules or amendments thereto for final adoption by the rank and file of the party, voting directly at a party referendum, as it is called. The platform, also, may only be adopted provisionally by the state convention, subject to final ratification by the members of the party. Secondly, the convention may nominate candidates for public office, but the nominations are subject to ratification by the membership. Thirdly, the members of the principal party committees are elected directly by the members of the party, and may be recalled at any time by a majority of those voting on the question when submitted to the members. The question of recall must be submitted when ordered by the requisite number of local associations. Fourthly, the local associations may initiate amendments to the constitution and rules and platform, and a majority of the members throughout the state voting thereon can adopt them. Thus, though the Socialist party organization is as highly centralized as that of any other party, the acts of those in authority are subject to control by the majority of the members, or at least are supposed to be subject to such control, through the operation of the initiative, referendum, and recall.

The Socialists have not only adopted a radical redivision of powers between the representative organs of party government

[1] F. J. Goodnow, *op. cit.*

[2] During and since the World War, the Socialist party was greatly weakened by schism and internal dissension. However, the skeleton of the organization remains and for that reason is described here. In 1924, the party had nineteen organized state branches with a total dues-paying membership of about eighteen thousand.

and the rank and file; they have also made some fundamental changes in the character of party administration. The most important officer in the Socialist party organization is not the chairman of the state committee, as in other parties, but the state secretary. This officer, though usually elected directly by the membership, is regarded as an employee rather than as a leader of the party, and is expected to devote all his time to its service. Instead of being left to secure his reward for party service by obtaining election or appointment to public office or otherwise, as in other parties, he is paid a fixed salary. The necessary funds for salaries and other expenses of organization are raised by the sale of stamps to the members. These stamps are furnished each month by the national secretary to the state secretaries, one for each member of the party in good standing within the state, at the rate of ten cents apiece. The state secretary retails them to the secretaries of the party locals at twenty-five cents apiece. The local secretaries dispose of them to members at fifty cents each. Thus the national, state, and local organizations are expected to secure a stable and regular revenue and the members of the party to feel a personal interest in the conduct of party affairs between as well as during the campaigns. The Socialist party organization is thus more complete than that of any other party, for no other party makes provision for the regular employment of paid officials and the regular collection of membership dues. On paper it is more democratic than that of any other party. Whether it is so in fact, and whether it is as efficient as democratic, are questions to which only experience can afford an answer.

Test of Party Affiliation.

The test of party membership before the legal recognition of the political party was generally left to the discretion of the official party committees. This system still obtains in a few states. Thus in Rhode Island [1] the rules of the Republican party provide that town and city committees shall be chosen biennially at the caucuses or conventions which elect delegates to the state convention for the nomination of a candidate for governor and other state officers, or at the caucuses or conventions for the

[1] Rules of the Republican State Central Committee of Rhode Island, revised to September 15, 1924.

nomination of representatives to the general assembly. These town and city committees shall, when occasion requires, secure voting lists to be used in local Republican caucuses and shall determine what voters are eligible to vote in such caucuses. When two local caucuses in any town or city claim to represent the Republican party, the executive committee of the state central committee shall determine which one to recognize. Moreover, the state central committee in its discretion may disqualify any one or all of the members of a town or city committee, and choose others to fill such vacancies. The state central committee is elected biennially by the state convention and the committee in turn elects the state chairman. The latter appoints the state executive committee. In this way party management is effectively centralized, and the supreme authority in party affairs is vested in those who control the central organization. The right of the individual member of the party to participate in the government of the party and the nomination of party officers and candidates is dependent primarily upon the will of the local party committee, ultimately upon that of the officers of the state organization.

In a few states, the test of party membership, instead of being left to the discretion of party officers, either local or central, is clearly defined in the party rules. Thus in South Carolina [1] the rules of the Democratic party provide that the applicant for membership in the party must be a white Democrat, or a negro who voted for General Hampton in 1876 and has voted the Democratic ticket continuously since then. Moreover, such a negro may not vote in a Democratic primary unless he produces a written statement, signed by ten "reputable" white men, who shall swear that they know of their own knowledge that the negro in question has voted the Democratic ticket continuously since 1876. In other words, the test of party membership is mainly one of race. In South Carolina, as in Rhode Island, the enforcement of the test is vested primarily in the local committee, subject to appeal to the county committee.

The Socialist party has adopted the most stringent test of party affiliation. The voter who would be accepted as a "comrade" must first sign the party's official declaration of faith, and there-

[1] Rules of the Democratic Party of South Carolina, as adopted by the state convention, May 21, 1924.

after he must regularly pay his party dues. Failure to observe the constitution and rules of the party will entail expulsion from the organization, and failure to pay the dues will be punished by suspension from the privilege of participation in the government of the party. The test of membership in the Socialist party, however, is not arbitrary and contingent upon the good will of the officers of the organization, as is the case of such an organization as that of the Rhode Island Republicans, and it is not discriminatory against any class of persons (except those who do not believe in the "class war"), as in the case of the Democratic organization in South Carolina. It is a test defined by the supreme representative organ of the party, subject to the express approval of the majority of the members, and embodied in a known and fixed rule. The number of persons regularly enrolled in the party organization as dues-paying members is, however, only a small proportion of those who support the party tickets at the polls. In general the party enrolment ranges between five and twenty per cent of the party vote. There is no evidence that the number of persons enlisted in the organizations of other minor parties is any greater than in the case of the Socialists, although the requirement of financial support from the rank and file is made by no other party. Indeed, there is no evidence that the number of partisans actively enlisted in the organizations of any of the parties, major or minor, is greater than five to twenty per cent.

Open *v.* Closed Primaries.

Since the legal recognition of the political party, the test of party membership has often been fixed by the law of the state. This is now the general rule in the states in which the system of direct nomination at primary elections has been substituted for the delegate convention system. The tests established by law are of several kinds.[1] They may be based upon the voters' past or present political affiliations, or they may be based upon their intentions with respect to political affiliations in the future, or they may involve a combination of two or more of the foregoing. Thus, the law may be satisfied with a mere declaration, unsubstantiated by proof, that the voter has in the

[1] See Miller McCintock, "Party Affiliation Tests in Primary Election Laws," *American Political Science Review*, xvi, pp. 465-467 (1922).

past generally supported the candidates of the party of his choice. Wherever the secret ballot is established at general elections, such a test is practically no more effective in excluding undesirable persons from the party than a test based on a mere declaration of intent to support the party's candidates in the present or future. By either test, such a voter is free to decide for himself at the time of the primary with which party he will affiliate for the time being, and with either test the system may well be described as one providing for an open primary. At present, such open primary systems are established in about one-third of the states in which the direct primary has been made mandatory by law.[1]

The alternative to an open primary is one in which the primary of each party is effectively closed to all except *bona fide* members of the party in good standing for some definite period of time. A closed primary system is most effectively established by requiring that all those who would take part in making partisan nominations must be publicly enrolled in advance. In Massachusetts, under the primary law of 1911, the voter became enrolled simply by attending a primary election and voting with some recognized political party. Thereafter, so long as he should regularly attend the primaries, he remained a member of that party, unless he went before the town or city clerk or election commissioners at least ninety days before the date of the primary election at which he should desire to affiliate with a different party, and requested that the desired change be made in his official enrolment. In New York and most states requiring an official party enrolment, the voter is required to designate his party affiliation when he registers, and from the registrars' records the lists of enrolled party voters are made up for the ensuing year. Either of the above-described systems of party enrolment presents an effective barrier to unpremeditated changes of party membership during the heat of a political campaign.

[1] The widest open primary system exists in Wisconsin and Colorado. In those states, no party test whatever is imposed. At the time of voting, the voter receives the primary ballots of all the parties and, in the secrecy of the polling booth, marks the ballot of the party whose candidates he wishes to help nominate. During recent years, the direct primary has tended to become more and more effectively closed to all except *bona fide* party members. (McClintock, *op. cit.*)

Nature of the Party System.

The results of the official enrolment of partisans in the states which provide for party enrolment illustrate the strength and character of the party system in American politics. The following are typical.

Party	New York 1922	Louisiana 1922	California 1922	Oregon 1922
Republican	1,267,436	2,547	927,046	230,098
Democrat	1,130,944	188,781	305,658	85,557
Socialist	32,534	159	22,511	3,968
Prohibition	22,987	....	21,260	3,146
Farmer-Labor	9,141	....	....	....
Miscellaneous	803,200 [1]	....	3,019	10,286 [1]
Independent	....	300	....	....
Refused to state party affiliation	....	....	172,799	....
Total registration prior to general election	3,266,242	191,787	1,452,293	333,055

[1] The chief elements in the "miscellaneous" group in New York and Oregon were the independents and those who refused to state their party affiliations, with possibly a sprinkling of adherents of minor parties not shown on the list.

In each state it is evident that the great majority of the voters are partisans. In New York, more than three-fourths of the voters indicated their party affiliation; in Louisiana, more than 99 per cent; in California, almost nine-tenths; and in Oregon, over 96 per cent. Not only are the great majority of the voters partisans, but also the great majority of them belong to one or the other of the two major parties. In New York, 73.4 per cent of the registered voters were enrolled as Republicans or Democrats in 1922; in Louisiana, 99.6 per cent; in California, 84.8 per cent; and in Oregon, 94.7 per cent. The number of organized parties in the states usually ranges from four to six, but it is seldom that more than two of them are of major political importance. In a considerable number of states, including most of those of the South, a large majority of the voters profess to belong to a single party, as in Louisiana, California, and Oregon.

The official party enrolments, however, do not show the number of partisans actively enlisted in the party organizations. The most important work of the parties is the making of nominations, but examination of the primary election returns in different states reveals the fact that there is no uniformity in the attendance of partisans at the primaries of their respective parties. The extent to which partisans affiliated with the major organizations actively participate in the making of nominations depends upon the political importance of their party and varies with the chances for the success of their candidates at the general elections. Where election is certain, as in the case of the Democratic candidates in many southern states, the attendance of partisans at the primaries is usually larger than at the general elections. It is often proportionately as large as the attendance of all voters at the general elections in states where the issue is doubtful. Where defeat is certain, the attendance at the primaries is commonly small, sometimes so small as to be merely nominal. When neither election nor defeat is certain, the results are various, depending mainly upon the personality of the candidates for nomination and the closeness of the contests between them.

The official returns of primary elections further show that party ties rest lightly upon a considerable proportion of the voters. Whilst in Oregon, for example, two-thirds of all the voters are enrolled Republicans, and have been such ever since the adoption of the system of party enrolment in 1904, they have nevertheless chosen two Democratic governors and two Democratic United States senators during this period, and cast the electoral vote of the state once for the Democratic candidate for the presidency. Either many voters are Republicans mainly for the purpose of participating in the Republican primaries, since Republican nominations are usually much more important than those of any other party, or else partisan principles are frequently subordinated at the polls to other considerations of a personal, or, at least, non-partisan character. The same conditions exist in most northern states in which one of the major parties is much more numerous than the other. In the close states, on the other hand, party ties seem in general to be less lightly regarded by the voter. The evidence indicates, however, that the strongest motive impelling a considerable number of voters to become partisans is the desire to make their votes count for as much as possible, rather than an enduring loyalty to any particular party creed or organization. What attracts them to the primary is not the spirit of partisanship, but the opportunity which the primary system affords of choosing twice among the candidates for office. Such voters are partisans chiefly in name.

WORKING OF PARTY SYSTEM

The existing partisan system, regarded as a system of organizing the electorate, is, like the system of electoral districts, an artificial creation. The party organizations which are recognized by law for the purpose of making nominations for state offices are also recognized for the purpose of making nominations for federal offices. The same has been true as to local offices; but in this field a contrary tendency has recently appeared. Where official party enrolment is provided for, the same enrolment serves as the basis for participation in the state and federal primaries, and in many localities also for the local primaries. State and federal primaries generally, with the exception of the presidential primaries, and local primaries less generally, are held on the same day. Thus the same partisan system which is employed for the organization of the state electorates is made to serve the purposes of the voters in federal politics, and in many cases in local politics also. State, federal, and local, legislative, executive, and judicial nominations are all made by the same electoral associations. But where the same party organizations represent the same groups of voters in the selection of so many different candidates, there inevitably ensues a great confusion of ideas. State, federal, and local issues, legislative, administrative, and judicial issues, are by no means identical. There are usually at least two sides to each issue, and the chances that any large number of voters will be on the same side all along the line of issues are not very great. In order that an electoral association of the existing American type may have a fair prospect of success at the polls, each member must subordinate many of his personal views for the sake of joining his party associates on common ground. Party organization necessarily involves some compromise of private opinions in the interest of agreement upon a general program, and under the existing conditions in American politics it involves an unparalleled degree of such compromise.

Effects of Partisan System in State Politics.

The confusion of issues and compromises of opinions inherent in the established party system has unfortunate consequences on the operation of the system in the states. In the first place, the importance of principles of any kind in the actual conduct of party government is unduly diminished. The difficulty of singling out the paramount issue in a campaign and securing the support of the whole party upon that issue stimulates an overemphasis of the other features of party association, the local prejudices, the private and special interests, the purely personal loyalties, the evil consequences of party irregularity. The taking of sides upon important issues is avoided as far as possible. Platforms tend to become an inscrutable compound of undisputed generalities, trivial details, and vague promises. If issues must be faced, it is usually easier for a major party to be obstructive than constructive. A recent writer has justly observed: "Their [the two leading parties] success as partisan organizations depends on the willingness of their members [that is, those who are not merely nominal members] to sacrifice individual convictions in the interests of party unity. The party is to them a very real and valuable thing, whose preservation is worth the subordination of their private opinions. Republicans and Democrats are held together more by personal loyalty, by the habit of association, by common interests, and by the fear of the consequences of independence, than by common convictions. Every party whose chief purpose is to control the government must be bound together by a cement of this kind."[1] Indeed, a great and successful party becomes a political entity, a being with a separate existence of its own, with a character to maintain, a personality to inspire, a destiny to fulfill. A party without principles would be a mean and unlovely and, in the long run, ineffective creature, but it takes more than principles to make a party. It is not surprising, therefore, that many who describe themselves as partisans hold their party ties lightly. Men of the highest principles and men of no principle at all make poor partisans.

Secondly, the issues which in practice are most likely to be compromised for the sake of party solidarity are those peculiar to the states. This is clearly indicated by the results of the elections. Viewing the Union as a whole, the two leading parties divide the voters with extraordinary evenness, and have done so with some temporary interruptions for a long period of years. Only one candidate for the presidency has ever succeeded in gaining the support of as many as three voters out of five. The most sweeping presidential victories were those of Jackson in

[1] *The New Republic*, Aug. 14, 1915, p. 30.

1828, Lincoln in 1864, Grant in 1872, Roosevelt in 1904, Harding in 1920, and Coolidge in 1924. Harding, who received the largest proportion of the popular vote ever cast for any candidate, received only 60.3 per cent of the total vote. On the other hand, through the division of the opposition, Wilson was elected in 1912 with 43 per cent of the total vote, and Lincoln was elected in 1860 with only 39.9 per cent. In order to avoid such minority elections most voters normally support at presidential elections the candidates of one of the two leading parties. Ordinarily the successful candidate for the presidency polls between 48 per cent and 52 per cent of the popular vote, and the leading unsuccessful candidate not less than 40 per cent to 45 per cent. Since the final establishment of the national convention in 1840, there have been only five presidential elections at which more than two parties have had votes in the electoral college. Ordinarily no minor party can carry a state. But any equally even division of the voters in the several states does not exist. There are ten southern states which the Democrats, since the suppression of the negro vote, have never failed to carry for their candidate for president. There is an equal number of northern and western states which the Republicans, during the same period until the split in the party in 1912, never failed to carry for their candidate for president.[1] That is to say, federal issues must be generally deemed more important than state issues, or at least the choice of federal officers must be regarded as more important than the choice of state officers. Were it otherwise, the state electorates rather than that of the Union as a whole would be evenly divided by the parties, for the major party organizations are created to win elections, especially the most important elections, and an electoral association which desires to win will not remain in a permanent minority in a state unless its members regard state issues as of secondary importance.

The subordination of state issues in the interests of party solidarity increases the artificiality of the partisan system as it operates in the states. The members of a major political organization in a state may have little or no basis for common action, so far as state issues are concerned, and different factions within the party in a state may be more widely separated from one

[1] See the diagrams and tables in Holcombe, *The Political Parties of To-day*, ch. iv, *passim*.

another on state issues than from the opposition. Under such circumstances more important issues, so far as the state is concerned, may be at stake in primary elections than in the general elections. Such indeed is the case in all states where one of the major parties dominates state politics. Moreover, in such states, since the party nomination for state office is ordinarily equivalent to election, the members of the minority party are excluded from any effective share in the government of the state. Since the control of the nominating machinery in the dominant party will give control of the general elections, those members of the dominant party who control the nominating machinery may control the government of the state. In the states where the major parties are more evenly matched, the control of the nominating machinery in both parties, if held by politicians willing to work together, may likewise give practical control of the government of the state. In such states the members of both parties may be practically excluded from any effective share in the government of the state, if they are excluded from effective participation in the nominating process. Whether the majority of a party may be so excluded depends upon the nature of the nominating process and the purposes of the permanent party officers.

Working of Convention System.

Under the delegate convention system the process of nominations was such as to facilitate the control of the nominating machinery by the active members of the party organizations. The test of party affiliation was framed and applied by the regular party committees, and participation by the rank and file in the primaries and caucuses was consequently more or less contingent upon the favor of their official leaders. Partisans rarely voted directly for the candidates of their choice, and consequently could express their preference only through the medium of delegates to the conventions. If all genuine members of a party, and no others, were admitted to a primary, if the primary were honestly conducted and a correct return made of the votes cast therein, if the delegates to the conventions were loyal to their pledges, or, in case they had made no pledges, were sincerely desirous of nominating the best candidates, and if the conventions were honestly conducted, the process of nomination was likely to represent the will of the majority of the party. But if the primaries and conventions were conducted arbitrarily and unfairly, the wishes of the rank and file would have little influence upon the result. In practice, the permanent party committeemen not only judged the qualifications of participants in the primaries, but also prepared the slates of delegates to the conventions, conducted the primary elections, passed provisionally upon contests between rival slates of delegates for the credentials, made up the temporary rolls of accredited delegates, selected the temporary officers, and arranged for the permanent organization of the conventions. Under these circumstances, it is not surprising that the rank and file were often unable to prevent the nomination of candidates to whom the majority were strongly opposed.

The true character of the process of nomination under the delegate convention system was recognized almost from the beginning. John C. Calhoun, writing in 1844, declared: "The further the convention is removed from the people, the more certainly the control will be placed in the hands of the interested few. . . . At each successive remove the voice of the people will become less full and distinct, until at last it will become so faint and imperfect as not to be audible."[1] The existence of the two-party system in national politics made the position of the professional party managers almost impregnable, so long as the process of nomination remained unchanged. If unscrupulous party committeemen chose to disregard or defeat the will of the rank and file, the theoretical check upon their abuse of power was to "bolt" the nominations and support other candidates at the polls. But such a course meant the desertion of the party, at least temporarily, and in the period before the introduction of the secret ballot might have caused the forfeiture of all claims to participate in future nominations. Where the nominations of both parties were made without due regard for the preferences of the majority of their members, a "bolt" from one party to the other would have been futile. The organization of an independent party on short notice was impracticable, except in local campaigns. Though an independent party could be organized

[1] From his statement refusing to permit his name to be presented to the Democratic national convention at Baltimore in 1844 as a candidate for the presidency.

on a national scale, if time were permitted, it could not become of major importance without displacing one of the existing major parties. So long as the bipartisan system prevailed, and the process of nomination remained as established under the delegate convention system, the principal check upon the conduct of affairs by the active members of the party organizations was in practice their own sense of responsibility to their followers.

Influence of "Machines" and "Bosses."

The permanent party officers were not without a motive for seeking to control the nominations.[1] In the first place, control of the nominating machinery enabled those who held the control, the "machine" as they may be described, to dispose of the nominations for private gain. This gain might take the form of advancement of their personal political fortunes, or it might even take the form of money. In some cases, particularly in the case of the more conspicuous offices, payment for nominations might be made under the guise of contributions to campaign funds. In the case of less conspicuous offices, such as minor places on the state ticket, and minor administrative and judicial nominations, the sale and purchase of nominations could be more open. In some states at certain periods such disposition of nominations was brazen.[2] Occasionally vendors of nominations have been convicted of corruption in the courts. Convictions, however, for obvious reasons, could hardly be expected in the greater proportion of the cases. There can be no question that the deliberate sale of a nomination for money is corrupt, but the line is not easy to draw between a proper and an improper disposal of nominations, not for money, but for the advancement of the political interests of the members of the "machine." Personal and party success in such cases easily become identified, and a disposition of nominations in such a way as to advance the fortunes of the party and incidentally of the party managers is less open to criticism, at any rate so long as the party is regarded as a private association, and its managers are left to their own devices to secure compensation for the undoubted services they are required

[1] For an excellent discussion of the subjects treated in this section, see C. E. Merriam, *The American Party System* (New York, 1922), chs. iv-vii.

[2] See W. M. Ivins, *Machine Politics and Money in Elections in New York City* (New York, 1887).

to perform. It is often said that party managers and workers should be public-spirited enough to perform their party duties without compensation, but such a point of view overlooks the fact that much of the work connected with the conduct of party affairs and the getting out of the vote on election day is menial drudgery, demanding heavy sacrifices of time and effort, and offering little compensation in the way of public honors or esteem.

Secondly, control of the nominations enables the "machine" to influence the public conduct of those officials who owe their nominations to "machine" support in the primaries or conventions. By using such influence with members of a state legislature, the "machine" can promote or obstruct the enactment of legislation desired or opposed by private interests to whom the members of the "machine" may be indebted for political or personal favors. Tax exemptions or appropriations, or franchises or other special legislation, if not prohibited by the state constitution, and special consideration in connection with public general legislation, are the not infrequent objects of such influence. By using such influence with administrative officials the "machine" can affect the appraisal or assessment of property, the awarding of contracts, the inspection of machinery and buildings, and the enforcement of law generally. By using such influence with the judiciary the "machine" can affect appointments to receiverships, masterships, refereeships, and so forth, and in general it can affect the use of the power of appointment to office and the distribution of the public patronage. A "machine" may include a large number of active politicians, but in general on important questions of "machine" or party policy the advice of a few of the more experienced leaders is followed. If there be some one among these whose advice is especially valued, that one is commonly described as a "boss."[1] There has been much indiscriminate abuse of "bosses" in American politics, but there is a clear necessity for discrimination between good and bad "bosses." The distinction indeed is similar to that drawn many centuries ago by Aristotle between the good king and the bad king or tyrant. The good king was a leader whose power was exercised for the common welfare. The tyrant was one whose power was exercised

[1] For a good discussion of the social background, the personal qualities, and the technique of a typical state political boss, see Harold F. Gosnell, *Boss Platt and His New York Machine* (Chicago, 1924). See also W. B. Munro, *Personality in Politics* (New York, 1924).

for private ends. In fact the line between the two was not always easy to draw, for many rulers showed a mixture of the good and the bad. It is the same with the modern "boss." If the word must be used only in a bad sense, it should be understood that those who have the power of a "boss" may use it for public as well as private ends, and if they use it chiefly for public ends are entitled to a better name.

Under the delegate convention system, however, the business of party management too often fell into the hands of professional politicians intent rather upon personal gain than upon the promotion of the common welfare. In any state where one of the major parties dominated the political situation, if the party itself was dominated by self-seeking professional politicians, the government of the state likewise tended to become vested in the hands of the "machine." Where the major parties were more evenly matched in state politics, the voters at least had a choice of evils, and consequently a somewhat more effective position in the conduct of party and public affairs. The situation that could exist in a boss-ridden state has been vividly described by no less a person than the president of the last constitutional convention in the state of New York in a speech before that body.[1] "What is the government of this state? What has it been during the forty years of my acquaintance with it? The government of the constitution? Oh, no. . . . From the days of Fenton, and of Conkling, . . . down to the present time the government of the state has presented two different lines of activity, one of the constitutional and statutory officers of the state, and the other of the party leaders,—they call them party bosses. They call the system—I didn't coin the phrase; I adopt it because it carries its own meaning—the system they call 'invisible government.' For I don't remember how many years Mr. Conkling was the supreme ruler in this state; the governor did not count, the legislatures did not count; comptrollers and secretaries of state and what not did not count. . . . Then Mr. Platt ruled the state . . . and the capital was not here, it was at 49 Broadway. . . . The ruler of the state during the greater part of the forty years of my acquaintance with the state government has not been any man authorized by the constitution or by the law, and, sir, there

[1] Elihu Root, Speech in New York Constitutional Convention, Aug. 30, 1915.

is throughout the length and breadth of this state a deep and sullen and long-continued resentment at being governed thus by men not of the people's choosing." This charge was not successfully disputed either in the constitutional convention or outside.

The Need for Reform.

The delegate convention system doubtless might have been greatly improved by the adoption of certain reforms. The chief of these were:—[1] (1) the adoption of a uniform primary day and the holding of a joint primary for all political parties at the regular polling places; (2) the official enrolment of all members of recognized political parties; (3) the direct election of all delegates to all conventions, so-called intermediate conventions being abolished; (4) the direct election of party committeemen as well as delegates to conventions at the primaries; (5) the printing of an official primary ballot, the names of all candidates for choice as delegates to conventions or as committeemen to be filed with appropriate public officials a reasonable length of time before the primaries; (6) the fixing of the dates of all political conventions and the regulation of procedure therein by law; (7) the certification of the election of all delegates by public officials and the determination of contests between rival delegations by the state courts; (8) the abolition of the secret ballot in conventions and the nomination of all candidates by open roll call; (9) the regulation of the basis of representation in conventions and upon party committees by known and fixed party rules; and (10) the extension to primary elections of the laws relating to corrupt practices at general elections. Nowhere, however, were the party managers willing to consent to extensive reforms, until the demand for the abolition of the convention system and the establishment of the system of direct nominations at the primaries had become so strong that the reform of the convention system was no longer acceptable.

The delegate convention system, so far as nominations for state office are concerned, has now given way in most states to the system of direct nominations at the primaries, or as it is commonly called, of direct primaries. This system has been in

[1] See *Report of the Joint Committee of the Legislature of New York on Primary and Election Laws*, 1910, p. 217.

operation for many years in various localities for the nomination of candidates for local office, and for a number of years in the South for the nomination of Democratic candidates for state office.[1] Its use for the nomination of candidates for state office in the North and West is more recent, but already Wisconsin and Oregon, the first northern and western states to adopt the state-wide direct primary, have employed the system for over twenty years. It is not too soon to inquire to what extent the system has justified the hopes of its originators.[2]

Working of the Direct Primary.

A candidate for nomination under the direct primary system ordinarily secures a place on the official primary ballot by filing a petition. This petition bears not less than a prescribed number of signatures, varying with the size of the electoral district and the importance of the office sought. In states where there is an official party enrollment the signatures must be of enrolled members of the party whose nomination is sought. Experience has indicated that the collection of signatures, at least by candidates early in the field, is mainly a matter of money, although since the process of signature collecting serves to a certain extent to advertise the candidacy, it is not altogether a waste of money. A few states have faced the situation more candidly by providing that a filing fee shall be paid to the public treasury in lieu of a petition.[3] In some of these states, however, the requirement of a fee has been declared unconstitutional, on the ground that it sets up a requirement for election to public office not authorized by the Constitution. The logic of these decisions is difficult to appreciate, since the requirement of a petition amounts to the same thing. In general, the process of getting on the primary ballot is not difficult, and the establishment of the direct primary has undoubtedly tended to increase the number of active candidates for party nominations wherever there has been a fair chance of success at the general election.

[1] See E. Meyer, *Nominating Systems* (1st ed., 1902).

[2] The best collection of articles dealing with the direct primary in all its phases is to be found in the *Annals of the American Academy of Political and Social Science*, cvi (1923). For an excellent study of the operation of the direct primary in a particular state, see R. S. Boots, *The Direct Primary in New Jersey* (New York, 1917).

[3] A filing fee is also required in a number of other states but not as an alternative to the petition.

The establishment of the direct primary has also tended to alter the methods of campaigning for nominations. Under the convention system the object of the candidate was to secure the support of the delegates, and his activity was necessarily directed towards securing the favor of those whose influence with the delegates might be supposed to be greatest. This influence might rest with the voters, by whom the delegates to the lowest order of conventions were at least nominally elected, or it might rest with the professional party managers, by whom such delegates might be actually selected, and by whom the delegates to the higher orders of conventions commonly were actually selected. Under the direct primary system it is the support of the voters themselves that must be secured. This support may be obtained by direct appeals to the voters in the case of all nominations in which the interest of the voters can be aroused by such appeals. In other cases it may be necessary, as under the convention system, to enlist the interest of the party managers, or to combine with a candidate for nomination to a more conspicuous office and form a "slate." "Trading" votes in a direct primary, however, is not so easy a process as "trading" votes in a convention. The candidates must generally be more dependent upon "publicity," that is, upon the dissemination of information concerning their personality, their record, their purposes, and their associations. If a party is united upon its principles, primary campaigns must inevitably turn chiefly upon personalities, but where, as frequently happens, a party is not united upon state issues, the primary campaign may provide a more effective opportunity for the public discussion of such issues than the general election itself. Such is generally the case in many parts of the South, and in not a few of the northern and western states.

The result of the increase in the number of active candidates for the important nominations and of the change in the character of primary campaigns, taken together with the consciousness on the part of the voters of the greater power that may be theirs under the system of direct nominations, has been to increase the interest of the rank and file in the making of nominations. This increase of interest in nominations, however, has not taken place equally with respect to all nominations. There has been a general tendency to neglect the primaries of parties with little chance of success at the general election, the members of such parties often taking more interest in the primaries of the dominant party than in their own. Not infrequently, even in northern and western states, the attendance at the primary of the dominant party closely approaches and occasionally surpasses the party vote at the general election, whilst the attendance at the primaries of the opposition is but a small fraction of their vote at the polls. In the primaries of parties with good prospects of success at the general election, the interest of the voters depends upon the importance of the nominations which are to be made and the closeness of the contest between the several candidates for nomination. When a close contest is waged for an important nomination, the interest of the voters is much greater than it commonly was in similar cases under the delegate convention system. But contests for minor places on the state ticket, including high judicial offices, and for minor administrative and judicial offices generally, often fail to arouse any lively public interest. A candidate for nomination for such a position as secretary of state or judge of a circuit court has ordinarily a great deal of difficulty in getting the rank and file of the party to think about his candidacy at all, to say nothing of forming any intelligent opinion of the requirements of the office and the qualifications of the various candidates for nomination thereto.

Effect on Party Spirit.

The unequal development of popular interest in nominations which results from the establishment of the direct primary system has had important consequences upon the character of party leadership. The influence of the regular party managers or "machine" upon nominations for the conspicuous offices has been diminished, for "machine" candidates must secure the approval of the rank and file, expressed directly in the primary, and under such circumstances as tend to encourage independent candidates to repudiate the leadership of unworthy "bosses." A candidate for governor or United States senator, fresh from popular endorsement in the primary, is far stronger with reference to the powers of the "invisible government" than a candidate for a similar position nominated under the convention system could ordinarily have been. To the extent that the offices for which nominations are sought are conspicuous, the effect of the direct primary is to establish "visible" party leadership in place of "invisible" leadership. But, as has been pointed out, many of the offices for which nominations are commonly made in the direct primary are not conspicuous. The voters are not generally interested in them, or well informed with respect to their requirements and the qualifications of those who seek them. In such cases, when there is no official "slate" prepared by the regular party managers, a common practice is for a candidate for a conspicuous nomination to make a slate of his own by pooling his interests with those of the candidates for other nominations whose coöperation is likely to prove most useful. Thus the result of the primary election, so far as those other nominations are concerned, is likely to be an endorsement of a certain slate-maker, either the "machine" or the successful candidate for the most conspicuous nomination, rather than of the several other candidates in particular. If the "machine slate" is endorsed, the primary system is only partially successful in substituting visible for invisible party leadership. In either case, so-called direct nominations are much less direct in fact than they may be made to appear.

If primary nominations for all offices are actually direct, the results may be even less satisfactory than when they only appear to be direct. One of the chief advantages of the popular election of large numbers of administrative and judicial officers, from the standpoint of the professional politician, is the facility it affords for placating all sections of a heterogeneous party by distributing the minor nominations among the different elements within the party. But in the direct primary it becomes possible for any members of a party to make an appeal to that element which is most numerous, geographical, racial, or religious, as the case may be. If this is done by some candidate for each place on the ticket, it may happen that all the successful candidates will represent the dominant element in the party. Such lack of balance in the party ticket may lead to grave dissatisfaction among the other elements within the party, and thereby imperil the integrity of party loyalty and the effectiveness of party discipline. This menace to the solidarity of party organization is much more serious under the direct primary than under the convention system, for in a convention the delegates can easily select candidates for the minor places on the ticket with a view to their effect on the strength of the ticket as a whole. Moreover, an active direct primary campaign seems more likely to arouse bitter personal enmities than a campaign for convention delegates. At least it makes such enmities better known to the public, and hence more difficult to settle after the heat of the campaign. The results upon party unity in the ensuing campaign for election can more easily be unfortunate than under the convention system. An active primary campaign, too, is likely to lay more stress upon the issues with respect to which the party is divided than upon those with respect to which it is united. Where the former are the more important, it is well that it should be so, but the former may not be the more important. Supporters of unsuccessful candidates for nomination may more easily than under the convention system come to undervalue the principles upon which the members of the party are agreed. In short, the direct primary system, though it greatly increases the interest of voters in party nominations, at least in those for the more important offices, and to a corresponding extent increases also the sense of responsibility on the part of the leaders to the rank and file, is less favorable than the convention system to the maintenance of party harmony, and consequently to the efficiency of the existing bipartisan system.

Effect on Party Organization.

Moreover, the direct primary system, in its prevailing form, includes not only the direct nomination of candidates, but also the direct election of party committeemen. Under the convention system, as has been pointed out, the most important committees, particularly the state central committees, were chosen only indirectly by the rank and file of the parties, usually through the instrumentality of the conventions. Where the system of "invisible government" was established, the convention was more likely to be controlled by the committee than the committee by the convention. The only committeemen chosen directly by the members of the party were the local committeemen, and they were dependent for their positions not only upon their ability to control their districts by carrying the primaries or caucuses, but also upon their ability to obtain "recognition" by their superiors in the "organization." District leaders as a rule could not command the confidence of their followers unless they were "regular," and they could not indefinitely maintain their regularity unless they also enjoyed the confidence of their superiors. Thus even the local committeemen, since they could not serve two masters, tended to become "organization" men, and the power of the "machine" was consolidated from top to bottom. The direct election of all committeemen profoundly affects this internal relationship of the "machine," for it makes each committeeman's title to office as good as any other's. It is no longer possible for any one, whether a local or central committeeman, to challenge the regularity of another. All are equally dependent upon the rank and file of the party, and equally independent of one another. The result is to decentralize the structure of party organization, and thereby to diminish the power of unofficial party managers to combat the enemies of party harmony by the time-honored methods.

The effect of the direct primary upon the relations between committeemen and candidates has been as notable as its effect upon the relations between the different orders of committeemen. It is the duty of committeemen to manage election campaigns in the interest of all the candidates, and it is the duty of candidates to work for the success of the party as a whole. In other words, it is necessary that candidates and committeemen should work together in harmony. Under many primary laws, however, committeemen do not take office until the beginning of the year following their election. Consequently they do not manage the campaigns of the candidates nominated in the same primaries in which they are elected, unless they happen to be chosen to succeed themselves. In other words, the candidates nominated at a direct primary find the party machinery in the hands of committeemen chosen as a rule not less than two years before. Now if there has been no change during this period in the control of the party, this arrangement may not prove unsatisfactory, but if the candidates and committeemen who carry the primaries are out of sympathy with the committeemen who carried the preceding primaries, dissensions will arise. It can hardly be expected that a candidate will have much confidence in a committee whose slate perhaps has just been repudiated in the primary, or that a committee will be zealous in support of a candidate who has just smashed the official slate. Under the convention system, either the committeemen were responsible to the candidates who had carried the convention, or the candidates were responsible to the committeemen who had manipulated it. Under the direct primary system the convention can no longer serve as the instrument of party harmony, and ordinarily nothing is substituted for it. Thus the direct primary may be the means of making party committeemen more responsible to the rank and file of the parties than before, but at the cost of a more or less serious division of authority between the several orders of committeemen and the candidates. In other words it tends to disorganize the major parties.

The experience of the last twenty years in the direct primary states indicates that the new system alone will not prevent the control of nominations by minorities. Where any member of a party may contest for a nomination, there is nothing to prevent any number of persons from so doing, and in general, as already pointed out, the most important nominations are likely to be sought by several candidates. Now the greater the number of candidates for a nomination, the less the likelihood that any one of them will secure a majority of all the votes cast in the primary. There is a constant temptation for each candidate to seek to divide the potential following of his leading opponent by inducing several candidates to appeal to the same following. The result may be, and frequently is, that the successful candidate for the nomination receives less than a majority of all the votes cast. This in itself is of no great importance, provided that the successful candidate is not a person to whom the majority of the party are actually opposed. It occasionally happens, however, that there is a definite issue between the majority and the minority of a party, and the candidate of the minority wins through the division of the majority among several candidates. In general, the candidate favored by the "machine" has a big advantage over his competitors, because the "machine" is generally the most adept in holding its following together, and the most efficient in getting out the vote in the primaries. A "good machine" doubtless will ordinarily not intervene in the primaries on behalf of any of the candidates, at least not on behalf of those for conspicuous nominations, but will remain impartial until after the nominations have been made. But the direct primary was not introduced on account of "good machines" but on account of "bad machines." Where no great issue is at stake in the nominations, and the questions are mainly of personality, the "machine" seems generally able to prepare a "slate," especially for the less important offices filled by election in the state at large and in the unwieldier sort of districts, and procure its endorsement in the primaries. It is not surprising that the direct primary has not been the instrument of any general overthrow of the established leaders in the major parties.

Effect on State Government.

The effect of the establishment of the system of direct nominations upon the character of the candidates actually nominated for public office is difficult to estimate. During the comparatively short period that the direct primary system has been in general operation, the political situation has been too confused to permit the discovery of any definite change either in the ability or in the moral character of the candidates of the major parties. In a few states the introduction of the state-wide direct primary was followed by a change in the personnel of the party leaders, in the other states no change took place. Doubtless some men have been nominated who would not have been nominated under the former system, or at least would not have been nominated so easily, but it cannot yet be affirmed that the type of man who is successful in politics has been materially altered. The evidence is clearer with respect to the effect of the direct primary upon the conduct of the men nominated and elected to public office, at least in the case of men elected to the more conspicuous offices. These men seem generally to display more initiative in office, more independence of unofficial party leaders, and more confidence in the support of public opinion than similar men in similar positions were wont to display when nominated under the convention system. Above all the establishment of the direct primary has strengthened the position of the governor as the leader of his party and thereby tended to make party leadership more "visible" and hence more responsible. Political issues have been presented more directly to the members of the several parties, and thus the whole electorate has been compelled to think more continuously and more accurately about public affairs. The minor officeholders are at least less dependent upon unofficial party leadership than they were under the unregulated convention system, and the undue influence of special interests operating through secret arrangements with professional party managers and "bosses" must likewise have been somewhat diminished.

The general establishment of the direct primary system has thus been followed by notable improvement in all conditions with respect to which the delegate convention system had become objectionable.[1] It must not be inferred, however, that all the credit for the improvement is due to the change from indirect to direct nominations. The direct primary system could not be established without the adoption also of many of the reforms suggested for the improvement of the convention system. Direct nominations have meant the holding of joint primaries for all major parties on a uniform primary day under the management of public election officials in accordance with rules laid down by law, subject to appeal to the courts for the determination of the rights of partisans in general and particularly of candidates for nominations. They have meant also the abolition of all intermediate conventions, the direct election of delegates to the state conventions, and the direct election of all important party committeemen. Finally, they have meant the extension to the primaries of most of the provisions of law intended to protect the purity of the general elections. All these reforms could have been adopted without the abandonment of the delegate convention system, had the party managers and bosses consented; and, if adopted, they would have produced at least a part of the improvement in political conditions which has actually taken place since the introduction of the direct primary. Actually, however, the whole improvement in the conditions under which nominations are made is associated in the minds of the voters with the introduction of the system of direct nominations, and under the circumstances such an association of ideas is not unjustified.

FURTHER REFORM OF NOMINATING METHODS

The direct primary system, nevertheless, must be regarded as an imperfect instrument for the selection of partisan candidates. In the first place, no satisfactory test of party affiliation has yet been devised. The true purposes and motives of voters who seek recognition as members of a particular party are

[1] See *ante*, ch. iv.

beyond the reach of public primary officials acting in accordance with rigid rules of law. The establishment of an official party enrolment, based on the declaration of the voter at primary or registration day, is at best a mechanical arrangement, tending to prevent honest voters from changing their affiliation promptly in response to changes in their political opinions or in the nature of the paramount issues, but by no means ensuring that none but genuine members of a party shall participate in the making of its nominations. Indeed in localities where one of the major parties dominates the local political situation, the closed primary system inevitably fosters an unnatural concentration of voters of divergent political sympathies in the locally dominant party. In states where the primary of the dominant party is more important than the general election, a like tendency may be discovered, and in all states there is a more or less general impression on the part of the voters that the primary is to be considered as a preliminary public election rather than a private or purely partisan affair. Any effective test of party affiliation or system of enrolment is accordingly felt to be an interference with the secrecy of the ballot. Where the so-called open primary has been established, however, the invasion of the primaries of one party by the members of another for the purpose of procuring the nomination of the weakest candidates may easily become a serious menace to the integrity of party nominations. Where several candidates are contesting for an important nomination in the primary of one party and there are no important contests for nominations in the primary of the other party, the exercise of an improper influence upon the nominations of the first party by voters who do not expect to support its candidates at the ensuing election is the subject of not infrequent complaints. There is no agreement as yet, however, upon the proper test of party affiliation, if any, and no decision has been reached as between the open and the closed primary.[1]

The Non-Partisan Primary.

The most obvious alternative to the existing partisan primary systems is a non-partisan primary system. At a non-partisan primary the voter is free to choose among all the candidates for

[1] Recently, however, there has been a tendency toward the more effective types of the closed primary. McClintock, *op. cit.*, p. 466.

any nomination, regardless of his or their party affiliations. The two candidates receiving the greatest and second greatest number of votes, respectively, for any nomination become the official candidates for the office at the ensuing election. No party labels, nor, as a rule, descriptions of any sort, are printed either on the primary ballot or on that used at the general election. By the abolition of party designations on the primary ballot, and the decision at a second election between the two leading candidates at the primary, the state can avoid many of the perplexing questions inseparable from the attempt to regulate partisan nominations by law. It becomes unnecessary to define the test of party affiliation, for the state by refusing to recognize party designations relieves itself of the responsibility for maintaining the integrity of the party organizations. Under the non-partisan primary system, voluntary electoral associations may still make their nominations before the primaries, if they wish, but control of the nominating machinery, whatever it may be, no longer carries with it such enormous advantages as under the former delegate convention system prior to the establishment of the direct primary. Control of the nominating machinery under the delegate convention system, as formerly established, carried with it an excessive influence upon elections, because the electoral system was a *plurality* electoral system. The non-partisan primary system is in effect a *majority* electoral system, under which the voter has two votes, a first-choice vote expressed in the primary, and a second-choice vote expressed at the ensuing general election. In case the voter's first choice is one of the two leading candidates at the primary, his second choice can be cast and counted for him again at the final election. Otherwise he is free to make a second choice between the two candidates most generally preferred at the primary. If it be provided that any candidate at the primary who receives a majority of all the votes cast shall thereupon be declared elected without the formality of a second election,[1] the non-partisan primary system becomes substantially identical with the majority electoral system which formerly prevailed in France and Germany and is still used in French local elections.

There is a distinct tendency in recent primary legislation to reject both forms of the partisan primary and adopt the non-

[1] This is the plan followed in the Chicago aldermanic elections.

partisan primary.[1] This tendency first appeared in connection with municipal elections. The separation of local from state and national issues was especially desired in municipal affairs and the abolition of party designations, which were mainly national and state party designations, seemed the most direct way of bringing about the desired separation. The non-partisan primary was first applied to the selection of candidates for state office in connection with judicial nominations. The briefest experience with the direct primary made it evident that purely judicial issues had no place in ordinary partisan controversies, and that judges ought not to be compelled to procure their nominations by partisan appeals on issues with which impartial judges should have no concern. The non-partisan judicial primary now exists in about one-fourth of the states.[2] The next step in the development of the non-partisan primary was its extension to the nomination of local officers other than those in cities. In California and Minnesota, the non-partisan primary system was adopted for all county nominations in 1913.[3] In Minnesota, the system was also applied to the selection of candidates for the state legislature in 1912, while North Dakota in 1923 provided for the non-partisan nomination and election of all elective state officers, including members of the legislature. However, in Nebraska, a constitutional amendment designed to apply the principle to both state and local offices was defeated by the voters in 1924.[4]

It would seem clear that the state should either protect the purity of partisan nominations by establishing an effective test of party affiliation, or abandon the attempt to regulate the selection of candidates by political parties, and frankly treat the primary as a preliminary public election. The so-called open primary is a hybrid system which has fewer advantages than either the closed primary or the non-partisan primary, and most

[1] See R. E. Cushman, "Non-Partisan Nominations and Elections," *Annals*, cvi, pp. 83-96 (1923).

[2] It has been abandoned in Kansas, Iowa, and Pennsylvania. Cushman, *op. cit.*, pp. 86-87.

[3] The same action was taken by North Dakota in 1919. A number of other states apply the non-partisan principle to the nomination and election of particular county officials such as school superintendents and county judges. Cushman, *op. cit.*, p. 84.

[4] A similar amendment, adopted by the California legislature in 1915, was rejected at the polls.

of the disadvantages of both. The closed primary is the least objectionable to party leaders and "bosses" because it is least menacing to the solidarity of party organization. The non-partisan primary would be most favorable to the influence of the rank and file of the parties, provided the ballot were "short" enough to enable them to dispense with the party label as a guide to intelligent voting. So long, however, as there are many comparatively unimportant, or at least inconspicuous, offices to be filled by popular election, especially in unwieldy or highly artificial election districts, the mere voter dares not dispense with the party label as a guide through the maze of meaningless names on the ballot. The reform of the process of nomination, like so many other reforms in the machinery of government, cannot be completed by itself alone.[1] It can be effectively accomplished only as a part of a general scheme of reform, which shall simplify the whole process of election. Such a general scheme of reform in its turn is dependent upon a radical reorganization of the whole structure of state government. a topic which is further discussed in the concluding chapter.

Other Proposed Primary Reforms.

Various methods have been employed in different states to diminish the evils of primary nominations by minorities of the parties. In some states it has been provided that no nomination shall be made by less than some specified portion of the party, such as 35 or 40 per cent, and that in case of a failure to nominate in the primary the nomination shall be made by a convention or party committee. In other states it has been provided that in case there is no nomination by a majority of the voters attending the primary, a second primary shall be held, at which the members of the party shall choose between the two leading candidates at the first. This system, which in effect is a non-partisan primary within a partisan primary, has been favored in several southern states where the Democratic nomination is equivalent to election, and where accordingly the regulation of the process of nomination is as important as the regulation of the whole electoral system in many states. A number of states have experimented with preferential voting by providing for the expression of first and

[1] See *post*, ch. viii.

second choice votes on one ballot at a single primary.[1] Thus, if no candidate is the first choice of a majority of the voters, their second choices may be ascertained without the trouble and expense of a second primary. Where the nomination is equivalent to election, this procedure is substantially the same as would be the abolition of the primary in many states, and the holding of a single non-partisan election at which the preference of a majority of the voters could be ascertained by means of a preferential ballot. Such a non-partisan electoral system, avoiding or at least diminishing the evils of plurality elections by means of the preferential ballot, would be less expensive to the state, less laborious to the voter, less exhausting to the candidate, and less demoralizing to the party, than any primary system requiring a second election to determine the will of the majority. Preferential voting is thus apparently sound in theory. Nevertheless, the experience of the states with the preferential primary ballot has not been altogether satisfactory. The fault lies chiefly with the voters themselves who, in many instances, simply do not take the trouble to register their second choices. In view of the long ballot used at so many primary elections, they are scarcely to be blamed for their neglect. But even with a short ballot, it is by no means certain that the system will work as intended. The fact that six states have tried preferential voting in their primaries and have given it up is significant.[2]

Further Reform of Party Organization.

The most serious objection to the direct primary, from the standpoint of the practical politician, is its tendency to disorganize the major parties. In order to secure a contested nomination a candidate must build up a more or less elaborate personal organization. Candidates for important nominations in extensive districts, such as a gubernatorial nomination in one of the larger states, must build up elaborate organizations, or

[1] Oklahoma (1925) is the most recent addition to the list. See Harry A. Barth, "Oklahoma Adopts Preferential Voting in the Primary," *National Municipal Review*, xiv, pp. 410-413 (1925). See also B. H. Williams, "Prevention of Minority Nominations for State Offices in the Direct Primary," *Annals*, cvi, pp. 111-115 (1923).

[2] Idaho, Indiana, North Dakota, Louisiana, Washington, and Wisconsin. See Williams, *op. cit.*, pp. 112-113. In this connection, the experience of Cleveland with the preferential or "Mary Ann" ballot is instructive. *American Political Science Review*, xvi, pp. 84-86 (1922).

must possess a well-organized following, if they are to have much chance of success. Once nominated, such a candidate is not unlikely to put more trust in his personal organization than in the official party organization. The latter may indeed have opposed his candidacy, unless he was originally the "organization" candidate. Thus, one consequence of the direct primary system is the creation of numerous personal campaign committees, which may conduct more or less independent campaigns, each on behalf of its own candidate, even after the primaries. The authority of the official party committees is thereby impaired and the solidarity of party organization undermined. Moreover, for reasons already pointed out, the nature of the primary campaign is such as to foment internal dissensions within a party to a greater extent than campaigns for nomination under the convention system, and to make the subsequent restoration of party harmony more difficult. Finally, as has also been previously stated, the direct election of the party committees in the primaries tends to decentralize the organization of the major parties. The effect of decentralization is to facilitate independent action by factions within a party, and thus to render even more difficult the maintenance of party unity by the state leaders or "bosses." In short, the direct primary system, at least in its present form, tends to break down the bipartisan system in state politics.[1] Whether the direct primary can be so reformed as to preserve the existing degree of popular control

[1] If the direct primary weakens the bipartisan system in one way by lessening the authority of the party leaders, it strengthens it in another because it discourages the formation of more than two parties. "Instead of forming an independent party to promote their special interests, the voters who care greatly about the men or measures that will serve their interests best, have the option of entering the primaries of a major party and bringing about, if possible, the nomination of their favorite leaders as the party candidates and the adoption of their favorite measures as the party policies. If unsuccessful in this, an active primary campaign may at least advertise their cause as well as any third party could do. Participation in the primaries of a major party offers the additional advantage that success in the primaries automatically brings to their side many who have been indifferent to their propaganda and not a few who have been opposed to it but are willing to abide by the decision of their party. Failure, on the other hand, to impose their opinions on a major party does not deprive the individual members of a special group of their freedom of choice at a general election. The members of the major parties consequently have two opportunities to influence the results of the electoral process, while those who adhere to a third party have but one." Holcombe, *The Political Parties of To-Day*, pp. 317-318.

over party nominations, whilst removing its tendency to disrupt the major party organizations, is therefore a question that must be considered before final judgment can be passed upon the primary system itself.

The disorganization of parties, which the direct primary in its present form seems calculated to produce, may be somewhat relieved by either of two reforms. The first is the appointment of party committeemen after the primaries by the successful candidates for nomination; the second, the designation of candidates for nomination by party committeemen before the primaries, subject to responsibility for their designations at the primaries. The former course might seem the more consistent with the theory of direct nominations, but that solution of the problem is rendered difficult by the fact that in each district there are ordinarily so many candidates on the ballot that it would be impracticable for them all to join in the appointment of committeemen, and unfair to leave such appointments to any one of them. The other solution implies the legal recognition of a duty on the part of the regular committees to make official "slates" for the guidance of the voters at the primaries and to retire from office at once in case their "slates" are repudiated. This was substantially the plan advocated by Charles E. Hughes when governor of New York in 1910, a plan which was based upon the principle that harmony must exist between candidates and committeemen.[1] There is no assurance that such harmony will exist where both are chosen independently at the primaries, the committeemen generally two years in advance of the candidates. If it be thought unwise to secure harmony by authorizing committeemen to designate "slates" under suitable restrictions, then some procedure should be devised by which candidates may designate committeemen. Such procedure could be devised more easily, if the number of offices filled by election were not so great. The necessity of improving the forms of party organization, if the system of direct nominations is to be made more satisfactory, constitutes one of the strong arguments in favor of the electoral reform known as the short ballot.

In general, the development of the direct primary has been

[1] For a more recent elaboration of Mr. Hughes' views, see his article entitled, "The Fate of the Direct Primary," *National Municipal Review*, x, pp. 23-31 (1921).

in the direction of the second of the above reforms. This is especially evident in the rise of pre-primary conventions.[1] Such conventions and party gatherings have often functioned as informal and extra-legal bodies and, in a few instances, they have been given a definite legal status in the scheme of nominations. Thus, in South Dakota, the law provides for county and state proposal conventions whose composition, procedure, and duties are carefully regulated by statute. One of the functions of these party conventions is to select a list of candidates for submission to the voters at the party primary. One additional list may likewise be submitted by the dissatisfied minority members of the convention. From these two lists together with any other nominations which may have been made by the usual petition method, the party voters at the primary select the nominees of their party.[2] Thus the law attempts to impose a certain measure of official responsibility upon the party organization without at the same time discouraging the more independent members of the party from entering the primary as candidates for the party nomination.

Future of Bipartisan System.

None of the plans for party reorganization hitherto tried has operated in a satisfactory manner,[3] and the problem of the proper relation between candidates and permanent officers cannot yet be regarded as solved. Apparently popular control of the nominating process cannot be secured except by some means no less menacing to the solidarity of the major party organizations than the existing direct primary. At all events the tendency of recent legislation with reference to nominations seems to be in the direction of a further weakening of the major party organizations. Neither the growing dislike of the closed primary nor the growing dislike of minority nominations augurs well for the maintenance of the bipartisan system in its traditional form and vigor. The direct primary in its present form seems unlikely to give permanent satisfaction, and yet no plans of further reform

[1] Schuyler C. Wallace, "Pre-Primary Conventions," *Annals*, cvi, pp. 97-104 (1923).

[2] For a good discussion of the South Dakota law, see C. A. Berdahl, "The Operation of the Richards Primary," *Annals*, cvi, pp. 158-171.

[3] See for descriptions of novel plans of party organization adopted in Colorado and South Dakota, *The American Year Book* for 1912, pp. 60-61.

are in sight except such as threaten even more seriously the solidarity of the major parties. In short, the judgment to be pronounced upon the direct primary system itself seems finally to depend upon the judgment to be pronounced upon the bipartisan system in state politics. If the bipartisan system be on the whole a necessary and proper instrument for rendering more effective popular control over governmental agencies, as its advocates contend, then further changes in the direct primary should be made with a view primarily to the strengthening of the major party organizations. Such changes would necessarily be in the direction of a restoration of power to the conventions. This view has prevailed in New York and Idaho, where the power to nominate candidates for offices filled by election in the state at large has been restored to the state convention. But if the bipartisan system be on the whole an impediment to an effective popular control of governmental agencies, then the primary should be further developed along the lines of least resistance, or supplanted by some system of proportional representation which would make public regulation of the process of nomination less important. This is what is proposed in the most noteworthy of recent plans of state constitutional reform.[1] Whether the bipartisan system should be further fortified, or further undermined, is a question that cannot be answered without further consideration of its effects upon the legislative, executive, and judicial branches of state government.

[1] See *post.*, ch. xvi.

CHAPTER VIII

THE ELECTORAL PROCESS

The first step in the conduct of elections is the preparation of the ballot. Prior to the introduction of the Australian or official ballot, the ballot was theoretically prepared by each voter for himself. Actually it was in most cases prepared for the voter by his local party managers. There was ordinarily a separate form of ballot, therefore, for each local electoral district and for each political party. The ballots were generally distributed at the polls by party officials, and were publicly dropped into the ballot boxes by the voters. Such a system was ruinous to the independence of the voters and the honesty of elections. The independent voter was first put to the inconvenience of preparing his own ballot. He was then compelled to disclose his independence to an unsympathetic world. Intimidation by the exercise of economic or social pressure was thus made easy. Bribery was also made easy, for the party worker could always know whether or not a purchased vote was actually delivered.

THE ELECTORAL MACHINERY

The Official Ballot.

The introduction of the official ballot brought about an enormous improvement in the conduct of elections. As originally employed in Australia, the official ballot contained the printed names, with addresses but without party designations, of all avowed candidates for the office to be filled at the election, together with a blank space in which the voter might write in any other name for which he might wish to vote. These ballots were prepared and distributed by public officials and marked by the voters in secret. The Australian ballot was introduced in Great Britain in 1872, and thus brought to the favorable attention of Americans. Beginning in 1888, it was rapidly introduced in the United States, and now exists in some form in forty-seven states.[1] In all these states, however, the official ballot has lost its original Australian simplicity. The practice of holding a multitude of elections simultaneously and of nominating party tickets of candidates for all elective offices makes the American ballot much longer than the Australian or English. It becomes a "blanket" ballot. Nevertheless, here as abroad, the independent voter has been protected by its introduction. Intimidation and bribery have been made more difficult. The temptation to the corrupt use of money has been diminished. A heavy item in the cost of running for office has been eliminated. Probably no reform in electoral technique has worked a greater improvement in the conduct of elections than the official ballot.

The extent of the improvement, however, has depended upon the form of the official ballot. The first form is the office-column or office-block ballot. Originally introduced in 1888 in Massachusetts, this type contains the names of all the candidates for each office separately, arranged generally in alphabetic order. The groups of candidates for the several offices are arranged according to the supposed importance of the offices. For the convenience of the voters in identifying the candidates of their choice, the name of each candidate is followed by the name of the party by which the candidate was nominated. In order to vote such a ballot, it is necessary for the voter to place a cross-mark in the square opposite the name of each candidate for whom he wishes his ballot to be counted. Thus, the use of the office-column ballot involves the making of a separate mark for each office for which the voter has a choice among the candidates. Since it will take an equal length of time to vote a "straight" ticket, that is, for all the candidates of any one party, and a "split" ticket, that is, for candidates of different parties for different offices, a party watcher at the polls cannot ascertain by the length of time the voter is occupied in marking his ballot whether he is "regular" or votes independently. The office-column ballot, therefore, is the form most favorable to the independence of the voter and the honesty of elections. Moreover, such a ballot cannot be voted at all by an illiterate voter without the aid of some mechanical device prepared in advance which will enable him to locate the names of the candidates for whom he

[1] E. C. Evans, *History of the Australian Ballot System in the United States* (Chicago, 1917).

wishes to vote by their position upon the printed ballot. In practice, therefore, the introduction of the office-column ballot is almost equivalent in itself to the establishment of a literacy test for the suffrage.

The second form of the official ballot is the party-column ballot which differs from the office-column type in two important respects. In the first place, the names of the candidates are arranged on the ballot according to the parties by which they are nominated instead of according to the offices for which they are nominated. The candidates of each party appear in a vertical column, and the several party columns usually are arranged in the order of party importance, measured by the party vote at the last preceding election. Secondly, at the head of each column, usually just above the name of the party, appears a square or circle, surmounted by a party emblem. In order to vote a "straight" ticket by means of such a ballot it is necessary merely to place a single mark in the party square or circle at the head of the party column. The illiterate voter is enabled to place his mark properly by the presence of the emblem, an eagle, or a rooster, or a star, or a fountain, or a flaming torch, as the case may be, which he readily learns to recognize. To vote a "split" ticket it is generally necessary to mark a cross opposite the name of each candidate for whom the voter wishes his ballot to be counted, even if all but one are members of the same party. Where the ballot contains the names of candidates for a large number of offices, for example, thirty-four in Chicago, Illinois, in 1924 (not counting twenty-nine presidential electors), it takes much more time and effort to vote independently than to vote a regular party ticket. This tends to discourage independent voting, and also to disclose to party watchers the identity of the independent voters. Moreover, it is ordinarily impossible for the illiterate voter to vote anything but a straight ticket. The party-column form of ballot is obviously more desirable from the standpoint of the party politician, and probably for that reason was more widely adopted than the original Massachusetts form.[1] Whether it is also more desirable from

[1] At present, the party-column ballot exists in half of the states but, in eleven of these, the party emblem is not used. The office-column ballot is found in ten states. The remaining states have various intermediate types. For example, the office-column ballot is sometimes modified by the addition of party squares or circles, as in Pennsylvania, and the party-column ballot by the elimination of the same, as in Georgia.

the standpoint of the public, however, depends upon other considerations.

Office-Column *v.* Party-Column Ballot.

The original advocates of ballot-reform in the United States [1] preferred the office-column form of the ballot. This preference was based partly on the ground that the office-column ballot more closely resembled the Australian model, but mainly on the ground that its use would make it as easy to vote a "split" as a "straight" ticket, and would thereby tend to encourage independent voting.[2] This argument assumed that the habit of party regularity ought not to be artificially stimulated. There was some foundation for such an assumption. One of the most gifted critics of American politics, writing at the time of the introduction of the Australian ballot, observed with reference to the two major parties: "Neither party has, as a party, . . . any clean-cut principles, any distinctive tenets. Both have traditions. Both claim to have tendencies. Both have certainly war cries, organizations, interests, enlisted in their support. But those interests are in the main the interests of getting or keeping the patronage of the government. Tenets or policies, points of political doctrine and points of political practice, have all but vanished. They have not been thrown away, but have been stripped away by time and the progress of events, fulfilling some policies, blotting out others. All has been lost, except office or the hope of it." [3] If it were true that the major parties are so unprincipled as this, the case against anything tending to stimulate the habit of party regularity would seem to be well founded. Bryce's pessimistic view, however, sounds strangely similar to that penned by De Tocqueville, a half-century earlier, and already quoted in these pages.[4] Yet history, as Bryce himself knew, had shown the inaccuracy of De Tocqueville's analysis of the party system, for Bryce admits that the parties at least had traditions. While De Tocqueville was in the act of writing, the Jacksonian Democracy was engaged in ham-

[1] See J. H. Wigmore, *The Australian Ballot.*

[2] For a discussion of ticket-splitting and other forms of irregular voting, see A. C. Millspaugh, "Irregular Voting in the United States," *Political Science Quarterly*, xxxiii, pp. 230-254 (1918).

[3] James Bryce, *The American Commonwealth*, pt. iii, The Party System, ch. 54, The Parties of To-day.

[4] See *ante*, ch. iv.

mering out a distinctive policy which served it well for a generation: a strict construction of the constitution, a tariff for revenue only, internal improvements at state, not at federal, expense, an independent treasury and a severance of relations between the government and the banks, and no interference by Congress with the domestic institutions of the states. So likewise, while Bryce was penning his strictures of the American party system, the campaign of 1888 was taking shape. This was to end in the effective control by the Republicans of all branches of the federal government for the first time in half a generation, and in the enactment of a series of measures reflecting the distinctive tenets of the dominant party. But it is easier for the critic to recognize established traditions—for unless they were generally recognized they would not be traditions—than to discern those that are in the process of making. Mariners on the high seas cannot discern whether the tide is rising or falling, yet it continually rises and falls. When the facts of party history are placed in their proper perspective, the case against the habit of party regularity does not seem so clear, at least so far as candidates for federal office are concerned. The vindication of national party organizations against the charge of lack of principle, however, does not of itself vindicate the use of national party designations by candidates for state and local office.

The arguments in favor of the party-column ballot, nevertheless, are not without some weight. In the first place, under existing conditions the great majority of the voters ordinarily prefer to vote a "straight" rather than a "split" ticket. This preference is clearly indicated by the election returns of the states which possess the office-column ballot. Now the form of ballot which is most convenient for the great majority of the voters is the one which ought to be used, other things being equal. Secondly, under existing conditions the great majority of the voters need some assistance in the task of voting. This need is recognized even by the advocates of the office-column ballot, for that form, like the party-column form, is arranged to show the party affiliation of each candidate whose name is printed on the ballot. Both forms of ballot, therefore, tend to stimulate the habit of party regularity, though doubtless the party-column form does so to a greater degree. Under existing conditions it is necessary to affix a party label to each candidate, for without the label the voter would often be at a loss how to mark his ballot. At every general election there are so many obscure candidates for so many inconspicuous offices that few voters can form a personal opinion with respect to the qualifications of all of them.[1] Now if the form of the ballot is to correspond to the needs of the existing electoral system and to the facts of human nature, the voter must be enabled to make his ballot count in the main as a vote of confidence in some political party, which selects his candidates for him, rather than in the particular candidates themselves. These for the most part he would try in vain to select for himself, if he were left wholly to his own knowledge for a guide. But if the voter is really in most instances indicating his choice between parties rather than between candidates, why compel him to go through the motions of marking a cross against the name of a candidate for each office, when one mark might serve equally well? If other things were equal, particularly if the time required to vote a "straight" and "split" ticket were the same, the case in favor of the party-column form of ballot would be strong.

The Need for Further Ballot Reform.

The chief criticism of the form of the official ballot applies to both the prevailing forms alike. It is that the state, which compels the voter to rely so largely on the party label as a guide through the intricacies of the ballot, does so little to guarantee

[1] The Chicago, Illinois, ballot, already referred to, contains the names of the candidates of nine different parties for the following offices (exclusive of the twenty-nine presidential electors to be chosen): United States senator, two representatives in Congress from the state at large, one representative in Congress from the district, governor, lieutenant-governor, secretary of state, auditor of public accounts, state treasurer, attorney-general, three trustees of the University of Illinois, one state senator, three representatives in the state house of representatives, one judge of the circuit court of the county, two judges of the superior court of the county, state's attorney, member of county board of review, two members of the county board of assessors, county recorder of deeds, clerk of circuit court, clerk of superior court, coroner, county surveyor, three trustees for the sanitary district of Chicago, clerk of the municipal court, bailiff of the municipal court. Fortunately, not all the parties made nominations for all the offices, but enough nominations were made to bring the total number of names (exclusive of the candidates for presidential elector) to 132. Without the guidance of the party label, it is safe to assert that few voters would have been able to indicate their choice for every office on that ballot, and that many voters would have been practically disfranchised with respect to most of the thirty-four elections for which, in addition to the presidential election, that ballot was made to serve.

the integrity of the label. At most the primary and ballot laws of the several states ensure nothing more than that the label is borne by candidates whose nomination is "regular" in form. Concerning the substance of their creed and the purposes of their candidacy the official party label signifies little or nothing, except in the case of presidential electors. Congressmen may be nominated in districts where the majority of the party is out of sympathy with the policies professed by a majority of the delegates in the national convention. Under most primary and ballot laws they are nevertheless as much entitled to the party label as the candidate for president himself. Likewise in the case of candidates for state office the legal right to the party label may indicate little or nothing with respect to the principles and purposes of the candidate. Federal and state governments alike operate directly upon the people, through their own agents, and the principles to which a party professes allegiance in the nation at large need have no connection with those which it undertakes to advance in a particular state.

In most states which have established the direct primary, special efforts have been made to provide for the formulation of the party issues in such a way as to reflect the wishes of a majority of the party. The state platforms are usually adopted by conventions or party councils in which the candidates for office who have been successful at the primaries are expected to wield the chief influence. But platforms as a rule actually reflect the principles and purposes appropriate to candidates for political offices; that is, offices through which policies are to be executed with respect to which the voters may be expected to have opinions of their own.[1] Many of the offices for which partisan candidates are nominated do not fall within this category.[2] A

[1] See Ralph S. Boots, "Party Platforms in State Politics," *Annals*, cvi, pp. 72-82 (1923); and Burton Y. Berry, "The Influence of Political Platforms on Legislation in Indiana, 1901-1921," *American Political Science Review*, xvii, pp. 51-69 (1923).

[2] For example, of the thirty-four offices, exclusive of presidential electors, which the voters of Chicago were required to fill or help fill by election in 1924, the following were hardly suitable for administration upon either national or state party lines: secretary of state, auditor of public accounts, state treasurer, trustees of the University of Illinois, judge of the circuit court, judges of the superior court, state's attorney, member of the county board of review, members of county board of assessors, recorder of deeds, clerk of circuit court, clerk of superior court, trustees of the sanitary district of Chicago, coroner, county surveyor, clerk of municipal court, bailiff of municipal court.

state convention or council, meeting to draft a platform for a state campaign, ordinarily reflects the principles and purposes of the successful candidate for the party nomination for governor. That these principles and purposes are not always the same as those of the most conspicuous party candidate, the candidate for president, is revealed by the fact that a state occasionally chooses presidential electors of one party and at the same time a governor of another party. In states with the party-column ballot, such as New Hampshire, Ohio, and Indiana, this has not happened so frequently as in states with the office-column, such as Massachusetts, Minnesota, and Oregon, but it has happened often enough to indicate that the same party label may mean different things as applied to candidates for different offices on the same ballot. It may also mean nothing at all, except that a nomination is "regular" in form. The meaninglessness of the national party label in state and local politics is most conspicuously revealed in the cases, not infrequent, of candidates who secure in the "regular" manner the nominations of both major parties (and sometimes of minor parties as well) for the same office.

The use of the party label on the official ballot may be indispensable when thirty-four offices are to be filled by the voters at one operation, but under existing conditions it is nevertheless objectionable. Either the number of offices to be filled by election at any one time should be so reduced that the voters can manage the operation without the use of a label, or the state should supplement the label with such other information concerning the candidates for election as will enable the voters to know in each case what stands behind the label. In other words, it is not the form of the ballot, but the system of filling so many and so diverse offices at the same time without proper provision for informing the voters concerning the character and purposes of the several candidates, thereby making the habit of party regularity indispensable, that is fundamentally at fault. The full advantages of the official ballot will not be realized until either party designations can be abolished without confusion to the voter, or the state can undertake to furnish the voter not only with the party designation of each candidate, but also with a separate statement of the principles and purposes professed by each.[1] In other words, the further improvement of the form of the ballot involves either the further reform of the general structure of state government or a radical change in the methods of conducting political campaigns.

The Actual Conduct of Elections.

The further steps in the conduct of elections are the casting and counting of the ballots,[2] and the canvass and declaration of the returns. Originally these duties were placed upon the regular local and state officials, and seem to have been performed in a fairly satisfactory manner. With the growth of party spirit, however, the original system became less satisfactory. Local officials were not unlikely to belong to one party. Under such circumstances, even if honest men, they were subject to the temptation to favor the candidates of their own party in the decision of questions involving the exercise of administrative discretion, such as the right of a challenged voter to cast his ballot, or the validity of a ballot prepared or marked in an irregular manner. Prior to the registration of voters and the adoption of the official ballot, the purity of elections depended in no small part on the exercise of a wise discretion by the officials charged with the conduct of elections, and the records are filled with contested election cases in which party spirit clearly got the better of discretion. If the local officials were not honest, particularly if they were supported by a majority or a well-organized minority of the local electorate, there was almost no limit to their power to prevent a free ballot, a fair count, and a full return. Thus the notorious Boss Tweed of New York City is reported to have said: "I don't care who does the voting, so long as I do the counting."

The conduct of elections has been improved by the application of two principles: publicity, and bipartisanship. First, all political parties, in some cases, all candidates, are now generally authorized to be represented at the polls by watchers. The watchers are entitled to see everything that is done by the election officials, both at the casting and at the counting of the

[1] In Oregon, North Dakota, and Florida, official publicity pamphlets for candidates are prepared and mailed to the registered voters prior to the election. P. O. Ray, *An Introduction to Political Parties and Practical Politics* (3rd ed., New York, 1924), pp. 197-199.

[2] Voting-machines are now used in a number of states but with varying degrees of success. See Ray, *op. cit.*, pp. 275-278, and T. David Zukerman, "The Case for Mechanical Balloting," *National Municipal Review*, xiv, pp. 226-233 (1925).

ballots. The canvassing of the returns from the several election districts and the declaration of the results is also generally done by the officials charged with those duties in the presence of watchers or of the public at large. Provision is generally made for the public inspection of ballot boxes at the opening of the polls, for the security of the ballots before and after the count, and for an official recount at the request of any candidate. If the count is correctly and publicly made, there is little opportunity for further error in the canvass of the returns and declaration of the results. Secondly, instead of leaving the conduct of elections to the regular local officials, special election officials are now commonly provided in such a manner that each of the two major parties will be equally represented. The appointments of election officials, though generally made by the regular local officials, are made from the party lists, not infrequently from nominations by the local party committees. Election judges and clerks act in pairs, one of each pair belonging to each of the major parties. Thus the two parties are enabled to check and balance one another in the conduct of elections. So far as the interests of the public coincide with the interests of one or the other of the major party organizations, the system works well.

The system of bipartisan control breaks down at the point where the interests of the major party organizations cease to coincide with those of the public. So far as the public is interested in minor parties, the system is defective, though not seriously so in cases where the minor parties can afford to maintain their legal quota of watchers. The system is more seriously defective with respect to the purity of elections at which measures, not men, are at stake, especially in cases where both major parties are interested in the adoption or defeat of the same measures. Most states make no provision for watchers in behalf of measures which may be submitted to the electorate, and where provision is made it is not always easy to take advantage of it. In such cases the party machines may conspire to falsify the counting or return of the ballots without much risk of detection, or at least of conviction for any crime. This was done, for example, in Michigan in 1912, in the case of the woman suffrage amendment, in certain election districts, notably in Detroit. Likewise when the interests of the two machines are identical with respect to candidates for election, the possibility of collusion and fraud is never absent under the bipartisan system of control. In the main, however, elections are now honestly conducted, or may be honestly conducted, if the public will take the trouble to enforce their rights under the laws, especially their right to know who is registered and how the votes are cast and counted. If the public, however, leave the protection of their interests to the major party organizations, they cannot expect their interests to be better protected than the interests of the major parties themselves. In short, the principal imperfections in the election machinery to-day are the consequences of the imperfection of the bipartisan political system. In general, the conduct of elections is now much more honest than fifty or even twenty-five years ago. Serious faults in the contemporary electoral process are more manifest in connection with the registration of the voters and the conduct of campaigns than in the conduct of the elections themselves.

Registration.

All states provide, either in the constitution or by statute, that a list of qualified voters be prepared to serve as the evidence of the voters' right to vote when they appear at the polls on election day. There are two principal methods of preparing the list of qualified voters. Under the older method, which still obtains in a few states, the list of qualified voters is prepared by the selectmen, as in Vermont, or by the poll-tax collectors, as in Arkansas, or by some similar body of local officers. The newer method, first introduced in New York and California in 1866, and adopted during the last thirty years in more than forty of the states, is the method of personal registration. The prospective voter is required to visit the registrars of voters in person, and establish his right to vote by producing satisfactory evidence of his possession of the legal requirements. In a few states and in most large cities personal registration is required of all voters at regular intervals, generally every year or every other year, but in most states it is sufficient that the voter establish his right once in person, either on coming of age or on acquiring a new legal residence. Thereafter his name will remain upon the list until death, or removal from the district, or disqualification for crime or other valid reason. At the time of registration various items of information about the voter, designed to establish his identity in case of challenge at the polls, are recorded. This information always includes the ordinary facts of name and residence, and in some cases, particularly in large cities where voters are often unknown to their own neighbors, much more than that. Thus in New York the registry of voters shows the following information: full name and place of residence; age; length of residence in state, county, and election district; country of birth, and date of naturalization, if naturalized, and designation of court issuing the certificate of naturalization; location of last preceding voting-residence; date when registered; occupation; location of employment; and signature of each voter. If the voter is unable to write, the signature is omitted and a record made of his answers to a series of questions of a personal nature. In some states a description of the voter's personal appearance is required, the object being to prevent impersonation of a registered voter by one not entitled to vote. In the states where personal registration is required at periodic intervals, the voter is often put to considerable trouble in order to keep his name upon the registry and the requirement is in substance an addition to the regular qualifications for the exercise of the suffrage, having the effect of disfranchising shiftless or indifferent voters.[1]

The proof of a registration law is in the enforcement. In 1913 a registration law was adopted for the first time in Indiana, one of the last states to provide for the registration of voters, and one of the states in which corrupt practices at elections, particularly bribery, personation, and repeating, had long been more notorious than in most states. This law was in effect during the electoral campaign of 1914. In 1915 the mayor of Terre Haute and 115 other local politicians were indicted and tried for corruption at the preceding election. Of the accused,

[1] A number of American cities, such as Boston, Omaha, Madison, Minneapolis, St. Paul, and Duluth, are experimenting with an improved type of permanent registration. The advantages claimed for such permanent registration are that it lessens the time and trouble required for the voting process, it reduces the number of errors in the lists of registered voters, it costs less, and, finally, is not more open to fraud than the prevailing systems of personal, periodic registration. See F. L. Olson, "Permanent Registration Successful in Minneapolis," *National Municipal Review*, xiii, pp. 488-492 (1924). For a criticism of permanent registration, see Frank H. Riter, "Permanent Registration for Elections Unsuitable for Large Cities," *National Municipal Review*, xiv, pp. 532-535 (1925).

89 confessed and the others were convicted. The evidence in the case indicated that the registration law had been made a farce. One witness testified to the frequent registration of non-residents and of dead men, and in one case even of a pet dog. On election day these fraudulent registrations were voted on by hired repeaters and thugs. One witness, who was under twenty-one years of age, testified that he voted fourteen times; another, twenty-two times. A saloon-keeper testified that the mayor demanded that almost double the number of legal voters be registered in one precinct, and that on election day the mayor threatened to put him out of business unless he got out the full registered vote. A watcher testified that in one precinct where eighteen colored voters resided she saw between three and four hundred colored men vote. This is one of the most extreme cases of corruption on record in American politics, and it happened in a city where there was a modern registration law. However, the guilty were punished. In general, it seems probable that false registration, personation, and repeating can be prevented, or at least reduced to comparatively small proportions, under a proper registration law, supported by local public opinion. When elections are held on the day of registration, however, as is done in some states in the case of measures submitted to the people, opportunity for fraudulent voting is afforded by the fact that there is no time to examine the voting lists before the votes are cast, and hence no time to challenge the "floaters."

In most states the self-interest of the party organizations is the principal guarantee of the integrity of the process of registration. Registration officers are chosen equally from the two major parties. Appointment is a common mode of rewarding petty party workers. In New Jersey, by the registration law of 1911, an attempt was made to improve the process of registration by improving the character of the registration officials. The law provided that the party committees or any group of citizens might nominate candidates for appointment as registration officers to the civil service commission. The commission then examined the candidates both with respect to their ability to perform the simple clerical duties of the office and with respect to their general record and moral character. From the list of those who were declared to be qualified, the actual officials were selected by lot. However, these provisions of the act of

1911 were repealed in 1920. In general, whether any such abandonment of the principle of bipartisanship in the appointment of registration officials will improve the administration of registration laws would depend probably upon the ability and character of the civil service commission itself. If the civil service commission were influenced by partisanship, the system might be more partisan than the ordinary bipartisan system. But if the civil service commission maintained its independence of partisanship, the system should afford protection against those abuses to which any bipartisan system is necessarily exposed.

THE ELECTORAL CAMPAIGN

There are four principal methods of reaching the voters. The first and most direct is by personal canvassing. The candidates or their representatives interview the voters, so far as possible, and solicit their support. This may be done by calling on the voters at their residences or by buttonholing them in public places. In rural districts enterprising candidates, especially candidates for local offices, frequent the post offices around mail time, and at other times cover the countryside as best they can. In recent years, automobiles and good roads have tended to increase the radius of rural canvassing. In the cities canvassing has to be done more largely at night. In former times, the saloon was the principal scene of political activity. In 1884, of 1002 primary meetings and local district conventions held in New York City prior to the presidential election, 633 were held in saloons, and 86 next door to saloons.[1] No method of political campaigning is so effective as personal canvassing. No method makes such great demands upon the resources of the candidate. Except in the smallest districts, personal canvassing is impracticable without the expenditure of large sums of money or the support of an established political organization. In the former case the candidate can build an organization of his own. In the latter, unless he is a candidate for an important and conspicuous office, he becomes a mere cog in the machine.

The second method of reaching the voters, and the only other method of reaching them individually, is by mail or by the dis-

[1] See W. M. Ivins, *Machine Politics and Money in Elections in New York City*, p. 21.

tribution of hand-bills from house to house. To reach the individual voter by mail involves the expenditure of from two to ten cents each, according as the candidate sends merely a postal card or a more or less elaborate personal letter. In a gubernatorial campaign in New York State such a method would involve the expenditure of from $80,000 to $400,000 for a single communication. The distribution of hand-bills would be no less expensive, but might be more satisfactory to the candidate, since the payment of the distributors might secure their votes as well as their services. The distribution of literature is much less effective than personal canvassing, partly because it is difficult to adapt the literature to the temperament and circumstances of the individual voter, and partly because it is by no means certain that the voter will read the literature after it is delivered to him.

The other principal methods of reaching the minds of the voters aim to reach them *en masse.* One method of reaching the voters *en masse* is by public meetings. This method involves the hiring of halls, and usually also some expense for speakers, music, and advertising. Meetings in halls are commonly attended only by partisans of the candidates in whose interest the meetings are arranged. They are probably of little value for the purpose of winning over doubtful voters or opponents. Such meetings are useful chiefly for the purpose of arousing the enthusiasm of the faithful, and inciting them to greater activity in the campaign. Street meetings and meetings at factory gates during the noon hour are more valuable for the purpose of reaching indifferent and doubtful voters in the cities and industrial districts, and in the rural districts addresses at grange meetings and the agricultural fairs serve the same purpose. The broadcasting of political speeches by radio was first used in the presidential campaign of 1924 and there is every reason to believe that radio broadcasting will be even more widely employed in future campaigns. Another method of reaching the voters *en masse* is by advertising, in the newspaper, on the "movie" screen, and on the ubiquitous billboard, to say nothing of the political possibilities of aeroplane "sky-writing" or "smoke-writing" as now practiced by the manufacturers of certain well-known cigarettes. In so far as such publicity may be secured without cost, as by letters and statements to the press, interviews with reporters, and editorial support, it is the cheapest and easiest method of campaigning. It cannot be so effective as personal canvassing, and need not be relied upon by candidates in small districts or with well-organized support. But in larger districts all candidates for nomination at the primaries, unless on an organization slate, and independent candidates for election are mainly dependent upon such publicity, unless they are supplied with adequate campaign funds. In short, under modern electoral conditions, the support of an elaborate party organization or the command of extensive funds is indispensable for any effective campaign for public office, except in the case of purely local offices. If the candidate is supported by an organization, then the burden of raising the funds may be shifted from the shoulders of the candidate to those of the organization, but in any case the funds must be raised.

Corrupt Practices.

These various methods of campaigning are all subject to abuse, though in different degrees. The method of personal canvassing is most subject to abuse, because it is most secret and direct. Bribery, intimidation, and the exercise of undue influence generally, whether by the use of money, by promises of employment or appointment to office, by threats of dismissal, or otherwise, may be safely accomplished only through direct and secret contract with the voter. The employment of canvassers and handbill distributors is also subject to grave abuse, since such employment can be made the pretext for payments to men whose chief service to the candidate may be the casting of their votes for him. Where the intent of the candidate in employing such workers is primarily to secure their votes rather than their services, the payment partakes more of the nature of a bribe than of a wage. Treating likewise may easily become a means of undue influence and corruption. The methods of reaching the voters *en masse* may also be used corruptly. Halls may be hired for meetings with the intent of influencing the proprietors as well as the general public. Newspapers may be bought; though, if the ownership is not concealed, such a use of money cannot ordinarily be regarded as improper.[1] A graver evil is the secret

[1] But cf. Graham Wallas, *Human Nature in Politics*, p. 97, for a discussion of circumstances when such purchase might be regarded as improper.

purchase of newspaper space and editorial support. But the most serious forms of corruption when the voters are dealt with *en masse* are more subtle:—promises of future benefits, to be conferred by legislation or otherwise, which those who make the promises have no intention or no reasonable hope of fulfilling; appeals to religious, racial, and social prejudices and passions; unmerited personal abuse of opponents, misrepresentation, slander, and libel.

It is not money alone that is the source of all evil in electoral campaigns. Intimidation, undue influence, unworthy and insincere arguments, slander, and libel are evils with which the corrupt use of money has nothing to do. Some of these evils, such as slander and libel, may be directly attacked by appropriate legislation. Unfortunately such legislation is difficult to enforce. In general a strong and healthy public opinion must be the main protection of candidates against such intangible abuses as the publication of unworthy and insincere arguments, the private circulation of false and malicious gossip, and the exercise of any undue influence otherwise than by the use of money. It is only because the body of voters is in the long run a good judge of the character of men that the representative system can be made to work at all well. The use of public patronage for corrupt purposes is a more tangible evil. This, however, can be dealt with more effectively by indirect means than by direct prohibition. The introduction of the "merit" system in place of the "spoils" system will be more fully discussed in connection with the consideration of the administrative systems of the states. When all is said, it remains true that the misuse of money in electoral campaigns is the chief tangible source of evil. The prevention of corrupt practices is correctly associated in the public mind with the regulation of the expenditure of money.

The Prevention of Corruption.

American legislation designed to prevent corrupt practices during electoral campaigns, like American legislation designed to improve the conduct of elections, was inspired by the example of England. Like the British ballot act of 1872, the British corrupt and illegal practices act of 1883, together with its subsequent amendments, set up a standard which Americans were not slow to appreciate.[1]

The English law is founded upon the distinction between acts which are declared to be corrupt and those which are merely illegal. Corrupt acts include bribery, treating, undue influence, personation, and failure to make the required returns of campaign expenditures. Illegal acts include the payment of money by or on behalf of a candidate for the conveyance of voters to the polls, for the use of property for the posting of bills, for the use of election committee rooms in excess of the authorized number in the district, for music, torches, flags, banners, cockades, ribbons, etc., and for the use of any premises where liquor is sold as a committee room, and the payment of money for any purpose in excess of the maximum amount permitted by law. The acts declared to be corrupt are carefully defined. Illegal acts are for the most part acts which may easily be made the pretext for corruption, although not in themselves corrupt. In order further to guard against corruption, the law defines the objects for which expenditures may lawfully be made. Thus the candidate may employ one election agent, one deputy in each election district, one polling agent at each polling place, and a limited number of clerks and messengers, depending upon the character of the district and the number of voters. No paid employee is permitted to vote. No money may be expended except for the following purposes: (1) the payment of the personal expenses of the candidates; (2) advertising, printing, and distributing addresses, circulars, and notices; (3) stationery, messengers, postage,[2] and telegrams, including telephone; (4) public meetings; (5) expense of maintaining headquarters. Finally, the maximum of legal expenditure is limited, exclusive of a schedule of personal expenses and fees allowed the candidate, to 14 cents per registered voter if a county constituency, and to 10 cents per registered voter if a borough constituency.

The law fixes the responsibility for the use of money during the campaign upon a person known as the election agent. Each candidate is required to designate an election agent at the be-

[1] The act of 1883 applies only to parliamentary elections. Separate but similar legislation was enacted for local elections.

[2] However, each candidate is allowed a limited franking privilege for the purpose of sending a statement of his platform and claims to his constituents.

ginning of the campaign and to make all expenditures, except those classed as personal, through his agent. The candidate may act as his own agent, but ordinarily he employs a professional campaign manager. Within five weeks after the election, the agent must file a return with the local election officials showing: (1) all payments made through his agency on account of the candidate; (2) all personal expenses of the candidate; (3) all disputed claims, so far as known; (4) all unpaid claims; (5) a complete statement of all receipts, whether from the candidate or from any other person. In case of contributions from any other than the candidate, the name of each contributor and the amount of the contribution must be separately shown. Both agent and candidate must also severally declare under oath that they will not pay nor promise anything further on account of the election than shown in the return. The return must include vouchers for all payments in excess of ten dollars, and all bills are presumed to have been paid within four weeks after the election. Summaries of these returns for all the candidates are published by the election officials at the expense of the candidates in at least two papers of general circulation in the district, with an indication of the place where the original returns may be inspected by the public.

The penalties for violation of the law are extremely severe. Any person guilty of a corrupt practice is liable to a heavy fine and disfranchisement. Any candidate guilty of committing a corrupt practice is punished by disqualification forever for membership in Parliament from the district. If a corrupt practice has been committed by his agent without his knowledge or consent he is disqualified for seven years. Any candidate, guilty directly or through his agent of an illegal practice, is punished by disqualification for the life of the ensuing Parliament. Charges of corruption or illegality may be preferred by any voter, but must be prosecuted at the instance of the attorney-general. The trial takes place before a special court of two judges, and the proceedings are thoroughly non-partisan. The act has wrought a revolution in the character of electoral campaigns in Great Britain. Prior to its passage, British elections were notorious for their venality. Money was used lavishly, corruption was brazen. In some districts it is said that the greater part of the voters were under pay by one or both of the candidates. Since then, money has been much less lavishly used. Corruption by candidates or their agents has been reduced to trivial proportions. In the words of one of the closest observers of British politics: "The old electoral abuses have been very much reduced. . . . Bribery in England is disappearing. In by far the greatest number of constituencies it does not exist, and the elections are on the whole pure." [1] The system is doubtless not without its defects. For instance, it does not regulate the use of money independently by private persons or associations, such as tariff reform leagues or brewers' associations. This defect grows more serious as the political activity of such associations increases. But the system has greatly checked the particular evils at which it was aimed, and has clearly demonstrated what a salutary change in the habits of men can be brought about by wise and forceful legislation.

Complexity of the Problem.

The merits of the British corrupt and illegal practices act of 1883 were quickly perceived by intelligent Americans.[2] The need for effective legislation against similar practices in American electoral campaigns was a matter of common knowledge.[3] It was not practicable, however, to incorporate the British act bodily into the election laws of the American states and obtain the same results as in Great Britain. The differences between the British and American electoral systems are too fundamental.

In the first place, a general election in an American state is a much more complex operation than a parliamentary election in Great Britain. In Great Britain there is but a single office to be filled by election in each district. The candidate for Parliament is the sole representative of the cause of his party in the district. For the duration of the campaign his personal election agent is the head of the local party organization. Usually, indeed, the candidate selects as his election agent the secretary of the local party association. The interests of the party become identified with those of the parliamentary candidate. In an American state a general election is really a multitude of elections held

[1] A. L. Lowell, *The Government of England*, i, 237.

[2] See W. M. Ivins, *Machine Politics and Money in Elections in New York City*, New York, 1887.

[3] See, for example, the discussion of the party system in James Bryce, *The American Commonwealth*, pt. iii.

simultaneously. There are many offices to be filled by election in each district. No one candidate for office is exclusively the representative of his party. All candidates on the same party ticket, from presidental electors down to coroners, are served by the same election agents, the regular party committees. The interests of the party are not identified with those of any particular candidate for office. If a voter is bribed, he is ordinarily bribed to vote for a party, not for a single candidate. Corruption generally inures to the benefit of all candidates on the same ticket. Some may have connived at it, others may have been ignorant of it, or may even have opposed it. To penalize all the beneficiaries of corruption, as in England, would mean to void the election of a president or governor, because of the corruption of a few voters in a single district, perhaps primarily in the interest of a local candidate. In England it is just to void the election of the candidate for Parliament because of the corrupt acts of his election agent, since the agent serves that candidate alone. But in the United States it is not ordinarily practicable to trace corruption, for which a party committee is directly responsible, back to any particular candidate. Party committeemen themselves might be disqualified for future service as committeemen or as public officials. Such a penalty would be appropriate in cases where the committeemen control the candidates. It would be inadequate, however, in cases where they are merely the agents of the party. In short, the multiplicity of elective offices and the separation of party management from the personal fortunes of particular candidates make the prevention of corrupt practices a much more difficult undertaking in the United States than in Great Britain.

Secondly, in the United States the process of nomination is much more complicated than in Great Britain. In the latter country the rivalry for parliamentary nominations is much less keen than that for most elective offices in the United States. The personality of the candidate is of minor importance. Primary elections are unknown. In the United States, in cases where nomination is equivalent to election, the contests for nomination cause the expenditure of more money than the elections themselves. In all cases where nominations are attractive, the candidates for nomination, unless supported by party organizations, must conduct personal campaigns before the primaries. Primary elections tend to take on the aspect of preliminary general elections. Effective corrupt practices acts in this country must regulate the expenditures in primary as well as in general elections. Moreover, the choice of party officials is an integral part of the electoral process in the United States. Like the nominations for public office, the party offices may be hotly contested. The choice of delegates to the principal conventions, and, in states where party committeemen are elected directly by the rank and file of the parties, the election of members of the principal committees, often involve the decision of much more momentous issues than the personality of the candidates or the character of the platforms in the next campaign. In a struggle between different factions for the control of a party organization the whole future of the party itself may be at stake. Special interests which expect to profit through the control of the organization by a particular faction may well prefer to sacrifice temporary success at the polls for the sake of maintaining their grip on the organization. So long as the bipartisan system of politics endures, the permanent control of the organization is much more important for many purposes than temporary control of the government itself. Consequently effective corrupt practices acts in this country must regulate the use of money in the election of party committeemen as well as in the nomination and election of public officials.

Thirdly, the regulation of the sources of campaign funds is more important, as well as more difficult, in the United States than in Great Britain. In the latter country the parliamentary candidate is as a rule expected to finance the entire campaign in his district. That is one reason why there is less rivalry for parliamentary nominations than might be expected by an American. If a desirable candidate cannot afford to finance as vigorous a campaign as is required, he may be assisted by a grant from the central campaign fund of the party. Ordinarily there is little of that effort, so characteristic of American politics, to finance the local campaign in each district by contributions from those who expect to support the party's candidates at the polls or hope to profit in some way by their success. This may be explained partly by the fact that party organization, except in the case of the Labour Party, is less democratic than in the United States, and partly by the fact that special interests cannot hope to profit by the success of particular candidates to such an extent as in the United States. The separation of politics from public administration is so effectively accomplished in Great Britain that opportunities for private profit through the favor of elective officials are much rarer than in the United States. But whatever be the explanation, the supply of funds for the conduct of campaigns by persons who are not themselves candidates for election is a much more common practice in the United States than in Great Britain. Just as the expenditure of money by candidates may exercise an undue influence over voters, so the contribution of money to campaign funds by special interests may exercise an undue influence over candidates. The candidate whose election or the organization whose success in general is made possible by financial support from railroads, public service corporations, or bootleggers is hardly more disinterested than one who has accepted an acknowledged retainer. It is not strange that the link between visible and "invisible" government was located by the "muck-rakers" in the methods of party finance.

Development of Corrupt Practices Acts.

The American states have been much slower to follow the example of Great Britain in regulating the use of money in elections than in regulating the form of the ballot. Bribery and the other forms of gross corruption have always been penalized here as there. But prior to 1890 there was no recognition in any American state of what the English law of 1883 defined as illegal practices. In that year the same group of reformers who had been the first advocates of the Australian ballot in this country succeeded in putting through the first feeble imitation of the English corrupt and illegal practices act. The demand for reform was strongest in New York and Massachusetts. As the first Australian ballot law was enacted in Massachusetts, so the first modern legislation for the regulation of the use of money was enacted in New York. The New York law of 1890 provided merely that candidates for election should file a return after the close of the campaign showing the nature and amount of their expenditures during the campaign. The Massachusetts law of 1892 went further, providing that no candidate should pay or promise any money to promote his election except for personal expenses and to political committees. Personal expenses were defined as writing, printing, and distributing letters, circulars, etc., stationery and postage, telegraph, telephone and messenger service, traveling, and other petty personal services. No return of the nature or amount of personal expenses was required. In addition, voluntary contributions might be made in any amount to political committees. A political committee was defined as any three or more persons acting together to promote the success or defeat of a party principle or candidate. Every political committee was required to have a treasurer, through whom all receipts and expenditures were to be made. Political committees might receive contributions from any source and in any amount, and might spend money in any amount for any lawful purpose. After the close of the campaign, the treasurer was required to file a return with a city or town clerk, provided the total expenditures exceeded twenty dollars, showing in detail the nature and amount of all expenditures and the source and amount of all contributions. Any individual, not a member or agent of a political committee, spending more than twenty dollars, was also required to file a return of expenditures.

The scope of this early legislation was manifestly inadequate. Neither the New York nor the Massachusetts law imposed any new restrictions upon the nature of political expenditures. Neither limited their amount. Neither could afford the public any real protection against the corrupt use of money. The New York candidate could easily evade the New York law by making his expenditures through political committees. The Massachusetts candidate could easily evade the law in his state by alleging that his expenditures were personal. The definition of personal expenditures was so broad that almost any expenditure was covered. The means of enforcement and the penalties were equally inadequate. The returns were merely filed, not published, and convictions of violation of the acts, if anybody were interested to secure them, would have been exceedingly difficult to obtain. The penalties were comparatively small fines or short terms of imprisonment. Despite the unpromising character of this pioneer legislation, similar laws were enacted in a number of states. In 1893 Missouri first introduced a limitation upon the amount of expenditures by candidates and committees. In 1897 several states began the limitation of the sources of campaign funds by prohibiting contributions from corporations. The gradual introduction of civil service reform measures also involved, among the other things, the prohibition of political assessments upon officers under the merit system. In 1903 the extension of the principle of publicity of campaign expenditures to the primaries was begun in the South, where the primaries were the most important phase of the electoral process. Yet it must be admitted that down to 1904 legislation providing for publicity in the financing of political campaigns had accomplished little for the purification of American politics. Less than half of the states had adopted any such legislation. Practically all the legislation that had been adopted was so defective in scope or in means of enforcement that little could be expected from it. Even had convictions for violations been practicable, nobody was interested to secure convictions, because nobody could profit thereby. Defeated candidates, even if their own hands were clean, could not immediately profit by convicting their successful opponents of violations, because their opponents would still hold the offices to which they had been elected. They could never profit by such convictions unless public opinion could be enlisted in support of those who would respect the law. For this public opinion seemed unready. It is not surprising, therefore, that during this period there were few prosecutions for violations of these laws, and fewer convictions.

A great change in the opinion of the public set in after the presidential election of 1904. There were four causes for this change. The first and most conspicuous was the revelation of the huge sums of money contributed in recent campaigns, particularly that of 1904, by large corporations, and by individuals with large corporate connections. The revelation of the contributions by the great New York life insurance companies made the deepest impression upon the mind of the public, for these contributions consisted of money which in a way was the policyholders' money and was used to promote causes of which many of the policyholders did not approve. But the revelation of the contributions made by certain railroad, traction, and financial magnates was equally disquieting, for such heavy contributors could not fail to exercise an undue influence upon the party organizations which they supported. Certain corporate interests, indeed, were found to support both organizations,—a course which could not but seem to honest party men utterly unprincipled. As Perry Belmont, treasurer of the Democratic national committee and one of the heaviest contributors to the campaign of 1904, observed: "The great captains of industry have been induced or compelled, or they have permitted themselves on one pretext or another, to endeavor to control political agencies and organizations by the use of money."[1] The people were now becoming convinced of this ugly truth. The truth frightened them, for it meant that control of their institutions was slipping away from them into the hands of an oligarchy of wealth.

The other causes of the change in public opinion were no less significant. The second cause was clearly indicated by the chairman of the Democratic national committee, who observed: "We are all familiar with what has been going on in the use of money in state, local, and national campaigns. We all know that it is not only a menace to the country, but to the political parties themselves."[2] And the party leaders were bound to take notice of a condition that menaced the parties. Moreover, campaign managers were finding that where so much money was known to be available for political purposes, they were at the mercy of any unscrupulous person who possessed political influence and wanted cash. "People who accept five, ten, or one hundred dollars a day to work at the polls would not accept it, if there was danger of its being made public."[3] Thirdly, the growing increase in the cost of elections threatened the political future of all men who could not command the necessary funds. As President Gompers of the American Federation of Labor observed: "The use of money, particularly to the extent it has been used in the last decade, has made it practically impossible for a wage earner to become a member of either state legislature or the Congress of the United States."[4] Finally, the large contributors themselves were to a certain extent the victims of the evil system their own unfortunate practices had fostered. Compulsory and effective publicity, it was pointed out, "gives the corporation that does not want to contribute an excuse for not giving, and a majority of them in my opinion are practically coerced into

[1] Minutes of First Meeting of National Publicity Bill Organization, Washington, January 17, 1906, p. 3.

[2] Norman E. Mack, *loc. cit.*, p. 11.

[3] *Loc. cit.*, p. 16.

[4] *Loc. cit.*, p. 18.

giving—black-mailed, in fact."[1] In the face of attack from so many quarters the traditional American system of secret party finance had to give way.

Further Regulation of the Use of Money.

Effective regulation of political campaign funds requires legislation by Congress as well as by the state legislatures. Congress inaugurated the new era in 1907 by prohibiting all corporations from contributing to funds used to promote the election of federal officers, and national banks and corporations engaged in interstate commerce from contributing to state and local campaign funds. It took the next step in 1910 by requiring the filing after the close of the campaign of a sworn statement of receipts and expenditures by national and congressional committees and all other political committees spending money in two or more states for the purpose of influencing federal elections. In 1911 it took a further and much more important step. The principle of publicity was extended to contributions and expenditures in the primaries, publicity was made continuous throughout the campaign instead of being confined to a single statement filed after the close of the campaign, and the amount that might be spent by a candidate in the primary and general election campaigns together was limited to five thousand dollars in the case of a candidate for the House of Representatives and to ten thousand dollars in the case of a candidate for the Senate.[2] Meanwhile similar legislation was being enacted by the states. By 1911 nearly half of the states had enacted legislation prohibiting campaign contributions by corporations, and three-fourths of the states had enacted legislation providing for filing returns of

[1] Ex-Congressman Lamb, *loc. cit.*, p. 17.

[2] In the Newberry case (Newberry *v.* United States, 256 U. S. 232, decided in 1921), the Supreme Court of the United States, by a vote of five to four, decided that the act of 1910 could not apply to senatorial primaries. Four of the judges were of the opinion that the Constitution merely authorized Congress to regulate "the manner of holding elections," and not the nominating process, while a fifth thought Congress had no jurisdiction over senatorial primaries prior to the adoption of the Seventeenth Amendment. Following this decision, Congress enacted a new law (1925) which was substantially the same as the act of 1910 but which applied only to "a general or special election" and not to a primary election. One other act of Congress deserves to be mentioned in this connection. A statute of 1918 imposes penalties upon any person who promises to give anything of value to anyone to secure his vote at a congressional election and upon any person who accepts such gifts in return for his support.

contributions and expenditures. Some of this legislation marked little or no advance over the pioneer legislation in New York and Massachusetts. Much of the later legislation, however, was of a more effective character.

The most significant of the later acts were those adopted in Oregon through the direct popular initiative in 1908, and in Wisconsin in 1911. These acts go much further than any previous legislation in the American states in regulating the nature as well as the amounts of campaign expenditures. In both respects they marked a closer approximation to the English model than the earlier legislation in this country. The Wisconsin act of 1911 is most clearly based upon the English principle that all expenditures are illegal except those expressly authorized by law. Expenditures by candidates, whether in connection with a primary or general election, are prohibited except (*a*) for personal hotel and traveling expenses; (*b*) for payments to the state required by law; (*c*) for contributions to duly registered personal campaign committees; (*d*) for contributions to party committees; and (*e*) for actual personal expenses of public speakers. No bills or claims presented later than ten days after the close of the campaign are to be paid. No payments whatever may be made on account of services rendered on primary or general election day, or for the transportation of voters to the polls.

The Wisconsin act of 1911 provides for periodic returns both by candidates and by committees throughout the campaign, and forbids the printing of a candidate's name upon the ballot unless the proper returns have been filed. Maximum limits are placed to the amounts that may be spent by or on behalf of candidates for nomination and election, and to the amounts that may be spent by the state central committees in excess of sums paid in on behalf of candidates and included in the statements of their personal expenditures. A similar though less drastic limitation was adopted in Massachusetts in 1914, when maximum limits were placed to the amounts that might be contributed to campaign funds or spent for campaign purposes by persons not themselves candidates. In that state, however, no limit was placed upon the total sums that might be raised and spent by the state central committees. Charges of non-compliance with the Wisconsin law are tried before a special election court. Conviction, except in the cases of candidates for Congress or the state legislature, is to be followed by forfeiture of office. In the excepted cases a record of the conviction is to be transmitted to the appropriate body for such action as that body may choose to take. The exceptions are required by the federal and state constitutional provisions that Congress and the state legislatures respectively shall be the judges of the election and qualifications of their own members. Trial before a special election court and forfeiture of office in case of conviction, subject to the exceptions above noted, are also provided for by the Oregon legislation of 1908 and the Massachusetts legislation of 1914.

Working of the Corrupt Practices Acts.

Testimony concerning the operation of the American corrupt practices and campaign publicity acts is conflicting. Some of those who ought to know assert that the laws are generally observed, that they tend to reduce the cost of running for office, and to prevent the corrupt use of money in elections. Others assert that they are not generally observed, that they have not reduced the cost of running for office, and that they do not prevent the corrupt use of money in elections. Their chief effect, according to the hostile critics, where they produce any effect at all, is to encourage the practice of perjury. This conflicting testimony can be partly explained by the fact that the laws are very different in different states, some being much more defective than others. The statutes passed during the earlier period of legislation were most defective. It is doubtful whether they were generally observed. Certainly they did not reduce the cost of running for office nor prevent the corrupt use of money in elections. They were often held in open contempt by candidates and party workers. They were universally disregarded by non-political associations, having occasion to expend money independently in political campaigns, notably by liquor dealers' associations. Some of the later statutes ought to produce better results.[1]

It is clear, however, that the best American statutes cannot be expected to accomplish so much for the purification of elections as was accomplished by the British act of 1883. There are so many more candidates and elections in this country, the location

[1] See for an excellent discussion of these laws James K. Pollock, jr., *Party Campaign Funds* (New York, 1926).

of responsibility is so much more difficult, and the attention of the public is subject to so many more demands during campaigns, that the enforcement of laws depending mainly upon publicity and public opinion for their effectiveness is far less easy than in Great Britain. In some respects the best American laws are superior to the British. Continuous publicity throughout the primary and election campaign should be more effective than publicity after the campaign has closed. On the other hand, the returns under the British act must be published in full in at least two local newspapers at the expense of the parties. In the United States returns are merely filed with some public official. The voters know nothing of their contents except in so far as they may be voluntarily informed by newspapers or public speakers. Such information, at least during the campaign, is likely to be partisan and ineffective. The laws of the American states are also more imperfect than the British act with respect to the limitation of the objects of campaign expenditures. Few of them define with sufficient accuracy the legitimate objects of expenditure. This is necessary to prevent evasion. Very few absolutely forbid the expenditure of money on the day of election. This is indispensable to the purification of elections. The most important aspect of these laws is their enforceability in the courts by prosecution for violations. Few of them make any effective provision for such enforcement. Those few fail to deal effectively with candidates for legislative office. In general, responsibility for violations of the laws cannot be fixed with such certainty as in Great Britain. Hence the severe penalties enforced in Great Britain are probably impracticable in national and state elections here. They will remain impracticable, so long as the American electoral system remains as complex as at present.

Some good results of the recent legislation nevertheless may already be detected. There has undoubtedly been a decrease in the contribution of funds to political campaigns by large corporations and corporate interests. This was clearly revealed by the investigations of the special sub-committee of the United States Senate Committee on Privileges and Elections during the presidential campaign of 1912. The immediate effect has been to diminish the total amount of the campaign funds raised by the regular party committees and to increase the efforts of campaign committees to raise funds by popular subscription. The ultimate effect must be to popularize party finance to an extent that would have seemed visionary to politicians of the period of Mark Hanna and Matthew S. Quay. The popularization of party finance means the democratization of party management. It means the curbing of the power of "invisible" government, so far as that power arises from its financial support of the party organizations. It is doubtful, however, whether the total expenditure of money in campaigns has been diminished. The increased reliance of candidates upon personal campaigns and the increased need for publicity on a large scale, resulting from the introduction of the direct primary and the awakening of public interest in the business of party management, have created an increased demand for legitimate campaign expenditures. This increased demand can only be met by increased contributions by the candidates themselves, or by their followers and personal friends. The increased expenditure of money by personal campaign committees in primaries and elections may more than offset the decrease in expenditures by the regular party committees. The legitimate expense of running for office to-day, except in the states where a limit is fixed by effective legislation, is probably greater than ever before. It is certainly greater for candidates without organized support, compelled to finance their own fight for nomination and election. It might be supposed that the increase in the legitimate demands for money, combined with the increased difficulty of raising campaign funds, would tend to reduce the amounts available for illegitimate uses. It may be surmised that the use of money for corrupt purposes, at least in national and state campaigns, has diminished in recent years. But this cannot yet be proved.

Much remains to be done before the methods of conducting campaigns can be regarded as satisfactory. The problem of dealing with the grosser forms of corruption has existed from the beginning of popular government and can never be solved by legislation alone. But some of the newer problems arising out of the growing complexity of modern civilization can be dealt with effectively by prudent legislation. Particularly the problem of the use of money for legitimate campaign purposes needs further study in the light of modern electoral conditions. It is clear that unless some limit is placed on the amounts that may be spent by individuals, whether candidates or not, rich men will possess an undue advantage over poor men in politics. It is equally clear that if excessively low limits are placed upon the use of money for legitimate purposes, the candidates with newspaper support [1] or strong organizations behind them will possess an undue advantage over their opponents. Hearst with his papers and Tammany with its organization are much less dependent upon campaign funds than the reformers can ordinarily hope to be. Then there is the interest of the voters to be considered. If no limit is placed on the amounts that may be spent in campaigns, they may be unduly subject to corrupt influences. But if the limits are excessively low, they may be deprived of due information concerning the nature of the issues and the merits of the candidates.

The Need for Further Reform of Campaign Methods.

Compared with the limits imposed by the British act of 1883, the limits imposed upon the amount of expenditures for legitimate purposes by many American states seem unduly low. Thus the Oregon law of 1908 permits the candidate to spend not more than twenty-five per cent of the salary of the office sought by him. The candidates for governor may accordingly spend $1250 each, whilst candidates for minor offices on the state ticket, who secure much less free publicity from the newspapers, must finance their campaign with smaller sums. The gubernatorial candidate's allowance works out to about one-third of a cent per voter. In California the law of 1909 permitted the expenditure of $250 for the first five thousand voters in a district, two dollars for each additional one hundred voters up to 25,000, one dollar for each further one hundred up to 50,000, and fifty cents for each one hundred voters thereafter. At that rate a gubernatorial candidate could now spend almost ten thousand dollars. This sum would enable him to send a postal card to less than one-third of the voters of the state.

These limits seem absurdly low compared with those fixed by the British act. So they would be, if the candidates for governor alone were considered. But an American campaign is financed

[1] A few states, however, attempt to restrain various abuses of newspaper publicity by requiring political advertisements to be properly labeled, paid for at the standard rate for advertising space, etc.

by the joint expenditures of all the candidates for all the offices, national, state, and local, supplemented by the sums raised from other sources by the party committees. Prior to 1918, the total expenditure in British elections averaged about one dollar per vote cast. The exact total expenditure here is unknown.[1] The investigations of the subcommittee of the Senate Committee on Privileges and Elections in 1912, taken together with what is known about expenditures by local candidates, show that in localities where the contest is close the total expenditure per vote cast must generally far exceed the total in a British campaign.

The heaviest single item in the cost of campaigns is the cost of getting out the vote on primary and election day. The proposal is not infrequently made that this item could be greatly reduced by making voting compulsory, that is, by penalizing those who fail to vote.[2] It is argued that if the voter were subject to a small fine for failure to exercise his franchise, the party organizations would not be put to so much trouble and expense in getting him to the polls. This argument overlooks two important considerations. First, there may be a good reason for failure to attend the polls. The voter may be absent from the locality in which his right to vote must be exercised. Absence may result from the nature of his occupation, as in the case of fishermen, sailors, actors, commercial travelers, and railroad employees, or from the removal of his actual residence when it is too late to change his legal residence also before the next election. Absence may also result from physical disability, and from opposition or even mere indifference to all the candidates who have any chance of election. Secondly, voters who would be induced to attend the polls solely by the prospect of a small fine for absence are not the kind who are wanted at the polls. The indifferent voter should be cured of his indifference by a wider diffusion of political intelligence

[1] The Kenyon Committee gives the total expenditure of the two major parties in the presidential election of 1920 as $14,318,542.92. (*Senate Report No. 883, 66th Cong., 3rd Sess.*) This sum includes the expenditures on behalf of candidates during the primaries preceding the national conventions and the expenditures of the national, congressional, senatorial, and state committees of the two parties. Professor Merriam estimates that the total outlay of the major parties in a presidential election is $20,000,000, plus $10,000,000 from public funds for election costs, plus unknown public costs for the various primaries. (*The American Party System*, p. 335.)

[2] The constitutions of North Dakota and Massachusetts authorize the legislature to provide for compulsory voting but thus far no use has been made of these constitutional provisions.

and more effective methods of campaigning. The mercenary voter is not wanted at all. A small fine would not discourage the neglect of electoral duties by any voters except those to whom the fine would seem big. What is needed is a plan which will encourage voting by those who would not be influenced by the prospect of a small fine.[1]

There are several better proposals for reducing the cost of political campaigns than that of compulsory voting. One is the improvement of election machinery. In most states absent voters are now permitted to vote by mail, or at the nearest voting-place, wherever they may be, or in advance before they leave home.[2] Absent-voting should reduce somewhat the cost of political campaigns, although any saving of transportation expenses by the party is partly offset by the additional expenditure from the public treasury for the administration of the absent-voting law. Moreover, where periodic registration is required, it would be well to experiment with a carefully safeguarded system of permanent registration, thus lessening the voter's burden and at the same time decreasing the expenses of registration. Another good proposal is the prohibition of all payments by candidates or political parties for services rendered on election day, and the assumption by the state of those election-day expenses which are necessary and proper. Thus, the state already assumes the entire cost of printing and distributing the ballots,—a heavy item to candidates and parties before the introduction of the Australian ballot. It should also assume the cost of transporting to the polls all voters who really need such assistance. A larger use of public buildings for political meetings is also possible and, if necessary, halls might be provided at public expense for the conduct of rallies. A few states, led by

[1] See A. B. Hart, The Exercise of the Suffrage, in *Practical Essays in American Government.*

[2] See *ante*, ch. vi. Thus far, the results of absent-voting have not been particularly impressive. In the Chicago mayoralty election of 1923, with a total vote of approximately 723,000, only 226 votes were cast *in absentia.* And yet, of the 5,000 non-voters interviewed, 20 per cent of those who were registered but did not vote declared that they were out of town on election day. (Merriam and Gosnell, *op. cit.*, pp. 63-72.) However, in Indiana, in the Beveridge-Ralston senatorial election of 1922, 38,711 absent-voters' ballots were used in a total vote of 1,071,680 or 3.6 per cent. See also James K. Pollock, jr., "Absent Voting with particular Reference to Ohio's Experience," *National Municipal Review*, xv, pp. 282-292 (1926). The disappointing results of absent-voting laws seem to be due to lack of effective publicity concerning their provisions, and the red tape which surrounds the whole process of absent voting.

Oregon, have undertaken the publication and distribution of official campaign bulletins in order that candidates and parties may make at least one statement to every voter at the least possible cost. These pamphlets are usually published once before the primary and once between the primary and election, and contain copies of the party platforms, campaign lives and portraits of the candidates, and other matter. Only a few states have yet appropriated public money directly to the use of political parties. In Colorado a law enacted in 1909 granting a sum to each party in proportion to its voting strength was declared unconstitutional in 1911. In Oregon the presidential primary law of 1910 provided that the delegates to national conventions, chosen to express the preference of the voters of the state between the candidates for the presidential nominations, should receive their necessary traveling expenses from the state. This statute was repealed in 1915. Similar legislation in Minnesota and Idaho has likewise been repealed.

How far the state should go in financing political campaigns cannot be determined upon any general principles. If the political party is to be treated as one of the organs of government, as is implied in the legal regulation of the process of nomination, the use of public money for partisan purposes can be justified as a public use. How much public money should be so used would depend upon how much private money candidates and party organizations are to be permitted to use. That in turn depends in part upon such factors as the number of offices to be filled by election at any one time, the size of election districts, and the nature of the electoral process. Thus the question of the use of money in elections and campaigns, like so many other political questions, cannot be settled by itself alone.

CHAPTER IX

THE STATE LEGISLATURE

The constitutional history of the states, as has been previously shown, reveals two principal tendencies in the development of the legislatures: the standardization of form and the limitation of powers. The standard form is the bicameral. Each state now has a legislature consisting of two separate houses. No legislation can be enacted without the separate consent of each house. The powers of the two houses have been strictly limited. So far as the enactment of ordinary legislation is concerned, the limitations upon the two houses are the same. This is true of the limitations both upon legislative powers and legislative procedure. There is only one exception. The power to originate money bills is generally conferred exclusively upon the lower house. The power to amend such bills, however, is vested in the upper house. Under the guise of amendments the upper house can originate such bills almost as freely as if the power were expressly granted. Regarded simply as legislative bodies, therefore, the two houses possess substantially equal authority. The executive powers conferred upon the legislatures are vested chiefly in the upper houses. The power of appointing executive and judicial officers, possessed so extensively by the first state legislatures, has been largely taken away. The power of confirming executive appointments, originally vested in special executive councils, has been transferred to the upper houses alone. The judicial powers of the legislatures remain divided between the two houses as originally planned. The lower houses possess the sole power to impeach; the upper houses, to try impeachments. Whilst the vesting of the power of confirming executive appointments and trying impeachments in the upper houses would seem to indicate a greater degree of confidence in those bodies, no such partiality has been shown with reference to the exercise of purely legislative powers. With respect to these the two houses have been treated alike.

The principal questions that now arise are these. First, is the bicameral system the best system under existing conditions? Secondly, has the limitation of powers proceeded as far as is necessary and proper, or should the powers of the legislatures be further limited?[1]

THE WORKING OF THE BICAMERAL SYSTEM

The bicameral system, as has been shown, was originally advocated on a number of grounds. These are all reducible, however, to two principal grounds. The first is that the legislative branch of the government should represent the whole people, not merely a majority. Under a representative system by which each man has one vote and representatives are chosen directly by a majority of voters in local electoral districts, the body so chosen is likely to represent merely a majority of the people. Those who cast their votes for unsuccessful candidates have no representative of their own choosing. They may be represented indirectly by successful candidates in other districts, provided that the classes of voters who are in a minority in some districts are in a majority in other districts. But if there is any class of voters which is in a minority in all districts, that class will be entirely excluded from any share in the representation. Now an aristocracy, whether it be one of birth, or wealth, or intellect, or character, is always in a minority. If it is not in a minority, it is not an aristocracy. Sanguine democrats, like Jefferson, believed that the majority in each locality would naturally choose the best men for their representatives. Less sanguine men, like Adams and Jay, believed that the majority would choose men of their own sort. They feared that the aristocracy would not be properly represented under a system of unbalanced majority rule. They advocated the bicameral system, in order that the aristocracy might have special representation in a separate house. Thus the senates would represent the minority. The lower houses would represent the majority. The legislatures as a whole would represent the people as a whole. For

[1] On the working of particular state legislatures, see the excellent series of articles entitled "Our Legislative Mills," *National Municipal Review*, xii, xiii, *passim* (1923-1924). The best study of the working of the legislative system in any particular state is that of the Illinois legislature, made by the Illinois Legislative Reference Bureau for the use of the Constitutional Convention of 1920. See *post*, Appendix D.

practical purposes, however, the defenders of aristocracy accepted wealth as the test of aristocracy. Their senates were designed to protect the rich against the poor. If the separate assent of both houses were required for the enactment of laws, there could be no legislation which was not acceptable to the rich as well as to the poor.

In most of the original states this form of the aristocratic theory of government was rejected. Not all men were considered fit to vote, but all who were considered fit were permitted to vote for both senators and representatives on equal terms. The bicameral system was accepted because it was believed to insure a more deliberate procedure in the enactment of laws. Hasty and ill-considered legislation, unnecessary and corrupt legislation, was believed to have less chance of passing two houses than one alone. Senators might be required to possess higher qualifications with respect to experience, even with respect to wealth. They might even be chosen by a different electoral process. But they were generally chosen by the same electorates as the representatives. They were expected to review the acts of the lower house with a jealous eye, but not to thwart the will of the majority of the people.

Methods of Legislative Apportionment.

It is necessary to inquire, first, whether the former reason for the bicameral system justifies the maintenance of the state legislatures in their present form. The existing legislatures consist as a rule of an upper house of from thirty to fifty members and a lower house of from fifty to one hundred and fifty.[1] In most states the members of the lower house are from two to three times as numerous as the members of the upper.[2] Thus the senates are more select bodies than the lower houses. The greater dignity of the senates is further secured in a majority of the states by the choice of senators for longer terms than representatives.

[1] The smallest senates are those of Delaware and Nevada with seventeen members each; the largest is that of Minnesota with sixty-seven members. The smallest lower house is that of New Mexico with thirty members; the largest are those of New Hampshire and Connecticut with 418 and 262 respectively.

[2] In five states, Colorado, Idaho, Minnesota, Montana, and New Mexico, they are less than twice as numerous. In Vermont, on the other hand, they are more than seven, and in New Hampshire, more than seventeen times as numerous.

In many states, however, senators and representatives are chosen for identical terms, generally two years. Differences in the electorates of the two houses, in the qualifications of their members, and in the process of election, so far as they ever existed, have generally been abolished. At present, therefore, in most states the principal differences in the character of the two houses result chiefly from differences in their size and in the manner of apportioning their members.[1]

The basis of representation in the lower houses of the legislatures, except in New England, is the county. The simplest form of county representation is that whereby each county is a separate representative district. The total number of representatives is apportioned among the counties as nearly as possible in proportion to population, but no county receives less than one representative. The representatives from each county are elected in the county at large. Such a system of representation prevails in most of the southern states and in several of the northern and middle western states, notably in New Jersey, Ohio, and Iowa. In the more sparsely settled states, it is not possible to give separate representation to each county without making the lower house too large or the representation of the people too unequal. In such states counties may be grouped together, if necessary, to form a single district. Sometimes a comparatively populous county is entitled to one representative of its own and is grouped with other counties for the purpose of choosing another representative. In a few states where the county serves as the representative district, notably Louisiana [2] and Maryland, populous urban counties are subdivided into special electoral districts for the choice of representatives. In nearly a dozen states the practice has been adopted of dividing the whole state into special electoral districts, as nearly as possible equal in population, returning one member each. In some of these states, however, each county comprises at least one district. In others counties may be grouped as well as divided in order to form equal single-member districts. In New England the town is the basis of

[1] See Robert Luce, *Legislative Assemblies* (Boston, 1924). See also A. Z. Reed, *The Territorial Basis of Government Under the State Constitutions* (New York, 1911). See, further, *Bulletins for the* (*Massachusetts*) *Constitutional Convention*, No. 29, "The Basis of Apportionment of Representatives in the Several States" (Boston, 1918).

[2] In Louisiana the parish is the local equivalent of the county.

representation. The systems of apportionment, however, are as diverse as in other parts of the country. In Massachusetts, for example, the local communities are divided or grouped together as may be necessary in order that the people may be represented as nearly as possible according to their numbers. In Connecticut and Vermont, on the other hand, the old colonial practice by which each town or city, regardless of its size, sends an equal number of representatives, still prevails almost unchanged.

The basis of representation in the upper houses is more uniform. In most states single-member districts are formed by grouping or dividing counties, generally with a view to approximate equality of population. In a few states, of which Ohio is the most notable, populous counties, entitled to more than one senator, are not divided into single-member districts. In such counties, senators like representatives are elected at large. In a very few states, of which New Jersey is the most notable, each county is entitled to an equal number of senators, regardless of population. In some states the apportionment of senators and representatives is based upon the distribution of some special class of persons, rather than upon that of the total population. Thus in New York it is based upon the distribution of citizens, regardless of the alien population. In certain southern states it is based on the distribution of qualified electors, regardless of the negro population. Except in a few of the oldest and smallest states, a reapportionment of members is made by each legislature every ten years. Some states place constitutional restrictions upon the power of apportionment, requiring that legislative districts be as compact in form and as nearly equal in size as practicable. Two of these states expressly provide for the judicial review of legislative apportionments for the correction of errors,[1] and doubtless in others the courts have the power to set aside arbitrary and unreasonable apportionments.

Over-representation of Majority Parties.

It is apparent that the existing standard form of legislature cannot be justified on the ground that it represents the whole people.[2] The lower house does in most cases represent the ma-

[1] New York and Oklahoma.

[2] The two houses certainly do not afford separate representation to the rich and poor. The only difference between the two houses tending to make one more representative of the rich than the other is the differ-

jority, as it was intended to do. The upper house, however, does not represent the minority. It also represents the majority. Indeed, the principal effect of the maintenance of an upper house is to give the majority party a stronger hold on the state government than it would have, if there were no upper house. Since the upper houses are smaller than the lower, their members are usually chosen in larger electoral districts. Now the larger the electoral districts into which a state may be divided, the more favorable the results of elections will be to the majority party. There are two reasons for this. First, the effect of any system of representation based upon plurality elections in local districts is to magnifiy the importance of the majority. Writers upon the subject of proportional representation have frequently pointed this out, and quote copious statistics to prove it. It is obvious without statistical proof. If all the representatives of the people were chosen on a general ticket in the state at large, all would be chosen by the majority. This is what happens under the present system of choosing presidential electors. The smaller the districts, the more closely the distribution of representatives among the several parties corresponds to the relative popular strength of the parties. In a state where the majority party is strong, comprising, say, 55 to 60 per cent of the total vote, it may secure all the representatives in Congress, nearly all the state senators, and more than its share, though not so much more, of the members of the lower house. Secondly, the disproportionate representation of the majority party may be further enhanced by the practice of gerrymandering.[1] A gerrymander is an arrangement of electoral districts which enables the majority party to carry the greatest possible number of districts with the least possible number of votes. The larger the districts into which a

ence in size. From this it follows that in most states senators are chosen in larger districts than representatives. Hence the cost of election is likely to be greater. To a certain extent this greater cost of election may serve as a property qualification for senators. In most states this tendency cannot be of great importance. A more important consequence of the difference in size is the effect upon the representation of parties.

[1] For a study of gerrymandering in Missouri, Kentucky, and Tennessee, see C. O. Sauer, "Geography and the Gerrymander," *American Political Science Review*, xii, pp. 403-426 (1918). In 1925, the Democratic members of the state senate of Indiana fled to Ohio in an endeavor to break the quorum and thus prevent the Republican majority from enacting a gerrymander bill. The Republican members of the Rhode Island Senate fled to Massachusetts in the preceding year to prevent the Democrats from correcting a gerrymander.

state is to be divided, the greater the possibility of the gerrymander. Willful and deliberate discrimination against the minority party is consequently most notorious in the formation of congressional districts. A gerrymander, however, may be perpetrated in the interest of particular individuals as well as in that of the majority party. In fact one of the most grotesque congressional gerrymanders of recent years was perpetrated in South Carolina,[1] where discrimination against the minority party could hardly have been an object.

The over-representation of the majority party in the state legislatures is consistently defended by the supporters of the existing bipartisan political system. Since ours is a government by parties, it is urged, it is necessary that the governing party possess power commensurate with its responsibility. So long as the people look to the majority party to carry out the program to which it has pledged itself in its platform, the people must trust the majority party with adequate control of the legislative machinery. Frequently, however, a majority party comprises but a slight majority of the total number of voters. Sometimes the vote cast for its candidates may even be less than a majority of the total vote. Unless the majority party could secure a disproportionate share of the seats in the legislature, a comparatively few members would hold the balance of power. In close states a majority party which possessed no more than its proportionate share of representatives would have a slender and dubious hold upon the legislature. In order to possess an efficient working majority, the party must have not only a bare majority, but also a margin of safety. In short, the system of government by party requires that the majority party have effective control of the legislature. Ordinarily in close states effective control cannot be secured without over-representation. Whether such a system is a good system depends upon the manner in which the majority party uses its power. Certainly it is not the system contemplated by the framers of the original state constitutions.

Discrimination Against Urban Districts.

A secondary effect of the bicameral system is to facilitate discrimination against the inhabitants of the large cities in the

[1] See J. R. Commons, *Proportional Representation* (2d ed.), p. 55.

apportionment of representatives.[1] Discrimination against the large cities may be accomplished in various ways. Since the total number of senators and representatives is usually fixed in the state constitution, a requirement that each county receive at least one senator or representative will generally give to the less populous counties more than their proportionate share of the total number. Such a requirement actually produces under-representation of the large cities in one or both houses in a considerable number of states. The requirement that each county receive an equal number of senators or representatives produces a much more inequitable discrimination against the cities. In New Jersey the counties are equally represented in the senate; the people are proportionately represented in the lower house. Thus the senate is controlled by the county districts, whilst the house is controlled by the cities. In Connecticut the reverse is true. The senators are apportioned according to population, whilst the lower house represents the towns without regard to population. In this state the most extraordinary discrimination occurs.[2] New Haven, Bridgeport, Waterbury, and Hartford, with a combined population in 1920 of 535,843, have only eight representatives in the lower house of the legislature. The four towns of Union, Hartland, Killingworth, and Colebrook, with a combined population of 1728, also have eight representatives. Discrimination against the large cities may also be brought about by the lack of provision for periodic apportionments. In some cases discrimination is explicitly required by the constitution. Thus in New York the constitution seeks to preserve rural domination of the legislature by providing that no county (with one exception) shall have less than one representative in the lower house and that no two contiguous counties (by which New York City is meant) shall have more than half of the total

[1] See J. M. Mathews, "Municipal Representation in State Legislatures," *National Municipal Review*, xii, pp. 135-141 (1923). For a discussion of the rotten borough system in Rhode Island and the "gas attack" of 1924 in the state senate, see C. C. Hubbard, "Legislative 'War' in Rhode Island," *ibid.*, xiii, pp. 477-480 (1924). In 1925, the city council of Chicago adopted a resolution in favor of the metropolitan area seceding from Illinois and forming a separate state. See editorial, "Yes, We'd Like to Pull out of Illinois," *Chicago Tribune*, June 26, 1925; see also C. M. Kneier, "Chicago Threatens to Revolt," *National Municipal Review*, xiv, pp. 600-603 (1925).

[2] See Lane W. Lancaster, "Rotten Boroughs and the Connecticut Legislature," *National Municipal Review*, xiii, pp. 678-683 (1924).

number of senators. In most of the states the rural districts retain a hold upon one of the houses out of all proportion to their numerical strength. In two of them, Rhode Island and Delaware, gross discrimination against the cities exists in both branches of the legislature.[1]

Discrimination against the inhabitants of the cities in both branches of a legislature can hardly be justified upon any principles of government at present accepted by Americans. Discrimination against the cities in one branch is defended by representatives of the rural communities on the ground that they are fairly entitled to control at least one branch. Originally the country districts, that is, the agricultural classes, controlled both branches of all state legislatures. With the growth of cities, however, and the rise of an urban industrial class, the political supremacy of the farmers was threatened. In many states conflicts of interest arose between city and country. In all states rural and urban prejudices clashed. In states where the urban voters are a majority, a discrimination against the cities which enables the rural districts to control one branch of the legislature establishes a check upon the power of the urban majority to dominate the rural minority. Thus the bicameral system facilitates the maintenance of the balance of power between city and country. Such a system may be advocated as a mode of protecting the rights of the rural minority. But it is inconsistent with the modern theory of party government. This is clearly apparent in those cases where one party represents the cities, and the other the rural districts. In such cases the effect of discrimination against the cities is to interfere with the effective control of legislation by the majority party, whenever the city party is in a majority in the state as a whole. Such discrimination raises many fundamental questions. Are not the rights of rural minorities adequately protected by the courts? If not, could they not be adequately protected by some suitable system of rural "home

[1] The discrimination against the cities in the apportionment of members of the legislature goes far to explain the opposition in the legislatures of these states to all political changes designed to increase the power of the "people," that is, of a numerical majority of the voters. The direct nomination of candidates for state office in the primaries is opposed in such states as Rhode Island because the abandonment of the convention system would mean the end of the control of such nominations by the rural districts. Direct legislation by the people is objectionable because it would nullify rural control of the legislatures. It is not a theory, but a condition, that confronts the rural voters of those states.

rule"? If not, would it not be better to abandon the present system of representing only local majorities in the legislatures, and to adopt a different system of representation, a system frankly designed to represent all the people?

The Problem of Legislative Procedure.

The second ground for the adoption of the bicameral system was the supposed value of a second chamber as a means of protecting, not the minority, but the majority itself against the enactment of undesirable legislation. With only one house, there was believed to be insufficient security for due deliberation. The separate consideration of proposed legislation in two houses was advocated merely as a method of legislative procedure. It becomes necessary, therefore, to inquire next what are the present methods of legislative procedure,[1] and to what extent the existence of the second house ensures due deliberation.

The rules of procedure in the state legislatures have developed in response to four principal influences: the volume of legislation, the number of members, the limitations of time, and the exigencies of the party system. The volume of legislation has grown enormously, is still growing, and threatens to continue to grow. In 1923, the legislatures of forty-four states met in regular or special sessions and adopted approximately 16,500 acts and resolves.[2] The total number of bills introduced into the legislatures of these states was of course much greater, ranging from several hundreds in the smaller states to 3862 in New York.[3] In most of the states, the time that may be devoted to the consideration of this mass of proposed legislation is strictly limited by the constitution. In Indiana, for instance, the total number of measures introduced into the legislature of

[1] An excellent monograph on this subject is H. W. Dodds, "Procedure in State Legislatures," *Annals*, lxxvii, Supplement (1918). See also Robert Luce, *Legislative Procedure* (New York, 1922).

[2] The legislatures of the four remaining states met in 1924 and passed 1400 acts. The 16,500 measures referred to above do not include 122 constitutional amendments which were favorably acted upon by the legislatures, nor do they include the scores of resolutions which were adopted but which did not have the force of law. In 1925, forty-one legislatures passed 11,364 acts. See American Bar Association, *1925 Report of the Committee on Noteworthy Changes in Statute Law*, p. 51.

[3] During the six years (1916-1921) a total of 18,662 bills were introduced into the New York legislature, of which 5,680 were passed by both houses. See New York Judiciary Constitutional Convention, 1921, *Report*, Exhibit E.

1923 was 957, a comparatively moderate number. The session was limited to sixty-one days.[1] If every measure were to be considered separately on the floor of each house, and the houses were to sit for five hours each day, a maximum allowance if due time be allowed for other necessary legislative work, each house would have to dispose of a measure every nineteen minutes. If each member were to speak but once on each measure, senators could speak for twenty-three seconds each, and members of the house of representatives, half that period. In large states like Massachusetts, New York, Illinois, and Pennsylvania, although there is no fixed limit to the duration of a session, the volume of proposed legislation is so much greater than in Indiana that the pressure on the time of the legislature would appear to be about the same.

Under actual conditions, the pressure upon the time of legislative bodies is greater than these calculations indicate. The beginning of every regular session is inevitably given over to organization and the introduction of bills. The middle part, as will be made clear hereafter, is likely to be devoted to committee work, trading, and manipulation. There remains only the last part of the session for actual legislation. One legislature which sat for one hundred and thirty-two days passed four hundred and forty-eight general laws, three hundred and twenty-eight special laws, and sixty-two joint resolutions, a total of eight hundred and thirty-eight, or an average of more than six a day. One half of the total were passed in the last fifteen days, nearly thirty a day. Nearly one hundred were passed on the last day.[2] This crush of legislation at the close came in a legislature where there was no time limit. Where there is a time limit, the crush is worse. If any considerable number of members were opposed to a measure, were free to debate it at length, and chose to do so, the enactment of the measure would be impossible. If each member of the minority party were free to speak at length on each measure, and chose to do so, the majority could not carry on the government of the state.

[1] In fact, the legislature, by adjourning over the week-ends, sat for only forty-five working days.

[2] S. P. Orth, "Our State Legislatures" (reprinted from the *Atlantic Monthly*, Dec., 1904), in P. S. Reinsch, *Readings on American State Government*, pp. 41-56. A very interesting article on the personnel and work of the legislatures.

Methods of Legislative Procedure.

All legislative bodies therefore make some provision for the classification of their business, the regulation of their time, and the restriction of the freedom of debate. These provisions vary greatly among the several states, but certain essentials are found everywhere. In the first place, all proposed legislation is classified according to its nature, and all measures in each class are referred to an appropriate committee. The nature of the classification, and consequently the number of committees, varies, but the rule that every measure shall be referred to a committee before being considered by the whole house is in general effect. Secondly, a regular order of business is established by a standing rule, and in the absence of a special rule or order each measure is considered in its regular order. No bill may be adopted by either house until it has been read three times, and by the constitutions of many states the readings must be on separate days. The rules of procedure provide for the progress of bills through their several stages, including their several readings and reference to committees, and for the consideration of business in the various stages at appointed times. Finally, debate may be limited in different ways. First, limitations may be placed upon the freedom of debate in general. Thus, in most legislative bodies no member may speak twice to a question until all who wish have spoken once. In some bodies no member may speak to any question for more than a prescribed length of time. In all houses there are certain questions to which a member may not speak for more than a prescribed period of time. In the case of a number of questions the prescribed time may be very short, ten, five, or three minutes. Certain motions, particularly the motion to adjourn, are not debatable at all. Secondly, limitations may be placed upon the freedom of debate upon particular measures. Thus, a motion may be adopted to fix a time at which the discussion of a pending measure shall be terminated and the vote shall be taken. Finally, in most legislative bodies debate may be terminated at any time by the adoption of the previous question, that is, of a motion that the main question be now put to a vote. The adoption of the previous question puts an end to debate at once, though generally the member in charge of the bill is granted a few minutes in which to make a closing statement before the taking of the vote.

The rules of procedure are adopted by each house when it first convenes. Subject to the limitations of the constitution, the members may then adopt such rules as they please. For the first and last time they are completely their own masters. Each member is the peer of any other. By the adoption of rules, each member and the house as a whole put on shackles. The shackles are riveted by the choice of officers. The organization of the house is then completed. In some states, as has already been pointed out, the constitutional limitations upon legislative procedure are numerous and salutary. This is notably the case in New York. The rules of procedure incorporated in the constitution of that state carefully regulate the manner of passing bills. Special restrictions are placed upon the procedure with respect to private and local bills, and tax and appropriation bills. On the final passage of financial bills, the ayes and noes must be taken, and a special quorum is prescribed. In all states where new constitutions have recently been adopted, similar, though generally less complete, provisions designed to prevent hasty and disorderly proceedings in the state legislatures have been adopted. Unfortunately, as will be explained hereafter, the practices of bringing in special rules to govern procedure with respect to matters in which the legislative leaders are concerned, and of doing almost anything by unanimous consent, tend to bring the constitutional limitations into contempt.

The Influence of the Speakership.

The most powerful officer in the lower houses of the state legislatures is the speaker. The first source of the speaker's power is the power of recognition. No member may address the house for any purpose unless he has first been recognized by the speaker. By refusing to recognize a member the speaker can reduce that member to comparative impotence. By ascertaining in advance for what purpose members will desire recognition, and by arranging to grant recognition in a certain order or only for certain purposes, the speaker can control the course of business. By habitually recognizing certain members for certain purposes the speaker can raise those members to positions of the greatest influence in the conduct of affairs. In states where party lines are sharply drawn and party spirit runs high, the speaker is ordinarily selected before the beginning of the session at a party caucus.

At the same time a party floor leader may be selected, whom the speaker will regularly recognize for the purpose of making the motions necessary for the management of the house by the majority party.

The second source of the speaker's power is the power to rule. An appeal may be taken from a ruling of the speaker to the house as a whole, but his rulings will ordinarily be sustained by the majority, if they are in the interest of the party. Through the possession of the power to rule, the speaker possesses the further powers of declaring the presence of a quorum, and of refusing to entertain dilatory and obstructive motions. By the use of these powers a masterful speaker may do much to prevent a minority of members from impeding the enactment of the measures desired by the majority.

The third source of the speaker's power is the power of appointment. By appointing members of his own party to a majority of the places on committees, he insures the control of committees by his party. By appointing his most trusted associates to the chairmanship of the most important committees, he determines the character of the party leadership. By appointing insurgent members of his party to unimportant and inconspicuous committees he further fortifies the power of the regular party leaders.

The fourth source of the speaker's power is the power of reference. By referring important measures to committees controlled by the party leaders he may determine the fate of the measures. Unimportant measures may be referred to the committees which from the standpoint of the "organization" are less reliable. Committees manned by able but independent members of the party may be heavily burdened with routine business of a non-partisan character. Committees manned by less capable members may find little to do.

The fifth source of the speaker's power is the power to control the committee on rules. This power does not exist in all legislatures, and is important only in those where the committee on rules is highly privileged. In general, however, the powers of the speaker are the same in all the states. The president of the senate, who is usually the lieutenant-governor *ex officio*, exercises the powers of recognition, ruling, and reference, but does not always make appointments to committees or control the committee on rules. In the senates the most important member is likely to be the floor leader of the majority party.

The Influence of Legislative Committees.

In many respects, as has already been suggested, the rules of procedure adopted by the legislative bodies of the states vary greatly. State legislatures might be classified in a number of ways, according to the nature of the variations in their rules. The most significant classification is that based upon the extent to which special privileges are granted to the regular standing committees. Upon this basis of classification the legislative bodies fall into three divisions.

The first division comprises those states in which comparatively few privileges are granted to the committees. In Massachusetts, the principal state in this class, the only important privilege granted to the committees is that of examining measures referred to them prior to their consideration by the house as a whole. Each committee is accustomed to give a public hearing to the advocates and opponents of each bill which has been referred. Each committee is required to report each bill, after public hearing and before an appointed day, to the house or senate, as the case may be. With one or two exceptions, all committees to which proposed legislation is referred on introduction, are joint committees of both houses. Both public hearings and committee deliberations are attended by the members from each house before reports are made to either house. Bills are generally reported to the house in which they were first introduced. If passed by that house, they may be considered at once by the other house without further consideration in committee. The reports of committees are received and acted upon in order, and the regular order cannot be changed without the consent of four-fifths of the members of the house. None of the committees among which the business of the house is originally divided enjoys any special privileges, either with respect to the consideration of their reports or with respect to the control of debate. The most important committee is that on ways and means. To this committee are referred the governor's budget proposals which serve as the basis for the comprehensive general appropriation bill and for the supplementary general appropriation bill. The executive estimates are subjected to careful revision with ample opportunity for hearings. All proposed new legislation entailing the expenditure of public money is also referred to the committee on ways and means, before it is placed on the order of second reading, so that there may be a report on its relation to the state finances. Thus there are two reports on such a measure, one from the committee to which it was originally referred on its general merits, the other from the committee on ways and means on its relation to the state budget plans.

The Massachusetts system of legislative procedure has many advantages.[1] The holding of a public hearing on every bill affords an excellent opportunity for the ventilation of real and imaginary grievances, and for gauging the extent of the public demand for proposed legislation. It educates both the legislators and the public. It also compels the proponents of ill-considered and undesirable legislation to run the gantlet of pitiless publicity. The requirement that every bill be reported to the whole house prevents committees from pigeonholing desirable legislation and compels them to justify their action in each case. The establishment of a regular order, which cannot be set aside except by a four-fifths vote, and which must be completed before the legislative session can end, insures that every measure will be duly considered by at least one house. Thus the majority of the legislature can effectively control the course of legislation, for they cannot be prevented from adopting any bill which they desire to adopt, nor from defeating any bill to which they are opposed. The use of joint committees instead of separate committees of each house for the initial consideration of proposed legislation saves much time on the part of legislators, and much effort on the part of proponents and opponents of legislation. It also tends to remove needless friction between the two houses. The Massachusetts system of procedure is seen at its best in the case of appropriations. The centralization of legislative responsibility for all appropriations in the hands of the ways and means committee has enabled that committee to play an intelligent and important part in the successful operation of the Massachusetts budget system, established by constitutional amendment in 1918.

[1] For a good article on the organization, procedure, and work of the Massachusetts legislature, see A. C. Hanford, "Our Legislative Mills: Massachusetts, Different from the Others," *National Municipal Review*, xiii, pp. 40-48 (1924).

The restrictions upon the power of this committee to originate appropriations, and the requirement that its reports be considered separately in the regular order, enable the legislature to deal with each appropriation on its individual merits. The late Professor Reinsch justly observed: "The General Court[1] of Massachusetts is in all respects nearest the people, and most responsive of any American legislature to intelligent public opinion."[2] But there is one feature of this system of procedure which, as things now stand, would be considered undesirable in all states, and in most of them constitutes an insuperable objection to its adoption. The legislature ordinarily cannot dispose of its business in less than five or six months.[3]

The Ascendency of the Privileged Committees.

The second division of states comprises those in which legislative committees are more highly privileged than in Massachusetts. In these states committees are privileged to grant or refuse public hearings on referred bills at their discretion. In states where committees meet at the call of their chairmen, the chairman of each committee can decide in most cases whether or not a hearing shall be held. Committees are privileged to report bills to the house or to kill them by refusing to report. In most states the majority, under the rules, can discharge a committee from further consideration of a bill, but in many of these such action is difficult in practice. In some states the reports of important committees are privileged under the rules, and entitled to prior consideration out of the regular order. More frequently, however, special consideration is obtained for the reports of such committees through the collusion of the speaker and the committee chairman or the floor leader. The speaker recognizes the member in charge of the report, to the end that the member may move that the report be made a special order for consideration at an appointed hour. In such states the regular order may generally be set aside by a majority vote, and unless the majority is ready to repudiate the regular legislative leaders it will adopt

[1] The constitutional name of the Massachusetts legislature.

[2] P. S. Reinsch, *American Legislatures and Legislative Methods*, p. 174.

[3] For a full description of legislative procedure in Massachusetts, see L. A. Frothingham, *A Brief History of the Constitution and Government of Massachusetts*, ch. vii (2nd ed., 1925). Doubtless the length of the legislative session could be materially reduced by the adoption of certain minor changes in the rules of procedure.

any special order proposed by them. If, as is the case in most of these states, the legislative session is strictly limited by the constitution, there is inevitably a tremendous press of business in the last days of the session. Under such circumstances, the speaker and the chairmen of the principal committees are nearly omnipotent. They may not be able to force through to enactment all the measures which they favor, but they can certainly prevent the adoption of measures to which they are opposed. The general knowledge that they possess this power increases their power to secure the adoption of the measures which they favor. Measures go through in blocks, without discussion and often without examination by the body of members, practically by unanimous consent.

The existence of separate committees in each house serves further to strengthen the position of the "organization" and to weaken the general body of members. A common practice, where a bill is passed by one house and amended in the other, is to appoint a special conference committee, composed of the leading members of the regular standing committees having jurisdiction over the bill in each house, to agree on a compromise measure and report it in identical form to each house. These reports are always privileged, and receive immediate consideration regardless of the regular order. If they are made towards the close of the session the two houses must adopt them as made, or accept responsibility for the defeat of the legislation. Where the leaders wish to control the action of the legislature on a measure, a favorite plan is to procure the adoption of conflicting committee reports in each house and the reference of the measure to a conference committee. The latter committee they are sure to control and they are consequently able to rewrite the measure, if they wish, and to bring it to pass that it shall be adopted, if at all, on terms satisfactory to themselves. In some legislatures where there is a time limit, a special committee on the revision of the calendar (that is, the list of pending measures in their regular order) is appointed towards the close of the session. The membership of this committee is, of course, dictated by the "organization," and it determines what measures shall thereafter be considered, and the order of consideration. Such a committee, consisting as a rule of not more than five members of the lower house and three of the upper, practically controls the business of the legislature for the rest of the session. It is in itself a bicameral legislature in miniature, in favor of which the larger body abdicates its constitutional powers.

A specimen of this type of procedure at its worst is afforded by the rules of the Illinois legislature.[1] In 1923, there were in the house thirty-one standing committees, the largest, the committee on appropriations, having forty-nine members. Few of the committees had less than nineteen members. On the average, members of the house served on from four to six committees each. In the same session, there were thirty-nine standing committees in the senate, having on the average more than eighteen members each but ranging in size from two to forty-two. Some members served on seventeen or eighteen committees and the president of the senate pro tem. was on twenty-five. Such a situation has been aptly described in the following language: "The committee system of Illinois makes normal legislative action all but impossible. The natural result is that political ringsters find a fertile field for their work. To push legislation through, power must be concentrated in the hands of a few, who are governed by no rules and cannot be held responsible by the honest but unorganized majority. Business cannot be carried on under the rules, so it is rushed through under 'suspension of the rules,' and the actual procedure even at other times bears only a faint resemblance to that pictured by the regulations."[2] In at least three-fourths of the states the legislative committees are too large and too numerous. Under such circumstances it is difficult, even when an honest majority are trying to control legislative proceedings, to secure a full attendance at committee meetings and prompt action. Almost universally the actual work of committees is done in secret or "executive" session, and there is no provision for roll-calls on contested measures, or for any record of committee proceedings. In those states where the committees are not required by standing rule, and cannot easily be required by special order, to report all bills, a bill may be killed in committee, and every man in the legislature could

[1] See Leonard D. White, "Our Legislative Mills: The Legislative Process in Illinois," *National Municipal Review*, xii, pp. 712-719 (1923). See also, "The Legislative Department," *Illinois Constitutional Convention Bulletins*, no. 8 (1919).

[2] C. L. Jones, *Statute Law Making in the United States*, pp. 18-19.

claim to have supported it. Nothing to the contrary could be shown from the record. A more irresponsible procedure could not be devised.[1]

This system of procedure, which may be described as the normal system because it exists in the greater number of states, substitutes the rule of the committees for the rule of the majority. This result was first clearly pointed out by the distinguished author of the brilliant study in American politics, entitled *Congressional Government,* written forty years ago, when the system prevailed in Congress as well as in most of the states. "I know not how better to describe our form of government in a single phrase," he wrote, "than by calling it a government by the chairmen of the standing committees. . . . This disintegrate ministry . . . has many peculiarities. In the first place, it is made up of the elders of the assembly, for by custom seniority in . . . service determines the bestowal of the principal chairmanships; in the second place, it is constituted of selfish and warring elements, for chairman fights against chairman for use of the time of the assembly . . . ; in the third place, . . . it consists of the dissociated heads of forty-eight 'little legislatures' (to borrow Senator Hoar's apt name for the committees); and in the fourth place it is instituted by appointment from Mr. Speaker. . . . It is highly interesting to note the extraordinary power accruing to Mr. Speaker through this pregnant prerogative of appointing the standing committees of the house. . . . The most esteemed writers upon our constitution have failed to observe, not only that the standing committees are the most essential machinery of our governmental system, but also that the speaker of the house of representatives is the most powerful functionary of that system. So sovereign is he within the wide sphere of his influence that one could wish for accurate knowledge as to the actual extent of his power. But Mr. Speaker's powers cannot be known accurately, because they vary with the character of Mr. Speaker."[2]

[1] See Nebraska Legislative Reference Bureau, Bulletin No. 3, *Legislative Procedure in the Forty-Eight States*, pp. 16-17.

[2] Woodrow Wilson, *Congressional Government* (ed. of 1900), pp. 102-104. For an account of the origin of the committee system in American legislatures, see J. F. Jameson, "The Origin of the Standing Committee System in American Legislative Bodies, *Pol. Sci. Quart.*, ix, 2.

The Predominance of the Committee on Rules.

Since the publication of *Congressional Government* a striking change has taken place in the operation of the committee system in Congress, and a similar change has taken place in a few of the states. In Congress the power of the speaker grew steadily greater, until at last, in 1910, it had become so great that it was insupportable. The chief source of the increased power of the speaker was his control of the committee on rules, and the gradual extension of the highest privileges to this committee. The speaker controlled the committee on rules because he was the chairman of the committee and held the decisive vote. The other four members were evenly divided between the two major parties. The committee on rules had become highly privileged because, with the increase in the membership and business of Congress, party exigencies demanded an increase in the power to control its deliberations. The power which had once been distributed among a number of semi-independent committee chairmen needed to be centralized. The committee on rules was accordingly privileged to meet at any time, even during the sittings of the house, to report at any time, interrupting the consideration of the regular order, and to obtain immediate consideration for its reports. The committee was granted exclusive jurisdiction over all proposals to change the rules or to adopt any special order of business, and was authorized to bring in a special rule at any time without waiting for a proposal for such a rule to be referred to it by the house. Special rules reported by the committee were made effective, if adopted by a majority of the house, but without a special report from the committee the house could not depart from the regular order except by a two-thirds vote. Thus the committee on rules practically controlled the order of business, at least so far as contentious matters were concerned. Non-contentious matters, usually disposed of, if at all, by unanimous consent, could be controlled by the speaker alone. In short, the combination of the power of recognition, appointment, and control of the committee on rules made the speaker a veritable dictator in the house of representatives. A similar development in the influence of the speaker took place in those states where business was heavy, where members were numerous, where time was short, and where party lines were closely drawn. This was notably the case in the state of New York.

The dictatorial power of the speaker became objectionable in Congress for three reasons. First, it menaced unduly the interests of the minority party. The minority leaders found that, under the operation of special rules reported by the committee on rules for the purpose of rushing party measures through their several stages to enactment, they were deprived of adequate facilities for criticism of the majority's measures and for exposition of their own. Secondly, it was oppressive to the unprivileged members of the majority party. Insurgent members in particular found that the means of coercion in the hands of the speaker were so effective as to reduce them to impotence unless they supported the party program. Thirdly, it threatened to destroy the liberty of ordinary members, without regard to their party affiliation, with respect to the promotion of private and local measures. In 1910 the speaker was removed from the committee on rules, the committee was enlarged, and the members were elected by the house itself. In 1911 the power of appointment was taken from the speaker and conferred upon the committee on ways and means. The majority party members of this committee were chosen by the party caucus, and the caucus adopted the practice of considering the more important pieces of proposed legislation before they were reported out of committee, and instructing the party leaders what action should be taken. These reforms accomplished little for the protection of the minority party and the individual members, but they transferred the control of the legislative machinery from the speaker to the party caucus. The reform of the rules in the national house of representatives stimulated the reform of procedure in the state legislatures, but no state went so far as Congress in curbing the power of the speaker and in developing the authority of the party caucus. In New York the speaker remains chairman of the committee on rules. In that state the congressional system, as it existed prior to the reform of 1910-11, still holds sway.

Effects of Methods of Procedure.

The normal system of legislative procedure and what may now be described as the New York system have much in common. Under either system the speaker is the dominant personality in the business of legislation. Under either system a handful of privileged members outweigh all the rest. Under either system the unprivileged member finds himself a mere cog in a machine, so far as the enactment of legislation is concerned. The more mechanically he performs the duties required of him by the legislative leaders, the more successful he can hope to be in serving the special interests of his own district. A new member especially (and a substantial portion of the membership of every legislative body is always new) is helpless without the favor of the "organization." As former Speaker Smith of the New York assembly once candidly confessed: "Unquestionably no matter how able he may be, he cannot possibly understand the rules . . . in one year."[1] It is not surprising that under such circumstances members seem to be chiefly interested in special rather than in general legislation. Elihu Root declared in his valedictory address to the New York constitutional convention of 1915: "We found that the legislature of the state had declined in public esteem, and that the majority of members of the legislature were occupying themselves chiefly in the promotion of private and local bills, of special interests, . . . upon which apparently their reëlections to their positions depended, and which made them cowards and demoralized the whole body."[2] The responsibility for the action of the legislature on important matters is assumed by a few experienced leaders. The cement which holds their following together is the control of the distribution among the districts represented by their followers of public money and of special privileges of various sorts.

The principal difference between the normal and the New York systems of procedure concerns the relations between the little band of leaders. Under the New York system the leaders are more closely banded together than under the normal system. Committee chairmen are less independent of one another and are more effectually subordinated to the authority of the speaker and the committee on rules. Under the normal system the "organization" is in control, but it is loosely articulated. Under the New York system the "organization" is closely articulated. Its decisions may be swiftly formed, and promptly executed. The New York system is consequently more favorable to effective party action. Under the normal system of committee government, each committee is, as the late Senator Hoar

[1] New York Constitutional Convention of 1915, *Record*, p. 1213.
[2] *Ibid.*, p. 4458.

of Massachusetts observed a generation ago, a "little legislature" by itself. Within its special field it reigns supreme. Each decides for itself what the interests of the people and of the party require of it. Under the New York system the speaker and committee on rules make the final decision as to what the interests of the people and of the party require. In fact, in most states the interests of the parties are involved in but a very few of the measures that come before the legislatures. As has already been pointed out, the parties in America are essentially national parties. They are divided mainly upon national issues. It is difficult for them to take sides upon purely state issues. The members of most legislatures are elected upon party lines that have little connection with the bulk of the legislative business. The committees comprise members of both parties, and normally their reports reflect the compromise of various individual opinions regardless of party. The custom by which only majority party members attend committee meetings on public general bills, which is growing in Congress, has not been established in the states. In most state legislatures party measures are few, and party voting either in committee or on the floor of the two houses infrequent.[1] New York, as might be expected in view of the procedure which has developed there, is an exception to the general rule.

Party lines indeed are much less important in the state legislatures than is frequently asserted. In general the party "boss," if there be one, or the party caucus, rarely dictates the action of party members on public questions. As President Lowell of Harvard has pointed out, the "boss" usually controls only a portion of the members of the party, and is usually disinclined to meddle with general legislation. To attempt to dictate to his followers on general legislation would only weaken his authority over them. He confines his attention to the distribution of the "spoils," to laws that bear upon electoral machinery, and to such bills as affect the persons from whom he derives his revenue.

[1] See A. L. Lowell, "The Influence of Party upon Legislation in England and America," plate iv., in the *Annual Report of the American Historical Association* for 1901, i, pp. 319-542. For a more recent study of voting in the lower house of the New York legislature, see Stuart A. Rice, "The Behavior of Legislative Groups," *Political Science Quarterly*, xi, pp. 60-72 (1925). For a similar study involving twenty-one state legislatures, see Stuart A. Rice, *Farmers and Workers in American Politics* (New York, 1924).

"The very position of the boss depends upon the fact that parties exist for public objects, while he exists for private ones."[1] Parties in the state legislatures do not as a rule caucus on public questions, because they have too little cohesion. No member need feel bound by the vote of a party caucus unless he goes into the caucus and participates in the vote. No member need go into a party caucus unless he expects to be satisfied with the result. He is not so much dependent upon the good will of his nominal party associates as upon the support of his own district. Consequently the authority of the speaker, supported as it is by genuine power to reward and to punish, is far more important than that of any party caucus. But, as President Wilson said long ago: "Mr. Speaker's powers cannot be known accurately, because they vary with the character of Mr. Speaker." If a forceful presiding officer, whether in the lower house or in the senate, coöperates to the full extent of his ability with a masterful governor, a party program can be put through the house or senate with certainty and celerity. But if the presiding officers of the two houses are out of sympathy with the governor, party programs, so far as the governor may stand sponsor for them, are likely to fail. If the presiding officers of the houses are chiefly interested in private and local measures and indifferent to the common welfare, jobbery and the abuse of patronage will hold sway. In such matters party lines are of little account.

Effects of the Bicameral System.

Under either the normal or the New York system of procedure, the division of the legislature into two separate houses is one of the less important factors affecting the character of legislation. The general results of the bicameral system can be discerned from the record of legislation in the states. In Michigan, for example, during the regular legislative session of 1923, there were 342 bills introduced into the senate, and 550 into the lower house. Of the bills originally introduced into the senate 119 were killed in committee, 12 on the floor, and 53 passed that body and were killed in the other house, mostly in committee. Of the bills originally introduced into the lower house, 245 were killed in committee, 38 on the floor, while 67 which passed the house were killed in the senate, mostly in committee. The re-

[1] A. L. Lowell, *op. cit.*, p. 349.

maining measures passed both houses. The legislative record of Michigan is typical of that of most states where the normal procedure is established. It is clear that the division of the legislature into two houses is of less consequence than the division of each house into committees. Altogether 120 of the 892 measures introduced into the two houses, after having passed one house, were killed in the other. It does not follow, however, that this action was in every case in the public interest. A favorite trick of politicians who wish to avoid the adoption of popular, but to them objectionable, legislation is to procure the introduction in each house of different measures ostensibly designed to accomplish the same purpose. Each house can then pass its own measure and kill that passed by the other house. Every legislator who needs to placate public opinion in his district can vote for one of the measures and help kill the other. Thus a majority of the whole legislature can get on record in favor of the legislation without finally adopting any legislation at all. The bicameral system enables unrepresentative or corrupt legislatures to defeat by chicanery legislation which they would not have the courage to kill openly. It enables the "organization" to divide the responsibility for unpopular work between two sets of committees.

The operation of the bicameral system in New York has been made the subject of a careful study.[1] "When considering the final argument for the bicameral principle, that it serves as a check to hasty, ill-considered, and careless legislation, there is danger of becoming confused by the great mass of measures with which a legislature has to deal. There are so many bills that careful and adequate consideration is exceedingly difficult in the short period of the session, and with the many demands upon the time of most legislators. The bicameral system permits consideration by two different bodies. Two hasty considerations may not be as good as one thorough one, but they may be better than one hasty one. The effect of a second consideration is shown by the fact that 19 per cent of the bills passing one house were killed in the second, and 15 per cent of the bills passing both houses were amended in the second. However, it has been noted that most of the bills defeated were comparatively unimportant

[1] D. L. Colvin, *The Bicameral Principle in the New York Legislature* (New York, 1913).

ones. The number would probably have been considerably less if the first house had accepted full responsibility. Two considerations do not necessarily mean a double consideration. There is a tendency to assume that a subject has been considered in the other house when the consideration has been very inadequate; or sometimes one house passes a bill with the expectation that the other house will deal with it more carefully. There is frequently a shifting of responsibility. It is also customary to advance bills advocated by the party leaders. The important bills are determined upon by the party leaders and upon these the second chamber is of little additional usefulness in furnishing consideration. The present system tends to make the party boss or group of party leaders the determiners of what shall be passed, as it is the party's function to control both houses." [1]

The operation of the bicameral system in states where party organization is less coherent than in the New York legislature has never been studied with equal thoroughness. Doubtless the system operates in various ways under different conditions.[2] In many states where the normal procedure prevails, the results appear to correspond closely to those noted in the case of New York, except that the legislative machine is even less responsible than in New York. In all these states the chief barrier to the flood of bills is the system of committees. Indeed, many of the bills which are introduced are never expected to get further than the committee stage. Of the bills that are favorably reported from committee comparatively few fail to pass. In a few states, where the number of legislators and the volume of business is relatively small, the importance of the committees is less, and that of discussion on the floor of the legislative halls greater. In Arizona, for example, of the 203 bills introduced into the house during the session of 1923, only 15 were killed in committee while 90 were killed on the floor of the house and 52 in the senate. Of the 158 bills introduced into the senate, 10 died in committee, 86 were defeated on the floor of the senate, and 33 were killed in the house. With a small legislature like that of Arizona, coupled with a small volume of legislative business, the

[1] D. L. Colvin, *The Bicameral Principle in the New York Legislature*, pp. 187-188.

[2] This conclusion is verified by the *National Municipal Review's* series of articles on the state legislatures. For a recent defense of the bicameral principle, see Robert Luce, *Legislative Assemblies* (Boston, 1924), pp. 34-42.

committees are naturally of less importance. In most states such deliberate procedure is impracticable under existing conditions. Control of time and business has to be exercised by somebody. In practice it is exercised by the speaker and committee chairmen, acting as a rule less as party leaders than as mere "organization" or "machine" men. Between the interests of the party and of the "organization" there may be, and often is, a wide gap. In none of these states is the process of legislation, as President Wilson phrased it, "a straightforward thing of simple method, single, unstinted power, and clear responsibility." In all these states the division of the legislature into two separate houses makes the process of legislation less straightforward. It stints every power of the legislator except that to evade responsibility.[1]

The Need for Further Reform.

The abolition of the bicameral system and the establishment of unicameral legislatures would not of itself sufficiently improve the process of legislation.[2] It is only a single thorough consideration of measures, not a single hasty one, which can be expected to be much better than two hasty considerations. In order to secure one thorough consideration of measures, five other changes would be necessary in most states. The first is to increase the time allowed for the transaction of legislative business.[3] No leg-

[1] It might seem that the two houses would exert a more useful check upon one another in such states as Massachusetts, but in practice the system of joint committees tends to neutralize the normal effects of the bicameral system.

[2] In recent years, constitutional amendments providing for a unicameral legislature have been proposed in a number of states but no such amendment has thus far been adopted.

[3] The quadrennial session of the Alabama legislature is limited to fifty days. The difficulties involved in this constitutional limitation have been somewhat lessened by the practice of holding split sessions. Under this arrangement, the legislature meets for a few weeks, bills are introduced, and then a recess of several months is taken, after which the legislature formally re-assembles and completes the allotted fifty days. The theory of the recess is that it will enable both the legislators and their constituents to become familiar with the measures introduced. The split session of Alabama is wholly at the discretion of the legislature and is not specifically authorized by the constitution. By constitutional amendment of 1918, the Massachusetts legislature was authorized to establish split sessions but thus far the legislature has preferred to remain in continuous session. On the other hand, in California (1911) and West Virginia (1920), the split session has been made mandatory by constitutional amendment. In the opinion of Professor West, the device has been "reasonably successful" in California (see Victor J. West, "Our Legislative Mills: California—the Home of the Split Session," *National Municipal Review*, xii, pp. 369-376 (1924), but it is not certain that the same can be said of West Virginia.

islature with its session limited to forty or sixty days can ever become a genuine deliberative body.[1] The existence of the fixed time limit is a standing invitation to all those who hope to gain by avoiding due deliberation to postpone every important measure to the last minute, when deliberation is impossible. A second necessity is the adoption of rules of procedure which will ensure the careful consideration of every important measure by the main body of legislators. A combination of the rules adopted in Massachusetts to ensure the consideration of all measures by the main body of legislators and of those adopted in New York to ensure due deliberation in their proceedings would be required. Thirdly, it is necessary to keep the membership of the legislatures within the limits which permit of deliberation. Large bodies of legislators must inevitably delegate their task of deliberation to smaller bodies which can handle it. The legislature must be small enough for the whole number to be accommodated in a hall where each member can be readily heard by his associates. Fourthly, it is necessary to pay legislators a living wage. Three, four, or five dollars a day is totally inadequate compensation for men who in most cases must leave their homes and neglect their private businesses. The high cost of nominations and elections makes a bad matter worse. Unless legislators are to supplement their official wages by prostituting their public position to purposes of private gain, the only men who can afford to go to most legislatures are those so poor that they have nothing to lose or so rich that they need not care how much they lose. The substitution of a single house with a limited membership for the present arrangements would enable most states to pay their legislators a suitable salary without any increase of cost to the people.

THE PROBLEM OF LEGISLATIVE POWERS

Finally, it is necessary to limit the volume of legislative business. The work which falls upon the legislatures of most of the states is too great to permit the bulk of it to be disposed of except by summary process. The legislatures are attempting to do

[1] Even if limited legislative sessions are retained, the amount of time available for deliberation could be measurably increased by substituting electrical voting devices for the present method of roll-calls. Beginning with Wisconsin in 1915, two other states, Iowa and Texas, have adopted electrical voting.

altogether too much. Relief must be secured by the further limitation of legislative powers.

Complexity of Legislative Work.

The strictly legislative work of the state legislatures falls into four classes. The first relates to the selection of matters concerning which there shall be legislation. To a certain extent this function is assumed by the state conventions of the political parties. The party platforms generally promise legislative action on a few matters. These promises unfortunately are frequently too vague to be of much practical assistance to the legislatures. To a greater extent the state governors have assumed the function of leadership in the formulation of legislative programs. Their messages to the legislatures at the opening of the session generally contain some indication of matters to be considered with a view to action. Since the governor is armed with the appointing and veto powers, his recommendations are bound to be considered, regardless of his party affiliation. If he is disposed to make vigorous use of these powers in order to promote a legislative program of his own, he becomes a more influential legislator than any single member of the legislature itself, not even excepting the speaker. Public recognition of this fact has caused the governor to accept a responsibility, which the framers of the original state constitutions would have regarded as unconstitutional, for the action of the legislature upon the principal public issues. Executive usurpation of legislative prerogatives has been sanctioned by public opinion, because the governor has tended to stand for the interests of the state as a whole, being elected in the state at large, whilst the members of the legislatures have only too often stood for local and private interests within their several districts. The bad judgment of the legislatures in the selection of matters concerning which there should be legislative action has been one of the principal causes of that decline in the public esteem which has been noted by every critical observer of the state legislatures from the time of the Federal Convention of 1787 down to the present time.[1]

The second class of legislative work relates to the collection

[1] The contemporary attitude is evidenced by such comments as these: "Political Mess Marks Legislature's Closing," *Philadelphia Public Ledger*, April 17, 1925; "Thank Heaven It's Over," *Illinois Manufacturers' Association Bulletin*, June 25, 1925.

of the information upon which intelligent legislative action must be based. No legislator can be well informed by his own study or experience concerning more than a small proportion of the many matters which he is called upon during the course of a session to consider. The notion that legislators are omniscient citizens, who can pass judgment upon any subject after a short debate on the floor of the house, is as obsolete as powdered wigs. Like the jury, which was once composed of men who knew all about the case at bar and has come to be composed of men who know nothing about it, the legislature must now for the most part be instructed concerning the matters upon which they are to act by those who know. In default of further information, the general body of members must ordinarily accept the opinion of the committee which has the matter in charge, or of the party leaders. There are three principal methods of obtaining further information. First, in cases of unusual importance or difficulty, the legislature may appoint a special investigating committee, or authorize the appointment by the governor of a special commission to make all necessary and proper investigations.[1] Such investigating bodies may be armed with the power to subpoena witnesses, administer oaths, and take testimony generally. Secondly, the legislature may direct some administrative official or department to present a report on a designated subject. This method is appropriate in cases of ordinary importance or difficulty. In general, however, the legislatures rely mainly upon the third method. This method, in many states not formally recognized at all, is that commonly called lobbying.

The lobby is the collective name for the men and women who make it their business to instruct members of the legislature.[2] Not all lobbyists are undesirable factors in the legislative process. Persons seeking to influence the course of legislation may be animated by the most disinterested motives. Their assistance may be invaluable to conscientious legislators in search of reliable information about pending measures. Chambers of commerce, boards of trade, employers' associations of various kinds, trade unions and labor organizations of various kinds, farmers'

[1] See Luce, *Legislative Procedure*, pp. 175-180.

[2] For a woman's criticism of "respectable lobbying" by women's organizations, see George Madden Martin, "The American Women and Representative Government; an Evolution of the Lobby," *Atlantic Monthly*, cxxxv, pp. 363-371 (1925).

alliances, and philanthropic societies, as well as business corporations and private interests, send their representatives to the halls of legislation. Lobbyists, however, do not ordinarily engage in this business merely as a pastime. Their professional success depends in the long run, no matter whom they may serve, upon the fate of the measures they are engaged to promote or oppose. Their advantages over the ordinary private member are very great. Being either past members of the legislature, or at least experienced in legislative work, they know the rules better than he. Being picked men, they are either abler or more unscrupulous than he. Being personally interested, they are far better informed on the subject than he. Being supported in many cases by powerful business organizations, they are not unlikely to be more influential with the legislative "organization." By collusion with the leaders they may compel the ordinary members to support their measures. Or they may compel the leaders to support their measures by manipulation of the ordinary members. Even without actual corruption, the lobby may easily exercise an undue influence upon the course of legislation. In fact, with or without the use of corrupt practices, the lobby has exercised an undue influence upon legislation, and the knowledge of this fact is the second of the principal causes for the decline of the state legislatures in public esteem.

The third class of legislative work relates to the drafting of bills.[1] With respect to the former classes of legislative work the failure of the legislatures is to a certain extent a matter of opinion. With respect to the drafting of legislation their incompetence is plainly recorded in the statute books. Crude, almost illiterate, legislation is constantly coming to light through the proceedings of the state courts; laws which cannot be intended to mean what they say, and laws which mean nothing, are not uncommon. A regulation found in the road law of one state that no one shall operate a political steam roller or band wagon on the highway doubtless was put there in jest, but there is nothing funny about a provision, found in the same state, that proprietors of hotels shall keep the walls and floors of their rooms covered with plaster. In Massachusetts, where things are supposed to be done better, one legislature, in trying to prevent the display of the red flag of anarchy upon the highway, succeeded in forbidding

[1] See Luce, *Legislative Procedure*, ch. xxiv, "The Wording of Laws."

Harvard students from carrying their college banner to the football field. The most astonishing revelation is contained in an address of a former governor of Kansas. "Notwithstanding the fact my executive clerk and the attorney-general did their best to scrutinize all the bills, chapters 177 and 178, and chapters 174 and 175, respectively, are duplicates. Chapter 75 of the laws of 1911 was repealed three times. . . . Chapter 318 of the laws of 1913 was immediately amended by chapter 319 of the laws of 1913. Chapter 82 of the laws of 1911 was repealed by section 7 of chapter 89 of the laws of 1913, and after being repealed was then amended and repealed by chapter 108 of the laws of 1913."[1] "What is commonly called the *technical* part of legislation is incomparably more difficult than what may be called the *ethical*. In other words, it is far easier to conceive justly what would be useful law than so to construct that same law that it may accomplish the design of the lawgiver."[2]

The fourth class of legislative work relates to the actual consideration and enactment of legislation. This class of work is, indeed, the prime function of legislative bodies. But the task of considering proposed legislation has been largely delegated, as the study of legislative procedure shows, to the committees. The final enactment of laws, though formally executed by the whole body of members, in many cases amounts to little more than the registration of the decision previously reached by the legislative "machine." Where the legislative "machine" is also to a sufficient extent a partisan machine, as in New York, such a practice is not wholly irresponsible. But where the legislative machine cannot be successfully identified with anything which can be brought to account by the state electorate as a whole, as is the case in most states possessing the normal type of procedure, such a practice is highly irresponsible. It readily lends itself to the control of legislation by the "invisible government." It is not surprising, therefore, that much legislation has been enacted by the state legislatures, which the people did not want and which was not in their interest, and much legislation has been defeated, which the people did want and which would have been in their interest. The irresponsibility of the legislatures in the

[1] Address of Governor Hodges before the House of Governors, Colorado Springs, August 26, 1913.

[2] Quoted from John Austin by Governor Hodges in the address cited above.

consideration and enactment of legislation is the final cause of their decline in public esteem.[1]

The Necessity of Relief from Non-Essential Work.

The decline of the state legislatures in public esteem, as has been shown, began at the very beginning of the independence of the states. It has proceeded ever since without any interruption. The methods which have hitherto been employed to check that decline [2] have failed to accomplish their purpose. The limitation of legislative procedure by constitutional provisions has generally been beneficial so far as it has gone. But it cannot go far enough to afford an adequate remedy. The limitation of the forms of legislative action must be supplemented by the chastening of its spirit. The limitation of legislative powers has mitigated a number of specific evils. But such a remedy is necessarily imperfect. It throws a burden upon the constitution-amending organs, the conventions and electorates, which those organs were not designed to bear. It cannot prevent the legislatures from all wrongdoing without preventing them from doing anything at all. It is a remedy that cures disease only by killing the patient. The object of legislative reform should be, not to prevent the legislatures from legislating badly, but to permit them to legislate well. Upon this principle the limitation of the length of legislative sessions is manifestly unsound. That extreme remedy has in fact, as has been shown, merely aggravated the evil. Legislation is a necessary function of the state. There can be no better organ of legislation in a populous state than a rightly organized representative legislature. But the existing legislatures cannot be expected to rehabilitate themselves so long as they remain overburdened with non-legislative duties. The most promising method of restoring the legislatures to their

[1] The evidence of recent dissatisfaction with the work of the state legislatures is abundantly set forth in the writings of those political critics who have collectively come to be known as "muckrakers." The classic period of "muckraking" extended from 1904, the date of publication of Lincoln Steffens's *The Shame of the Cities*, to 1910, when Speaker Cannon of the national House of Representatives was deposed from the chairmanship of the Committee on Rules. The work of the "muckrakers" was of very unequal value, and much of it was ephemeral. A well-balanced, though unduly pessimistic, criticism of the state legislatures, antedating the era of "muckraking," is E. L. Godkin's "The Decline of the State Legislatures," in *Unforeseen Tendencies in Democracy* (N. Y., 1898).

[2] See *ante*, ch. v.

rightful place in public esteem is to relieve them of such classes of work as are not inseparable from the consideration and enactment of laws, and permit them to concentrate their powers upon the performance of their proper duties.

The first three classes of legislative work described above are necessary preliminaries to the work of legislation, but they are not inseparable from it. The selection of the matters concerning which there shall be legislation has already, to a slight extent, been taken out of the hands of the legislatures. The process can be further extended. Party initiative in state legislation may be encouraged and party responsibility made more effective by the separation of state from national party organization. Executive initiative may be encouraged by a readjustment of relations between executive and legislature. Executive responsibility may be made more effective by a reorganization of the executive branch of the state governments. These suggestions will be discussed more fully in later chapters. The collection of information also has already to some extent been taken out of the hands of the legislatures. This process likewise can be further extended. The appointment of special investigating commissions where special investigations are necessary, the assistance of the permanent administrative officers in matters subject to their jurisdiction, the support of legislative reference libraries[1] for the supply of general information: these are means of procuring information which are coming more and more to be freely employed. In particular, legislative reference agencies are now well established institutions in a great majority of the states.[2] The technical part of legislation, the drafting of bills, has been improved in some states by the employment of professional draftsmen, usually in connection with the legislative reference libraries.[3] This should be done in all states. As John Stuart Mill wisely said: "There is hardly any kind of intellectual work which so much needs to be done not only by experienced and exercised minds, but by minds trained to the task through long and laborious study."[4] Few members of the state legislatures

[1] Charles McCarthy, *The Wisconsin Idea*, pp. 214-218. See also, F. C. Howe, *Wisconsin, an Experiment in Democracy*, p. 47.

[2] See John A. Fairlie, "Legislative and Municipal Reference Agencies," *American Political Science Review*, xviii, pp. 303-308 (1923).

[3] See Nebraska Legislative Reference Bureau, Bulletin No. 4, *Reform of Legislative Procedure and Budget in Nebraska*, pp. 24-26.

[4] J. S. Mill, *Representative Government*, ch. v.

are adequately prepared to do this kind of work. None should be needlessly burdened with it.[1]

Regulation of the Lobby.

The most difficult of the problems that must be solved, if the legislatures are to regain their rightful prestige, is that created by the pernicious activities of the lobby.[2] With the growing recognition of the legitimate functions of the lobby, doubtless the pernicious activities are less pronounced than formerly but the problem is still far from solved. Many just indictments have been drawn of the insidious and corrupting influence of unscrupulous lobbyists. It is enough to cite one of the most deliberate of these indictments. Said Governor Russell of Massachusetts in a message to the legislature of that state: "There exists in this state, as in other states, an irresponsible body known as the lobby, representing or preying upon special interests, which professes and undertakes for hire to influence or control legislation. Its work is wholly distinct and different from advocacy of one's cause in person, or by counsel or agent, which is the constitutional right of every one. It seeks often to control nominations and elections, and to subject the legislator, directly or indirectly, to secret and improper influences. It throws suspicion upon the honest and temptation in the way of the dishonest. Professing greater power than it has, it frequently extorts money as the price of its silence or unnecessary assistance. It has initiated legislation, attacking the interests of its clients in order to be hired to defend those interests. It has caused the expenditure of large sums of money to obtain or defeat legislation. It cares little for the merits of a measure or the means employed to make it successful. In my judgment improper measures have, by its influence, been made law, against the public interest, and just measures have been defeated. These criticisms have not been based upon rumor or conjecture, but upon facts reported after most thorough investigation by your

[1] For a general discussion of the topics treated in the above paragraph, see Luce, *Legislative Procedure*, ch. xxv, "Help for Lawmakers." See also Ernst Freund, *Standards of American Legislation*, especially ch. vii (Chicago, 1917).

[2] See Luce, *Legislative Assemblies*, ch. xvii, "The Lobby."

predecessors, who denounced the evil in unsparing terms and diligently sought a remedy."[1]

It is far easier, as Governor Russell candidly confessed, to state the evil than to suggest the remedy. "Clearly it is impossible and improper to prevent a constituent or any other person from having the freest access to a legislator. This constitutional right guaranteed to the people gives opportunity to the lobby to do its work. Prevention by non-intercourse is therefore impossible."[2] Prevention by publicity is constitutionally possible. Indeed provision had already (1890) been made in Massachusetts for the publication of the names of lobbyists and the sums of money paid to them. This act for the regulation of the lobby was based upon a distinction between different kinds of lobbyists. Lobbyists employed merely to appear before legislative committees and make oral arguments were denominated legislative counsel. Lobbyists employed not only to make oral arguments before committees but also to interview individual legislators were denominated legislative agents. Legislative counsel and agents, before doing any lobbying, were required to register their names on separate lists with the sergeant-at-arms, stating the names of their employers and the titles of the bills in connection with which they were employed. Within thirty days after the close of the session legislative counsel and agents were required to file separate statements, showing the total sums of money received as compensation for their services. Their employers were likewise required to report the sums of money paid to lobbyists for the purpose of influencing legislation. Governor Russell believed that good would come from this act, if fairly and thoroughly enforced, but that it fell short of being a sufficient remedy. It would make public the names of hired lobbyists, but not in the case of "agents" the nature of their activities.

[1] Message to Legislature, January, 1891. Reprinted in P. S. Reinsch, *Readings on American State Government*, p. 79. See also "Report of the Committee to Investigate Methods used for and against Legislation concerning Elevated Railroads and to inquire into the Conduct of Members of the House in connection therewith, with the Evidence taken at the Hearings of the Committee and Arguments of Counsel." *Massachusetts Legislative Documents*, House No. 585, 1890. This committee recommended the enactment of a law for the regulation of the lobby, which was done. This report can be matched by similar reports and findings in every part of the Union. The best known of these, and the most instructive, is the report of the Hughes investigation into the political expenditures of life insurance companies in New York, 1905.

[2] *Ibid.*

It would make public the expenses incurred, but too late to affect the legislation in connection with which they were incurred.

Experience has shown that Governor Russell's opinion of the Massachusetts act for the regulation of the lobby was sound. The mere registration of the names of lobbyists amounts in itself to little. It enables the press to know more readily who are employed to influence legislation, and by whom. The legislators themselves are likely to know this anyway in every case in which the agent would be willing voluntarily to reveal the identity of his principal. Every year after the close of the session, too late, as Governor Russell pointed out, to affect legislation, the public is furnished with a quantity of obsolete information concerning the revenues of the members of the lobby. But no more is known than before about the use to which the lobbyists devoted their revenues. The means of checking up untruthful returns are inadequate, and in general the enforcement of the act leaves much to be desired. Like the early legislation designed to prevent corrupt practices at elections by publicity of campaign funds, the Massachusetts law to regulate the lobby is a good deal of a sham. Governor Russell suggested that it be strengthened by empowering some public officer, before a measure finally becomes law, to demand under oath a full and detailed statement concerning the expenditure of money by lobbyists and their employers; but this has never been done. The Massachusetts plan for the regulation of the lobby has been adopted in a few states,[1] but in general the regulation of corrupt practices in connection with legislation is left mainly to the courts.

The courts have shown themselves unable to cope with the situation. They have recognized that it is the right of every citizen who is interested in any proposed legislation to employ a paid agent to collect evidence and facts, to draft his bill and explain it to any committee or to any member thereof or of the legislature fairly and openly; and that lobbyists' services which are intended to reach only the reason of those sought to be influenced are not improper, provided that the lobbyists' agency is disclosed. Contracts for secret lobbying and personal solicitation have generally been held to be illegal, but the evils of lobby-

[1] See M. A. Schaffner, *Lobbying* (Comparative Legislation Bulletin, No. 2, Legislative Reference Department, Wisconsin Free Library Commission).

ing are little affected by making certain lobby contracts illegal and void. Such contracts become subjects of litigation only when the system of lobbying is imperfectly organized. The real menace arises when principal and agent work harmoniously together against the public interests for private ends.[1] The late Robert M. LaFollette, when governor of Wisconsin, was the most conspicuous among a group of reformers who urged more drastic legislation against the lobby.[2] Governor LaFollette's suggestion was that hired lobbyists should be forbidden to attempt personally and directly to influence any member of the legislature to vote for or against any measure affecting the interests represented by such lobbyist. He believed that "every legitimate argument which any lobbyist has to offer, and which any legislator ought to hear, can be presented before committees, before the legislators as a body, through the press, from the public platform, and through printed briefs and arguments placed in the hands of all members and accessible to the public." To permit more than that, he urged, gives an undue advantage to the interests that can afford to maintain a permanent lobby throughout the session, to say nothing of the temptation to corruption inseparable from any system which permits personal solicitation of legislators by lobbyists. LaFollette's suggestions were, in the main, adopted and embodied in the Wisconsin act of 1905.[3]

The Need for Further Limitation of Legislative Powers.

The legislature cannot reform the lobby, unless it first reforms itself. Doubtless the state legislatures are now on the whole somewhat less venal than a generation ago. Observers who have been in the best position to know say so.[4] Certainly not a little has been done by the legislatures in recent years tending to correct some of the worst abuses. The adoption of laws or rules

[1] See Marshall *v.* Baltimore and Ohio Railroad, 16 Howard, 314, and Trist *v.* Child, 21 Wall, 441. But cf. Foltz *v.* Cogswell, 86 Cal., 542, where "honest personal solicitation" is held not to be illegal.

[2] See his Annual Message to the Legislature of 1905. A special message of the same governor, dealing more fully with the same subject, is reprinted in Reinsch's *Readings on American State Government*, pp. 81-84.

[3] For detailed accounts of the working of the lobby system, see Lynn Haines, *The Minnesota Legislature of 1909*, and *The Minnesota Legislature of 1911*, and F. Hichborn, *Story of the Session of the California Legislature of 1909*, and the same, 1911, and 1913.

[4] Perhaps as good an opinion as any on this matter is that of Theodore Roosevelt. See his *Autobiography*, pp. 76 ff.

forbidding members of the legislature to accept fees for their advocacy of measures before legislative committees has corrected a gross abuse in many states. The adoption of anti-pass laws, designed to prevent the railroads from furnishing legislators with free transportation, has struck a heavy blow at a principal source of the undue influence of the railroad lobby.[1] The better regulation of nominations and elections has tended to make more difficult one of the methods employed by lobbyists for influencing the action of legislators. The establishment of public service commissions, with jurisdiction over the rates and services of railroads and public utilities, has mitigated another evil. It has not only relieved the legislatures of the responsibility for the details of regulation. It has also, so far as such corporations are concerned, deprived dishonest legislators of any reasonable pretext for the introduction of "strike" legislation, that is, of bills not intended to be passed but merely to serve as a means of extortion from the corporations. The further development of reliable administrative agencies for the regulation of corporate affairs, where the regulation of technical details is necessary, will do much to diminish the opportunity for corruption in legislative bodies.

If the state legislators are more honest than was formerly the case, are they likewise more able than in times past? It must frankly be admitted that no satisfactory answer can be given to this question.[2] If the occupations of the individual members are examined, it will be found that the professions, especially the lawyers, are predominant, and that other groups and divisions of the population are under represented. In the agricultural states a good many farmers get into the legislature, especially the lower house, but industrial wage-earners are everywhere conspicuously scarce.[3] On the basis of their educational attain-

[1] For an interesting revelation of another side of the evil of free passes, see a letter from an official of the Pennsylvania Railroad to the president of the New York State Constitutional Convention of 1894, a dozen years before the enactment of the anti-pass laws, reprinted in C. A. Beard, *Readings in American Government and Politics*, pp. 478-481.

[2] For a defense of legislators, see Luce, *Legislative Assemblies*, ch. xiv; for a scathing but overdrawn denunciation, see H. L. Mencken, "Politics" in *Civilization in the United States; an Inquiry by Thirty Americans* (New York, 1922).

[3] The lower house of the Pennsylvania legislature of 1925 contained 41 lawyers, 18 clerks, 17 merchants, 13 farmers, 12 manufacturers, 8 contractors, 6 publishers, 5 insurance men, 5 realtors, 5 physicians, 5 "retired,"

ments, the state legislators, while not usually men and women of marked distinction, are, nevertheless, well above the general average of the people as a whole. If the legislators seem lacking in ability and are inefficient, the fault lies chiefly with the legislative system and not with the personnel.

No scheme for the restoration of legislative prestige is worth much which does not attempt to make the legislative system more efficient. Much of the work now attempted by the state legislatures is work for which large representative bodies are not fitted.[1] No inconsiderable portion of the output of legislation, so-called, consists of measures of an administrative or quasi-judicial character. Practically all private and local legislation is of this character. Fully half the time of the legislative committees is devoted to the consideration of such measures. In states like Massachusetts, where there are comparatively few restrictions upon legislative powers and procedure, hundreds of bills are introduced every year on such petty matters as, for example, whether John Smith, having been discharged for cause, shall be reinstated in the Boston Fire Department.[2] In states like New York, where legislative powers and procedure are more strictly limited by the constitution, the situation is scarcely less discreditable.[3] Such constitutional limitations as those providing that only one subject shall be contained in any one bill, and that that subject shall be clearly expressed in the title, tend to diminish the opportunity for legislative corruption. But they do little to increase legislative efficiency. Such constitutional limitations as those providing that legislatures shall not legislate at all on certain subjects make more work for constitutional conventions and state electorates. But they do not help the legislatures to act more wisely upon those matters which are left to legislative discretion. The most promising plan for the

8 bankers, 3 salesmen, 3 managers, 3 teachers, together with 20 other occupations having one or two representatives each. The women members included a farmer, an insurance broker, a housekeeper, and three housewives.

[1] See (*Illinois*) *Constitutional Convention Bulletins*, No. 8, "The Legislative Department," pp. 527, 578, 587 (Springfield, 1919).

[2] See *Bulletins for the* (*Massachusetts*) *Constitutional Convention*, No. 34, "Special Legislation" (Boston, 1918).

[3] From 1899 to 1920 inclusive, the New York legislature enacted 15,585 laws. Of this number, 8093 were special or local in character. In 1923, the legislature of Florida enacted 246 general acts and 658 special and local acts. In the same year, the legislature of Tennessee enacted 122 "public" acts and 711 "private" acts. The private acts filled two stout volumes containing 1400 and 1169 pages respectively.

further improvement of the character of legislation is the adoption of such further limitations on legislative powers and procedure as, without restricting the scope of legislative action, will permit the more systematic use of administrative and quasi-judicial methods and machinery in the process of legislation.

CHAPTER X

THE STATE EXECUTIVE

The progress of democracy during the first half of the nineteenth century, as has been shown, had two principal effects upon the development of the state executive. The first was the establishment of executive independence of the legislature. The second was the decentralization and disintegration of the executive. The direct popular election of the principal executive officers made them more independent of the legislatures than they ever could have been under the original system of legislative election. The abolition of executive councils chosen from and by the legislatures further secured the independence of the executive. The direct popular election of the principal executive officers, however, at the same time that it rendered them more independent of the legislatures, also rendered them more independent of one another. The governor, secretary of state, treasurer, attorney-general, and other central officers became supreme, each in his own department. They became severally and equally responsible to the people. In a word, the executive branch of the state governments became what is technically known as a plural executive. The direct popular election of subordinate and local administrative officials produced a similar effect. The sheriff, county clerk, county treasurer, prosecuting attorney, and other similar officials became supreme, each in his own department. They became severally and equally responsible to the people. Thus the state executive was decentralized as well as disintegrated. By the middle of the nineteenth century this process had gone as far as it could in most states. There remained few important administrative offices, either central or local, which were not filled by popular election.

THE DISORGANIZATION OF THE EXECUTIVE

Primary Effects.

The effect of executive decentralization and disintegration during the first half of the nineteenth century was to make the governor the chief executive in name only. The strictly executive powers originally conferred upon him, as has been shown, were not great. He could command the militia. Beyond that, he could do nothing without calling a meeting of his council. With the advice and consent of his council, he could appoint all officials not elected by the legislature or by the people, and in general could order and direct the affairs of state according to the constitution and laws. His principal duty was to take care that the laws were properly enforced. To this end he could direct his attorney-general to prosecute offenders. In case of need he could also call out the militia. But his main reliance for the enforcement of law was placed in the sheriffs and justices of the peace. By the appointment of vigilant and energetic sheriffs and of prudent and independent justices of the peace he could secure a spirited and efficient administration. Now the developments of the first half of the nineteenth century left him practically no means of enforcing the laws except by calling out the militia. This was too drastic a weapon for ordinary use. The direct election of subordinate and local administrative officials deprived the governor of his control over the executive branch of the government. The attorney-general, and especially the sheriffs and local prosecutors, became the real executives, so far as responsibility for the enforcement of the laws was concerned. The governor had ceased to be much more than a figurehead in the conduct of state administration.

The effect of executive independence of the legislature was to increase the importance of the legislative functions of the executive. This was inevitable under the circumstances. The direct election of the governor by the people made him the most conspicuous representative of the whole people. The development of the party system made him the most important party leader holding office in the state government. The development of the veto power made him a member of the law-making organ of the state. The disorganization of the executive branch of state government left him no effective means of controlling his nominal subordinates except through the enactment of special legislation. Executive orders had to be issued in the form of statutes. Since the people were prone to hold the governor responsible for the enforcement of law, despite the weakness of his position as an administrative officer, he was inevitably driven to employ his legislative authority for purely administrative purposes. Since the rank and file of the party were prone to hold the governor responsible for the redemption of the promises in the party platform, despite the nominal separation between legislative and executive powers, he was inevitably driven to employ his legislative authority also for purely legislative purposes. In states where the veto power reached its fullest development, a governor gifted with the qualities of leadership was not only a member, but the most powerful single member, of the legislative branch of the government. In short, the office of governor was removed from the field of administration to the field of legislation. The governor was transformed from a chief executive into a chief legislator of the state.

Secondary Effects.

The transformation of the governor into a legislator left the political party as the principal bond of union between the different members of the executive branch of the state governments. This bond was totally inadequate for the purpose of enforcing a systematic and efficient conduct of affairs. Candidates for state and local administrative offices on the same party ticket were bound to make common cause with one another during the campaign. After election, however, their community of interest centered around the problem of reëlection rather than around the work of public administration. Party ties had their place in purely political affairs, but except for the governor the administrative officers had no legitimate connection with affairs of that nature. State or county administrative officers might form rings for their mutual political benefit, but they rarely formed rings for the benefit of the public. Between state and local officials, party ties as such were of even less use in promoting systematic and efficient administrative action. The local officials were primarily responsible to the party only within their own localities. Under such circumstances the party could serve as an instrument of administrative organization only in so far as there was an extra-legal party organization to which partisans in public office could be held responsible. The leaders of the party organizations, the "bosses," whether or not also the occupants of the principal executive offices, were the men who could exert most influence upon the course of administration. But such influences, as has been pointed out, were more commonly exerted for private than for public ends. In general, the state or local official who was elected by the people was left free to determine for himself how the duties of his office should be performed. The disorganization of state administration was in striking contrast to the centralization and integration of party management.

The principal force making for unity and coherence in the conduct of state administration was the judiciary. As early as 1830, De Tocqueville with his usual sagacity detected the importance of the judiciary in administrative affairs. Noting that "there is no point which serves as a center to the radii of the administration," he inquired: "How then can the government be conducted on a uniform plan? and how is the compliance of the counties and their magistrates, or the townships and their officers, enforced?" His answer was: "The courts of justice are the only possible medium between the central power and the administrative bodies; they alone can compel the elected functionary to obey, without violating the rights of the elector. The extension of the judicial power in the political world ought, therefore, to be in the exact ratio of the extension of the elective power: if these two institutions do not go hand in hand the state must fall into anarchy or into servitude."[1] The courts of justice, however, could only command the administrative officer to perform acts required of him by law, in cases of negligence on his part, or enjoin him from performing acts not authorized by law, in cases of usurpation of power on his part. They could not compel him to do with energy and zeal what he was inclined to do listlessly and with indifference. They could not compel him to act at all in cases where action or inaction was a matter of administrative discretion. The courts themselves could not act upon their own motion, but only upon the suit of a citizen or another administrative officer, or upon presentment or indictment by a grand jury. The courts could at most produce compliance by particular administrative officers with the letter of the law governing their particular offices. They could not produce spirited and efficient coöperation between the various members of the administrative branch in general. By the middle of the century, after the adoption of the direct

[1] De Tocqueville, *Democracy in America,* i, ch. v.

popular election of judges, they themselves had become responsible to the same electorates as the administrative officials. The extension of the judicial power in the political world, as De Tocqueville would say, was no longer in the same ratio as the extension of the elective power.

It must not be supposed that the results of this administrative anarchy were very injurious to the public. Under the conditions that then existed they were not. In the middle of the nineteenth century there was little need for an elaborately organized administrative system under the direct control of the state governments. For the most part the federal government had undertaken the services which could not well be performed by the local authorities in towns and counties. It was an individualistic age. Every man was taught to look to the courts for the protection of his personal rights, and to the legislatures for the redress of general grievances. Little was expected of the administrative branch of the state government, and that little was done tolerably well. Politicians able to procure their nomination and election to state administrative offices were necessarily men of some initiative and resourcefulness. Men who lacked those qualities were not likely to shoulder their way to the front. In addition to initiative and resourcefulness, common honesty was the principal qualification for holding such offices. The burden of administration fell upon the local authorities, and so long as the requirements of local administration were not too technical, they were capable of giving satisfactory service. As De Tocqueville very justly observed, the administrative effects of the decentralized system of administration were of less consequence than the political.[1] Popular elections and rotation in office gave many citizens an opportunity to participate in the actual conduct of affairs. If their work was not done so well as it might have been by professional administrators, at least it was their own, and they loved it. The people had an affection for such a system, which they could not have felt so strongly for one more efficient but imposed from above. That affection was diffused over all the agencies and processes of government; the citizen was warmly attached to the state, and proud of it as a bigger and better self.

[1] De Tocqueville, *Democracy in America*, i, ch. v.

The Need of Executive Reconstruction.

Before the process of democratizing and thus disorganizing the executive branch of the state governments had been completed, a need for the reconstruction of the executive began to develop. The first cause of this new development was the impulse to state enterprise resulting from the success of the Erie Canal and the refusal of the national government, after the accession of the Jacksonian Democracy to power, to undertake internal improvements at national expense. A more profitable field for state enterprise in most states was presently found in the development of free public education, and later of the higher education. Both DeWitt Clinton and Horace Mann inspired many imitators. With the coming of the railroad the policy of internal improvements at state expense was generally abandoned, but the policy of state enterprise in the field of education has become more firmly established with the passage of the years. A second cause was the growth of new forms of industry and of industrial organization requiring a radical extension of the police power of the state. The development of banking and insurance, of railroading and the supply of monopolistic public services of various kinds, compelled the individual to look to the state for active assistance by special administrative officials in order to prevent irreparable frauds and oppressions. The local officials could not, and the courts did not, afford the protection that was needed. The growth of the factory system of industry and the development of a permanent wage-earning class of large dimensions has forced a corresponding growth of a new social conscience, and the development of new instrumentalities for the maintenance of social and industrial justice. The advancement of science brought a new knowledge of methods of conserving human and natural resources, and created a demand for the services of experts in public health administration, in the supervision of industry, and in the promotion of agriculture. The local governments could not afford to employ such experts. The organization of expert service by the state became necessary and proper. Above all, the progress of humanity brought a demand for better care for defectives, dependents, and delinquents. More ample provision and more specialized treatment were demanded for the sick and the insane, for the aged and the destitute, for the petty offenders and the criminals. The state has assumed to an ever-growing extent the support of charities, hospitals, and corrections. In a word, "the old order changeth."[1] A new age dawns. The people of the states feel new responsibilities and demand new instrumentalities for their discharge.

The most conspicuous sign of the new age was the growing number of separate state administrative agencies. In Massachusetts, one of the first states in which the tendency towards the development of new administrative agencies appeared, the process began in 1837 with the establishment of the state board of education. The office of bank commissioner was established in 1838, the state board of agriculture in 1853, the office of insurance commissioner in 1855, the state board of charity in 1863, the office of tax commissioner in 1865, the commission on fisheries and game in 1866, the state board of health, the railroad commission, and the bureau of labor statistics in 1869, and the office of corporation commissioner in 1870. Since then the creation of new offices, boards, and commissions has proceeded apace. Before the consolidation of 1919, there were more than one hundred separate administrative agencies of the central government charged with the direct enforcement of law or with the supervision of the activities of local administrative authorities.[2] In Illinois, prior to enactment of the civil administrative code in 1917, there were also more than one hundred separate state offices, boards, and commissions, created by statute, in addition to those created by the constitution. Less than a fourth of these statutory bodies were created before 1870 and more than a third were created between 1900 and 1915.[3] In New York, there were in 1925 nearly two hundred separate state administrative agencies.[4] A similar but less numerous

[1] See the very interesting and suggestive book, bearing that title, by William Allen White (New York, 1909). For a more complete and scientific statement, see Herbert Croly, *The Promise of American Life* (New York, 1909). See also Walter E. Weyl, *The New Democracy* (New York, 1912).

[2] See Report of the Massachusetts Commission on Economy and Efficiency on the Functions, Organization, and Administration of the Departments of the Executive Branch of the State Government, 1914.

[3] See Report of the Illinois Efficiency and Economy Committee, 1915, p. 7.

[4] See Report of Reconstruction Commission to Governor Alfred E. Smith on Retrenchment and Reorganization in the State Government (Albany, 1919), and Report of the State Reorganization Commission (Albany, 1926). The latter was prepared by a commission under the chairmanship of Charles E. Hughes at the instance of the Legislature. See *post*, Appendices E and F, for extracts from these two important documents.

multiplication of agencies has taken place in other states so that to-day there is no state where the organization of the executive branch of the government retains its early nineteenth-century simplicity.

A less conspicuous but more important sign of the new age was the growing tendency to increase the powers, both direct and supervisory, of the state administrative agencies. This tendency towards the centralization of power will be considered in the following chapter, where the present relations between the central and local administrative authorities in the principal departments of state administration are examined.

Another significant sign of the new age was the economy and efficiency movement, which culminated in administrative reorganization and budgetary reform. Logically carried out, these reforms greatly strengthen the power of the governor. Hence, they may conveniently be discussed in connection with an analysis of the position and authority of the governor, first, in matters of state administration, and second, in his relations with the legislature.

THE GOVERNOR AS CHIEF EXECUTIVE

By the middle of the last century the governor had practically ceased to be the chief executive in the governments of the states. The process of decentralizing and disintegrating state administration had gone as far as it could. Moreover, the development of new agencies of administration at first had little effect in strengthening the power of the governor, since he was not usually authorized to make appointments to the newly created offices. In the middle of the nineteenth century there were in most states no offices of importance not filled by election, either by the legislature or by the people. However, as the number of administrative officials and boards continued to increase, this situation began to change. Legislative selection became more and more discredited and was largely superseded by popular choice or by gubernatorial appointment. Popular election in turn brought with it the "long ballot" and placed an undue burden upon the electorate. The logic of events favored a growth of the governor's appointing power so that more and more important administrative positions came to be filled by the designation of the governor.

Nevertheless, the increase in the number of such appointive officers did not bring a corresponding increase in the administrative importance of the governor. Several obstacles tended to prevent the governor from becoming the real executive head of the state. In the first place, his power of appointment and removal was not made commensurate with his nominal responsibility for the conduct of state administration; secondly, in many states, the governor was hampered by an unduly short term of office; and, finally, the administrative services of the state were not correlated and integrated into a single harmonious system.

Power of Appointment and Removal.

The power to appoint and remove subordinate administrative officers is one that would seem most necessary and proper for a chief executive as a means of controlling and directing the administration.[1] It has never been fully conferred, however, upon the governors of the states. This fact was well brought out by a survey made in New York ten years ago.[2] At that time, there were, in addition to popular election, at least sixteen different ways of appointing the heads of state departments, bureau chiefs, and other principal officeholders and members of commissions. Of those appointed directly by the governor, some were appointed by him alone, others only with the advice and consent of the senate. Of the department heads and major officials holding office in 1915, just about one-half were appointed by the governor with the advice and consent of the senate. Only five department heads, beside the governor, were elected by the people. In most states a much larger proportion of the total number of department heads are elected by the people. However, in four states,[3] the governor is now the only state executive officer elected at large. The tenure of office of department heads is almost as various as the manner of appointment. In New York,[4] some officials hold office for a fixed term coin-

[1] With reference to minor officials and employees, the appointing power should be restricted by adequate civil service regulations. See *post*, ch. xi.

[2] See New York Bureau of Municipal Research, *The Constitution and Government of the State of New York*, charts i, ii, iii, and iv.

[3] Maine, New Hampshire, New Jersey, and Tennessee.

[4] The above lines with reference to New York were written before the adoption of the consolidation amendment in November, 1925. Enabling legislation to carry out the amendment will doubtless produce some changes in the methods of appointment and removal.

ciding with that of the governor, a larger number for a fixed term not coinciding with that of the governor, and in many cases exceeding that of the governor in length. All these officials may be removed by impeachment and some in no other way, though all who hold offices created by ordinary law may be legislated out of office by so-called "ripper" bills, which destroy the office in order to get rid of the incumbent. Some may be removed by the governor at will, others upon the preferment of charges deemed by the governor sufficient to justify removal, others only after a public hearing upon such charges, others only upon recommendation by the senate, others by some other method not subject to the control of the governor. Altogether, there are at least seven different methods, besides impeachment, of removing department heads and other principal officials. Less than half of the total number may be removed by the governor upon his own individual responsibility. In other states the situation is much the same. Under such circumstances, the actual chief executive is not the governor but the multitude of department heads, bureau chiefs, and other principal officeholders, and members of boards and commissions.

Although there are various methods of appointment now in use in the states, the one most generally prevalent, so far as important officials are concerned, is that of executive nomination subject to senatorial confirmation. The rule of senatorial confirmation dates back to the beginnings of the state governments when the early distrust of executive power resulted in the requirement that gubernatorial appointments be approved by the executive council. With the adoption of the practice of electing the principal executive officers directly by the people, with the general acceptance of the doctrine of checks and balances and the consequent transfer to the state senates of the authority to confirm nominations to inferior offices, so far as these were not vested in independent department heads, the governor's power of appointment declined to a minimum. Under such conditions the maxim, "To the victor belong the spoils," was more than a candid confession of faith by politicians flushed with success at the polls. It was a fair statement of the normal operation of the constitutional arrangements for filling administrative offices under the state governments. So far as concerns those offices which are filled by popular election, the maxim was obviously sound. The spoils, that is, the offices, certainly fell into the hands of the successful candidates. In the middle of the nineteenth century, the principal state offices were of that character. The distribution of these "spoils" was directly controlled by those who controlled the nominating machinery of the political parties. Thus the leaders of the party organizations acquired the habit of looking upon all the patronage as theirs to be used for the good of the organizations. Having "had enough experience in politics to know how valuable workers are when the campaign is on and how difficult it is to find suitable rewards for all the deserving," it was natural to use what little patronage there was at the disposal of the elective state officials to reward "deserving" party workers.[1] In short, the appointing power came to be intimately associated with the organization of parties and the conduct of elections.

Patronage and the "Invisible Government."

The power of appointment consequently tended to fall into the hands of the leaders of the party organizations. It is not difficult for the party leaders to control appointments vested in minor elective state officials, wherever they can control the nomination of such officials. To control the appointments of the governor, however, it is necessary to control a majority of the confirming body, the state senate. As a state organization comprises the district leaders in the senatorial districts, the leaders of a state organization are likely to control the senate whenever their party is in power. Thus a party leader need not himself be governor in order to control the distribution of the patronage. Indeed, the separation of party leadership from official administration has been one of the most conspicuous features of the traditional system of state politics. Under such a system the interests of "organizations" are not identical with those of the parties for which the organizations assume to act, just as the interests of parties are not identical with those of the people as a whole. When party organizations are managed primarily in the interests of the leaders or "bosses," that is, when corrupt "machine rule" prevails, the interests of the bosses of the two

[1] See Letter of W. J. Bryan to W. W. Vicks, American Collector at San Domingo, August 20, 1913.

major parties become fundamentally identical.[1] "The most undesirable bosses do not hold the offices which they control, yet they really form the all-powerful invisible government which is responsible for the administration and corruption of the public offices of the state."[2] Bipartisan "machine rule" seems to have prevailed at times in more than one state. In general, however, the power of a boss, whether he be a desirable or an undesirable boss, is indeterminate, depending much on the personalities of the official and unofficial leaders. It is, on the whole, exceptional for a single boss to hold undisputed sway, or to hold any sway for long. The power is more commonly divided among several leaders, and the limits of their power and the duration of their tenure are ill-defined.

The Authority of the "Bosses."

The manner in which a well-defined boss system operates with respect to executive appointments was clearly brought out by the evidence in the Barnes-Roosevelt libel case. Roosevelt testified that, when governor, he habitually consulted Senator Platt, the Republican state boss, before making appointments. In recommending men for appointment to positions allotted to the minority party, the evidence showed that Platt in his turn was accustomed to consider the wishes of Croker, the Democratic boss. When asked why he consulted Platt, Roosevelt answered that he had to, if he wanted to have his nominations confirmed. *Question:* "That is, you had to be in alliance with the invisible government, so-called, to get the nominations confirmed?" *Answer:* "To get the nominations confirmed I had to have the support of the senate, and the senate was responsive to Mr. Platt's wishes." Ordinarily Roosevelt made no appointments of any kind, even those not dependent upon senatorial confirmation, until he had ascertained that they would not be objectionable to the boss. Yet Roosevelt was not a subservient governor. In Senator Platt's autobiography, published five years before the Barnes-Roosevelt trial, it is stated that "Roosevelt had from the first agreed that he would consult me on all questions of appoint-

[1] It was Theodore Roosevelt's charge that the interests of the Republican leader Barnes and the Democratic leader Murphy were fundamentally identical, which led to the libel action of Barnes *v.* Roosevelt, tried at Syracuse, N. Y., in April and May, 1915.

[2] Quotation from the alleged libelous speech by Roosevelt.

ments. . . . He religiously fulfilled this pledge, although he frequently did just what he pleased. . . . Roosevelt told me, for instance, that he proposed to remove Lou Payn. I protested, but he was removed, and I was consulted about the appointment of his successor."[1]

Broadly speaking, there are three types of state governor. First, there are those who humbly accept the leadership of the heads of the party organization and dutifully perform their part in the operation of the "machine." Secondly, there are those who recognize the power of the organization but treat a boss as an associate rather than as a master. Thirdly, there are those who seek themselves to become bosses. These types, however, are not always clearly defined. Sometimes the same governor appears in one character at one time, in another at another. In short, the actual relations between governors and legislatures in the matter of appointments are exceedingly uncertain and obscure. In general, however, the power of appointment, subject to senatorial confirmation, seems to be a source of weakness rather than of strength to state governors. So long as these conditions persist, it is scarcely possible for the governor to be in full measure the responsible, directing head of the administration.

The Need of Longer Terms for Governors.

But even if full power of appointment and removal were conferred upon the governor, it does not necessarily follow that he would thereby become the efficient head of an efficient administration. In more than one-half of the states, the gubernatorial term of office is fixed at two years. This period is altogether too short to achieve satisfactory and permanent results in administration.[2] Of course, such a defect may be partially offset by reëlection for one or more additional terms. Reëlection is a fairly common practice in some states but in others, particularly those which are classed as "doubtful," it is much less certain. In those states, the continuity of administration may be seriously disturbed by the frequent alternation in power of the parties.

[1] See *Autobiography of Thomas Collier Platt*, compiled and edited by Louis J. Lang, pp. 374-375. See also Harold F. Gosnell, *Boss Platt and His New York Machine*, ch. viii.

[2] See Report of the **(New York) State Reorganization Commission** (Albany, 1926), pp. 5, 6.

The present tendency is to increase the governor's term of office to four years. By thus lengthening the term, the chief executive will be enabled to devote more attention to the development of administrative leadership since he will be relieved of the burden of conducting a biennial campaign for reëlection.

The removal of the present restrictions on the appointing power and the lengthening of the term of office will do much to develop the administrative authority of the governor. But unless these reforms are accompanied by a thoroughgoing reorganization of the numerous existing administrative agencies, they will fall short of accomplishing their purpose. The necessity for this third reform produced the recent movement for administrative reorganization.

The Need of Administrative Reorganization.

As a result of the development of new administrative agencies during the period from 1850 to 1915, the executive branch of state government became an exceedingly complicated mechanism. The various parts of the mechanism were created at different times in a haphazard fashion to deal with new economic and social problems or merely to provide "spoils" for faithful party workers. The larger problem of securing a proper correlation of the various agencies was almost completely neglected by the legislature until that problem became so pressing that it could no longer be avoided. The consequences of this long continued process of multiplying independent offices, boards and commissions became more and more apparent as time went on. There was waste and inefficiency due to the duplication of efforts and the overlapping of functions. Responsibility was diffused and effective control, whether by the legislature, the governor, or the people, was rendered extremely difficult. Moreover, the cost of maintaining the ever-expanding administrative services of the state resulted in a heavier and heavier burden of taxation. Public officials found themselves in a dilemma. On the one hand, the citizens as users of the public services continued to demand that the state undertake new functions, and enlarge and extend the old; on the other hand, the citizens as taxpayers complained more and more loudly at the growing expense of government. These conditions were not peculiar to the state governments but appeared to a greater or less degree in all governmental units, especially in the cities.[1] The rise of large-scale industry produced somewhat analogous problems in the business world and led to a quest for greater efficiency. In short, the time was ripe for the beginning of a new science of administration both in the field of industry and in that of government.

The science of business administration in the United States is largely a development of the period since 1903 when Frederick W. Taylor first announced the principles of scientific management. A similar development of the science of governmental administration may be said to date from the establishment of the New York Bureau of Municipal Research in 1906. This bureau was a conspicuous leader in the great movement of the past two decades designed to place the administrative branch of federal, state, and local governments upon a more efficient and economical basis.[2] The New York Bureau met such a need and was so successful in its work that other bureaus of like character were established in various parts of the country. The value of these private research organizations for the scientific study of administrative and other governmental problems was so apparent that they were soon supplemented by temporary or permanent public agencies supported at public expense. One of the earliest and most important of these was President Taft's Efficiency and Economy Commission, organized in 1910 under the chairmanship of Dr. Frederick A. Cleveland. In more than a third of the states, beginning with New Jersey in 1912, similar official investigating bodies have since been appointed. Thus the next decade was an era of efficiency and economy commis-

[1] The magnitude and urgency of American municipal problems made city government one of the first objects of reform and reconstruction. The advent of the commission form of government in 1901 marked the end of the "Dark Ages of American municipal history" and the beginning of the "Municipal Renaissance." See W. B. Munro, *Municipal Government and Administration*, i, ch. v (New York, 1923).

[2] It should also be kept in mind that the cause of scientific public administration has been greatly aided by the writings of scholars and publicists such as F. J. Goodnow, J. A. Fairlie, and Herbert Croly, by the increasing attention given to courses in administration in colleges and universities, and by the efforts of many civic, philanthropic, and professional organizations such as the National Municipal League (1894), the American Association for Labor Legislation (1907), the National Tax Association (1907), etc. See W. F. Willoughby, "The Modern Movement for Efficiency in the Administration of Public Affairs," written as an introduction to Gustavus A. Weber, *Organized Efforts for the Improvement of Methods of Administration in the United States* (New York, 1919).

sions.[1] Out of their investigations came the parallel movements for administrative reorganization and for budget reform,—movements which have been outstanding developments in state government during recent years.

The Program of Administrative Reorganization.

Postponing for later consideration the question of budget reform, it may now be asked what the program of administrative reorganization involves. As the movement has progressed, certain general principles have been evolved, which have been well summarized by a recognized authority on the subject.[2] In the first place, all administrative agencies should be consolidated into a few orderly departments, each comprehending a major function of government such as finance, education, or public works. The internal organization of each department should be such as to allow closely related activities to be grouped under appropriate bureaus and divisions. Secondly, definite lines of responsibility should be established for all administrative undertakings. Each department should be headed by a single official appointed and removed at the discretion of the governor and hence responsible to the governor who in turn is responsible to the people for the entire state administration.[3] A similar re-

[1] See Raymond Moley, *The State Movement for Efficiency and Economy* (New York, 1918); see also Gustavus A. Weber, *op. cit.*

[2] See A. E. Buck, "Administrative Consolidation in State Governments," National Municipal League pamphlet (3d ed., 1924), pp. 3-4. There is a vast body of literature on administrative reorganization and consolidation. Current developments are usually noted and discussed in the *American Political Science Review* and the *National Municipal Review*. Of special importance is the pamphlet by A. E. Buck, cited above, which is brought down to date by his article, "Recent Steps toward Administrative Consolidation in State Governments," *National Municipal Review*, xiv, pp. 672-680 (1925). See also John M. Mathews, "State Administrative Reorganization," *American Political Science Review*, xvi, pp. 387-398 (1922). For an acute criticism of the principles of administrative reorganization and of their application, see F. W. Coker, "Dogmas of Administrative Reform," *ibid.*, pp. 399-411.

[3] The application of this principle would result in electoral as well as administrative reform since it would introduce the "short ballot." The governor and an independent auditor or comptroller would be the only elective executive officials; even in the case of the auditor, provision might be made for his appointment by the legislature. The National Short Ballot Organization (now merged with the National Municipal League) was founded in 1909 to champion the following principles: (a) Public offices should not be filled by popular election unless they are important enough to attract public attention, *i.e.*, unless they are policy-determining offices. Since the governor is the only policy-determining official in the state executive, it follows that

sponsible relation should be maintained between the department head and his bureau and division chiefs. Interdepartmental coöperation should be secured through the medium of the governor's cabinet, a body consisting of the department heads and advising the governor in administrative and financial matters. Thirdly, the term of office of the principal administrative officials should be coördinated with that of the chief executive. It is desirable that such officials be designated to serve at the governor's pleasure, but, if this is not politically practicable, then their terms should not be longer than that of the governor, who should be elected for a four-year period and should be eligible for reëlection. However, for members of boards or commissions having quasi-legislative, quasi-judicial, or advisory powers, where continuity of personnel is of importance, it may be preferable to provide for longer and overlapping terms. Finally, boards or commissions should not be used for purely administrative work, but where quasi-legislative, quasi-judicial, advisory, or inspectional functions are involved, a board may advantageously be attached to the department to perform such functions.[1]

It was one thing for efficiency and economy commissions to propose a thorough-going reorganization and consolidation of administrative agencies on the basis of the above principles,—and, in fact, some of the investigating commissions made no such comprehensive proposal. It was quite another thing to secure the legislation necessary to put a reorganization plan into effect. Legislators and politicians hesitated to make changes which might unfavorably affect the supply of party patronage. Office-holders feared that their positions and power might be abolished or curtailed. The strengthening of the governor's appointing power was looked upon with real or feigned suspicion and the old dread of executive tyranny and iniquity was re-affirmed.

he should be elected and the rest appointed. (b) Very few offices should be filled by election at any one time so as to permit adequate and unconfused public examination of the candidates. Short ballot reform is thus designed both to lighten the electorate's burden and to secure a better integration of the administrative services, but the emphasis is placed upon the former object.

[1] For a further discussion of this topic, see *post*, ch. xi. See also Appendix E. Governor Lowden of Illinois (1917-21) did much to popularize these principles. Cf. Frank O. Lowden, "Reorganizing the Administration of a State," *National Municipal Review*, xv, pp. 8-13 (Jan., 1926).

In particular, the abolition of the ancient practice of senatorial confirmation was regarded with disfavor and distrust. Considering the bad character of some of the recent state governors, this desire to retain a check upon the appointing power of the chief executive was not based solely upon reasons of prejudice or patronage. If the governor is to be made the real head of the administration with a lengthened term of office, then more effective ways than now exist for holding him responsible will have to be devised.[1] Furthermore, the problem was not simply one of persuading the legislature to pass the necessary consolidation bill. In most states, complete reorganization was not possible without constitutional amendment,—a fact which proved a substantial barrier, particularly in those states where the amending process is difficult.

The Practice of Administrative Reorganization.

Confronted with such obstacles, it is not surprising that the movement for administrative reorganization has thus far failed to reach all, or even a majority, of its objectives. There is great variation from state to state in what has been done, but existing schemes of reorganization may usually be classified under one of three heads: (1) piecemeal consolidation, (2) reorganization without materially increasing the power of the governor, and (3) reorganization designed to make the governor more clearly the head of the state administration.[2]

First in point of time came consolidations of previously independent agencies functioning in the same field. At a relatively early period, the policy of having a separate and independent managing board for each of the charitable or correctional institutions of a state was recognized as unbusinesslike. To secure better coördination, general supervisory boards, and, later, central boards of control were created. Thus the Massachusetts state board of charities, established in 1863, was given a general power of supervision over the state institutions.[3] From supervision, it was but a short step to substitute single for multiple management. The principle of single management is exemplified

[1] See *post*, ch. x.

[2] W. F. Dodd, *State Government*, pp. 246 ff.

[3] R. H. Whitten, "Public Administration in Massachusetts," *Columbia University Studies in History, Economics, and Public Law*, vii, pt. 4 (1898), p. 45.

in the Iowa board of control which was set up in 1897 to take over the functions of the various separate boards which had previously administered the thirteen charitable institutions of the state.[1] Similar consolidations were made in many other states. A like process went on in other fields, particularly in those relating to labor and agriculture. In 1901, New York consolidated the work of the bureau of labor statistics, the board of mediation and arbitration, and the department of factory inspection under a single commissioner; and by further legislation enacted in 1913 and 1915, the labor agencies of that state were brought under a department of labor, headed by an industrial commission. In much the same way, consolidated labor departments under industrial commissions were created in Wisconsin (1911), Ohio and Pennsylvania (1913), and Colorado (1915).[2] Desirable as these consolidations were, they did not go very far in reorganizing state administration. The problems of interdepartmental relations and of responsibility to the governor were but little affected. Moreover, since the legislature at each session was apt to create more new bodies than it consolidated or abolished existing ones, the number of administrative agencies continued to grow. Until the era of efficiency and economy commissions, consolidations everywhere were of this piecemeal and fragmentary character. In short, the problem of administrative reorganization had not yet been envisaged as a whole by legislators and by the general public.

The New Jersey Type of Reorganization.

As a result of the investigations of the various efficiency and economy commissions, the policy—if such it may be called—of piecemeal consolidation tended to be enlarged into that of general administrative reorganization. As noted before, in some states, a more or less general reorganization was carried out without strengthening the power of the governor to any extent; in other states, reorganization resulted in a substantial increase of the governor's authority and control over the state administration. Of the states in the first category, New Jersey affords

[1] H. M. Bowman, "The Administration of Iowa," *ibid.*, xviii, pt. 3 (1913), p. 112.

[2] John R. Commons and John B. Andrews, *Principles of Labor Legislation* (rev. ed., New York, 1920), p. 472.

a striking illustration. A partial consolidation was put into effect in New Jersey by laws enacted in 1915, 1916, and 1918. This legislation established consolidated departments of commerce and navigation, conservation and development, taxes and assessments, shell fisheries, labor, agriculture, institutions and agencies (i.e., charities and corrections), and fish and game.[1] Most of these new departments are headed by a board rather than by a single official and, in some cases, the boards are required to be bipartisan in personnel. The members of the various boards are appointed by the governor with the advice and consent of the senate for overlapping terms which are usually longer than the three-year period for which the governor is elected. For example, the board of conservation and development consists of eight members, "not more than four of whom shall be members of the same political party." This board is a continuous body; its members are appointed for a four-year term and two retire each year.[2] Since the governor may not remove board members from office, it is obvious that with senate confirmation and the bipartisan requirements, the mere power of appointment for a term longer than his own gives him little control over the department. The chief executive officer of the board is the director of conservation and development who is appointed by the board but who may be removed by the governor after a hearing, "provided, that charges against him have been submitted in writing, signed by a majority of the members of the board; and provided further, that the governor find such charges to be true in fact; and their nature such that, in his opinion, the best interests of the state demand the removal of said executive."[3] What is true of the department of conservation and development is true of most of the other departments. In the case of the state board of agriculture, gubernatorial appointments are limited to persons nominated by certain organizations. The department of labor, however, is headed by a single commissioner chosen by the governor for a five-year term with the confirmation of the senate.

[1] The department of conservation and development is a consolidation of six previously separate agencies, the department of shell fisheries of seven, and the department of commerce and navigation of four. The other departments likewise represent consolidations of two or more agencies.

[2] New Jersey *Session Laws*, 1915, ch. 241.

[3] *Ibid.*, sec. 10.

It is apparent that reorganization in New Jersey has been in the direction of creating a group of administrative commissions substantially independent of any one governor. The result is that the governor continues to be the chief executive in name more than in fact. A further barrier to gubernatorial control of administration in New Jersey is to be found in the budget act adopted in 1916.[1] In some states, as will be pointed out later,[2] budget reform legislation has been of great assistance in strengthening the administrative power of the chief executive, but this is not the case in New Jersey. There, the legislature is free to disregard the governor's budget recommendations if it chooses, and in practice it does so freely. The executive veto, which includes the item veto, may be set aside by a majority vote in each house, which makes it difficult for the governor to defend his estimates against legislative increases. It, therefore, avails little for the governor to attempt to control a department by scaling down the appropriations requested by that department. Moreover, after the general appropriation bill has been enacted, the governor has little supervision over the funds thus voted. He is not authorized to permit transfer of items within appropriations granted to any department; this power is conferred upon the state house commission consisting of the governor, state treasurer, and state comptroller, the two latter officials being chosen by the legislature. The state house commission also has control over the distribution of the emergency funds[3] and supervises the work of the state purchasing agent. However, the purchasing agent is appointed by the governor with the consent of the senate for a term of five years and is removable by the governor at any time for the non-performance of his duty.

While the framers of the New Jersey reorganization legislation were not willing to make the governor the coördinating, responsible head of the administration, they realized that a certain amount of interdepartmental coöperation was desirable. Hence,

[1] *Session Laws*, 1916, ch. 15.

[2] See *post*, ch. x.

[3] For example, the legislature of 1925 appropriated an emergency fund of $250,000 to "meet any conditions of emergency until legislation appropriate therefor shall be enacted." New Jersey *Session Laws*, 1925, ch. 237. Disbursements from the emergency fund may be made only upon the written authority of each and every member of the state house commission.

it was provided by law [1] that there should be a monthly meeting of executive officers representing six named departments together with the representatives of such other agencies as the governor might designate. The governor was made ex-officio member and chairman of this group. The group was empowered to make recommendations to the legislature for the purpose of promoting efficiency and preventing duplication, especially in the engineering work of the state. Departmental coöperation was also facilitated by a law permitting the interchange of expert personnel and special apparatus between departments, provided that temporary transfers of "loans" of this sort could be made without detriment to the work of the lending department. The same law likewise provided that "two or more departments may unite in coöperative work in lines germane to the duties of said departments and the heads thereof may agree between themselves for the distribution of the expense to be incurred." [2] This last provision is made easier to accomplish because the legislature allowed the departments considerable flexibility in determining their own internal organization and arrangement of activities. To refer again for illustration to the department of conservation and development, the board of conservation and development is granted power to create bureaus and divisions, to appoint chiefs of such agencies, and to fix the salaries of all employees. Any unnecessary office or position may be abolished by the director of conservation and development with the approval of the board. A number of the other reorganized departments possess similar powers.

The above description of administrative reorganization has been given in some detail because it exemplifies a type of consolidation which, although containing desirable features, does not increase the governor's executive authority. No other state has gone as far as New Jersey in this direction, but in Wisconsin and Michigan the administration is organized upon somewhat similar principles.

The Illinois Type of Reorganization.

The third type of administrative reorganization and the one most comprehensive in scope is that which is designed to make

[1] *Session Laws*, 1915, ch. 190.
[2] *Ibid.*, 1916, ch. 49.

the governor more clearly the directing head of an integrated administrative system.[1] The first state to introduce this type was Illinois, where, following the very able report of the efficiency and economy committee in 1915 and under the energetic leadership of Governor Frank O. Lowden, the "civil administrative code" was enacted in 1917.[2] The code provided for the abolition or absorption of more than one hundred statutory agencies and consolidated their functions under nine departments, as follows: finance, agriculture, labor, mines and minerals, public works and buildings, public welfare, public health, trade and commerce, and registration and education.[3] In spite of the sweeping changes which were made, the reorganization was not complete. The code, being merely a statute, naturally had little effect on the status of the various offices provided for in the constitution, such as the secretary of state, auditor of public accounts, treasurer, superintendent of public instruction, and attorney-general who continued to be elected. Moreover, there were over twenty statutory bodies which were not, and, up to

[1] There is a fourth type of administrative reform which has been adopted in a number of states. This plan does not involve a consolidation of existing agencies, but it does seek to strengthen the administrative authority of the governor. For example, in 1911, California created a state board of control of three members who were to be appointed by the governor without the consent of the senate and who were to serve at the pleasure of the governor. (*Session Laws*, 1911, ch. 349.) The state board of control was intended to be the instrument by which the chief executive might supervise the state administration. It was empowered to examine the books and records of all state agencies, to require reports from such agencies, to visit and inspect the state institutions, to approve warrants drawn on the state treasury, to hear claims against the state and to report to the legislature as to whether or not such claims should be allowed, to establish a uniform accounting system for state offices, boards, and departments, and to approve contracts for the purchase of supplies. With the consent of the governor, the board was authorized to create deficiencies. Thus, without a consolidation of existing agencies, the governor's administrative power was strengthened through the creation of a general supervisory body which was placed completely under his direction. In passing, it should be mentioned that, under the consolidation plan adopted in 1921, the state board of control became the head of the newly created department of finance. Boards similar to the one established in California in 1911 have also been set up in Alabama, Kansas, North Dakota, West Virginia, and a few other states.

[2] *Session Laws*, 1917, "The Civil Administrative Code," pp. 2-36; see also John M. Mathews, "Administrative Reorganization in Illinois," *National Municipal Review*, ix, pp. 737-756 (1920); A. E. Buck, "The Illinois Civil Administrative System," *ibid.*, xi, pp. 362 ff. (1922); Frank O. Lowden, "Reorganization in Illinois and Its Results," *Annals*, cxiii, pp. 155-161 (1924).

[3] There are now eleven code departments, the 1925 legislature having created a department of conservation and a department of purchases and construction. *Session Laws*, 1925, pp. 585-600.

the present, have not been included in or attached to one of the code departments. In this class are the trustees of the University of Illinois, the civil service commission, the adjutant general and the national guard, the legislative reference bureau, and the state library.[1]

Each code department is headed by a single director appointed by the governor, subject to confirmation by the senate, for a term of four years coinciding with that of the governor. Each director has under him an assistant director and various bureau chiefs, also appointed by the governor and senate, although under the immediate control of the department head. For the performance of quasi-legislative or quasi-judicial duties, salaried boards are provided, the members of which are appointed by the governor with the senate's approval. Their terms of office are likewise four years, except in the case of the tax commission and the normal school board where six-year overlapping terms obtain. In all cases, these boards are attached to the appropriate code departments; for example, the industrial commission is attached to the department of labor, the commerce commission (the state regulatory body for public utilities) to the department of trade and commerce, and the food standards commission to the department of agriculture. Although these commissions have been nominally departmentalized, each of them is in fact largely independent of control by the director of the department to which it has been allocated. They are, however, under the general financial supervision of the director of finance, since the code provides for an extensive system of financial and budgetary control. To assist the directors and the governor in determining questions of policy, unpaid advisory boards are also provided in six departments. But these advisory commissions have no power over actual administration and full responsibility rests squarely on the department heads.

With reference to the internal organization of the reorganized departments, the Illinois plan is very similar to that used in New Jersey except that the former does not empower the departments to create and abolish bureaus and divisions. Although the Illinois code does provide for the principal subordinate offi-

[1] The elective state board of equalization was abolished in 1919 and was replaced by a state tax commission which was attached to the department of finance.

cers within the departments, it does not attempt to define the exact duties of such officers. These duties, together with the distribution and performance of departmental business, are covered in detail by rules formulated by the several directors.[1] Likewise, each department may appoint its necessary employees, subject to the state civil service regulations, and may determine their compensation in cases where it is not already fixed by law.[2] Other sections of the code prescribe the standard working day, the number of hours per day during which each office shall keep open for public business, etc.

The Illinois code also deals with the problem of interdepartmental relations. It is provided that "the directors of departments shall devise a practical and working basis for coöperation and coördination of work, eliminating duplication and overlapping of functions. They shall, so far as practicable, coöperate with each other in the employment of services and the use of quarters and equipment."[3] Under certain circumstances, the departments may require necessary assistance from each other and a department head may, with the consent of the superior officer of the employee, request an employee of another department to perform any duty which he might assign to his own subordinates. Moreover, the department of finance is authorized to "investigate duplication of work of departments and to formulate plans for the better coördination of departments."[4] Since the law specifies that all directors shall have offices in the state capitol building, the governor is enabled to keep in close personal touch with the activities of the code departments and to organize the directors into a cabinet if he chooses to do so. The code contains other important provisions in addition to those already discussed. Thus, provision is made for a centralized purchasing system, for a uniform accounting system, and for an executive budget. These provisions will be considered in subsequent pages.[5]

Results of Administrative Reorganization.

The Illinois civil administrative code was not only the first comprehensive plan of administrative consolidation but, with the possible exception of Tennessee, it has continued to be the most

[1] Code, sec. 16.
[2] *Ibid.*, sec. 20.
[3] *Ibid.*, sec. 26.
[4] *Ibid.*, sec. 36, par. 15.
[5] See *post*, ch. x, xi.

comprehensive plan in actual operation. The movement for administrative reorganization has now reached a point where twelve other states,—Idaho, Nebraska, and Massachusetts in 1919, Washington, Ohio, and California in 1921, Maryland in 1922, Pennsylvania, Tennessee, and Vermont in 1923, Minnesota and New York in 1925,—have introduced more or less comprehensive reorganizations of the third, or Illinois, type. The Massachusetts, California, and Maryland reorganizations are the least comprehensive of the group and have been criticized as being merely "paper consolidations." Except in Massachusetts and New York, the administrative changes in the states mentioned above rest upon a statutory basis rather than upon constitutional amendment. In Massachusetts, a constitutional amendment adopted in 1918 merely directed the legislature to organize the administration into not more than twenty departments.

Of much greater importance was the reorganization amendment adopted in New York in November, 1925. This amendment had had a long and interesting history, dating back to the proposals made by Governor Charles E. Hughes in 1910.[1] It provided for the consolidation of the administrative agencies of the state into not more than twenty departments and also shortened the ballot by abolishing the elective offices of secretary of state, state treasurer, and state engineer. The legislature may reduce the number of departments below twenty, but may create no new departments. When new functions are undertaken, they are to be placed under one of the existing departments. With certain exceptions, the heads of all departments are to be appointed by the governor subject to confirmation by the senate. In order to work out the details of the reorganization, an unofficial commission of fifty-six leading persons from all parts of the state and representing various interests was organized under the chairmanship of Charles E. Hughes. This commission reported a notable plan to the 1926 legislature.[2]

Significant features of other administrative reorganizations might well be noted, if space permitted; but even a brief descrip-

[1] On the history of reorganization in New York, see F. C. Crawford, "New York State Reorganization," *American Political Science Review*, xx, pp. 76-79 (1926).

[2] See Report of the State Reorganization Commission, February 26, 1926. Legislative Document (1926), No. 72. See also *post*, ch. xvi, and Appendix F.

tion of what has been done in the other states which have followed the example of Illinois is impracticable. Without further description, therefore, we may inquire concerning the result of all these changes and consolidations. It must be frankly admitted that what has thus far been accomplished is only a small portion of what remains to be done. The administrative branches of many state governments are still substantially unreformed and even in states like Illinois and Tennessee, where reorganization has gone furthest, there are conspicuous omissions and defects. The question then is, has state administration been improved and rendered more efficient and economical by such consolidations as have been put into effect? The answer to this question will depend upon many factors such as the thoroughness of the reorganization scheme, the character and ability of the administrative personnel and especially of the governor, the presence or absence of other related reforms such as the executive budget system, adequate civil service regulations, the centralized purchasing of supplies, etc. After a due allowance is made for these factors, the consensus of opinion among careful students is that administrative reorganization and consolidation have generally produced increased efficiency and economy, although the increase has probably not been so great as some of its advocates had anticipated. A second result has been to strengthen the administrative power of the governor in those states where reorganizations of the Illinois type have been put into effect. An important beginning has thus been made in creating a real chief state executive, to whom all departments may be subjected and department heads held responsible. But if the governor's authority is thus increased, ought not additional means to be provided for holding him responsible for the use of his authority? This fundamental question cannot be answered until the relations between the executive and the legislature have also been examined.

THE GOVERNOR AS CHIEF LEGISLATOR

The change in the character of the office of governor, resulting from the reformation of the original state governments and the redistribution of powers among their several branches, has brought about a corresponding change in the normal relations between the executive and the legislature. By the middle of the nineteenth century, as has been indicated, the governor had been shorn of most of his administrative responsibilities and had become primarily a legislator. The subsequent development of new agencies of administration in response to changing social and economic conditions, until the recent consolidation movement, did not operate to restore the administrative character of the gubernatorial office. It rather tended to enhance the importance of the governor's legislative powers, and to diminish the gap that once was supposed to separate the chief executive from the legislature.

The Executive Veto.

The principal source of the present legislative authority of the governor is the veto power. In 1923, when forty-four legislatures met in regular or special sessions, more than eleven hundred separate bills and more than one thousand parts of bills were disapproved by the executive.[1] In the forty-four states, about 7 per cent of the total number of bills submitted to the governors were vetoed. This percentage does not include the bills which were negatived in part. The use of the veto was very much greater in some states than in others. The governor of California disapproved 411 measures out of the total of 890 acts passed by the legislature and he also vetoed or reduced 49 items of appropriations. In New York, 196 bills out of 1098 and 18 items, and in New Jersey, 78 out of 251 bills were the objects of executive disapproval. At the other extreme there were two vetoes in Florida and Vermont, three in Massachusetts, and four in Iowa. Doubtless many factors affect the use of the veto by the state governors, but the most important is the nature and scope of the constitutional provisions conferring the power. Vetoes are in general effective. Comparatively few measures are re-enacted by

[1] Owing to the lack of complete records, the authors were not able to determine the exact number of separate bills and resolutions which were vetoed. The available data indicate that 1120 measures were disapproved in their entirety, but the total number was probably over twelve hundred. The total number of parts of bills which were negatived amounted to 1041. With few exceptions, these parts consisted of items of appropriation which were vetoed or reduced. However, in Washington, the governor may disapprove sections in bills other than appropriation acts and there were ten such sections eliminated by the executive in 1923. In Oregon, the governor may negative emergency clauses and thus preserve to the people the right of popular referendum if they care to exercise it; in 1923, one emergency clause was thus stricken out.

the legislatures after they have been returned without the approval of the executive. In 1923, there were only eleven states out of the forty-four in which any bills or parts of bills were passed over the governor's veto. Out of a total of more than eleven hundred acts disapproved, 104, or 9 per cent, were overridden by the legislatures; out of the 1041 parts of measures negatived, 40, or about 4 per cent, were restored by the legislatures. Most of the unsuccessful vetoes occurred in four states, in each one of which there was a pronounced lack of harmony between the executive and legislative branches.[1]

The effectiveness of the veto power as a means of executive control of legislation is increased by the rules adopted in many states governing the use of the so-called "pocket" veto. By the Federal Constitution the President is allowed ten days in which to examine congressional enactments and affix his signature to those he approves. A bill becomes law without his approval, if he fails to return it within that period to the house in which it originated with a statement of the reasons for his disapproval. But if Congress adjourns within ten days after sending a bill to the President, and his signature is not affixed before adjournment, the bill does not become law. Failure on the part of the President to sign such a bill before the adjournment of Congress operates therefore as an absolute veto, and is called the "pocket" veto. A similar rule existed in many of the states and was found to work badly. Because of the constitutional limitations upon the length of legislative sessions and practice of adopting most legislation in the closing days of the session, the governors had insufficient time in which to examine the bills submitted to them for

[1] Four states,—Kansas, Maine, New Jersey, and Ohio,—contributed 85 out of the 104 unsuccessful vetoes. In Ohio, Governor Donahey wielded the veto "axe" so vigorously that he received the sobriquet "Veto Vic." The percentage of vetoes over-ridden in 1923 was somewhat larger than is usually the case. For example, in 1915, out of a total of 1066 bills which were disapproved in whole or in part, only 22 were re-enacted.

The relative effectiveness of the veto power in different states is shown in the following table.

		Total Bills Vetoed	Total Bills Passed Over Veto	Total Parts Vetoed	Total Parts Passed Over Veto
Pennsylvania	(1899–1919 inclusive)	1396	0	2588	0
New York	(1900–1920 inclusive)	4083	2	2401	4
Massachusetts	(1900–1918 inclusive)	205	31	Not authorized.	
South Carolina	(1900–1920 inclusive)	112	25	134	81
Washington	(1901–1921 inclusive)	87	22	147	23

approval. Consequently they were forced either to sign many bills which, could they examine them with care, they would veto, or else to run the risk of "killing" measures which might on careful examination prove unobjectionable. In order to remove this difficulty, many states have provided that bills shall become law unless vetoed by the governor within a specified period after the adjournment of the legislature. This period extends from five days in several states to thirty days in Pennsylvania and a few others. Such a rule gives the governor more opportunity to examine the legislative output and enables him to exercise his absolute veto more deliberately and confidently. In a few states, notably New York and California, the governor's power is even stronger. He is allowed thirty days for the examination of bills enacted at the close of the session, and no bill becomes a law unless signed by him within that period. In such states the governor sits after the close of the legislative session practically as a third chamber. He grants hearings to advocates and opponents of measures which have received legislative approval, refers legal and financial questions to his attorney-general or other advisers, and in general does what he can to determine for himself whether the measures adopted by the legislature should be enacted. In such states as New York, Pennsylvania, and California, the legislative output is so great that even in thirty days the governor cannot examine it all for himself. He must delegate a part of the task to others, organize a council of revision, so to speak, and rely in many cases upon the advice of his informal councilors. Thus ancient practices reappear under modern forms.

Effect of Development of Veto Power.

The increase in the effectiveness of the veto power has reacted upon the general position of the governor and his relation to the legislature. His influence over legislation is much greater than is indicated by the number of bills actually vetoed by him. Many bills which it is known the governor will not approve will not be adopted by the legislature, or will be amended in the hope of removing the grounds of executive disapproval.[1] Legis-

[1] Bills which have passed both houses and have been transmitted to the governor are frequently recalled by the legislature by means of a concurrent resolution. In some cases, the recall is suggested by the governor in order to avoid a formal veto, or to secure the incorporation of amendments favored

lators may even support measures known to be favored by the executive in order to avoid executive disapproval of private and local bills in which they may be especially interested. Since the effectiveness of the veto power is a matter of common knowledge, the promoters of legislation often seek executive approval for proposed legislation before its introduction into the legislatures. The governors are induced, if possible, to endorse important projects of legislation in their annual messages to the legislatures, or to assist them by sending in special messages. The executive messages are looked to by the people of the states as legislative programs, and consequently exert a greater influence upon the course of legislation than any speeches that may be pronounced by ordinary members on the floor of either house. Members are prone to look to the governor not only to outline the legislative program, but also to prevent the adoption of undesirable legislation which it may be inconvenient for them to defeat. This shifting of responsibility has gone so far in some states that the governor exerts a more powerful and beneficial check upon legislation adopted by both houses than either house does upon that adopted by the other. This seems to be the case, for example, in New York.[1] In California, an instance is recorded where the legislature passed two contradictory bills dealing with the same subject, with the expectation that the governor would approve the better of the two and disapprove the other.[2] In short, the veto power, especially in the states where it exists in its most effective form, has enormously enhanced the authority of the governor in his dealings with the legislature.

The growth of the legislative authority of the governor has

by the executive, or merely to give the governor more time to consider the measure in question. Moreover, the haste with which the legislature works often makes it necessary to recall bills upon its own initiative. The recall is wholly an extra-legal device since the governor is not legally bound to comply with such a resolution, and the legislature is under no legal obligation to adopt a recall resolution at the suggestion of the governor.

In Alabama, Virginia, and Massachusetts, the executive is authorized by the constitution to return bills to the legislature with proposed amendments in lieu of vetoing them outright. The effect of this provision has been to reduce the number of vetoes. In Alabama, from 1903 to 1915, 27 acts were negatived before adjournment while 156 acts were returned by the governor with proposed amendments; in only six cases were these amendments rejected.

[1] See D. L. Colvin, *The Bicameral Principle in the New York Legislature*, p. 112.

[2] See P. S. Reinsch, *American Legislatures and Legislative Methods*, p. 284.

been accompanied by a change in the conception of the office itself. Originally the governor was armed with the veto power primarily in order that he might protect his own office and the executive department generally against legislative encroachments. It seems to have been anticipated that such encroachments were most likely to come in the form of unconstitutional enactments, which the veto power might help to avert. The use of the veto power to control legislation not directly relating to the interests of the executive was a secondary consideration.[1] At present, however, few vetoes are for the purpose of defending the constitutional prerogatives of the executive. Only a small proportion of the vetoes apply to important public general acts. Most of them deal with ill considered or badly drawn public acts of minor importance, private and local measures, and appropriations, particularly for salaries and special objects of various kinds. Governor Hughes of New York headed his omnibus veto message of 1910, covering 118 bills which he declined to approve after the close of the session, as follows:—"The following bills are not approved because they are either duplicates or unnecessary, or are defectively drawn, or are embraced in or conflict with bills already signed, or are unconstitutional, or are for purposes which can be suitably accomplished under general laws, or should be provided for, if at all, by amendments to the general law, or are objectionable and inadvisable by reason of proposed changes."[2] In short, the office of governor tends to be regarded as an agency for supplying the deficiencies in the legislative branch of state government which result from the defective organization of the legislatures and from defective legislative procedure.

Executive Influence Upon Appropriations.

The enlargement of the veto power through the adoption of the item veto has thrown upon the governor in more than two-thirds of the states important duties in connection with the revision of appropriations after they have been made by the legislature. But the states have been much slower to give the governor a voice in the preparation of appropriation bills before

[1] See *The Federalist*, No. 73.

[2] See D. L. Colvin, *The Bicameral Principle in the New York Legislature*, p. 115. The omnibus veto is regularly used in New York and the form of the veto message has become standardized.

they are acted upon by the legislature. The natural jealousy of executive authority at the time of the Revolution caused the people of the original states to put complete control of public finance in the hands of the legislature, and, subject to the veto power, there it remained until modified by the recent movement for budgetary reform. Like the movement for administrative reorganization, budget reform in the states is a development of the last ten years. The significance of the changes wrought by the budget legislation of the past decade cannot be fully appreciated without devoting some attention to the methods, or lack of methods, by which the appropriations of the state governments were formerly made.

In the nineteenth century and in the early part of the present century, the traditional practice of the American states with respect to the voting of appropriations was thoroughly consistent with a decentralized and disintegrated administrative system. Appropriations for certain purposes were required, the amounts of which were, and still are, frequently fixed by the state constitutions. Chief among these were the salaries of the members of the legislature, of the principal executive officers, and of the judiciary. Other appropriations were determined by the legislature. In a dozen states, including several of the largest, all appropriations were limited to two years. Elsewhere the legislature might make appropriations for such periods as it chose with the result that, in a few states, permanent or continuing appropriations were provided for the principal objects of expenditure.[1] Special appropriations for private and local objects were often made without any limit of time. With these exceptions, appropriations for general governmental purposes usually expired at the close of the fiscal year, and unexpended balances reverted to the state treasury. Each department of administration ordinarily reported directly to the legislature upon the expenditure of its appropriation, and transmitted in the same manner its estimates of the appropriations necessary and proper for the ensuing year, or, in the case of states where the legislature

[1] Continuing appropriations authorize the expenditure of fixed sums annually until those amounts are changed or revoked by specific legislative act. At present, Wisconsin is the most notable example of a state that has a system of permanent appropriations. Seven states have recently abandoned the system. See A. E. Buck, *Budget Making* (New York, 1921), pp. 151-154.

met biennially, two years. Generally, neither the governor nor any other executive officer had anything to do with any departmental estimates save his own. However, in some states, a more orderly practice grew up. Thus, in Massachusetts, department heads submitted their estimates in advance of the meeting of the legislature to the state auditor. He then arranged them in some systematic order, together with a comparative statement of departmental expenditures for the preceding years, and submitted the whole as one report to the legislature.

The legislature referred the departmental reports and estimates to standing committees but there were considerable differences in procedure and practice in the various states. In some, there were several committees with jurisdiction over different classes of appropriations. In others, all appropriation bills were referred to a single committee. In some states, there were separate appropriation committees in each house; in others, there was a single joint committee. In a number of states, bills that carried appropriations, not required to cover departmental estimates, might be reported by various committees without consulting either the departments concerned or the appropriation committee. However, in most states, such bills were referred before final action by the house to the appropriation committee. Thus there was some centralized control over the appropriation measures in most legislatures. The department heads were required to appear before the appropriation committee and to demonstrate the necessity and propriety of the appropriations for which they asked. The chief difficulty with this procedure was that they appeared independently, each working solely for his own department and responsible in no way for other departments or for the size of the state appropriations as a whole. Since every active department head normally wanted to expand the services of his own department and was likely to overrate its importance as compared with others, departmental estimates tended to increase year by year, without much regard to the general growth of public expenditures and revenues. In consequence, the legislature was confronted with the difficult task of reducing the estimates in order to keep the total appropriations within reasonable compass. Such a task was made more difficult by the number and magnitude of the special and local "pork" appropriations which many districts wanted their representatives to procure for them in addition to the appropriations for regular departmental work.

This system inevitably bred extravagance and inefficiency. The departmental reports ordinarily presented no clear picture of the fiscal operations of the state as a whole, the estimates of the various department heads were likely to be excessive, and their recommendations unrelated to one another or to any co-ordinated administrative policy. The officer, if any, who collected the estimates and transmitted them to the legislature had no control over them, the departmental heads themselves had no constitutional right to defend their estimates, and in practice, the legislature might disregard them. The result tended to be perfunctory work on the part of the state fiscal officers. Intelligent planning for the future by the administration was almost impossible. Even the balancing of current appropriations and revenues was made difficult. The states sought to correct these evils by constitutional limitations upon the power to contract debts, but such remedies were unsatisfactory. They did not necessarily curb extravagance and waste, but too often merely operated to curtail important activities of the state administration, while money was squandered upon objects in which the legislature was more directly interested. Under such circumstances, the departments with the most political influence were likely to receive the most favorable treatment at the hands of the legislature. If that influence was created by the use of departmental funds in accordance with the desires of influential members of the legislature or of party leaders, politics and administration became confused to the detriment of the public interest.

Effect of Item Veto.

Under such circumstances, it was not surprising that the strong hand of the governor wielding the veto power was welcomed as a means of controlling such an unbusinesslike system. This fact is strikingly evidenced by the increasing number of states which have conferred upon the chief executive the authority to negative individual items of appropriation as well as complete bills. Originally, as has been indicated,[1] the primary purpose of the item veto was to prevent improper or unconstitu-

[1] See *ante*, ch. v.

tional expenditures rather than to restrain expenditures which were merely excessive in amount. But in time, owing to the increasing cost of government, the lack of financial policies and planning, and the extravagant habits of legislatures, the original intent of the item veto became subordinated to a demand that the governor extensively use his veto power as a means of compelling the state to live within its income. How effective this use was is shown by the experience of New York. There, in 1910, the appropriations were reduced thirteen times as much by the executive veto as by the veto which the upper house possessed over money bills originating in the lower.[1] In the same state, in 1914, the governor disapproved 60 separate appropriation acts and 209 items, totalling in all $7,272,000, or 15 per cent of the total amount passed by the legislature.

In an endeavor to limit the wholesale employment of the item veto, legislatures tended to resort to improper itemization. Since the definition of what constitutes an item is primarily a matter for the lawmaking branch to determine, the practice arose of putting necessary and unnecessary expenditures together in large lump-sum items, the theory being that the constitution did not allow the governor to reduce such items but merely permitted him to approve or disapprove them in their entirety. Faced with this difficulty, the governors sought to reduce as well as to strike out appropriations. In 1885, the governor of Pennsylvania, without specific constitutional authority, first ventured to reduce items of appropriation; in 1901, this practice was upheld by the state supreme court and thenceforth was employed on a large scale. Thus, in 1913, 516 appropriation bills were enacted by the Pennsylvania legislature; of these, 110 were negatived in their entirety, 147 bills, each of which contained only one item, were reduced, 410 items in 139 measures were disapproved or reduced, while the remaining 120 acts were signed by the executive without change. The aggregate amount vetoed was over $21,000,000 or 23 per cent of the total appropriated by the legislature.[2]

The Pennsylvania plan of an enlarged item veto for a time enjoyed considerable popularity. Many governors and publicists advocated its adoption. In about a dozen states besides Penn-

[1] See D. L. Colvin, *op. cit.*, p. 113. See also E. E. Agger, *The Budget in the American Commonwealths*, ch. ii and iii.

[2] See R. H. Wells, "The Item Veto and State Budget Reform," *American Political Science Review*, xviii, p. 784 (1924).

sylvania, the chief executives attempted likewise to reduce items or to disapprove parts of items. Their efforts were not very successful because the courts, in the absence of specific constitutional authority, were inclined to hold such action void. Moreover the item veto, both in its original and modified forms, was generally opposed by the new school of budget reformers which began to develop at about that time. The budget advocates, led by the New York Bureau of Municipal Research under the directorship of Dr. Frederick A. Cleveland, presented in lieu of the Pennsylvania plan a counter proposal which found complete expression in the New York budget amendment of 1915 (rejected by the voters) and the Maryland budget amendment of 1916. According to the budget reformers, the veto and the item veto as applied to appropriation bills were illogical and ineffective. They were illogical because they reversed the relation which should exist between the governor and the legislature. Instead of the executive initiating appropriations subject to the revision of the legislative department, which was supposed to control the purse, the opposite situation prevailed. The veto and the item veto were ineffective because responsibility for expenditures was divided. They encouraged extravagance on the part of the lawmaking branch so that it came to rely upon the governor to make ends meet and produce financial order out of chaos. Moreover, it was not enough for the executive merely to negative large sums. What was often needed was a general reduction all along the line, and it was not easy to secure a balanced outlay simply by disapproving a bill or an item here and there. Finally, in many states, the major appropriation acts were generally passed at the end of the session. If executive action on them were required before adjournment, the governor had too little time for careful scrutiny; on the other hand, if he were allowed to negative appropriation measures and items after adjournment, his veto was usually final. It was subject neither to legislative reconsideration nor to adequate public criticism, and it might be used to reward or punish members of the legislature through the approval or disapproval of "pork" projects.

The Need for Budgetary Reform.

Such criticisms as these made it increasingly clear that the veto power, when used alone, was neither sufficient to cope with the mounting cost of state government nor was it able to produce a unified and orderly system of state finance. As noted before, the efficiency and economy commissions of the past decade helped to focus attention on this fact as well as on the need of administrative reorganization. The investigations of President Taft's Commission on Economy and Efficiency were especially noteworthy in calling the attention of the whole country to the importance of the budget problem. The outcome was a budget reform movement which swept the United States and led to significant financial changes in nation, state, and city. Beginning with Wisconsin in 1911, every state except Missouri enacted and put into force some kind of budgetary legislation. In six of these states [1] the budget systems thus established were based upon constitutional amendments. It is necessary, next, to examine the budget systems which have been established and to inquire concerning the results of a reform which has been characterized as "the most marked improvement that we have made in state administration since the turn of the twentieth century." [2] At the outset, it may be well to indicate more precisely what is meant by the word "budget," since that term is used with several different meanings. As applied to governmental or public bodies, it may be described as a systematic plan of proposed expenditures and estimated revenues for a definite period prepared and submitted by a duly authorized agency for the approval of the legislature. But however defined, the essence of the budget idea is merely that of careful financial planning, planning such as will

[1] Maryland, West Virginia, Massachusetts, Nebraska, Louisiana, and California.

[2] W. B. Munro, *The Government of the United States* (2d ed., New York, 1925). Among the books on state budgets, the following may be noted: Harry A. Barth, *Financial Control in the States with Emphasis on Control by the Governor* (Philadelphia, 1923); A. E. Buck, *Budget Making* (New York, 1921); F. A. Cleveland and A. E. Buck, *The Budget and Responsible Government* (New York, 1920); Luther H. Gulick, *Evolution of the Budget in Massachusetts* (New York, 1920); W. F. Willoughby, *The Movement for Budgetary Reform in the States* (New York, 1918). The number of articles dealing with state budgets is large, only a few of which can be mentioned here. Of special value are A. E. Buck's excellent summaries of state budget progress printed in the *National Municipal Review* as follows: "The Present Status of the Executive Budget in State Governments," viii, pp. 422-435 (1919); "State Budget Progress," x, pp. 568-573 (1921); "Progress in State Budget Making," xiii, pp. 19-25 (1924); "Recent Steps toward Administrative Consolidation in State Governments," xiv, pp. 672-680 (1925). In a recent volume of the *Annals* ("Competency and Economy in Public Expenditures," cxiii, 1924), there are several valuable articles dealing with various phases of the state budget problem.

give a comprehensive but intelligible picture of the government's finances, coupled with such processes as are necessary to secure for the plan due consideration.

Types of Budget Systems.

The existing state budget systems are of three principal types, classified according to the person or agency legally responsible for the initiation of the budget. (1) In one state, Arkansas, a legislative budget system is used, under which the budget is framed and presented to the legislature by a joint legislative committee; (2) thirty-three states have the executive type of budget in which the governor is made primarily responsible for its formulation; (3) while in thirteen states, the board or commission type prevails. The budget boards or commissions in this last group of states are variously constituted, in some cases being entirely composed of administrative officers, either acting ex-officio or appointed specially for that purpose, or both. In other cases, they consist of both administrative officers and representatives of the legislature. For example, the Louisiana state board of affairs, which prepares the budget, is made up of six members appointed by the governor with the consent of the senate. The New York board of estimate and control consists of the governor, comptroller, and chairmen of the assembly ways and means and senate finance committees. In West Virginia, the budget authority is the board of public works, consisting of the governor and six other elective officers. However, the general tendency in the states is towards the executive type of budget. A considerable number of states which have experimented with the other types have recently adopted executive budget systems. This tendency is both sound in principle and thoroughly in accord with the historical evolution of state government. Since the budget involves financial planning, such planning is likely to be better performed under the responsibility of one man rather than of several. But mere planning of itself alone is not sufficient; means must be provided to insure that the plan, if adopted, is actually carried out. Hence, the individual who assumes responsibility for the planning of the budget should also be made responsible for its execution. Both of these functions are essentially executive functions and should be placed upon the governor as chief executive. Thus the planning and execution of the budget is but a logical step in the development of the governor's control over appropriations.

Main Features of Executive Budget System.

Since, therefore, the executive type of budget tends more and more to prevail, the attention of the reader may be directed primarily to the main features of that system.[1] Although under such a system, responsibility for the budget is placed upon the governor, it is manifestly impossible for him to do personally the great amount of careful, continuous, and detailed work necessary in budget planning. Accordingly, he is usually provided with special staff agencies upon whom he may rely for assistance. When this assistance is lacking or is inadequate in character, the budget of even the best-intentioned governor suffers accordingly. Thus, in Illinois, under the civil administrative code, the chief executive is assisted in the preparation of the budget by the director of the department of finance and, more particularly, by a bureau in that department under a superintendent of the budget. In Virginia, the staff consists of a director of the budget and special assistants, all of whom are appointed by the governor and are under his immediate supervision.

The first step in the process of budget-making consists in the preparation of estimates of expenditure by the several state departments and the filing of these estimates with the governor or with his budget staff agency. In a few states, such as New Jersey, the law lays down detailed rules as to the form of these estimates and the data to be included. More generally, the character of the detailed information required in the estimates is determined by supplementary regulations issued by the budget authority. In either case, on or before a prescribed date, the estimates are transmitted to the governor or to his staff agency for review, revision, and compilation, together with revenue estimates which are usually supplied by the state auditor or comptroller.

The extent to which the governor may revise the estimates varies. Usually the law requires that all proposed expenditures must be reviewed, but only in a few states may all such proposals be actually revised by increasing, decreasing, or striking out

[1] See A. E. Buck, "The Present Status of the Executive Budget in the State Governments," *National Municipal Review*, viii, pp. 422-435 (1919).

items. Frequently, the estimates of the legislative and judicial departments are specifically exempt from executive revision and must be transmitted to the legislature without change. However, even in these cases, there is nothing to prevent the governor from making such recommendations and suggestions as he sees fit. In order to facilitate the work of revision and compilation, the governor or his budget representatives may investigate the necessity for the various requests and hold departmental and public hearings. If departmental needs are continuously investigated throughout the year and not simply as an incident of budget compilation, the data thus secured are likely to be much more useful in revising the estimates.

The outcome of these labors is the budget or comprehensive financial plan, which is transmitted to the legislature. The budget statute or constitutional amendment may prescribe the exact form in which that document shall be submitted, as in Maryland, or it may contain no specific provisions concerning the contents of the budget, as in New Jersey. There is considerable variation concerning the date for presenting the budget to the legislature. In some states, it must be transmitted at the opening of the session; in others, within ten, twenty, or thirty days thereafter. It is important that the legislature receive the budget at the earliest possible moment, particularly in those states where the legislative session is limited. On the other hand, if too little time is allowed for preparation, a governor-elect may find himself seriously embarrassed in his endeavor to comply with the budget requirements. Some states have attempted to meet these difficulties but thus far not with great success. Such difficulties cannot be fully overcome until the election calendar, the legislative calendar, and the fiscal calendar are better articulated with each other.

The budget message with its supporting information is necessarily not in a form suitable for direct enactment into law. It requires translation into appropriation, revenue, and, in some cases, borrowing measures. This distinction is recognized in law or practice in nearly all the states. Thus, in Maryland, the governor must accompany his budget with a bill containing all the proposed appropriations clearly itemized and classified. In other states, particularly those in which the constitution requires separate appropriation acts for certain purposes, several appropriation bills may be introduced. It is desirable, as far as possible, to incorporate all expenditures proposed in the budget in a single general appropriation bill since this facilitates the work of the legislature and preserves the unity of the budget plan. Revenue and borrowing measures are not usually recommended in the form of bills, but are merely outlined in the governor's message.

Among the most important provisions of a budget system are those which prescribe what action may be taken after the budget has been transmitted to the legislature. Too many budget statutes fail to deal adequately with this phase of the problem. In a number of states, however, fairly satisfactory provisions are found. For example, in Maryland, the governor and administrative officers may, and, at the request of either house, must appear before the legislature to defend or explain the budget.[1] In Virginia, the standing appropriation committees of the legislature must within five days meet jointly and hold public hearings on the estimates. At these hearings, the governor and his representatives and the public are authorized to be present and to be heard. Where the executive is specifically directed to submit an appropriation or budget bill, the general rule is that this measure must be finally acted upon by the legislature before other appropriation bills are passed. The California budget amendment of 1922 stipulates that "until the budget bill has been finally enacted, neither house shall place upon final passage any other appropriation bill, except emergency bills recommended by the governor, or appropriations for the salaries, mileage, and expenses of the senate and assembly." Of course, this type of restriction by itself will not prevent special appropriation bills from being passed unless the legislature fails to enact the budget until adjournment. However, such special acts are not only given a deferred status but in a number of states are limited in other ways. Here again, Maryland furnishes the most extreme case. In that state, every supplementary appropriation must be

[1] Similar provisions appear in the budget amendment proposed in New York by the State Reorganization Commission of 1926. The text of this amendment, which is the most elaborate and in many ways the most promising of recent plans for budgetary reform, is reprinted in Appendix F. See also the proposals for a "capital budget," recommended by the Special Joint Legislative Committee on Taxation and Retrenchment, likewise reprinted in Appendix F. For further discussion of these proposals, see *post*, ch. xvi.

embodied in a separate bill limited to a single purpose, must directly or indirectly provide the revenue to meet the appropriation, must be passed by a majority of all the members elected to each house, and, finally, is subject to the executive veto. In other states, the procedural and substantive limitations on the legislature's power are generally much less stringent and the principal check is afforded by the gubernatorial veto.

The extent to which the budget figures may be amended by the governor or the legislature after the budget has been introduced varies. In California, the executive may at any time after its introduction amend or supplement the budget and propose amendments to the budget bill before or after its enactment. This is a fairly common provision. In most cases, the legislature may increase, decrease, add, or omit items, or even may completely disregard the budget recommendations, but in Maryland and West Virginia, the legislature, with certain exceptions, is limited to striking out or reducing items.[1] In Nebraska, decreases or eliminations may be made by an ordinary vote but increases require a three-fifths vote of each house and such increases may not be vetoed by the governor. Since budget reform is not designed to destroy the legislature's ultimate control of the purse but rather to provide conditions under which such control may be effectively exercised, it hardly seems wise to impose undue restraints upon the legislature's right to amend the budget bill. If the governor retains the veto power and that power be enlarged so as to allow the reduction as well as the disapproval of items of appropriation, as has been done by the budget amendments of Massachusetts and California, he will have adequate means of defending his recommendations against legislative increases.[2] Then, if the legislature proceeds to set aside such vetoes, the responsibility for the appropriations thus made rests with the lawmaking branch and not with the executive.

The enactment of the general appropriation bill or bills together with the necessary revenue measures is too often regarded as the end of the budget process, whereas it is really only the

[1] In Maryland and West Virginia, the budget bill becomes law without further action by the governor and the executive veto is abolished in that connection.

[2] If the legislature increases the appropriation of a department which is under the control of the governor, the governor may direct the head of the department not to spend the full amount appropriated.

point at which the budget plan is ready to be put into execution. The methods by which the state's financial plan is carried out involve, or should involve, adequate systems of accounting, auditing, and reporting, centralized purchasing of supplies or at least central supervision of purchases and contracts, the expenditure of departmental appropriations according to an allotment plan and subject to the approval of the governor or of some specially designated financial agency, provisions for the transfer of items of appropriation and for the use of emergency funds, etc. These topics are discussed in the following chapter and hence require no further consideration in this connection.

Effects of Introduction of Executive Budget.

In conclusion, a brief summary of the results of the movement for state budgetary reform may be given. Here, as in the case of administrative reorganization, it will be found that there are wide differences from state to state. Considering the universality of budget legislation, the achievements thus far realized are disappointing. It has been said, and can probably still be said, that "a large majority of the states are no better off from the standpoint of financial planning and control than they were before they provided for the establishment of a budget system."[1] This condition is due, not so much to defects in the budget statutes, as to the inertia of state officials, the shifting of responsibility for budget planning, and the frequent deadlocks which occur between the legislative and executive branches of state government. Of even greater importance is the fact that state administration is still far from being thoroughly reorganized and consolidated.[2] How can a governor frame and be responsible for a comprehensive financial plan when numerous department heads, whom he did not appoint and cannot remove, may appeal to the legislature, if the governor reduces their estimates of proposed expenditure? This defect is partially offset in a few states where the executive has complete supervision of the enforcement of the state budget. For example, in Nebraska, no appropriation becomes available for use until the spending agency has submitted quarterly estimates and has had these estimates approved by the

[1] A. E. Buck, "State Budget Progress," *National Municipal Review*, x, p. 568 (1921).

[2] *Ibid.*, pp. 571-573.

governor. Under such circumstances, even without administrative consolidation, an adequate executive budget system might measurably increase the administrative authority of the governor. Nevertheless, the two reforms logically belong together and the maximum effectiveness of each will be impaired without the presence of the other. Serious as these shortcomings are, they are not irremediable and even now are partially counterbalanced by the positive results which budget reform has brought. In those states where budget legislation has been honestly and consistently applied, the old, chaotic financial practices have largely disappeared and substantial economies have been obtained. As for the other states which are still "no better off," it may be said in partial justification that the budgetary movement is a very recent development and that in this, as in many other things, governments proceed slowly. Even though many states at present have only "paper" budget systems, such states have at least recognized the validity of the budget principle. Sooner or later, there is a strong likelihood that these paper plans will be vitalized, improved, and put into actual practice. Then an important step in the reconstruction of state government will have been consummated.

THE ENFORCEMENT OF EXECUTIVE RESPONSIBILITY

The development of the authority of the governor, both as a legislator and as an administrator, has emphasized the perennial question: How shall the governor be held responsible for his powers, so that he may not abuse them to the detriment of the public good? Shall responsibility be enforced through the ancient process of impeachment, or through that modern device, the recall, or shall some other method be employed?

The Power of Impeachment.

Originally, the power of impeachment was deemed an important instrument for the defense of the legislatures and the people against executive encroachments and possible usurpation. However, it has not proved of much actual importance. In most of the original states the governors were chosen by the legislatures for short terms, and there was no real need of the power of impeachment to maintain the supremacy of the latter. Since the general adoption of direct popular election of governors for longer terms and the development of the executive veto, a legislature which could not override a veto would have little chance of successfully impeaching a governor on the ground that he had refused his assent to laws deemed by the legislature to be for the public good. So long as the executive branch of state government was decentralized and disintegrated, there was little occasion to use the power of impeachment to remove governors for abuse of their administrative authority. In fact, there have been only ten cases of the impeachment of governors in the entire history of the states. Five of these cases occurred in the South during the period of reconstruction after the Civil War. In each case governors who were attempting to maintain the civil or political rights of the freedmen were impeached by legislatures under the control of the party bent on asserting white supremacy in state politics. One governor was removed from office, one resigned to escape removal, and in the other cases the charges were dropped. Two governors were impeached in northern states during the same period. One was acquitted, and the other was removed from office on account of embezzling state funds.

The most recent cases of impeachment were those of Governor Sulzer of New York in 1913, Governor Ferguson of Texas in 1917, and Governor Walton of Oklahoma in 1923. Governor Ferguson made war on the state's institutions of higher learning, which in reprisal led to an investigation of the gubernatorial office. The investigation disclosed numerous financial irregularities and the governor was accordingly impeached and removed from office. Governor Walton resorted to a dubious employment of the state militia in his violent controversy with the modern Ku Klux Klan. The outcome of the conflict was unfavorable to the governor, as he was removed from office following impeachment proceedings. Governor Sulzer was nominally removed from office on account of filing an incorrect return of his campaign expenses and suppressing evidence sought by a legislative committee appointed to investigate his alleged misconduct. He was really impeached because he had defied the political "machine" to which he owed his nomination and election and had sought to make himself leader of the "organization." Such a use of the power of impeachment reacts injuriously upon the whole party, and cannot be regarded as a normal mode of maintaining the supremacy of the organization over those whom it puts in office. In general, the power of impeachment must be regarded as an extraordinary remedy for official misconduct. It plays no important part in upholding the existing balance of power between the executive and legislative branches of the state governments.

The Recall.

The recall has sometimes been advocated as a substitute for the power of impeachment. It is argued that, since the process of impeachment is so difficult to operate, the power to deprive an executive of office before the expiration of his term by a popular vote will accomplish the same purpose more directly. Usually, however, the recall is advocated on the general ground that the voters should have the power to retire legislators and executives from office whenever they lose confidence in them. Executive officers can be impeached only for high crimes and misdemeanors, misfeasance or gross misconduct in office. Legislators cannot be impeached at all, and the legislatures are the sole judges of the elections and qualifications of their own members. Consequently, neither legislators nor executives can be removed from office on account of failure properly to represent the people in matters of policy or on account of general loss of popular confidence in their integrity or capacity. When annual elections prevailed, the shortness of the term of office made the discontinuity of popular control unimportant. With the extension of the terms of elective officers, the establishment of continuous popular control became more important. The longer the terms of elective officers, possessing the power to determine the policy of the state, the more important does the power of popular recall become.

In fact, however, little use of the recall has been made for the purpose of retiring state officers. The most striking instance occurred in 1921 when the governor (Lynn J. Frazier), the attorney-general, and the commissioner of agriculture of North Dakota were recalled from office because of their connection with certain issues growing out of the Non-Partisan League movement. In the following year, however, ex-Governor Frazier was elected by the people to the United States Senate. In this same year (1922) two members of the Oregon public utility commission were recalled because unpopular rate increases had been authorized by the commission. Though the recall has been not infrequently employed in municipalities, its use in the states, especially for the retirement of officers selected in the state at large, involves much greater effort and expense. In states where terms of office are long, the recall doubtless gives to the voters a feeling of greater security against possible misgovernment, and to legislators and executives a feeling of more immediate responsibility. Apparently, therefore, it must be regarded as an extraordinary remedy whose chief value lies in its potential rather than in its actual use, "a gun behind the door," as it has been aptly described.

It is generally recognized that both the impeachment and the direct popular recall are cumbersome weapons for enforcing official responsibility. In the Model State Constitution proposed by the National Municipal League,[1] the interesting suggestion is made that the legislature be empowered to recall the governor by a two-thirds vote of its members. Like the popular recall, the legislative recall could be invoked for any reason which seemed valid to the legislature; it could be employed in very much the same way as a motion of "want of confidence" is used under a parliamentary form of government. The National Municipal League does not propose cabinet government for the states, but it does seek to bring the executive and legislative branches into more harmonious relations.[2] Under its proposed model constitution disagreements between the executive and the legislature with reference to particular bills may be settled by the use of the popular referendum. Where the lack of harmony is more serious and persistent, then the presumption is that the legislature will invoke the right of legislative recall and thus end the deadlock. With such provisions as these, the governor could continue to be elected by the people to serve as chief legislator as well as chief administrator of the state and yet the legislature would possess adequate means for checking the abuse or unwise use of power.

[1] See Appendix C.

[2] See *post*, ch. xvi.

CHAPTER XI

STATE ADMINISTRATION

The subject of state administration is so broad and so important that it may profitably be studied from many points of view. In it, the historian finds reflected the material, intellectual, and moral changes of American life. State administration is also of vital interest to the economist and sociologist, the business man, the worker, and the whole body of citizens generally, since the contemporary economic and social institutions of the United States are in large measure fostered, modified, or restrained by the numerous administrative services of the state governments. The political scientist must necessarily adopt a more limited scope for his inquiry. While not neglecting the other aspects of the subject, his chief task is to analyze and appraise the various state administrative functions and the agencies through which they are performed.

In the preceding chapter, there was a general summary of the development of new administrative agencies in the states, of the relations between the governor and the state administration and between the governor and the legislature, and of the recent movements for administrative reorganization and budget reform. It now remains to examine in turn the organization and powers of the principal administrative departments, to devote some attention to the present relations between the state and local administrative authorities, and to consider certain personnel, matériel, and financial problems which have been incidentally referred to in the earlier portions of the book.

EDUCATION

At the present time, the most important department of state administration is that of education.[1] In the beginning, there was

[1] For a general survey of American public school administration, see E. P. Cubberley, *Public School Administration* (rev. ed., Boston, 1922). Much useful information on educational finance is contained in a series of monographs published during 1924 and 1925 by the Educational Finance Inquiry

little provision for popular education at public expense. The states in which colleges existed at the time of the Revolution gave them little aid, and even less attention was paid by the state governments to local common schools. Outside of New England, there were few localities which maintained common schools. Nowhere was attendance compulsory, nor tuition free except for those who could not afford to pay. Since that time, free common schools have been established in all the states and attendance at the public schools or at private schools of equivalent grade [1] has been made compulsory. The further development of state systems of free public education has also involved the establishment of local secondary schools, of evening and continuation schools for the further general education of young wage earners, of trade and industrial schools for special training in the arts and crafts, of state normal schools for the better training of common school teachers, of state universities, agricultural, mechanical, and professional (except theological) schools for higher education, of special schools for the training of defectives and delinquents, and of state libraries and travelling institutes for the further education of adults. This development has by no means been uniform throughout the states. The differences in state common school systems are clearly reflected in the rates of illiteracy. The census of 1920 indicates that the rate for Louisiana is eighteen times the rate for Iowa. The differences in the secondary, higher, and more specialized school systems are equally great, though not so easily measured. However, with the exception of the New England states, the state governments as a rule now spend more money on education than on any other single branch of state administration.

Centralization of Educational Administration.

The growth of the educational systems of the states has been marked by a progressive shifting of control from local to central educational authorities. In the beginning, there were no special

Commission. A recent summary of existing educational legislation in the states is to be found in a bulletin (No. 47, 1924) of the United States Bureau of Education.

[1] An Oregon statute of 1922 which compelled all children between the ages of eight and sixteen years to attend only the public schools has been declared unconstitutional by the United States Supreme Court. Pierce v. Society of the Sisters of the Holy Names of Jesus and Mary, 268 U. S. 510 (1925).

educational authorities except the local school boards and committees. At present, practically all the states have an independent department of education under an executive head, known usually as the state superintendent of public instruction. Most of them have also a state board of education with a general educational jurisdiction, and many of them have special boards for the control of special institutions, such as normal schools, training schools of various kinds, and state universities. The division of control of educational matters between the central and the local authorities varies greatly. There are still a few states in which the control is vested almost exclusively in the local authorities. In such states, the central authorities have little more than advisory powers. There are also a few states in which the local authorities are little more than the agents of the central authorities. In such states, the central authorities may prescribe the curriculum in the local schools, select the textbooks, examine teachers for certification as to their qualifications, and exercise extensive powers of appointment and removal of county superintendents and other local authorities. They may administer the state school lands, apportion the state school funds, and, in some cases, withhold grants from local authorities which fail to reach a prescribed standard of efficiency.[1] They may appoint inspectors of local schools, regulate the construction and maintenance of school buildings, especially in such matters as ventilation and sanitation, and operate the educational institutions directly under the control of the state. Most of the states fall between these two extremes. The centralization of educational administration has proceeded more rapidly in some states than in others, but everywhere the tendency is the same.

The centralization of educational administration has increased the number and powers of the state educational authorities, but has not yet brought about the general adoption of a uniform plan of organization. Every state has a state superintendent of

[1] The conditional subsidy is becoming an increasingly important means of strengthening central control over education. This method is employed, not only by the states in dealing with their own local authorities, but also by the federal government in dealing with the states. Thus, Congress, by the Smith-Lever Act of 1914 and by the Smith-Hughes Act of 1917, has made substantial appropriations to the states for agricultural extension work and for vocational education, subject to compliance with the conditions and standards laid down by Congress. Attempts have recently been made to extend federal grants-in-aid to matters of general education but these attempts have thus far been unsuccessful.

public instruction, or an officer of the same character under another title. In thirty-four states he is elected by the people, but in six he is appointed by the governor (usually with the approval of the senate), and in eight he is appointed by the state board of education. The terms, salaries, and powers of these officers vary greatly. In a few states, of which New York is the best example, he enjoys security of tenure, an attractive salary, and broad powers. In a few states, such as Massachusetts, his powers are less, but his actual influence has been very great. In most states, he has relatively little power and not much influence. State boards of education exist in forty-six states but, in four of these states, the boards have no functions relating to the common schools, They are organized in various ways, and differ in power and influence no less widely than the superintendents of public instruction. In size, they vary from three to thirteen members. Some boards are composed entirely of state officials, serving *ex officio;* some are composed of members elected by the legislature; some are composed of members appointed by the governor; some, of members obtained by a combination of these and other ways. Only in Michigan are the members elected by popular vote. In some states, the powers of the board are very small. In others, they may have charge of state school funds, elect a secretary or commissioner who acts as state superintendent, appoint county superintendents and school boards, select textbooks, and prescribe curricula. In several states they manage the normal schools, besides performing all the preceding functions, and in a few, of which Oklahoma is the best example, they act as boards of control for all state educational institutions. A larger number of states divide these functions among several independent bodies, creating separate boards for the adoption of textbooks, the administration of school lands or funds, the management of special schools, the examination of teachers, etc., in so far as these matters are not reserved to the local authorities. There is no common rule for the division of power between the different central educational authorities, and, in general, no systematic arrangements for effective coöperation between them.

It is apparent that there is a real need for reorganization and consolidation in the field of state educational administration. As yet, however, little has been accomplished towards meeting this need. Partly because the office of state superintendent of public instruction is generally made elective by the constitution and partly for other reasons, the reorganization movement has left the central educational agencies substantially unchanged.[1]

CHARITIES AND CORRECTIONS

The second department of state administration in order of present importance is that which relates to the care of delinquents, defectives, and dependents.[2] At the time of the Revolution, prisoners of all kinds, hardened criminals, petty offenders, persons awaiting trial, without distinction of age, sex, or other conditions, were placed in the custody of the sheriff, and kept by him in such manner as he should see fit, commonly at a charge to the county of so much per capita, like livestock in a pound.[3] Defectives were not accepted as public charges unless they had committed some offense or were incapable of self-support. In the former case, they were treated like other lawbreakers; in the latter, they were dealt with like ordinary paupers, unless supported by their relatives. In general, the deaf and dumb, the blind, the feeble-minded, and the insane were maintained by their nearest relatives in their homes. Paupers were a recognized charge upon the locality in which they had their residence. Temporary destitution might be relieved by special aid ("outdoor relief") granted under the supervision of the local overseers of the poor. Permanent paupers were entitled to maintenance at public expense in almshouses. "Indoor relief," however, in an age which tolerated imprisonment for debt, was likely to be even less desirable, from the standpoint of the victim, than imprisonment.

A deeper knowledge of the nature and causes of poverty and crime, and a broadening sympathy with the pauper and the transgressor, has brought about a great change in the methods

[1] Even the thorough Tennessee reorganization of 1923 did not result in a completely unified department of education. See A. E. Buck, "Administrative Consolidation in State Governments," *op. cit.*, pp. 26-29.

[2] On charities and public welfare, see "Public Welfare in the United States," *Annals Am. Acad. Political and Social Science*, cv., no. 194 (January, 1923), especially pt. iv; J. L. Gillin, *Poverty and Dependency* (New York, 1921); and the (annual) *Proceedings of the National Conference of Social Work*. On corrections, see L. N. Robinson, *Penology in the United States* (New York, 1921) and F. H. Wines, *Punishment and Reformation* (New York, 1919).

[3] See Allan Nevins, *The American States during and after the Revolution, 1775-1789* (New York, 1924), pp. 461-465.

of dealing with them. In the first half-century after the Revolution, the dawn of a more scientific and a more humane age was ushered in by the work which, in prison reform, is associated with the names of the English reformers, John Howard and Elizabeth Fry. In America, imprisonment for debt was abolished, jails and prisons were made more decent, and the establishment of penitentiaries and reformatories, as the names indicate, marked the adoption of more enlightened views concerning the purposes of punishment. In the treatment of poverty, there came a conviction that society should undertake more than the mere relief of destitution. The duty of preventing poverty, so far as possible, began to be recognized. In America, during the first half of the nineteenth century, the most conspicuous expression of this growing conviction was the founding of Washingtonian Societies for the promotion of temperance in the use of alcoholic liquors. This movement culminated in 1850 in the so-called "Maine idea," the idea of state-wide prohibition by law.

The reformation of the original system of charities and corrections has been based upon two fundamental principles: the break-up of the old poor law and the old penal system, and the provision of specialized treatment for the different classes of dependents and delinquents. The poor may be divided roughly into two main classes, those whose poverty seems to be due to causes more or less within their own control, and those whose poverty is due to other causes. The belief is growing that the latter class should be relieved according to the nature of the cause. Systematic and effective provision can be made for the relief of the victims of industrial accidents, occupational diseases, casual sickness, and disability due to old age by the adoption of workmen's compensation acts and the development of general systems of social insurance. Destitution of the able-bodied due to involuntary unemployment can be diminished by the regularization of industry. Where relief is necessary, it can be provided more scientifically and more humanely by the shifting of the cost of maintenance during unavoidable and predictable periods of unemployment to the industry in which the unemployment occurs. Destitution of the able-bodied due to inefficiency, so far as it results from lack of skill and training, can be met by the further development of education. Destitution of the deaf and dumb and of the blind can also be met by the further development of the system of education. Their cases should be treated as an educational, not as a charitable, problem. The former class of poor, those whose poverty seems to be due to causes more or less within their own control, should not only be relieved. They should be so treated as to help them to become self-supporting. Ordinarily punishment, such as by incarceration in workhouses (distinguished from almshouses by the fact that relief is deliberately connected with work), is insufficient. Drunkards, for example, should be helped to become temperate by treatment designed to strengthen their will. This cannot be accomplished by breaking their pride with harsh treatment. Vagabonds and the "work-shy" should receive special treatment. The feeble-minded and incurably insane should be segregated.

Centralization of Administration.

The growing recognition of these principles has brought about, especially in recent years, an unparalleled demand for the creation of new agencies of relief and correction. This demand can only be met by the development of a more specialized administrative organization. In many cases, the local authorities do not carry on charitable and correctional work on a broad enough scale to make the necessary subdivision of labor possible. They cannot afford to employ the proper kinds of expert administrators. The states have consequently been forced to assume an ever growing share in the management of charitable and correctional institutions. For example, the care of the insane, of the feeble-minded, of special classes of offenders such as the criminal insane, juvenile delinquents, and alcoholics, and the treatment of the tuberculous poor, is supervised or supported to an ever increasing extent by the central authorities. The development of modern methods of punishment has caused a further growth of central control. Boards of pardon and parole have been established in order to assist the governor in the exercise of his power of pardon, and to supervise the conduct of offenders whose sentences have been suspended during good behavior. Boards of prison industries have been created in order to bring about a better use of the prisoner's time while under restraint. Contract prison labor, and the production of goods, whether within or without prison walls, to be sold in competition with the products of free labor, tend to give way before the development of prison industries which supply the needs of state institutions and teach the prisoner a trade. Workmen's compensation acts might conceivably be enforced through the county or district courts. They are usually administered by special state commissions. Mothers' pension acts are more generally administered by local authorities, but all the proposed plans for general schemes of social insurance contemplate their administration by the central authorities. In short, charitable and penal administration, and the administration of those new public activities for the conservation of human resources which are neither charitable nor penal, such as the relief of the victims of industrial accidents, tend more and more to fall into the hands of the central administrative authorities of the states.[1]

The centralization of charitable and penal administration, like that of educational administration, has not yet brought about the general adoption of any uniform plan of organization.[2] There are several types of organization corresponding to different stages in the process of centralization of control. First, there may be a separate board of managers for each charitable and penal institution, over which there may be one or more central boards, with power to inspect public institutions under their jurisdiction, and to make recommendations to their managers. Such central boards may have jurisdiction over private as well as public charities.[3] These central supervisory bodies are usually interested mainly in the questions of general policy arising in connection with institutional management, but they may also supervise the details of fiscal administration. In California, there is a single state board of control, with full power of supervision in fiscal affairs over all public institutions, and with no power of supervision in other respects. Secondly, there may be local boards of managers for each institution, subject to general supervision by one or more central boards, as in the first case. In addition, the central board or boards or an independent officer may also be intrusted with full control over financial matters, such as the letting of contracts for construction and the pur-

[1] At present, there are only three states, Mississippi, Nevada, and Utah, which have no state agencies, either advisory or administrative, for charitable and correctional activities.

[2] See S. P. Breckinridge, "Summary of the Present State Systems for the Organization and Administration of Public Welfare," *Annals*, cv. (January, 1923), pp. 93-103.

[3] On state supervision of private charitable agencies and on the general relations of public and private agencies, see J. L. Gillin, *op. cit.*, chs. xiv-xvi.

chase of supplies. In New York, there is both a state board of charities and a state superintendent of purchase, a state commission of prisons and a state superintendent of prisons. There is also a state hospital commission for the administration of the insane hospitals, and a variety of minor state administrative agencies, such as the state commission for mental defectives, the prison industries board, the building improvement commission, the state probation commission, and the state commission for the blind, with jurisdiction over special phases of the subject. Finally, there are two private associations, the Prison Association of New York and the State Charities Aid Association, empowered by law to inspect the public institutions and to report to the state administrative authorities or to the legislature.[1] Thirdly, there may be one or more central boards with full and exclusive jurisdiction over the administration of public charitable and penal institutions. Where a single board controls directly all the institutions of this general character, as is the case in Iowa and a number of other states, the process of centralization is almost complete. The one step yet remaining is to replace the single board by a single commissioner and this step has been taken as a result of general administrative consolidations in some of the states. Thus, the Illinois reorganization of 1917 abolished the supervisory charities commission, the board of administration, and the independent boards of trustees of the penal and reformatory institutions and transferred substantially all their powers and duties to the director of the department of public welfare, appointed by the governor. Nine other states have recently created similar departments[2] but not all of these have followed the principle of "one man control."[3] The present tendency seems to be toward the more general adoption either of the single board of control type or of the single commissioner type. There is wide disagreement among the experts as to which of these two forms is the more desirable but it is not unlikely

[1] The list of New York agencies given above will be changed to a considerable extent when the reorganization required by the constitutional amendment of 1925 is put into effect. See *ante*, ch. x.

[2] Some of these consolidated departments exercise both welfare and health functions.

[3] For the arguments for "one man control," see C. E. McCombs, "State Welfare Administration and Consolidated Government," *National Municipal Review*, xiii, pp. 461-473 (Supplement, August, 1924). The single commissioner type does not preclude the use of one or more advisory boards.

that the latter form will be more and more widely adopted in the future.

PUBLIC HEALTH ADMINISTRATION

Public health administration at the time of the Revolution had two principal objects: the establishment of quarantines against contagious diseases, and the abatement of nuisances. Social and economic changes and the progress of medical science in the nineteenth century have greatly enlarged the scope of public health administration, but the activities of the public health authorities are still associated with one or the other of those two objects. For the purpose of preventing the spread of disease, and abating nuisances of various kinds, prejudicial to the public health, very extensive though unequal powers have been conferred upon administrative officials in all the states. Among them are the following: (1) the power to investigate (a) the causes of disease, for example, by the establishment of cancer research laboratories, (b) the prevalence of disease, for example, by the establishment of registration areas for the recording of vital statistics, and (c) the location of disease, for example, by the inspection of factories, tenements. etc. (2) Compulsory isolation of the sick at home or in hospitals. (3) Free medical treatment and nursing, for example, in cases of tuberculosis. (4) Public preventive medicine by the preparation and distribution of vaccines, antitoxins, etc. (5) Medical examination of immigrants and school children. (6) Care of dead bodies, if necessary, in connection with transportation and burial. (7) Free diagnosis of disease in public laboratories. (8) Disposal of sewage, garbage, dust, ashes, smoke, etc. (9) Suppression of offensive trades and of offenses against the public health or morals. (10) Ventilation and illumination of factories and workshops, protection of workers against dangerous machinery and industrial processes injurious to health, regulation of the hours of labor of men, in certain occupations, and of women and children, and eventually of wages as well. (11) Prevention or suppression of unsanitary housing conditions by building laws and inspection. (12) Control of the manufacture, transportation, and sale of explosives and fireworks. (13) Control or suppression of the sale of impure foods, poisonous drugs, alcoholic liquors, tobacco (to minors), unclean milk, etc., and protection of the purity of water supplies. (14) Public instruction in personal and social hygiene, and the suppression of advertisements and printed matter detrimental to public health and morals. (15) Regulation of the practice of all professions connected with the public health, such as medicine and surgery, nursing, undertaking and embalming, dentistry, optometry, pharmacy, veterinary medicine, plumbing, etc.[1]

This enormous expansion in the activities of the state in relation to health has entailed the organization of an elaborate system of public health administration. In the beginning, there were no special agencies, either state or local, for the protection of the public health. In general, the ordinary local authorities were expected to take such action to prevent the spread of disease as local public opinion and the medical knowledge of the times demanded. In case of extraordinary epidemics, the governor could go to the assistance of the local authorities, but this was rarely done. The abatement of nuisances was largely left to private initiative by means of actions in the courts of law. In 1787, Massachusetts led the way in the improvement of public health administration by providing that each town should establish a local board of health. Many towns, however, neglected to do this. It was not until after the Civil War that the need was recognized for regular state-wide supervision of the public health by special state officials, and for systematic coöperation between the central and local health authorities. In 1869, Massachusetts again led the way by the establishment of a state board of health. Since then, central public health authorities have been established in all the states. But these state boards of health have been granted jurisdiction over only a part of the general field of health administration. Special administrative boards or offices have been created from time to time in the several states, as the need happened to arise, for the purpose of dealing with special problems relating to public health. Thus, boards of education frequently were authorized to enforce the laws relating to the health of school children, boards of charity and of insanity were

[1] See R. C. Cabot, "The Administration of Public Health," in the *Cyclopedia of American Government*, ii, pp. 117-121. See also Harry H. Moore, *Public Health in the United States* (New York, 1923); and M. P. Ravenel, ed., *A Half Century of Public Health* (American Public Health Association, Jubilee Historical Volume, 1921). For current legislation, see *State Laws and Regulations pertaining to Public Health*, published annually by the United States Public Health Service.

generally created or charged to administer the laws relating to the health of dependents, special food and dairy commissioners were often appointed to enforce the laws relating to the inspection of foods and milk, the enforcement of liquor laws was left to the sheriffs and local constables, boards or commissioners of agriculture were generally charged with the enforcement of the laws relating to the health of domestic animals, the inspection of tenements, factories, workshops, and other buildings, mines, elevators, boilers, etc., was frequently confided to separate bureaus or departments, and the enforcement of laws relating to the hours of labor and wages of wage-earning men and women was entrusted to factory inspectors, boards of conciliation and arbitration, minimum wage commissions, or various combinations thereof. The regulation of the conditions for entrance into the professions connected with the public health and the examination of applicants has generally been divided among a number of separate boards. In some states, there are half a dozen or more such boards, each independent of the others. The result has been an extraordinary subdivision of authority and diffusion of responsibility among a confused array of central agencies for the administration of laws relating to health.

This condition has been somewhat improved as a result of the recent consolidation movement. Various agencies have been consolidated under a state board of public health, as in Delaware and Washington, or under a single commissioner or director, usually assisted by an advisory board or council, as in Illinois, Ohio, and Tennessee. But much remains to be done.

Centralizing Tendencies.

Despite the confusion resulting from the division of public health administration among so many independent bodies, there has been a steady drift toward the centralization of control over health administration in the hands of the state authorities. This tendency can be observed most clearly in the evolution of the powers of the original state health authorities. Three separate stages may be discerned. The first state boards of health were authorized to make investigations, publish reports, and offer advice to the local authorities. The second stage was reached when the state was divided into health or sanitary districts, and the central board was empowered to appoint district inspectors with wide powers of direct action within their districts. This stage is best represented by the existing organization of the state departments of health in Massachusetts, New York, and Pennsylvania. The third stage was reached when the central authorities were granted the power not only to supervise but also to control the work of the local authorities. In more than a dozen states, the central authorities may appoint the local health officers, if the local governments fail to appoint them, and may remove them, if they neglect their duties or are incompetent to perform them. In Vermont and Florida, the local authorities are regularly appointed by the central authorities and act as their agents. In several states, local health regulations must be approved by the central authorities before becoming effective. In New York, the central health authorities are authorized to enact and from time to time to amend a sanitary code for the whole state with the exception of New York City, and the local authorities are required to enforce it under the supervision of the district health inspectors. Moreover, the central authorities may themselves, if they choose, enforce the health laws in localities where no local authorities have been appointed. Thus a high degree of centralization in public health administration is reached.[1] But the jurisdiction of these state departments of health is ordinarily limited to matters of general concern.

LABOR LAW ADMINISTRATION

The most important division of public health administration, not commonly placed under the jurisdiction of the state health departments or boards, is the enforcement of health and safety legislation designed for the special protection of wage earners.[2] In this branch of administration, there has also been a constant tendency to increase the powers of the central authorities. The first state administrative agencies charged primarily with the

[1] This centralization is further increased by the granting of state subsidies to the local authorities for various kinds of health work. Congress, by the Sheppard-Towner Act of 1921, applied the conditional subsidy principle to the promotion of maternity and infant hygiene and welfare in the states. At present, forty-three states have accepted the provisions of this act and are receiving grants-in-aid from the federal treasury.

[2] On labor legislation and administration, see J. R. Commons and J. B. Andrews, *Principles of Labor Legislation* (rev. ed., New York, 1920). For a compilation and digest of state labor laws, see *Labor Laws of the United States with Decisions of Courts relating thereto*, published by the United States Bureau of Labor Statistics (Bulletin 370, 1925).

protection of wage earners were the bureaus of labor statistics, the earliest of which was that of Massachusetts established in 1869. Like the original state boards of health, the duties of these bureaus were merely to make investigations, publish reports, and give advice. The next step was to provide for state inspection of factories and workshops in order to prevent the maintenance of conditions dangerous to life and limb or injurious to the general health of the workers. Under various laws, all the states, to a greater or less degree, have made provision for the inspection of fire hazards, boilers, mines, dangerous machinery and processes of manufacture, lighting, heating, ventilation, and sanitation, and for the enforcement of laws limiting the hours of labor and other conditions of employment.

Moreover, the enforcement of labor legislation is something more than a special phase of public health administration. It involves such functions as the fixing of minimum wages, the settlement of industrial disputes, the administration of workmen's compensation acts and other forms of social insurance, and the operation or supervision of employment agencies. The states have made considerable progress in regulating labor conditions in these respects as well as in connection with the protection of the health of wage earners. For example, more than a dozen states, beginning with Massachusetts in 1912, have enacted minimum wage laws of various kinds applicable to women and children workers.[1] However, at present the future of such laws is uncertain. Recent decisions by the United States Supreme Court holding mandatory minimum wage statutes to be unconstitutional as applied to adult women have gone far to nullify this type of legislation.[2] These decisions are broad enough to cover all existing acts except that of Massachusetts which relies upon publicity rather than penalties to secure the observance of minimum wage awards.

Beginning with Maryland in 1878, practically all the states have established one or more public agencies for the peaceful settlement of industrial disputes through mediation, conciliation, and voluntary arbitration. Valuable as these agencies have been,

[1] The Kansas act of 1920 applied also to men.

[2] Adkins *v.* Children's Hospital of the District of Columbia, 261 U. S. 525 (1923); Sardell *v.* Murphy (Arizona minimum wage law), decided October, 1925. The points of constitutional law involved in these and other labor cases are discussed in ch. xiii.

they have been far from successful in preventing industrial warfare. In spite of this fact, the states have hesitated to take more drastic measures. This hesitation is due partly to constitutional restraints and partly to very real practical difficulties. However, two states have endeavored to surmount these difficulties. Colorado in 1915 provided for compulsory investigation of labor disputes by the state industrial commission and forbade strikes, lockouts, or any change in the terms of employment until after the hearing and report of the commission. The commission's finding or award is not made mandatory upon the parties to the dispute. Five years later, Kansas enacted a drastic compulsory arbitration statute applicable not only to public utilities but also to industries concerned with the production and distribution of food, clothing, and fuel. Strikes and lockouts in these industries were prohibited and disputes not settled by peaceful action of the parties involved were to be adjudicated by a court of industrial relations consisting of three judges appointed by the governor and senate. The awards of this court were made mandatory and might cover working conditions, hours of labor, and minimum or standard wages, together with other phases of the business affected. Furthermore, in cases where production and operation were suspended as a result of a dispute, the court might take over and operate directly the industries in question. This Kansas law aroused great controversy and did not long remain in effect. Its most important provisions were declared unconstitutional by the United States Supreme Court,[1] and, in 1925, the court of industrial relations was abolished by the legislature.

Contemporary labor legislation also includes schemes for social insurance since such insurance is designed primarily for the benefit of the wage earning classes and their dependents. The principal types of social insurance found in the states are the workman's compensation acts and various forms of mothers' pensions. Beginning with Maryland in 1902, forty-two states now have workmen's compensation laws, most of which are administered by special state boards or commissions. More recently, workmen's compensation has been supplemented by

[1] Wolff Packing Co. *v.* Court of Industrial Relations, 262 U. S. 525 (1923),—unconstitutional as to fixing of wages in meat packing establishments; *ibid.*, 267 U. S. 552,—unconstitutional as to compulsory arbitration in a competitive business not affected with a public interest.

legislation providing for the vocational rehabilitation of industrial cripples. By the Industrial Rehabilitation Act of 1920, Congress granted conditional subsidies to the states to be used in restoring to civil employment persons injured in industry or in any legitimate occupation. At present, thirty-nine states have accepted this act and are receiving federal grants-in-aid for rehabilitation work. Mothers' pension laws are found in forty-two states. As noted previously, such laws are generally administered by the local authorities, but, in half the states, the local authorities are subject to some form of state supervision. Three states authorize old age pensions and these, likewise, are primarily under local administration.[1] No state has, as yet, attempted to meet the problem of unemployment by establishing a system of unemployment insurance. In so far as this problem has been dealt with by the states, it has been through state regulation of private employment agencies so as to reduce or eliminate the abuses to which such agencies subjected applicants for work; through the establishment of free public employment agencies by the state, and through more or less sporadic attempts to provide for the construction of public works during periods of industrial depression so as to give employment to large numbers who are out of work.[2]

From the brief survey which has just been given, it is apparent that the labor legislation of the states covers a wide range of subjects. Much of this legislation involved the creation of special enforcement agencies, each substantially independent of the others. Here, as in other branches of state administration, there consequently developed a real need for administrative reorganization and consolidation. Beginning with Wisconsin in 1911, more than one-fourth of the states have established con-

[1] Nevada (1923), Montana (1923), Wisconsin (1925). The old age pension laws of Arizona and Pennsylvania were declared unconstitutional by the supreme courts of those states in 1921 and 1925 respectively. The Nevada law, as amended in 1925, provides that old age pensions are to be wholly administered by the county authorities. The Wisconsin statute of the same year permits counties to adopt old age pensions which are to be administered by the county judges, subject to the approval of the state board of control.

[2] A majority of the states have regulated private employment agencies and have established state employment agencies. A few states have tried to plan their public works construction programs so as to correlate with the business cycle. Thus a California law of 1921 provides for the extension of state construction projects during periods of extraordinary unemployment caused by temporary industrial depression.

solidated departments of labor. These departments are headed by an industrial commission, as in Wisconsin, Minnesota, and California, or by a single director, as in Illinois, New Jersey, and Tennessee. Some of these departments were created as a part of a general reorganization of the state administration; others were the outcome of piecemeal consolidations including only the state's labor law enforcement agencies.

AGRICULTURE

The same tendencies appear in the administration of the laws designed for the special benefit of farmers and stock growers.[1] In many states, the activities relating to the interests of agriculture, horticulture, dairying, and stock growing are more important and more diversified than those relating to the interests of industrial wage earners. Some of the activities associated with public administration in relation to agriculture and allied interests are the following: the collection of rural statistics, the holding of agricultural fairs and farmers' institutes, the analysis of soils and fertilizers, the registration of livestock, the study and suppression of animal and plant diseases, pests, etc., the inspection of herds and meat products, dairy products, apiaries, etc., the grading of cotton, wool, grain, etc., the preservation and propagation of fish and game, the conservation of natural resources in general, especially of forests, and reforestation, drainage of swamp lands, and irrigation, the encouragement of agricultural experimentation and poultry and stock breeding, the supervision of warehouses and commission merchants and of the supply of agricultural labor, the examination and licensing of veterinarians, the inspection of fruits and seeds, trees, shrubs, and plants, and the regulation of cold storage. The result has been the creation of an even greater number of separate administrative agencies than in the case of labor law administration. Among the more important administrative agencies of this character are the following: state boards or commissioners of agriculture, state veterinarians, entomologists, chemists, foresters, fish and game commissioners, food and dairy commissioners, inspectors of fertilizer, hides, apiaries, etc., state fair and cattle

[1] On state agricultural administration, see Edward Wiest, *Agricultural Organization in the United States* (Lexington, Kentucky, 1923), especially ch. xiv.

commissioners, and trustees of agricultural experiment stations. Protection of the public health comprises manifestly but a small part of the activities of these authorities. They are expected to assist in the development of better methods of raising and marketing crops, to stimulate the breeding of improved grades of stock, and, in general, to encourage rural industry and enrich country life.

In the administration of the laws relating to rural as well as urban industry, there has been a constant tendency to increase the powers of the central administrative authorities. The first state boards of agriculture had advisory powers only. They were expected to stimulate rural industry in a general manner, and, in particular, to patronize the county agricultural fairs. Subsequently, these state boards were granted greater powers of supervision. For example, they were in some cases authorized to apportion state funds in aid of county fairs on condition that the fair managers complied with certain requirements intended to make the fairs more serviceable to the farmers. Eventually, in a few states, they were themselves authorized to manage state fairs, and endowed with other powers of direct control. More frequently, however, as the need for direct central control of rural services was recognized, instead of conferring additional powers upon the original boards of agriculture, special agencies were created wholly independent of the boards of agriculture. Gradually, as in the administration of the laws relating to urban industry, the need for closer relations between different administrative agencies was recognized. The movement began for the organization of departments of agriculture, which, like the departments of labor, should more effectually correlate the activities of all state agricultural authorities. This movement first appeared in the South, starting with Georgia and Tennessee in 1874 and 1875 respectively. Many other states have taken similar action, especially during the last ten or fifteen years when so many plans for general administrative reorganization have been carried out or attempted. In about two-thirds of the states, there are now organized agricultural departments in which are united a considerable number of services. These departments are usually placed under the direction of a single commissioner rather than under the earlier type of agency, a state board of agriculture. This is notably the case in Pennsylvania,

Ohio, and California, to mention only a few examples. As for the remaining states, the division of power among numerous separate administrative authorities still obtains. Even in those states which have established consolidated departments of agriculture, it is not unusual for such functions as the protection of fish and game and the promotion of forestry to be placed under the jurisdiction of a separate department of conservation or a department of fisheries and game. But, in general, it appears that, in the administration of the laws relating to rural industry, there has been a substantial measure of centralization of control and also a considerable degree of integration of organization.

PUBLIC WORKS

At the time of the Revolution, the principal public works constructed and maintained by the states were those of a military character. The states still spend considerable sums of money upon armories for the use of the militia. The growth of state transportation enterprises in the first part of the nineteenth century has left a few states with more or less useful canals on their hands.[1] Of these, New York is the chief. At present, the principal public works of the states fall under the following heads: highways; waterworks of various kinds, including storage reservoirs for urban supply and irrigation, river and harbor improvements, drainage, and flood prevention;[2] state parks and reservations;[3] and public buildings and monuments. To administer these various kinds of public works, a corresponding variety of administrative agencies has been created. For the most part, the administration of the public works of the states is completely centralized in the hands of the state authorities, but no pronounced tendency is apparent towards the organization of con-

[1] Only one state, Georgia, now owns a railroad, and that road is leased to a private company. See Carl D. Thompson, *Public Ownership* (New York, 1925), pp. 77-78.

[2] Water supply problems and projects are being increasingly dealt with in recent years by joint state action. Two notable interstate agreements are now pending, the Colorado River Compact involving seven southwestern states, and the Delaware River Compact involving New York, New Jersey, and Pennsylvania.

[3] Sixteen states have established state forest reserves and twenty-six states have established state parks. The movement for state parks has been greatly stimulated by the widespread use of automobiles. See Harold A. Caparn, "State Parks," *National Municipal Review*, x, pp. 581-600 (Supplement, November, 1921).

solidated departments of public works with a general jurisdiction over works of different kinds. In states where so-called state departments of public works have been created, the department generally has charge of some one public work, such as a canal or a system of state roads, which happens to be of exceptional importance. However, the more thorough of the recent administrative reorganizations have resulted in placing the principal types of public works under the control of a single department. This is notably the case in Illinois, Ohio, and Tennessee.[1] The questions concerning the relations between state and local authorities, which have played so important a part in the development of other branches of state administration, here have been raised urgently only in connection with the construction of internal improvements, especially those of a local character, at state expense. From this point of view, the most important division of public works administration is that of the highways.

Highways.

The study of state highway administration reveals the same tendencies that have been observed in the development of other branches of state administration.[2] In the beginning, the construction and maintenance of highways was left entirely to the local authorities. Almost without exception, this continued to be the situation until the last decade of the nineteenth century. In 1891, New Jersey began the movement for building improved roads with the aid of state appropriations and with state supervision. Massachusetts followed in 1893, California and Connecticut in 1895, and New York in 1898.[3] The introduction of the automobile has greatly increased the radius of traffic everywhere, and has correspondingly increased the demand for good roads. As a result, the highway problem has ceased to be

[1] In 1925, the jurisdiction of the Illinois department of public works and buildings was somewhat narrowed by a law which vested certain of its functions in a new department of purchases and construction. The New York reorganization amendment of 1925 contemplates a consolidated department of public works.

[2] See G. R. Chatburn, *Highways and Highway Transportation* (New York, 1923). On the history of highways and highway administration as exemplified in a typical state, see W. C. Plummer, *The Road Policy of Pennsylvania* (Philadelphia, 1925). Useful information on highways and highway finance is contained in "The Automobile: Its Province and Its Problems," *Annals*, cxvi (November, 1924).

[3] See J. A. Fairlie, *Local Government in Counties, Towns, and Villages* (New York, 1906), pp. 264-267.

purely local in character and has become statewide and national in its scope. In consequence, both the state and the federal governments are now spending huge sums upon road construction. As early as 1906, New York, by popular vote, authorized a bond issue of $50,000,000 to be used in building a state highway system. Within the last ten years, many other states have likewise borrowed heavily in order to execute comprehensive road schemes. These schemes have been adopted upon the theory that the state as a whole has an interest in the improvement of the main routes of travel. The interest of the federal government in highway development has received striking expression in the Federal Highway Act of 1916 and its amendments, which provide for large conditional subsidies to the states. This legislation "transformed road construction throughout the United States. Every state in the Union accepted its provisions, and, in the year following its passage, more constructive highway legislation was placed upon the state statute books than had ever before been enacted in a similar period in the history of the country. Prior to 1916 the federal government took no active part in road building; to-day about one-half of all highways in course of construction are receiving federal aid, and are subject to the inspection and approval of federal engineers."[1]

Under such circumstances, it is not surprising that state highway departments or equivalent agencies have been established in all the states. As noted before, the state highway agency may be a separate department or it may be a part of a department of public works which is charged with other duties as well. The principal functions of state highway agencies may be classified according to the order of their historical development as follows: first, the inspection of local roads and the giving of advice to local authorities as to how to improve them; secondly, the allocation of state highway money among local authorities, coupled with more or less state supervision of its expenditure; and thirdly, the actual construction of roads by the state highway department itself. This third function is the one most generally exercised wherever the state goes into the roadbuilding business on any extensive scale, although the problem of locating

[1] A. F. Macdonald, *Federal Subsidies to the States* (Philadelphia, 1923), p. 69. See also the annual reports of the Chief of the Bureau of Public Roads, United States Department of Agriculture.

the state roads causes many difficulties on account of local jealousies. In addition to the building of roads, the state highway authorities often have charge of the examination and licensing of automobile drivers, and regulate the use of state roads by the public. In general, the tendency is strongly towards the centralization of control over local roads and road construction.

SUPERVISION OF CORPORATIONS

Business corporations were originally chartered by special acts of the state legislatures. At the time of the Revolution, there were very few such corporations in the United States, and the method of regulation by special act seemed to afford adequate security to the public against the abuse of corporate privileges by their promoters and proprietors. The development of industry in the first half of the nineteenth century, particularly of banking, insurance, and transportation, greatly increased the demand for corporate privileges in general and the value of certain special privileges, such as those of issuing notes with a limited liability for redemption and of taking property by right of eminent domain. Corrupt means were not infrequently employed to secure the grant of such special privileges, and, in many corporate charters, state legislatures failed to insert proper safeguards for the interests of the public. In 1819, the decision of the United States Supreme Court in the Dartmouth College case showed that the states would be unable to correct, without the consent of the promoters or proprietors, the errors that might appear in badly drawn or corruptly obtained charters. Thereupon, there arose a widespread popular demand for stricter regulation of the practice of incorporation, and for closer supervision of the operations of corporations. Most states provided that charters should not be issued except under authority of general laws, and that corporations of certain kinds—principally, at first, banks and insurance companies—should be subject to continuous supervision by special officials. After the Civil War, the increasing dependence of the public upon the railroads, and, in the cities, upon urban public utilities, created a demand for special regulations to secure adequate service at reasonable rates without discrimination. The right of the state legislatures to regulate such corporations in these respects was affirmed by the

United States Supreme Court in the Granger cases[1] and has been exercised in one form or another by practically all the states. A recent development in the regulation of corporations has been the enactment by about forty states, beginning with Kansas in 1911, of the so-called "blue-sky" laws. These laws are based upon the assumption, which is amply justified by the facts, that the regulation of the issue of corporation securities by the states in which the corporations are created is imperfect, and that there is need for the regulation of the sale of such securities to investors in other states. Consequently, the vendors of corporate securities are required, before making any sales within the state, to submit their offerings to inspection by a special official and procure a license. But no states have yet dealt effectively with the issue of securities, except in the case of public service corporations.

The growing recognition of the necessity of regulating corporations has been reflected in a corresponding growth of administrative agencies for purposes of regulation. The administration of the general laws regulating corporations was at first imposed upon the secretaries of state. Special administrative machinery, however, was soon created for the supervision of special classes of corporations. Commissioners of banking and of insurance, railroad and warehouse commissions, special boards for the regulation of municipal utilities, and general corporation commissions or commissioners have been created from time to time as various needs were recognized. There has been a constant tendency to extend the powers of central control over the various classes of corporations. Commissioners of banking and insurance at first generally possessed merely the power to receive reports and make them public. Subsequently, they received ever broadening powers to examine the books and records of banks and insurance companies, audit their accounts, require the maintenance of certain reserves, and the investment of funds in approved securities, and to exclude undesirable enterprises from the further conduct of business within the state. Jurisdiction has been frequently extended over private and fraternal banking and insurance as well as over ordinary corporations. In several states of the South and West, the state authorities are authorized to engage to a limited extent in the business of banking,

[1] See Munn *v.* Illinois, 94 U. S., 113 (1876).

for such is the effect of the bank deposit guarantee laws enacted in those states.[1] Under the influence of the Non-Partisan League, North Dakota has established a state-owned bank, the Bank of North Dakota.[2] In one state, Wisconsin, the state authorities have been authorized to engage in the business of life insurance, while five states have provided systems of state hail insurance.[3]

Regulation of Public Utilities.

The most striking example of the growth of the power to control business corporations is afforded by the regulation of public service corporations.[4] The Massachusetts railroad commission of 1869 had power merely to investigate, issue reports to the public, and make recommendations to the railroads. The Massachusetts gas and electric lighting commissioners of 1885 were authorized to issue orders to the corporations under their jurisdiction, to forbid the construction of unnecessary competitive plants, and to regulate the creation of new securities as well as the rates and conditions of service. The Wisconsin railroad commission of 1905 was authorized not only to exercise all the foregoing powers, but also to appraise the physical property of the railroads and determine its true value. Two years later the Wisconsin public utilities commission was created with similar jurisdiction over local railway, light, and power companies; and in the same year the New York public service commissions were established. Thereafter the Wisconsin and New York plans of regulating public service corporations spread rapidly throughout the Union. State regulation of municipally owned public utilities has gone as far as that of privately owned utilities.

[1] Kansas, Nebraska, South Dakota, North Dakota, Mississippi, Washington, and Texas. The Oklahoma law of 1907, the first of the bank deposit guarantee statutes, was repealed in 1923. The experience of the other states, especially during the post-war depression, has not been particularly happy. See Thornton Cooke, "The Collapse of Bank-Deposit Guaranty in Oklahoma and Its Position in Other States," *Quarterly Journal of Economics*, xxxviii, pp. 108-139 (1923-24).

[2] See Alvin S. Tostelbe, *The Bank of North Dakota; an Experiment in Agrarian Banking* (Columbia University Studies, cxiv, New York, 1924). During the first half of the nineteenth century, there were fifteen states which owned and operated one or more banks.

[3] Montana, Nebraska, North Dakota, South Dakota, and Oklahoma.

[4] See M. L. Cooke, ed., *Public Utility Regulation* (New York, 1924). Motorbus companies are the latest addition to the list of public service corporations and are being more and more brought under state regulation.

The tendency to increase the powers of the administrative authorities charged with the supervision of corporations is much more general than the tendency to establish any uniform type of administrative organization. The granting of charters to domestic corporations, and the admission of foreign corporations for the transaction of general business within the state, still remain in most states duties of the secretary of state. The consolidation of jurisdiction over all classes of public service corporations in a single public utilities commission has been accomplished in most of the states, beginning with Wisconsin in 1907. Massachusetts at one time had three separate commissions regulating the rates and service of public utilities. In addition to its public service commission, New York has a separate commission with jurisdiction over transit in the city of New York. Most states still maintain separate departments for the supervision of banks and insurance companies. A few states, however, notably Virginia and South Carolina, have consolidated all the offices and boards having jurisdiction over the organization and activities of business corporations into a single state corporation commission. These corporation commissions act also as state boards of assessors for the assessment and taxation of certain classes of corporations. In general, however, the taxation of corporations is controlled by an entirely different set of officials from those who supervise their operations, and in many states there may be two wholly distinct valuations placed upon the property and business of corporations, one for the purpose of regulating rates or other features of their business, another for purposes of taxation. The single state corporation commission represents one type of consolidated department. A more recent development is the department headed by a single commissioner, a type which has been adopted in a number of states as a result of a general administrative reorganization. Thus, in Ohio, the department of commerce, under a director, enforces the laws dealing with banking, building and loan associations, insurance, "blue-sky" securities, oil inspection, and fire prevention, while the public utilities commission is attached to the department for administrative purposes. On the other hand, the Minnesota reorganization of 1925 provides for a similar department headed by a commission of three members. No standard practice has yet developed.

MILITIA AND STATE POLICE

At the time of the Revolution, the most important department of state administration was the military.[1] All the original state constitutions made some provision for the organization and control of the militia. In the constitution of Massachusetts, military administration was regulated with special care. The governor was declared to be the commander-in-chief of the army and navy and of all the military forces of the state, by sea and land, and was entrusted with all the powers of a captain-general and commander-in-chief and of an admiral, subject only to the constitution of the state and the law of the land. After the Revolution, however, the state maintained no military forces except the militia, and the actual power of the governor over the militia was strictly limited by the constitutional provisions governing its organization. Militia captains and subalterns were elected by the "train-band and alarm list" of their respective companies, regimental field officers were elected by the captains and subalterns, and brigadiers by the field officers. The major-generals were appointed by the legislature, the two houses voting separately. No militia officer could be removed except by address of both houses to the governor or by court-martial. Thus, the militia organization was completely decentralized, and the authority of the governor was not much more than nominal. A similar form of organization was originally adopted in most of the states. During the course of the nineteenth century, the militia tended to become somewhat less decentralized in character. In particular, the power of the governor as commander-in-chief was often strengthened by giving him authority to appoint militia officers, at least those of the higher ranks. This step, however, did not necessarily improve the military character of the militia; political and social, rather than military, considerations continued, as before, to play too large a part in state military administration.

In recent years, the character of the militia as a military body has been considerably improved. By the Federal Constitution of 1787, Congress was authorized to employ the militia to

[1] For a good discussion of the activities of the states in the recent war with Germany and her allies, see Charles G. Fenwick, *Political Systems in Transition* (New York, 1920), ch. ix.

execute the laws of the Union, suppress insurrections, and repel invasions, and, to that end, was empowered to provide for its organization, equipment, and discipline, reserving to the states the appointment of officers and the training of the men according to the discipline provided by Congress. Prior to the Militia Act of 1903 and the National Defense Act of 1916, Congress made little effective use of these powers and the states were given practically a free hand in the organization and control of their military forces. However, as a result of this legislation, an efficient system of national supervision over the military establishments of the several states was developed and the militia, or "National Guard," became a coördinated national organization supplementary to the regular army of the United States.[1]

Desirable as these changes were from the standpoint of federal authority, they did not materially help the states in their internal problems of maintaining law and order. The ordinary state agencies for the preservation of the peace were mainly the local sheriffs and constables in the rural districts and the municipal police in the cities.[2] For extraordinary occasions, such as severe strikes and riots, where special police protection was required, reliance was placed upon the militia acting under the governor as commander-in-chief.[3]

Recent Tendencies in Law Enforcement.

As a result of the great economic and social changes in American life during the last fifty or seventy-five years, both the militia and the local police have tended to become ineffective instruments of the police power of the state. It is apparent that the militia is too clumsy an organization to be of any value in the performance of minor police duties, such as the apprehension of ordinary criminals. On account of the slowness with which it is mobilized, the great expense involved, and the danger of using either too much force or too little force, the militia often fails to give satisfaction in the performance of major police

[1] See Macdonald, *op. cit.*, ch. vi.

[2] In case of need, these agencies might be supplemented by a posse comitatus summoned by the sheriff.

[3] The governor's control of the militia is ordinarily exercised through the adjutant general, an officer who is usually appointed, and sometimes also removable, by him.

duties, such as the preservation of order in serious labor disputes. Under circumstances of this sort, the presence of bayonets, machine guns, tear gas bombs, and barbed wire may only serve to inflame the strikers to more desperate measures. Moreover, the use of the militia in connection with labor troubles has operated to discredit every form of military service among wage earners. In the case of local police agencies, these have likewise been unsatisfactory instruments for enforcing state law and order. Being locally elected or appointed, urban and rural police officers have in the past been subject to little or no central control, in consequence of which, state legislation has been frequently nullified through non-enforcement. The state constitutions usually direct the governor to "take care that the laws be faithfully executed," and yet, on account of the extent to which administrative decentralization has been carried, he has had comparatively little control over the local officials upon whom he must largely depend for the regular enforcement of state laws.

The efforts of the states to deal with this phase of administrative decentralization and its resulting evils have been along four principal lines.[1] In the first place, as noted before, certain types of laws such as those dealing with education, health, and labor, are either enforced directly by specially constituted state agencies or by local officials subject to continuous and increasingly effective state supervision. Direct administration is especially evident in connection with prohibition legislation and has frequently resulted in the creation of state prohibition commissioners and state prohibition enforcement units. Secondly, in a number of jurisdictions, the governor has been given a limited authority to remove local officers charged with the general administration of state law. Thus, in New York, Michigan, Wisconsin, and elsewhere, the governor may remove sheriffs, district attorneys, and certain other local administrative officials for neglect of duty or inefficiency. This power is valuable so far as it goes but its use is apt to be restricted to the most conspicuous cases of neglect or inefficiency. Thirdly, beginning with New York City in 1857, the policy of actual state control over police departments in the larger cities made considerable

[1] See W. F. Dodd, *State Government*, ch. xi, for a good discussion of the methods and agencies for the enforcement of state law.

headway for a time. This policy, however, did not prove permanent. It was regarded as an undue infringement upon the principle of municipal home rule and the subsequent improvement in the character of city police forces made such extreme control less necessary.[1] The last and most recent development is the creation of state police forces, armed with general powers of law enforcement and authorized to operate throughout the whole state.[2]

State Police.

The general movement for state police is a product of the period during and since the World War, but the idea itself is not new. The Texas Rangers, originally organized in 1835 to patrol the Mexican border, represent the earliest form of state police. The first state to provide for state police officers with general police powers was Massachusetts, where in 1865 a few state constables were appointed. Much later in point of time, but far more important as a precedent and as an example, was the establishment of the Pennsylvania State Constabulary. This was organized in 1905 on the general model of the Royal North West Mounted Police of Canada, and consisted of four troops of fifty men each.[3] As a result of the legislation of the last ten years, state police forces now exist, or have existed, in one form or another, in about one-fourth of the states. The principal factors in this development have been summarized[4] as follows: the need for some kind of temporary or permanent protective body to replace the regular militia which was drafted into the federal service in 1917; the increased mobility of the criminal due to the use of the automobile; the "crime wave" in the aftermath of the war, and the consequent inability of local sheriffs and constables to furnish adequate police service to rural areas; the desire to prevent disorder in industrial disputes without resorting to that clumsy and expensive weapon, the militia;

[1] Baltimore, Boston, Kansas City, and Saint Louis are the only important cities having state controlled police forces at the present time. See W. B. Munro, *Municipal Government and Administration*, ii, pp. 189-191.

[2] On state police, see Bruce Smith, *The State Police* (New York, 1925) and Milton Conover, "State Police Developments: 1921–1924," *American Political Science Review*, xviii, pp. 773-781 (1924).

[3] See Smith, *op. cit.*, pp. 37 ff.

[4] See Conover, *op. cit.*, p. 773.

the necessity for traffic regulation on the state highways; the difficulty of securing uniform enforcement of prohibition legislation; and the recognition of the efficiency of a small, mobile, professional police organization performing continuous patrol duty.

The jurisdiction of the state police is very broad. Its members are vested with all the general police powers possessed by local peace officers and these powers may be exercised anywhere within the state, subject, in a number of instances, to certain restrictions as to strike and riot duty in cities.[1] In addition, the state police force coöperates with the various state departments in many ways and is sometimes charged with the execution of a considerable number of collateral functions such as elevator and building inspection, censorship of Sunday entertainments, inspection of the pollution of streams by industrial refuse, and examination of applicants for automobile drivers' licenses. There is danger that the continued increase of such duties will hamper the state police in carrying out the primary purposes for which the agency was established.

In such states as Pennsylvania, New York, and New Jersey, the state police organizations are headed by a superintendent appointed by the governor and senate, responsible directly to the governor, and removable by the governor. Thus, the chief executive is provided with an efficient instrument for insuring a better and more uniform enforcement of the laws of the state. In other states, such as Connecticut, Michigan, and West Virginia, the state police bodies are more or less controlled by administrative boards and the lines of responsibility are not so clearly fixed.

As a rule, the state police forces have proved to be very useful additions to the states' administrative machinery. They have, in large measure, been successful in meeting the needs which called them into existence. However, the course of the state police has not been altogether clear sailing. Organized labor, fearing the use of strong-arm methods in strikes, has maintained a distinctly hostile attitude. State police forces

[1] In a few states, such as Delaware, Maryland, and Washington, the so-called state police is, in reality, merely a special highway police force devoting its attention primarily to motor vehicle control. Illinois, in 1925, extended general police powers to its state highway maintenance patrol.

have also been opposed as an infringement upon the province of local government. The state police organization has frequently been a political issue and, in four states,[1] it has been abolished. Nevertheless, in spite of these unfavorable developments, the merits of the state police far outweigh its defects and its future development seems reasonably secure.

STATE FINANCE

Expenditures.

The development of the activities of the state governments has entailed a great increase in state expenditures. This increase has been especially marked since the beginning of the present century. In 1903, the states spent $182,631,000; in 1913, $379,-098,000; and in 1924, $1,513,628,000.[2] Between 1913 and 1924, the expenditures of the states almost quadrupled. The real increase, however, was not as great as these figures would seem to indicate since they do not take into account increases in wealth and population and changes in the purchasing power of money. If the expenditures for 1913 and 1924 are reduced to a per capita basis and those for 1924 are further translated into dollars with a purchasing power as of 1913, it will be found that the expenses of the states have only somewhat more than doubled.[3] But even after these allowances have been made, the increase is indeed large.

In 1924, the per capita expenditures of the states upon the different branches of state administration were as follows: [4]

[1] Arizona, Colorado, Idaho, and New Mexico.

[2] United States Bureau of the Census, *Report on Wealth, Public Debt, and Taxation, 1913*, ii, pp. 40-42; *ibid.*, *Financial Statistics of States, 1924*, p. 17.

[3] See A. F. Macdonald, "The Trend in Recent State Expenditures," *Annals*, cxii, pp. 8-15 (May, 1924). From 1912 to 1922, it has been estimated that the national wealth increased 72 per cent. (See "Estimated National Wealth," *Reports on Wealth, Public Debt, and Taxation, 1922*, p. 19.) From 1913 to 1923, state expenditures increased 245 per cent. For a valuable study of expenditures with special reference to New York State, see Clarence Heer, *The Post-War Expansion of State Expenditures* (New York, 1926). See also "State Expenditures, Tax Burden, and Wealth," *A Report by the (New York) Special Joint Committee on Taxation and Retrenchment* (Albany, 1926).

[4] *Financial Statistics of States, 1924, passim.* See the text discussion in the report for an explanation of the table reprinted on p. 368.

State Governmental Cost Payments Per Capita, 1924

	All States	Massachusetts	New York	Minnesota	South Carolina	Arkansas	Nevada	California
Current expense of all general departments...	$9.00	$10.31	$10.95	$12.34	$5.26	$4.68	$26.32	$14.14
General government...	0.67	1.11	0.84	0.62	0.54	0.43	2.06	0.73
Protection to person and property	0.46	0.71	0.63	0.60	0.20	0.17	1.53	0.78
Development and conservation of natural resources	0.48	0.24	0.53	1.26	0.43	0.26	3.79	1.25
Health and sanitation.	0.21	0.43	0.16	0.32	0.13	0.13	0.71	0.17
Highways	1.11	1.42	1.78	1.63	0.12	0.64	3.88	2.23
Charities, hospitals, and corrections	1.49	3.05	2.12	1.74	0.73	0.54	2.87	2.08
Education	3.34	1.16	4.22	5.64	2.61	1.80	10.72	6.65
Recreation	0.02	0.06	0.07	0.02	*	*	*	0.01
Miscellaneous	1.24	2.13	0.59	0.51	0.49	0.70	0.76	0.26
Expense of public service enterprises	0.10	0.05	....	....	....	....	....	0.50
Interest	0.50	0.44	1.00	0.48	0.20	0.09	1.06	1.03
Capital outlays	4.00	1.62	2.85	4.90	1.70	1.16	36.46	3.92
Total	$13.61	$12.43	$14.79	$17.71	$7.16	$5.93	$63.84	$19.58

* Less than one-half of one cent.

From the above table, it will be observed that there is a wide variation in per capita expenditures from state to state. The per capita cost for Arkansas, the lowest in 1924, was only a little less than one-half of the average for all the states, while the per capita cost for Nevada, the highest in 1924, was more than four times the average. How are these differences to be explained? In recent years, most of the states have borrowed heavily for capital outlays, but these outlays are not uniformly distributed from year to year. Consequently, because of outlays in a particular year, the average of a state may be considerably increased above the per capita costs of the preceding and following years. Again, in a state like Nevada which has a large area and a small population, a certain minimum of state activity is necessary regardless of the population, and these "overhead costs" are reflected in an unduly large per capita expenditure. Even if two states are approximately equal in size and number of inhabitants and are otherwise similarly situated, the public demand for state services may vary substantially. In this connection, it is well to bear in mind the possibility of differences in the distribution of governmental expenditures between the states and their respective local governments. What is primarily a local charge in one section of the country may be a state expense in another. The subsidy principle introduces another qualification. Some states have accepted large subventions from the federal government; others have been inclined to refuse such grants-in-aid because of the conditions attached to them. If the subsidy is for a purpose which would not otherwise be undertaken or would be undertaken on a smaller scale, the per capita cost to the state is increased accordingly. The same result is produced whenever subventions are granted from the state treasury to the local areas, and, here again, these grants are more widely used in some states than in others. Finally, the lack of uniform methods of accounting and reporting makes comparisons of the expenditures of the states somewhat uncertain.

Another indication of the development of the administrative activities of the states is afforded by the estimates of the value of their public properties. In 1924, the value of the lands, buildings, and equipment of the states used or held for specified purposes was estimated as follows: [1]

1. Charities, hospital. and corrections	$552,127,938
2. Education	457,348,065
3. General government	228,853,455
4. Public service enterprises	86,150,506
5. Development and conservation of natural resources	60,553,752
6. Highways	46,022,375
7. Protection to person and property	43,939,654
8. Recreation	41,977,922
9. Miscellaneous	34,115,391
10. Health and sanitation	28,208,074
Total	$1,579,297,132

A more complete picture of state expenditures for a particular year requires that capital outlays be classified according to the branches of administration in which they were incurred. The following table shows the per capita current expense, the per capita expense for outlays, and the total per capita expense of state functions during 1924.[2]

[1] *Financial Statistics of States, 1924*, pp. 122-125.

[2] *Ibid., passim.* The census report does not attempt to allocate interest charges according to the purpose for which the debt was incurred.

	Current Expense	Outlays	Total Expense
1. Highways	$1.11	$3.20	$4.31
2. Education	3.34	0.34	3.68
3. Charities, hospitals, and corrections	1.49	0.24	1.73
4. Miscellaneous	1.24	0.01	1.25
5. General government	0.67	0.07	0.74
6. Development and conservation of natural resources	0.48	0.05	0.53
7. Protection to person and property	0.46	0.03	0.49
8. Health and sanitation	0.21	0.02	0.23
9. Public service enterprises	0.10	0.03	0.13
10. Recreation	0.02	0.02	0.04
Total	$9.10	$4.00	$13.10

From the standpoint of money cost, both current and capital, it thus appears that the three most important activities of the states are those having to do with the administration of highways, education, and the care of the defective, dependent, and delinquent classes. However, the real importance of the several branches of state administration is not to be judged solely by a money standard. There must also be taken into account the degree of necessity of the service, the direct results obtained, and the indirect consequences which may ensue.

Revenues and Tax Administration.

The growth of state expenditures in recent years has made necessary a corresponding increase in state revenues. At the close of the Revolution, the principal sources of state revenue were three in number. First, there were the customs duties which each state could impose upon imports or exports from or to other states and foreign countries. Secondly, there were the excise duties which each state could impose upon domestic trade and industry. Thirdly, there was the general property tax from which both the state and the local governments derived a revenue. In some states, the poll tax also was an important source of revenue. The Federal Constitution of 1787 took away the first source of state revenue. The second source was not interfered with, but there was a general tendency to rely upon the third. In the eighteenth century, the general property tax was an excellent source of state revenue.[1] Under the economic and social

[1] On the general property tax, see H. L. Lutz, *Public Finance* (New York, 1924), ch. xviii, and J. P. Jensen, *Problems of Public Finance* (New York, 1924), chs. xv and xvi.

conditions of the period, it was fairly proportional to the ability of the taxpayer to pay, it was clear and certain in its operation, it was easy to collect and convenient for the taxpayer, the cost of collection was low, the amount to be raised could be varied at will, and the exact amount desired could always be obtained. During the course of the nineteenth century, the original advantages of the general property tax gradually diminished. The enormous development of intangible personal property, especially of the securities and stocks of business corporations, made evasion more easy. The unprecedented growth of the rate of taxation, especially for local purposes, greatly increased the temptation to evasion. By the concealment of intangibles, especially of corporate securities and stocks, the undervaluation of properties difficult to appraise accurately, and the declaration of fictitious debts, unscrupulous men succeeded in evading more or less completely their fair share of the general property tax. The result was the penalization of honesty, lack of uniformity in assessments, double taxation of some properties as compared with others, and the general demoralization of the taxpayer, particularly with respect to the taxation of intangibles.

This result was even more unsatisfactory from the standpoint of the state than from that of the local tax authorities. Since the local assessments served as the basis for the apportionment of the state tax between the different localities (towns and cities in New England, counties elsewhere), differences in the practice of local assessors caused the state tax to bear unequally upon different localities. The first demand, therefore, was for the equalization of assessments as between the different localities, in order that the state tax might be justly apportioned throughout all parts of the state. With the continued increase, however, in the tax rate and in the amount of intangible personalty escaping taxation under the general property tax, there came a demand for further reform. The process of reform has followed two separate channels: the reform of the administration of the general property tax, and the reform of the tax itself.

The next step in the reform of the administration of the tax, after making provision for the equalization of assessments in different localities, was to increase the powers of the assessors to prevent the evasion of the tax. A good example of such a reform was the Ohio tax inquisitor law of 1885. Such laws, however, failed to accomplish their purpose. A further step was taken by the enactment of the Ford franchise tax law in New York in 1899, and by the enactment in Massachusetts of the law for the taxation of the corporate excess. The former provided that the value of the franchise of a public service corporation should be assessed and taxed as if it were real estate. The latter provided for the assessment by central tax authorities of all the properties of business corporations of every kind in excess of the value of real estate and tangible personalty assessed locally. The next steps in the reform of tax administration carried the process of centralization further. Wisconsin, in 1903, provided for the assessment of the tangible property of all steam railroads located within the state by central tax authorities. The example of Wisconsin has been followed in about two-thirds of the states.[1] In 1913, Ohio and Montana provided for the assessment of all property by agents of the central tax authorities. This was the longest step in the process of centralization yet taken, but two years later these laws were repealed.

The general property tax itself was meanwhile being subjected to a process of reform. Two leading principles seem to underlie recent attempts to reform the general property tax as a source of state revenue. The first is the classification of property for the purposes of taxation. The second is the separation of the sources of state and local revenues. The development of the first principle may be conveniently traced in the legislation of New York. It began in 1906 with the exemption of mortgages from the general property tax. In 1910, the bonds of business corporations generally were exempted. In the following year, the exemption was extended to secured debts of all kinds. In 1915, the constitutional convention proposed a change in the constitution which would have permitted the development of this principle to its logical conclusion.[2] The legislature was to have power to classify property for purposes of taxation and to provide for the assessment of all personalty under the direction of the state tax authorities. Proposals to authorize the classification of

[1] Wisconsin, however, was by no means the first state to take this step. As early as 1873, New Jersey created a commissioner of railroad taxation to assess the real property of railroads.

[2] Article x, in which these changes were proposed, was submitted separately to the people, and rejected by them.

property for purposes of taxation have been submitted to the people in several states in recent years and adopted in a few of them. In several states also, special provision has been made for the taxation of certain kinds of real property, such as urban building sites and forest lands, at different rates or upon different principles than property in general.

The separation of the sources of state and local revenues may be brought about chiefly in two ways.[1] First, property exempted from the operation of the general property tax may be subjected to separate taxation under special laws. An example of this is the so-called flat or low-rate tax law for the taxation of intangibles, which imposes a rate of usually three or four mills per annum upon the value of such property. The state supervises the collection of this flat or low-rate tax, surrendering to the local authorities as a rule the major portion of the proceeds. Such laws have been adopted in several states. Secondly, the states are developing new sources of revenue from new kinds of taxes. One example of this is the levying of special franchise or business taxes on railroads and other public service corporations, as is the practice in many states, or upon all business corporations, as is the practice in a considerable number of states.[2] These taxes may be assessed upon some external indicia of ability to pay, such as capitalization, or miles of track or wire, or number of messages transmitted, or upon gross earnings, or upon net earnings. In the latter case, the tax approximates a limited income tax. Beginning with Wisconsin in 1911, about a dozen states have carried this idea further and have established a state tax either on personal incomes or on all incomes, both personal and corporate.[3] These income taxes are assessed and

[1] See Mabel Newcomer, *Separation of State and Local Revenues in the United States* (Columbia University Studies, lxxvi, 1917). As an important principle of financial reform, the separation of the sources of state and local revenues no longer commands the support that it did ten years ago. A certain amount of separation is desirable but complete separation brings disadvantages both to the state and to the local governments. See Lutz, *op. cit.*, pp. 251-252. See also "A Plan of a Model System of State and Local Taxation," *Proceedings of National Tax Conference, 1919*, xii, pp. 426-470. This plan was prepared by a committee appointed by the National Tax Association, and was discussed at length by tax officials and experts at several national tax conferences. See *Proceedings*, xii, pp. 401-425; xiii, pp. 273-329; xiv, pp. 66-98; xv, pp. 285-328.

[2] See E. R. A. Seligman, *Essays in Taxation* (9th ed., New York, 1921), chs. vi-viii.

[3] See Alzada Comstock, *State Taxation of Personal Incomes* (Columbia University Studies, ci, 1921-1922).

collected under the direction of the central tax authorities and the proceeds are generally reserved for the use of the state, but in Massachusetts, New York, and Wisconsin, a distribution is made between the state and the localities. All the states except Alabama, Florida, and Nevada now have the inheritance tax as a source of state revenue and, in most of these states, the proceeds are not shared with local governments.[1] In recent years, as state highway expenditures have mounted, the automobile has been singled out as an important object of taxation. All the states have so increased their motor vehicle licenses that they are in effect special property taxes and forty-four states have levied a tax of from one to five cents a gallon on gasoline.[2] However, not until 1924 did the general property tax cease to be the largest source of income for the state governments.

The relative importance of the different sources of revenue is shown by the following table: [3]

State Revenue Receipts Per Capita, 1924[4]

	Total	Per Capita	Per Cent
From taxes			
general property tax	$351,604,364	$3.16	25.7
special taxes	226,771,320	2.04	16.6
poll taxes	3,622,032	0.03	0.3
business and non-business licenses	435,462,771	3.91	31.8
From special assessments and from special charges for outlays	23,865,844	0.21	1.7
From fines, forfeits, and escheats	8,043,643	0.07	0.6
From subventions and grants, donations, and pension assessments	133,595,444	1.20	9.8
From highway privileges, rents, and interest	61,477,536	0.55	4.5
From earnings of general departments	113,045,661	1.02	8.3
From earnings of public service enterprises	12,577,403	0.11	0.9
Total	$1,370,066,018	$12.32	...

[1] See Seligman, *op. cit.*, ch. v.

[2] See Harry A. Barth, "State Taxation of Passenger Automobiles," *National Municipal Review*, xiii, pp. 641-651 (1924) and James W. Martin, "The Administration of Gasoline Taxes in the United States," *ibid.*, pp. 587-600 (Supplement, October, 1924). Illinois, Massachusetts, New Jersey, and New York are the only states which do not levy a gasoline tax.

[3] *Financial Statistics of States, 1924, passim.* For an explanation of the above classification of receipts, see the text discussion of the report. For a summary of state tax and revenue laws, see United States Bureau of the Census, *Digest of State Laws relating to Taxation and Revenue, 1922.*

[4] Compare with table on p. 368.

The progress of reform in the revenue systems of the states has been marked by a corresponding development of central administrative agencies. Both the reform of the administration of the general property tax and the reform of the tax itself have made necessary the creation of special tax authorities and the constant enlargement of their powers. First, the attempt to equalize local assessments compelled the establishment of state boards of equalization. This development began in some of the New England states as early as 1820 and in Ohio in 1825.[1] Next, the assessment of property directly by the state governments brought about the creation of such offices as those of tax and corporation commissioner or of state boards of assessors, or the enlargement of the powers of the state boards of equalization. State excise and license fees were originally levied and collected by the state treasurers. In the nineteenth century, the states began to employ license fees more and more as a means of regulating social and industrial conditions. State legislation for the control of the liquor traffic, for example, incidentally opened up a new source of state revenue, which, in a few states, was seized by the state governments. The general practice has been to relieve the state treasurers from responsibility for the enforcement of such laws by the creation of special excise commissions or commissioners. Moreover, such state offices as those for the supervision of banks and insurance companies and other corporations are in some instances supported entirely or largely by fees, paid directly to the heads of those offices. Thus, the state revenues may be collected by a number of state officials. Recently, a strong tendency has appeared towards the consolidation of various authorities concerned with the collection of state revenues. The first step in this process of consolidation has usually been the merging of separate state boards of equalization and of assessors into so-called state tax commissions. Beginning in Indiana in 1891, state tax commissions or similar agencies have been established in most of the states, with constantly increasing powers over the assessment of property for purposes of taxation, both local and state, and for the collection of state corporation, business, inheritance, and income taxes, and other revenues.[2]

[1] In New England, the practice of equalizing local assessments by legislative committees had been established much earlier.

[2] See H. L. Lutz, *The State Tax Commission* (Boston, 1918). Central administrative supervision over local assessments is simply one phase of

The general reorganization movement of the past decade has brought about a further consolidation in which the state tax commission is sometimes attached to or placed under the jurisdiction of the department of finance.

Debts.

The power to borrow money is generally recognized as a necessary governmental attribute but the exercise of that power is very susceptible to abuse. The truth of this statement is well illustrated from the history of the states.[1] A hundred years ago the state legislatures were not restrained in the incurrence of indebtedness by any constitutional limitations. However, the disastrous financial experiences of the states in the era of internal improvements together with subsequent abuses of the borrowing power led to the writing of debt restrictions in the state constitutions. Beginning with Florida in 1838, more or less stringent limitations and regulations have been adopted in every state except Connecticut, New Hampshire, and Vermont. Without analyzing in detail these various constitutional restrictions, it is sufficient to say that they may involve one or more of the following: absolute prohibition of debt incurrence for certain purposes or in excess of specified limits;[2] special procedural requirements for passage by the legislature; approval by popular referendum; regulation as to the form of the debt, term of years

state supervision over local finance generally. Other phases of this topic include local tax and debt limits, control of budgets as to form, procedure, and objects of expenditure, uniformity as to auditing, accounting, and financial reporting, etc. Space will not permit a discussion of these subjects, but reference may be made to the following: "State Supervision of Local Finance," Reports of the Round Table on Public Finance at the Second and Third National Conference on the Science of Politics, *American Political Science Review*, xix, 144-149 (1925); *ibid.*, xx, pp. 147-152 (1926); J. A. Fairlie, *Local Government in Counties, Towns, and Villages* (New York, 1906), ch. xv; R. C. Atkinson, *The Effects of Tax Limitation upon Local Finance in Ohio, 1911 to 1922* (Cleveland, 1923); Lane Lancaster, *State Supervision of Municipal Indebtedness* (Philadelphia, 1923); Wylie Kilpatrick, "State Supervision of Municipal Accounts," *National Municipal Review*, xii, pp. 247-254 (1923), and "State Supervision of Municipal Finance in New Jersey," *ibid.*, xiv, pp. 490-501 (1925); Philip Zoercher, "The Indiana Scheme of Central Supervision of Local Expenditures," *ibid.*, xiv, pp. 90-95 (1925).

[1] On state debts, see *Illinois Constitutional Convention Bulletins*, No. 4, "State and Local Finance," pp. 288-303 (Springfield, 1919), and *Massachusetts Constitutional Convention Bulletins*, No. 15, "Constitutional Restrictions on State Debts" (Boston, 1918).

[2] The debt limits do not usually apply to loans approved by popular referendum.

for which it may run, and rate of interest; mandatory tax levy sufficient to pay the interest and retire the principal at maturity; sinking fund administration, etc.

Constitutional limitations undoubtedly prevent or lessen the more serious evils connected with the borrowing power but they go only a little way towards securing a wise and moderate use of the public credit. As a matter of fact, the tendency in recent years has been to relax these restrictions by constitutional amendment or to incur large debts by popular referendum under existing constitutional provisions. But limitations or no limitations, the states have had little difficulty in borrowing large sums as is shown by the following table:

TOTAL AND PER CAPITA NET DEBT OF STATES [1]

YEAR	TOTAL	PER CAPITA
1890	$211,210,000	$3.37
1902	234,965,000	2.99
1912	345,942,000	3.57
1915	424,154,000	4.31
1919	519,886,000	4.95
1924	1,183,467,433	10.64

The above statistics indicate a large increase in state debts during the period since the war. However, this increase has by no means been uniform throughout the states. There was only a single state, Nebraska, which reported no net indebtedness in 1924. From 1912 to 1922, there were eight states [2] which actually decreased their net total indebtedness but, in about half of the states, the increase amounted to over 300 per cent at the end of that decade. The net debt of Oregon rose from $31,000 in 1912 to $41,552,377 in 1924 while the net per capita debt jumped from $0.64 to $49.95, the highest per capita in any state. Pennsylvania had no net indebtedness in 1912; the debt of that state in 1924 was $48,130,099. As a rule, the chief cause of such increases is to be found in the highway programs of the states. In 1924, 47.1 per cent of the gross indebtedness of the

[1] The statistics for 1890, 1902, and 1912 are taken from "Public Debt," Bureau of the Census, *Reports on Wealth, Public Debt, and Taxation*, 1922; p. 10; those for 1915, 1919, and 1924 from *Financial Statistics of States, 1924*, p. 42. The statistics given in the remainder of the paragraph are likewise taken from these two sources, *passim*.

[2] Arizona, Connecticut, Georgia, Kansas, Massachusetts, Oklahoma, Virginia, and Wisconsin.

states was accounted for by highway loans. The only other purpose which accounted for more than 10 per cent was the relief of war veterans through bonuses, homes, and other forms of assistance. Veteran relief had caused 10.9 per cent of the gross debt of the states.[1]

Financial Administration and Control.

Two phases of state financial administration have already been discussed, namely, the preparation and adoption of the budget plan, and tax and revenue administration. The present section, therefore, will be devoted to treasury administration and to certain problems centering around the execution of the budget.

The oldest state financial office is that of treasurer, an office which now exists in all the states and is usually made elective by the state constitution. The original duties of the state treasurer related principally to the receipt, custody, and disbursement of public funds and these duties have continued down to the present time.[2] In the performance of these functions, grave evils and abuses have often arisen which the states have sought to remedy by increasingly drastic constitutional and statutory requirements.[3] Even when treasury administration is honest, it is nevertheless true that "the states have lagged far behind the efficient and economical methods of great semi-public and private corporations." [4]

The major problems of treasury administration center around the safekeeping of state funds, economical management of treasury balances, and the investment and management of funds.[5] With reference to the custody of funds, all the states now use the "bank depository system" instead of the earlier "inde-

[1] For a valuable study of the debt of a particular state, see "The Debt of the State of New York, Past, Present, and Future," *A Report by the Special Joint Committee on Taxation and Retrenchment* (Albany, 1926). This committee recommended the adoption of a "capital budget" and, as far as possible of a "pay-as-you-go" policy in financing recurrent public improvements. See Appendix F.

[2] These are by no means the only duties of the treasurer. He is frequently an *ex-officio* member of various boards, some of which may not deal with financial matters.

[3] A recent case in point is that of Governor Len Small of Illinois. In December, 1925, the state supreme court handed down a decision directing Governor Small to account for approximately one million dollars of interest money withheld by him while state treasurer.

[4] M. L. Faust, *The Custody of State Funds* (New York, 1925), p. 4.

[5] The paragraphs on treasury administration are mainly summarized from Faust, *op. cit., passim.*

pendent treasury system." Except for relatively small amounts of vault cash, the funds of the state are deposited in one or more duly qualified banks within the state. The selection of particular depositories may be made by law, by the governor or treasurer, by a state depository board, or by other similar agencies. The patronage value of a judicious distribution of state funds has been and still is well recognized in practical politics. However, depository legislation usually attempts to impose certain general requirements, such as distribution on the basis of the financial strength of the depositories, or on the basis of the security pledged to safeguard the state against loss from the insolvency of the bank, or on the basis of the state revenues which are collected in the localities, or on the basis of the interest rates which the banks agree to pay, or on a combination of these and other provisions.

The second major problem of treasury administration has to do with the economical management of treasury balances. The treasurer should have the absolute right to receive and deposit according to law all the money paid to the state. Unfortunately, this ideal is far from realized under prevailing conditions. Revenue collecting agencies, both local and central, do not promptly turn their collections into the state treasury, a practice which may make it necessary for the state to borrow temporarily or to pay interest on warrants. Where a department collects fees for its services and is legally authorized to expend those fees for its own expenses, treasury supervision over the custody of such funds is rendered very difficult. Even without the receipt of fees, a department or institution may have its own separate treasury to which lump sum appropriations are paid by the state treasurer and from which departmental expenditures are made without central treasury control. Economical treasury management also requires the securing of an adequate interest income for the use of state funds without impairing their security. Thanks to court decisions and to statutory prohibitions, the "honest graft" of state treasurers in pocketing all or part of the interest on state deposits is less common now than formerly. Most states have legislation requiring bank depositories to pay interest on state deposits at not less than a minimum specified rate or at a rate fixed by a system of competitive bidding. Another uneconomical form of treasury administration is the very common habit of creating many separate funds among which the state revenues are apportioned. The states very much need a Consolidated Fund such as William Pitt established for England long ago. The practice of having many separate funds —there are no less than twenty-eight in Pennsylvania—makes for complexity of treasury accounts, immobility of cash balances, and unnecessary temporary borrowing with interest expense. Even where temporary borrowing is necessary, a number of the states resort to unwise methods of doing it, with a consequent increase of interest charges.

The management of permanent and trust funds, represented principally by sinking funds and school funds, constitutes a third phase of treasury administration. The prevailing method of retiring the funded indebtedness of the states is through sinking funds which may be held on deposit until needed or invested in approved securities. The investment of such funds is usually entrusted to a special administrative board consisting of the treasurer and certain other named officials. The actual administration of state sinking funds leaves much to be desired. Too often, the legislature has failed to appropriate to the fund or has appropriated money from the fund for other purposes, the possibility of peculation or unwise investment is not always completely guarded against, and there may be a loss of interest due to failure to invest sinking funds promptly, to say nothing of the complicated accounting problems which may arise. The serial bond, which is retired in installments over a period of years out of the proceeds of current revenues, requires no sinking fund and largely avoids the difficulties just mentioned. Though serial bonding is being more and more widely used by local governments, New York is the only state where the serial type has been made compulsory for state purposes. Trust funds for educational and other purposes are handled in much the same way as sinking funds and present similar problems of administration.

In general, treasury administration suffers from inadequate and unintelligible publicity. Such publicity should include not only the customary statements of receipts and expenditures, but also the names of the banks in which state funds are deposited, the average balances maintained by the state in those banks, interest receipts, information as to the kind and amount of security pledged to protect the deposits, the real surplus or deficit in sinking funds and other permanent funds, etc. Obviously, treasury publicity is closely connected with questions of accounting[1] and auditing and these topics may now be considered with reference to the state treasurer and also with reference to the execution of the budget plan.

The relation of accounting and auditing to budgetary practice is one that has only recently been developed, but the auditing function itself is an ancient one. In its early form, it was represented by the audits which legislative committees made of the accounts of the state treasurers. With the growth of state revenues and expenditures in the nineteenth century, and the general adoption of biennial sessions of the legislature, the necessity arose for continuous supervision of state finances by a special permanent official. The office of state auditor or comptroller was therefore created.[2] With the general adoption also of direct popular election of state administrative officers, including both state treasurers and auditors or comptrollers, the existing system of independent audit came into operation. The powers and duties of the auditing officer vary greatly in different states. As a rule, the state treasurer may not pay any bill or claim against the state without the previous approval of the auditor. The auditor is required to examine the treasurer's accounts once a year or oftener and to report periodically to the legislature. In a few states, the auditor's accounts are in turn audited by legislative committees, and everywhere the legislature may investigate the accounts of the state at any time. There is a tendency also to give the auditor power both to supervise the accounts of state institutions and to prescribe uniform systems of accounting. In some states, however, as already indicated, special officials have been appointed to supervise the accounts of certain state institutions, and, in a few states, central boards of control supervise or administer the finances of all state institutions. The powers and duties of the auditor have been variously affected by the recent budgetary reform movement. Where the board type of budget organization has been adopted, the auditor is usually included as one of the board members. However, in

[1] On governmental accounting problems, see Francis Oakey, *Principles of Government Accounting and Reporting* (New York, 1921).

[2] All but three states have such an official and, in most of these states the office is created by the constitution and is filled by popular election.

the executive type, the planning and execution of the budget is entrusted to the governor or to some specially created agency placed directly under his control. Since the auditor is normally a constitutional elective officer independent of the chief executive, there may be a certain amount of conflicting and overlapping duties as between the auditor and the executive budget agency. This is not necessarily undesirable. A good executive budget system presupposes, not only that the governor shall have staff assistance to see that the budget is carried out, but also that the legislature shall have the means of maintaining a continuous and independent check on the governor and the spending agencies. Such a check can best be developed through the office of auditor and, to that end, the auditor should cease to be an elective officer and should be appointed by the legislature. This has long been the practice in New Jersey and Tennessee.

The Execution of the Budget.

The execution of a budget requires continuous fiscal supervision and control by some responsible agency.[1] This gives rise to important personnel problems, since there can be no efficient financial planning and operation without some standard of efficiency and some system of efficiency ratings in the public employment of the state. Important matériel problems also result, notably that of the economical purchase of supplies. These problems will be reserved for discussion in a later portion of the chapter. The execution of a budget also raises problems of administrative accounting. Such accounting must be distinguished from the control-accounting under the direction of the auditor. The latter is primarily a matter of keeping expenditures within the appropriations and involves the determination of all questions concerning the legal authority to spend money. Administrative accounting, on the other hand, should include such matters as cost accounts and operation accounts. These the governor and budget agency need for purposes of information and should have as a means of keeping in touch with what is being done.[2]

[1] See Barth, *Financial Control in the States with Emphasis on Control by the Governor*, *passim;* Buck, *Budget Making*, ch. xi; and "Competency and Economy in Public Expenditures," *Annals*, cxiii (May, 1924), pt. iii.

[2] See Buck, *op. cit.*, pp. 185-190.

The administrative machinery set up for the execution of the budget, as has already been pointed out, varies greatly in the several states. Among the better states, Ohio is a conspicuous example.[1] By the general administrative reorganization of 1921, a department of finance was created under a director appointed by the governor and senate. In addition to preparing the budget for the governor and serving as a permanent agency for efficiency and economy, the department has power to control the financial transactions of all the executive departments (1) by prescribing and requiring the installation of a uniform system of accounting and reporting; (2) by requiring itemized statements of expenditures proposed for any specified future period to be submitted to the department for approval or disapproval in whole or in part; (3) by requiring orders, invoices, claims, vouchers or payrolls to be submitted to the department, where such submission is required by law or deemed necessary by the governor, with a similar power of approval or disapproval of such items; (4) by supervising and examining accounts, and expenditures and receipts of public money, and the disposition and use of public property in connection with the administration of the budget; (5) by prescribing uniform rules governing forms of specifications, advertisements for proposals, opening of bids, making of awards and contracts in connection with the purchase of supplies and performance of work; (6) by reporting to the attorney-general for appropriate action all facts showing illegal expenditures of public money or misappropriation of public property; and finally, where proposed expenditures have been wholly or partially negatived by the department, the department may notify the auditor, who is thereupon obliged to withhold the necessary authorization for such expenditures. Under certain circumstances, transfers between appropriation items in the budget are allowed. These transfers require the sanction of a special controlling board consisting of the governor, attorney-general, auditor, and the chairmen of the finance committees of the legislature. Having such an agency as this department of finance under his control, the governor has an effective instrument not only for preparing the budget but also for controlling its execution. No other state has gone so far as Ohio in the development of agencies for the

[1] See R. E. Miles, "Fiscal Control in Ohio," *Annals*, cxiii, pp. 105-112.

control of expenditures,[1] but the tendency is steadily towards more stringent methods of fiscal regulation.

Centralized Purchasing.

The development of the various branches of state administration has involved ever increasing expenditures for the purchase of supplies and materials.[2] It has been estimated that from one-fifth to one-half of the current expenses of the state governments is thus incurred.[3] Twenty years ago, the prevailing rule was for each state agency to do its buying independently of other agencies. From the standpoint of the state, the results of this decentralized policy were distinctly disadvantageous. Separate departmental and institutional purchasing meant piecemeal purchases, orders too small to receive large discounts on wholesale lots, lack of standardization in goods bought, and greater opportunities for favoritism, collusive bidding, and other evils. Centralized purchasing aims to overcome or lessen these evils by "the concentration of purchasing power, permitting goods to be bought in large quantities at the lowest and best prices under competitive bidding and promoting prompt delivery, inspection, and payment for goods with the minimum inconvenience to dealers; the standardization of supplies, eliminating unnecessary range in kinds of goods, also unduly expensive grades; and the development of an expert purchasing staff, acquainted with the details and skilled in the methods of the several phases of purchasing, inspecting, testing, and storing goods."[4]

Centralized purchasing in the states first appeared in connection with the administration of penal and charitable institutions. When the separate boards of managers of these institutions were superseded or placed under the direction of a single board

[1] The Ohio department of finance was modeled upon that created in Illinois by the civil administrative code of 1917. This department, according to Governor Lowden, was "the key-stone of the structure." See Frank O. Lowden, "Reorganizing the Administration of a State," *National Municipal Review*, xv, p. 13 (Jan., 1926). See also the plan for an executive department, recommended by the New York State Reorganization Commission of 1926, *Report*, pp. 6-20.

[2] On centralized purchasing, see "Competency and Economy in Public Expenditures," *Annals*, cxiii, pt. vii; Buck, *Budget Making*, pp. 177-185; Milton Conover, "Centralized Purchasing Agencies in State and Local Governments," *American Political Science Review*, xix, pp. 73-82 (1925); A. G. Thomas, *Principles of Government Purchasing* (New York, 1919).

[3] See Buck, *op. cit.*, p. 177.

[4] See Buck, *op. cit.*, pp. 177-178.

of control, the purchasing function was frequently entrusted to this new board. As early as 1897, Iowa established such a board of control with authority to supervise the buying of all supplies for the penal and charitable institutions of the state, while Texas, in 1899, created a state purchasing agent for its charitable institutions. However, the real impetus to centralized purchasing dates from the era of efficiency and economy commissions and is closely connected with administrative consolidation and budget reform. Administrative consolidation necessarily meant fewer buying agencies. Budget reform focussed attention on economical methods of purchase. In consequence, during the last ten or fifteen years, centralized purchasing systems have been widely adopted. At the present time, about three-fourths of the states have established a central purchasing agency for the various departments, or for the state institutions, or for both. In a majority of these states, the central agency does the buying for all branches of the state government.[1]

However, this widespread development has not evolved a uniform type of purchasing organization.[2] In New Hampshire, the office of purchasing agent is an independent office under the governor, while in Oklahoma, the state board of affairs, consisting of three members, not only acts as a board of control for the state institutions but also makes the actual purchase of supplies for all state purposes and uses. The purchasing agent in Illinois is under the department of purchases and construction, and in Ohio the superintendent of purchases and printing is a subordinate of the department of finance. Nebraska has two separate central purchasing agencies, each functioning independently of the other,—the purchasing bureau in the department of finance serving the executive departments and the state board of control buying for the public institutions. These types of agency indicate the variety of administrative mechanism which the states have set up for centralized purchasing. There is much difference of opinion as to which type is best. However, because of the close connection between purchasing and the planning and execution of the budget, it would seem logical to place the purchasing office under the department of finance or under a

[1] In such states, however, there are frequently minor exceptions to the above rule.

[2] See Russell Forbes, "Centralized Purchasing in Governments of United States and Canada," *Annals*, cxiii, pp. 272-286.

similar budget agency. This step would enable the standard specifications used in centralized purchasing to be readily followed in preparing the budget estimates and would provide the budget authority with easily accessible data concerning changes in the prices of supplies and materials, expenditures for various kinds of goods, and the prospective needs of the state departments and institutions in the preparation of the budget.

STATE PERSONNEL ADMINISTRATION

In the preceding chapter, the "spoils" system was discussed in connection with the power of appointment. It now remains to consider the efforts which the states have made to correct the evils of the "spoils" system by introducing the "merit" system and reforming personnel methods generally.[1] The development of new administrative agencies since the middle of the nineteenth century has greatly increased the number of appointive positions in the state service. In New York, there are about twenty-two thousand state officers and employees, while Massachusetts and Illinois each have more than ten thousand names on the state payroll. Many of these appointees hold posts requiring exceptional training or skill. The centralization of state administration, especially in such departments as education, charities and corrections, and health, has created an unprecedented demand for experts in the public service. Many more hold subordinate positions requiring no exceptional training or skill. In such positions, the principal requirements are attention to work and fidelity to the public interests. The treatment of such positions as "spoils," making the tenure of office dependent upon the fluctuating fortunes of political parties, or even of different factions within the same party, demoralizes the public service. Competent experts will not accept public employment upon these terms. Diligence and zeal among the rank and file are discouraged. Moreover, "the use of govern-

[1] On civil service reform and state personnel administration, see "Competency and Economy in Public Expenditures," *Annals*, cxiii, pts. vi, viii; W. C. Beyer, "Employment Standardization in the Public Service," *National Municipal Review*, ix, pp. 389-403 (1920); Milton Conover, "Merit Systems of Civil Service in the States," *American Political Science Review*, xix, pp. 544-560 (1925); Lewis Meriam, *Principles Governing the Retirement of Public Employees* (New York, 1918); A. W. Proctor, *Principles of Public Personnel Administration* (New York, 1921); Paul Studensky, "Pensions in Public Employment," *National Municipal Review*, xi, pp. 95-124 (1922).

ment offices as patronage is a handicap difficult to overestimate from the standpoint of those who strive to get good government. Any effort for reform . . . results in the reformers immediately finding themselves face to face with an organized band of drilled mercenaries who are paid out of the public chest to train themselves with such skill that ordinary good citizens when they meet them at the polls are in much the position of militia matched against regular troops. . . . Civil service reform is designed primarily to give the average American citizen a fair chance in politics." [1]

The evil results of the "spoils" system, as applied to purely administrative offices, were recognized as soon as the administrative work of the state governments began to become important. The agitation for the introduction of the "merit" system began shortly after the Civil War, and was at first directed chiefly towards the reform of the federal civil service, in which the evils of the "spoils" system were most serious, and most notorious. The assassination of President Garfield by a disappointed office seeker accelerated the adoption of the reform by Congress, and, since the enactment of the first civil service law in 1883, the "merit" system has been extended throughout a large part of the federal service. Its progress in the states has been much slower.[2] It was established in New York in 1883 and in Massachusetts in the following year. Twenty years passed before any other states adopted the reform. Since 1905, however, it has been introduced in nearly one-fourth of the states.[3]

The object of the "merit" system is to fill administrative offices with the fittest persons available without regard to political affiliations. This object is sought by classifying subordinate positions in the public service according to their character and giving public notice of vacancies in each class. Any qualified

[1] See Theodore Roosevelt, *Autobiography*, pp. 146-147. The entire chapter entitled "Applied Idealism" is an excellent exposition of the object and nature of civil service reform.

[2] However, the "merit" system is widely used in cities.

[3] The list of states is as follows: New York, Massachusetts, Wisconsin, New Jersey, Illinois, Colorado, Ohio, California, Connecticut, Kansas, and Maryland. In 1921, the Connecticut legislature abolished the "merit" system and the Kansas legislature failed to appropriate funds for its continuance. A number of other states have adopted improved methods of personnel administration without formal commitment to the "merit" principle.

citizen may apply for appointment, and the relative fitness of all applicants is determined, so far as practicable, by competitive examinations. Candidates are rated according to their fitness, and the names of those with the highest ratings are certified to the appointing officers whenever appointments are to be made. Appointing officers are required to make all permanent appointments from the certified lists, though they generally have some latitude of choice. The practice varies with respect to the tenure of civil service appointees. In some states, no permanent officeholder within the classified service may be dismissed without the filing of charges and a formal hearing before the civil service commissioners. In others, the power of dismissal, except for political or religious affiliations, is unrestricted. In the latter states, it is assumed that when the appointing officer cannot replace a discharged civil servant except from the official list of eligible applicants, there will be little incentive to dismiss any employee except for inefficiency or misconduct. In general, however, the weight of opinion seems to be in favor of further restricting the power of dismissal.[1]

Operation of the "Merit" System.

The "merit" system has improved the conduct of state administration wherever it has been administered in good faith. It has reduced political influences in the appointment of subordinate officials and employees. It has eliminated the unfit from the civil service. But it has not always been administered in good faith. If the civil service commissioners themselves owe their positions to political influences, they may feel unduly dependent upon the power which controlled their appointment. There are many ways in which they can connive at evasions of the spirit of the system in the interests of a partisan "machine." Sometimes the civil service law seems expressly devised to deprive the commissioners of the necessary independence. Thus, the Colorado law, as amended in 1915, provides that the terms of all the commissioners shall expire simultaneously at the beginning of the term of each governor. In general, the system does not go far enough to secure the best results. Promotions are un-

[1] See the "Standard Civil Service Law for States and Cities," drafted by the National Civil Service Reform League. It is reprinted in A. W. Procter, *op. cit.*, Appendix 2, pp. 201-234.

certain, and stop altogether before the most responsible positions are reached. Increases of salary are often dependent upon special legislation, and the principal administrative offices remain outside the classified service and are filled by political appointments. Consequently, there is little incentive for the most capable and ambitious to enter or long remain in the service. The distinction between administrative and political offices needs to be carried further towards the top than is actually the case in any of the states which have yet adopted the "merit" system. In other states, some of the advantages of the "merit" system are secured by the creation of independent department heads in the most important branches of state administration. Thus, the organization of the departments of education in many states is such that the appointment of subordinates is comparatively free from ordinary political influences. But as a rule, the reform of the civil service under the state governments has lagged behind civil service reform in the nation and in the cities.

Recently, however, there has been a noticeable improvement in the civil service of the states. The rise of the science of employment management or personnel management in private industry has helped to focus attention on the positive aspects of the "merit" system instead of on its negative phases as was formerly the case. It is being more and more realized that a satisfactory recruitment of personnel is only the beginning and not the end of the problem. In consequence, better methods of examining applicants for the public service are being devised, efficiency records and ratings are being developed, positions are being more logically classified according to the nature of the duties performed, salaries are being more nearly standardized so as to give equal pay for equal work, and civil pensions and retirement systems are coming into use.[1] In short, civil service reform is being gradually transformed into the science of public personnel administration. The value of such changes is indeed great. For example, a simple but adequate classification of positions facilitates the work of examining candidates, simplifies the keeping of efficiency ratings and the handling of promotions,

[1] Beginning with Massachusetts in 1911, eight states now have state-wide retirement systems for public employees. About one-half of the states have established state-wide retirement systems for their public school teachers. See H. H. Baish, "Retirement Systems and Morale in Public Service," *Annals*, cxiii, pp. 338-350.

makes possible salary standardization, and is almost indispensable in thorough budget planning.[1]

There is considerable variety in the type of administrative machinery which the states have set up to handle their personnel problems. Originally, the "merit" system was under the control of a civil service commission usually consisting of three members appointed by the governor for overlapping terms. This is still the prevailing form. However, here as elsewhere, administrative reorganization has brought about a tendency towards "one man control." Two states, Maryland and California, now have a single civil service commissioner instead of a commission. There is also a tendency towards placing certain phases of personnel administration under a consolidated department of finance. This may result in divided control, as is the case in Massachusetts. In that state there is, in addition to the civil service commission in the department of civil service and registration, a director of personnel and standardization under the commission of administration and finance. This difficulty is avoided in the Minnesota reorganization of 1925. In that state, the department of administration and finance, which is headed by a commission of three, is both a budget, a purchasing, and a personnel agency. "The duty of classification, fixing salary scales, and controlling all the factors of employment, such as recruiting, morale, and promotion, are devolved upon the commission acting through the director of personnel." [2] Thus in Minnesota the closely related functions of budget planning and execution, centralized purchasing, and personnel administration are all entrusted to one department. The principle upon which this reorganization is based seems to be thoroughly sound.

A majority of the state civil service commissions are concerned only with the recruiting and control of employees in the state

[1] See Lewis Meriam, "The Uses of a Personnel Classification in the Public Service," *Annals*, cxiii, pp. 215-220. About a dozen states have recently taken steps towards a better classification of employees and a greater standardization of salaries. Following the administrative reorganization of 1923, Pennsylvania achieved notable results along these lines. See C. L. King and Richard Lansburgh, "Pennsylvania Classifies Her Employees," *National Municipal Review*, xiii, pp. 15-19 (1924).

[2] J. S. Young, "Reorganization of the Administrative Branch of the Minnesota Government," *American Political Science Review*, xx, p. 75 (1926). The central purchasing and personnel powers of the department of administration and finance do not, however, extend to the state institutions. These continue under the board of control.

service. In five states, however, the state commissions are vested with a greater or less degree of supervision and control over the personnel of local governments. Thus, in Massachusetts, no city has its own civil service agency. All municipal officials and employees in the classified service are under the jurisdiction of the state commission. The same relationship exists in Maryland and New Jersey for such of the local subdivisions as have adopted the "merit" system. On the other hand, in New York and Ohio, local civil service commissions exist, but they are subject to a certain amount of supervision by the state commission.

MISCELLANEOUS ADMINISTRATIVE OFFICES

The organization and activities of the principal administrative departments of the state governments have now been described. It remains to mention briefly certain offices and agencies which have thus far not been considered. These include three of the older state officials, the lieutenant-governor, the attorney-general, and the secretary of state, together with a number of the newer boards and commissions.

The constitutions of thirty-five states provide for a lieutenant-governor elected by the people. As a rule, the only duties of this officer are to succeed the governor in the event of the latter's death, removal, absence, disability, or impeachment; and to preside over the state senate. From this, it is apparent that his executive functions are not actual but potential while his normal duties are those of a legislative character. In the states which have not established a lieutenant-governor, various other arrangements are made for the gubernatorial succession. There would be little loss in abolishing the office of lieutenant-governor and providing that the immediate succession to the governorship should go to one of the principal officials appointed by the governor.

The office of attorney-general exists in all the states and is usually filled by popular vote. However, in six states, the attorney-general is chosen by the governor, by the legislature, or by the state supreme court. In any case, he occupies an important place in the general conduct of administration, since he is not only the principal prosecuting officer of the state, but also the legal adviser of the governor and the department heads. In most states, the authority of the attorney-general as public prosecutor is still seriously curtailed by the powers granted to the county or other local prosecutors in their respective districts. His powers as legal adviser are more important on account of the volume and character of state legislation. The opinions of the attorney-general are relied upon by the department heads for guidance through the intricacies of the statute books. Where the conduct of administration is prescribed by law with infinite and not always intelligible detail, as is the practice in most states, the department heads may be more dependent upon the opinions of the attorney-general than upon those of the governor himself. Owing to the fact that the office is established by the constitution, the reorganization movement has had relatively little effect on the status of the attorney-general. However, in recent years, his authority has been somewhat strengthened. Whereas formerly state agencies were sometimes authorized to employ their own counsel, a few states have now specifically directed that all legal business of the state shall be conducted by the attorney-general or under his direction. Furthermore, there is a tendency to increase his powers of supervision and control over local prosecuting officials. This is notably the case in Louisiana, where the constitution of 1921 provides for a state department of justice, headed by the attorney-general.

Every state has a secretary of state or secretary of the commonwealth. This official is usually elected by the people but, in nine states, he is appointed by the governor and senate or chosen by the legislature. The secretary of state originally performed duties now in most states divided between the governor's private secretary and the clerks of the legislative houses. At present, he is charged with a great variety of duties, mostly of a perfunctory sort, relating to the conduct of elections, the state printing, the distribution of public documents, the supervision of corporations, including the issuance of certificates of incorporation and the enforcement of "blue-sky" laws, the issuance of motor vehicle licenses, the custody of public records, etc. He (and also the attorney-general, auditor, and treasurer) is frequently called upon to serve as an *ex officio* member of one or more boards. Unlike the office of attorney-general, the secretary's office usually requires little or no exercise of discretionary authority on the part of its incumbent. But like the attorney-general, the secretary of state rests upon a constitutional pedestal and hence is ordinarily excluded from consolidation plans and proposals. The New York reorganization amendment of 1925 is an outstanding exception to this rule. By this amendment, the secretary of state ceases to be an elected official and the legislature receives full power to organize a department of state.

The remaining state administrative agencies are so diverse as almost to defy classification. The list includes election or canvassing boards, fire marshals or commissioners, examiners in accounting, law, and other callings which are not under the jurisdiction of the state health or educational authorities, boards of censors (chiefly for moving pictures), athletic commissions, racing commissions, etc. In general, these are detached agencies, created to carry into effect various specially significant laws, and destined under any systematic scheme of administrative reorganization to be incorporated into the appropriate executive departments.

TYPES OF DEPARTMENTAL ORGANIZATION

In the preceding sections of this chapter, it has been pointed out that the administrative machinery of the states is of various types. Since this is a topic requiring further analysis, the remainder of the chapter will be devoted to comparing and contrasting these types and to noting their respective merits and defects.

Elective Department Heads.

At the present time, there are three principal types of departmental organization in which the department head is elected by the people, and five principal types in which the department head is selected in some other way. The three types of departmental organization with a popularly elected head are the following: (1) a single-headed department; (2) a multi-headed department, the members being elected in the state at large by all the voters; and (3) a multi-headed department, the members being elected by districts. The first type is the most common. The second type is best illustrated by the boards of regents of the state universities in certain states; the third, by several railroad commissions and state boards of equalization. The third type has proved very unsatisfactory in a number of cases, partly because of the tendency of the members of such boards and commissions to place the local interests of their respective districts above the general interests of the whole state. The second type has, in most cases, proved less unsatisfactory, partly, it may be suspected, because few states have entrusted much power to such bodies. The first type has proved least unsatisfactory. Under the system of making nominations for elective office by delegate conventions, the nominations for such places as commissioner of agriculture or labor, where elective, were commonly awarded by the managers of the major parties to candidates known to be acceptable to the farmers or to organized labor, as the case might be, and the nominees were commonly supported by all partisans without question. Under the direct primary system, the distribution of the nominations in a manner generally acceptable to the interests most concerned is less certain. Hence the results, particularly in states where extensive powers have been conferred on the elective officials, have been less satisfactory. In general, with the exception of the attorney-general, the most important administrative offices are those of comparatively recent creation and are not filled by popular election.

The unsystematic character of state administrative organization is clearly revealed by the illogical application of the principle of popular election to the choice of administrative officials. Almost everywhere, attorneys-general, secretaries of state, treasurers, and auditors are elected by popular vote. Yet some of these are administrative officers with important discretionary powers, while others have perfunctory duties involving little or no exercise of discretion. In all states there are appointed officers who have far greater authority than the popularly elected secretary of state. In most states, too, some officers are elected by the people, who in other states are chosen in some other way. Why should the members of the state board of equalization have been elected by the people in Illinois,[1] for example, although the members of the far more important tax commission are not so elected? Why should state railroad and warehouse commissioners be elected by the people, when the far more important public utilities commissioners are not so elected? Why should superintendents of public instruction be elected by the people in many

[1] The Illinois state board of equalization was abolished in 1919 and replaced by a state tax commission which is appointed.

states, while the far more important commissioners of education in other states are not so elected? If commissioners of agriculture are to be popularly elected, as is still the practice in some states, why should not commissioners of public health and workmen's compensation commissioners be similarly elected, as is the practice in no state? If the principle of popular election be sound, why so many exceptions? If unsound, why should it not be abandoned? Recently, such questions as these have been raised with increasing frequency. Short ballot reform and administrative reorganization both look to the abandonment of the direct popular election of administrative officials. In consequence, the present trend is strongly against the use of the elective principle under such circumstances and the states are gradually reducing the number of administrative offices which the people are called upon to fill. The most notable step towards a shorter ballot was the New York reorganization amendment of 1925, which removed from the ballot the secretary of state, the treasurer, and the state engineer and surveyor.

Non-elective Department Heads.

The passing of the elective principle has not thus far led to any general agreement as to the form of organization which should replace it. Where the department head is not elected by the people, there are many types of departmental organization, the principal of which are as follows: (1) the department with a single head appointed by the governor, usually with the consent of the senate; (2) the department with a single head appointed not by the governor but by a separate board or commission, usually unpaid, which exercises, however, only advisory powers in addition to the powers of appointment; (3) the department with a multiple head, consisting of a board or commission, usually unpaid, which exercises its powers mainly through the instrumentality of a paid expert secretary; (4) the department with a multiple head, consisting of a board or commission, usually paid, which exercises its powers directly through its own members; and (5) the department with a single head appointed by the governor, with or without the consent of the senate, but dependent upon the advice of an advisory council for the exercise of certain of his powers. The first type is found in all the states and is commonly employed where the duties of the department are largely of a ministerial character. Such, for example, is the type of organization generally adopted for departments of banking and insurance. This type of organization is also beginning to be used for the performance of functions which involve a considerable degree of discretion. For example, the single state tax commissioner or civil service commissioner performs duties of a quasi-legislative or quasi-judicial nature and the same is true of the heads of some of the reorganized departments in other branches of administration.

The second type of departmental organization is comparatively rare. It is employed most frequently for the organization of state departments of education. The best illustration of this form is the department of education of the state of New York. In that state, the legislature chooses each year one member of the state board of regents for a term of twelve years. The compensation is nominal, and the powers of the board are practically limited to the choice of commissioner of education. This officer is well paid, and serves during the pleasure of the board as the active head of the public school system of the state. The manner of appointing the regents protects them against ordinary political influences, since it would require seven years to change a majority of the board, and thus enables them to choose the commissioner of education solely with a view to his professional attainments and administrative skill. Such a system has the advantage of taking the management of the schools as completely "out of politics" as is possible. In most states where a similar type of organization has been adopted for the department of education, the members of the board which selects the commissioner are appointed by the governor for comparatively long terms, and as the terms are ordinarily so arranged that not more than one expires in any one year, the independence of the educational department is well safeguarded. Where it is highly important, as in the management of the public schools, to reduce ordinary political influences to a minimum, this type of organization has heretofore possessed distinct advantages over the first.

The third type of departmental organization closely resembles the first. In this type, there is both an unpaid board and a well-paid expert official at the head of the department, but the division of authority between them is different from that existing in the second type. The unpaid board not only chooses the paid expert, but actively directs the administration of the department. The paid expert is nominally the agent of the board, and the latter is the principal in the conduct of affairs. Actually the relations between principal and agent will be largely determined by the character of the men themselves. An active and capable secretary of such a board will often exercise as much real influence as the commissioner in the second type of organization. Active and capable members of boards, however, may exercise much more influence than in the second type. This system has the advantage of combining the enthusiasm and personal enterprise of intelligent amateurs with the experience and skill of the professional administrator. Under the most favorable conditions, it brings together in one harmonious organization the public-spirited citizen and the bureaucrat. It is a more economical type of organization than the second or fourth types, and seems particularly well adapted for the conduct of pioneer work in new fields of administration. It was a type frequently adopted when the state governments first turned their attention to educational, agricultural, charitable, and public health administration. It has been more generally employed in some parts of the country, notably in New England, than in others. Under this type of departmental organization, for example, Horace Mann developed the work of the Massachusetts state board of education, and F. B. Sanborn that of the board of charity.

The fourth type of departmental organization is commonly employed in those branches of administration which combine administrative, quasi-legislative, and quasi-judicial powers.[1] The members of this type of board or commission, unlike those of a board of the third type, are expected to devote most or all of their time to the duties of the office, and receive suitable compensation. Their secretary is distinctly a subordinate, and, unlike the secretary of a board of the third type, receives a smaller

[1] Quasi-legislative and quasi-judicial functions are most frequently found in connection with the work of tax commissions, public utilities commissions, and industrial commissions. The nature of these quasi-legislative functions is discussed in the following pages. The quasi-judicial duties are exemplified by the action of state tax commissions in hearing and deciding appeals from local assessments and by the action of state industrial commissions in deciding whether or not an injured workman is entitled to compensation under the terms of the workmen's compensation law. This kind of activity is the subject of further discussion in ch. xiii.

salary than his chiefs. The power and responsibility are combined in the hands of the board or commission itself. The earliest examples of this form were the boards of equalization created in several states prior to the Civil War. Most of the early boards of equalization, however, consisted of other state officials, *ex officio*, or were elected by the people. After the Civil War, this type of organization was adopted for the railroad and warehouse commissions of the Granger period, and is now regularly employed for public service commissions except those which are popularly elected. Recently, it has been applied to several other branches of state administration, notably the administration of health and labor laws. Modern health and labor laws contain numerous provisions to the effect that the conditions of employment shall be reasonably safe and wholesome, that employees shall be adequately protected against the danger of industrial accident and disease, or that due care shall be taken to preserve the health and safety of industrial wage earners. The enforcement of laws couched in such general terms was found to be exceedingly difficult, unless the generalities of the law were translated into specific instructions for the guidance of industrial inspectors. The legislatures were unable to do this work themselves, for it required more time and more specialized skill than they commonly possessed. The practice of leaving to the courts the interpretation of these general provisions in particular cases was slow, vexatious, and inadequate. The need arose for the determination in advance of fixed and definite sanitary and industrial rules which should serve as guides both to the official inspectors and to the public. The power to adopt such rules, like the power to regulate the rates of public utilities, seemed too broad to confide in a single administrative official. In 1911, Wisconsin, which had led the way in the creation of modern tax and public utility commissions, established a state industrial commission with a comprehensive jurisdiction over the enforcement of labor legislation of all kinds. This method of dealing with such matters came to be known as the Wisconsin idea, and has been copied in many states, particularly in the Middle and Far West, where there has been much legislation in recent years relating to social and industrial welfare. Several of these commissions, notably in the Pacific Coast states, have been named industrial welfare commissions, and have received very broad powers for the regulation of hours of labor, rates of wages, and other social and industrial conditions.

The fifth type of departmental organization resembles that originally adopted for the organization of the executive department. After the abolition of the original governor's councils, except in three of the New England states, this type of organization fell into disuse. It has recently been revived and adopted for departments which exercise important quasi-legislative and quasi-judicial, as well as ordinary administrative, powers. The first instance of its renewed use seems to have been in the Massachusetts department of boiler inspection organized in 1907. The chief boiler inspector was charged with the duty of seeing that steam boilers were reasonably safe. The legislature was unable to define by law with sufficient accuracy the tests of safety to be applied to all kinds of boilers under all sorts of conditions. Consequently, it provided for the creation of a board of boiler rules, which was charged with the duty of preparing standard specifications for the testing and licensing of steam boilers. This board was composed of four persons, one representative of boiler manufacturers, one representative of boiler users, one representative of stationary engineers and firemen, and one representative of boiler insurance companies, together with the chief boiler inspector who acted as chairman. Since that time, this form of departmental organization has been adopted in other cases where wide discretionary powers were delegated to administrative officials, notably in the organization of the New York and Massachusetts departments of health in 1913 and 1914, respectively, and in the organization of the New York and Pennsylvania departments of labor in 1913. There have been some changes in these departments since 1913 but the principle upon which they are now organized is still substantially the same. The Ohio reorganization of 1921 employs a similar principle in the departments of commerce, finance, and industrial relations.

Under this form of organization a single commissioner, appointed by the governor, is charged with the enforcement of all the laws, which fall within the jurisdiction of the department, and also with the enforcement of the codes elaborated by the advisory board or council. These councils are composed of representatives of the various interests most directly concerned in the work of the departments, appointed by the governor, together with the commissioner. They exercise no purely administrative powers but are limited to the quasi-legislative function of making rules and regulations. Under certain circumstances, they may also act as a quasi-judicial body in hearing cases which arise under the law or under their administrative rules. The commissioner is paid a suitable salary, and the members of the council are paid a smaller sum, proportioned to the work they do. This form of organization gives a more logical application than any of the others to the old maxim, "Many heads for council, one for action." It is possible to make the advisory councils more representative of the different interests concerned than administrative commissions can ordinarily be, without sacrificing administrative efficiency on the part of the commissioners for the sake of securing their representative character. It is also possible to hold the single administrative head more strictly responsible for the good conduct of administration than can be done where there are several commissioners of equal authority.

The Working of Different Organization Types.

Most of the recent administrative reorganizations have proceeded upon the theory that the best type of departmental organization is that characterized by a single non-elective head with or without an advisory council, depending upon the kind of work to be done. Former Governor Frank O. Lowden of Illinois has done more than any other state executive to popularize this theory. "When I became governor of Illinois," he is reported to have said in a recent address,[1] "there were something over one hundred and twenty-five independent and unrelated agencies of the state government, sometimes composed of boards, sometimes commissions, and sometimes individual officials. . . . The problem was to gather up the scattered agencies and to reorganize them into departments of government. . . . The question then arose as to whether these departments should be under the control of individuals or of commissions. In acquiring the habit of creating a board or a commission to take care of governmental work, we have assumed that if something important was to be done, it would be best done if done by a body of men, and not an individual. The fact is,—as all who have had experience in busi-

[1] Frank O. Lowden, "Reorganizing the Administration of a State," *National Municipal Review*, xv, pp. 9-10 (1926).

ness of any kind know—that it is the individual who does things, not a board or a commission. There is no commission anywhere, there is no board anywhere, that does things affirmatively unless it is dominated by one man, and the only benefit from the other members of that body is in their advisory capacity." Elaborating the idea, he continued: "There are some who have assumed that large responsibility could be more safely deposited in a body of men than in a single man. Experience has not justified this. Where the responsibility is upon the individual, he cannot shirk it. Where it is placed in a body of men, the individual can find shelter behind that body, when called to account for the manner in which he has exercised his power. There is also a deadly inertia in a board or commission which is not so likely to be found in the individual. . . . For these reasons, in Illinois we placed at the head of each of the nine departments an individual, whom we called a director, and not a board or commission."

The authors of the Illinois civil administrative code recognized, however, the need of systematic arrangements for supplying the department directors with information and advice. "It may happen," Governor Lowden pointed out,[1] "that the head of a department, upon some important question of policy, would like the advice of able and experienced men. We, therefore, provided advisory committees. The members serve without pay. We have found that many of the ablest men in Illinois are perfectly willing to serve upon an advisory committee without pay, although they could not be induced to take a salaried position. In this way we availed ourselves of the best talent within the state upon the various subjects of state administration." The authors of the code recognized also that the department directors should have a free hand in the assignment of duties to the division chiefs within their departments. The code consequently provides for the various subordinate departmental officers, but does not attempt to define their duties with precision. The distribution of authority is governed by departmental rules formulated by the directors. According to Governor Lowden there was much debate among the authors of the code over this proposition. "It was objected that this conferred too much power upon the individual head of a department. Many thought that the code should define precisely the duties of the heads of divisions in the

[1] *Ibid.*, p. 10.

several departments. In my judgment, to have adopted that theory would have greatly impaired the efficiency of the code."

The principles embodied in the Illinois civil administrative code, though widely approved, have not yet gained universal acceptance. Speaking of the Ohio administrative reorganization of 1921, which was modelled upon that of Illinois, a well-informed critic said: [1] "The principles upon which this and other recent reorganizations are based are clear and familiar. There is, first, the principle of economy. . . . No serious exception can be taken to this principle. . . . Secondly, there is the more fundamental principle of concentration of power and responsibility. . . . However valid the theory may be in certain of its applications, it may be subject to more substantial and radical qualifications than our leaders in administrative reorganization are allowing. . . . First, in the matter of the single-headed administrative department, is it true that for all such departments unity of power and responsibility is of more importance than continuity of policy and the maintenance of relations of mutual respect and confidence between staff and head? . . . Secondly, are we not in danger of carrying too far the idea that popular control is advanced chiefly by placing vast powers in one elected officer [referring to the governor], with the expectation that this officer will feel responsibility so certainly fixed upon him, that he will be more sensitive to public opinion than he would be if he possessed a narrower allotment of power? . . . Are we not greatly exaggerating the ability of public opinion . . . to keep constant observance upon its representatives and to pass satisfactory judgment upon them periodically?"

"These recent systems of reorganization," according to this critic,[2] "give too little weight to such needs as the following: (1) the need of securing continuity of policy in administrative departments having work of a technical and regulation-establishing character; (2) the need for facilitating the establishment of customs and traditions of non-interference by periodically changing political officers; (3) the need for eliciting the participation of disinterested citizens serving on unpaid boards, exercising powers of investigation, advice, and publicity; (4) the need for

[1] F. W. Coker, "Dogmas of Administrative Reform," *American Political Science Review*, xvi, pp. 408-409 (1922).

[2] *Ibid.*, pp. 410-411.

placing legal authority and responsibility in the particular offices most likely to develop a sense of professional responsibility and pride in connection with the work of such offices; (5) the uselessness of extending the scope of power of any officer beyond the limits of what that officer can actually devote his attention to. Both reason and experience show that, for the administration of many functions, diffusion, rather than concentration, of authority, secures not only more efficient but also more democratic administration."

There is room in state administration for both theories, that of the concentration and that of the diffusion of power and responsibility. Their applicability must depend somewhat upon the circumstances, which are not the same in all the states. The recent report of the state reorganization commission in New York proposes the consolidation of all administrative agencies into eighteen departments.[1] Two of these, if the suggestions of the commission are adopted, the department of audit and control and the department of law, will be headed by elective officers, the comptroller and attorney-general, respectively. Five are to be single-headed departments under appointive officers, namely, the executive department, and the departments of state, public works, banking, and insurance; while six are to be single-headed departments under appointive officers, assisted by advisory councils. These are the departments of taxation and finance, conservation, labor, health, mental hygiene, and prisons. Three departments are to have boards or commissions at their heads, operating for the most part through permanent expert administrators chosen by themselves. These are the departments of agriculture and markets, education, and charities. Finally, two departments are to be headed by commissions, constituting the active executives in charge, namely, the departments of public service and of civil service. Thus, in this most deliberate of administrative reorganizations, both the principle of the concentration of power and responsibility and that of their diffusion are recognized, but it is the former which clearly tends to prevail. To what extent it will be practicable to carry that principle in the government of any particular state must depend largely upon the

[1] Report of the State Reorganization Commission, 1926, *passim*. The recommendations of the commission were adopted in the main by the legislature of 1926.

general political condition of the state and the public interest in problems of administration. In most states it should be possible to secure greater economy and efficiency in the conduct of public affairs by carrying the principle of concentration farther than has yet been done; in some, it could apparently be carried much farther to the advantage of the public.

CHAPTER XII

THE STATE JUDICIARY

The constitutional history of the judicial branch of the state governments, like that of the legislative and executive branches, is a history of the progress of democracy. Like that of the executive branch, it is also a history of the growth of power. The democratization of the judiciary profoundly affected the character of judicial organization, just as the democratization of the executive affected the character of the executive organization. The growth of power profoundly affected the relations of the judiciary with the coördinate branches of government, just as the growth of power in the case of the executive affected its relations with the legislative branch. The democratized executive ultimately was found to require reconstruction in the interest of efficiency. The first question that arises in connection with the work of the courts is whether there also any reconstruction is required in the interest of efficiency. The growth of executive power at the expense of the state legislatures was necessary to establish a better balance between the two branches. Its propriety has been justified by the result. The present tendency in the development of the state executives is toward a further increase of executive power at the expense of the legislatures. The second question that arises in connection with the work of the courts is whether there also the growth of power was necessary to establish a better balance between the three branches, in other words, whether the propriety of the redistribution of powers has been justified by the result. With a view to attempting an answer to these questions the work of the courts may be divided into three classes: (1) the administration of justice by the adjudication of ordinary civil and criminal causes; (2) the enforcement of constitutional limitations upon the legislatures by the exercise of the power of judicial review; and (3) the enforcement of both constitutional and statutory limitations upon the executive by the same means. In this chapter the first of these three classes of judicial work will be considered.

THE ADMINISTRATION OF JUSTICE

The original organization of the state courts was partly an unconscious development of colonial institutions, partly a conscious adaptation of those of contemporary England. But colonial judicial organization was the most defective branch of colonial government, and the English model at the time of the Revolution was itself badly in need of reform. The administration of justice in the American colonies had been by no means clearly distinguished from other branches of administration. The supreme court in the chartered colonies was the governor and his court of assistants, subject in important cases to appeal to the general court, that is, to the representatives of the freemen. The grounds for appeal from the decisions of the ordinary magistrates were ill-defined, and the temptation for the legislatures to meddle in judicial business was strong. In the proprietary and crown colonies the governor was in a better position to maintain the supremacy of the executive in judicial affairs. A regular system of independent courts hardly arose until the eighteenth century. Even then everyday justice was administered mainly by local magistrates. These magistrates, usually justices of the peace, were unlearned in the English common law, and relied mainly upon their own common sense. After the Revolution came the real reception of the common law and the endeavor to construct a systematic judicial system. English judicial organization, as set forth in the *Commentaries* of Blackstone, was archaic, complicated, and arbitrary. Certain general principles of organization were discoverable, however, upon which the Fathers builded their several systems. The principal features of the early state judicial organizations were:—(1) local peace magistrates and local inferior courts for petty causes; (2) a central court of general jurisdiction at law and over crimes, with provision for local trial of causes at circuit and review of civil trials in bank in the central court; (3) a central court of equity, in which causes were heard in one place, though testimony might be taken in the locality; and (4) a supreme court of review. Generally, indeed, the second and third courts were merged.[1]

The development of the state judiciaries, like that of the state

[1] See Roscoe Pound, "Organization of Courts," in Bulletin vi, *Publications of the American Judicature Society*, pp. 11-12.

governments in general, was until recently largely molded by the needs and ideas of the frontier. Pioneer communities needed above all else certainty, quickness, and cheapness in the administration of justice. Cheapness was necessary because the frontier was poor. Quickness was necessary because the frontier was rough and impatient. Certainty was necessary because the frontier was self-taught. These needs directly controlled the development of judicial institutions in the pioneer states and indirectly affected judicial institutions in all the states. More recently, the growth of cities and the increasing complexity of urban life has subjected judicial institutions to new tests. The great industrial communities need more nicety and refinement in the law, more expertness in the judges, and a higher degree of specialization in the organization of courts and the administration of justice. The influence of the old frontier and of the new social and industrial order upon the present organization and practical working of the state courts is seen alike in the law itself, in the organization of the courts, and in the forms of procedure.

THE DEVELOPMENT OF THE LAW

The influence of the frontier upon the body of the law resulted in a rapid renovation of the English common law into an acceptable American system. The democratic spirit of frontier life was incompatible with the maintenance of the English tradition, in which the law was a strange and inscrutable thing, and lawyers a class apart from common men. Democracy demanded a system of law such that every man might be, if he wished, his own lawyer. The social and economic basis of frontier life was simple; the relationships of men did not require that the law should be refined. The conditions of life as well as the spirit of democracy were thus favorable to a revolution in law as well as in government. As it happened, the year of the American declaration of political independence of England was also a year of declarations of independence in England itself. In 1776 Adam Smith published his epoch-making treatise on the *Wealth of Nations,* inaugurating a revolt against the obsolescent doctrines of mercantilism. In the same year, Bentham published his *Fragment on Government*, inaugurating a revolt against the anachronisms of the English common law. Both Smith and

Bentham were pioneers whom the people of the states could appreciate. Bentham's work especially made a deep impression in America. This impression is most apparent in the demand for the codification of American law, of which so much was heard in the middle of the nineteenth century. Codification, Bentham argued, would assist both in the study and in the administration of law. It would express the whole body of law in the fewest possible rules, and would set it forth in a logical order and in a uniform and intelligible terminology. It would eliminate the need for learned commentaries and endless reports of cases. These claims appealed to the frontier democracy. To it, codification meant the realization of the dream that every man should be his own lawyer, and, when his turn came, should hold judicial as well as political and administrative office. In short, Bentham's theory of the law was well suited to the American frontier. Thus the reception of the English common law after the Revolution was closely followed by the reception of the ideas of the English law reformers.

The influence of the new social and economic order has been directly contrary to that of the old frontier. During the formative period of American law the influence of the judges, as pointed out by De Tocqueville, was very great. After the reception of the common law, all legal education began, and much ended, with the study of Blackstone. In each jurisdiction the judges were engaged in adapting the principles of the common law to the facts of American life. So far as Americans were concerned, much of the law was unwritten. Courts as well as people were engaged in pioneer work. Both in the development of the unwritten law, and in the interpretation of that which was written, each state judiciary was equally free to apply the utilitarian test in the light of local conditions. Law was copiously made or as people often preferred to say, discovered, by the judges themselves. Under any system of judge-made law the force of precedent becomes great, and in the course of time the law itself tends to become rigid. On account of the differences in local conditions in different states, it also tended to become diversified. Popular recognition of these tendencies was the signal for an increase of legislative activity in the field of ordinary civil and criminal law. The development of the new social and economic order stimulated the demand for the more rapid readjustment by legislation of the judge-made rules to the changing conditions. The growth of a new social conscience brought with it an assumption by the state of new social responsibilities. It was less generally expected that each man should be his own lawyer, and that the law should be so simple that any man might administer it. The demand for codification abated. Closer business relations between the states created a demand for greater uniformity in the laws of the states. The volume of legislature-made law greatly increased. The law itself became more complex, more refined, more remote from the comprehension of the layman. Justice became more uncertain, slower, and more expensive.

Recent Criticism of the Law.

In recent years criticism of the law, both civil and criminal, has become more and more frequent. At first, to be sure, adverse criticism was badly received, especially by the lawyers themselves. There was a disposition to regard the legal system as something too venerable to be touched by profane hands. When Roscoe Pound ventured to address the American Bar Association in 1906 upon "The Causes of Popular Dissatisfaction with the Administration of Justice," his was a voice crying in the wilderness. Most of his hearers seemed incredulous, and some were indignant that the perfection of their system should be so much as questioned. But the critics were not to be silenced. In the ordinary administration of the civil law it was the wage-earners and the poor who seemed most to suffer. The most notorious of the grievances of the former arose out of the operations of the law of master and servant as applied to the case of employees injured while at work. The demand for reform of the employers' liability law led presently to the complete abandonment of the old law and the adoption of modern workmen's compensation acts based on entirely different principles. But there was growing dissatisfaction with many phases of the labor law. It was dramatically expressed by Samuel Gompers, for many years the president of the American Federation of Labor, when testifying before a New York legislative committee, in the oft-quoted remark: "God save labor from the courts!" It was more soberly reflected in the report of the United States Commission on Industrial Relations, which found one of the principle causes of industrial unrest to be "denial of justice in the creation, in the adjudication, and in the administration of law." [1]

More serious in the long run, though not so immediately menacing, was the denial of justice to the poor. "Of all the questions which are before the American people," said William H. Taft in an address before the Virginia Bar Association, "I regard no one as more important than the improvement of the administration of justice. We must make it so that the poor man will have as nearly as possible an equal opportunity in litigating with the rich man, and under present conditions, ashamed as we may be of it, this is not the fact." [2] And Elihu Root, in his introduction to R. H. Smith's significant study of the work of legal aid societies in the United States, remarked: "Nor can any one question that the highest obligation of government is to secure justice for those who, because they are poor and weak and friendless, find it hard to maintain their rights. This book shows that we have not been performing that duty very satisfactorily, and that we ought to bestir ourselves to do better." [3] Mr. Root added: "I do not think we should be overharsh in judging ourselves, however, for the short-comings have been the result of changing conditions which the great body of our people have not fully appreciated. We have had in the main just laws and honest courts to which the people—poor as well as rich—could repair to obtain justice. But the rapid growth of great cities, the enormous mass of immigrants (many of them ignorant of our language), and the greatly increased complications of life have created conditions under which the provisions for obtaining justice which were formerly sufficient are sufficient no longer."

The Failure of Criminal Justice.

Most serious of all, in recent years, has been the failure of criminal justice. In the nineteenth century it was upon the frontier that the administration of criminal justice was most unsatisfactory. But in the twentieth the "crime wave" appeared in the large cities. In 1914 Alderman Merriam's Committee

[1] See Summary of Report, p. 5. (Washington, 1915).

[2] Quoted by R. H. Smith, *Justice and the Poor*, p. 6.

[3] R. H. Smith, *Justice and the Poor, A Study of the Present Denial of Justice to the Poor and of the Agencies making more Equal their Position before the Law*, p. ix. (New York, 1919.)

on Crime reported to the Chicago City Council that the treatment of crime in Chicago was wholly inadequate.[1] They found that many professional criminals escaped the penalties of the law, and preyed at will upon society, that poor and petty criminals were often punished more heavily than was just, that the treatment of those sentenced to penal institutions was pitifully ineffective, and that practical methods of preventing crime were not applied as extensively as experience showed to be possible. They found also that crime was rapidly increasing, that professional criminals had built up a "crime trust" with an elaborate organization, that there was collusion between members of the detective force and the criminals, that political influence, favoritism and graft exerted a pernicious influence upon the police force, tending to demoralize especially the detective branch of the service, that in many cases professional bondsmen and unscrupulous criminal lawyers perverted the course of justice, and that many criminals suffered from serious physical and mental disorders and required hospital treatment rather than ordinary punishment. In view of these and other findings, the Commission made forty-five specific recommendations for the improvement of conditions. Some of these recommendations were adopted, but the "crime wave" continued. It was evident that the failure of criminal justice presented a problem of extraordinary difficulty.

The first step in the solution of the problem was the study of the facts. A noteworthy beginning was presently made in Cleveland, Ohio, under the auspices of the Cleveland Foundation, a community trust, providing means for the distribution of bequests left by men and women interested in the welfare of the city. This Foundation had already made comprehensive surveys of public education and recreation facilities in the city, and in 1921 turned its attention to the problem of crime. A systematic investigation was made of the local police administration, the system of prosecution of criminals, the operations of the criminal courts, correctional and penal treatment, the relations between medical science and criminal justice, legal education in Cleveland, and the influence of the newspapers upon criminal justice. The report concluded with a general analysis of the problem of

[1] Report of the City Council Committee on Crime, p. 9 (Chicago, 1915).

criminal justice in American cities by Dean Roscoe Pound.[1] The survey showed that Cleveland with approximately 800,000 population in 1920 had six times as many murders as London with 8,000,000 population. "For every robbery or assault with intent to rob committed during this same period in London there were seventeen such crimes in Cleveland. . . . There are more robberies and assaults to rob in Cleveland every year than in all England, Scotland and Wales put together."[2] The investigators made numerous suggestions for the improvement of criminal justice, ranging from the reorganization of the police department to the incorporation of the bar.[3] Special stress was laid upon the necessity for the reorganization of the courts and the reform of judicial procedure. In conclusion, however, Dean Pound struck a note of optimism. "Our judicial organization is much better," he wrote, "as a foundation on which to build than that which was left to us by the Colonies, or than the eighteenth-century English organization which was the only other model. Our law is better organized, more accessible, and much more complete than that on which Marshall and Kent and Story labored. The bar is better taught and in far better public esteem than it was at the close of the eighteenth century. . . . Determination on the part of the present generation of lawyers to make over the institutions of rural America for the predominantly urban America of today . . . will make the first half of the twentieth century a classic period in American law no less truly than was the first half of the nineteenth."[4]

The Cleveland survey did not fail to bear fruit. The local bar association, together with other civic organizations, formed the Cleveland Association for Criminal Justice to carry the recommendations of the Survey into effect. It proposed particularly to exercise a constant surveillance upon the processes of justice, to assist those in authority to make improvements in the organization and operation of the agencies of criminal justice, and to furnish means for an intelligent public appraisal of the efficiency of law enforcement. Improvements in the administration of justice were immediately apparent. The probation

[1] *Criminal Justice in Cleveland*, published by the Cleveland Foundation. pp. ix, 729. (Cleveland, 1922.)

[2] *Criminal Justice in Cleveland*, p. 3.

[3] *Op. cit.*, pp. 649-651.

[4] *Op. cit.*, p. 652.

department of the local judicial establishment was reorganized, the prosecutors' offices were greatly improved, the grand jury system was made more efficient, the bar association intervened more effectively in order to secure the reëlection of tried and capable judges whose terms had expired, and, most remarkable of all, there was a decrease in the amount of crime.[1]

The method pursued in Cleveland was so manifestly sound and promising that it gave new impetus to the study of crime and law-enforcement everywhere. In Missouri a similar survey was instituted in 1925. It revealed, according to preliminary reports, the amazing facts that in St. Louis in the course of a single year there were 149 cases of homicide and only 25 punishments, 2701 burglaries and 107 punishments, 2075 robberies and 85 punishments. The chances of escaping the penalty for murder were five in six in St. Louis and ten in eleven in Kansas City; for burglary, 24 in 25 in St. Louis and 99 in 100 in Kansas City. Meanwhile a National Crime Commission had been organized to give direction and force to the awakened public sense of insecurity. The long period of growing distrust in the quality of law-enforcement approached its culmination.[2] It had become evident that, whatever the cure for the scandal of lawlessness might be, the only hope for its application lay in an aroused public opinion. It was evident also that one source of crime was the law itself, insofar as it set up standards of conduct which public opinion was not ready to support with the necessary firmness. Thus the next step in the solution of the problem of administering justice efficiently was recognized to be the study of the law.

The Reform of the Law.

Many agencies are now coöperating in the systematic study of the law. Foremost among them is the American Bar Association. Organized in 1878, this association has always devoted itself primarily to the advancement of the science of jurisprudence and to the promotion of the efficient administration of justice throughout the Union. One of its early enterprises was to encourage greater uniformity of legislation among the states. Largely

[1] Raymond Moley, *An Outline of the Cleveland Crime Survey*, pp. 63-64. (Cleveland, 1922).

[2] See R. W. Child, *Battling the Criminal.* (New York, 1925.) See also *Report Crimes Survey Committee*, Law Association of Philadelphia, 1926.

through its efforts the first state commissioners for the promotion of uniformity of legislation were appointed in New York in 1890, and presently most of the states had followed suit. A national conference of commissioners on uniform state laws is held annually, and models for uniform legislation by the states have now been prepared, covering such branches of the law as negotiable instruments, warehouse receipts, sales, bills of lading, stock transfers, etc., and have been enacted into law in a growing number of states. The annual report of the president of the American Bar Association, containing summaries of the new legislation of the states, has also been helpful in promoting better informed legislation in the various sections of the country. Another effective agency for the study and improvement of the law is the American Institute of Criminal Law and Criminology, organized in 1909. The Association of American Law Schools has also brought to bear upon the problem of law reform the concerted efforts of the teachers of law in the leading universities. Recognizing the need of more systematic efforts to bring about such a restatement of the law as will bring certainty and order out of the wilderness of precedent, these organizations joined in 1923 in founding the American Law Institute. As one of its first tasks, the institute undertook, in collaboration with a committce of the National Conference of Commissioners on Uniform State Laws, to draft a model code of criminal procedure. When completed, this will doubtless be recommended to the state legislatures throughout the Union for adoption. The Federal Government is also contributing the force of its example to the movement for the revision of the law. The Federal Arbitration Act, effective January 1, 1926, provides a model system for the arbitration of commercial disputes. The awards rendered in such arbitration proceedings are made enforceable in the federal courts. Already two states have adopted similar acts, applying to commercial arbitrations within their jurisdiction, and other states seem likely to do the same. In consequence of these unparalleled activities, the outlook for the further improvement of the law appears brighter than ever before.[1]

[1] See, for a learned and suggestive discussion of the whole subject, B. N. Cardozo, *The Growth of the Law* (New Haven, 1924).

THE ORGANIZATION OF THE COURTS

The influence of the frontier upon the organization of the courts resulted in the democratization of the administration of justice. This meant more than the mere introduction of popular elections of judges. It meant the bringing of justice directly to every man's door. In a country of long distances, in a period of slow communication and expensive travel, the central courts of general jurisdiction caused intolerable expense to litigants. Popular election of judges was accompanied by the creation of local judicial districts and fixed local courts, the erection of intermediate appellate courts between the trial courts and the courts of final review, and the establishment of special municipal courts at the bottom. The details of judicial organization vary greatly among the states, yet with all this variety of detail there is upon the whole a distinct and characteristic type. This general type of judicial organization contains four separate sets of courts. First, there is a supreme tribunal composed of a fixed number of judges, sitting only in that tribunal, and exercising mainly or exclusively appellate jurisdiction. Frequently, also, there is an intermediate court of a similar kind, interposed between the highest appellate court and the superior courts of first instance, thus creating to a certain extent a system of double appeals. Secondly, there is a set of superior courts of first instance with a general jurisdiction at law, in equity, and over felonies and the more serious misdemeanors. Thirdly, there is a set of probate courts, usually one in each county, often manned by laymen. Fourthly, there is a set of magistrate's courts, held by one magistrate for each locality, or as separate courts by several magistrates for each town or county. They have usually a petty civil and criminal jurisdiction, and power to bind over graver offenders to the superior court of first instance.[1]

The details of state judicial organization may be readily obtained from various convenient compilations.[2] At present the membership of the highest state courts ranges in number from three in half a dozen of the western states to sixteen in New Jersey. In most of the states the number of judges in

[1] See Pound, *op. cit.*, pp. 14-17.

[2] See, for example, *The American Year Book, A Record of Events and Progress, Year 1925*, p. 182. (New York, 1926).

the highest court, however, is seven or five. Their terms range from two years in Vermont to twenty-one in Pennsylvania, six and eight year terms predominating. In Massachusetts, however, judges serve during good behavior, as in the federal courts, in New Hampshire during good behavior or until they reach the age of seventy, and in Rhode Island for life or until removed by the legislature. Their salaries range from $3000 in South Dakota to $18,000 in New Jersey. They are appointed by the governor, with the consent of the legislature, or of the senate, or of the executive council, in six of the eastern states; they are elected by the legislature in four other states. Elsewhere they are elected by the people, voting by districts in four states and at large in the remaining thirty-four. Similar diversity exists in the composition of the lower courts, and in the tenure, compensation, and mode of selection of their judges. Outside of the northeastern states, however, popular election is the rule. The various district and circuit courts are consequently separate and independent of each other. In most states, therefore, judges may still remain inadequately employed in some districts, while in others the business of the courts may be heavily in arrears. In short, the democratization of the administration of justice has resulted in the decentralization and disintegration of judicial organization in the same manner, though not to the same extent, as the democratization of state administration in general has resulted in decentralization and disintegration.

The Need for Judicial Reorganization.

The influence of the new social and economic order upon the organization of the courts has as yet been much less than its influence upon the law itself. Intermediate appellate courts are still being interposed between trial courts and those of final review, and municipal courts are still being added at the bottom. Juvenile courts, domestic relations courts, night courts, land courts, workmen's compensation commissions, industrial welfare commissions, public service commissions, all armed with limited judicial powers, attest the growing need of greater specialization in the administration of justice. Courts and judges have been multiplied, but the organization of the judicial systems has been neglected. Nevertheless, the recent movement for the consolidation of state administrative agencies could not fail to extend to the agencies for the administration of justice. In a few states, notably Massachusetts, the superior courts had never been disrupted and the same necessity for consolidation does not exist as in most states. Despite the manifest advantages of the Massachusetts system, however, the movement for judicial consolidation has made little progress in the superior courts. A beginning has been made, however, in the municipal courts. Detroit furnishes the most noteworthy example of a consolidated municipal court, but other cities are following in the same path.[1] The Cleveland Survey recommended a similar consolidation of the local courts in that city, and the American Judicature Society, organized a few years earlier to promote the efficient administration of justice, drafted a model plan of consolidation for use everywhere. This plan was adopted by the Illinois constitutional convention of 1922 for the city of Chicago, but unfortunately failed of approval by the people along with the rest of the work of that convention.[2]

The plans of the American Judicature Society for the reorganization of the courts were broad enough to cover not only the municipal courts but also the entire judicial system, and merit further attention. The model judiciary article was originally prepared at the instance of the National Municipal League to form part of the model state constitution which that organization undertook to draft in 1919. Subsequently revised, it remains the most systematic and complete project of judicial reform which has yet been brought forward. The principal objects of the proposed reorganization of the courts were: (1) to effect a unification of the courts, and (2) to restore to the courts control of practice and procedure through the rule-making power. The former object was to be accomplished by consolidating all the ordinary courts into three main departments: (1) one for appellate business; (2) one for trials of all kinds; and (3) one for the special convenience of each separate county. The model article then provided for the management of the entire judicial establishment by a council of judges, representing each of the

[1] "Criminal Justice and How to Achieve It," Supplement to the *National Municipal Review*, xi (March, 1922). See also *Journal of the American Judicature Society*, v (October, 1921), and vi (April, 1923).

[2] American Judicature Society, Bulletin IV-B *Second Draft of Metropolitan Court Act*, and Bulletin VII-A, *Revised Draft of State-Wide Judicature Act*.

three main kinds of courts. The judicial council was to be empowered to make the rules of practice and procedure, and to control the work of the clerks of the courts and other administrative officers attached to the judicial establishment. It would also control the calendars of cases pending in the several courts, and make the assignments of judges so as to avoid congestion in any of the courts and equalize the work of the judges. At the head of the council and of the judicial system as a whole would stand the chief justice, a real and not merely a nominal chief judicial officer.[1]

The movement for the general reorganization of the state judiciary has not yet borne fruit in any state. In several states, however, noteworthy steps have been taken in the direction indicated by the judicial reformers. The Massachusetts judicature commission of 1919-21, after careful study of the general problem of judicial organization and procedure, recommended the creation of a permanent judicial council, and such a body was instituted in that state in 1921. Similar judicial councils were established in Ohio and Oregon in 1923, and in North Carolina in 1925. In California a proposed constitutional amendment creating a judicial council has received the approval of the legislature and will be submitted to the people in 1926. These bodies should be able to bring about substantial improvements in the conduct of judicial business and to furnish the public with more accurate and comprehensive information on the administration of justice than has hitherto been available. The dearth of reliable judicial statistics, indeed, has been one of the contributing causes of the inefficiency in the administration of justice, and has been a leading cause of public helplessness in the face of growing dissatisfaction with the work of the judiciary. In New York a constitutional amendment adopted in 1925 provided among other improvements in the administration of justice that judicial statistics, both civil and criminal, should be compiled and published annually. These measures promise well for the future, but as yet the movement for judicial reorganization lags far behind that for the reorganization of the executive branch of the state governments.

[1] For the full text of the Model Judiciary Article, with explanatory comments, see *Journal of the American Judicature Society*, vi (August, 1922), pp. 48-58.

The Selection and Tenure of Judges.

The most significant result of the new order upon the organization of the courts is the growing dissatisfaction with the popular election of judges. Popular election undoubtedly made the judiciary more independent of the legislative and executive branches of government, but it also made them more dependent upon the party organizations. In local judicial districts, especially in rural districts, popular elections seem to have generally resulted in real choices by the voters. But this has not generally been the result in the larger cities and districts, and in the election of judges by the voters of a whole state. In such cases the voters may elect, but the actual selection is likely to be done by others. In most states, while the delegate convention system of party organization lasted, the actual selection probably rested with the party leaders. In some states special arrangements were established by custom. Thus, in several states nominations for the more important judicial offices were made by the lawyers of the state at special "bar" primaries, and were commonly accepted by the major party leaders. In many states it was customary for both parties to renominate retiring judges, regardless of their party affiliation. On the other hand, not infrequently judicial nominations were openly disposed of by party leaders for partisan or personal ends, and quite generally elevation to the bench was possible only for those who served the regular apprenticeship in the party organization. The direct primary brought confusion to all these arrangements. The importance of excluding the judiciary from the ordinary partisan primary was quickly realized. As has been pointed out, several states have already established special non-partisan primaries for the nomination of judges, and provided special non-partisan ballots for use in judicial elections. But these devices have not brought about the desired improvement in the character of the judiciary.[1]

The most efficient state judiciaries are those of which the judges are not elected by the people. In Massachusetts and New Jersey, for example, where judges are appointed by the governor, there is less criticism of the work of the courts than in New York, where they are elected by the people. The prestige of the courts, as reflected in the authority of judge-made law,

[1] See R. E. Cushman, "Non-Partisan Nominations and Elections," *Annals of the American Academy of Political and Social Science*, cvi (March, 1923).

seems on the whole to have been higher prior to 1850 than subsequently in many of the states which then introduced popular elections.[1] It is the political power of the courts, not their efficiency in the administration of justice, that has been enhanced by popular elections. In the administration of justice, as in other branches of state administration, there is a growing need in most states for the employment of specialists and experts, and hence for greater security of tenure, more adequate compensation, more centralized and better integrated organization. How such reorganization shall be accomplished, without diminishing popular control of those courts which exercise important political functions, is a question which, in recent years, has been receiving increased attention.

No aspect of the problem of judicial reorganization gave the framers of the model judiciary article of the American Judicature Society more concern than that dealing with the selection and tenure of judges. The judicial reformers agreed that direct popular election was inimical to efficiency in the administration of justice, but they could not be blind to the popular preference for that system of choice. The caution displayed by the constitutional conventions which have had the opportunity in recent years to propose plans of judicial reorganization indicates the general reluctance to abandon a system which enjoys the prestige of long-continued popular favor.[2] In the original draft of the model judiciary article, as published by the Judicature Society,[3] no particular mode of selecting judges was prescribed. It was pointed out that the greatest defect in judicial administration was the lack of coördination of the judicial system and that the greatest need was to unify the system. The plan for the unification of the courts was suitable for any form of selection, and it seemed of the utmost importance that conflicts of opinion concerning the best mode of selecting judges should not overshadow the immediate task of reorganization. In the commen-

[1] See *Preliminary Report on Efficiency in the Administration of Justice*, prepared by Charles W. Eliot, Louis D. Brandeis, Moorfield Storey, Adolph J. Rodenbeck, and Roscoe Pound for the National Economic League, pp. 8-12.

[2] See, for example, *Bulletins for the Massachusetts Constitutional Convention of 1917-18*, No. 16, "The Selection and Retirement of Judges," and No. 36, "The Removal of Judges in Massachusetts"; and compare *Illinois Constitutional Convention Bulletins*, No. 10, "The Judicial Department," prepared by Professors W. F. Dodd and J. A. Fairlie. (Springfield, 1919.)

[3] See its *Journal*, vi, no. 2, p. 52.

tary on the model draft, however, a plan approved by the Illinois constitutional convention of 1922 for Cook County (Chicago) was singled out as particularly promising. Under this plan, if approved by the people, county judges were to be appointed by the governor from a list to be made up by the supreme court. The terms of judges so appointed were to be for the usual period of six years, at the end of which time the voters of the county should determine whether they should continue to serve. A judge who should fail to receive the approval of the voters at such an election would be ineligible for reappointment for another term. Others should be reappointed by the governor.

The National Municipal League, which incorporated the model judiciary article into its model state constitution, was bolder in its treatment of the problem of selection of judges.[1] It provided simply that the chief justice and the justices of the supreme court should be appointed by the governor for terms of ten years, subject to the consent of a majority of the legislature, and that the judges of the lower courts should be appointed by the governor for like terms without the necessity of legislative consent. The legislature, however, was to have power to remove any judge, upon due notice and after opportunity to be heard, with the concurrence of two-thirds of its members. Since the grounds upon which removal might be made were not stipulated in the constitution, this would give the legislature a freer hand in the matter of removals than under the ordinary process of impeachment. But, while the judicial reformers would generally prefer the appointment of judges by the executive, there is no sign of a growing disposition in the states where popular election prevails to give up that time-honored, though dubious, practice.[2]

THE FORMS OF PROCEDURE

The influence of the frontier upon the forms of procedure resulted in the limitation of judicial powers to regulate the business of the courts. The conduct of trials, especially, was hedged about with close restrictions. A strong tendency developed to convert the trial judge into a mere umpire, whose function it should be to hold an even balance between the contending

[1] *A Model State Constitution*, secs. 60 and 69. See Appendix C.

[2] Cf. W. S. Carpenter, *Judicial Tenure in the United States; with special references to the Tenure of Federal Judges.* (New Haven, 1918.)

parties, that is, between the lawyers for the parties. For example, serious limitations were placed upon the power of the presiding judge to charge the jury. Often the judge was forbidden to comment on the evidence, or was required to reduce his instructions to writing, or permitted to give instructions only at the request of counsel. Indeed, in a very few states, the presiding judge was deprived of all power to control the conduct of cases by counsel. This tendency to dethrone the trial judge and exalt the lawyers and jury had existed from the time of the Revolution, and by 1850 was the dominant tendency in most states. In some states the juries were made judges of the law as well as the facts at issue in a cause. Elsewhere the judges were held to the strictest responsibility for the correct determination of questions of law arising in the course of litigation. Appeals were freely allowed whenever errors were alleged to occur in the rulings of the trial judge, and reversal by the court of appeal of a ruling by a trial judge was made sufficient cause for a new trial, even if the merits of the case were not affected by the ruling. Judicial procedure became overladen with technicalities, and the legislatures fell into the habit of constantly amending the rules of procedure, even at the behest of litigants seeking an advantage in particular cases. The codification of the rules of procedure should have prevented this confusion, but the legislatures in states where codes were adopted could not refrain from tinkering with them. In New York, the code of civil procedure adopted in 1848 was so altered by amendment that a new code had to be adopted in 1876. The second code contained between three and four thousand provisions, and has been amended nearly five hundred times in the course of a single decade. In short, the regulation of judicial procedure by the state legislatures was perhaps a logical result of the spirit of the frontier, but it tended to defeat its own object, for it tended to make justice less certain, less speedy, and more costly.[1]

The Reform of Judicial Procedure.

The influence of the new social and economic order upon the regulation of judicial procedure has been no greater, as yet, than upon the organization of the courts.[2] There is still too much

[1] See Moorfield Storey, *The Reform of Legal Procedure* (New Haven, 1911).

[2] See *Preliminary Report on the Administration of Justice*, pp. 18-29.

legislation concerning the details of procedure. There is still a tendency to treat the rules of practice as giving to parties procedural rights which they may vindicate through appeal, although their substantive rights are not affected. There is still a tendency for courts of appeal to try cases upon the letter of the record instead of upon the real facts. There is still an overemphasis of formal issues instead of essential issues in litigation, of the technicalities of procedure instead of the merits of controversies. There is still too much appellate procedure, and in general too many trials and retrials. Such a system affords too much advantage to the litigant with the shrewdest counsel and the longest purse. Imperfections of procedure contribute to inefficiency in the administration of justice to a very unequal degree in different states for there is the greatest diversity of procedure in the different states. "Jurisdictions whose procedure is admirable in some respects are very backward in other respects. But few generalizations are possible. . . . In other words, while there are general evils which exist throughout the United States, the problem of procedural reform is largely local, and must be studied specially with reference to the conditions that obtain in each state." [1]

These generalizations are confirmed wherever careful study is made of the working of the state judicial systems. In Massachusetts, a state where the administration of justice has long been in the hands of able and respected judges, a judicature commission was appointed in 1919 to make a thorough investigation of the organization, procedure, and practice of the courts. This commission reported that the organization of the courts was generally satisfactory, but that there was "a waste of judicial power at both public and private expense." [2] It recommended no less than twenty-six separate acts for the improvement of the administration of justice.[3] In New York a similar investi-

[1] *Preliminary Report, op. cit.*, p. 18.

[2] Massachusetts Judicature Commission, *Second and Final Report*, 1921. Legislative Documents, House No. 1205, p. 10.

[3] A number of these were adopted by the legislature, including the act for the establishment of a judiciary council, already mentioned above. The commission discussed the plan of the American Judicature Society for the unification of the courts, and rejected it, on the ground that such a radical change was not needed in Massachusetts. It also discussed and rejected the proposal that the entire power to regulate the practice and procedure of the courts should be turned over to the courts themselves, as urged by some judicial reformers. The commission stated that it believed the proposition

gation was made by the so-called judiciary constitutional convention of 1921. This body consisted of thirty of the most eminent judges and lawyers in the state. It reported that the judicial system of the state had proved "reasonably satisfactory and successful as a whole," but that "many reforms of procedure are desirable." [1] The complaint so often heard of the uncertainty, delay, and expense of the law the convention ascribed "to litigants and the profession [of the law] itself, to constant legislative tinkering with our procedure in many objectionable ways . . . and to the failure to enact scientific and accurate remedial legislation." [2] It recommended a long list of minor changes in the organization and procedure of the courts, some of which were adopted by the legislature, and others in the form of constitutional amendments by the people. The principal constructive proposal to be adopted was that providing for the collection and publication of more adequate judicial statistics.[3]

The principal procedural defects in the administration of justice have been ably analyzed by R. H. Smith in his very significant book, *Justice and the Poor*.[4] "The body of the substantive law," he writes, "is remarkably free from any taint of partiality." In the administration of the law, on the contrary, he found grave defects. The first of these defects was excessive delay. Delays were mainly of two sorts: first, those encountered in getting a case heard and decided; and secondly, those occasioned by taking appeals on points of law to the higher courts. Excessive delay caused injustice in two ways: first, by making the time required for the final disposition of a case so long that persons with a grievance are discouraged from seeking justice in the courts;

to be sound in principle, but that its adoption was unnecessary in Massachusetts. See pp. 28-32, esp. at p. 30.

[1] New York Judiciary Constitutional Convention of 1921, *Report to the Legislature*, January 4, 1922, pp. 7-8. This body, like the Massachusetts judicature commission, considered the proposals for the unification of the courts, advanced by the American Judicature Society, and for the transfer of the rule-making power from the legislature to the courts, but rejected them. See pp. 6 and 43.

[2] Report, p. 8.

[3] See *Journal of the American Judicature Society*, v, pp. 142-3 (February, 1922).

[4] Published by the Carnegie Foundation for the Advancement of Teaching, with the sub-title "A Study of the Present Denial of Justice to the Poor and of the Agencies making more Equal their Position before the Law with particular Reference to Legal Aid Work in the United States." See esp. Part I. (New York, 1919).

and secondly, by forcing unfair settlements on persons unable to afford the time and money necessary to fight their case to a finish. The second defect was excessive court costs and fees. The average daily cost to the state for a trial with jury was variously estimated at from fifty to one hundred and fifty dollars.[1] But the fees charged to litigants bore no relation either to the state's expense in maintaining the judicial organization, or to the actual disbursement of the parties. "They are too low to deter the rich, but high enough to prohibit the poor." The third defect, according to Smith, was the expense of counsel. "The lawyer is indispensable to the conduct of proceedings before the courts, and yet the fees which he must charge for his services are more than millions of persons can pay."[2] Smith estimated that there were over thirty-five million people in the United States whose financial condition rendered them unable to pay any appreciable sum for lawyers' services. An impressive showing can be made of the agencies which have been created to bring justice within reach of the poor, notably the small claims courts, domestic relations courts, administrative tribunals such as the workmen's compensation commissions and industrial accident boards, conciliation and arbitration agencies, assigned counsel, and public defenders in criminal cases, to say nothing of the legal aid societies in the larger cities. But much still remains to be done.[3]

The Reform of Trial by Jury.

The most significant result of the new order upon the regulation of judicial procedure is the growing dissatisfaction with the traditional system of trial by jury. De Tocqueville, as has been shown, and all other early observers, reported that the jury system worked well. The principal difficulty in pioneer communities lay in procuring the requisite number of jurors. A majority of the states consequently made provision for reducing the number required for the petty jury in certain courts or classes of cases.[4] A lesser number have limited or dispensed with the

[1] Smith, *op. cit.*, p. 23.
[2] *Ibid.*, p. 31.
[3] *Ibid.*, p. 249.
[4] The first recorded case since the Revolution in which a statute was declared unconstitutional was that of Holmes *v.* Walton, decided in New Jersey in 1780. The ground for the decision was that the legislature had no right to reduce the number of the jury from twelve, as fixed by the common law, to six, as contemplated by the legislature.

use of the grand jury.[1] But more recently there has been evidence of loss of confidence in the juries. In civil cases arising out of complicated business relations the judgment of ordinary juries is distrusted. There is a pronounced tendency to waive the right of trial by jury in such cases and to refer the determination of facts to a referee or master, who reports his findings to the court. Most significant of all, there is a tendency to do away with the requirement of unanimity in civil trials. A growing number of states have provided that civil juries which fail to agree upon a unanimous verdict within a reasonable time may return a verdict by a five-sixths, or a three-fourths, or even by a two-thirds vote. In criminal cases, also, there is a tendency to distrust the judgment of ordinary juries. This is reflected in the abuse of the right to challenge prospective jurors, and in the difficulties and delays that arise in the empanelling of juries in important cases. The use of equitable remedies in certain classes of cases, notably those arising from labor disputes in which strikers threaten to damage the property of their employers, in effect reduces the value of the jury system in criminal cases. Judges may imprison strikers for contempt of court without trial by jury, although the alleged offense for which the striker is adjudged to be in contempt may be a crime. Thus he is in effect punished for crime without the benefit of a jury trial. In short, the democratization of the administration of justice in the middle of the nineteenth century tended to exalt the jury, and especially the lawyers, at the expense of the judge, but the influence of the new order seems to be in the opposite direction.

The Need for Further Reform.

In the administration of justice, as in other branches of state administration, the need of the times is for more specialization of function and for better utilization of expert personnel. This is most evident in the administration of criminal justice. To an ever greater extent the public demands not only that criminals be apprehended and punished to the end that the public safety be assured, but also that the criminal be so treated as to make

[1] The right of the people of a state by constitutional amendment to dispense with indictment by grand jury was affirmed by the United States Supreme Court in a case involving the constitutionality of such a provision in the California constitution of 1879 (Hurtado *v.* California, 110 U. S., 516).

him as far as possible an asset rather than a liability to the state. This involves in the first instance the classification of offenders, and the segregation of the young, the physically handicapped, and the mentally defective. Hence, the increasing employment of psychiatrists, medical examiners, and child specialists; hence, also, the increasing development of special facilities for the treatment of juvenile delinquents, state farms and tuberculosis camps for adults, and hospitals for the criminal insane. All the states now make more or less extensive use of the indeterminate sentence, the suspended sentence, and parole, and possess more or less developed systems of probation. It is clear that in the treatment of juvenile offenders, the modern methods are working a substantial improvement.[1] The effects of the newer methods, especially parole and probation, upon older offenders are less clear. Certainly much remains to be done, especially in the treatment of the habitual criminal and the mentally defective.[2]

REPRIEVES AND PARDONS

The development of modern methods in the administration of justice has reduced the importance of the ancient practices of reprieve and pardon.

The power to grant reprieves and pardons, vested in the state executives, was originally deemed, like the power of impeachment vested in the legislatures, one of the essential factors in the establishment of a proper balance between the three departments of government. Just as the power of impeachment was expected to provide a means of preventing executive and judicial officers from playing the tyrant in general, so the power to grant reprieves and pardons was relied on to prevent the perpetuation of injustice in particular cases.

It cannot be said that the history of the reprieving and pardoning power has justified the anticipations of the Fathers, any more than has that of impeachment. But it has been a very

[1] See Miriam Van Waters, *Youth in Conflict* (New York, 1925). See also W. Healy, "The Practical Value of Scientific Study of Juvenile Delinquents," U. S. Children's Bureau Publication, no. 96, 1922; and Lenroot and Lundberg, "Juvenile Courts at Work," *ibid.*, no. 141, 1925.

[2] R. W. Child, *Battling the Criminal*, chap. x. Cf. J. L. Gillin, *Criminology and Penology*, (New York, 1925). See also S. S. Glueck, *Mental Disorder and the Criminal Law*, (Boston, 1925); T. M. Osborne, *Prison and Common Sense*, (Philadelphia, 1924); Frank Tannenbaum, *Wall Shadows, A Study in American Prisons.* (New York, 1922).

different history. The power of impeachment has been so little used that it has become almost obsolete. The power of reprieve and pardon, on the contrary, has been used too much. It early became evident that governors were under great temptation to use it with excessive liberality, and that in practice the power was seriously abused.[1] It has sometimes been used for purely political purposes. Thus, the governor of Arkansas a few years ago pardoned some three hundred prisoners at one time, with most dramatic effect, expressly in order to call public attention to the iniquity of the contract labor system then employed in that state. It has probably been used more frequently for partisan and personal ends. Governor "Ma" Ferguson of Texas, who was inaugurated in 1925, issued above one thousand pardons during the first ten months of her term. Over a hundred more were granted to take effect on Thanksgiving Day. Such unparalleled liberality in the exercise of executive clemency threatened to become a scandal. Indeed scandals in connection with the use of the pardoning power have been too frequent.[2] Many states therefore have provided that the governor may grant pardons only upon the recommendation of a special board or "in conjunction with" a board of which he may be a member.[3] In general it is clearly desirable that proceedings in connection with pardons should be surrounded with at least as much publicity as in the case of proceedings before boards of parole and similar agencies.

The gradual decrease in the severity of penal methods, and more recently the introduction of the practice of parole, have tended to deprive the pardoning power of its reason for being. At the present time the power to pardon plays no part in the maintenance of the balance between the departments, and it is doubtful whether there is any good reason for vesting such a power in the hands of an officer, like the governor, primarily political in character. Properly constituted boards of parole are proving far more reliable agencies for the exercise of a judicious clemency than the governors ever have been. With

[1] See Francis Lieber, "Reflections on the Present Constitution of New York," 1867, in his *Miscellaneous Writings*, ii, pp. 185-189.

[2] See Christen Jensen, *The Pardoning Power in the American States* (Chicago, 1922). Governor Davis of Kansas was arrested after his term of office had come to an end in 1925 and tried on a charge of accepting money for a pardon, but was acquitted.

[3] See *Massachusetts Constitutional Convention Bulletins*, No. 4, "The Pardoning Power."

the increasing public recognition of the value of their work it would seem desirable to abolish the power of pardon altogether. In the states where capital punishment has been abolished it is doubtful whether there is much better reason for retaining longer the power of reprieve.

CHAPTER XIII

JUDICIAL REVIEW OF LEGISLATION AND ADMINISTRATION

The power of the courts to review the constitutionality of legislation and to refuse to enforce that which they declare unconstitutional is formally a judicial power. It springs from the duty of the courts to determine what law applies in cases where there is a conflict of law. But cases involving conflict between statutes and the law of the constitution are different from ordinary cases of conflict of laws. Expounding a constitution is a different kind of work from construing a statute.[1] It is essentially political in character. To the student of politics, as distinct from administration, the exercise of the power of judicial review and veto is the most important part of the work of the courts.

JUDICIAL REVIEW OF LEGISLATION

There are two sources of the veto power exercised by the state courts. First, it is implied, as already shown, in the very nature of the system of constitutional government in the states. Secondly, it is expressly conferred by the Federal Constitution. The implied power of judicial veto is the power merely to refuse to enforce state legislative enactments in conflict with the state constitution. The expressed power is the power to refuse to enforce any state enactment, whether in the form of an ordinary act of legislation or in that of a clause of the state constitution, which is in conflict with the Constitution of the United States, or with a law made in pursuance thereof, or with a treaty made under the authority of the United States. In the former class of cases the decision of the highest court of the state is final. In the latter the decision of the Supreme Court of the United States alone is final. Prior to 1915, however, there was no provision for appeal to the United States Supreme Court from decisions

[1] See W. F. Dodd, "The Problem of State Constitutional Construction," *Columbia Law Review*, xx, pp. 635 ff. (1920).

of state courts in cases involving alleged conflict between state legislation and the supreme law of the land, unless the state courts refused to protect the rights claimed under the supreme law. Since 1915 it has been possible to procure from the United States Supreme Court a final decision in all cases involving alleged conflicts between the supreme law and the constitutions and laws of the states. The exercise of the power of judicial veto in the government of the states, therefore, falls under two heads: (1) the veto by the state courts of ordinary state legislation in conflict with a state constitution or of any state legislation in conflict with the supreme law of the land; and (2) the veto by the federal courts of state legislation, statutory or constitutional, in conflict with the supreme law of the land.

Exercise of Judicial Veto.

The power of judicial veto was at first exercised infrequently and with great caution. Haines, in his work, *The American Doctrine of Judicial Supremacy,* lists only eighteen cases in which statutes were rendered null and void by the refusal of the state courts to enforce them during the forty odd years from 1776 to 1819.[1] This list is not complete, but it indicates accurately enough the extent to which the power was used at that period. Down to the Civil War the practice of invalidating legislative acts seems to have been confined mainly to a few states, and to have been infrequently indulged in even in those few.[2] Thereafter the practice rapidly became more common. During the six years from 1903 to 1908, inclusive, nearly four hundred state laws were declared unconstitutional by the state courts.[3] Making due allowances for the increase in the number of states and in the volume of state legislation, it is evident that the importance of the veto power possessed by the state courts has greatly increased. The power to veto state legislation originally possessed by the federal courts, like that originally possessed by the state courts, was exercised sparingly. Only thirty-seven state acts were declared unconstitutional by the federal courts from their organization to the Civil War. Since

[1] See Haines, *op. cit.*, p. 228.

[2] See E. S. Corwin, "The Establishment of Judicial Review," *Michigan Law Review*, ix, p. 314.

[3] See New York State Library Legislative Bulletins, 1903-1908, summarized in Haines, *op. cit.*, p. 307.

then the federal courts, like the state courts, have exercised the judicial veto much more freely. From 1860 to 1910 the federal courts declared one hundred and eighty state acts unconstitutional.[1]

The more frequent use of the judicial veto since the middle of the nineteenth century can be partly explained by the constitutional changes which took place at that time. In New York, for example, 285 acts or parts of acts had been declared unconstitutional by the state courts down to the year 1912. Of these barely one per cent were enacted under the original constitution of 1777, and not much over two per cent under the second constitution of 1821. Of the balance about three-fifths were enacted under the constitution of 1846, and about two-fifths under the constitution of 1894.[2] The exercise of the judicial veto by the New York courts falls almost entirely in the period since the adoption of the popular election of judges and of stricter constitutional limitations upon legislative powers and procedure. The same is true of most of the states. The more frequent use of the judicial veto by the federal courts since the Civil War can likewise be partly explained by the effects of constitutional changes. The adoption of the thirteenth, fourteenth, and fifteenth amendments to the Federal Constitution greatly increased the jurisdiction of the federal courts over state legislation.[3]

The increased use of the judicial veto since the Civil War cannot be wholly explained by changes in the written constitutions of the states and nation. The adoption of the reconstruction amendments did not greatly increase the constitutional limitations upon acts of Congress. Yet the more frequent use of the judicial veto against congressional legislation in the last half century is as marked as its more frequent use against the legislation of the states. Prior to 1860 only three acts of Con-

[1] See B. F. Moore, *The Supreme Court and Unconstitutional Legislation*, in *Columbia University Studies in History, Economics, and Public Law*, liv, no. 2, appendix iii. (New York, 1913.)

[2] See H. A. Davis, *The Judicial Veto*, appendix. In recent years the judicial veto has been exercised more vigorously than ever before. A count of state legislation (including constitutional provisions and municipal ordinances as well as ordinary laws) invalidated by U. S. Supreme Court decisions between 1910 and 1922 by B. B. H. Meyer of the Library of Congress showed a total of 166 such cases in the eleven years, or about fifteen per annum. See *Congressional Record*, vol. 64, pt. 5, pp. 4566-4570.

[3] See, especially, C. W. Collins, *The Fourteenth Amendment and the States* (Philadelphia, 1912).

gress had been declared unconstitutional. Between 1860 and 1910 no less than thirty such acts were vetoed by the federal courts, and since 1910 acts of Congress have been set aside at the rate of more than one a year. The federal courts, moreover, have no greater jurisdiction over state legislation in one state than in another. From the beginning down to 1910 they declared unconstitutional only two acts of the state of Massachusetts, only four acts of the other five New England states, two New Jersey acts, and none at all of Delaware. Yet during the same period they declared unconstitutional twelve Tennessee acts, thirteen Missouri acts, sixteen each of the states of Louisiana and New York, and seventeen of Pennsylvania.[1]

There can be no doubt that, along with the increase in the independence of the state judiciary and the enlargement of its jurisdiction over state legislation, there came a change in public sentiment towards the judiciary generally. The people began to look more confidently to the courts for protection against abuses of power by the legislatures. The courts were encouraged to use their powers more vigorously. This tendency was most marked in the states where the courts were originally weakest and where the legislatures had been guilty of the greatest abuse of power. There was also greater need to use the judicial veto against the legislation of such states. But the change in public sentiment occurred everywhere. In other words, the political importance of the state courts was enhanced directly by popular distrust of the state legislatures, as well as indirectly through the increase of constitutional limitations upon legislative powers and procedure. The federal courts shared with the courts of the states the growing sense of power, despite the loss of prestige resulting from certain unpopular decisions, such as those in the Dred Scott, legal tender, and income tax cases.

Effect of Judicial Veto.

The effect of increased jurisdiction over state legislation and of growing popular favor is reflected in the character of judicial

[1] See Moore, *op. cit.*, appendix iv. Since 1910 the continued invalidation of state laws by the U. S. Supreme Court has raised the total number of measures thus set aside to 28 for Kentucky, 25 for Louisiana, 24 for New York, and 21 for Pennsylvania. Five states, on the other hand, have never enacted any laws held to be in conflict with the Federal Constitution, namely, Rhode Island, Connecticut, Delaware, Wyoming, and Idaho. See *Congressional Record*, cited above.

vetoes. Of the eighteen acts listed by Haines which were declared unconstitutional by the state courts prior to 1820, a majority related to the organization or duties of the courts, judicial procedure, or trial by jury. Only one act was declared unconstitutional on account of defective legislative procedure in its enactment. In other words, the judicial veto was originally employed by the state courts principally to protect their own constitutional rights. Since 1860 a great change has taken place in the nature of the legislation most frequently vetoed by the courts. Of the four hundred acts declared unconstitutional by the state and federal[1] courts in the years 1903-1908, fifty-five were vetoed because the subjects of the acts were not clearly expressed in their titles, fifty-three on the ground that they were special or class legislation, when their objects could have been attained under existing general acts or should have been secured by new general acts, forty-nine because, if enforced, they would have deprived persons of liberty or property without due process of law, and thirty-six because they denied the equal protection of the laws. That is to say, nearly half the total number of acts vetoed by the courts were declared unconstitutional on account of defective legislative procedure or because, if enforced, they would have accomplished their purpose "without due process of law." Only thirty-two of these acts were vetoed by the courts on account of interference with the constitutional rights of the judiciary.[2] In short, whilst the state courts originally used the judicial veto principally to protect their own constitutional rights, they now use it largely to condemn the fruits of incorrect legislative procedure and to maintain the integrity of "due process of law." Originally the state courts were on the defensive. Now the effect of the judicial veto in the states is to put the legislatures on the defensive.

A similar change has occurred in the use of the judicial veto by the federal courts. All the cases in which provisions of state constitutions and statutes, territorial statutes, and municipal ordinances have been vetoed by the Supreme Court of the United States down to the year 1910 have been classified according to the clauses of the Federal Constitution with which these enactments came in conflict.[3] From this classification it appears that

[1] All but 28 of these vetoes were by the state courts.

[2] See Haines, *op. cit.*, p. 307.

[3] See Moore, *op. cit.*, appendix v.

nearly one-third of all these enactments were declared unconstitutional on the ground that they conflicted with that clause of the Federal Constitution which grants to the federal government the power to regulate interstate and foreign commerce, and that almost another third conflicted with the provision forbidding any state to pass any law impairing the obligation of contracts. About one-tenth of the vetoed enactments conflicted with the clause of the fourteenth amendment forbidding any state to deprive any person of life, liberty, or property without due process of law, or to deny any person the equal protection of the laws. There was no considerable number of conflicts with any other single provision of the Federal Constitution. Prior to the Civil War the greater portion of the state laws declared unconstitutional by the federal courts conflicted with the commerce clause of the Federal Constitution, or tended in some other way to impair the supremacy of the federal government within its constitutional sphere. Since then an increasing portion have conflicted with the clauses limiting the supremacy of the state governments in their constitutional spheres. The "due process of law" clause has become particularly important during the last quarter century. In other words, the judicial veto was originally used by the federal courts against state legislation primarily in order to maintain the supremacy of the federal government in the conduct of national affairs. Latterly it has tended to be used more and more to enforce federal constitutional limitations upon the conduct of local affairs by the state governments.

Due Process of Law.

Both the more frequent use of the judicial veto by the state courts and the increasing interference in the domestic affairs of the states by the federal courts have been greatly facilitated by the construction which has been placed upon the "due process of law" clauses in both state and federal constitutions. Prior to the Civil War due process of law in the states was guaranteed only by the state constitutions, and the guarantee, as already pointed out, was commonly understood to mean a guarantee of the right to law.[1]

[1] See *ante*, ch. iii. Cf. E. S. Corwin, "Due Process of Law before the Civil War," *Harvard Law Review*, xxiv, p. 375.

The principal case, prior to the Civil War, in which the term was interpreted more broadly arose out of the enforcement of the New York state-wide prohibitory liquor law of 1855.[1] In this case a law which prohibited the sale of intoxicants after a certain date was declared unconstitutional, on the ground that in effect it deprived those who owned intoxicants at that time of their property without due process of law. The court's objection to the law was caused, not only by the procedure prescribed for the confiscation of intoxicants offered for sale after the law went into effect, but also by the substance of the law itself. In the case of intoxicants in the possession of inhabitants of the state prior to the date when the act became effective and offered for sale thereafter, the court declared their confiscation by any procedure whatever to be unconstitutional. In general, however, the "due process" clause was not at that time supposed to limit the power of the legislature in the enactment of substantive law. Its purpose was believed to be to secure a government of law rather than of men, not to control the content of the law. When the federal courts were first charged by the fourteenth amendment with the duty of enforcing due process of law upon the state governments, they still adhered to this view.[2]

It was inevitable that the courts, both state and federal, when once they began to feel their power, should take a more aggressive view of their duty under the "due process" clause. If ours is to be a government of law, not of men, it follows that members of a state legislature are not free to act arbitrarily and oppressively any more than other men who may happen to hold public office. In other words, they may not accomplish an arbitrary and unreasonable purpose by expressing it in the form of a statute and calling it law. Should a legislature enact such a law, it would be the duty of the court to interpose with a judicial veto. The original Massachusetts constitution, for example, explicitly provides that the law-making power of the legislature extends only to the enactment of "wholesome and reasonable" measures. The same limitation is implied in all the state constitutions. Thus the constitutional guarantee of due process of law comes to mean a guarantee of reasonable law, or what in the opinion of

[1] Wynehamer *v.* The People, 13 N. Y., 378 (1856).
[2] See the Slaughter-House Cases, 16 Wall, 36 (1873).

the court is reasonable law. Doubtless, the authority of a court to declare a statute unconstitutional on the ground of unreasonableness is a delicate one, not to be exercised by inferior courts, nor by any court unless the unreasonableness of the act is clear beyond a doubt. Indeed, the very existence of such power was long denied by leading writers on constitutional law.[1] The attitude of the state and federal courts, however, toward much recent legislation relating to social and industrial conditions cannot be explained except upon the theory that such a power exists. But it is clear that the courts themselves in the exercise of this power are also subject to the rule of reason, and that between courts and legislature the ultimate judges must be the people.[2]

The Rule of Reason.

The first important case in which the rule of reason was applied by the federal courts against state legislation was decided the year after the decision of the Slaughter-House cases.[3] In this case the United States Supreme Court was asked to enforce the payment of interest due on bonds issued by a municipal corporation under a state law authorizing cities and counties "to issue bonds for the purpose of building bridges, aiding railroads, water-power, or other works of internal improvement." The bonds in question were issued for the purpose of aiding a company to establish an iron-bridge works. It was conceded that the steps required by the act prerequisite to the issuing of the bonds were regular, and that the language of the statute was sufficient to justify the action of the city authorities, if the statute itself was within the constitutional competency of the legislature. The Supreme Court held that "the theory of our governments, state and federal, is opposed to the deposit of unlimited power anywhere. . . . There are limitations on such power which grow out of the essential nature of all free governments, implied reservations of individual rights, without which the social compact could not exist, and which are respected by all governments

[1] See Thomas M. Cooley, *A Treatise on the Constitutional Limitations which rest upon the Legislative Power of the States of the American Union* (7th ed.), ch. vii, "The Circumstances under which a Legislative Act may be declared Unconstitutional."

[2] See A. N. Holcombe, *The Foundations of the Modern Commonwealth*, ch. viii. (New York, 1923.)

[3] Loan Association *v.* Topeka, 20 Wall, 655 (1874).

entitled to the name. . . . There can be no lawful tax which is not levied for a public purpose." In this case the court believed that a tax levied for the purpose of meeting the interest charges on bonds issued in aid of a private iron-bridge works was not levied for a public purpose. In effect by this decision the right of the city to repudiate the bonds was sustained. In a dissenting opinion a minority of the court declared that "courts cannot nullify an act of the state legislature on the vague ground that they think it opposed to a general latent spirit supposed to pervade or underlie the constitution, where neither the terms nor the implications of the instrument disclose any such restriction. . . . Such a power is denied to the courts because to concede it would be to make the courts sovereign over both the constitution and the people, and convert the government into a judicial despotism. . . . Unwise laws and such as are highly inexpedient and unjust are frequently passed by legislative bodies, but there is no power vested in the circuit court to determine that any law passed by a state legislature is void, if it is not repugnant to their own constitution nor the constitution of the United States." The opinion of the minority was consistent with the theory of judicial review generally acted on by the courts prior to that time, but it was the opinion of the majority that has since then prevailed.

Another step in the judicial application of the rule of reason was taken in connection with the regulation of railroads and other so-called "businesses affected with a public interest." In the leading case [1] the United States Supreme Court noted the contention "that the owner of property is entitled to a reasonable compensation for its use, even though it be clothed with a public interest, and that what is reasonable is a judicial and not a legislative question," and rejected it, saying: "As has already been shown, the practice has been otherwise . . . it has been customary from time immemorial for the legislature to declare what shall be a reasonable compensation under such circumstances. . . . We know that this is a power which may be abused; but that is no argument against its existence. For protection against abuses by legislatures the people must resort to the polls, not to the courts." This was the view expressed by the minority in the Topeka bridge-works case. Though temporarily revived, it

[1] Munn *v.* Illinois, 94 U. S. 113 (1876).

was becoming old-fashioned, and was vigorously denounced in a dissenting opinion by a minority of the court. The minority view soon came to prevail, and eventually was stated by an undivided court as follows: "A state enactment, . . . establishing rates for the transportation of persons and property by railroad that will not admit of the carrier earning such compensation as under all the circumstances is just to it and to the public would deprive such carrier of its property without due process of law . . . , and would therefore be repugnant to the fourteenth amendment of the constitution of the United States. While rates for the transportation of persons and property within the limits of a state are primarily for its determination, the question whether they are so unreasonably low as to deprive the carrier of its property without such compensation as the constitution secures, and therefore without due process of law, cannot be so conclusively determined by the legislature of the state . . . that the matter may not become the subject of judicial inquiry." As the court further remarked, "the idea that any legislature . . . can conclusively determine for the people and for the courts that what it enacts in the form of law . . . is consistent with the fundamental law, is in opposition to the theory of our institutions."[1]

A notable assertion of the power of the courts to reject unreasonable acts of legislation, or so to restrict their application as to avoid consequences which seem to the courts unreasonable, is found in connection with the judicial interpretation of the antitrust acts. The Sherman antitrust act of 1890 is entitled, "an act to protect trade and commerce against unlawful restraints and monopolies," and declares every contract, combination in the form of trust or otherwise, or conspiracy, in restraint of trade or commerce among the several states, to be illegal. At first the United State Supreme Court held every contract or combination found by them to be in restraint of such trade to be forbidden by the act. Then in the Northern Securities case[2] one of the five judges, who joined in the decision that the Northern Securities Company was an illegal combination, stated that he could not assent to the view that every contract or combination that might be found to be in restraint of interstate trade

[1] Smyth *v.* Ames, 169 U. S. 466, 526 (1898).
[2] Northern Securities Co. *v.* United States, 193 U. S. 197 (1904).

would be illegal. The only contracts and combinations which in his opinion should be declared illegal were those imposing an unreasonable restraint upon interstate trade.[1] Finally, in the Standard Oil and American Tobacco Company cases, decided seven years later, this view was accepted by eight of the nine members of the court.[2] The manner of applying the rule of reason to state antitrust legislation is well illustrated by two recent cases involving the so-called Harvester trust.[3] In one of these cases a Missouri act, forbidding "all arrangements . . . between two or more persons, designed to lessen, or which tend to lessen, lawful trade or full competition . . . ," or "which are designed . . . to increase, or which tend to increase, the market price of any product . . . ," was sustained by the United States Supreme Court. In the other case, the Kentucky antitrust acts, which had been construed by the state supreme court to make any combination for the purpose of controlling prices lawful, unless for the purpose or with the effect of fixing a price greater or less than the real value of the article, were declared unconstitutional. The United States Supreme Court held that the expression "real value," defined by the state supreme court as "market value under fair competition and under normal market conditions," was in the given case nothing more than an illusory form of words, and that the law as construed by the state court prescribed an unreasonable standard of conduct. Doubtless, however, if the state supreme court had not been trying to construe the law in such a way as to apply to foreign combinations like the Harvester Company and not to apply to domestic combinations like the tobacco growers' association, they could have given the law what would have seemed to the United States court a reasonable meaning.

The rule of reason was first applied to labor legislation in a decision of the New York court of appeals in 1885.[4] In the preceding year the legislature enacted a law "to improve the public health by prohibiting the manufacture of cigars and preparation of tobacco in any form in tenement houses" in certain cities, namely New York and Brooklyn. The constitu-

[1] See case cited, at p. 361.
[2] 221 U. S. 1, 106.
[3] International Harvester Co. *v.* Missouri, 234 U. S., 199, and International Harvester Co. *v.* Kentucky, 234 U. S. 216; both decided in 1914.
[4] *In re* Jacobs, 98 N. Y. 98.

tionality of the act was immediately attacked on the ground that it would deprive the manufacturers of cigars and other tobacco products in tenement houses of liberty and property without due process of law. The court declared that "the constitutional guarantee that no person shall be deprived of his property without due process of law may be violated without the physical taking of property. . . . Any law which . . . takes away any of its essential attributes deprives the owner of his property. . . . So too one may be deprived of his liberty and his constitutional rights thereto violated without the actual imprisonment or restraint of his person. Liberty . . . as understood in this country, means the right, not only of freedom from actual servitude, imprisonment, or restraint, but the right of one to use his faculties in all lawful ways, to live and work where he will. . . . Generally it is for the legislature to determine what laws and regulations are needed to protect the public health and secure the public comfort and safety, and while its measures are calculated, intended, convenient, and appropriate to accomplish these ends, the exercise of its discretion is not subject to review by the courts. But they must have some relation to these ends. Under the mere guise of police regulations, personal rights and private property cannot be arbitrarily invaded, and the determination of the legislature is not final or conclusive. If it passes an act ostensibly for the public health, and thereby destroys or takes away the property of the citizen, or interferes with his personal liberty, then it is for the courts to scrutinize the act and see whether it really relates to and is convenient and appropriate to promote the public health. It matters not that the legislature may in the title to the act, or in its body, declare that it is intended for the improvement of the public health. Such a declaration does not conclude the courts, and they must yet determine the fact declared and enforce the supreme law. . . ." The court thereupon determined that the act in question was not a health law and that it had no relation whatever to the public health. Consequently, the act was declared unconstitutional, being in the opinion of the court an unreasonable exercise of the police power.

Since this decision in the Jacobs case, the judicial veto has been invoked on the ground of unreasonableness more frequently against labor laws than against any other single class of measures. Laws designed to protect industrial wage-earners and thereby also the people as a whole against the injurious effects of employment in factories, mills, mines, and other work-places for excessively long hours, or under unwholesome conditions, or at wages inadequate to meet the cost of the necessaries of decent living, or in other respects to regulate the conditions of employment in modern industry in the interest of the employees, must be defended, if at all, as necessary and proper uses of the police power. The police power may be defined as the power of promoting the public welfare by restraining and regulating the use of liberty and property.[1] Its use therefore in every case involves some deprivation of liberty and property, and gives the courts the opportunity to decide whether such deprivation has been accomplished by due process of law. In the opinion of the courts, many laws limiting the hours of labor of men and women, regulating employment under unwholesome conditions, prohibiting the payment of wages in anything but lawful money, requiring the payment of wages at frequent and regular intervals, forbidding deductions from wages on account of imperfect workmanship, requiring compensation for industrial accidents at specified rates, prohibiting discrimination against workmen on account of membership in trade unions, or in other respects limiting the freedom of contract between employer and employee, have been unreasonable, and consequently have been vetoed by them.[2] The courts have set up a new right unknown prior to 1885, namely the right to freedom of contract, and in many cases have declared to be unconstitutional, state enactments in the interest of industrial wage-earners interfering therewith.[3]

Criticism of Rule of Reason.

The unreasonableness of the legislation to which the rule of reason has been applied is, however, a matter of opinion. The enactment of such laws in itself is evidence of a strong and, at least in the legislature, preponderant opinion that they are reasonable. Naturally, the courts have not escaped adverse criticism for their use of the judicial veto to defeat such legislation. The practice of vetoing laws because they seem to the courts

[1] See E. Freund, *The Police Power.*
[2] See F. J. Goodnow, *Social Reform and the Constitution.*
[3] See R. Pound, "Liberty of Contract," *Yale Law Journal*, xviii, p. 454.

to be unreasonable is particularly vexatious when the courts are closely divided in their opinion. Of seventy-eight cases in which statutes were vetoed by the United States Supreme Court between 1901 and 1907, twenty-nine decisions were rendered by a vote of five to four, forty-six by a vote of six to three, and three by a vote of five to three.[1] Of 166 cases, in which state legislation was vetoed between 1910 and 1922, at least twenty-five were decided by a closely divided Court, with three or four of the judges dissenting.[2] Mr. Bryan, in his famous Chicago convention speech of 1896, voiced the thoughts of many, when he exclaimed: "They criticize us for our criticism of the Supreme Court of the United States. My friends, we have not criticized, we have simply called attention to what you already know. If you want criticisms, read the dissenting opinions of the court."

The courts, indeed, have found the severest critics of the application of the rule of reason among the judges themselves. One example, so far as its application to labor legislation is concerned, will serve as well as many. In 1905, the United States Supreme Court vetoed the New York bakers' ten-hour law. This law had been enacted to protect the health of employees in bakeries, and had been sustained by the state courts on the ground that it was a reasonable exercise of the police power. Altogether eight of the thirteen judges who pronounced judgment upon the act during its passage through the state courts, and four of the nine members of the United States Supreme Court, were of the opinion that the act should be upheld as a valid health law. Five members of the latter court, however, declared that "there is in our judgment no reasonable ground for holding this to be necessary or appropriate as a health law. . . ." And again, "There is no reasonable ground for interfering with the liberty of person or the right of free contract by determining the hours of labor in the occupation of a baker." This decision has been freely condemned by the critics of the courts, but by none more effectively than by the dissenting members of the Supreme Court itself. Justice Harlan said: "It is enough for the determination of this case, and it is enough for this Court to know, that the question is one about which there is room for debate and for an honest difference of opinion. There are many reasons of a

[1] See Haines, *op. cit.*, p. 327.
[2] *Congressional Record*, vol. 64, pt. 5, pp. 4566-4570.

weighty substantial character . . . in support of the theory that, all things considered, more than ten hours' steady work each day, from week to week, in a bakery or confectionery establishment, may endanger the health and shorten the lives of the workmen, thereby diminishing their physical and mental capacity to serve the state and to provide for those dependent upon them. If such reasons exist, that ought to be the end of this case, for the state is not amenable to the judiciary in respect of its legislative enactments, unless such enactments are plainly, palpably, beyond all question, inconsistent with the Constitution of the United States."

Justice Holmes registered a separate protest against the decision of the majority of the court. "This case," he declared, "is decided upon an economic theory which a large part of the country does not entertain. If it were a question whether I agreed with that theory, I should desire to study it further and long before making up my mind. But I do not conceive that to be my duty, because I strongly believe that my agreement or disagreement has nothing to do with the right of a majority to embody their opinions in law. . . . The fourteenth amendment does not enact Mr. Herbert Spencer's Social Statics. . . . A constitution is not intended to embody a particular economic theory, whether of paternalism and the organic relation of the citizen to the state or of *laissez faire*. It is made for people of fundamentally differing views, and the accident of our finding certain opinions natural and familiar or novel and even shocking ought not to conclude our judgment upon the question whether statutes embodying them conflict with the constitution of the United States." There can be no doubt that Justice Holmes expressed correctly the duty of the courts in the exercise of the power of judicial review.[1] The Federal Constitution explicitly guarantees to the people of the states a republican form of government, but it does not guarantee the conduct of state affairs according to any particular theory. Certainly it does not guarantee the conduct of state affairs according to the theory of *laissez faire*. Socialism itself would be constitutional, if a social revolution were necessary for the protection of the people, and if that particular kind of a social revolution were appropriate to

[1] See A. N. Holcombe, *The Foundations of the Modern Commonwealth*, p. 325.

the occasion. Should such a revolution be brought about by "due process of law," the judiciary would have no more right, under any sound interpretation of the American constitutional system, to interpose with a judicial veto, than they had to attempt to settle the question of slavery by the Dred Scott decision.

Criticism of the courts for the injudicious application of the rule of reason dates from the first time when the courts applied the rule. In the first important case, the New York prohibitory liquor law case, decided in 1856, the majority of the court said, "Liquor is not a nuisance *per se,* nor can it be made so by a simple legislative declaration." Since prohibitory liquor laws had been enacted and were then in full force in ten or a dozen other states, there was a good deal of criticism of this decision. The court would doubtless have been correct in saying that liquor had not been considered a nuisance under the common law, but whether or not liquor was considered a nuisance by the people of New York in 1855 was certainly a question which the people could decide for themselves through their regular representatives better than the court could decide it for them. When the same question subsequently arose in another case and was eventually brought before the Supreme Court of the United States, that court was of the opinion that "the courts cannot, without usurping legislative functions, override the will of the people as thus expressed by their chosen representatives."[1] The New York courts received a similar rebuff from the United States Supreme Court in the oleomargarine case. In 1885 the New York court of appeals declared unconstitutional "an act to prevent deception in sales of dairy products," which prohibited the sale of oleomargarine. This decision was made on the ground that the anti-oleomargarine act was arbitrary class legislation, unreasonably sacrificing the rights of the oleo manufacturers to the interests of the butter makers.[2] When a similar statute, enacted by the legislature of Pennsylvania, came shortly afterwards before the Supreme Court of the United States, the court said: "It cannot adjudge that the defendant's rights of liberty and property, as thus defined, have been infringed by the statute of Pennsylvania, without holding that, although it may have been enacted in good faith for the objects expressed in the title,

[1] Mugler *v.* Kansas, 123 U. S. 623 (1887).
[2] People *v.* Marx, 99 N. Y. 277 (1885).

namely, to protect the public health and to prevent the adulteration of dairy products and fraud in the sale thereof, it has in fact no real and substantial relation to those objects. The court is unable to affirm that this legislation has no real or substantial relation to those subjects."[1] A dissenting judge of the Supreme Court pointed out the conflict between this decision and that of the New York court, vetoing the similar act of the New York legislature, but the majority repudiated that precedent.

Dissatisfaction with the use of the judicial veto by the federal courts in cases involving the rule of reason has on the whole, particularly in recent times, been much less than with its use by some of the state courts. There have been several instances in which similar legislation has been attacked in the courts of a number of states, and has been pronounced unconstitutional by some state courts and constitutional by others. In most of these cases the United States Supreme Court has taken the more sympathetic view of the reasonableness of these laws. For example, to consider only the field of labor legislation, laws prescribing the mode of weighing coal in order to fix the compensation of coal miners have been held invalid in Illinois, Missouri, Colorado, and Kansas, but not in Tennessee, nor, on appeal in the last case, by the federal Supreme Court. Laws designed to prevent extortion at company stores by requiring employers to pay wages in money have been declared unconstitutional in several states, and constitutional in several other states and in the United States. In one state the courts denied the power of the legislature to enact a mandatory workmen's compensation law, but similar laws have been enacted in many other states and also by Congress without incurring judicial condemnation. Probably nothing has injured the prestige of certain state courts more seriously than their refusal to enforce laws, involving an alleged unreasonable exercise of the police power, which the courts of other states and of the United States have declared constitutionally unobjectionable. The result of such decisions in many states has been to create grave uncertainty as to the limits of legislative power to deal with social and industrial conditions and to cause excessive delay in putting into effect remedial legislation demanded by a strong and preponderant opinion among the people. The modern development of the rule of

[1] Powell *v.* Pennsylvania, 127 U. S. 678 (1888).

reason has doubtless greatly increased the scope and importance of the judicial veto, but its injudicious use has seriously impaired popular confidence in the courts, particularly in certain states.[1]

Judicial Review of Legislative Procedure.

A second source of the recent growth in the political power of the courts, which also has occasioned criticism of their use of the judicial veto, is to be found in the constitutional limitations upon the forms of legislation and legislative procedure. The principal limitations upon the forms of legislation are the provisions that the subject of an act shall be expressed in the title, and that the act shall not embrace more than one subject, found in about two-thirds of the constitutions, and the provisions forbidding the amendment of acts by mere reference to title, found in nearly half of the constitutions. These limitations were adopted to protect honest legislators against fraud and surprise, and to stop the practice of logrolling.[2] They undoubtedly inculcate a sound legislative practice, and if not construed too literally by the courts, tend to encourage clearness as well as honesty in legislation. Unfortunately they have been construed too literally by the courts of some states, giving rise to an enormous amount of litigation, and leading to the nullification of beneficial as well as undesirable statutes. An eminent authority notes that "while the courts lean to a liberal construction, they have in a minority of cases been indefensibly and even preposterously technical." [3] In recent years there has been an astonishing number of acts vetoed by the courts on account of purely formal defects, especially in certain states of the South and West. On the whole, however, the limitations upon the forms of legislation have been of less consequence, as applied by the courts, than those upon legislative procedure.

The principal procedural requirements are these: that bills shall be read three separate times, or that they shall be read on three separate days, or that they shall be read three times in full; that they shall be referred to legislative committees and duly reported by the same; that they shall not be introduced

[1] See Jane Addams, in *American Journal of Sociology*, xiii, p. 772.

[2] See *ante*, ch. v.

[3] See E. Freund, "The Problem of Adequate Legislative Powers under State Constitutions," in *Publications of the New York State Constitutional Convention Commission*, Papers on Special Topics, pt. i, p. 107.

after a stated period; that rejected measures shall not be reintroduced in the same session; that a motion to reconsider shall not be entertained on the same day; that bills shall not be so amended as to alter the subject thereof; that bills and all amendments shall be printed; that they shall be on the desks of members in their final form three days before their final passage; that a majority of all the members be required for passing a bill; that the final vote be by yeas and nays and be entered on the journal; and that the signature of the presiding officer must be affixed in open session. Some of these provisions are salutary, and their fulfillment can be readily verified by examining the journals, such as the requirements relating to the final vote on the passage of a bill. Others, however, are impracticable, and in practice are regularly evaded, such as the requirement that a bill be read three times in full. Compliance with the constitutional requirement in such cases becomes perfunctory or is frankly ignored. In the latter case the necessary fraud may be covered up by a false entry on the journal. The requirement that no amendment be entertained which alters the subject of a bill gives rise to exceedingly difficult questions of construction, which are highly unsuitable for judicial review. In many states the judicial veto is freely employed to condemn measures for procedural defects, often without much or any regard for their real merits.[1] In Alabama and Mississippi, for example, during a recent period of only five years, for which the official reports were searched by the writer, nearly two score of legislative acts were declared unconstitutional by the state courts, mostly on account of formal or procedural defects.

A recent and judicious critic of the work of the courts suggests that the trouble lies in the constitutions themselves as well as in the courts.[2] "The sound policy of constitution-making is to impose procedural requirements only under the following conditions: (1) that they serve an object of vital importance; (2) that they can be complied with without unduly impeding business; (3) that they are not susceptible of evasion by purely formal compliance or by false journal entries; (4) that they do

[1] For a particularly flagrant case of the judicial veto on technical grounds, contrary to the merits, see Koehler and Lange *v.* Hill, 60 Iowa, 543 (1883). cited in Thayer's *Cases on Constitutional Law*, i, p. 252.

[2] See E. Freund, *op. cit.*, p. 104.

not raise difficult questions of construction; and (5) that the fact of compliance or non-compliance can be readily ascertained by an inspection of the journal. The application of these tests would lead to the discarding of most of the existing provisions. . . . As to those retained, the judicial power to enforce compliance should be limited." Professor Freund's suggestions for the limitation of the power of judicial review are, that the validity of a statute should not be questioned on account of procedural defects after the expiry of a short period from the date of its enactment, or that no statute should be questioned at all for procedural or formal defects, if the attorney-general, prior to approval by the governor, has certified that the form and procedure are constitutionally correct. In short, relief from the evils of the injudicious use of the judicial veto on account of technicalities should be sought by increasing executive responsibility for the technical perfection of legislation.

Limitation of Judicial Veto.

Many of the critics of the state judiciaries have demanded more drastic remedies for the abuse of the judicial veto. The belief that technical justice too frequently was substituted for substantial justice, and especially the belief that the rule of reason, as applied by the courts, too frequently was unreasonable, culminated in a demand for more direct popular control of the judiciary. The first method of direct popular control advocated by the critics of the judiciary was the recall of judges. As has already been stated, seven of the ten states which have adopted the popular recall of state officials included judges among the officials subject to recall. Hitherto, however, the recall has been utilized to remove judges from office even less than in the case of other state officials. No judge has yet been recalled because of popular dissatisfaction with a decision involving any question of constitutional interpretation. The first instance of the popular recall of a judge occurred in California. The judge of a lower court reduced to a nominal sum the bail originally required of a prisoner awaiting trial for a serious offense. Thereupon the prisoner fled. The judge was charged with collusion in the prisoner's escape, and was recalled by the indignant people of his district. The recall has not yet even been invoked against a member of any superior or supreme court. In short, the recall of judges, like the recall of state officials generally, seems likely to be little used.

Another method of direct popular control was suggested by Theodore Roosevelt in an address before the Ohio constitutional convention of 1912. This was the so-called recall of judicial decisions. The term was a misnomer. Roosevelt's proposal was not to reverse the action of the judiciary in a case once decided by them, but to prevent such action from becoming a precedent for the decision of future cases arising under the same law, if the people were of the opinion that the rule of reason had been unreasonably applied in that case to that particular law. In Colorado this proposal was adopted in the form of a constitutional amendment, authorizing the people, by the same procedure as that provided for the direct popular initiative, to order the enforcement of a statute, which had been duly enacted by the legislature and approved by the governor, but vetoed by the supreme court, if the majority so desired. This amendment, however, was itself declared unconstitutional by the supreme court of the state.[1] In New York the decision of the state supreme court, adverse to the constitutionality of the workmen's compensation act, was recalled by the ordinary process of constitutional amendment. In this instance the amendment adopted by the people specifically provided that the "due process of law" clause should not thereafter be construed to forbid the enactment by the legislature of a workmen's compensation act. In general, those states which possess the direct popular initiative, applying to constitutional amendments as well as to ordinary statutes, already possess all the machinery necessary for precisely that "recall of judicial decisions" which Roosevelt advocated, and in any state where the process of constitutional amendment is reasonably easy there would be little time gained by the adoption of any special procedure for the recall of decisions. In states where the process of constitutional amendment is slow and inconvenient the general reform of that process is what is most immediately important. It is not surprising, therefore, that the "recall of decisions" made little progress under that name.

The agitation over the judicial veto, however, was not without effect. The Ohio constitutional convention, where the plan

[1] People *v.* Western Union Telegraph Co., 198 Pac. 146 (1921).

for the "recall of decisions" was first broached, recognized the evil which Roosevelt sought to relieve, and provided a remedy of its own. The Ohio plan, adopted by the people in the same year, provided simply that statutes should not be declared unconstitutional by the lower courts, nor by the supreme court unless at least six of the seven judges concurred in the decision.[1] This plan should effectually prevent the nullification of legislation by the state courts unless its repugnance to the constitution is actually clear beyond a reasonable doubt. Another good result of the agitation over the judicial veto was the adoption by Congress in 1915 of an amendment to the federal judiciary act, providing that appeals might be taken from the state courts to the United States Supreme Court in all cases involving the interpretation of the Constitution of the United States, even when the rights claimed under the Federal Constitution were protected by the state courts. Thus it should be possible hereafter for the federal courts to establish a uniform interpretation of the Federal Constitution throughout the country in all cases involving the exercise of the rule of reason under the "due process of law" clause. The most important result of the agitation over the judicial veto was the change it produced in the attitude of the courts towards legislation enacted under the police power for the protection of industrial wage earners against the hazards of their employments. The Illinois supreme court, for example, which in 1895 denied the power of the legislature to limit the hours of labor of women employed in industry, reversed that decision in 1910.[2] The New York court of appeals, which in 1907

[1] A similar plan was submitted to the people of Minnesota in 1914 and approved by a majority of those voting thereon, but failed of adoption because of the failure of a majority of all those attending the polls to vote for it, as required by the constitution of that state. See *American Year Book* for 1914, p. 62. In North Dakota a constitutional amendment was adopted in 1918 providing that acts of the legislature should not be declared unconstitutional in that state without the concurrence of at least four of the five judges of the supreme court. The advocacy of a similar limitation upon the power of the U. S. Supreme Court to invalidate acts of Congress by Senator Borah and the late Senator LaFollette has caused a good deal of discussion. For recent defenses of the existing practice, see Robert von Moschzisker, *Judicial Review of Legislation*, published by the National Association for Constitutional Government (Washington, 1923), and Charles Warren, *Congress, the Constitution, and the Supreme Court* (Boston, 1925). See also R. E. Cushman, "Constitutional Decisions by a Bare Majority of the Court," *Michigan Law Review*, xix, pp. 771-803 (1921).

[2] Ritchie *v.* People, 155 Ill. 98 (1895); Ritchie *v.* Wayman, 244 Ill. 509 (1910).

denied the power of the legislature to prohibit the employment of women in industry at night, reversed that decision in 1915.[1]

Judicial Ideas of Liberty and Justice.

The truth is that a profound change has been taking place in the dominant conceptions of liberty and justice. In the latter part of the nineteenth century the courts came much more completely than at any previous time under the influence of the individualistic social philosophy of the English utilitarians. They seem to have been especially impressed with the later form of that philosophy, formulated by Herbert Spencer. This influence is clearly revealed in numerous judicial opinions and legal writings, and was well expressed by the then leader of the American bar, James C. Carter.[2] "There is a guide," he wrote, "which, when kept clearly and constantly in view, sufficiently informs us what we should aim to do by legislation and what should be left to other agencies. This is what I have so often insisted upon as the sole function both of law and legislation, namely, to secure to each individual the utmost liberty which he can enjoy consistently with the like liberty to all others. . . . To leave each man to work out in freedom his own happiness or misery, to stand or fall by the consequences of his own conduct, is the true method of human discipline." Such a conception of liberty and justice made it possible for intelligent men sincerely to denounce plans "to equalize the inequalities which the rights of free contract and private property have brought about," that is, for example, laws levying a progressive income tax or regulating the hours of labor, as involving "confiscation or the destruction of the principle of private property."[3] This is a negative conception which was probably never consciously accepted by the American people as a whole, certainly not without important qualifications. If held at the time of the Civil War, it would have left the freedmen, for example, to relapse into peonage under the guise of liberty of contract. It is this negative conception of liberty and justice that was repudiated by

[1] People *v.* Williams, 189 N. Y. 131 (1907); People *v.* Schweinler Press, 214 N. Y. 395 (1915).

[2] J. C. Carter, *Law, its Origin, Growth, and Function*, p. 337.

[3] See W. H. Taft, "Recent Criticisms of the Federal Judiciary," in *Report of the American Bar Association*, 1895, p. 246.

Justice Holmes in the dissenting opinion, already quoted, in the New York bakers' case.

The twentieth century has brought a more positive conception of liberty. It is coming to mean more than the mere absence of physical restraints upon the physical person, or of statutory restraints upon the legal person. Real liberty is not the antithesis of social control. Rather, rightly directed and effective social control is the condition of such liberty. Thus the modern conception of liberty is bound up with the modern conception of social justice, and social justice is understood to be an end in itself, not merely another name for justice to individuals. It involves the idea of the state itself as a person, as a subject of rights, the only idea of the state consistent with the origin of the American states and the nature of their political institutions. Thus it becomes possible for intelligent men sincerely to advocate plans to equalize at least some of the inequalities which the rights of free contract and private property have brought about, without doing violence to their faith in the fundamental principles of American government. Liberty of contract, in particular, that late nineteenth century product of juristic reasoning, now tends to be conceived, not as an inalienable part of the citizen's constitutional liberty, but as a means to such liberty, to be protected only in so far as it effectually serves that end. State legislatures are now enacting more freely than ever before measures restricting in various ways the liberty of contract, and these measures in increasing numbers are successfully withstanding the process of judicial review. The supreme court of Oregon, to mention only one of the states, has sustained statutes providing for the fixing of minimum wages for women employed in industry and prescribing a maximum limit upon the hours of labor of wage-earning men.[1] Time was when such statutes would doubtless have been summarily vetoed by the courts in every state in the Union. Though there is still much uncertainty in the attitude of the courts towards statutes involving limitations upon liberty of contract, on the whole the twentieth century con-

[1] See Stettler *v.* O'Hara, 69 Ore. 519 (1914), and State *v.* Bunting, 71 Ore. 259 (1914). Cf., F. Frankfurter, "Hours of Labor and Realism in Constitutional Law," *Harvard Law Review*, xxix, p. 353.

ception of liberty tends to prevail in the halls of justice as well as in those of legislation.[1]

[1] This passage has been left substantially as originally written ten years ago. It must be confessed, however, that the tendency of the courts to accept newer conceptions of liberty and justice does not seem so clear now as then. The Supreme Court of the United States, which in 1917 permitted the Oregon minimum wage law to stand, through the lack of a majority for a decision either for or against it, subsequently declared unconstitutional a similar law enacted by Congress for the protection of women employed in the District of Columbia. See Adkins *v.* Children's Hospital, 261 U. S. 525 (1923). Four of the judges dissented in this case. Chief Justice Taft wrote a dissenting opinion, in which he declared that he had supposed that the decision of the Court in the New York ten-hour law case (Lochner *v.* New York) was no longer acceptable as a precedent in such cases; and Justice Holmes in a separate dissent reiterated his well-known views in favor of a more tolerant policy on the part of the Court towards legislative experiments in the use of the police power to bring about a larger measure of social justice. An extraordinary feature of this decision was the circumstance that, if the case had come before the Court a year earlier, it would probably have been decided the other way. See T. R. Powell, "The Judiciality of Minimum Wage Legislation," reprinted in *The Supreme Court and Minimum Wage Legislation,* published by the *New Republic* (New York, 1925), p. 12. This volume is the best commentary on the judicial review of state legislation under the police power that has appeared in recent years. Dean Pound in his *Introduction* puts his finger on the weakness in the exercise of the power of judicial review when he says: "One of the chief sources of difficulty in judicial treatment of social legislation has been the tendency to treat the 'reasonable' as something absolutely given." *Ibid.*, p. xxii. Other cases in recent years in which the older view of constitutional liberty has prevailed against the newer conception are the Washington compulsory state employment agency law case, Adams *v.* Tanner, 244 U. S. 590 (1917), the Kansas compulsory arbitration law cases, Wolff Packing Co. *v.* Court of Industrial Relations, 262 U. S. 525 (1923) and 267 U. S. 552 (1925), the Arizona minimum wage law case, Sardell *v.* Murphy, decided October 19, 1925, and two current cases not yet reported, one concerning a Pennsylvania anti-shoddy law and the other a Wisconsin act imposing death duties on gifts made in anticipation of death.

On the other hand, the newer conception has prevailed also in several cases. Noteworthy among these are the decisions sustaining the constitutionality of the New York and Washington "state fund" workmen's compensation acts, New York Central *v.* White, 243 U. S. 188, and Mountain Timber Co. *v.* Washington, 243 U. S. 219 (1917), and the decisions sustaining the New York rent-control and sedition acts, Marcus Brown Holding Co. *v.* Feldman, 256 U. S. 170 (1921), and Gitlow *v.* New York, 268 U. S. 652 (1925). See, for cogent statements of the newer conception, Ernst Freund, *Standards of American Legislation* (Chicago, 1917), and Benjamin N. Cardozo, *The Nature of the Judicial Process* (New Haven, 1921). "The criterion of reasonableness," Freund writes, "may be the only one available; but if so, it means that adequate scientific or conventional tests have not yet been developed. To oppose legislative discretion by undefined judicial standards of reasonableness is to oppose legislative by judicial discretion, and constitutional doctrines so vaguely formulated cannot be expected to command confidence." *Op. cit.*, p. 5. And Judge Cardozo, noting that liberty was once conceived as something "static and absolute," finely adds: "Gradually . . . a new conception of the significance of constitutional limitations in the domain of individual liberty emerged. . . . It is the dissenting opinion of Justice Holmes [in the Lochner case], which men will turn to in the future as the beginning of an era. In the instance,

The American doctrine of judicial review is fundamentally sound.[1] In times like the present, however, when public opinion on matters of vital interest is undergoing a radical change, the judiciary are put to a severe test. They are not expected to be the first by whom new ideas are introduced. It is their function to compel due deliberation on the part of legislators and of the people when new social and economic conditions seem to demand new principles of legislation. But neither should the courts be the last to lay the old ideas aside. The judicial veto is one of the greatest of political powers and should be exercised with corresponding caution. It is easy for learned judges to believe that they have a mission to save the people from the consequences of their own supposed folly but they should not forget that both the state and federal courts have not generally been happy in their boldest political decisions. In general, the people profit most from their own experience with unwise legislation, and will find an effective remedy at the polls. The courts may properly defer the enforcement of legislation that seems to them clearly unreasonable, when passed in response to a quickly formed and untested public opinion, until that opinion has been seasoned by further reflection, but the strong and preponderant opinion of the people must, without too much delay, be able to prevail. Since the time of Lincoln it has been settled that the people themselves must be the final arbiters of their own constitutions.

it was the voice of a minority. In principle, it has become the voice of a new dispensation. . . ." *Op. cit.*, pp. 76-81. Nearly a score of years ago, a statesman of brilliant intuitions and deep perceptions caught an early glimpse of the new age. "The chief law-makers in our country may be, and often are, the judges, because they are the final seats of authority. Every time they interpret contract, property, vested rights, due process of law, liberty, they necessarily enact into law parts of a system of social philosophy; and as such interpretation is fundamental, they give direction to all law-making. The decisions of the courts on economic and social questions depend upon their economic and social philosophy; and for the peaceful progress of our people during the twentieth century we shall owe most to those judges who hold to a twentieth century economic and social philosophy and not to long out-grown philosophy, which was itself the product of primitive economic conditions." Theodore Roosevelt, "Presidential Message to the Congress," December 8, 1908, *Congressional Record*, vol. 43, pt. 1, p. 21. Apparently the courts, in the exercise of their power of reviewing the constitutionality of legislation, are today the battle-ground upon which is being fought the decisive contest between the time-honored but increasingly inappropriate philosophy of the old frontier and the newer conceptions springing from the altered circumstances of a city-dweller's world.

[1] For a judicious statement of the modern doctrine of judicial review, see E. S. Corwin, "Judicial Review in Action," *University of Pennsylvania Law Review*, lxxiv, pp. 639-671 (May, 1926).

In recent years the courts have been freely criticized for their slowness to discard the late nineteenth century conception of liberty and justice. It was right, however, that they should be somewhat slower than the legislatures in adopting the new principles of legislation. It was also right that they should be criticized for their slowness, for in the exercise of their political powers they are amenable, like the other organs of government, to public opinion, and ultimately must be guided by it.

The Value of Advisory Opinions.

The system of judicial organization under which the judges exercise their political powers most effectively and with least friction is that originally adopted in Massachusetts. Appointment by the governor and tenure during good behavior have proved well suited for the maintenance of an able and impartial judiciary. The system of removal by the governor upon address by a majority of the legislature has worked better than the usual process of impeachment. It has facilitated the retirement of a few undesirable judges without undermining the independence of the judiciary.[1] The system of advisory opinions has also worked well. The Massachusetts supreme court vetoes fewer legislative enactments than the supreme court of any other of the larger states. This relatively infrequent use of the judicial veto may be partly explained by the absence of most of the constitutional limitations upon legislative powers and procedure which abound in the constitutions of many states. But it is to no inconsiderable degree the result of the legislative and executive practice of calling upon the supreme court for their opinion concerning the constitutionality of proposed measures, when their constitutionality is questionable, in advance of their enactment into law. Often there are several such requests for advisory opinions in the course of a single legislative session. The opinion of the court is invariably accepted. When the opinion is adverse to the constitutionality of a proposed measure, the legislature may, if it chooses, proceed thereafter by means of a constitutional amendment. This has been done in several cases. More frequently the measure is dropped.

[1] See L. A. Frothingham, *A Brief History of the Constitution and Government of Massachusetts*, pp. 32-38. (2nd ed., Boston, 1925.)

Doubtless, it would not be desirable to require the courts in most states to pass upon all the constitutional questions that might arise prior to final action in the legislature or by the executive. Questions concerning the form of legislation or legislative procedure might better be disposed of in some more summary way, for example, upon the opinion of the attorney-general, as already suggested. But prior to final legislative action in any state upon those measures which on other grounds may incur a judicial veto, the opinion of the judges would often be timely and helpful.[1]

JUDICIAL REVIEW OF ADMINISTRATION

The power of the judiciary to review the acts of administrative officers is fundamentally the same as that to review acts of legislation. But there are certain important differences in the manner in which the power of judicial review is exercised in the two classes of cases.

First, the legislatures derive all their powers directly from the state and federal constitutions, but administrative officers derive their powers in part directly from the constitutions and in part through legislative enactments. Consequently the courts, when they review the validity of an administrative act, have to consider not only the constitutional but, in most cases, also the statutory powers of the officer responsible for the act. Besides the specific constitutional limitations upon legislative power and procedure which must be considered by the courts when they review the validity of the acts committed by administrative officers under authority of legislative enactments, there are also two general limitations of very great importance. The first is the prohibition against the delegation of legislative powers to non-legislative bodies. The Federal Constitution expressly declares that "all legislative powers herein granted shall be vested in a congress of the United States." Likewise in the states all legislative powers, unless otherwise ordered by the constitution, must be exercised exclusively by the state legislatures. The second general limitation is the prohibition against the vesting of judicial powers in administrative officers or of admin-

[1] See A. R. Ellingwood, *Departmental Coöperation in State Government*, pp. 248-257.

istrative powers in the judiciary. The judiciary, therefore, in inquiring into the validity of any administrative act which has become the subject of litigation, must first of all determine whether it is in fact an act of administration.

Control of Administrative Discretion.

Though a legislature may not delegate its purely legislative powers to administrative officers, it may lay down general rules of action under which administrative officers may proceed, and it may require such officers to apply those rules to particular cases. Thus, a legislature may not authorize a public service commission to regulate the rates of a public service corporation upon any principles and in any manner the commission pleases, but it may declare that rates in general shall be just and reasonable and that a commission shall determine what rates in particular cases are just and reasonable. But the action of that commission is subject to the rule of reason, just as would be the action of the legislature itself, if the legislature sought to exercise directly the power to prescribe specific rates. The courts may set aside the findings of such a commission, if in the opinion of the courts the findings are excessively unreasonable and arbitrary, just as they might set aside legislative enactments under similar circumstances. The tests of reasonableness in the regulation of rates may be defined in detail in legislative enactments. In practice they are generally left to be worked out by the commissions, subject to the approval of the courts. As yet neither the courts nor the commissions have reached any final conclusions concerning the tests that should be applied. Doubtless partly for that reason, the courts have disapproved many of the findings of the commissions and have refused to enforce the orders based thereon. But in the review of the findings of administrative bodies of longer standing and more settled practice than the public service commissions, the courts exercise their veto less freely. They are less likely, for example, to set aside a valuation fixed by a state board of assessors than one fixed by a public service commission, although the findings of the former may be no more conclusive in law than those of the latter. It is impossible to lay down any general rule indicating how far the courts will go in reviewing the reasonableness of the determinations of administrative officers.[1] But, though the courts have not often refused to review decisions rendered in the first instance by executive officers, they rarely consent to exercise jurisdiction when their decisions are reviewable by administrative officials.

There is really nothing new in the modern theory of the judicial review of administrative determinations by administrative bodies, such as railroad and public service commissions. The fundamental principles are the same as those underlying the review by the courts of the validity of the acts of any administrative officer. The action of the policeman who is charged to do whatever is necessary and proper for the maintenance of the peace, and who uses force against disturbers thereof, is just as much subject to review by the courts as that of the public service commission which orders a reduction of rates. The public service commission, like the policeman, is a great convenience to the public, because it relieves the ordinary citizen of responsibility for the performance of duties which he is not specially qualified to perform, and because it can devote its undivided attention to problems to which he can devote at best only an intermittent attention. If there were no public service commissions, a citizen might order a public service corporation possessing a virtual monopoly in his locality to reduce excessively high rates to a reasonable level, just as a citizen, if there were no policeman at hand, might order a trespasser off his premises. In either case, if a dispute arose, there would be an opportunity for appeal to the courts for the protection of the rights of either party. A trustworthy public service commission, however, like a policeman, is more serviceable in such cases than the courts, for its authority can be more easily and more speedily invoked, its operations are subject to fewer procedural restraints, and its decisions are or ordinarily ought to be equally acceptable to both parties. The corner loafer has as much right to appeal from an order of a traffic policeman to move on as the public service corporation from that of a commission to reduce its rates. If he

[1] The federal courts, for example, have said they will not review at all the decisions of immigration officers with respect to the citizenship of persons applying for admission to the United States (U. S. *v.* Ju Toy, 198 U. S. 253), but they will take extraordinary pains in reviewing the decisions of patent officers with respect to the patentability of inventions (U. S. *v.* Butterworth, 112 U. S. 50; U. S. *v.* Duell, 172 U. S. 576). See T. R. Powell, "Conclusiveness of Administrative Determinations in the Federal Government," in *Am. Pol. Sci. Rev.*, i (1907).

exercises his right less frequently, the reason is either that the decisions of the policeman are more trustworthy than those of the public service commission, or that the authority of such commissions is comparatively new and business men are not yet accustomed to it, or that the public service corporations expect to gain more by delay than they can lose by litigation.

There are important differences in effect, if not in law, between the decisions of policemen and public service commissions. The decision of a policeman, dealing with a disturbance of the peace, must be made and enforced immediately. That of the public service commission, dealing with an application for a reduction or increase of transportation rates, may be delayed until all pertinent facts have been examined with care. The policeman must rely solely on his own knowledge and judgment. The commission can obtain assistance from trained accountants and engineers and experts of all kinds. The decision of the policeman is informal and applies only to the particular case. That of the commission becomes a matter of record and may serve as a precedent for future cases of similar character. Thus the commission tends to become a rule-making body, whose orders operate like the ordinances of a municipal corporation. Indeed, many executive officers and boards, created in recent years, have been expressly authorized to issue special regulations or ordinances with the force of law. For instance, health and labor laws, providing that living and working conditions shall be reasonably safe and wholesome, may be put into practical effect through sanitary or industrial codes adopted and promulgated by authority of state boards of health, or public health councils, or industrial welfare commissions, or other similar administrative bodies. There is no more significant feature in the recent history of public administration in the states than the rapid development of such rule-making administrative bodies, either composed of experts in the branches of administration confided to their care or able to command the services of experts. Had the original state executive councils generally survived, they might have developed into rule-making bodies of this type. Actually, however, the need for machinery for the elaboration of general rules of law into special rules of administrative action has been met by the creation of a series of special administrative boards.

Working of Judicial Review of Administration.

The chief difference between the judicial review of the administrative decisions of public service commissions and those of policemen is not in the theory but in the practice. Appeal from the decision of a policeman, when taken at all, is taken after the decision has been executed, and the material facts in the case are reëxamined and finally determined by a jury. Appeal from the decision of a public utilities commission is usually taken before the decision is executed, and the material facts in the case are determined by the judges. The former class of cases consists of common law actions of tort or arises under the criminal law. The latter consists of applications for extraordinary equitable remedies, chiefly by means of writs of mandamus or injunction. In general the practice is more important than the theory. The motorist, who violates a speed regulation issued by a highway commission, is summarily prosecuted under the criminal law, but a bill-poster, who erects an advertising sign in such a manner as to violate an anti-billboard regulation issued by a park commission, is more likely, if the sign be one of value, to apply for an injunction to restrain the agents of the commission from interfering therewith until the highest courts have pronounced judgment upon the matter. On the other hand, if the sign be a mere handbill of little value, apparently it may be summarily destroyed by agents of the commission without any judicial process whatsoever.[1]

In cases where the reasonableness of an administrative decision is finally determined by a jury, the exercise of judicial control over administration becomes a mere incident in the ordinary administration of justice. But in cases where the reasonableness of an administrative decision is finally determined by the judges themselves, the exercise of judicial control over administration may, and in many modern cases does, involve the judges in exceedingly complicated and technical investigations. In general, however, judges who find themselves compelled to investigate the facts, in the light of which the reasonableness of an order is to be determined, are too busy to make the necessary investigations. Thus, the review of the order of a railroad commission that a certain rate, declared to be unreasonable, be

[1] Lawton *v.* Steele, 119 N. Y. 226. Cf. F. J. Goodnow, *Principles of the Administrative Law of the United States*, pp. 356-366.

reduced or of a health or dairy commission that the use of a certain food or drug, declared to be impure, be discontinued throws a burden upon the courts which they cannot bear. The facts are highly technical, their own training has been along other lines, and they cannot come to a proper decision without assistance. Either they must rely on the reports of special referees or masters, appointed by themselves to ascertain the facts and to recommend findings for their approval, or they must rely on the judgment of the regular administrative officers. In some classes of cases, where till recently judges have been comparatively quick to question the reasonableness of administrative determinations, notably in cases involving the orders of public service commissions, the courts now seem more disposed to rely upon the findings of the regular administrative officers. This is undoubtedly a wholesome tendency in all cases where the administrative officials are appointed on the ground of fitness and protected against undue political influence.

The question of the finality of administrative determinations of fact became most acute in connection with the regulation of railway rates by state commissions. After a struggle, the right of the courts to exercise the power of review was universally conceded. In some states, however, it is wisely confined to the highest court in the state. Thus much time and expense is saved by the elimination of trials in the lower courts, from which in important cases appeals are almost certain to be taken to the court of last resort. In some states the decisions of state commissions may be reviewed only by writs of error or certiorari or by direct appeal from the order of the commission. Thus the final decision may be reached promptly without awaiting the issue of litigation over attempts to enforce the administrative order by the regular judicial process. Many states limit the period after the issuance of an order during which judicial review thereof may be sought. Many hasten the final determination of such appeals by granting them preference over other classes of cases. Most of the states declare the findings of the commissions to be *prima facie* reasonable, so that the burden of proving their unreasonableness lies upon the party which refuses to accept them. Some provide that no evidence may be presented to the courts which has not been first presented to the commission, and that cases in which new evidence is introduced in court shall be remanded to the commission for disposition in accordance with the new evidence. In a few states, corporations which refuse to accept an order of a commission are liable to a heavy fine for each day that they fail to follow the same, provided that the order is ultimately sustained by the courts, or are required to file a bond sufficient to repay the difference between the old rate and the new to all shippers or passengers who pay an excessive rate after a commission has ordered a reduction. But in many states an appeal to the courts operates to stay the order of the commission.[1] In general, there is a distinct tendency to discourage the courts from exercising too aggressively the power of reviewing on the ground of unreasonableness the validity of administrative findings and orders.

Besides the substantive limitations upon the power of administrative officers and bodies to issue ordinances and perform special administrative acts, there are also certain procedural limitations which may not be disregarded without impairing the validity of such action. Public service commissions, for example, are bound to grant a hearing to all parties to be directly affected by a proposed order. This hearing must be adequate and fair. The findings must not be contrary to the evidence. The order must be supported by the facts as found.[2] Parties must have proper notice of proceedings which may directly affect them, must be apprised of the evidence submitted or to be considered in the case, and must be granted opportunity to cross-examine witnesses, to inspect documents, and to offer evidence in further explanation or rebuttal.[3] The procedural limitations upon administrative officers and bodies vary widely in different cases. In many cases they are prescribed by statute. In others they are left to the judgment of the officers, subject to judicial review and the nullification of arbitrary and unlawful acts. Perhaps in no case are the limitations more rigorous than in that of public service commissions. Certainly in no case are they so rigorous as in that of a strictly judicial tribunal. Administrative action is designed to be more summary and more

[1] See Maxwell Ferguson, *State Regulation of Railroads in the South*, pp. 212-217.

[2] See Interstate Commerce Commission *v.* Louisville and Nashville Railroad, 227 U. S. 88 (1913). See also Bruce Wyman, "Jurisdictional Limitations upon Commission Action," *Harvard Law Review*, xxvii, p. 565.

[3] See Wyman, *loc. cit.*, p. 567.

flexible than that of the courts. But the rights of the people may not be determined by mere administrative fiat. No administrative officer or body can set itself up as a benevolent despotism. Administrative action, like the action of the coördinate branches of government, must be justified as one phase of the reign of law.

Limitations upon Judicial Review.

Another important difference between the review of judicial administration and of legislation results from the judicial practice of dividing administrative acts into two classes, discretionary and ministerial. It is not at all clear just where the line of division runs.[1] In a general way it may be said, that in the performance of acts of discretion administrative officers are unrestricted within the limits of their constitutional and statutory powers, except by the requirement of due process of law and the rule of reason. But in the performance of ministerial acts administrative officers have no discretionary authority. In the famous case of Marbury *v.* Madison, for example, the United States Supreme Court held that the signature of the commission of a justice of the peace in the District of Columbia by the President of the United States completed the act of appointment, and that the delivery of the commission to the person named therein was a purely ministerial act, which it was the duty of the Secretary of State to perform. Apparently Chief Justice Marshall would not have hesitated to command Madison to deliver the commission, had he not found that the act of Congress giving the Supreme Court original jurisdiction over the case was unconstitutional. Thus it becomes possible for the courts to control administration, not only by refusing to give legal effect to administative acts unauthorized by the constitution or the laws, but also by commanding administrative officers to perform or not to perform such acts as in the opinion of the courts they have no right to refuse or to attempt to perform.

[1] Cf. Kendall *v.* United States, 12 Peters, 524, and Stokes *v.* Kendall, 3 How. 37. See also F. J. Goodnow, *Principles of the Administrative Law of the United States*, pp. 399-400. This treatise contains the best summary of the law governing judicial control of administration. See especially books v and vi.

Such control, however, is suitable only for inferior administrative officers, and is rarely exercised in other cases.[1]

Discretionary administrative acts may be further divided into two classes, those which are purely administrative and those which are political in character. With the action by competent executive officers in the latter class of cases the federal courts at least will not interfere at all. Thus the President may decide which of two contesting state governments shall be recognized as the constitutional government of the state, and the Supreme Court will grant no relief to those who question the reasonableness of his decision.[2] The same rule applies to certain decisions by state authorities. For example the Indiana legislature provided by an act adopted in 1911 for the submission of a new constitution to the people of the state at the general election of 1912, although the existing constitution granted no authority to the legislature to submit a general revision of the constitution to the people and prescribed a different procedure for the submission of specific amendments. Upon suit by a taxpayer to enjoin the governor and other members of the state board of elections from submitting the proposed new constitution, the state supreme court granted the injunction. An appeal was taken to the Supreme Court of the United States on the ground that the judgment of the state court in effect denied to the state the republican form of government, since the interference of the judiciary with the action of the coördinate branches prevented the people from adopting, if desired, the proposed new constitution. The federal Supreme Court declared that the claim that the decision of the state court denied to the state a republican form of government did not present a justiciable controversy, and dismissed the case for want of jurisdiction.[3] Thus the governor was apparently free to obey either the command of the legislature expressed in the form of the statute or that of the state supreme court expressed in the form of an injunction. Whichever horn of the dilemma had been chosen by him, the federal court would not have interfered. But the line of division between political and administrative acts is no clearer than that between discretionary and ministerial acts.

[1] J. A. Fairlie, "The State Governor," in *Michigan Law Review*, x, nos. 5 and 6, under caption, "Judicial Control of the Governor."

[2] Luther *v.* Borden, 7 How. 1.

[3] Marshall *v.* Dye, 231 U. S. 250.

Advantages of Administrative Justice.

It has already been pointed out that until recently judicial control of administration had long been the principal centralizing force in state administration. Its limitations, as a means of imparting spirit and vigor to administration, have also been indicated.[1] The truth is that the courts are not fitted to perform all the duties that have fallen upon them in connection with the interpretation and enforcement of modern economic and social legislation. Judges must be specially learned in the principles of the law, and cannot hope to become equally expert in all the branches of public administration. The regulation of the rates and conditions of service of public utilities, of the construction and manner of operation of factories, shops, and mills, of the production and sale of food and drugs, to mention only a few of the rapidly growing subjects of modern economic and social legislation, requires special technical knowledge and skill. The requirements of such branches of public administration can be adequately met only by specially trained men as administrators, just as the efficient administration of justice in ordinary litigation requires specially trained men as judges. The real problem is to procure such men for the public service. The habit of looking to the courts for the final determination of important administrative questions does not solve the problem. It merely shifts its location. The courts have been just as much puzzled in trying to administer this modern legislation as other bodies of men without proper technical training. The Supreme Court of the United States, for example, to say nothing of the state courts, has been on both sides of several of the difficult questions that have arisen in the administration of the laws regulating railroad rates.[2]

It is necessary to relieve the excessive strain which the power of judicial review under the changing conditions of modern society has thrown upon the courts. If one were compelled to state the most important experiment in the administration of justice in the twentieth century, the answer, according to one of the most searching of recent students of the work of the

[1] See *ante*, ch. x.

[2] Cf. for instance, Minneapolis and St. Louis Railway *v.* Minnesota, 186 U. S. 257 (1902) and Northern Pacific Railway *v.* North Dakota, 236 U. S. 585 (1915).

courts, would unhesitatingly be the attempt to secure justice through administrative channels.[1] The possibilities of this method of administering justice are best indicated by the work of the public service commissions and industrial accident commissions. They have simplified procedure, reduced costs, made lawyers less indispensable, accelerated the despatch of business, increased the employment of technical experts in the adjudication of cases, and made justice more certain. The success of these administrative tribunals has had good results both upon the legislatures and the courts. It has enabled the legislatures to rid themselves of much detail in the development of modern social policy, which they were unfitted to handle. This has tended to improve the quality of the work which has remained for the legislatures. It has also enabled the courts to concentrate more effectively upon the tasks for which they are best fitted. More and more they tend to emphasize the importance of the strictly procedural limitations upon the powers of administrative tribunals, while leaving them free to exercise their discretion within the bounds prescribed by the rule of "reason." The test of "reasonableness" is as difficult to apply in reviewing the acts of administrative tribunals as in reviewing those of the legislatures, but the disposition to tolerate differences of policy seems no less developed in the one field of action than in the other.

Thus the same result is reached in the study of judicial review of administration as in that of the judicial review of legislation. No plan for correcting the defects of the existing system is sound which proposes to destroy the power of judicial review. The activity of the state courts in the control of administration springs from excessive administrative weakness, not from excessive judicial strength. No plan is adequate which proposes merely to increase the responsibility of the state judiciaries to the electorates. The action of the state courts is itself subject to review by the federal courts in all cases involving any alleged deprivation of liberty or property without due process of law, and the federal courts cannot be touched by any state reform such as the recall of judges or of judicial decisions. The most

[1] R. H. Smith, *Justice and the Poor*, p. 83. For a suggestive brief discussion of the problems presented by the growth of administrative tribunals and administrative offices vested with wide discretionary authority, see chaps. xii and xiii of this excellent work.

promising plan for correcting the defects of the existing system is to increase the efficiency of the administrative branch of the state governments. This can be done best by the further development of administrative tribunals, by the further reform of the methods of selecting administrative officers, and by the further centralization and integration of state administration.

FEDERAL CENTRALIZATION AND JUDICIAL REVIEW

The last important result of the judicial review of state legislation and administration has been the centralization of power in the government of the Union at the expense of the governments of the states. In one of the boldest of the decisions, in which Chief Justice Marshall defined the limits between state and federal powers, a Maryland statute imposing a tax upon the operations of the Second Bank of the United States was declared unconstitutional.[1] The power to create, declared Marshall, implies a power to preserve. The power to destroy, if wielded by a different hand, is hostile to, and incompatible with, the powers to create and to preserve. Where such hostility and incompatibility exists, the authority which is supreme, that is, the federal government, must control, not yield to, that over which it is supreme, that is, the state governments. The power to tax involves the power to destroy by taxation. Hence the Supreme Court of the United States, the special guardian of the rights of the federal government, could not admit that the states had any power to tax the operations of the Bank of the United States, an institution necessary and proper for carrying into execution certain powers delegated to the federal government. Some forty years later the federal government in its turn levied a tax upon certain operations of state banks, namely, the issue of bank-notes, avowedly designed to destroy that branch of their business, and thereby so far as possible to destroy the banks themselves, in order that the field might be free for the creation of the new national banking system. But the Supreme Court of the United States declined to extend to the state banks the protection which it had not hesitated to extend to the ill-fated United States Bank. On the contrary it again asserted the supremacy of the purposes of the federal government

[1] McCulloch *v.* Maryland, 4 Wheat, 316 (1819).

and of the powers of its agents in case of conflict between the agencies of the state and federal governments.[1]

The tendency of the federal Supreme Court to prefer the interests of the United States to those of the states is most clearly revealed in the long series of cases defining the limits between the federal and state powers to regulate commerce. Time was when the federal courts inclined to the view that, in default of action by Congress to regulate commerce between the states in some respect, the state governments themselves might prescribe necessary and proper regulations. More recently they have inclined rather to the view that the failure by Congress to use its power to regulate interstate commerce in a particular respect is to be construed as a command that there be no regulation of such commerce in that respect. To-day for instance, as is clearly shown by the decisions in the railroad rate cases, no state may use its power to regulate purely intra-state commerce in such a manner as to interfere with the efforts of Congress to regulate interstate commerce.[2] While the decision in the first federal child labor law case indicates that the Supreme Court will keep the commerce power of the Congress within limits of some sort, and in general presumably will try to preserve for the states some suitable field of action, the tendency is for the federal Supreme Court, since it serves as the court of appeal from all the states in all cases involving due process of law, more and more to establish the principles of legislation which the states must carry into effect, if they act at all. If, under the guise of enforcing the due process clause of the fourteenth amendment, the underlying principles of modern legislation and administration, state as well as federal, are to be determined at Washington, the relations between the Union and the states must undergo a revolution. In the long run this may prove to be the most important effect of the judicial review of legislative and administrative action.

[1] Veazie Bank *v.* Fenno, 8 Wall. 533 (1869).

[2] See especially Dayton-Goose Creek Railway Co. *v.* United States, 263 U. S. 456 (1924).

CHAPTER XIV

THE CONSTITUTIONAL CONVENTION

In the beginning, as has been shown, there was no uniform practice with respect to the organization and powers of the constitutional convention.[1] In some of the original states, as in Virginia, the first independent state constitution was enacted in the same manner as an ordinary statute, and possessed no higher sanction than that placed by public opinion upon the proceedings of a Revolutionary provincial legislature. In others, as in Pennsylvania, it was prepared by a Revolutionary provincial legislature or convention, and was then expressly submitted to public opinion for approval before final adoption. In others, as in New York, it was prepared by a legislative body which had explicit authority from the voters to draft a constitution and put it into effect without any further consultation of the people. Finally, in Massachusetts and in New Hampshire the original state constitutions were prepared by special constitutional conventions, called by the ordinary legislatures in response to special popular votes, and they were then submitted to the voters for their express approval. The ordinary legislatures of these two states participated in the work of constitution-making only to the extent of submitting to the voters the question whether or not they would call a special constitutional convention, and, upon discovering the will of the people in the matter, issuing the call and providing for the election of delegates. This was the beginning of the constitutional, as distinct from the Revolutionary, convention in American constitutional history.

In the beginning, moreover, it was uncertain whether or not the constitutional convention would become a permanent element

[1] On constitutional conventions, see W. F. Dodd, *The Revision and Amendment of State Constitutions*, chs. i, ii, iii (Baltimore, 1910); R. S. Hoar, *Constitutional Conventions: Their Nature, Powers, and Limitations* (Boston, 1917); *Illinois Constitutional Convention Bulletins*, Nos. 1, 3 (Springfield, 1919); J. A. Jameson, *A Treatise on Constitutional Conventions* (4th ed., Chicago, 1887); *Massachusetts Constitutional Convention Bulletins*, Nos. 1, 35 (Boston, 1918).

in the government of the states. Only four of the thirteen original states, or including Vermont, five states, recognized the constitutional convention as a regular organ of government. Although only three states made express provision for the amendment of their original constitutions by legislative action, the legislatures of the other six possessed by implication similar powers of amendment as well as the power of general revision. Jefferson, one of the most earnest advocates of the constitutional convention as a permanent organ of government, feared for a time lest the legislatures, particularly that of his own state, should usurp the powers of constitutional amendment and revision, thus taking away from the people the direct control of the fundamentals of their government. Furthermore, as the event proved, the special provision made for the constitutional convention in Massachusetts proved inadequate, that made in Pennsylvania worked badly, and that made in Georgia did not work at all. Nevertheless, the constitutional convention proved to be a political device thoroughly in harmony with the spirit of American government. Its survival has demonstrated its fitness. During the one hundred and fifty years that have elapsed since the dawn of American independence there have been over two hundred constitutional conventions, or, upon the average, one convention in each state in each generation.

ORGANIZATION OF CONVENTIONS

The state constitutional conventions have invariably been unicameral bodies. In the beginning, as has been shown, the bicameral principle was adopted in most of the states for the organization of the legislatures, and eventually it was adopted for that purpose in all. But it has never been applied to the organization of constitutional conventions. Since class legislation was not apprehended from a body created solely to consider changes in the frame of government, there was felt to be no need of a division into upper and lower houses in order to give separate representation to upper and lower classes of the population. Since the constitutional convention possessed no power to tax or to make appropriations, there was no need of a second chamber in order to give special representation to taxpayers. Since the constitutional convention exercised no executive or judicial powers, there was no need of a second house to which those powers might be separately entrusted. For protection against the adoption of hasty or ill-considered measures, the people at first relied upon the slower and more deliberate procedure pursued by the Revolutionary assemblies and early conventions in considering fundamental changes in the frame of government. Subsequently, the development of the referendum enabled the electorate directly to forbid undesired changes in the fundamental law. In short, those considerations which were supposed to justify the adoption of the bicameral system for the ordinary legislative bodies did not fit the case of the constitutional convention.

The state constitutional conventions have generally been organized upon the model of the lower houses of the state legislatures. Indeed, the original constitutional conventions, as has been shown, were in most states the identical provincial assemblies, which, through the instrumentality of the constitutions framed by themselves, were transformed into the lower houses of bicameral legislatures. Subsequent constitutional conventions were organized upon the same model, because they were intended to represent the whole people rather than any privileged class, and the lower houses of the legislatures were considered more representative of the whole people than the upper. Since the Civil War, however, there has been a tendency in the larger states to modify the basis of representation. Thus, the Illinois constitution of 1870 provided that future conventions in that state should be chosen by senatorial districts, two delegates from each district. The New York constitution of 1894 contains a similar provision, with three instead of two delegates to be chosen from each senatorial district, plus fifteen delegates to be chosen from the state at large. The Pennsylvania convention of 1872 was organized in a similar way, ninety-nine delegates being chosen by senatorial districts and twenty-eight in the state at large. For the Massachusetts convention of 1917-1918, it was provided that a number of delegates equal to the number of representatives in the state legislature should be chosen from the regular representative districts, and that, in addition, four delegates should be chosen from each of the sixteen congressional districts into which the state was divided and sixteen from the state at large. The Missouri convention of 1922 consisted of two delegates from each senatorial district and fifteen from the state at large. The purpose of election by senatorial or congressional districts was to reduce the influence of petty local interests in the constitutional convention. The addition of delegates chosen in the state at large tended still further to enhance the influence of state-wide as contrasted with merely local considerations.

There have likewise been attempts in recent years to regulate or so far as possible to exclude ordinary partisan influences. The Pennsylvania convention of 1872 was elected under a system of limited voting by which it was intended that the minority party should be assured a due share of the delegates. Each voter was permitted to vote for only fourteen delegates at large, although twenty-eight were to be elected, and for only two senatorial district delegates, where three were to be elected. Consequently, the dominant party was not able to elect much more than half the total number of delegates at large and two-thirds of the district delegates. Furthermore, a provision that one-third of the delegates might require the separate submission of any proposed amendment afforded additional protection to the minority party. More recently, since the introduction of the system of direct nominations, several states have proposed plans for the nomination of delegates at non-partisan primaries and their election without any party labels, obviously suggested by the systems of non-partisan judicial nominations and elections. The Massachusetts convention of 1917-18 was elected under such a plan. The Ohio convention of 1912 was also chosen so as to eliminate the regular partisan divisions. In general, the personnel of constitutional conventions is superior to that of the ordinary legislatures. The importance of the work to be done attracts able men to the conventions, and the publicity of their proceedings puts delegates on their best behavior. Constitutional conventions have by no means been generally free from partisanship, but partisan influences have usually been confined to their legitimate field, the formulation of a program of revision and the recommendation of appropriate amendments for adoption by the electors.

PROCEDURE OF CONVENTIONS

The procedure of constitutional conventions is also generally modeled upon that of the lower houses of the state legislatures. Thus, the New York convention of 1915 was dominated by the president, the committee on rules, and the recognized leaders of the dominant party in precisely the same manner as the legislative assembly. In other states the ordinary committee system generally prevails. But the greater publicity that attaches to the work of conventions makes their actual procedure more deliberate than that of legislatures. Moreover, the limitations upon the length of sessions which seriously impair the efficiency of so many state legislatures do not apply to conventions at all. Although conventions have to finish their work in season for submission to the electors at the next election, there is ordinarily time for due deliberation.[1] Where constitutional revisions are submitted to the electorates *en bloc* there is more opportunity for the evasion of responsibility, than where each proposed change is submitted separately. Moreover, such a submission tends to combine in one opposition all those who for any reason are opposed to the revision. These difficulties are avoided where the convention directs that each change shall be separately voted upon by the electorate. However, if numerous amendments are proposed in this way, a heavy burden is placed upon the voters. Under such circumstances, the best plan is that followed by the New York convention of 1915 which submitted a few specially important or highly controversial proposals separately and all others *en bloc.*

More important is the effect of the strict limitation of the functions of conventions. Though the conventions have power to make any recommendations they please to the electors for adoption, and though in practice they do recommend ordinary legislative measures in ever increasing quantity, they are largely free from the kind of business which is chiefly responsible for the discredit into which the ordinary legislatures have fallen. They

[1] Where careful preliminary investigations are made in preparation for the convention, the proceedings and deliberations of that body are greatly facilitated. For example, before the Massachusetts convention of 1917-1918, a special research committee was appointed, under the chairmanship of Professor W. B. Munro, to compile information and data for the use of the delegates. (See *Massachusetts Constitutional Convention Bulletins*, Nos. 1-37 (Boston, 1918). A similar service was rendered the Illinois convention of 1920-1922 by the legislative reference bureau, the research work being under the immediate charge of Professor W. F. Dodd. (See *Illinois Constitutional Convention Bulletins*, Nos. 1-15 (Springfield, 1919). A more formal type of agency is the constitutional commission. Such a commission may not only make preliminary investigations but may also recommend specific proposals and changes for the subsequent consideration of the legislature or of a regular constitutional convention. The constitutional commission was used in New York (1872), Michigan (1873), Vermont (1919), and Pennsylvania (1920).

have little occasion to deal with private and local measures. They do not make appropriations at all. Their patronage is slight, and nothing of importance can be done without the approval of the electorates. Under these circumstances delegates can concentrate their attention upon matters of constitutional and legislative policy, and decide questions more strictly upon their merits than is ordinarily possible in the legislatures.

WORKING OF THE CONVENTION SYSTEM

It is not surprising, therefore, that the constitutional convention, considered as an organ of state government, has been more successful than the legislature. There have been comparatively few instances where the work of conventions has been totally rejected by the electorates. Notable examples of this kind were the revisions submitted by the Massachusetts convention of 1853, the Illinois conventions of 1862 and 1920-1922, the New York conventions of 1867 and 1915, and the Arkansas convention of 1918. Most of the general revisions submitted to the electorates for approval have been accepted by a majority of those voting thereon. Conventions which have submitted their proposed amendments separately have also fared well at the hands of the voters. The Ohio convention of 1912 considered five hundred and two questions and finally submitted forty-one separate amendments to the electorate. Thirty-three of these were adopted and eight were rejected. The record of the Nebraska convention of 1920 is even better; forty-one amendments were submitted separately and all were adopted. On the other hand, of the twenty-one amendments proposed by the Missouri convention of 1922, fifteen were rejected. Such records as these compare favorably with those of the legislatures in the submission of amendments to the electorates. Conventions have sometimes refused to submit their work to the electorates when popular approval by the existing electorate seemed likely to be withheld. For example, several recent conventions in southern states, bent on disfranchising negro voters, declared their revisions effective without popular approval. Other conventions, bent on extending the suffrage, have submitted their work to electorates including the new voters whom the convention proposed to enfranchise. Without doubt, in the absence of constitutional provisions clearly defining the powers of a constitutional convention, there is always a possibility of arbitrary action by such bodies. But where the practice of submission to the existing electorates is definitely established, the popular veto appears to be an adequate check against the usurpation of power by conventions.

The success of the constitutional convention raises the question whether the legislatures might not do more satisfactory work if their organization and procedure more closely resembled that of the conventions. The legislatures of several of the states in the Swiss Confederation are organized in much the same manner as the constitutional convention. In Berne, for example, the legislature consists of a single house, elected for four years. This house has broad legislative powers, subject to the referendum at the option of a certain proportion of the electors. Proposals to amend the constitution, however, must in any case be submitted to the electors for their approval, as in the American states. In practice comparatively few measures have to be submitted to the electorate for approval, unless there is a sufficient demand for popular review, because the constitution contains little matter of an ordinary legislative character. A constitutional convention in Berne is chosen in precisely the same manner as the ordinary legislature. When the people wish to choose a convention, they simply recall the whole legislature and choose a new one. The members of the recalled legislature are eligible for reëlection. One effect of this arrangement is to provide more continuous popular control over the constitution than can be exercised in this country through occasional conventions meeting only at specified intervals or when the legislature can be induced to submit a call to the electorate. Another is to maintain a higher standard for the personnel of the legislature than can be maintained for the members of American legislatures with their limited legislative powers and excessive burden of non-legislative duties.

Whether or not in the American states a single unicameral legislative body could be safely entrusted with all the powers of both constitutional convention and legislature would depend mainly upon two factors. The first is the extent to which the legislatures can be relieved of the excessive burden of non-legislative duties which now so encumber their deliberations. The second is the extent to which the power of popular review over legislation can be effectively exercised by the state electorates. The relief of the legislatures from non-legislative duties is contingent upon the development of independent and reliable administrative agencies. The effective exercise of the power of popular review is contingent upon the development of satisfactory methods for direct legislation, subject to suitable restrictions, by the electorates.

CHAPTER XV

DIRECT LEGISLATION BY THE ELECTORATE

Many arguments have been put forth in support of direct popular participation in law-making, but they are all reducible to not more than two.[1] The nature of these two general arguments was well explained by John Stuart Mill, when discussing the criterion of a good form of government. "The first element of a good government," he declared,[2] "being the virtue and intelligence of the human beings composing the community, the most important point of excellence which any form of government can possess is to promote the virtue and intelligence of the people themselves. The first question in respect to any political institutions is, how far they tend to foster in the members of the community the various desirable qualities. . . . The government which does this the best has every likelihood of being the best in all other respects, since it is on these qualities, so far as they exist in the people, that all possibility of goodness in the practical operation of the government depends. We may consider then as one criterion of the goodness of a government, the degree in which it tends to increase the sum of good qualities in the governed, collectively and individually; since, besides that their well-being is the sole object of government, their good qualities supply the moving force which works the machinery. This leaves, as the other constituent element of the merit of a government, the quality of the machinery itself; that is, the degree in

[1] On direct legislation, see J. D. Barnett, *The Operation of the Initiative, Referendum, and Recall in Oregon* (New York, 1915); W. F. Dodd, *The Revision and Amendment of State Constitutions* (Baltimore, 1910); *Illinois Constitutional Convention Bulletins* (Springfield, 1919), No. 2, "The Initiative, Referendum, and Recall"; A. L. Lowell, *Public Opinion and Popular Government* (New York, 1913), pt. iii and appendices; *Massachusetts Constitutional Convention Bulletins* (Boston, 1918), No. 6, "The Initiative and Referendum"; E. P. Oberholtzer, *The Referendum in America* (rev. ed., New York, 1912). For periodical summaries and discussions of initiated and referred constitutional amendments and statutes, see the *American Political Science Review*, *American Year Book*, *National Municipal Review*, and *Political Science Quarterly Supplement*.

[2] *Representative Government*, ch. ii.

which it is adapted to take advantage of the amount of good qualities which may at any time exist, and make them instrumental to the right purposes. . . . Government is to be judged by its action upon men, and by its action upon things; by what it makes of the citizens and what it does with them; its tendency to improve or deteriorate the people themselves, and the goodness or badness of the work it performs for them, and by means of them. Government is at once a great influence acting on the human mind, and a set of organized arrangements for public business. . . ." The first general argument, therefore, which may be advanced in behalf of the submission of measures to the electorates, is that the practice of voting on measures affords a beneficial educational discipline.

The second general argument is that the direct participation of the electorate in the process of law-making will improve the quality of legislation. Improvements may be brought about, it is urged, either directly through the action of the electorates themselves, or indirectly through the increased sense of responsibility which the legislators will feel when subject to effective control by those whom they represent.

THE COMPULSORY CONSTITUTIONAL REFERENDUM

These theoretical considerations need to be put to the test of experience. For the purpose of applying this test the work of the electorates in passing judgment upon measures can most conveniently be divided into three classes: the first, comprising all measures which are submitted to the electorate upon the initiative of some official representative body, a constitutional convention or legislature; the second, comprising all measures which are first adopted by a representative body but are subsequently referred to the electorate by popular petition; and the third, comprising all measures submitted to the electorate upon the initiative of some of the voters themselves with or without the intervention of a representative body.[1] Of the first class of measures the great mass are constitutional amendments, and the action of the electorates on these may be taken as typical of the action of the electorates upon all measures submitted upon the initiative of representative bodies.

[1] The direct initiative makes no provision for the intervention of the representative legislative body; the indirect initiative does make such provision.

The first class of measures has been hitherto by far the most numerous. During the ten years from 1899 to 1908 inclusive, four hundred and seventy-two constitutional questions were submitted to the electorates of forty-three states, *i.e.*, all the states then in the Union except Delaware and Vermont. On the average, there was more than one constitutional amendment each year in every state.[1] Since then, the rate of submission has tended to increase. From 1919 to 1925 inclusive, over six hundred constitutional questions were drafted by legislatures and by constitutional conventions and were voted upon by the electorates of forty-eight states.[2] The second and third classes of measures are of more recent origin and are less widely used. The popular referendum was first put into practice in Oregon in 1906 and down to the close of 1925 had been employed altogether one hundred and seventy-three times in sixteen states. The popular initiative was used for the first time in Oregon in 1904 and down to the close of 1925 had been employed altogether four hundred and forty times in eighteen states. Of the four hundred and forty questions involved, two hundred and fourteen were initiated constitutional amendments and two hundred and twenty-six were initiated statutes.[3] Taking the Union as a whole, it is evident that the work of the electorates, so far as it relates to action upon measures, is indeed extensive.

The work of the electorates, however, is not evenly distributed among the states. According to Dodd's investigations, fifty-one proposed constitutional amendments were referred to the electorate in California in ten years, fifty in Louisiana, and thirty in Missouri. On the other hand, in each of thirty states, fewer than ten amendments were referred by the legislature during the same period. Since 1910, when Dodd's study was published, there have been similar variations between the states. The explanation must be sought partly in the differences in the political conditions in the several states, but mainly in the character

[1] See Dodd, *The Revision and Amendment of State Constitutions*, p. 268. Constitutional questions include constitutional amendments and proposals to hold constitutional conventions.

[2] The statistics for 1919-1925 were computed from the periodic summaries in the *National Municipal Review* and the Supplement of the *Political Science Quarterly*, and from personal inquiry and investigation.

[3] The above figures on the initiative and referendum bring down to date the statistics given in the *Illinois Constitutional Convention Bulletins*, No. 2, p. 103.

of the constitutions themselves and of the processes of amendment. In Indiana, for example, the process of amendment is so difficult that despite persistent attempts it was not possible to secure final action on a single amendment during a long period of years. In Louisiana, on the other hand, the legislature is so limited in its powers to enact ordinary statutes, and the constitution itself is so encumbered with ordinary legislative matter, that, it is scarcely an exaggeration to say, the people's representatives are compelled to depend upon the constant coöperation of the electorate in order to legislate at all. The use of the direct popular referendum and initiative is distributed with similar unevenness. Nineteen of the one hundred and seventy-three instances of the use of the popular referendum to 1926 occurred in Oregon, and one hundred and twenty of the four hundred and forty instances of the use of the popular initiative occurred in the same state. It has often been urged as a special advantage of the federal system of government that the separate states can more easily undertake political experiments than a single consolidated government, and that, since each state can profit by the experiments of the others, progress in government is more certainly secured by the competition between the states in the adoption of improvements. The various arrangements in the several states with respect to the direct action of the voters upon measures furnish a conspicuous illustration of this advantage of federal government.

The character of the work performed by the state electorates can be ascertained only by inspection of the results of the votes upon the measures referred to them. It will be convenient to consider first the results of the voting upon constitutional amendments referred to the voters by the several state legislatures.

Working of Constitutional Referendum.

The first matter to be considered is the degree of interest displayed by the voters in the work put upon them by the compulsory constitutional referendum. During the ten years 1899-1908, the average vote upon the four hundred and seventy-two measures covered by Dodd's investigations amounted to less than fifty per cent of the total vote cast at the polls on the several occasions when the measures were put to the vote.[1] There was a marked variation, however, in the interest displayed in proposed constitutional amendments in the different parts of the country. In New York, less than a third of those who went to the polls cast their votes on the measures referred to them by the legislature. In New England and the northeastern states generally, the average vote was not much over forty per cent. In New Jersey, a series of important amendments relating to the reorganization of the state judiciary were submitted at a special election in 1903, and only 12 per cent of the normal vote of the state was cast upon them. In the West, the proportion of voters voting on constitutional amendments was also low, being on the average nearer 40 than 50 per cent of the total. In the central states, on the other hand, and in the South, the proportion was higher than in the other parts of the country, averaging above 50 and towards 60 per cent.[2] In short, there is great inequality in the size of the vote cast upon the various kinds of measures submitted to the voters under the compulsory constitutional referendum, and presumably there is a corresponding degree of inequality in the public interest in these measures.

The nature of the questions which the voters tend to regard as most important is revealed by an analysis of the measures upon which three-fourths or more of those attending the polls were sufficiently interested to vote. In general, with the exception of negro suffrage and the liquor question, the questions arousing the most interest on the part of the voters which most frequently arose under the compulsory constitutional referendum involved the methods of conducting public business, the use of public moneys, and the pay of the public servants. They touched the pocket-books rather than the feelings of the people. The action of the voters upon them was not reckless, but prudent, inclining rather to excessive caution than to the exhibition of the "gusts of passion" which some critics of popular institutions have apprehended.

A fair inference with respect to the character of the work of the state electorates, obtained by inspection of the results of popu-

[1] Since 1908, the vote upon constitutional amendments has usually continued to be light in comparison with the total vote cast.

[2] But in the South, if the degree of interest were calculated on the basis of the ratio between votes cast on measures and votes cast for candidates at the primaries, the comparative showing would not be so good.

lar referenda upon constitutional amendments, is that the voters are capable of discriminating between satisfactory and unsatisfactory measures. In no state are the constitutional amendments proposed by the legislature accepted mechanically by the electorate, and in no state are they mechanically rejected. Some are accepted and others are rejected. The proportion of measures rejected varies considerably among the states, but the election returns of all the states are alike in affording no evidence that the electorate is a mere machine for registering the decisions of other organs of government.

Action that is clearly unreasonable has been rare. In 1900, the voters of Oregon declined by a narrow majority to repeal the obsolete provision of their constitution excluding free negroes from the state. The provision had long ceased to have any legal effect, if it ever had any, and the majority of those who went to the polls failed to vote on it at all. In 1912, the voters of Ohio declined to ratify a proposition from their constitutional convention striking from their constitution another obsolete provision excluding negroes from the right of suffrage. This provision was not finally removed until 1923. But these instances of futile action prompted by prejudice are exceptional.

A more serious evil is the frequent adoption of measures with respect to which the election returns indicate that there is no clear public opinion at all. Many measures are adopted or rejected by majorities so small that it is impossible to determine whether the decision represents the will of the electorate or merely is the result of chance. Thus, in California during the years 1898-1908, there were half a dozen proposed amendments which were adopted or rejected by majorities of less than 1 per cent of the total vote cast thereon. The change of one voter in two hundred from one side to the other would have altered the result. For example, in 1904 a proposition permitting the revision of codes by single acts was rejected by a majority of 883 in a total vote of 118,983, and in 1908 propositions to repeal a provision regarding the taxation of mortgages and to increase the compensation of state officers were decided, the former negatively, the latter affirmatively, by majorities of 835 and two respectively in a total vote of over one hundred and eighty thousand. Similar cases can be found in other states. That any important question can be permanently decided by such majorities is unthinkable, and if the decision in close cases has been acquiesced in, the explanation must be that the public are indifferent concerning the result. In other words, there can be no real public opinion concerning the matters in question. The fact that a popular referendum could elicit from the electorate a languid expression of sentiment on such questions indicates a gratifying response on the part of many voters to the call of duty, but also indicates that the electorates ought not to be called upon to perform work in which they feel so little interest.

Indeed the most serious evil in the working of the compulsory constitutional referendum is the lack of interest shown in a large proportion of the measures. Ninety per cent of the measures are voted on by less than three-fourths of those who go to the polls. A majority are voted on by less than half of the voters. When the vote is small, there is no certainty that the decision is supported by any real public opinion, and when the vote is close as well as small, the decision may easily be produced by mere chance, or even by some more objectionable influence. The burdening of the ballot with trivial propositions constitutes a needless tax on the patience of the voter, and tends to breed contempt of his high function as final arbiter of public questions. The power to foist upon the voter the task of deciding unimportant but vexatious questions constitutes a harmful temptation to lazy and timid and dishonest legislators, and tends to foster slovenly and even pernicious practices in legislative bodies. On the other hand, where the public interest is lively, all the evidence tends to show that the submission of measures to the voters works well. In such cases the decision represents the expression of a genuine public opinion. This opinion may not always be the result of pure reason. Yet the state electorates show a readiness to change their opinions, once expressed, when proper reasons are furnished for so doing, and display no inconsiderable acuteness in discriminating between the merits of the different propositions lying within the field of their interest that are brought to their attention. Of course when there is a strong and greatly preponderant public opinion with respect to any matter, it is not necessary to refer a question relating thereto to the electorate. Honest and intelligent public officials are capable of reading the mind of the people for themselves. It is when public opinion is not altogether clear, as in regard to the regulation of the liquor traffic, or when the interest of the official is not identical with that of the people, as in regard to the powers or perquisites of office, that the value of the compulsory referendum is greatest. In such cases the referendum affords the most direct and the most certain means of testing public opinion. It provides the best security against the excessive violence of political controversy, and largely contributes to the stability of the governments of the states.

Reform of Constitutional Referendum.

The lack of interest on the part of the voters in many proposed constitutional amendments may be partly explained by the failure of the legislatures to make adequate provision for bringing proposed amendments to the notice of the electorates. In most states the legislatures are not constitutionally required to publish such measures in any other manner than ordinary legislative enactments, and in fact do not publish them except in the volumes of session laws. Unless the measures are specially discussed on the platform or in the newspapers, most voters will learn of their existence for the first time when they examine their ballots at the polls. Then they will be compelled to form a hasty judgment upon the evidence afforded by the bare titles of the measures on the ballot. In a few states it has been provided that measures should be printed on the ballot in full instead of by title. Few voters, however, are able to study a column or more of proposed legislation deliberately and intelligently in the polling booth. Still fewer will do so without feeling that to throw such a burden upon them without notice is an unreasonable imposition. Several states therefore have provided that proposed amendments shall be printed in full one or more times, at prescribed intervals prior to the election, in one or more newspapers in each county. The newspapers themselves are inclined to endorse this method of publication, for reasons some of which are obvious enough. Such publication undoubtedly does secure more or less publicity, especially in rural districts where the county papers of the major parties are recognized political institutions. No state, however, prior to the introduction of the optional referendum, made any special provision for putting before the voter the reasons for a proposed constitutional amendment, and the discussions volunteered by the newspapers were likely to be partisan, and almost certain to be one-sided. Matters touching the interests of the newspapers themselves, such as, for example, proposals to establish a better system of publicity, could hardly be expected to receive much consideration upon their merits. At best this mode of publication is a casual rather than a systematic attempt to inform the electorate about the merits of the proposals upon which it is required to vote, and the interest it may be expected to arouse will be casual rather than systematic. Matters not spontaneously felt by the voters to be of major importance will not receive general public attention. Nevertheless the neglect of the states to provide proper procedure for arousing the interest and assisting the judgment of the voters does not explain all the indifference to proposed constitutional amendments which has been shown to exist.

In recent years it is certain that the practice of the compulsory constitutional referendum has left much to be desired. It is frequently asserted that the cause lies in the number of measures referred to the voters, and that if the number were restricted the public interest would increase. Several states have acted upon this assumption, placing arbitrary limits upon the number of amendments that may be proposed at the same time. Thus Illinois provides that amendments may not be proposed to more than one article of the constitution at a time, nor to the same article more than once in four years.[1] Vermont does not limit the number, but forbids the proposal of any amendments except at intervals of ten years. The Vermont provision seems clearly unreasonable, since the objection is not that the voters are required to express an opinion in too many different years, but that they are required to express too many opinions in the same year. The Illinois provision tends rather to discourage than encourage the submission by the legislature of important amendments only, because it is so easy for opponents of action on the important matters to combine in order to force the submission of unimportant matters, thus blocking the path for the others. This has actually occurred in recent years in that state and has been the cause of much criticism.

The cause of the lack of interest in so large a proportion of the

[1] A "gateway amendment" designed to liberalize the amending article of the Illinois constitution was defeated in 1924 through failure to receive an affirmative majority of all votes cast at the election.

proposed amendments in recent years has not only been their excessive number, but also the excessive triviality of many of them. A superficial remedy for this evil consists in the provision existing in a dozen states that no proposed amendment shall be adopted unless it receives the affirmative votes of more than a bare majority of those voting thereon. In Rhode Island the requirement is a three-fifths, in New Hampshire a two-thirds, vote. The more common practice is the requirement that a measure, to be adopted, must receive a majority, not merely of all the votes cast thereon, but of all the votes recorded at the election at which the measure is voted on. This is in effect a rule that all voters who attend the polls and do not vote either for or against a proposed amendment shall be counted against it. Such a rule is illogical, for the presumption in their case is not that they are opposed to the measure but that they are willing to abide by the decision of those who hold an opinion strongly enough to take the trouble of expressing it. It also works badly. During the years 1898-1908, there were seventy-five measures referred to the voters in twelve states upon which a special majority was required for adoption. Twenty-five of these measures received the affirmative votes of a majority of all those participating in the elections at which they were severally referred, and were consequently adopted. Ten received more negative than affirmative votes and were rejected. The other forty were favored by a majority of those voting on them, but nevertheless failed of adoption, because of the number of voters who failed to express any opinion. Most of these measures were open to no serious objections. Many were not even controversial and should have been adopted. Thus in Minnesota a proposition to permit school funds to be invested in municipal and other local bonds was referred to the voters at three successive general elections before it was adopted, though it was never approved by less than seventy-five thousand majority. A proposition to establish a state road and bridge fund was also thrice referred, and, though regularly approved by even larger majorities, was never adopted at all. Finally, the rule can be easily evaded in practice, as has been done in certain cases in Oklahoma, by the simple but costly expedient of calling a special election.

Another remedy for the lack of interest displayed by voters in constitutional amendments referred to them by state legislatures has been tried in Nebraska and Ohio. This consists in a provision that proposed amendments may be formally endorsed or protested by political parties in state convention assembled. The voter may express his approval of the position of his party in general by a single cross on his ballot which then is counted as one vote for the straight party ticket. Thus his opinion is expressed for or against the various measures which have been referred to the people, as the case may be, without the necessity of his taking the trouble even to read their titles. This device may be a logical development of the party system, as established in many states, but it is an extraordinary manner of stimulating popular interest in voting on measures. In Nebraska the party which controlled the legislature, and hence the submission of constitutional amendments, regularly endorsed the propositions which were submitted. Thus, because of the general prevalence of the habit of voting a straight party ticket, a large number of votes were counted for the several propositions, although few votes were actually cast for them. The electorate was converted into a mere rubber stamp and finally, in 1925, this provision was repealed. In Ohio the system has worked in a similar manner. In 1903 nine-tenths of the voters were recorded on each of three propositions which had been acted upon by both political parties. A fourth proposition had neither been endorsed nor protested by any party and was actually voted on by less than one-sixteenth of those who went to the polls. Such a remedy is grasping for the shadow, and overlooking the substance. The official returns make a brave show, but the voters have little part in it.

The chief difficulty with the constitutional referendum does not lie in the smallness of the vote on many of the measures submitted, but in the smallness of the public interest in them; and the true remedy does not lie in attempting to enhance the size of the vote by mechanical devices, but in attempting to free the ballot from the burden of trivial matters. The most promising remedy is to substitute in whole or in part the optional for the compulsory referendum on constitutional amendments proposed by the state legislatures. Before considering the practicability of such a remedy, however, it is necessary to examine the operation of the optional referendum upon ordinary legislative enactments.

THE POPULAR REFERENDUM

The optional referendum upon legislative enactments, like the compulsory referendum upon proposed constitutional amendments, can best be studied by inspection of the results of the votes actually cast upon the measures thus referred to the electorates.

Working of Popular Referendum.

In the first place, popular interest in measures referred to the voters under the optional referendum is more general than in measures referred under the compulsory constitutional referendum. Of the one hundred and seventy-five constitutional amendments submitted by legislatures and by constitutional conventions to the electorates in 1924, one hundred and seven were voted upon by less than one-half of those who went to the polls while only eleven received as high as 75 per cent of the vote cast. Of the fourteen statutes submitted under the optional referendum in the same year, none received a vote of less than 53.5 per cent and only three were under 75 per cent.[1] From 1919 to 1925 inclusive, seventy-nine acts were submitted by means of referendum petitions and more than one-half of this number were voted upon by at least 75 per cent of those voting at the elections in question. In short, the optional referendum places upon the voters no such burden of deciding measures which do not interest them as is placed upon them by the compulsory constitutional referendum. At the same time, the electorates reject a larger proportion of the measures referred to them under the optional referendum than of those referred under the compulsory constitutional referendum. While it is unusual for as many as 50 per cent of the latter to be rejected, more than half of the bills referred under the optional referendum have been disapproved by the voters. In the sixteen states in which the optional referendum has been put to use down to the close of 1925, the popular veto was invoked against one hundred and seventy-three measures and was successfully exercised against one hundred and nine of these. In other words, under the optional referendum the voters are much less frequently required to vote upon meas-

[1] See Ralph S. Boots, "The Initiative and Referendum in 1923 and 1924," *National Municipal Review*, xv, pp. 42-65 (1926).

ures of which they do not disapprove than under the compulsory referendum. Thus, if the test of the popular referendum is its efficiency as a device for preventing the adoption of measures not satisfactory to the voters, the optional referendum upon legislative enactments is apparently a more efficient instrument than the compulsory referendum upon proposed constitutional amendments.

The greater efficiency of the optional referendum is indicated also by an examination of the nature of the measures referred to the electorates by petition. It has been shown that under the compulsory constitutional referendum many trivial matters can be disposed of only by reference to the voters, and that this condition will persist so long as the constitutions of many states are loaded with legislative detail. Under the optional referendum presumably no measure is referred to the voters unless a substantial number of voters is sufficiently interested to file a petition. In practice it appears that the measures referred by petition are usually not of a trivial character. Of the seventy-nine statutes referred to the state electorates by petition from 1919 to 1925 inclusive, fifteen related to parties, primaries, elections, and the suffrage, thirteen to the creation, reorganization, or abolition of state administrative agencies, ten to matters of local government, eight to problems connected with the prohibition of intoxicating liquors, and four to the relations of capital and labor, including workmen's compensation measures. The other referred bills dealt with a variety of topics ranging from an act prohibiting daylight saving time in Maine to an act establishing the Bank of North Dakota. None of these measures was of such an unimportant character as often appears under the compulsory constitutional referendum. Examination of the measures vetoed by the state electorates leads to the conviction that the legislatures enacting them were sometimes out of touch with, if not in direct opposition to, public opinion upon the matters concerned. Without exception, all the referred bills dealing with parties, primaries, and elections in general and with the repeal or modification of the direct primary in particular were negatived by the voters. Three acts directed against butter substitutes were decisively beaten. In Massachusetts, legislative attempts to establish a motion picture censorship and to levy a gasoline tax were overwhelmed at the polls. Some of the other measures which were vetoed included proposals to enforce prohibition, to give husband and wife equal property rights, to provide for a system of workmen's compensation, to make labor unions liable to suit, to create the office of state sheriff, to repeal and reënact a state housing code, and to define "Grade A" milk.

The evidence with respect to the voting upon measures referred to the people under the optional referendum tends to corroborate the inferences drawn with respect to the voting upon measures referred under the compulsory constitutional referendum. It indicates that with respect to the measures in which the voters are interested they are able to vote with discrimination. Since the voters are more generally interested in measures referred under the optional referendum than in those submitted under the compulsory constitutional referendum, it follows that on the whole the operation of the optional referendum is more satisfactory. There is indeed no logical reason why the voters should not be as capable of deciding the fate of statutes referred to them upon petition of a certain fraction of the electorate as of deciding the fact of constitutional amendments referred to them by mandate of the constitution itself. It is not the nature of the procedure under which the reference is made, but the nature of the measure, that determines the action of the voters. The value of right procedure for the selection of measures for reference to the electorate lies in the desirability of excluding from reference such measures as will not interest the voter. In the case of a measure referred by petition, there is at least the presumption that some of the voters are deeply interested in the measure. In the case of a measure referred by constitutional mandate, there is no such presumption. If the contents of the state constitutions had been restricted to the important matters which alone were originally inserted therein, there would have been such a presumption, but that has not been the case. Under the conditions that prevail in most of the states, the presumption is rather that the bulk of the proposed constitutional amendments will be such as the voters would be glad to leave to the discretion of their representatives if they could. There is, however, no way of doing this, except by abolishing the compulsory constitutional referendum, and extending the application of the optional referendum to all constitutional amendments proposed by the state legislatures.

Reform of Popular Referendum.

The substitution of the optional for the compulsory referendum on constitutional amendments is a change in the political system of the states that might well receive consideration. If the legislatures could adopt uncontested amendments without reference to the voters, they would be able to reduce the time required for amendments in such cases by from one to four years. There might often be a great gain to the public in such a saving of time, to say nothing of the advantage of relieving the electorate from a needless burden. The chief objections to the change spring from practical rather than theoretical considerations.

Emergency Legislation.

First, there is the difficulty under the optional referendum of giving to the legislature adequate power for dealing with emergencies without imposing undue restrictions upon the power of popular veto. An emergency exists whenever an important public interest demands immediate action, but immediate action may be prevented, if the necessary legislation is opposed by a number of voters sufficient to file a petition for a referendum. Either the power to refer a legislative enactment to the electorate, that is, to suspend the operation of a legislative enactment pending its approval or disapproval by the electorate, must be restricted, or the ability of the legislature to deal promptly and effectively with emergencies must be seriously impaired.

The states which have adopted the optional popular referendum may be divided into three classes with respect to the manner in which they have met this difficulty. The first class comprises those states which have chosen the first horn of the dilemma.[1] In these states the referendum is not applicable to measures enacted for the purpose of dealing with an emergency. Thus in South Dakota the referendum is not applicable to "such laws as may be necessary for the immediate preservation of the public peace, health, or safety, support of the state government and its existing public institutions." In Oregon, however, an emergency may be constitutionally declared only in the case of laws "necessary for the immediate preservation of the public

[1] South Dakota, Oregon, Montana, Oklahoma, Missouri, Michigan, Arkansas, Colorado, New Mexico, and Washington.

peace, health, or safety." All other measures, including bills making appropriations, except when passed in emergencies as above described, are subject to suspension when referendum petitions are filed against them. In each of the states of this class an emergency is defined in the terms of either the South Dakota or the Oregon constitution. The legislature itself, however, is the judge of the necessity of legislation in cases of alleged emergency, and may declare the existence of the emergency by an ordinary majority vote. If a declaration of emergency is contained in the preamble of a bill, the enactment of the bill serves itself as a declaration of emergency. Therefore, unless the legislatures can be constrained by the courts to give a very strict interpretation to the expressions "public peace," "health," and "safety," which is undesirable even if possible, this solution of the problem imposes extensive restrictions upon the power of popular veto.

The objections to such a solution of the problem are apparent. First, the power of a majority of the legislature to declare an emergency is liable to abuse, for the legislators are under strong temptation to declare an emergency whenever they have reason to fear that they have acted without the sanction of public opinion. Certain legislatures seem almost to have formed the habit of forestalling the exercise of the popular veto as much as possible by passing all measures under color of an alleged emergency, except where the lack of justification for such procedure is too palpable. Thus in South Dakota during the first twelve years after the adoption of the optional referendum the legislature enacted 1251 measures, of which 537 were declared to be emergency measures and hence not subject to the popular veto.[1] Whatever may be the results of such a practice in the case of statutory enactments, its impropriety in the case of constitutional amendments is beyond question. Unless some test of urgency can be devised which will not in effect leave the decision to the discretion of the legislature, the optional referendum cannot be considered a satisfactory substitute for the compulsory constitutional referendum. In some instances, the governor, by a threat of veto, has been able to restrain the legislature from abusing its power to declare emergencies. This idea has been carried to its logical conclusion in Washington and Oregon. In

[1] See A. L. Lowell, *Public Opinion and Popular Government*, p. 175.

the former state, the executive may disapprove any section in any bill and this of course includes emergency clauses or sections. Thus Governor Lister in 1915 negatived the emergency clauses in five bills and thereby compelled the legislature to be more discriminating in its declarations of urgency. Oregon in 1921, adopted a constitutional amendment specifically empowering the governor to veto emergency clauses in bills. Such an extension of the executive veto might well be adopted in all the states where the optional referendum exists.

A second objection to the mode of dealing with emergencies adopted in South Dakota and Oregon is that, even if the legislatures could be trusted not to abuse their power to pass measures in cases of acknowledged emergency, there is no agreement as to what constitutes an emergency. The South Dakota and Oregon provisions cannot both be right. In the latter state, for example, the power of the purse is fully reserved to the electorate, whilst in the former appropriation bills are not subject to the popular veto at all. If there are any doubts as to the propriety of permitting the review of certain classes of legislative enactments directly by the electorate, it would seem more consistent with the spirit of the referendum to authorize the voters to resolve those doubts for themselves. If a choice must be made between restricting the scope of the popular veto and impairing the ability of the legislature to deal promptly and effectively with an emergency, it would be surprising if no state chose the latter horn of the dilemma. In fact this choice has been made in Nevada, where all measures without any exception are subject to the optional referendum.

The legislature is not altogether deprived of the power to deal with emergencies, even if all measures are subject to the popular veto. In case of emergency, when the operation of a measure is suspended because of a referendum petition, the legislature or executive may order a special election to be held at once, and if the emergency be a genuine one, there should be no doubt as to the action of the voters, provided the proposed measure is really necessary and appropriate for the occasion. In fact, the actual abuse of the power to suspend the operation of an act by filing a referendum petition against it has been of an entirely different sort. Measures have been enacted with the support of a strong and clearly preponderant public opinion, against which referendum petitions have been filed, not so much in the hope that measures might ultimately be defeated, as in order to postpone for nearly two years the execution of an unwelcome public policy. In several states, for example, the enforcement of laws creating public service commissions or otherwise providing for the regulation of public utilities has thus been postponed through the filing of referendum petitions by representatives of the corporate interests to be affected thereby. In short, a satisfactory solution of the problem of emergency legislation is not to be found by grasping either horn of the dilemma.

The third class of states comprises those which have attempted to safeguard the power of the legislatures to deal with emergencies without unduly restricting the power of the electorate to veto legislative enactments.[1] The legislatures of these states are authorized to declare the existence of an emergency, but only by a two-thirds vote of all the elected members.[2] The operation of emergency measures may not be suspended by filing a referendum petition against them, but in three states[3] they may be disapproved at a subsequent election. In some of these states certain kinds of measures may under no circumstances be passed in the guise of emergency measures. In California, for example, no measure creating or abolishing any office, or changing any salary, term, or duties of any officer, or granting any franchise or special privilege, or creating any vested right or privilege, may be declared an "urgency" measure. Thus the popular veto power is not actually restricted, nor is the ability of the legislature to deal with real emergencies seriously impaired.

The Problem of Signatures.

A second practical difficulty with the referendum, it is sometimes asserted, arises from the necessity of protecting the public against the abuse of the referendum for the purpose of delaying the enforcement of measures which the electorate may be expected eventually to approve. In a few states there has been an attempt to prevent this abuse by requiring the signatures of a larger percentage of the electorate to referendum petitions de-

[1] Utah, Maine, California, Arizona, Nebraska, Ohio, North Dakota, Maryland, and Massachusetts.

[2] Three-fifths in Maryland.

[3] Maryland, Massachusetts, Nebraska.

signed to suspend the enforcement of a law than to those which provide for the reference of a measure to the voters without suspending its operation prior to the election. Thus in Montana the percentages required are 15 per cent in the former case and 5 per cent in the latter; in New Mexico they are 25 per cent in the former case and 10 per cent in the latter. The question of percentages, however, is an important one, and requires special consideration.

The requirement that a petition for the reference of a legislative enactment to the electorate for approval or disapproval be signed by not less than a stated number of voters serves several purposes. First, it is desirable that no measure should be referred to the voters unless there is some reason to suppose that the action of the legislature will not be approved by a majority of the voters. Secondly, it is desirable that no measure be referred unless there is some reason to suppose that the electorate will be sufficiently interested to express a genuine opinion thereon. Thirdly, it is desirable that no more measures be referred at any one time than the voters can reasonably be expected to consider on their individual merits. Evidently the question of how many signatures should be required on a referendum petition is one to which a final answer can be obtained only from experience. In most of the states the signatures of 5 per cent of the voters are required to complete a petition for the reference of a statute to the electorate for approval or disapproval. In some of the states there is a further requirement that the signatures be obtained in not less than a certain proportion of the counties of the state.[1] The latter provision is intended presumably to insure that the demand for an appeal to the electorate is not concentrated in a particular locality, but state-wide and general in character. Its chief effect is to favor the rural as against the urban voters.

In practice the collection of signatures to referendum petitions is not so managed as to throw much light on the real convictions of the voters. Whether signatures are collected by voluntary or by paid workers, many arguments are likely to be employed other than those pertaining to the merits of the measure in question, and many signatures are likely to be secured, not because

[1] Two-fifths, in Nebraska; two-thirds of the congressional districts in Missouri.

the signer desires to vote against the measure, or has indeed any definite opinion upon it, but because he desires to accommodate a friend, or conciliate a customer or business acquaintance, or get rid of an importunate caller, or simply thinks that the opponents of a measure are entitled to appeal to the electorate, if they wish, and should receive help from all voters who may sometime in their turn likewise desire to appeal to the electorate. In fact, signatures are generally collected by paid canvassers, whose compensation depends upon the number of signatures they obtain. At the rate of five cents per signature a referendum petition would cost from $1200 in a state like Oregon to $10,000 in a state like Ohio, and the requirement that such a petition be filed therefore amounts in such a case to a requirement that a corresponding amount of money be forfeited, so to speak, as a fee for the appeal to the electorate. If the money were actually paid as a fee to the state and expended under authority of the state in publishing authentic information concerning the measure, instead of in payment of the cost of collecting the signatures, it would seem likely that the electorate would be better informed concerning the merits of the measure than it is by oral discussions with canvassers for signatures, and that the evidence as to a public demand for a referendum on the measure would be no less convincing.

The value of a formal petition as a means of expressing public opinion has probably been overrated. The filing of a petition does not prove much concerning the real beliefs of those who sign it. When the number of signatures is fixed at a low figure, say, 5 per cent of the total electorate, the requirement apparently has not kept many measures off the ballot which opponents were determined should go to the voters.[1] When the number of signatures is fixed at a higher figure, on the other hand, the labor of securing additional names increases at a disproportionate rate, so that the cost of a petition signed by 20 per cent or 25

[1] As a rule, the percentages of signatures required for referendum petitions were fixed before the advent of woman suffrage. The enfranchisment of women practically doubled the size of the electorate and hence doubled the number of petitioners. Dodd suggests that this fact is one of the reasons for the lesser use of the initiative and referendum in Oregon since 1912. (See *State Government*, p. 515.) In any event, a percentage requirement becomes progressively more difficult as the electorate grows larger and larger. Massachusetts avoids this difficulty by stipulating that referendum petitions shall be signed by not less than fifteen thousand qualified voters.

per cent of the electorate will be much more than four or five times the cost of a 5 per cent petition. Indeed, what evidence there is—it is not much—suggests that the requirement of a 25 per cent petition is practically prohibitive. The existing system is superficially democratic. Actually, however, it operates to the advantage of permanent well-organized interests and to the disadvantage of those that can least afford to bear the burden of needless expense. Yet these are the kinds of groups whose appeals to the voters are most to be encouraged.

A better plan would seem to be to require persons proposing to appeal to the electorate for the veto of a legislative enactment to deposit with the state a sum sufficient to defray the cost of sending to all voters an adequate explanation of the nature of the measure to be referred to them, and of the reasons for which its opponents seek its defeat, subject perhaps to the proviso that if the measure is defeated, the money shall be refunded. Such a requirement would produce sufficient evidence of good faith on the part of the opponents, and if the governor has the power, as is the case in some states, to call a special election, when deemed necessary, there should be no serious abuse of the right to appeal to the electorate, simply for the purpose of delay.

Official Bulletins of Information.

Several of the states that possess the optional referendum have made provision for the publication of official bulletins for the better dissemination of information upon measures referred to the voters.[1] These bulletins contain copies of the referred measures, together with arguments thereon, prepared by the advocates and opponents of the measures, and are mailed to all registered voters several weeks before the election. The expense of printing the arguments is usually assessed upon those who prepare them, the state paying the balance of the cost. These "voters' text-books," as they are sometimes called, have proved a cheaper and more effective medium for reaching the electorate than newspaper advertising at public expense, which is the practice in a few states,[2] and have been instrumental in assisting the voters to vote upon measures intelligently. In Oregon and California,

[1] Oregon, North Dakota, California, Arizona, Montana, Nebraska, Ohio, Washington, Utah, Oklahoma, and Massachusetts.

[2] Colorado and Arkansas.

where the joint operation of the compulsory referendum on constitutional amendments and of the optional referendum on statutes has thrown a comparatively heavy burden on the voters, and where the official bulletins are said to be carefully read by many of them, there is far more evidence of discrimination between measures than in such a state as Missouri, where the burden of the referendum has also been comparatively heavy and where there has hitherto been no official bulletin of information.

It is not easy to determine just how effective the official campaign bulletins are as a means of educating the electorate. In Oregon the use of the pamphlet for the publication of arguments upon measures referred to the voters is optional with the supporters and opponents of the measures. In only a small proportion of cases are both affirmative and negative arguments published. Half of the referred measures have been published in the pamphlet without any arguments. Nor is there any relation between the publication of arguments and the results of the voting on the measures. Of the measures accompanied by affirmative arguments alone more were accepted than rejected, and of the measures accompanied by negative arguments alone, more were rejected than accepted. But the total number of measures referred to the electorate by means of the optional referendum is comparatively small, and the relation between the publication of arguments and the decision by the voters uncertain. There has been no perceptible tendency on the part of the opponents and supporters of measures referred to the voters by means of the optional referendum towards a more general use of the privilege of publishing arguments in the official bulletin. Apparently those who are most concerned have not yet been convinced by experience with the Oregon pamphlet that official publicity pays, nor have they been convinced that it does not pay. In California arguments on each side of every measure referred to the electorate must be published in the pamphlet, together with the text of the measures, and provision is made for the preparation of the arguments by members of the legislature or other responsible persons. A comparison of the California and Oregon pamphlets shows that the arguments and information laid before the voters in the former state are more complete and more adequate than in the latter, and the

California pamphlet is presumably a more effective aid to the voter.

Though the degree of effectiveness of the official bulletin as a medium of publicity cannot be accurately determined, and doubtless varies in different states according to the character and condition of the voters, it cannot fail to be of considerable value in the development of the referendum as an educational discipline. The clearest evidence of this is the marked increase in the proportion of voters attending the polls who have voted on constitutional amendments proposed by the legislature that has occurred since the adoption of the optional referendum and the publication of an official bulletin. In California during the ten years 1899 to 1908, the average vote on the fifty-one measures submitted by the legislature, indicated as a percentage of the total attendance at the polls, was forty-three per cent. In 1914, when the system of direct action upon measures by the electorate was subjected to the severest test ever imposed in any state, the result was as follows:

Number of Measures Submitted by Means of		Maximum and Minimum Vote on Measures	Average Per Cent of Total Vote for Governor
Initiative	17	$\left(\frac{890,317}{561,131}\right)$	73%
Optional referendum	4	$\left(\frac{755,450}{611,797}\right)$	73%
Legislative and compulsory constitutional referendum	27	$\left(\frac{674,420}{381,587}\right)$	60%

Despite the heavy burden laid upon the voters by the combined operation of the initiative and referendum, they voted more generally upon measures submitted by the legislature than ever before. In Colorado during the ten years 1899 to 1908, the average recorded vote upon the seventeen measures submitted by the legislature was thirty-seven per cent of the total recorded vote. The initiative and referendum were adopted in 1910, a year before their adoption in California, but there is no official bulletin or other provision for publicity except in the newspapers. The result of the voting on measures in 1914 was as follows:

Number of Measures Submitted by Means of		Maximum and Minimum Vote on Measures	Average Per Cent of Total Vote for Governor
Initiative	8	(247,606 / 121,620)	60%
Optional referendum	5	(129,304 / 101,266)	42%
Legislative and compulsory constitutional referendum	3	(111,262 / 104,560)	40%

Doubtless the greater increase of interest in measures submitted by the legislature in California than in Colorado since the adoption of the initiative and referendum cannot be explained wholly by the adoption of better means of publicity. The evidence, however, such as it is, tends to confirm the presumption that an official bulletin like that of California will materially help to arouse the interest and inform the intelligence of the voters.

The tendency among the states which have adopted the optional referendum is towards the adoption and further development of the official bulletin. Of the various types of bulletins now in use, that published in California is among the best, both in form and in substance.

Optional *v.* Compulsory Referendum.

Whether the optional referendum has yet so proved its worth as to justify the complete abandonment of the compulsory referendum may be questioned. With respect to various matters of detail the practice of the several states differs, and further experience may be necessary before a standard form of the optional referendum is developed. Yet it is already clear that the optional referendum, under the proper conditions and rightly used, satisfies the two tests of good government. As Mill phrases it, "government is to be judged by its action upon men and by its action upon things; by what it makes of the citizens and what it does with them." Judged by either test, the optional referendum upon legislative enactments has proved in the main a better governmental device than the compulsory referendum on constitutional amendments proposed by the state legislatures. It is a more efficient instrument both for the correction of misrepresentative action on the part of the legislatures and for the education of the voters themselves.

The substitution of the optional for the compulsory referendum upon constitutional amendments proposed by the state legislatures would have the effect of diminishing the existing distinction between constitutional and ordinary statute law. Now the process of constitutional amendment upon legislative initiative, as established in almost all states, requires the approval of all proposed amendments by the people. If that approval were dispensed with, except in the case of such amendments as should be brought before the electorate under the optional referendum, the status of amendments not referred to and formally approved by the electorate might seem less secure than that of those ordinary laws expressly approved by the electorate. To be sure, the legislatures are usually forbidden to propose constitutional amendments by bare majorities, but legislatures are also forbidden to adopt some kinds of ordinary legislation by bare majorities. In fact, the original distinction between constitutional and statutory law has already been so far impaired by the insertion of ordinary legislation in the state constitutions that the preservation of the distinction in its present form is of doubtful utility. It is for that very reason that it is proposed to substitute the optional for the compulsory referendum on constitutional amendments. The legislatures have shown themselves incapable of maintaining the distinction in any logical form, and for the revival of the traditional distinction, which is important, the public may confidently look to its more direct representative, the electorate. Whether the compulsory referendum should be retained for certain classes of amendments, as it now exists for certain classes of ordinary legislation, is a question that will be considered presently. It is enough to point out here that the vital distinction between constitutional and statutory law does not reside in the character of the procedure for its enactment, but in the importance attached to the substance of the law itself.

There can be no doubt that the referendum is now permanently established among the political institutions of the states. There is little question of abandoning it. The only questions concerning which there are still serious differences of opinion relate to the form in which, and the conditions under which, it shall be used. In the majority of states the referendum still exists only in the mandatory form, and is applicable only to constitutional amendments, and, in some of these states, to certain classes of ordinary legislation. In a large minority of the states it exists also in the optional form, and is applicable to most of the ordinary legislation. A comparative study of the operation of the referendum in each of its forms throws much light on the problems which still remain unsettled, and on the possibility of their solution.

The evidence indicates that the referendum, like any other political institution, is an imperfect instrument, which works better under some conditions than under others. The first limitation upon its most effective use is one of number. In 1924, the legislature of South Carolina submitted fifty-one constitutional amendments, most of which were of a local character. Only four of these amendments were adopted and the vote cast in no case equalled 50 per cent of the vote cast for governor. This is the greatest number of measures hitherto brought before the voters at one time by the operation of the referendum. In 1920, a constitutional convention in Nebraska submitted forty-one constitutional amendments at a special election, all of which were adopted. In 1912 a constitutional convention in Ohio also proposed forty-one amendments, which were submitted to the voters at a special election. In 1914 thirty-seven measures were submitted to the voters at a regular election in California. In at least some of these states the action of the electorate was generally conceded to have been deliberate and on most of the measures intelligent. Yet it was clear that the number of measures was greater than the voters could easily dispose of. There was a general opinion that the burden laid upon the electorate was excessive. The average number of measures brought before the voters by means of the optional referendum alone is not more than two or three, and the evidence indicates that this number of measures can be easily handled by the voters. When the number becomes excessive, the voters have a way of voting "no" on all or most of the measures without much regard to their several merits. This remedy has been most conspicuously applied in Missouri, where inadequate provision is made for the information of the electorate. In 1922, fourteen legislative measures were submitted by means of the optional referendum, only one of which was adopted. The others were defeated by large majorities, though some were apparently not without merit.[1] In short, beyond a certain point, any further increase in the number of measures submitted is not likely to bring a corresponding increase in the efforts of the electorate to understand the issues. Hence beyond that point, the greater the number of measures, the less satisfactory will be the result. It is not possible to determine just when that point is reached, and probably that point is reached more quickly in some states than in others. No two electorates are precisely alike with respect either to the distribution of interests or to habits of mind. The abuse of the optional referendum by submitting too many measures to the voters at the same time, however, is one for which the voters have the best remedy in their own hands. For that reason it is the compulsory rather than the optional referendum, the use of which should be curtailed in those states in which the total number of measures brought before the electorate by means of the referendum is felt to be excessive.

The second limitation upon the most effective use of the referendum is one of kind. The operation of the optional and, more clearly, that of the compulsory referendum reveals the reluctance of many voters to express an opinion upon matters outside the range of their personal experience. The mass of the voters, for example, will generally vote freely on measures relating to the organization or powers of juries, but not on measures relating to the organization or powers of the higher courts. They know whether or not they wish to prohibit the sale of intoxicating liquors, but are not so certain with respect to the desirability of concentrating the responsibility for the management of all charitable and penal institutions in a single state board of control. As President Lowell has said, "it would seem wiser, therefore, to confine the referendum to questions involving general principles alone, and to the class of matters where the public is normally familiar with the facts required for a decision, than to extend it promiscuously to questions where a rational opinion can be formed only by a knowledge of details with which the ordinary man does not readily become acquainted."[2] Experience shows that it is the compulsory rather than the optional form of the referendum which is mainly responsible for the submission of the

[1] However, it is only fair to point out that these measures were passed by a Republican legislature and were opposed by the Democratic state central committee for party reasons.

[2] A. L. Lowell, *Public Opinion and Popular Government*, p. 159.

wrong kind of measures to the voters, just as it is the compulsory rather than the optional form which is mainly responsible for the submission of the excessive number of measures. If the referendum is to be used under the most favorable conditions, therefore, it would seem to be necessary to restrict its use under the compulsory form and to extend its use under the optional form. In short, it would seem not only that the referendum has come to stay, but also that the optional form should tend more and more to prevail.

THE POPULAR INITIATIVE

The referendum is commonly connected in political discussions with the initiative. The literature relating to the subject almost invariably treats them as if they were inseparable. In practical politics also the two have generally been found together. Only two of the twenty-one states which have established the optional referendum have failed to establish the popular initiative.

The two devices, however, are distinct, and should be carefully distinguished in all discussions of the work of the state electorates. The referendum enables the electorates to disapprove and thereby annul a measure adopted by the legislature, and has on that account been termed, as has been said, the popular veto, or more properly, the electoral veto. The initiative enables the electorate itself to adopt a measure disapproved and therefore not adopted by the legislature. It has been accordingly termed the procedure for direct legislation by the people, or more properly, by the electorate. Ordinarily this expression is understood to include both the referendum and initiative, but such usage of the term is inaccurate and objectionable. The procedure for direct legislation by the electorate is necessarily completed by a popular vote, and to that extent the initiative resembles the referendum, but in all the earlier stages of the procedure the differences are more important than the resemblances. The vital distinction between them consists in the fact that under the referendum no measure can come before the electorate unless previously approved by the legislature, whilst under the initiative no measure comes before the electorate if it has been previously approved by the legislature.

So far as the procedure for direct legislation by the electorate is identical with that for the exercise of the electoral veto, it may be expected to operate in the same manner. Whether a measure originates within or without the legislature is in itself immaterial to the electorate. It is not the origin but the nature of the measure that concerns the voters, when it is submitted to them. If the voters can act intelligently on measures brought before them by means of the referendum, they can also act intelligently on measures submitted to their decision by means of the initiative, other things being equal. In other words, unless it can be shown that measures brought before the voters by means of the initiative tend to differ in some definite way from measures brought before them by means of the referendum, there is no reason to suppose that the electorate will be less capable of deciding wisely in the one case than in the other. The first question that arises, therefore, in connection with the initiative is not whether the voters can be trusted to use with discretion the power of direct legislation, but what, as a matter of fact, are the characteristic differences, if any, between initiated and referred measures.

Working of Popular Initiative.

If there were any marked differences between initiated and referred measures, it might be supposed that these differences would be reflected in the results of the voting thereon. If, for example, initiated measures, as a class, were generally felt to be less important than referred measures, the voting thereon should be less general. If the purposes of initiated measures were generally considered more objectionable, the election returns should show that a larger proportion of them are defeated. If their drafting and technical detail were generally found to be less perfect, the fact should appear in a growing distrust of initiated as contrasted with referred measures, and an increasing tendency to reject those which have failed to secure legislative approval.

In fact, the action of the electorates upon measures submitted by means of the initiative has hitherto not been markedly different from its action upon measures submitted by means of the optional referendum. In each case the interest in the measures brought before the voters, as indicated by the voting thereon, has usually been much greater than in measures submitted by means of the compulsory constitutional referendum. As in the case of the measures submitted by means of the optional referendum, nearly one-half of the measures submitted by means of the initiative have been voted on by not less than three-fourths of those who have gone to the polls, and only a small minority of the measures have failed to interest a majority of the voters.[1] The degree of interest shown by the voters in measures submitted by means of the initiative has been on the whole a little greater than that in measures brought before the voters by means of the optional referendum. This result, however, seems to be due mainly to the exceptional interest aroused by certain measures not infrequently brought before the voters by means of the initiative, rather than to any generally greater interest in initiated measures as such. The initiated measures which have aroused the most interest have related to such matters as prohibition and the liquor problem, taxation and the use of public credit, and formerly the extension of the suffrage to women. They have raised clean-cut issues, in the decision of which most voters have felt a direct personal interest. With the exception of the measures relating to taxation, they have generally involved questions of principle only, unconfused by questions of detail or of ways and means. Other matters with respect to which much legislation has been proposed by means of the initiative, and upon which comparatively large votes have been cast, are public education and improvements, the regulation of public utilities, the regulation of conditions of industrial employment, and the reform of systems of nomination and election to public office.[2] In short, the questions that have aroused most interest are substantially the same as those which have aroused most interest when raised by means of the optional referendum. So far as the degree of interest in initiated measures in general is an indication of their character, the evidence does not indicate that there are any marked differences in the character of initiated and referred measures respectively.

The evidence with reference to the relative acceptability of initiated and referred measures is shown by the following table

[1] Of the one hundred and twenty initiated measures voted upon from 1919 to the end of 1925, fifty-eight received a vote of not less than 75 per cent while only seven were under 50 per cent.

[2] Much use was made of the initiative and referendum by the supporters and opponents of the Non-Partisan League, particularly in North Dakota. In that state in 1920, five initiated measures aimed directly at the League were adopted by close margins, the total vote in each case being about 110 per cent of the total vote for presidential electors.

which covers the entire period from 1904 down to the beginning of 1926.

	Submitted	Adopted	Percentage Adopted
Laws referred on petition..........	173	64	37%
Amendments proposed by initiative	214	69	32%
Laws proposed by initiative.......	226	87	38%

It thus appears that constitutional amendments proposed by the initiative are somewhat less apt to be adopted than are initiated and referred statutes. The differences, however, between the three kinds of measures are not great enough to warrant any definite conclusions.

Theoretical Objections to Initiative.

Opponents of the initiative assert that certain characteristic differences are to be expected between measures originating outside of and not approved by the legislatures and those for which legislative approval is secured, and that if those differences are not yet clearly reflected in the election returns, it is because the initiative has not yet been in operation long enough for its full effects to become apparent. Ultimately, the less satisfactory operation of laws enacted by the people under the initiative will become apparent, it is urged, and the causes will be found to lie in the nature of the measures. In the first place, measures submitted to the electorate in accordance with the procedure of the initiative are devised and put forth by persons not acting in any official representative capacity and not responsible to anybody but themselves. The members of the legislature are chosen to provide for the common interests and promote the general welfare of the whole people, and have to deal with many measures, knowing that no two will be approved by precisely the same body of voters. The initiators of a measure to be submitted directly to the electorate are self-chosen, and need consider only the interests of a majority of those whom they expect to vote thereon. If they have no ambition to hold public office, they may utterly disregard the interests and beliefs of those whom they expect to vote against their measure. Therefore, it is to be feared that measures submitted under the initiative will tend to show less consideration for the rights of minorities than measures enacted by representative legislators. But without fair consideration for the rights of minorities, the peaceful operation of democratic institutions is impossible. In short, under such conditions the initiative, far from affording a beneficial educational discipline, would exercise, its opponents say, a profoundly demoralizing influence on the public mind.

Secondly, it is asserted by the opponents of the initiative that initiated measures, even if unexceptionable in principle, are more likely than legislative measures to be defective in detail. A legislative body is bound by rules of procedure intended to secure freedom of debate and adequate publicity for the reasons of its acts, as well as for the acts themselves. Its proceedings are intended to be deliberate, and to afford ample opportunity for the revision of immature proposals and for the amendment of those that are imperfect. The initiators of a measure to be submitted directly to the voters are bound also by rules of procedure, but these rules impose no restraint on secret deliberations and ordinarily afford no convenient opportunity for the revision of immature, or for the amendment of, imperfect proposals. Once a measure has been initiated, it must be accepted or rejected by the voters as it stands. Upon the electorate, therefore, there is more likely to be thrown under the initiative than under the referendum the difficult task of balancing an end that is good against a means that is doubtful, or of weighing the advantages of immediate action against those of acting more slowly with the aid of probably riper wisdom. In short, in so far as measures not approved by legislative bodies may be expected to differ from those which are so approved, they should be less rather than more perfect, it is argued, and the initiative therefore should tend to impair rather than improve the quality of legislation.

Its Educational Influence.

The first of these theoretical objections to the initiative may be partially tested by a further examination of the measures hitherto submitted to the electorates by means of the initiative. The following are the main classes of legislation in connection with which the rights of minorities seem most likely to be placed in jeopardy—taxation, the regulation of corporations, especially of public service corporations, the regulation of conditions of industrial employment, the regulation of social conditions involving vested business interests, as in the case of the liquor traffic, and legislation touching special racial or religious interests. The single tax is the most radical proposal in the field of taxation that has been brought before the electorates by means of the initiative. In several states single tax measures of various sorts have been brought to a vote, and have been defeated in every case by majorities varying from nearly two to one to more than five to one. In general the voters have shown themselves extremely cautious in adopting changes in their system of taxation, whether proposed by initiative or otherwise.[1] Measures relating to the regulation of public utilities have been brought before the voters in most states in which the initiative has been put to any considerable use, but not all the measures so submitted have been adopted, and no measures have been adopted by means of the initiative for which there was not precedent in the legislation adopted by other state legislatures. The same is true of labor legislation. No laws have been adopted by means of the initiative for which precedent cannot be found in the enactments of the state legislatures, nor do the voters adopt all the labor laws submitted to them. Thus, the eight-hour day for women when submitted by initiative in Oregon in 1914 was rejected, although it had been previously (1912) adopted by the legislature of California. With respect to prohibition and the liquor problem, the situation is the same. In 1914, for example, prohibition was submitted in five and adopted in four western states. In the fifth (California), where the measure submitted to the people contained some novel and comparatively oppressive provisions, the voters, though apparently friendly to prohibition, rejected the proposed measure. Among the four hundred and forty measures which have been submitted by means of the initiative down to the close of 1925, there have been only three cases which have raised a religious issue of any kind. These cases involved the proposal to compel all children to attend only the public schools and were directed against private schools in general and Catholic parochial schools in particular. The proposition was defeated in Michigan and Washington in 1924 but was adopted in Oregon in 1922, only to be declared unconstitutional by the United States Supreme Court three years later.[2] The principal measures which

[1] See especially, Oregon election returns, 1912, 1914.
[2] Pierce *v.* Society of Sisters of Holy Names, 268 U. S. 510 (1925).

have raised racial issues in the states possessing the initiative have been submitted by the legislatures, and they have been directed against aliens. The one conspicuous exception to this rule is the initiated California alien land law adopted in 1920. Experience in the "direct legislation" states indicates, so far as experience can yet indicate anything, that racial and religious questions will not be raised by means of the initiative, except under such circumstances as would probably cause them to be raised by the legislatures, if there were no procedure for direct legislation.

There is as yet no convincing evidence that the initiative has tended to demoralize the electorates by exposing casual majorities of voters to the temptation of abusing the rights of helpless minorities under the lead of irresponsible and reckless agitators. Either there have been legislative precedents for the radical measures submitted by means of the initiative, or they have been rejected at the polls. The best examples of the latter have been the single tax measures and those proposed by the Oregon reformers for the purpose of making over the constitution of that state. So far as proposals for radical reforms go, the chief effect of the initiative has been to secure for their proponents an earlier and wider hearing than would otherwise have been the case. Presumably this means that those proposals which are sound have a better prospect of speedy adoption by the legislature than if the initiative did not exist. Submission to the electorate by means of the initiative serves the double purpose of affording some beneficial educational discipline to the voters, and of revealing to the legislatures more clearly than can be done in any other way the state of the public mind. Where the result of the voting upon a measure shows a demand for action, even if the electorate itself refuses to accept the particular measure submitted to it, a wise legislature will act accordingly. The submission of so-called "blue sky" laws and their rejection by the electorates of three western states in 1912 and 1914 showed, first, that there was a public demand for the more effective protection of investors against fraudulent securities, and, secondly, that the voters were reluctant to approve legislation on the subject without further consideration. In one of the same states a "blue sky" law enacted by the legislature and submitted to the voters by means of the optional referendum was approved at the same time that an initiated measure was rejected. To secure the information concerning the state of the public mind afforded by the submission of these measures, the votes were well worth taking. Nor could the consideration of the measures have failed to be instructive to the voters. It is doubtless true that the full effects of direct legislation by the voters are not yet apparent, but the fears of those who assert that the initiative will exert a bad influence upon the electorates do not seem likely to be verified.

Its Influence on Legislation.

The second of the theoretical objections to the initiative may be partially tested in the same way as the first. There are many examples of initiated measures which raise for the consideration of the voters not only a main issue, consisting of some general principle of public policy, but also subordinate issues, arising out of the means proposed to give effect to the general principle of the measure. Now, the voters cannot decide at a single balloting on a given measure more than one of the issues that may be involved in it. Either they will lose sight of the general principle because of the superior importance attached to subordinate issues, or they will shut their eyes to defects of detail because of the engrossing interest of the general principle. For example, if a proposed law to prohibit the sale of intoxicating liquors should incidentally attempt to prohibit the growing of grapes or hops, grape and hop growers as a class would presumably take most interest in the features of the measure that concerned them most directly. A legislative system which does not permit the offering of amendments is bound to be inferior to one which does, so far as all but the simplest issues are concerned. Direct legislation by the voters, regarded solely as an educational discipline, may be more effective than legislation by representatives, but regarded from any other point of view, its utility will depend upon the nature of the issues involved in a given measure. A bill to abolish capital punishment may be effectively disposed of by the same voters, who find themselves at a loss how to vote on a measure to establish a public service commission and define its powers. Even if a majority of the voters are sure that they want more adequate regulation of the rates and service of public utilities, they may not be sure that a commission is the best means for securing that end, or that a commission of the particular sort, and armed with the particular powers, proposed in the measure submitted to them, is the kind of commission best fitted to carry out their purposes. Still less are the voters capable of voting intelligently on proposals to fix rates and conditions of service directly by law. The actual fixing of rates that will be just to all parties is dependent upon acquaintance with matters of fact about which it is unreasonable to expect many voters to be adequately informed.

It is also unreasonable to expect that those who prepare measures for submission to the voters will always be actuated by a desire to assist the voters to make their decision wisely. For example, in Colorado in 1914 a measure was submitted to the voters permitting juries to return verdicts by a three-fourths vote in civil cases, and also permitting women to serve on juries. As women vote in Colorado, this manner of putting the question may have seemed to its sponsors a good joke on the opponents of any departure from the established principle that the verdicts of juries shall be unanimous. The "joke," however, was too apparent, and the measure was rejected. But less conspicuous "jokers" may be deliberately inserted in lengthy technical bills, as when the Oregon single taxers initiated a measure to provide for the county regulation of local taxation and to abolish the poll tax.[1] Doubtless many of the devices for beguiling or deceiving members of legislative bodies, that have been employed by special interests to gain their private ends, will also be employed for the same purpose in connection with direct legislation by the people, though with less likelihood of success.

Improvement of Procedure for Popular Initiative.

In several of the states in which it has been proposed to establish the initiative, attempts have been made to improve the procedure for direct legislation. In California, the amendment adopted in 1911, by which the initiative was established, provided that bills might be submitted directly to the electorate on petition of 8 per cent of the voters, or that they might be submitted first to the legislature on petition of 5 per cent of the voters. If the legislature should fail to enact the measure as

[1] This measure was adopted by the voters in 1910, but two years later they repealed all of it except the part abolishing the poll tax.

proposed by the petitioners, it should be submitted to the electorate, but not otherwise. This plan was intended to prevent the needless submission of measures, but afforded no means by which an initiated measure, if amended in the legislature with the approval of its initiators, could be enacted without submission to the electorate. Even if convinced that the legislature had improved their measure, the initiators would, nevertheless, have no recourse but to let their original draft be submitted to the electorate and to urge the voters to reject it and accept the perfected bill referred as an alternative by the legislature. California thus has the indirect, as well as the direct, statutory initiative. Four other states [1] likewise have both the direct and indirect statutory initiative, while four states [2] have only the indirect form of the statutory initiative. The indirect form of initiative is the only form applicable to constitutional amendments in Nevada and Massachusetts. No state has both the direct and the indirect constitutional initiative.

The Massachusetts initiative and referendum amendment of 1918 contains some distinctive features which deserve special consideration.[3] In that state, a petition for an initiated bill is first signed by ten qualified voters and is thereupon submitted to the attorney-general for approval as to form and content. The attorney-general also furnishes a descriptive title for the measure in question. The petition is then supplemented by the signatures of twenty thousand additional voters, after which the bill is introduced in the legislature where it must be adopted without change or rejected. In the latter case, the legislature may submit to the people a substitute act. There must be a popular vote upon the original bill, if five thousand more signatures are secured. Before the vote takes place, a majority of the first ten signers may amend the original measure, subject to certification by the attorney-general. If the legislative substitute is satisfactory, there is no need to complete the petition and thus compel the submission of the original act. The procedure for initiated constitutional amendments is similar, but more complicated. The Massachusetts plan is calculated to exert the maximum of pressure upon the legislature with the minimum of effort on the

[1] Utah, Ohio, Washington, Massachusetts.
[2] South Dakota, Nevada, Maine, Michigan.
[3] Art. xlviii.

part of the electorate as a whole, and at the same time to provide for the incorporation of perfecting amendments in measures actually submitted to the people.

Yet when all this is done, the initiative remains a cumbersome piece of legislative machinery. Initiated bills must still be accepted or rejected by the voters in the exact form in which they are finally submitted. The electorate cannot revise and amend, like a law-making body which physically meets, and it can recommit a measure only by defeating it. In such an event, there can never be any certainty as to the grounds of the voters' objections, whether they approve the measure in principle and condemn the means employed to give effect thereto, or whether they condemn it in principle and in detail alike. It is as if an ordinary legislature had no option but to give an unqualified yes or no to every measure laid before it, as a jury can bring in no verdict but one of guilty or not guilty. As a means of improving the technical character of state legislation the initiative holds out little promise. The genius that would be required to perfect it, if devoted to the further improvement of methods of law-making in the state legislatures, should bring a much greater return.

Further Reform of Initiative.

The conditions under which the initiative operates to best advantage are the same as those under which the optional referendum operates to best advantage. The number of measures submitted at the same time must not be too great, and the nature of the measures must not be too technical or too remote from the experience of the voters. Not a few measures have been submitted to the voters by means of the initiative which have conspicuously failed to arouse general public interest. Among these have been a number of measures relating to purely local affairs, or to the general forms of local government when only special localities were really concerned. Some measures, indeed, of genuine public concern have been voted on by a surprisingly small number of persons. For example, in Colorado in 1912 measures were initiated to provide for trial by jury in cases of contempt of court and to place all appointed public officers under civil service rules. The former was rejected and the latter was adopted, only 28 per cent of the voters who attended the polls voting thereon. That was the smallest interest ever shown in initiated measures, yet the measures were not unimportant. In general there seem to be proportionately no more measures of trivial importance brought before the voters by means of the initiative than by means of the optional referendum. But the number of initiated measures has been excessive in several of the direct-legislation states,[1] and measures of an excessively technical or abstract character have been initiated in most of them. The Colorado measures noted above afford excellent illustrations of this. There were too many measures on the ballot in that state in 1912, the provisions for informing the voters about them were inadequate, and the particular measures noted above were technical in character and related to matters outside the experience of the mass of the voters.

The states which have introduced the official bulletin as a means of placing before the electorate the texts of referred measures, together with arguments thereon, have invariably made similar provision for publicity in connection with the use of the initiative. Thus one pamphlet contains all the matter relating to measures to be voted on by the electorate, regardless of the origin of the measures. In general what has already been noted concerning the value of the official bulletin as a means of publicity in connection with the referendum applies also to its use in connection with the initiative. The advocates and opponents of initiated measures, however, publish arguments in the official bulletins, the use of which for purposes of discussion is optional, much more freely than the advocates and opponents of referred measures. In no state does the available evidence indicate that the publication of arguments has any decisive influence upon the result of the vote. The arguments themselves vary widely in forensic power but are usually unexceptionable in tone and reveal a decent respect for the character of those to whom they are addressed. If it were certain that they were read by all the voters, it would be possible to bestow high praise upon the educational value of direct action by the electorate. The election returns demonstrate, however, that the direct action

[1] The tendency in recent years is generally away from an excessive use of the initiative and referendum. Thus in Oregon from 1906 to 1914 inclusive, the number of initiated measures submitted in the even years varied from ten to twenty-eight; from 1916 to 1924, inclusive, the number varied from three to eight.

of the electorate upon measures is an educational discipline of which a considerable minority of the voters do not as yet take advantage. Such voluntary disfranchisement of ignorant and indifferent voters, on the other hand, so far as voting upon measures is concerned, doubtless improves the operation of the initiative as an instrument of legislation.

Regarded as an instrument of legislation, however, the initiative is of limited value. It is not reasonable to expect that the electorate can enact directly more than a small fraction of the total mass of legislation demanded by the people of the states. In the main the people must continue to rely upon their less immediate representatives, the members of the legislatures. It is not reasonable to expect that the electorate can deal satisfactorily with any but the simplest issues, except temporarily until the legislature can be incited to action. Finally there are some matters over which the electorate should not be permitted to exercise an independent authority at all.

Limitation of Legislative Powers of Electorate.

In several states which have adopted the initiative, the power of the electorate has been restricted to the enactment of statutes. The power to adopt constitutional amendments without the previous approval of some other legislative body has been denied.[1] The objection to the constitutional initiative seems to be based upon the fear that the electorate cannot be trusted with direct legislative power and that the consequences of its abuse will be more serious in connection with constitutional amendments than in connection with ordinary legislation. A facile reply to this objection is that the nature of a measure under the conditions that exist in most states has no necessary connection with its status as constitutional or statutory, and that a discrimination against the use of the initiative for the adoption of such measures as happen to arise in the form of constitutional amendments is therefore not justified. This reply, however, does not wholly meet the objection. It can be seen by inspection of the election returns that most constitutional amendments are no less suited by nature for consideration and enactment directly by the electorate than ordinary legislation. There is one class of constitutional amendments, however, of which this is not true,

[1] South Dakota, Utah, Montana, Maine, Idaho, Washington.

namely, those which are intended to define or enlarge the powers of the electorate itself. It is natural for all persons, voters as well as those in more conspicuous places of authority, to strive for greater power. The electorate, if permitted to define its own powers, cannot be expected to resist the temptation unduly to enlarge them. The dangers that may result from the lack of any restrictions upon the power of electoral initiative in an American state are greatly diminished by the power possessed by the federal courts to veto state legislation in conflict with the Federal Constitution. The state electorates cannot destroy the republican character of established institutions, nor deny to any person the benefit of due process of law. The difficulties, however, that may result from the unrestricted initiative are not inconsiderable. For example, in Arizona a constitutional amendment was proposed by means of the initiative in 1914 for the purpose of depriving the legislature of the power to amend or repeal any statute adopted by the electorate. The needlessness of this proposal and the inconveniences that might be caused by it were pointed out in an able argument published in the official bulletin, but it was nevertheless adopted. The action of the electorate in this instance was not rational; it was instinctive, and action in such cases is more likely to be instinctive than rational. The electorate is not the people, and under our system of government it is just as improper for the electorate directly to define its own powers as for the legislature or the courts to define their own powers. The right of the legislature or courts to define their own powers is checked and balanced by the right of the other organs of government to do likewise. The same should be the rule for the electorate. The legal responsibility of the other organs to the electorate insures that the will of the voters, if well considered, will ultimately prevail.

There are some other limitations that should be imposed upon the direct popular initiative. When the electorate exercises the power of initiative, it acts as a legislative body, and is subject to many of the temptations that surround other legislative bodies. Experience has shown what these temptations are, and, to guard against them, many constitutional limitations have been imposed upon the ordinary state legislatures. In so far as these limitations regulate the procedure of the legislatures, they are mostly inapplicable to the electorates,—a fact which renders it impossible that the electorate can ever be a satisfactory independent agency for the enactment of the greater portion of state legislation. In so far as these limitations, however, relate to the powers of the state legislatures, they are applicable to the electorates. In Wisconsin, the proposed plan for direct legislation by the electorate, rejected by the voters in 1914, provided that the constitutional limitations upon the powers of the ordinary legislature should be imposed also upon the electorate, when acting as a legislative body. The Wisconsin plan showed a prudent recognition of the lessons of experience with American legislative bodies, but it was not altogether above criticism. The effect of constitutional limitations upon the powers of a state legislature, when properly enforced by executive and judiciary, is to prevent the enactment of the prohibited measures without the express approval of the electorate. It is not certain, however, that those kinds of measures which a legislature cannot be trusted to enact without the express approval of the electorate are identical with those which an electorate cannot be trusted to enact without the approval of the legislature. Nor, as has been pointed out, is it even certain that the existing limitations upon the powers of the legislatures are those which are most necessary and appropriate for legislative bodies. But in a general way it may be said that at the least such constitutional limitations should be imposed upon the electorates as will effectually prevent them from exercising executive or judicial powers under the guise of popular law-making.[1]

Conclusion.

Since 1904 when the initiative was first employed for the enactment of legislation directly by the voters, many popular measures have been adopted by the state electorates, which certainly would not have been adopted so soon, if the legislatures in those states had possessed a monopoly of the law-making power. The most

[1] The Massachusetts amendment of 1918 imposes numerous and important constitutional limitations upon the use of the initiative. Measures which make specific appropriations from the treasury, or which are inconsistent with certain constitutional rights of the individual, or which relate to religious matters, or which deal with the judiciary, or which are restricted in their operation to particular local subdivisions, are not subject to initiative petitions. Moreover, the limitations imposed upon the powers of the legislature are likewise imposed upon the legislative power of the electorate. Finally, the various limitations on the initiative are themselves not subject to change by the initiative.

notable illustration of the use of the initiative is afforded by the experience of Oregon. Among the measures that have been adopted in that state by means of the initiative are the following: the direct primary law, a local option liquor law, later state-wide prohibition, municipal home-rule, a railroad anti-pass law, several special corporation tax laws, the state-wide recall, a stringent corrupt practices act, the so-called Oregon plan for the direct election of United States senators (now superseded by the seventeenth amendment to the Federal Constitution), an employers' liability act, woman suffrage, extension of the public debt limit for road construction, the eight-hour day on public works, a public utilities commission law, prohibition of prison contract labor, and abolition of capital punishment. Nevertheless, regarded primarily as an instrument of government rather than as an educational discipline, the value of the initiative has consisted hitherto and must continue to consist principally in its efficacy as a mode of expressing public opinion. Modes of expressing the opinion of the voters which are advisory only cannot be as effective as those which are mandatory, and generally will be treated by them with comparative indifference. The operation of the Illinois public opinion law of 1901 has demonstrated this.[1] Under the initiative, the voters' knowledge that their opinions will have a certain effect brings out a fuller and more deliberate expression of opinion than under any other system. Whether initiated measures submitted to the voters are adopted or rejected, the value of the vote as an expression of opinion is equally great. The best effects of the popular initiative should be found, in the long run, not in the legislation placed by its use directly upon the statute books, but in the improvement of the legislation placed there by the legislatures.

[1] See, for an exception to the general rule, W. A. Robinson, "Advisory Referendum in Massachusetts on Child Labor Amendment," *American Political Science Review*, xix, pp. 69-73 (1925).

PART IV

CONCLUSION

CHAPTER XVI

THE FURTHER REFORM OF STATE GOVERNMENT

Two conclusions stand out clearly from the study of state government in the United States.

In the first place, it is evident that the governments of the states are now very different from what they were in the beginning. We are accustomed to look back at the institutions of the Fathers with veneration and awe. The truth is, so far as state government is concerned, that the institutions originally established were for the most part very imperfect. The people of all the states began with the same fundamental principles, popular sovereignty and the reign of law. But there was no agreement upon methods of reducing those principles to practice. Some of the methods originally employed were well devised and have endured. The government of Massachusetts, the most carefully planned and best constructed of the original state governments, is still carried on under the original constitution. In that state the character of the government has been much more affected by the growth of parties and the development of administrative activities than by the formal amendment of the constitution. In most of the original states, however, the first governments were not carefully planned and have been greatly altered by constitutional changes.

These changes have been many and various, but, as already indicated, they may all be classified under one or the other of two heads. The changes falling under the first head have to do with the democratization of the forms of government. The electorates have been made broader and more completely representative of the people. Their control over the other branches of government, legislative, executive, and judicial, has been strengthened. The changes falling under the second head have to do with the redistribution of powers between the legislative, executive, and judicial branches. The legislatures, practically supreme in most of the original states, have been subjected to more effective checks, and a better balance has been established between them and the coördinate branches. The result is that state government is now not only very different, but also on the whole very much better than it was in the beginning.

THE OUTLOOK FOR FURTHER REFORM.

The second conclusion to be drawn from the study of the government of the states is that the process of change by which the improvement of state government has been accomplished has not yet come to an end. The state governments are expected to do a great deal more for the people than in the beginning, and many things no doubt are now done much better. Nevertheless, it is generally believed that state government is not very efficient and in some cases not even decent. Whilst much of the dissatisfaction with the state governments must be ascribed to the imperfections of human nature, it is evident that the forms of government also still remain imperfect. The people have betrayed their dissatisfaction by the continual discussion of fresh expedients for further reform. In the years immediately preceding the World War the proposals which were most generally adopted tended chiefly to broaden the electorates and give them greater control over the conduct of public affairs. Most noteworthy among these were equal suffrage for women, the direct primary, the regulation of the use of money in elections, and, to a more limited extent, direct legislation and the recall. Since the War the favorite expedients have been those designed to impose further limitations upon the powers of legislatures and to increase the authority and usefulness of the executives and judiciary. Among these the reform of financial methods and budgetary procedure and the reorganization of executive departments and other administrative agencies have been most widely adopted. The former changes were advocated for the purposes of making state governments more popular; the latter, to make them more efficient.

Since the World War, as before, public opinion has seemed bewildered by the variety of reforms that have been recommended. There is no agreement yet concerning the proper qualifications for the suffrage or the best methods of making nominations and conducting elections. There is no agreement concerning the organization or powers of the legislatures, executives, and judiciary. There is no agreement concerning the functions of the electorates or the methods of changing the state constitutions. It is not surprising, therefore, that the discussion of the need for further reform has as yet been followed by a disproportionately small amount of actual achievement. There is no reason to suppose, however, that either the popular dissatisfaction or the discussion of plans for further reform will cease. State government in the future, as in the past, will probably be very different from what it is now. If the right expedients are now adopted, it ought also to be very much better.

But what are the right expedients?

If the laws governing the growth of state constitutions are consistent with those governing other political phenomena, the trend of constitutional development cannot be greatly altered as long as the underlying economic and social forces remain unchanged. Now the economic and social development of the United States has long proceeded in a well-defined course. There is no sign of any impending change of direction. Hence there is little prospect of a change in the direction of constitutional development. The further reform of state government will doubtless proceed along the same lines as in the past. The endeavor will continue to make those who direct the policies of the states more and more responsive to the opinion of their peoples. Efforts will not be abated to secure greater economy and efficiency in the conduct of public affairs. The trend of constitutional development may be less clear than the fact that changes do constantly occur. But its general direction must be substantially the same as before. This is clear enough when one takes a general view of the constitutional history of the states. If the changes that have occurred in the past have tended on the whole to make for better government in the states, that tendency must persist. The right expedients are those which can stand the test of time. This does not mean that no expedients are right except those which were approved and adopted by the Fathers. It means rather that new reforms, like those of former times, must meet the tests of expediency which the Fathers established. They must strengthen the sovereignty of the people; they must confirm the reign of law.

A PROPOSED MODEL STATE CONSTITUTION.

The problem of constitutional government in the states, now as in the beginning, lies in the discovery of methods of reducing these principles to practice. The judgment to be passed upon a particular proposal for reform must depend in part upon its relationship to the general plan of government. Most contemporary plans for further reform of state government, however, deal only with special cases of imperfection. Specific remedies are suggested for specific evils, regardless of their bearing on the government of the state in other respects. The messages of the governors, for instance, frequently contain suggestions for particular reforms, but plans for the systematic revision of a state constitution are rare, and do not go much beyond a proposal for calling a constitutional convention. Though there have been not a few such conventions in recent years, and some of them have recommended radical changes in governmental organization and procedure, they have quite properly devoted themselves to the redress of notorious grievances rather than to the elaboration of general schemes of reform. The most noteworthy projects during the period preceding the World War, which might fairly be described as general schemes of reform, were those brought forward by the Oregon People's Power League.[1] Since the War, the most comprehensive and deliberate scheme for the reconstruction of state government is that prepared by a Committee on State Government of the National Municipal League and submitted with the approval of the latter organization to the bar of public opinion.[2]

The National Municipal League's model state constitution contains several proposed reforms which seem at first glance to be not only radical innovations but also out of line with the previous trend of constitutional development in the state governments. First among these is the proposal to substitute a legislative body consisting of a single house for the traditional bicameral legislature. Secondly, the members of the legislature are to be elected under a system of proportional representation. Thirdly, there is to be a legislative council, consisting of a few

[1] For a description and discussion of these and other radical reforms proposed at that time, see the first edition of this book, pp. 449-477.

[2] See Appendix C. A Model State Constitution.

legislators elected by and from the whole body under the same system of proportional representation. Fourthly, the governor is to appoint all heads of departments without reference to any legislative body for its advice or consent, and is to have power to remove any of them at his discretion. Fifthly, all other executive and administrative officers are to be appointed under the merit system regardless of political considerations. Sixthly, the governor and the heads of departments are to have seats and a voice in the legislature, but without the privilege of voting therein. Seventhly, the responsibility for the preparation of the budget is to be fixed squarely upon the governor, and the legislature is to be authorized to require his attendance during its discussion. Eighthly, the judiciary are to be consolidated into a general court of justice, the popular election of judges is to be discontinued, and a judicial council is to be organized with power to make rules of pleading, practice, and procedure and to exercise general supervision over the business of the courts. Ninthly, cities and counties are to have wide powers of home rule. Tenthly, the electorate is to have power to adopt amendments to the constitution, to call a constitutional convention, and to enact ordinary laws without reference to the legislature, and also to disapprove and in effect veto measures adopted by the legislature.

Whether or not these proposals are out of line with the trend of state constitutional development may best be judged in the light of the criticisms which have always been brought against the state governments. One of the earliest and most influential of all the critics of state government was Thomas Jefferson. He was one of the earliest because he happened to live in a state which originally possessed one of the most imperfect constitutions and his own hard experience quickly revealed to him the nature of its imperfections. He was one of the most influential because he founded the political party whose principles of government were eventually accepted by the American people as the best principles of state government. In his widely read *Notes on Virginia*, written in 1782, he devoted a chapter to the constitution and government of that state. The constitution, he wrote, "was formed when we were new and unexperienced in the science of government. It was the first, too, which was formed in the whole United States. No wonder," Jefferson was moved to conclude, "that time and trial have discovered very capital defects in it."[1]

The Need for More Democracy in State Government.

The first capital defect Jefferson mentioned was that "the majority of the men of the state, who pay and fight for its support, are unrepresented in the legislature." This defect has been partially remedied in most of the states by the adoption of manhood suffrage. Indeed the recent extension of the franchise to women on the same terms as to men goes beyond anything Jefferson advocated. But the adoption of universal suffrage has not entirely corrected the defect. It may still happen that a majority of the qualified voters are unrepresented by persons of their own choice. This is the consequence of a development which Jefferson and his contemporaries could not, at least did not, foresee, namely, the development of the party system in American politics. If more than two parties take the field, and divide the voters nearly equally among them, a majority of the voters may easily fail to vote for winning candidates, and hence will be represented by persons not of their own choice. If there are only two parties of major importance, the same result may be brought about through the operation of the nominating system. The direct primary has given the partisan two choices instead of one. This, from his standpoint, may be an improvement over any system of election which gives him but a single choice. Nevertheless a sense of injustice is bound to remain as long as any considerable body of voters find themselves unable to secure representation to their liking. This feeling accounts for much of the dissatisfaction with state government which persists despite the democratization of the forms of government since Jefferson's time. Proportional representation with the single transferable vote should give every substantial group of voters a representative of their own choice. It would seem to be, therefore, a reform that is not out of line with the prevailing trend of constitutional development.

A second capital defect of the original Virginia government, according to Jefferson, was that "among those who share the representation, the shares are very unequal." The unit of repre-

[1] *Notes on Virginia*, p. 211; Ford's edition of the *Writings of Thomas Jefferson*, iii, p. 222.

sentation under the Virginia constitution, as in most of the other original states, was the county, and since the counties were very unequal in population the distribution of power in both branches of the legislature was very unequal. Jefferson emphasized the diversity of interests in different sections of the state and denounced the injustice of a system of representation which enabled certain favored interests to obtain a disproportionate share of power. At that time the favored interests were the great planters living on the shores of Chesapeake Bay and below the falls of the rivers. Although they had come to be outnumbered by the small farmers and pioneers living farther back from the coast and over the mountains, they still retained control of the legislature and, through the legislature, of the state government as a whole. Similar conditions existed in most of the other states. Since Jefferson's time the growth of cities and the development of sharp conflicts of interest between city-dwellers and those living closer to the soil has accentuated the difficulties resulting from a system of representation based upon territorial units. Though the methods of apportioning representatives in the state legislatures have been generally improved, there still remain many inequalities, and in several states there is gross discrimination against the inhabitants of cities. In some cases, notably in New York and Illinois, this has caused a rankling feeling of resentment among the people in the great cities which apparently makes the rural population less rather than more disposed to do them justice. Proportional representation would automatically relieve this situation as well as the similar evils resulting from partisan gerrymanders and other unfair legislative apportionments.

A third capital defect of the original Virginia constitution, according to Jefferson, was that "the senate is, by its constitution, too homogeneous with the house of delegates. Being chosen by the same electors, at the same time, and out of the same subjects, the choice falls of course on men of the same description." Jefferson believed this to be thoroughly unsound. "The purpose of establishing different houses of legislation," he declared, "is to introduce the influence of different interests or different principles. Thus in Great Britain it is said their constitution relies on the house of commons for honesty, and the lords for wisdom; which would be a rational reliance, if honesty were to be bought with money, and if wisdom were hereditary. In some of the

American states, the delegates and senators are so chosen, as that the first represent the persons, and the second the property of the state. But with us, wealth and wisdom have equal chance for admission into both houses. We do not, therefore, derive from the separation of our legislature into two houses, those benefits which a proper complication of principles is capable of producing, and those which alone can compensate the evils which may be produced by their dissensions." His own plan for a serviceable legislature, consisting of two houses, provided for the direct election of members of the lower house by the people and for the indirect election of senators by electoral colleges, consisting of electors chosen upon the same franchise as the members of the lower house. Thus he sought to secure special opportunities for wisdom, if not for wealth, in the organization of the government. This was then known as the Maryland plan. But this plan failed to win favor in his own state and despite his recommendation soon fell into discredit. The bicameral legislative system in the form which Jefferson condemned now prevails in all the states. Since the state legislatures have continued to be the least satisfactory parts of the state governments, the bicameral system continues to be the subject of adverse criticism. Proposals to abolish one of the houses certainly cannot be opposed on the authority of Jefferson.

The Need for the Better Distribution of Powers.

A fourth capital defect of the original Virginia constitution, to the discussion of which Jefferson devoted more space than to all the others, was "that all the powers of government, legislative, executive, and judiciary, result to the same legislative body." Such a concentration of power, he contended, "is precisely the definition of despotic government." The defect was the more serious, since the ordinary legislature "may alter the constitution itself" and may also determine "the quorum of their own body which may legislate for us." Thus there were no effective checks upon the power of the legislature, which could push its authority to the length, if it pleased, of establishing a dictatorship. The correct principle, Jefferson argued, was that "the powers of government should be so divided and balanced among several bodies of magistracy, as that no one could transcend their legal limits, without being effectually checked and restrained by the others." The means which Jefferson favored for establishing such a division and balance of powers were incorporated in his draft of a reformed state constitution, which he prepared in 1783 for submission to a proposed constitutional convention.[1] Not all Jefferson's expedients have been adopted. Indeed some of those from which he hoped for the greatest results have met with the least favor. Noteworthy among these were his proposals for an executive council and a council of revision.[2] Nevertheless, the constitutional history of the states from Jefferson's time to the present, as has been demonstrated, is largely a history of the application of the Jeffersonian principles. Not only have the forms of state government been made more democratic, but also there has been such a redistribution of powers as to put substantial checks upon the supremacy of the legislatures.

The principal innovations, contained in the model constitution of the National Municipal League, other than those designed to continue the process of democratizing the forms of state government, clearly fall in line with the tendency towards a more effective distribution of powers. The need for intelligent and energetic legislative leadership, which Jefferson recognized and hoped to satisfy in part through the improvement of the Senate, accounts for the League's proposal of a legislative council. Such a council, while avoiding the evils of an independent second chamber, should strengthen the influence of the most capable and experienced members of the legislature. The need for greater freedom on the part of the executive in the appointment of the principal administrative officers, and for greater protection against the abuse of the appointing power for political purposes in making minor appointments, which Jefferson recognized and hoped to satisfy in part by the establishment of an executive council, has been met in a different way by the framers of the League's model constitution. Their proposal is to give the governor an entirely free hand in the choice of the heads of departments, in other words, to permit him to choose his own executive council, but to take other appointments entirely out of politics through the extension of the "merit system" to all subordinate officers. The need for a stronger executive in order to make the general welfare of the state prevail over the local and special

[1] See Jefferson's Proposed Constitution for Virginia; *post*, Appendix B.
[2] See Appendix B.

interests represented in the legislature, which Jefferson recognized and hoped to satisfy in part through the creation of the council of revision, is reflected in the League plan for giving the governor and his department heads seats on the floor of the legislature with the right to speak but not to vote, together with a special responsibility for the preparation and explanation of the budget. The need for dissolving the legislative monopoly of the power to amend or revise the state constitution, which Jefferson recognized and hoped to satisfy by an ingenious, though hitherto untried, expedient,[1] is covered in the League's model constitution by the modern device of direct action by the voters.

The proposals relating to the judiciary and to local government may seem to be less directly connected with a general scheme for the more effective distribution of powers. Yet they clearly lie in the regular course of constitutional development.

The principal changes in the judicial system, proposed in the model state constitution, are in the organization of the courts. These changes, especially the consolidation of the courts and the creation of judicial councils, would remove many of the causes of legislative intervention in the administration of justice, and to that extent would make the judiciary more independent of the legislatures. They would clear the way for many improvements in the judicial system by introducing into that branch of administration the same principles of administrative organization which have proved their worth in the executive branch of state government. The trend toward such a reorganization of the judicial systems of the states is evident in all sections of the country. A judicial council, such as the model constitution proposes, was established in Massachusetts on recommendation of the judicature commission of that state in 1921, and similar councils were created in Ohio and Oregon in 1923. In Louisiana by the new constitution of 1921 a significant step was taken towards such a consolidation of the courts as is proposed by giving the supreme court important supervisory powers over the local courts and the state attorney-general greater authority over local prosecutors. The movement for a better integrated and more efficient judicial organization has in fact been going on for a long time, and would doubtless proceed more rapidly but for the difficulty of adjusting the necessary changes to the fundamental require-

[1] See Appendix B.

ment that the redistribution of powers between legislatures and courts shall not result in any ultimate impairment of popular control over the judicial process.

A similar situation exists with respect to the readjustment of the relations between the state legislatures and the local governments in county and city, especially in the larger cities. Municipal home-rule is one phase of the general process of limiting the excessive power of the legislatures and extending that of the electorates and protecting the rights of the people in the several localities to manage their own local affairs in their own way. But, as Professor McBain has clearly shown, this phase of the process is an intricate one, since the right of the people in the several localities of a state to manage their own affairs must be reconciled with the right of the people of the whole state to manage their affairs also. This cannot be satisfactorily accomplished merely by granting an unlimited measure of home-rule to any portion of the people. The adjustment of the relations between central and local authorities is one of the most important subjects in the whole field of state government. It is too big a subject to be disposed of incidentally in connection with a discussion of the reorganization of the central government of the states. It will suffice to say here that, though the growth of cities has gone far beyond anything foreseen by the framers of the original state constitutions, the measure of home-rule that should be extended to cities must be determined in accordance with the fundamental principles of popular sovereignty and the reign of law.

CRITICISM OF MODEL STATE CONSTITUTION

The framers of the National Municipal League's model state constitution would doubtless be the last to claim for their proposals anything more than such merit as belongs to a project which seeks to meet the needs of the present in the light of the experience of the past. Radical though the innovations may seem to be, which the League's proposals would require in state government, they are not unprecedented, and, all in all, form a project which is in thorough harmony with the historical trend of American constitutional development. Such a project may appear to have little chance of adoption, but, unless the existing state governments are to be pronounced beyond improvement, it is entitled to unprejudiced consideration. In the field of state constitutional reform the authority of Jefferson has never been surpassed, yet several of his most cherished proposals were not merely rejected by his contemporaries but consigned to all but utter oblivion. Certainly no modern reformer can expect a better fate. If, however, the proposals of the National Municipal League should be ignored by the politicians of the present day, they would still have a value, like Jefferson's model constitution of 1783, as evidence not only of the imperfections in the contemporary state governments but also of the current of thought among contemporary political reformers. If they are not adopted, reforms of a similar character probably will be adopted, unless the whole course of change, economic and social, as well as political, should turn in some new and unforeseen direction. The grounds upon which they are brought forward, therefore, as well as the objections that may be brought against them, deserve more careful examination.

The Unicameral Legislature.

The case for unicameral legislatures in the states may be briefly summarized. First, the abolition of one of the legislative houses would save money. Secondly, it would make for greater efficiency in the process of law-making. For instance, there would no longer be two sets of committees duplicating one another's work. Some states have already recognized the inefficiency of the dual committee system and made provision for joint legislative committees for the consideration of proposed legislation. But if joint committees are an improvement over the system of separate committees, why not joint sessions of the two houses, advocates of the unicameral legislature inquire, or better still, a single house? Thirdly, the abolition of one of the houses would put an end to the shifty practices by which each house may evade its proper responsibility for legislative action and would make the whole legislative process cleaner and freer from suspicion. Whatever advantages may once have been derived from the division of the legislature into two branches, capable of checking one another and thereby preventing hasty and ill-considered legislation, have become relatively unimportant since the adoption of more effective executive, judicial and popular checks upon legislative action than formerly existed. In short, the strengthening of the external checks upon the abuse of legislative power has made it possible to introduce a much simpler form of internal organization for the state legislatures than was originally deemed safe.

These arguments in favor of greater legislative economy, efficiency, and integrity have already brought about the downfall of the bicameral system in the government of cities. Separate boards of aldermen and common councils have largely given way to city councils, consisting of a single chamber. There is no sentiment in cities, which have made the change, in favor of a return to the former system. In truth, the bicameral system is largely an historical accident. It is as easy to justify separate representation for three or four special interests as for two, and in Europe the history of representative government affords more than one example of multicameral legislative bodies. If a bicameral legislature is a more convenient institution than one consisting of three or four houses, a unicameral legislature has a similar advantage over one consisting of two houses. But American political ideas, when not indigenous, were derived mainly from British sources, and in Great Britain the bicameral system seemed strongly established at the time of the American Revolution. Now that the House of Commons has acquired an all but complete monopoly of legislative power, the British tradition loses its earlier significance for Americans. Conservative British politicians continue to urge the reform of the House of Lords in order that it may be equipped to play a more vigorous part in the government of the realm, but the ablest constitutional reformers, like the late Lord Bryce, have been unable to suggest any scheme that could command the support of any influential section of the people. In the United States the bicameral system is established at Washington as part of a constitutional arrangement which puts the abolition of either Senate or House of Representatives beyond the bounds of practical politics. But in the individual states there is no similar barrier to the acceptance of the teachings of experience. The chief obstacle to the introduction of the unicameral system is the difficulty of securing agreement upon the particular type of legislature that is to be established. Is it the state senates that should be abolished, or the larger and less exclusive lower houses And if either is to be dispensed with, how should the other be chosen?

Proportional Representation.

What should be the proper size of a state legislature is a question to which the model state constitution offers no definite answer. It should be big enough, if possible, to give every substantial interest the opportunity of representation; but not so big as to render debate excessively formal and difficult. In general it is probably true that the bigger the district in which a representative is chosen, the bigger the representative tends to be; but also the less direct and intimate is his contact with the people of his district. These considerations, however, lose much of their force, if the representatives are chosen, as the model constitution proposes, by a system of proportional representation.

The advantages of proportional representation have been urged by numerous writers, from the time John Stuart Mill first gave them wide currency in his influential *Considerations on Representative Government* (1861) to the recent works on the subject by John H. Humphreys and by Hoag and Hallett.[1] It will not be necessary, they believe, to rely greatly upon the external checks for protection against legislative abuses, when the legislature itself is properly constituted. Under a representative system based on proportional representation, the legislature should represent the whole body of voters, not, as at present, that fraction which has been so fortunate as to cast their ballots for the successful candidates in the several representative districts. Thus each considerable group, holding like opinions, would secure a representative of its own, regardless of geographical distribution. Each representative, moreover, should be the best man available for selection by the group whose predominant opinions he shares. There should be no colorless, not to say unprincipled, compromise candidates, now so much in demand in doubtful districts; there would be no narrow restriction of candidacies by artificial residence requirements; there would be the promise of long-continued service for honorable and capable men. A legislature, so chosen and containing such a body of members, should produce legislation more acceptable to the people and technically more nearly perfect than that produced by the existing state legislatures. Since any group of voters would be free

[1] John H. Humphreys, *Proportional Representation* (London, 1911); C. G. Hoag and G. H. Hallett, *Proportional Representation* (New York, 1926).

to select their own candidates and any citizen would be free to appeal to his followers in all parts of the state, or at least in comparatively large districts, for support, there would be no need for elaborate systems of nomination, and therefore little likelihood of undue influence by any "invisible government." The artificial combination of the bulk of the voters into two major parties should give way to more numerous and more natural groupings, and party government should give way to popular government.

Partisanship in State Politics.

Before accepting the claims of the advocates of proportional representation, there are two queries to be considered. First, what is the justification of the existing bipartisan system in state politics? That is, what are the reasons for opposing such a splitting up of the major parties into minor groups as would result from the introduction of proportional representation, according to its advocates?

The case in favor of bipartisan politics in general has been strongly put by a writer who is himself an influential partisan politician,[1] Mr. J. Ramsay MacDonald, lately Prime Minister of Great Britain. Democracy, MacDonald argues, means voting for a general policy, not merely for an individual representative. This view may be illustrated by a case of a Prohibitionist, elected to membership in some representative body. He would have not merely to vote for temperance measures but to support or oppose all the measures of the administration or party in power. But in accordance with the theory of proportional representation, only on temperance is he a representative. Therefore proportional representation would weaken the representative character of legislation. The fundamental error of proportional representation, MacDonald concludes, lies in regarding the representative body merely as a mirror of opinion, whilst it is in fact the active will of the community it represents. "Thus a system of proportional representation will exaggerate rather than remove those dangers which arise from the fact that governments may not be really representative. It is a method of election for securing the representation of fragments of political thought and de-

[1] See J. R. MacDonald, *Socialism and Government*, published by the Independent Labour Party, London, 1909.

sire, and for inviting those fragments to coalesce after and not before elections. . . . It is rather in accordance with the requirements of popular rule that a government should be supported by such a majority as makes it absolutely responsible for its actions, rather than that it should have to effect compromises and coalitions which do not reflect popular wishes or arise from popular demands." [1]

"Democracy without a party would be a crowd without a purpose. Each person would follow the enticements of his own personal interests or his own personal will. . . . The people as a political agency have to develop a capacity to express their own will and to discover a method of carrying out their will. Party alone in some shape or form enables both these things to be done. . . . When political issues are pretty clear two parties are evidently enough. . . . A party is an organization of groups which find in it on the whole a better companionship than in any other combination, and a greater effectiveness than they would have were they not in the combination. . . . Under the party system new ideas easily permeate the active mass of party adherents. The party having to keep in touch with the whole of the nation is far more responsive to changes in popular outlook than is the group which only appeals to a special class or body of opinion. . . . Some . . . support the group system on the ground that it makes for the liberty of the electors. But this is a mistake. A majority must be found if responsible government is to exist, and no group can be inside that majority one day and outside it the next day. . . . On the whole it seems to me far better that the absorption of groups should take place outside Parliament than that they should combine inside. . . . Two parties will thus be formed, each with its center of gravity determined not by the bargaining of parliamentary managers and the barter of parliamentary office, but by public opinion. And so I return to the argument I advanced in a previous chapter: a group system of government is not so democratic as a party system because the latter to a greater extent than the former gives the electors a direct voice in saying what is to be the character of their government." [2]

This argument against proportional representation has been recently restated by another notable English writer, Mr. Harold

[1] MacDonald, *op. cit.*, i, pp. 164-167. [2] *Op. cit.*, ii, pp. 13-19.

J. Laski.[1] "On practically every issue in the modern state," he writes, "the serried millions of voters cannot do more than accept or reject the solutions offered. The stage is too vast to permit of the nice shades of quantitative distinction impressing themselves upon the public mind. It has rarely the leisure, and seldom the information, to do more than indicate the general tendency of its will. It is in the process of law-making that the subtler adjustments must be made. If this is true, it follows that a political system is the more satisfactory, the more it is able to express itself through the antithesis of two great parties. Each may contain a certain variety of opinion. Both may fail to attract in their ranks much more than that active minority which is willing to devote itself to political affairs. But the superiority of a two-party system over a multiplicity of groups is above all in this, that it is the only method by which the people can at the electoral period directly choose its government. . . . The group-system always means that no government can be formed until after the people have chosen the legislative assembly."[2] Thus Laski, like MacDonald, rejects proportional representation, despite its greater responsiveness to the variety of opinion among the electorate, because it tends to break up the major parties and to destroy the bipartisan system of politics.

The force of this general argument against proportional representation evidently varies according to circumstances. It is clearly greatest in the instance which both MacDonald and Laski had particularly in mind when they wrote, that of the British Parliament. In British politics the bipartisan system is highly serviceable, because the House of Commons is much more than a representative body for the consideration of proposed legislation. It is also an electoral college for the choice of the prime minister of the realm. The same circumstances which have made the presidential electors in the United States the passive instruments of the major parties in the choice of the chief executive tend to impose a similar rôle upon the British House of Commons. But in the United States the voters make an independent choice of presidential electors. They are ordinarily free to choose their representative in the Congress regardless of their preference

[1] See Harold J. Laski, *A Grammar of Politics* (New Haven, 1925), pp. 311-318.

[2] Laski, *op. cit.*, p. 314.

among candidates for the presidency. Hence the arguments advanced by MacDonald and Laski do not have the same force, when directed particularly against a proposal to adopt some system of proportional representation in the election of members of the popular branch of the American Congress. Moreover, neither the President nor the Senate is so dependent upon a partisan majority in the lower house as the British Cabinet is upon their partisans in the House of Commons. The will of the American people, as the writer has shown elsewhere,[1] so far as their preference between party programs is concerned, is as well, if not better, represented by the President than by his party associates in Congress.

The argument has the least force when applied to the problem of representative government in cities. The connection between national and municipal issues is remote, and the organization of the voters for the selection of municipal officers into two permanent groups upon the same lines as in national politics is not justifiable upon the particular grounds advanced by MacDonald and Laski. Their arguments can only justify the organization of two special municipal parties upon local issues. The maintenance of national party lines in local politics is commonly justified in the United States on different grounds. Thus the late Senator Platt, the "easy boss," is reported to have said: "For the doctrine of non-partisanship in local elections I had the sincerest and the profoundest contempt. I used to be amused at the that-settles-it air with which the question would be plumped at me: 'What has a man's views of the tariff to do with his capacity to give the people of New York City an honest and businesslike administration?'—as though my agreement that they had nothing to do with that matter involved a concession to the principle of local non-partisanship. It has everything to do with a man's ability to administer government, anywhere in the North or West, whether the influences about him are Republican or Democratic; and so strong is the predisposition of the American people in favor of a party as a political agent, and so strong is their prejudice against a multiplicity of parties, and so similar are the problems of administration, no matter what the political division to which they relate, that it is idle to attempt to create

[1] See A. N. Holcombe, *The Political Parties of To-Day* (New York, 2d ed., 1925), chap. xii.

municipal parties or factions. The success of such an attempt would have a demoralizing effect on party organization."[1] The growing success of non-partisanship in municipal government, however, has demonstrated the weakness of this old-fashioned argument. The recent experience of the cities indicates the value in local elections of any electoral system, whether "non-partisan" primaries, preferential voting, or proportional representation, which will discourage the maintenance of the same party divisions in both national and local affairs.

Now state government in the United States is a form of local government. In the state legislatures, as has been shown, national party lines are of secondary importance, especially since the election of United States senators has been transferred from the legislatures to the voters themselves. The majority party organizes the legislature, appropriates for its own members the speakership, the committee chairmanships, and the majority of the places on committees, and makes a partisan distribution of the legislative patronage. Thereafter little attempt is made, except in a few close states, to operate the machinery of legislation on a partisan basis, and members rarely vote on party lines. The party caucus ordinarily has nothing to do after the selection of the candidate for the speakership. It is the "organization" or the governor to whom members look for leadership. Neither of these relies for support exclusively upon the party majority, but accepts assistance wherever it can be found. It is only in the distribution of the patronage that partisanship upon national lines is the rule in state government. If state politics were separated from state administration by the removal from the ballot of non-political offices and by the general introduction of the "merit system," one of the principal difficulties standing in the way of state non-partisanship would be overcome. Non-partisanship in state and municipal elections does not mean the absence of partisanship. It means merely the repudiation of national party affiliations as the basis of action in state and municipal politics. Doubtless it would be more difficult to organize special parties upon state issues than it is to organize special parties upon municipal issues. For that reason the recognition of national political associations and the protection of the integrity

[1] *The Autobiography of Thomas Collier Platt*, compiled and edited by Louis J. Lang (New York, 1910), pp. 358-359.

of the major parties may be more suitable measures in the states than in the cities for making representative government responsible to the majority of the voters, but they are certainly less suitable than in the government of the nation. One of the chief arguments for proportional representation in municipal politics must be its tendency to release the voter from his bondage to the national parties. Likewise, though doubtless in lesser degree, proportional representation might be expected to give the voters a new freedom in state politics.

Group Action in State Politics.

The second query which must be considered before the claims of the advocates of proportional representation can be accepted is this. What is it that in actual practice under American conditions will be proportionally represented?

The advocates of proportional representation often appear to assume that it is groups of voters, united for the purpose of promoting the public interest upon some particular principle in which they are all agreed, which will be proportionally represented. Now, as Graham Wallas has so convincingly shown, "the origin of any particular party may be due to a deliberate intellectual process. . . . But when a party has once come into existence, its fortunes depend upon the facts of human nature of which deliberate thought is only one."[1] When the highly artificial major parties are broken up, as the advocates of proportional representation claim they will be, into smaller and more natural groups of voters, it is by no means certain that the lines of subdivision will be rational, that is, that "principles" will be the basis of union between the members of such groups. In Ashtabula, we are told, as a result of the first employment of proportional representation, "all sections and factions are represented in the new council." Though the seven councilors were elected in the city at large, regardless of the former division into four wards, "there were two from the first ward, one from the second, two from the third, and two from the fourth. . . . The 'drys' and the 'wets' are represented. The Protestants and Catholics; the business, professional, and laboring men; the Republicans, Democrats, and Socialists; the English, Swedes, and

[1] *Human Nature in Politics* (London, 1908), pp. 82-83.

Italians are all represented."[1] Now this was probably, as claimed by the advocates of proportional representation, the most representative body in the history of the city. But much besides "principles" was represented. Local, religious, partisan, social, and racial ties were likewise represented. Similar results were reported when proportional representation was subsequently tried on a larger scale in Cleveland and Cincinnati. To what extent, under such a system, voters will unite in the choice of representatives as a result of rational intellectual processes and to what extent as a result of impulses and instincts of which they may not be consciously aware, can be determined only by experience. Impulse and instinct, however, are not excluded from politics under the existing bipartisan system of representation. Moreover, the practice of electing men to represent particular localities in city councils because they are Republicans or Democrats in national politics, fails to insure that such representatives will actually represent their constituents on any local question. The defects of the existing representative system are serious, especially in populous urban localities, and the advantages claimed for proportional representation are substantial and important. The proposal is at least promising enough to merit further trial, not only in municipal elections but also in those of some of the states.

Executive Leadership.

Final judgment upon the proposals for the reorganization of the state legislature, which are contained in the model state constitution, must await further consideration of the proposals for the reorganization of the executive branch of state government and for the readjustment of the relations between executive and legislature. In the proposal for creating an executive cabinet, by giving the governor the power to appoint the heads of the principal departments, in that for establishing closer relations between executive and legislature, by giving the governor and his cabinet a voice in the legislature, and in that for developing more effective leadership in the latter body, by organizing a legislative council, there is much that suggests the British parliamentary system. Instead of the rigid separation of legislative and executive branches, practiced both at Washington and

[1] *Proportional Representation Review*, 3d series, no. 37, pp. 19-24.

in the state capitals, there would be a close association of executive and legislature. But it would be an association designed to bring only the political activities of the two into a closer relationship. The separation of administration from politics, if the "merit system" were established in the administrative activities of the state governments as proposed in the model constitution, would be more effectually secured than under the present system of separation of powers.

The Cabinet System.

The proposal to introduce certain features of the British cabinet system into the United States is not new. The founders of the Southern Confederacy were familiar with the defects of the traditional American practice, and when they came to adopt a constitution for the Confederate States they took advantage of the opportunity to make some changes in the established relations between executive and legislature. Reference has already been made to the increase of executive control over appropriations authorized in the Confederate Constitution. In addition, it was provided that "Congress may by law grant to the principal officer in each of the executive departments a seat upon the floor of either House, with the privilege of discussing any measure appertaining to his department." [1] A committee of the United States Senate in 1881 recommended a further step in the establishment of closer relations between executive and legislature.[2] It proposed that the members of the President's cabinet not only should have the right to participate in debates in either house of Congress, but also should be under the obligation to answer questions which might be put to them by members of Congress. This sounds much like the plan proposed in the model state constitution. But there are two important differences. First, the proposals of the Senate Committee of 1881 applied only to members of the president's cabinet, whilst those of the National Municipal League apply to the chief executive as well as to the members of his cabinet. Secondly, the Senate Committee further proposed that, immediately after the answer to the question should be made by the cabinet officer to whom it might be directed, and without any debate, there

[1] Art. i, sect. 6, par. 2.

[2] See Senate Report, no. 837, 46th Congress, 3d Session, Feb. 4, 1881.

should be a vote on the resolution upon which the question was based. Thus the proposal of the Senate Committee, if adopted, would have established a practice much more like that existing in the French parliament, known as the interpellation, than the English practice of questioning, proposed in the model state constitution.

The readjustment of the relations between the executive and the legislature, proposed by the framers of the Confederate Constitution, was never tried under normal conditions, and that proposed by the United States Senate Committee of 1881 has never been tried at all. But there has been much discussion of these proposals, especially the latter, by writers upon American politics. Woodrow Wilson's brilliant essay on *Congressional Government*, for example, was designed as a plea for closer relations between the two coördinate branches along the lines suggested by the Senate Committee. Among later writers who have looked with favor on these proposals, the general tendency has been to assume that their adoption would mean the introduction of some form of the British cabinet system. Thus Ford in his book, *The Rise and Growth of American Politics*,[1] bestows high praise on the Senate Committee report, and predicts that the ultimate type of government in the United States will be one in which "the actual management of affairs will naturally tend to pass into the hands of groups of statesmen trained to their work by gradations of public service, their fitness attested by success in coping with their responsibilities under the direct and continuous scrutiny and criticism of Congress. The presidency will tend to assume an honorary and a ceremonial character, and will find therein its most satisfactory conditions of dignity and usefulness."[2] And Kales, in his book, *Unpopular Government in the United States*, dealing particularly with state government, expresses more bluntly a similar conviction. Speaking of the time when the cabinet system is established in the form he advocates, he declares that "the method of selecting the single executive, whose principal function it is to place the executive power from time to time in the control of a proper council of state, selected from among the leaders of the majority of the

[1] See H. J. Ford, *op. cit.* (New York, 1898), pt. iv., "Tendencies and Prospects of American Politics."
[2] *Op. cit.*, p. 369.

legislature, is not very important."[1] The plans advanced by these writers for the introduction of the cabinet system, when examined closely, seem to contemplate the adoption of the form of the system existing in France, with its dignified but relatively unimportant president and its active ministry, responsible mainly to Parliament.

A little reflection will show that the proposal to introduce either the French or the British cabinet system into the government of the states runs counter to the whole course of their constitutional development. The constitutional history of the states is a history of the growth of limitations upon the authority of the legislatures and of the expansion of that of the executive. The governor in particular has gradually become the special object of popular confidence, and has been endowed with more important legislative powers than are vested in any other single officer. Now the introduction of the cabinet system in either the English or the French form means that the chief of the cabinet will not be the governor, elected by the people, but a member of the legislature, chosen by the majority of that body. It means therefore the enhancement of the authority of the legislature and the decline of that of the nominal chief executive. The latter indeed would be deprived of his leadership in state politics. Popular election of the governor, as Kales intimates, would no longer be worth while. Such a redistribution of powers between the legislature and the executive would be a reversal of the process that has been going on since the system of legislative supremacy was first questioned in the original states. It would cause the destruction of the existing balance between the departments of government. It has already been pointed out that there is no present need for the abandonment of the principle of the separation of powers in state government. What is needed is a more rational application of the principle. That means, more than anything else, the further strengthening of the executive branch of state government along the lines that have been pursued in the past, subject to an effective popular control.

Other advocates of the establishment of closer relations between executive and legislature contemplate the introduction of

[1] A. M. Kales, *Unpopular Government in the United States* (Chicago, 1914), p. 170. Cf., for an exposition of Kales' general plan of reform, chs. 14-16.

the cabinet system in a different form. Bradford, for example, in his book, *The Lesson of Popular Government*,[1] denied that the cabinet system, which he proposed for adoption, was an imitation of either the British or French system. He argued that the President's or governor's cabinet, though entitled to seats and a voice in the legislative branch, would not become responsible to the legislature, but remain responsible to the chief executive. Under the German imperial system, he pointed out, the chancellor and his associates were not responsible to the reichstag, though privileged to speak and obliged to answer questions in that body. They remained responsible to the emperor. In the United States, especially in the separate states, where the chief executive is elected by the people and can be called to account by them at comparatively frequent intervals, he believed that the introduction of the cabinet system, if no other changes were made in the organization and powers of the executive, would increase its authority instead of diminishing it. The results of the system would be greater publicity for legislative proceedings, greater opportunity for leadership, and more definite responsibility, not to the legislature, but to the people, on the part of the chief executive. Thus the introduction of the cabinet system was advocated on the ground that it would be thoroughly in harmony with the tendency in American politics to strengthen the chief executive in his relations with the legislature and to enhance his political authority as the special representative of the whole people.

The New York Plan.

It was this view of the situation which doubtless determined the New York constitutional convention of 1915 to adopt the plan submitted in that year to the people of New York.[2] Though rejected at the polls, the plan was not abandoned by its friends, and, after the War, Governor Smith, who had been a member of the convention, did much to revive public interest in its essential features. The Hughes commission of 1925-26 brought the plan forward again, developing its underlying principles more

[1] Gamaliel Bradford, *The Lesson of Popular Government* (New York, 1899), chs. 30-32. See also Chester H. Rowell's articles in *The World's Work*, December, 1924, and January, 1925.

[2] See the first edition of this book, pp. 473-476.

boldly and consistently than before. Important features of this plan have already been noted in connection with the discussion of the executive budget and state administrative reorganization. Particularly noteworthy in the present connection are the proposals for the creation of a limited number of departments, especially one to be known as the executive department—an innovation in state administrative reorganization—consisting of five divisions, that of the budget, of military and naval affairs, of standards and purchases, of inter-departmental relations, and of the state police, and for the establishment of closer relations between the executive and legislative branches of the government. The proposed executive department, which was to be placed in charge of the governor's chief secretary, taken together with the general consolidation of administrative agencies, was designed to give the governor the means of organizing a genuinely serviceable cabinet and becoming in fact as well as in name the chief executive of the state. The proposed budget amendment was designed to give the governor and his cabinet a voice in the legislature during the consideration of the budget, and at the same time give the legislature an opportunity to question cabinet members on financial matters not adequately covered by their budget statements.[1] The general purpose of the proposals was to strengthen the governor in the administration of public affairs and simultaneously to increase the power of the legislature to call the executive publicly to account. The New York plan has been described as an attempt to establish the cabinet system in American state government, but the development of the cabinet is clearly subordinate to the development of the gubernatorial office itself.

It would be a mistake to conclude that the New York plan is an attempt to introduce the British or French cabinet system into the United States. The direct election of the governor by the people and his resulting independence of the legislature are calculated to make him a more powerful, and also, from the viewpoint of the people, a more responsible political leader than the British prime minister. On the other hand, the executive veto makes the legislature less powerful, even within its restricted constitutional sphere, than the British House of Commons. The governor, to be sure, cannot hold the threat of dissolution over

[1] See Appendix F.

the legislature, as a prime minister can under the parliamentary system, but on the other hand, the legislature can remove the governor only by the difficult process of impeachment. The conditions under which the cabinet engrosses most of the executive powers in the British and French systems would not exist in the system proposed by the Hughes commission in New York. The British cabinet system is a system of undistributed powers, for those which the Parliament confers upon a ministry it can also take away. The cabinet is but a committee of Parliament. The New York plan contemplates a real distribution of powers, that cannot be altered except by the process of constitutional amendment, a process not wholly controlled by the legislature. Thus the New York plan resembles the former German rather than the French cabinet system, but it is not identical with either. The German was an irresponsible cabinet system, but the New York plan, if adopted, will leave the governor and his cabinet completely responsible to the people. It is really a logical development of the traditional American theory of government, a redistribution of powers on lines calculated to give more adequate recognition to the expert administrator and greater opportunity to the governor for political leadership than has hitherto been possible in any American state. It may better be described as a plan for the further development of the American principle of the separation of powers than as a plan for the introduction of the English cabinet system.

The fundamental differences between an independent cabinet system, like that proposed by the framers of the model state constitution and by the Hughes commission in New York, and the dependent cabinet system as developed in England, point towards different conclusions concerning the organization of the legislature and the party system. The report of the Hughes commission necessarily avoided the problem of legislative reorganization, but the framers of the model state constitution were not so restricted by the circumstances of their enterprise. They recognized that the strong independent executive, which they proposed, would have less need of the support afforded by highly organized political parties than the weaker governors under existing state constitutions. They could therefore view the subdivision of parties, which might be expected to follow the introduction of proportional representation, without concern. They made no provision for the regulation of nominations, evidently believing that legislative nominations would take care of themselves under the system of proportional representation which they advocated. Gubernatorial nominations might be made as at present in the party primaries, but the logic of the general plan contained in the model state constitution points toward open rather than closed primaries or toward a system of nonpartisan primaries such as has been established in many cities. This would mean less reliance upon the organizations of the national parties in state politics, and greater opportunity for political groupings responding more directly to state needs. There is little ground for believing that state and national politics can be divorced under present political conditions in the United States, but every measure which tends to separate them is a step toward a greater freedom and a more commanding authority for the peoples of the states.

The Proposed Legislative Council.

A more speculative feature of the model state constitution is the proposal for a legislative council. This body is designed to embrace the leaders of the legislature and to supply it with a continuous initiative in the development of legislative policy. It would supervise the collection of material for the guidance of the lawmakers, prepare the programs for the legislative sessions, and draft the measures necessary for carrying the programs into effect. The governor, though a member of the council, would not have the same authority there as in his own cabinet. The control would lie with the legislative members. Nothing perhaps shows more clearly the purpose of the framers of the model state constitution to propose a plan which should be in thorough harmony with the historical development of state government than this suggestion for a legislative council. There is no more convincing evidence of their desire to maintain a form of government characterized by a genuine separation of powers. Yet as long as the governor can pose as the chosen leader of the majority of the people and can support his pretensions by the use of an effective veto power, he has the means of asserting a more vigorous leadership than any group of councillors chosen by the legislature. The actual distribution of power between them will depend more upon the character of individuals than upon the kind of relationship formally prescribed in the constitution. But the scheme has at least the merit that it tends to bring the leadership of the legislature out of the murky recesses of committee rooms into the clear light of day.

Proposals for Direct Legislation.

The most dubious provisions of the model state constitution are those relating to direct legislation by the electorate. The procedure which is proposed for the reference of legislative enactments to the voters for their approval or disapproval, and for the submission to the voters of measures which the legislature has refused to enact, is based upon the practice of those Western states which have employed the process in its simplest and most direct form. Little attempt has been made to introduce the safeguards which experience has shown to be desirable to protect the public against hasty and ill-considered action by the electorate. A distinction is made between statutory and constitutional enactments, and the framers of the plan evidently intended that the adoption of the latter should be less easy than that of the former. But there is no such careful discrimination between the two processes as, for instance, under the Massachusetts plan for direct legislation, adopted in 1918, and no attempt is made to limit the constitutional initiative by excluding any classes of measures, such as those relating to religion, from its operation. Presumably the statutory initiative would be subject to the constitutional limitations which apply to the law-making power of the legislature, but in the absence of any effective distinction between the statutory and constitutional initiative these limitations lose much of their importance. Experience does not show good cause for vesting such extraordinary powers in the electorate. The Massachusetts plan is certainly more consistent with the fundamental principles of state government.

Within proper limits the procedure for direct legislation by the electorate is of unquestionable value, but those limits are narrower than was recognized by the pre-War Radicals. The Oregon People's Power League, whose agitation contributed so much to the spread of the initiative, referendum, and recall during the decade ending in 1915, cherished greater expectations from direct popular control of the legislative process than from the time-honored principle of separation of powers and the established system of checks and balances. But the experience of their own state, where their theories received the fairest trial, failed to furnish more than a partial support for their faith. The direct popular veto, if we may take the most conservative form of direct legislation by itself, cannot afford as much protection against legislative errors as the executive and judicial vetoes. In the first dozen years following the adoption of the initiative and referendum in Oregon six measures which had been enacted by the legislature and approved by the governor were vetoed by the Oregon electorate. During the same period eighteen measures were vetoed by the Oregon supreme court, and two hundred or more by the governor. The inference that the executive and judicial review of legislation will defeat more unwise laws than the popular review by the electorate is confirmed by the experience of the years since 1915. In Oregon, moreover, the courts have exercised the judicial veto with great caution, and the executive veto exists in by no means its most effective form. In states like California where the courts exercise their political powers more boldly and where the executive veto is more highly developed than in Oregon, the disproportion between the results of the executive and judicial vetoes and of the popular veto is greater than in Oregon. It is not so easy to compare the results of the direct popular initiative with those of executive leadership in the enactment of measures, but the evidence, such as it is, suggests that the state governors of merely average energy and enterprise have an immense advantage over the improvised and unofficial leadership for which the way is cleared by the direct popular initiative. In short, the actual workings of direct legislation by the electorates indicate the superiority of the carefully defined procedure adopted in Massachusetts over the more radical form of the system embodied in the model state constitution.

The framers of the model constitution introduced one innovation in connection with their proposed system of direct legislation which seems worthy of special notice. They provide that any bill, failing of passage by the legislature, may be submitted to a referendum by order of the governor, if at least one-third of all the members favored the bill while it was under consideration in the legislature, and also that any bill, which, having passed the legislature, is returned by the governor with objections and upon reconsideration is not approved by two-thirds of the members but is approved by a majority of them, may be referred by the legislature to the electorate. Thus it would be possible for deadlocks between the governor and the legislature to be broken by the electorate.

Such a procedure might well be of great value in certain cases, but in general too great store ought not to be set on the possibilities of direct action by the voters. As Walter Lippmann has convincingly argued in his books on *Public Opinion* and *The Phantom Public,* the electorate cannot do much more than align itself for or against the concrete proposals which are submitted to it by its leaders, official or unofficial. It cannot formulate an opinion of its own. "Somebody," Lippmann finely says, "must challenge arbitrary power first. The public can only come to his assistance." But the public, or the electorate, to speak more precisely, is not, when in action, a fixed body of individuals. It is merely those voters who are interested in an affair and care enough about it to support or oppose the principal actors. Students of government may recognize the compelling logic of Lippmann's analysis of the function of the public in politics without accepting unqualifiedly his enumeration of the objective tests for determining the scope of action by the public.[1] Lippmann indeed was not thinking particularly of the special case where the electorate deals directly with legislative measures. He was thinking rather of the ordinary situation in which voters have to choose between candidates for office. But surely Lippmann is close to the truth when he declares in effect that the voters act only by aligning themselves as the partisans of some one in a position of leadership, that they intervene from the outside upon the work of insiders, and that their judgment must rest on a small sample of the facts at issue. "It is the task of the political scientists," he concludes, "to devise the methods of sampling and to define the criteria of judgment. It is the task of civic education in a democracy to train the public in the use of these methods. It is the task of those who build institutions to take them into account."[2] Whatever may be thought of certain features of the model constitution's scheme of direct legislation by the electorate, the proposals for the settlement of deadlocks between legislature and executive seem to be founded

[1] See *The Phantom Public* (New York, 1925), p. 108.
[2] *Op. cit.*, p. 145.

on sound principles. Where the terms of office of legislators and executives are comparatively short, this process might not be of much practical value, but if the terms were lengthened, as well they might be in many states, it should prove highly serviceable.

Conclusion.

It is not necessary to discuss all the provisions of the model constitution in detail. A brief consideration of the main outlines of the scheme reveals its general character and demonstrates its consistency with the fundamental principles of state government in the United States. But the student of state government will have studied the workings of our institutions in vain, if he does not discover that the American political genius lies, not so much in its ability to grasp general principles, as in the capacity to take infinite pains in the practical solution of specific problems. It is doubtless important to organize the state legislatures in the best way that political theory can suggest, but it is more important that the existing legislatures should adopt the best forms of legislative procedure. More is to be gained by the careful comparison of legislative methods in the various states than by the contemplation of theoretical models. More is to be gained by the close scrutiny of budgetary practices than by speculation upon the principle of the separation of powers. The framing of the model constitution will be amply justified, if attention is thereby directed to the problems of contemporary practice which most require the thoughtful consideration of public-spirited citizens, and if their thinking is thereby turned into the channels most likely to lead to better government.

SUMMARY

The soundness of the original principles of state government, as understood by the Jeffersonian Republicans, has been demonstrated by the experience of more than a century. Popular control of the constitutions and governments of the states is now more firmly established, the distribution of powers is universally more effective, than in the beginning. Both the democratization of the forms of government and the redistribution of powers have made the state governments better instruments for the service of the people. But in most states popular control can be made more complete than it is now, and in all the distribution of powers can be made much more effective.

More complete popular control of government can be brought about in many states by the adoption of the referendum, initiative, and recall. But too much reliance should not be placed on these devices, and their use should not be made too easy. The procedure for direct legislation by the electorates should be subject to such safeguards as may be necessary in order to prevent the electorates from usurping non-legislative powers, which they are not fitted to exercise, and to insure due deliberation in the use of the powers which may properly be granted to them. In most states, however, what is most needed to bring about complete popular control of government is the simplification of the existing forms of government. A shorter ballot, more convenient methods of nomination of elective officers, the abolition of artificial electoral districts, more effective regulation of the processes by which the opinion of the electorate is formed: these are the reforms that offer the most promise. The removal of non-political officers from the elective to the appointive class, the consolidation of separate legislative chambers into a single house, the election of representatives, at least those from populous urban districts, by some form of proportional representation instead of the prevailing general ticket or single district systems, the abolition of official primary elections for the nomination of partisan candidates and the substitution, in cases where proportional representation is not suitable, of some form of preferential voting at the general election, the payment by the state of a larger share of the necessary cost of campaigns and elections, and the stricter regulation of the use of money by candidates and parties: these are some of the means by which the above reforms seem most likely to be accomplished.

The greatest defect in the government of the states has always been the abuse of power by the legislatures. After the experience of more than a century it should be clear that this defect cannot be cured merely by increasing the constitutional limitations upon legislative powers and procedure. It is in the organization of the legislature itself and in the readjustment of the relations between the legislature and the coördinate departments of government that the best hope for the future lies. The history of the constitutional convention shows how a legislative body may best be organized. The history of the growth of executive and judicial independence, of the separation of politics from administration, of the rise of the political influence of the governor and of the influence of the non-political expert in administration, shows how the relations between the legislature and the coördinate departments may best be adjusted. Indeed the greatest promise for the future lies, not in further changes in the forms of government, but in the further redistribution of powers. Additional checks upon the authority of the legislatures are needed. A better balance between the departments must be established by further strengthening both the executive department and the judiciary.

The strengthening of the executive seems most likely to be accomplished in two ways, by the further development of executive leadership in legislation and by the further reorganization of state administration. The more general use of administrative agencies for gathering information upon which legislation is to be based and in the preparation of legislative measures, the establishment of closer relations between the principal executive officers and the legislature, the further development of the executive veto, and above all the introduction of the executive budget: these are the most promising means by which executive leadership in legislation may be further developed. The extension of the "merit" system, the improvement of the methods of departmental organization, the further centralization and integration of administrative organization in general, the development of administrative tribunals, such as the public service commissions and other quasi-judicial bodies, and the wider recognition of the expert in the business of government: these are the most promising means of administrative reform. The proposals of the New York commission of 1925-26 for the strengthening of the executive, both on the legislative side by the establishment of the budget system and on the administrative side by the consolidation of boards and commissions and the creation of an executive cabinet, indicate the lines upon which the further strengthening of the executive may be expected to proceed. Municipal and county "home rule" and the delegation of broader legislative powers in local matters to the municipal governments are further means of relieving the legislatures from the demoralizing burden of special legislation.

The judicial branch of the state governments is that which has hitherto given the most acceptable service. In most states, however, the organization of the courts and the management of judicial business is by no means satisfactory, and the exercise of the power of judicial review of legislative and administrative acts too often imposes an undesirable burden upon the judiciary. In many states the development of better methods of legislation and of a more competent administrative system would go far to relieve the strain which legislative and administrative incompetence now throws upon the judicial system. In the administration of justice as well as in other branches of administration, the most promising reforms seem to be those designed to eliminate political influences, such as the adoption of better methods of selecting judges, and to promote economy and efficiency, such as the further centralization and integration of judicial organization and the granting to the courts of more power to regulate judicial procedure. The greatest defects have appeared in the administration of criminal justice, especially in large cities. The findings of the Cleveland and Missouri surveys best indicate the lines upon which further reform in this branch of judicial work may be expected to proceed. The National Crime Commission emphasizes the importance of minor changes in judicial procedure rather than major reforms in the body of the law and in the organization of the courts. Noteworthy among the proposals to which it has drawn attention are the following: that trial judges have more control over the abandonment of prosecutions by the public prosecutors and be allowed to comment on the evidence as well as to lay down the law, that prosecuting attorneys be allowed to draw inferences from the refusal of defendants to testify in their own behalf, that the activities of professional bondsmen be curtailed, that the qualifications for jury service be raised, that the practice of probation be more carefully regulated, and that the granting of pardons and paroles be surrounded with further safeguards. In general the improvement of criminal statistics and the organization of judicial councils should pave the way for the gradual introduction of more substantial reforms.

"Some men," wrote Jefferson,[1] several years after his retirement from public life, "look at constitutions with sanctimonious

[1] Thomas Jefferson to Samuel Kercheval, July 12, 1816.

reverence, and deem them like the ark of the covenant, too sacred to be touched. They ascribe to the men of the preceding age a wisdom more than human, and suppose what they did to be beyond amendment. I knew that age well; I belonged to it, and labored with it. It deserved well of its country. It was very like the present but without the experience of the present; and forty years of experience in government is worth a century of bookreading; and this they would say themselves were they to rise from the dead. I am certainly not an advocate for frequent and untried changes in laws and constitutions. I think moderate imperfections had better be borne with; because, when once known, we accommodate ourselves to them and find practical means of correcting their ill effects. But I know also that laws and institutions must go hand in hand with the progress of the human mind."

APPENDICES

APPENDIX A

CONSTITUTION OR FORM OF GOVERNMENT FOR THE COMMONWEALTH OF MASSACHUSETTS *

PREAMBLE

The end of the institution, maintenance, and administration of government, is to secure the existence of the body politic, to protect it, and to furnish the individuals who compose it with the power of enjoying in safety and tranquillity their natural rights, and the blessings of life: and whenever these great objects are not obtained the people have a right to alter the government, and to take measures for their safety, prosperity, and happiness.

The body politic is formed by a voluntary association of individuals: it is a social compact, by which the whole people covenants with each citizen, and each citizen with the whole people, that all shall be governed by certain laws for the common good. It is the duty of the people, therefore, in framing a constitution of government, to provide for an equitable mode of making laws, as well as for an impartial interpretation and a faithful execution of them; that every man may, at all times, find his security in them.

We, therefore, the people of Massachusetts, acknowledging, with grateful hearts, the goodness of the great Legislator of the universe, in affording us, in the course of His providence, an opportunity, deliberately and peaceably, without fraud, violence, or surprise, of entering into an original, explicit, and solemn compact with each other; and of forming a new constitution of civil government, for ourselves and posterity; and devoutly imploring His direction in so interesting a design, do agree upon, ordain, and establish, the following *Declaration of Rights, and Frame of Government,* as the CONSTITUTION OF THE COMMONWEALTH OF MASSACHUSETTS.

PART THE FIRST

A Declaration of the Rights of the Inhabitants of the Commonwealth of Massachusetts.

Article I. All men are born free and equal, and have certain natural, essential, and unalienable rights; among which may be reckoned the

* From the *Manual for the Use of the General Court* (Boston, 1926). The passages which follow are as originally adopted in 1780, except for one subsequent amendment, as noted below.

right of enjoying and defending their lives and liberties; that of acquiring, possessing, and protecting property; in fine, that of seeking and obtaining their safety and happiness.

Article II. It is the right as well as the duty of all men in society, publicly, and at stated seasons, to worship the SUPREME BEING, the great Creator and Preserver of the universe. And no subject shall be hurt, molested, or restrained, in his person, liberty, or estate, for worshipping GOD in the manner and season most agreeable to the dictates of his own conscience; or for his religious profession of sentiments; provided he doth not disturb the public peace, or obstruct others in their religious worship.

Article III.* As the public worship of GOD and instructions in piety, religion, and morality, promote the happiness and prosperity of a people, and the security of a republican government; therefore,........ all religious sects and denominations, demeaning themselves peaceably, and as good citizens of the commonwealth, shall be equally under the protection of the law; and no subordination of one sect or denomination to another shall ever be established by law.

Article IV. The people of this commonwealth have the sole and exclusive right of governing themselves, as a free, sovereign, and independent state; and do, and forever hereafter shall, exercise and enjoy every power, jurisdiction, and right, which is not, and may not hereafter be, by them expressly delegated to the United States of America, in Congress assembled.

Article V. All power residing originally in the people, and being derived from them, the several magistrates and officers of government, vested with authority, whether legislative, executive, or judicial, are their substitutes and agents, and are at all times accountable to them.

Article VI. No man, nor corporation, or association of men, have any other title to obtain advantages, or particular and exclusive privileges, distinct from those of the community, than what arises from the consideration of services rendered to the public; and this title being in nature neither hereditary, nor transmissible to children, or descendants, or relations by blood, the idea of a man born magistrate, lawgiver, or judge, is absurd and unnatural.

Article VII. Government is instituted for the common good; for the protection, safety, prosperity, and happiness of the people; and not for the profit, honor, or private interest of any one man, family, or class of men: Therefore the people alone have an incontestable, unalienable, and indefeasible right to institute government; and to reform, alter, or totally change the same, when their protection, safety, prosperity, and happiness require it.

Article VIII. In order to prevent those who are vested with authority from becoming oppressors, the people have a right, at such periods and in such manner as they shall establish by their frame of government, to cause their public officers to return to private life; and to fill up vacant places by certain and regular elections and appointments.

*** As amended in 1833.**

Article IX. All elections ought to be free; and all the inhabitants of this commonwealth, having such qualifications as they shall establish by their frame of government, have an equal right to elect officers, and to be elected, for public employments.

Article X. Each individual of the society has a right to be protected by it in the enjoyment of his life, liberty, and property, according to standing laws. He is obliged, consequently, to contribute his share to the expense of this protection; to give his personal service, or an equivalent, when necessary: but no part of the property of any individual can, without justice, be taken from him, or applied to public uses, without his own consent, or that of the representative body of the people. In fine, the people of the commonwealth are not controllable by any other laws than those to which their constitutional representative body have given their consent. And whenever the public exigencies require that the property of any individual should be appropriated to public uses, he shall receive a reasonable compensation therefor.

Article XI. Every subject of the commonwealth ought to find a certain remedy, by having recourse to the laws, for all injuries or wrongs which he may receive in his person, property, or character. He ought to obtain right and justice freely, and without being obliged to purchase it; completely, and without any denial; promptly, and without delay; conformably to the laws.

Article XII. No subject shall be held to answer for any crimes or offence, until the same is fully and plainly, substantially and formally, described to him; or be compelled to accuse, or furnish evidence against himself. And every subject shall have a right to produce all proofs that may be favorable to him; to meet the witnesses against him face to face, and be fully heard in his defence by himself, or his counsel, at his election. And no subject shall be arrested, imprisoned, despoiled, or deprived of his property, immunities, or privileges, put out of the protection of the law, exiled, or deprived of his life, liberty, or estate, but by the judgment of his peers, or the law of the land.

And the legislature shall not make any law that shall subject any person to a capital or infamous punishment, excepting for the government of the army and navy, without trial by jury.

Article XIII. In criminal prosecutions, the verification of facts in the vicinity where they happen, is one of the greatest securities of the life, liberty, and property of the citizen.

Article XIV. Every subject has a right to be secure from all unreasonable searches, and seizures, of his person, his houses, his papers, and all his possessions. All warrants, therefore, are contrary to this right, if the cause or foundation of them be not previously supported by oath or affirmation, and if the order in the warrant to a civil officer, to make search in suspected places, or to arrest one or more suspected persons, or to seize their property, be not accompanied with a special designation of the persons or objects of search, arrest, or seizure: and no warrant ought to be issued but in cases, and with the formalities prescribed by the laws.

Article XV. In all controversies concerning property, and in all suits between two or more persons, except in cases in which it has heretofore been otherways used and practised, the parties have a right to a trial by jury; and this method of procedure shall be held sacred, unless, in causes arising on the high seas, and such as relate to mariners' wages, the legislature shall hereafter find it necessary to alter it.

Article XVI. The liberty of the press is essential to the security of freedom in a state: it ought not, therefore, to be restrained in this commonwealth.

Article XVII. The people have a right to keep and to bear arms for the common defence. And as, in time of peace, armies are dangerous to liberty, they ought not to be maintained without the consent of the legislature; and the military power shall always be held in an exact subordination to the civil authority, and be governed by it.

Article XVIII. A frequent recurrence to the fundamental principles of the constitution, and a constant adherence to those of piety, justice, moderation, temperance, industry, and frugality, are absolutely necessary to preserve the advantages of liberty, and to maintain a free government. The people ought, consequently, to have a particular attention to all those principles, in the choice of their officers and representatives: and they have a right to require of their lawgivers and magistrates an exact and constant observance of them, in the formation and execution of the laws necessary for the good administration of the commonwealth.

Article XIX. The people have a right, in an orderly and peaceable manner, to assemble to consult upon the common good; give instructions to their representatives, and to request of the legislative body, by the way of addresses, petitions, or remonstrances, redress of the wrongs done them, and of the grievances they suffer.

Article XX. The power of suspending the laws, or the execution of the laws, ought never to be exercised but by the legislature, or by authority derived from it, to be exercised in such particular cases only as the legislature shall expressly provide for.

Article XXI. The freedom of deliberation, speech, and debate, in either house of the legislature, is so essential to the rights of the people, that it cannot be the foundation of any accusation or prosecution, action or complaint, in any other court or place whatsoever.

Article XXII. The legislature ought frequently to assemble for the redress of grievances, for correcting, strengthening, and confirming the laws, and for making new laws, as the common good may require.

Article XXIII. No subsidy, charge, tax, impost, or duties ought to be established, fixed, laid, or levied, under any pretext whatsoever, without the consent of the people or their representatives in the legislature.

Article XXIV. Laws made to punish for actions done before the existence of such laws, and which have not been declared crimes by preceding laws, are unjust, oppressive, and inconsistent with the fundamental principles of a free government.

Article XXV. No subject ought, in any case, or in any time, to be declared guilty of treason or felony by the legislature.

Article XXVI. No magistrate or court of law shall demand excessive bail or sureties, impose excessive fines, or inflict cruel or unusual punishments.

Article XXVII. In time of peace, no soldier ought to be quartered in any house without the consent of the owner; and in time of war, such quarters ought not to be made but by the civil magistrate, in a manner ordained by the legislature.

Article XXVIII. No person can in any case be subject to law-martial, or to any penalties or pains, by virtue of that law, except those employed in the army or navy, and except the militia in actual service, but by authority of the legislature.

Article XXIX. It is essential to the preservation of the rights of every individual, his life, liberty, property, and character, that there be an impartial interpretation of the laws, and administration of justice. It is the right of every citizen to be tried by judges as free, impartial, and independent as the lot of humanity will admit. It is, therefore, not only the best policy, but for the security of the rights of the people, and of every citizen, that the judges of the supreme judicial court should hold their offices as long as they behave themselves well; and that they should have honorable salaries ascertained and established by standing laws.

Article XXX. In the government of this commonwealth, the legislative department shall never exercise the executive and judicial powers, or either of them: the executive shall never exercise the legislative and judicial powers, or either of them: the judicial shall never exercise the legislative and executive powers, or either of them: to the end it may be a government of laws and not of men.

PART THE SECOND

The Frame of Government

The people, inhabiting the territory formerly called the Province of Massachusetts Bay, do hereby solemnly and mutually agree with each other, to form themselves into a free, sovereign, and independent body politic, or state, by the name of THE COMMONWEALTH OF MASSACHUSETTS.

[Here follows the frame of government.]

APPENDIX B

JEFFERSON'S DRAFT OF A CONSTITUTION FOR THE COMMONWEALTH OF VIRGINIA *

To the citizens of the commonwealth of Virginia, and all others whom it may concern, the delegates for the said commonwealth in Convention assembled, send greeting:

. . . .

We, therefore, the delegates, chosen by the said good people of this State, for the purpose aforesaid, and now assembled in general convention, do, in execution of the authority with which we are invested, establish the following constitution and fundamentals of government for the said State of Virginia.

The State shall forever hereafter be governed as a commonwealth.

The powers of government shall be divided into three distinct departments, each of them to be confided to a separate body of magistracy; to wit, those which are legislative to one, those which are judiciary to another, and those which are executive to another. No person, or collection of persons, being of one of these departments shall exercise any power properly belonging to either of the others, except in the instances hereinafter expressly permitted.

The legislature shall consist of two branches, the one to be called the House of Delegates, the other the Senate, and both together the General Assembly. The concurrence of both of these, expressed on three several readings, shall be necessary to the passage of a law.

Delegates for the general assembly shall be chosen on the last Monday of November in every year. But if an election cannot be concluded on that day, it may be adjourned from day to day till it can be concluded.

The number of delegates which each county may send shall be in proportion to the number of its qualified electors; and the whole number of delegates for the State shall be so proportioned to the whole number of qualified electors in it, that they shall never exceed three hundred,

* From *The Writings of Thomas Jefferson,* Ford's edition, iii, pp. 320-333. According to Ford, Jefferson drafted this proposed constitution some time between May 7 and June 17, 1783, and subsequently had it printed and eventually bound up with his *Notes on Virginia*, as an appendix, prefaced by the following statement: "In the summer of the year 1783, it was expected that the assembly of Virginia would call a Convention for the establishment of a Constitution. The following draught of a fundamental Constitution for the Commonwealth of Virginia was then prepared, with a design of being proposed in such Convention had it taken place."

nor be fewer than one hundred. Whenever such excess or deficiency shall take place, the House of Delegates so deficient or excessive shall, notwithstanding this, continue in being during its legal term; but they shall, during that term, re-adjust the proportion, so as to bring their number within the limits before mentioned at the ensuing election. If any county be reduced in its qualified electors below the number authorized to send one delegate, let it be annexed to some adjoining county.

For the election of senators, let the several counties be allotted by the senate from time to time, into such and so many districts as they shall find best; and let each county at the time of electing its delegates, choose senatorial electors, qualified as themselves are, and four in number for each delegate their county is entitled to send, who shall convene, and conduct themselves, in such manner as the legislature shall direct, with the senatorial electors from the other counties of their district, and then choose, by ballot, one senator for every six delegates which their district is entitled to choose. Let the senatorial districts be divided into two classes, and let the members elected for one of them be dissolved at the first ensuing general election of delegates, the other at the next, and so on alternately forever.

All free male citizens, of full age, and sane mind, who for one year before shall have been resident in the county, or shall through the whole of that time have possessed therein real property of the value of ———; or shall for the same time have been enrolled in the militia, and no others, shall have a right to vote for delegates for the said county, and for senatorial electors for the district. They shall give their votes personally, and *viva voce*.

The general assembly shall meet at the place to which the last adjournment was, on the forty-second day after the day of election of delegates, and thenceforward at any time or place on their own adjournment, till their office expires, which shall be on the day preceding that appointed for the meeting of the next general assembly. But if they shall at any time adjourn for more than one year, it shall be as if they had adjourned for one year precisely. Neither house, without the concurrence of the other, shall adjourn for more than one week, nor to any other place than the one at which they are sitting. The governor shall also have power, with the advice of the council of State, to call them at any other time to the same place, or to a different one, if that shall have become, since the last adjournment, dangerous from an enemy, or from infection.

A majority of either house shall be a quorum, and shall be requisite for doing business; but any small proportion which from time to time shall be thought expedient by the respective houses, shall be sufficient to call for, and to punish, their non-attending members, and to adjourn themselves for any time not exceeding one week.

The members, during their attendance on the general assembly, and for so long a time before and after as shall be necessary for travelling to and from the same, shall be privileged from all personal restraint and assault, and shall have no other privilege whatsoever. They shall receive, during the same time, daily wages in gold or silver, equal to the value of two bushels of wheat.

....

Of this general assembly, the treasurer, attorney general, register, ministers of the gospel, officers of the regular armies of this State, or of the United States, persons receiving salaries or emoluments from any power foreign to our confederacy, those who are not resident in the county for which they are chosen delegates, or districts for which they are chosen senators, those who are not qualified as electors, persons who shall have committed treason, felony, or such other crime as would subject them to infamous punishment, or who shall have been convicted by due course of law of bribery or corruption, in endeavoring to procure an election to the said assembly, shall be incapable of being members. All others, not herein elsewhere excluded, who may elect, shall be capable of being elected thereto.

Any member of the said assembly accepting any office of profit under this State, or the United States, or any of them, shall thereby vacate his seat, but shall be capable of being re-elected.

Vacancies occasioned by such disqualifications, by death, or otherwise, shall be supplied by the electors, on a writ from the speaker of the respective house.

The general assembly shall not have power to infringe this constitution; to abridge the civil rights of any person on account of his religious belief; to restrain him from professing and supporting that belief, or to compel him to contributions, other than those he shall have personally stipulated for the support of that or any other; to ordain death for any crime but treason or murder, or military offences; to pardon, or give a power of pardoning, persons duly convicted of treason or felony, but instead thereof they may substitute one or two new trials, and no more; to pass laws for punishing actions done before the existence of such laws; to pass any bill of attainder of treason or felony; to prescribe torture in any case whatever; nor to permit the introduction of any more slaves to reside in this State, or the continuance of slavery beyond the generation which shall be living on the thirty-first day of December, one thousand eight hundred; all persons born after that day being hereby declared free.

....

They shall have power to appoint the speakers of their respective houses, treasurer, auditors, attorney general, register, all general officers of the military, their own clerks and serjeants, and no other officers, except where, in other parts of this constitution, such appointment is expressly given them.

The executive powers shall be exercised by a *Governor,* who shall be chosen by joint ballot of both houses of assembly, and when chosen shall remain in office five years, and be ineligible a second time. During his term he shall hold no other office or emolument under this State, or any other State or power whatsoever. By executive powers, we mean no reference to those powers exercised under our former government by the crown as of its prerogative, nor that these shall be the standard of what may or may not be deemed the rightful powers of the governor. We give them those powers only, which are necessary to execute the laws (and administer the government), and which are not in their nature either legislative or judiciary. The application of this idea must be left to reason. We do however expressly deny him the prerogative powers of erecting courts, offices, boroughs, corporations, fairs, markets, ports, beacons, lighthouses, and sea-marks; of laying embargoes, of establishing precedence, of retaining with the State, or recalling to it any citizen thereof, and of making denizens, except so far as he may be authorized from time to time by the legislature to exercise any of those powers. The power of declaring war and concluding peace, of contracting alliances, of issuing letters of marque and reprisal, of raising and introducing armed forces, of building armed vessels, forts, or strongholds, of coining money or regulating its value, of regulating weights and measures, we leave to be exercised under the authority of the confederation; but in all cases respecting them which are out of the said confederation, they shall be exercised by the governor, under the regulation of such laws as the legislature may think it expedient to pass.

The whole military of the State, whether regular, or of militia, shall be subject to his direction; but he shall leave the execution of those directions to the general officers appointed by the legislature.

His salary shall be fixed by the legislature at the session of the assembly in which he shall be appointed, and before such appointment be made; or if it be not then fixed, it shall be the same which his next predecessor in office was entitled to. In either case he may demand it quarterly out of any money which shall be in the public treasury; and it shall not be in the power of the legislature to give him less or more, either during his continuance in office, or after he shall have gone out of it. The lands, houses, and other things appropriated to the use of the governor, shall remain to his use during his continuance in office.

A *Council of State* shall be chosen by joint ballot of both houses of assembly, who shall hold their offices seven years, and be ineligible a second time, and who, while they shall be of the said council, shall hold no other office or emolument under this State, or any other state or power whatsoever. Their duty shall be to attend and advise the governor when called on by him, and their advice in any case shall be a sanction to him. They shall also have power, and it shall be their duty, to meet at their own will, and to give their advice, though not required by the governor, in cases where they shall think the public good calls for it. Their advice and proceedings shall be entered in books to be kept for that purpose, and shall be signed as approved or disapproved by the members present. These books shall be laid before either house of assembly when called for by them. The said council shall consist of eight members for the present; but their numbers may be increased or reduced by the legislature, whenever they shall think it necessary; provided such reduction be made only as the appointments become vacant by death, resignation, disqualification, or regular deprivation. A majority of their actual number, and not fewer, shall be a quorum.

. . . .

They shall annually choose a *President,* who shall preside in council in the absence of the governor, and who, in case of his office becoming vacant by death or otherwise, shall have authority to exercise all his functions, till a new appointment be made, as he shall also in any interval during which the governor shall declare himself unable to attend to the duties of his office.

The *Judiciary* powers shall be exercised by county courts and such other inferior courts as the legislature shall think proper to continue or to erect, by three superior courts, to wit, a Court of Admiralty, a general Court of Common Law, and a High Court of Chancery; and by one Supreme Court, to be called the Court of Appeals.

The judges of the high court of chancery, general court, and court of admiralty, shall be four in number each, to be appointed by joint ballot of both houses of assembly, and to hold their offices during good behavior. While they continue judges, they shall hold no other office or emolument, under this State, or any other State or power whatsoever,

. . . .

These judges, assembled together, shall constitute the Court of Appeals, whose business shall be to receive and determine appeals from the three superior courts, but to receive no original causes, except in the cases expressly permitted herein.

A majority of the members of either of these courts, and not fewer, shall be a quorum. But in the Court of Appeals nine members shall be necessary to do business. Any smaller numbers however may be authorized by the legislature to adjourn their respective courts.

. . . .

There shall, moreover, be a *Court of Impeachments,* to consist of three members of the Council of State, one of each of the superior courts of Chancery, Common Law, and Admiralty, two members of the house of delegates and one of the Senate, to be chosen by the body respectively of which they are. Before this court any member of the three branches of government, that is to say, the governor, any member of the council, of the two houses of legislature, or of the superior courts, may be impeached by the governor, the council, or either of the said houses or courts, and by no other, for such misbehavior in office as would be sufficient to remove him therefrom; and the only sentence they shall have authority to pass shall be that of deprivation and future incapacity of office. Seven members shall be requisite to make a court, and two-thirds of those present must concur in the sentence. The offences cognizable by this court shall be cognizable by no other, and they shall be triers of the fact as well as judges of the law.

The justices or judges of the inferior courts already erected, or hereafter to be erected, shall be appointed by the governor, on advice of the council of State, and shall hold their offices during good behavior, or the existence of their courts. For breach of the good behavior, they shall be tried according to the laws of the land, before the Court of Appeals, who shall be judges of the fact as well as of the law. The only sentence they shall have authority to pass shall be that of deprivation and future incapacity of office, and two-thirds of the members present must concur in this sentence.

....

The justices or judges of the inferior courts may be members of the legislature.

....

In all causes depending before any court, other than those of impeachments, of appeals, and military courts, facts put in issue shall be tried by jury, and in all courts whatever witnesses shall give testimony *viva voce* in open court, wherever their attendance can be procured; and all parties shall be allowed counsel and compulsory process for their witnesses.

Fines, amercements, and terms of imprisonment left indefinite by the law, other than for contempts, shall be fixed by the jury, triers of the offence.

The governor, two councillors of State, and a judge from each of the superior Courts of Chancery, Common Law, and Admiralty, shall be a council to revise all bills which shall have passed both houses of assembly, in which council the governor, when present, shall preside. Every bill, before it becomes a law, shall be represented to this council, who shall have a right to advise its rejection, returning the bill, with their advice and reasons in writing, to the house in which it originated, who shall proceed to reconsider the said bill. But if after such reconsideration, two-thirds of the house shall be of opinion that the bill should pass finally, they shall pass and send it, with the advice and written reasons of the said Council of Revision, to the other house, wherein if two-thirds also shall be of opinion it should pass finally, it shall thereupon become law; otherwise it shall not.

If any bill, presented to the said council, be not, within one week (exclusive of the day of presenting it) returned by them, with their advice of rejection and reasons, to the house wherein it originated, or to the clerk of the said house, in case of its adjournment over the expiration of the week, it shall be law from the expiration of the week, and shall then be demandable by the clerk of the House of Delegates, to be filed of record in his office.

....

The members of the said Council of Revision shall be appointed from time to time by the board or court of which they respectively are. Two of the executive and two of the judiciary members shall be requisite to do business;

....

The benefits of the writ of Habeas Corpus shall be extended, by the legislature, to every person within this State, and without fee, and shall be so facilitated that no person may be detained in prison more than ten days after he shall have demanded and been refused such writ by the judge appointed by law, or if none be appointed, then by any judge of a superior court, nor more than ten days after such writ shall have been served on the person detaining him, and no order given, on due examination, for his remandment or discharge.

The military shall be subordinate to the civil power .

Printing presses shall be subject to no other restraint than liableness to legal prosecution for false facts printed and published.

Any two of the three branches of government concurring in opinion each by the voice of two-thirds of their whole existing number, that a convention is necessary for altering this constitution, or correcting breaches of it, they shall be authorized to issue writs to every county for the election of so many delegates as they are authorized to send to the general assembly, which elections shall be held, and writs returned, as the laws shall have provided in the case of elections of delegates of assembly, *mutatis mutandis,* and the said delegates shall meet at the usual place of holding assemblies, three months after date of such writs, and shall be acknowledged to have equal powers with this present convention.

. . . .

This convention being authorized only to amend those laws which constituted the form of government, no general dissolution of the whole system of laws can be supposed to have taken place, but all laws in force at the meeting of this convention, and not inconsistent with this constitution, remain in full force, subject to alterations by the ordinary legislature.

[Here follow sundry special and temporary provisions to introduce the new form of government.]

APPENDIX C

A MODEL STATE CONSTITUTION *

BILL OF RIGHTS

Section 1. All political power of this state is inherent in the people, and all government herein is founded on their authority.

Section 2. All men are by nature equally free and independent and have certain inherent rights; namely, the enjoyment of life and liberty with the means of acquiring and possessing property and pursuing and obtaining happiness and safety.

Section 3. No citizen of this state shall be disfranchised, or deprived of any of the rights or privileges secured to any other citizen, unless by the law of the land, or the judgment of his peers.

Section 4. There shall be no imprisonment for debt, except in cases of fraud, libel, or slander, and no person shall be imprisoned for a militia fine in time of peace. Laws shall be passed exempting for individuals a reasonable amount of property from seizure or sale for payment of any debt or liabilities.

Section 5. The privilege of the writ of habeas corpus shall not be suspended, unless, in case of rebellion or invasion, the public safety require it, and then only in such manner as shall be prescribed by law.

Section 6. The right of the people peaceably to assemble, and to petition the government, or any department thereof, shall never be abridged.

Section 7. Every person may freely speak, write and publish on all subjects, being responsible for the abuse of that liberty; and in all trials for libel, both civil and criminal, the truth when published with good motives and for justifiable ends, shall be sufficient defense.

Section 8. The right of the people to be secure in their persons, houses, papers and effects, against unreasonable searches and seizures shall not be violated; and no warrant shall issue but upon probable cause, supported by oath or affirmation, and particularly describing the place to be searched, and person or thing to be seized.

Section 9. The legislature shall make no law respecting an establishment of religion, or prohibiting the free exercise thereof.

Section 10. No public money or property shall ever be appropriated, applied, donated, or used directly or indirectly, for the use, benefit, or support of any sect, church, denomination, sectarian institution or asso-

* From the publications of the National Municipal League, 3rd (revised) edition, 1926.

ciation, or system of religion, or for charitable, industrial, educational, or benevolent purposes not under the control of the state.

Section 11. In all criminal prosecutions the accused shall have the right to appear and defend in person or by counsel, to demand the nature and cause of accusation, and to have a copy thereof; to meet the witnesses against him face to face; to have process to compel the attendance of witnesses in his behalf; and a speedy public trial in the county or district in which the offense is alleged to have been committed. The right of trial by jury in all criminal cases shall remain inviolate; but a jury trial may be waived by the accused in any criminal case or by the parties in any civil case as may be prescribed by law.

Section 12. No bill of attainder, ex post facto law, or law impairing the obligation of contracts, or making any irrevocable grant of special privileges or immunities shall be passed; nor shall private property be taken for a public use without just compensation.

THE LEGISLATURE

Section 13. There shall be a legislature of —— members who shall be chosen by the qualified electors of the state for a term of two years by the system of proportional representation with the single transferable vote. For the purpose of electing members of the legislature, the state shall be divided into districts composed of contiguous and compact territory from which members shall be chosen in proportion to the population thereof, but no district shall be assigned less than five members.

Section 14. Until otherwise provided by law, members of the legislature shall be elected from the following districts: The first district shall consist of the counties of —— and —— and shall be entitled to —— members. (The description of all the districts from which the first legislature will be elected should be inserted in similar language.) At its first session following each decennial federal census the legislature shall redistrict the state and reapportion the members in accordance with the provisions of section 13 of this constitution.

Section 15. The election of members of the legislature shall be held on the Tuesday next following the first Monday of November in the year one thousand nine hundred and ——— and every second year thereafter.

Section 16. Any elector of the state shall be eligible to the legislature.

Section 17. The term of members of the legislature shall begin on the first day of December next following their election. Whenever a vacancy shall occur in the legislature the governor shall issue a writ of appointment for the unexpired term. Such vacancy shall thereupon be filed by a majority vote of the remaining members of the district in which the vacancy occurs. If after thirty days following the issuance of the writ of appointment the vacancy remains unfilled, the governor shall appoint some eligible person for the unexpired term.

Section 18. A regular session of the legislature shall be held annually (or biennially) beginning on the first Monday in February. Special sessions may be called by the governor or by a majority vote of the members of the legislative council.

Section 19. The legislature shall be judge of the election, returns and qualifications of its members, but may by law vest in the courts the trial and determination of contested elections of members. It shall choose its presiding officer and determine its rules of procedure; it may compel the attendance of absent members, punish its members for disorderly conduct and, with the concurrence of two-thirds of all the members, expel a member, but no members shall be expelled a second time for the same offense. The legislature shall have power to compel the attendance and testimony of witnesses and the production of books and papers either before the legislature as a whole or before any committee thereof.

Section 20. For any speech or debate in the legislature, the members shall not be questioned in any other place.

Section 21. The legislature shall pass no local or special act in any case where a general act can be made applicable; and whether a general act can be made applicable shall be a judicial question. No local or special act shall take effect until approved by a majority of the electors voting thereon in the district to be affected, except acts repealing local or special acts in effect before the adoption of this constitution and receiving a two-thirds vote of all members of the legislature on the question of their repeal.

Section 22. A majority of all the members of the legislature shall constitute a quorum to do business but a smaller number may adjourn from day to day and compel the attendance of absent members. The legislature shall keep a journal of its proceedings which shall be published from day to day. A vote by yeas and nays on any question shall, at the desire of one-fifth of those present, be taken and entered on the journal.

Section 23. A secretary of the legislature shall be appointed in the manner hereinafter provided. The secretary shall appoint and supervise all employes of the legislature and shall have charge of all service incidental to the work of legislation. While the legislature is in session the secretary shall be under the control of that body.

Section 24. No law shall be passed except by bill. All bills, except bills for appropriations and bills for the codification, revision, or rearrangement of existing laws, shall be confined to one subject, and the subject, or subjects, of all bills shall be clearly expressed in the title. Bills for appropriations shall be confined to appropriations.

Section 25. No bill shall become a law until it has been read on three different days, has been printed and upon the desks of the members in final form at least three legislative days prior to final passage, and has received the assent of a majority of all the members. Upon final passage the vote shall be by yeas and nays entered on the journal; provided, that the employment of mechanical devices to record the votes of members shall not be contrary to this provision.

Section 26. Every bill which shall have passed the legislature shall be presented to the governor; if he approve he shall sign it, but if not he shall return it with his objections to the legislature. Any bill so returned by the governor shall be reconsidered by the legislature and if, upon reconsideration, two-thirds of all the members shall agree to pass the bill it shall become a law. In all such cases the vote of the legislature shall be by yeas and nays and entered on the journal. If any bill shall not be returned by the governor within ten days after it shall have been presented to him it shall be a law in like manner as if he had signed it, but if the legislature shall by adjournment prevent the return of a bill within ten days any such bill shall become a law unless filed by the governor, together with his objections, in the office of the secretary of the legislature within thirty days after the adjournment of the legislature. Any bill so filed shall be reconsidered by the next session of the legislature as though returned while the legislature was in session.

Section 27. Any bill failing of passage by the legislature may be submitted to referendum by order of the governor if at least one-third of all the members shall have been recorded as voting in favor of the bill when it was upon final passage. Any bill which, having passed the legislature, is returned thereto by the governor with objections and, upon reconsideration is not approved by a two-thirds vote of all the members but is approved by at least a majority thereof, may be submitted to referendum by a majority vote of all the members of the legislature. Bills submitted to referendum by order of the governor or legislature shall be voted on at the next succeeding general election unless the legislature shall provide for their submission at an earlier date.

Section 28. The legislature shall by a majority vote of all its members appoint an auditor, who shall serve during the pleasure of the legislature. It shall be the duty of the auditor to conduct a continuous audit of all accounts kept by or for the various departments and offices of the state government, and to report thereon to the legislative council quarterly and at the end of each fiscal year. He shall also make such additional reports to the legislature and legislative council, and conduct such investigation of the financial affairs of the state, or of any department or office thereof, as either of such bodies may require.

Section 29. There shall be a legislative council consisting of the governor and seven members chosen by and from the legislature. Members of the legislative council shall be chosen by the legislature at its first session after the adoption of this constitution and at each subsequent session following a general election. Members of the legislative council chosen by the legislature shall be elected by the system of proportional representation with the single transferable vote, and when elected shall continue in office until their successors are chosen and have qualified. The legislature, by a majority vote of all its members, may dissolve the legislative council at any time and proceed to the election of a successor thereto.

Section 30. The legislative council shall meet as often as may be necessary to perform its duties. It shall choose one of its members as chairman, and shall adopt its own rules of procedure, except as such rules may be established by law. The legislative council shall appoint the secretary of the legislature, who shall be ex-officio secretary of the council. The secretary shall be appointed for an indefinite term but may be removed by the council at any time.

Section 31. It shall be the duty of the legislative council to collect information concerning the government and general welfare of the state and to report thereon to the legislature. Measures for proposed legislation may be submitted to it at any time, and shall be considered, and reported to the legislature with its recommendations thereon. The legislative council may also prepare such legislation and make such recommendations thereon to the legislature, in the form of bills or otherwise, as in its opinion the welfare of the state may require. Other powers and duties may be assigned to the legislative council by law. The delegation of authority to the council to supplement existing legislation by means of ordinances shall not be deemed a delegation of legislative power.

Section 32. Members of the legislative council shall receive such compensation, additional to their compensation as members of the legislature, as may be provided by law.

THE INITIATIVE AND REFERENDUM

Section 33. The people reserve to themselves power by petition to propose laws and amendments to this constitution, and directly to enact or reject such laws and amendments at the polls. This reserved power shall be known as the initiative. An initiative petition shall contain the full text of the measure proposed, and, to be valid, shall be signed by at least —— voters of the state. Initiative petitions shall be filed with the secretary of the legislature, and the question of adopting any measure therein set forth shall be by him submitted to the voters at the first regular state election, held not less than four months after such filing.

Section 34. The people also reserve to themselves power to require, by petition, that measures enacted by the legislature be submitted to the voters for their approval. This reserved power shall be known as the referendum. A referendum petition against any measure passed by the legislature shall be filed with the secretary of the legislature within ninety days after the legislature enacting such measure adjourns sine die for a longer period than ninety days, and, to be valid, shall be signed by not less than —— voters of the state. The question of approving any measure against which a valid referendum petition is filed shall be submitted to the voters at the first regular or special state election, held not less than thirty days after such filing.

Section 35. A referendum may be ordered upon any act or part of an act, except acts making appropriations for the current expenses of the state government, and for state institutions existing at the time such act was passed, not exceeding the next previous appropriation for such purpose. When the referendum is ordered upon an act, or any part of an act, it shall suspend the operation thereof until such act, or part, is approved by the voters. The filing of a referendum petition against one or more items, sections, or parts of an act shall not delay the remainder of the measure from becoming operative. No act shall take effect earlier than ninety days after the adjournment of the legislature at which it was passed, except acts declared to be emergency measures. If it be necessary for the immediate preservation of the public peace, health, or safety that a measure become effective without delay, the facts constituting such necessity shall be stated in a separate section, and if, upon a yea and nay vote entered upon the journal, two-thirds of the members elected to the legislature shall declare the measure to be an emergency measure, it shall become effective without delay; but no act granting or amending a franchise or special privilege, or creating any vested right or interest, other than in the state, shall be declared an emergency measure.

Section 36. If a referendum petition be filed against an emergency measure, such measure shall be operative until voted upon, and unless approved by a majority of the voters voting thereon it shall be deemed repealed. Any referendum measure shall be submitted to the voters at a special election, if so ordered by the governor, or if the referendum petition be signed by —— legal voters. Any such special election shall be held not less than one hundred and twenty nor more than one hundred and thirty days after the adjournment of the legislature at which the act was passed.

Section 37. No measure shall be submitted to the people by the legislature except proposed constitutional amendments, and the veto power of the governor shall not extend to measures initiated by, or referred to, the people. Any measure submitted to a vote of the people shall become law or a part of the constitution only when approved by a majority of the votes cast thereon, provided that at least twenty per cent of those voting at the election vote in the affirmative, and shall take effect ten days after the completion of the official canvass, unless otherwise specified in the measure. If conflicting measures referred to the people at the same election shall be approved by a majority of the votes cast thereon, the one receiving the highest number of affirmative votes shall become law. Each measure shall be submitted by a ballot title, which shall be descriptive, but not argumentative or prejudicial. The ballot title may be prepared by the petitioner or by the secretary of the legislature, but in either event it shall be approved by the attorney general as to form, and shall be subject to court review.

Section 38. Only registered voters may sign initiative and referendum petitions. Such petitions may be circulated or presented in parts, but each part of any petition shall have attached thereto the affidavit of the circulator that all the signatures thereon were made in his presence, and that to the best of his knowledge and belief each signature is genuine and that of a registered voter. Petitions so verified shall be prima facie evidence that the signatures thereon are genuine, and no other affidavit or verification shall be required. The sufficiency of all petitions shall be decided in the first instance by the secretary of the legislature, subject to review by the court of last resort, which shall have original and exclusive jurisdiction over all such cases. If the sufficiency of any petition is challenged, such cause shall be a preferenced cause, and shall be tried and adjudicated without delay; but the failure of the court to decide prior to the legal date of certification of the ballot by the secretary of the legislature as to the sufficiency of any such petition shall not prevent the question from being placed on the ballot at the election named in such petition, nor militate against the validity of such measure if it shall have been approved by a vote of the people. In the event of legal proceedings to prevent giving legal effect to any petition upon any grounds, the burden of proof shall be upon the person or persons attacking the validity of the petition. If the secretary of the legislature shall decide any petition to be insufficient, he shall, without delay, notify the sponsors of such petition, and permit at least thirty days for correction and amendment.

Section 39. In the preparation of initiative and referendum petitions the services of the attorney general and of the legislative reference bureau of the state, if such shall exist, shall be at the service of the petitioners without charge, for consultation and advice as to constitutionality and form. Not more than one-fourth of the signatures on any completed petition shall be those of the voters of any one county. No law shall be passed to prevent giving or receiving compensation for circulating petitions, but laws shall be enacted prohibiting and penalizing fraudulent practices in the procuring or filing of petitions.

Section 40. At least fifty days prior to an election at which any measure is to be submitted to the voters, the secretary of the legislature shall cause to be printed and mailed to each voter, at the expense of the state, a publicity pamphlet containing a copy of all such measures, together with their respective ballot titles. Any citizen or citizens or officers of any organization of citizens may file with the secretary of the legislature for publication over their signatures, in such publicity pamphlet, arguments for or against any measure, and shall deposit at the time of filing such argument the proportionate cost, but no more, of the printing and paper for the space taken by them in such pamphlet.

The initiative and referendum provisions of this constitution shall be self-executing, and shall be treated as mandatory. Laws may be enacted to facilitate their operation, but no law shall be enacted to hamper, restrict or impair the exercise of the powers herein reserved to the people.

THE EXECUTIVE

Section 41. The executive power of the state shall be vested in a governor, who shall be chosen for a term of four years by the qualified electors of the state. An election for governor shall be held on the Tuesday next following the first Monday in November in the year one thousand nine hundred and —— and every fourth year thereafter. The governor shall hold his office for a term of four years from the first Monday in December next following his election. Any elector of the state shall be eligible to the office of governor.

Section 42. The governor shall, at the commencement of each session, and may at other times, give to the legislature information as to the affairs of the state, and recommend such measures as he shall deem expedient; and in case of a disagreement with respect to the time of the adjournment he may adjourn the legislature to such time as he shall think proper, not beyond the first day of the next regular session.

Section 43. The governor shall take care that the laws are faithfully executed. He shall commission all officers of the state. He may at any time require information, in writing or otherwise, from the officers of the executive department upon any subject relating to their respective offices. He shall be commander-in-chief of the military and naval forces of the state (except when they shall be called into the service of the United States), and may call out the same to execute the laws, to suppress insurrection or repel invasion.

He shall have power to grant reprieves, commutations and pardons, after conviction, for all offenses, subject to such regulations as may be provided by law relative to the manner of applying therefor.

Section 44. The governor and all civil officers, except such inferior officers as may by law be exempted, shall, before entering on the duties of their respective offices, take, and subscribe the following oath or affirmation: "I do solemnly swear (or affirm) that I will support and defend the Constitution of the United States and the Constitution of the State of ———, and that I will faithfully discharge the duties of the office of ——— to the best of my ability."

Section 45. In case of death, impeachment, or other disability of the governor, the powers and duties of the office shall devolve upon the presiding officer of the legislature for the remainder of the term, or until the disability be removed.

Section 46. There shall be such executive departments as may be established by law. The heads of all executive departments shall be appointed and may be removed by the governor. All other officers and employees in the executive service of the state shall be appointed by the governor or by the heads of executive departments as may be provided by law.

Section 47. The governor and heads of executive departments shall be entitled to seats in the legislature, may introduce bills therein, and take part in the discussion of measures, but shall have no vote.

Section 48. The legislature may, upon due notice given, and opportunity for defense, remove or retire the governor from office upon the concurrence of two-thirds of all the members elected to the legislature.

THE BUDGET

Section 49. Within one week after the organization of the legislature, at each regular session, the governor shall submit to the legislature a budget setting forth a complete plan of proposed expenditures and anticipated income of all departments, offices and agencies of the state for the next ensuing fiscal year (or biennium). For the preparation of the budget the various departments, offices and agencies shall furnish the governor such information, in such form and as he may require. At the time of submitting the budget to the legislature the governor shall introduce therein a general appropriation bill containing all the proposed expenditures set forth in the budget. At the same time he shall introduce in the legislature a bill or bills covering all recommendations in the budget for additional revenues or borrowings by which the proposed expenditures are to be met.

No appropriation shall be passed until the general appropriation bill, as introduced by the governor and amended by the legislature, shall have been enacted, unless the governor shall recommend the passage of an emergency appropriation or appropriations, which shall continue in force only until the general appropriation bill shall become effective. The legislature shall provide for one or more public hearings on the budget, either before a committee or before the entire assembly in committee of the whole. When requested by not less than one-fifth of the members of the legislature, it shall be the duty of the governor to appear before the legislature or to appear in person or by a designated representative before a committee thereof, to answer any inquiries with respect to the budget.

The legislature, by appropriate legislation, shall make this section effective.

Section 50. The legislature shall make no appropriation for any fiscal period in excess of the income provided for that period. The governor may disapprove or reduce items in appropriation bills, and the procedure in such cases shall be the same as in case of the disapproval of an entire bill by the governor.

Section 51. No money shall be drawn from the treasury except in accordance with appropriations made by law, nor shall any obligation for the payment of money be incurred except as authorized by law. No appropriation shall confer authority to incur an obligation after the termination of the fiscal period to which it relates.

THE JUDICIARY

Section 52. On and after January 1, 19—, the judicial power heretofore vested in the (here name all the courts of the state) shall be vested in the general court of justice, which shall have three departments, to be known as the supreme court, the district court, and the county court.

Section 53. The justices of the (here name the highest court of the state) and the judges of the (here name all the courts of the state except justice of the peace courts) holding office on said first day of January, 19—, shall constitute the first judges of the general court of justice, and shall continue to serve as such for the remainder of their respective terms and until their successors shall have qualified.

Section 54. The justices of the (here name highest court of state) shall become justices of the supreme court department of the general court.

Section 55. The judges of the district court (or circuit or superior court, as the case may be) and the judges of the (here name any special municipal courts which have a considerable trial jurisdiction) shall become judges of the district court.

Section 56. The judges of the county courts (or probate courts, if they are the only courts of county jurisdiction) shall become judges of the county court, and justices of the peace shall be attached as magistrates to the county court branch of the county in which they reside.

Section 57. The supreme court shall have and exercise (here insert all the powers and jurisdiction which it may be desired to confer upon the state's highest tribunal). The supreme court shall have power to sit in two or more divisions, when in its judgment this is necessary for the proper dispatch of business, and to make rules for the distribution of business between the divisions and for the hearing of certain cases by the full court.

Section 58. The district court shall have original jurisdiction in all cases, civil and criminal, except where exclusive jurisdiction is by this constitution or by law conferred upon some other department or division of the general court. It shall have such appellate jurisdiction as may be prescribed by general rules made by the judicial council, or by law.

Section 59. The county court shall have original jurisdiction to try all causes at the present time within the jurisdiction of the county court and justices' courts, unless or until otherwise provided by law. (If there is no court of county-wide jurisdiction, here define extent of county court's jurisdiction.)

Section 60. The chief justice and the justices of the supreme court shall be appointed by the governor for a term of ten years, subject to the consent of a majority of the legislature. The judges of the district court and the county court shall be appointed by the governor for a term of ten years.

Section 61. The chief justice shall be an additional justice of the supreme court and presiding justice thereof. He may sit in any division thereof. He shall preside over meetings of the judicial council, and shall be executive head of the general court of justice, exercising such powers as are herein expressed or may be hereafter conferred by rules, not in conflict herewith, made by the judicial council. It shall be the duty of the chief justice to organize the general court. The chief justice shall cause to be published an annual report which shall include statistics regarding the business done by each department of the general court, and the state of the dockets at the close of the year.

Section 62. Subject to alteration by the judicial council or by law, the state shall be divided into the following districts, namely:

First District: The first district shall comprise (and so forth).

Section 63. The district court judges shall be assigned by the chief justice to the several districts. As nearly as may be, each judge shall be assigned to a district containing all or a part of the district (or circuit) where he served regularly as a judge prior to the adoption of this constitution; but every such judge shall be eligible to sit under temporary assignment in any other district. Each district shall have a presiding justice who shall be appointed by the chief justice from among the judges over whom he is to preside, to serve as such until the end of the term of the chief justice, or until his retirement, or his removal as presiding justice by the judicial council. The presiding justice in each district shall have control over the calendars in the district and county courts in his district and the assignment of judges, subject to rules to be made by the judicial council.

Section 64. There shall be a judicial council, to consist of the chief justice, the presiding justices of the several districts, and two (or one) justices of the supreme court and two county court judges to be assigned for one year by the chief justice. The judicial council shall meet at least once in each quarter, at a time and place to be designated by the chief justice.

Section 65. The judicial council, in addition to other powers herein conferred upon it, or hereafter conferred by law, shall have exclusive power to make, alter and amend all rules relating to pleading, practice and procedure in the general court, and to prescribe generally by rules of court the duties and jurisdiction of masters and magistrates; also to make all rules and regulations respecting the duties and the business of the clerk of the general court and his subordinates, and all ministerial officers of the general court and all its departments, divisions and branches. The judicial council may reduce the number of justices of the peace in any county as vacancies occur.

Section 66. The rules in force at the time the general court shall be established, regulating pleading, practice and procedure in the courts consolidated by this constitution, which are not inconsistent herewith, whether the same be effective by reason of any or all acts of the legislature, or otherwise, are hereby repealed as statutes, and are constituted and declared to be operative as the first rules of court for the appropriate departments of the general court, but subject to the power of the judicial council to make, alter and amend such rules.

Section 67. There shall be selected, by nomination of the chief justice and confirmation of the judicial council, a clerk of the general court of justice, whose duties shall be prescribed by the judicial council. The supreme court reporter and clerks of all existing courts at the time of the establishment of the general court, shall continue in office until their terms expire or are terminated according to law, and shall be subject to the general supervision of the clerk of the general court. As vacancies occur in the offices of such clerks and supreme court reporter the places shall be filled in the manner provided above for the selection of the clerks of the general court, and the persons so selected shall hold for such terms and receive such salaries as the judicial council shall direct.

Section 68. Meetings of the judges of the supreme court and meetings of the district and county judges of the several districts shall be held separately at least once in each quarter, at times and places to be designated by the presiding justices. The chief justice shall be notified of all department and district meetings, and shall, in his discretion, attend, preside and take part in such meetings. The judges of all departments shall meet together and in departments once in each year, at a time and place to be designated by the chief justice. At all such meetings the judges shall receive and investigate, or cause to be investigated, all complaints pertaining to the operation of the courts in which they sit, and the officers thereof, and shall take such steps in reference thereto as they may deem necessary and proper. The judges shall have power at any meeting, and it shall be their duty, to recommend to the judicial council all such rules and regulations for the proper administration of justice as to them may seem expedient.

Section 69. The legislature may, upon due notice given and opportunity for defense, remove or retire from office any judge, upon the concurrence of two-thirds of all the members elected.

Section 70. All remuneration paid for the services of judges and court officials provided for under this constitution shall be paid by an appropriation by the legislature, and shall be reckoned as part of the expense of the judicial establishment under this constitution. The legislature may by law provide for the apportionment among the several counties of the state of the expense of the maintenance of the general court so far as the same may exceed the revenues received therefrom.

Section 71. Subject to alteration under rules made by the judicial council, the fees taxed shall be such as were at the establishment of the general court provided by law. All such fees and all masters' fees shall be paid to the clerk of the general court. All fines collected shall be paid to the clerk. All fees, costs and fines paid to the clerk shall be accounted for by him monthly and paid to the state treasurer.

SUFFRAGE AND ELECTIONS

Section 72. Every citizen of the United States, of the age of twenty-one years, who shall have been a resident of the state one year preceding the election, and of the county, township and ward (or precinct or election district) in which he resides, such time as may be provided by law, shall have the qualification of an elector.

Section 73. The legislature shall provide by law a system by which electors absent from their voting residence on election day shall not be denied the privilege of voting.

Section 74. For the purpose of voting, no person shall be deemed to have gained a residence by reason of his presence, or to have lost it by reason of his absence, while in the service of the United States, of the state government, or of a municipality of the state, or while navigating the waters of the United States or the high seas, or while a student of an institution, or while kept in an institution at public expense, or while confined in prison. The voting residence of a married woman shall be where she actually resides, and shall not be determined by the residence of her husband.

An American citizen otherwise qualified to vote shall not be deemed to have lost her voting privilege by marriage to an alien.

TAXATION AND FINANCE

Section 75. The power of taxation shall never be surrendered, suspended, or contracted away.

Section 76. The credit of the state or any civil division thereof shall not in any manner be given or loaned to or in aid of any individual, association or corporation.

Section 77. No debt shall be contracted by or in behalf of this state unless such debt shall be authorized by law for some single work or object to be distinctly specified therein; and no such law shall, except for the purpose of repelling invasion, suppressing insurrection, defending the state in war, or redeeming the present outstanding indebtedness of the state, take effect until it shall at a general election have been submitted to the people and have received a majority of all votes cast for and against it at such election; except that the state may by law borrow money to meet appropriations made for the next ensuing fiscal year (or biennium), in anticipation of the collection of taxes and revenues of such fiscal year (or biennium), and within fifty per centum of the amount of such anticipated taxes and revenues, but all loans contracted in anticipation of taxes and revenues shall be paid within one year.

MUNICIPAL CORPORATIONS

Section 78. Provision shall be made by a general law for the incorporation of cities and villages; and by a general law for the organization and government of cities and villages which do not adopt laws or charters in accordance with the provisions of sections 79 and 80.

Section 79. Laws may be enacted for the organization and government of cities and villages, which shall become effective in any city or village only when submitted to the electors thereof and approved by a majority of those voting thereon.

Section 80. Any city may frame and adopt a charter for its own government in the following manner:

The legislative authority of the city may, by a two-thirds vote of its members, and upon petition of ten per cent of the qualified electors shall forthwith, provide by ordinance for submission to the electors of the question, "Shall a commission be chosen to frame a charter?" The ordinance shall require that the question be submitted to the electors at the next regular municipal election, if one shall occur not less than sixty nor more than one hundred and twenty days after its passage, otherwise, at a special election to be called and held within the time aforesaid. The ballot containing such question shall also contain the names of candidates for the proposed commission, but without party designation. Such candidates shall be nominated by petition signed by not less than one per cent of the qualified electors and filed with the election authorities at least thirty days before such election, but the signatures of more than one thousand (1000) qualified electors shall not be required for the nomination of any candidate. If a majority of the electors voting on the question of choosing a commission shall vote in the affirmative, then the nine candidates receiving the highest number of votes (or if the legislative authority of the state provides by general law for the election of such commissioners by means of proportional representation, then the nine chosen in the manner required by such general law) shall constitute the charter commission and shall proceed to frame a charter. The legislative authority of the city shall, if so requested by the charter commission, appropriate money to provide for the reasonable expenses of the commission and for the printing of any completed charter and any separate and alternative provisions thereof and their distribution to the electors as required by Section 81.

Section 81. Any charter framed as provided in Section 80 shall be submitted to the qualified electors of the city at an election to be held at a time to be determined by the charter commission, but at least thirty days subsequent to the completion of the charter and its distribution among the electors and not more than one year after the election of the charter commission. Any part of such a charter, or any provision alternative to a part thereof, may be submitted to be voted upon separately. Not less than fifteen days before any such election the commission shall make provision for the distribution of copies of the proposed charter, and of any separate parts and alternative provisions thereof, to the qualified electors of the city. Any charter so proposed which is approved by a majority of the electors voting thereon, with the addition of such parts and as modified by such alternative provisions as may have been separately submitted and approved by a majority of those voting on any such part or provisions, shall become the organic law of the city at the time fixed in such charter, and shall supersede any existing charter and all laws affecting the organization and government of the city which are in conflict therewith. Within thirty days after its approval the election authorities shall certify a copy of the charter to the secretary of state who shall file it as a public record in his office and publish it as an appendix to the session laws enacted by the legislature.

Section 82. Amendments to any such charter may be framed and submitted by a charter commission in the same manner as provided in Section 81 for framing and adopting a charter. Amendments may also be proposed by a two-thirds vote of the legislative authority of the city, or by petition of five per cent of the electors; and any such amendment, after due public hearing before such legislative authority, shall be submitted to the qualified electors of the city at a regular or special election as in the case of the submission of the question of choosing a charter commission. Copies of all proposed amendments shall be sent to the qualified electors. Any such amendment approved by a majority of the electors voting thereon shall become a part of the charter of the city at the time fixed in the amendment and shall be certified to and filed and published by the secretary of state as in the case of a charter.

Section 83. Each city shall have and is hereby granted the authority to exercise all powers relating to municipal affairs; and no enumeration of powers in this constitution or any law shall be deemed to limit or restrict the general grant of authority hereby conferred; but this grant of authority shall not be deemed to limit or restrict the power of the legislature, in matters relating to state affairs.

The following shall be deemed to be a part of the powers conferred upon cities by this section:

(a) To levy, assess and collect taxes and to borrow money, within the limits prescribed by general laws; and to levy and collect special assessments for benefits conferred;

(b) To furnish all local public services; to purchase, hire, construct, own, maintain, and operate or lease local public utilities; to acquire, by condemnation or otherwise, within or without the corporate limits, property necessary for any such purposes, subject to restrictions imposed by general law for the protection of other communities; and to grant local public utility franchises and regulate the exercise thereof;

(c) To make local public improvements and to acquire, by condemnation or otherwise, property within its corporate limits necessary for such improvements, and also to acquire an excess over that needed for any such improvement, and to sell or lease such excess property with restrictions, in order to protect and preserve the improvement;

(d) To issue and sell bonds on the security, in whole or in part, of any such excess property, or of any public utility owned by the city, or of the revenues thereof, or of both, including in the case of a public utility, if deemed desirable by the city, a franchise stating the terms upon which, in case of foreclosure, the purchaser may operate such utility;

(e) To organize and administer public schools and libraries, subject to the general laws establishing a standard of education for the state;

(f) To adopt and enforce within their limits local police, sanitary and other similar regulations not in conflict with general laws.

Section 84. General laws may be passed requiring reports from cities as to their transactions and financial condition, and providing for the examination by state officials of the vouchers, books and accounts of all municipal authorities, or of public undertakings conducted by such authorities.

Section 85. All elections and submissions of questions provided for in

Sections 79 to 82, inclusive, or in any charter or law adopted in accordance therewith, shall be conducted by the election authorities provided by general law. (Where the practice is for cities to provide their own systems of municipal elections this practice should be continued.)

COUNTIES

Section 86. No new county shall be created and no existing county shall be subdivided unless the question is submitted to the duly enrolled or registered voters of the district or districts affected, at a regular or at a specially called election, and is approved by a majority of such voters voting thereon in the district or districts affected.

Section 87. The general powers and duties of county government shall be defined by general law, applicable to all counties, and optional plans for the organization of county government may be provided by law, to be effective in any county when submitted to the legal voters thereof and approved by a majority of those voting thereon.

Section 88. Any county shall have the power to frame, adopt and amend a charter for its government and to amend any existing law relating to its local organization, such charters and amendments to take effect when submitted to the legal voters of the county and approved by a majority of those voting thereon. The manner of exercising the powers herein granted may be regulated by general law.

Section 89. Any county with a population of over —— may be authorized by law to provide in its charter for a consolidated system of municipal government, providing for the powers and duties of county, city and other municipal authorities within the county and abolishing all officers whose powers and duties are otherwise provided for.

THE CIVIL SERVICE

Section 90. Appointments and promotions in the civil service of this state and of all civil divisions thereof, including counties, cities and villages, shall be made according to fitness, to be determined, so far as practicable, by examination, which, so far as practicable, shall be competitive.

PUBLIC WELFARE

Section 91. The maintenance and distribution, at reasonable rates, of a sufficient supply of food or other common necessaries of life, and the providing of shelter, are public functions, and the state and municipalities therein may take and provide the same for their inhabitants in such manner as the legislature shall determine.

Section 92. The conservation development and utilization of the agricultural, mineral, forest, water and other natural resources of the state, are public uses, and the legislature shall have power to provide for the taking, upon payment of just compensation therefor, of lands and easements, or interests therein, including water and mineral rights, for the purpose of securing and promoting the proper conservation, development, utilization and control thereof and to enact legislation necessary or expedient therefor.

Section 93. Advertising on public ways, in public places and on private property, within public view, may be regulated and restricted by law.

Section 94. The state, or any municipality thereof, appropriating or otherwise acquiring property for public use, may, in furtherance of such public use, appropriate or acquire an excess over that actually to be occupied by the improvement, and may sell such excess with such restrictions as shall be appropriate to preserve the improvement made. Bonds may be issued to supply the funds in whole or in part to pay for the excess property so appropriated or acquired; and such bonds, when made a lien only against the property so appropriated or acquired, shall not be subject to the restrictions or limitations of amount of indebtedness of the state or any municipality prescribed by this constitution or by law.

AMENDMENTS

Section 95. Amendments to this constitution may be proposed by the initiative as hereinbefore provided, or by the legislature at any regular or special session. Any such amendment presented in the legislature and agreed to by a majority of all the members shall be entered on the journal, with the yeas and nays, and shall be submitted to a vote of the electors by the secretary of the legislature at the first regular or special state election, held not less than three months after the date of adjournment. All proposed constitutional amendments shall be submitted on a separate, non-partisan ballot, and any amendment approved by a majority of the qualified electors voting on that amendment shall be declared adopted, provided that at least twenty per cent of those voting at the election be recorded in the affirmative. Any amendment so adopted shall become effective as part of the constitution ten days after the completion of the final canvass of the votes thereon unless a different date be specified in the amendment.

Section 96. The legislature, by vote of a majority of all the members entered by yeas and nays on the journal, may at any regular or special session call for a constitutional convention to amend or revise the constitution. The question, "Shall there be a convention to amend or revise the constitution?" shall be submitted to the qualified voters of the state in the manner prescribed in Section 95 for amendments proposed by the legislature, and if affirmed by a majority of the voters voting on said question, provided that at least twenty per cent of those voting at the election vote in the affirmative, the legislature shall at its next session provide by law for calling the same. Such convention shall assemble one month after the election of delegates. Delegates to the convention shall be chosen at a special election to be held not less than three months nor more than six months after approval of the proposition to call a convention. They shall be elected in the same manner as members of the legislature, by the system of proportional representation with a single transferable vote, except that the election of delegates shall be on a non-partisan ballot. As many delegates shall be elected from each legislative district as there are representatives in the legislature. The amendments or revision of the constitution shall be submitted to a vote of the people at a special election not less than three months nor more than six months after the adjournment of the convention, and if approved by a majority of the qualified voters voting thereon shall be published by the governor and become effective from the date of publication.

Section 97. The question, "Shall there be a convention to amend or revise the constitution?" may be proposed by petition. Such petition shall be signed by —— qualified voters, provided that in at least half of the counties of the state a number of qualified voters equal to five per cent of the total votes cast for governor at the last election sign the petition for a convention. The petition shall be filed with the secretary of the legislature, who shall canvass the same to ascertain whether it has been signed in accordance with the above requirements, and shall then publish the question in the manner prescribed in Section 95 except that the date of filing the petition shall take the place of the date of adjournment of the legislature prescribed therein. If the question be affirmed by a majority of the qualified voters voting thereon, provided that at least twenty per cent of those voting at the election vote in the affirmative, the convention shall be held in accordance with the provisions of Section 96.

Section 98. The provisions of the constitution affecting its amendment or revision shall be self-executing, but legislation may be adopted to facilitate their operation. If conflicting measures submitted to the people at the same election shall be approved, the one receiving the highest number of affirmative votes shall thereby become law as to all conflicting provisions.

APPENDIX D

THE LEGISLATIVE PROCESS *

X. ANALYSIS OF PRESENT LEGISLATIVE ORGANIZATION AND WORK.

A state legislature is essentially the affirmative organ of the state government for the development of new policies, or for the establishment of new principles. The executive has little or no authority to establish new policies, and the courts have less power to do so. The legislature, as the organ of the state government for affirmative action, should of course be so organized that it may operate effectively for this purpose.

During certain periods in the development of English law, legislative action was perhaps the most decisive influence in the development of the principles of private law. However, on the whole, the English legal system has in its main lines developed as a result of judicial action, and the legislature has normally limited itself to the meeting of new problems which could not be satisfactorily handled by the courts, or to the problem of restating in statutory form the results of judicial action. Occasionally important acts, such as the negotiable instruments act, the uniform sales act, and the uniform partnership act, are enacted by the General Assembly summing up and seeking to codify the existing law, with such changes as may seem desirable. Such an effort at legislative restatement of the whole law upon a particular subject is not frequent; and within the field of private law a session of the Illinois General Assembly ordinarily deals with only a small number of problems in which some specific difficulty may have presented itself.

The work of the Illinois General Assembly may, therefore, be said not to relate primarily to the development of rules for the regulation of relations between private individuals. Sir Courtney Ilbert remarked some time ago of the English Parliament that not one-tenth of the work of a session related to matters of private rights, and that the remainder related to matters primarily administrative in character. The same statement may be made regarding the work of the Illinois General Assembly. The great mass of its work relates to matters other than those which have to do with the relations between private individuals. Of course, the appropriations for the support of the state government and legislation regarding the administrative functions of the state and of the local subdivisions of the state are equally as important to the citizen as is legislation regulating the private rights of one citizen

* From the *Illinois Constitutional Convention Bulletins*, No. 8, "The Legislative Department," pp. 588-597. Compiled and published by the Legislative Reference Bureau (Springfield, 1919).

as against another. However, legislation which is primarily administrative in character involves problems of a distinctly different sort from that with respect to matters of private right.

An analysis of the legislative work of the General Assembly of Illinois in 1917 and 1919 indicates that of the 338 laws enacted by the General Assembly at its regular session in 1917, only seventeen can be classed as regulating primarily the private rights of parties among themselves. Of the 429 laws enacted at the regular session of the Illinois General Assembly in 1919 only fourteen belong to this class. A table is given below indicating in a rough fashion the types of matters dealt with by legislation in Illinois at these two sessions:

	1917	1919
State appropriations	63	67
Laws relating to state administrative matters	150	177
Laws relating to local administrative matters	108	171
Laws relating to purely private rights	17	14

Acts containing new substantive matter of legislation and merely containing appropriations incident thereto are not classified as appropriation acts. It is difficult to make a distinction between state and local administrative matters, and doubts have been resolved in favor of classification as local matters. The numerous acts readjusting local tax rates in 1919 are responsible for the large proportion of laws for that year classified as relating to local administrative matters.

This table probably indicates with sufficient clearness that the problems of legislation are primarily problems connected with the operation of state and local governments, and not problems having to do primarily with the rights of private individuals among themselves. In the case of state appropriations and of substantially all legislation regarding state administration, the information upon which legislation is to be based must be obtained primarily from the existing executive governmental agencies of the state, and with a better organization of the executive government the information for such legislation will be much more easily available than at the present time.

For matters relating to local administration, information again must to a great extent come from the state executive offices which have a general supervision over the different functions of local government. For example, with respect to schools and with respect to local charitable administration, a good deal of the impulse for legislation may come from the local communities, but this centers largely upon the state executive offices having supervision over these matters. Comment is made later in this discussion upon the fact that there is no constitutionally recognized relationship between the General Assembly and the executive department with respect to the enactment of legislation, although perhaps fully nine-tenths of the work of the General Assembly at each of its sessions must be devoted to legislation or proposed legislation having to do with the administration of government.

The chief problems of legislation coming before the General Assembly are problems of a technical character, requiring information regarding the actual operation of government and regarding the operation of similar institutions elsewhere. Legislation is a technical expert task and in the states of this country it is performed by a body, the length of whose session is in most cases narrowly limited. In Illinois where there is no constitutional limit, the General Assembly meets for five or six months in each two years, and the members during that five or six months' period return home ordinarily at the end of each week.

The executive veto operates as a purely negative check, and even as a negative check is exercised in the main in such a manner that defects in proposed legislation detected by the governor cannot be corrected by the General Assembly. As has already been suggested, substantially all bills come to the governor at the end of the session, and his action upon these bills is reported to the legislative bodies which have met merely in a formal manner and ordinarily without a quorum.

The whole development in the states of this country has been that of throwing limitations around the performance of legislative function, and of reducing the periods within which the legislature may act. Attention has already been called to the fact that annual sessions of legislatures have almost ceased in this country and also to the fact that legislative sessions are in most states limited to a fairly brief period. No limitations upon the legislative session exist in Illinois, and normally the General Assembly sits from January until close to the first of July, taking a recess a sufficient time before that date for the governor to act upon bills, and for laws to come into effect on the first of July, as now required by the constitution. Legislative bodies have not only been restricted in the frequency and length of their sessions, but their power has also been limited in this and other states by the development of the executive veto. The function of legislation is the affirmative task of laying down new policies, and the executive veto has come to be primarily a negative check.

Detailed limitations as to its procedure and as to the things which it may do have been placed around the legislature in such a manner that pitfalls exist in substantially every direction. Even the most carefully drafted legislation may have overlooked some one of the pitfalls which has been planned by the constitution, and even if such pitfalls have all been carefully avoided there is great danger of violating some constitutional provision as to procedure in the numerous steps of its cumbersome legislative process through which every bill must pass before it becomes law. Legislation has therefore become a hazardous occupation.

Distrust of legislatures developed very early after the independence of this country, and that distrust has led to a hampering of the legislative function in so many respects that effective and valid legislation has become an extremely difficult thing. Little has been done as yet in this country toward the working out of plans by which the General Assembly may be made a responsible legislative body for the affirmative enactment of state policies. Substantially all of the development has been toward limiting and restricting the General Assembly's power for evil, upon the apparent assumption that a legislative body is merely a necessary evil. Naturally little has been accomplished under this theory in the bettering of legislative organization.

The legislative body under the constitution of Illinois is and can be in no sense a body of lawmaking experts. Members of the General Assembly are elected from all walks of life for the purpose of giving ordinarily not over six months out of each two years of their time to the business of legislation. They may well represent under the plans now in existence the sentiment of the community with respect to broad matters of public policy, but such broad matters are rather infrequent as compared with the more detailed and more technical matters which must be dealt with by legislation.

XI. CONCLUSIONS

The principle of the separation of powers is formally embodied in the constitution of Illinois, but is expressly subject to all of the exceptions made in the text of the constitution itself. This principle was announced in the constitution of 1818, but the constitution of that year did little toward establishing the principle in practice. From 1818 to 1848, the legislative department was predominant and largely controlled the executive and judicial departments. Such a predominance of the legislative department characterized all state governments after the declaration of independence, and independent spheres of executive and judicial departments gradually became established in the fifty years following 1776. The increased power of the executive and judicial departments has come about primarily through the vesting in these departments of power at first regarded as legislative.

In a discussion earlier in this pamphlet upon the relations of the General Assembly with other departments of the state government, attention has been called to the express constitutional provisions bearing upon relationships with other departments. A number of exceptions have already been made to the principle of the separation of powers and perhaps the greatest exception to this principle in actual operation is that as to the relationship between the governor and the two houses of the General Assembly, when the executive and legislative branches of the state government are in accord. Much the greater part of legislative business bears upon the operation of government and it is essential that the executive and the legislative departments should work in close harmony upon these problems, for the executive is not only the body which will know most about the operation of existing laws (which it is itself administering) but it is also the body which will administer or supervise the administration of all new administrative legislation. It is essential that the General Assembly obtain from the executive department a large mass of information upon which new legislation may be based, and when the governor and the two houses of the General Assembly are in accord it is also natural that the governor as the head of the executive department should have a large influence with the legislative department in the final determination as to what legislation shall be enacted. Such an affirmative relationship between the governor and the General Assembly is now recognized by Article V, Section 7 of the constitution. The governor is required to give the General Assembly information as to the condition of the state and to recommend such measures as he shall deem expedient.

The theory that the governor and the legislature must be absolutely distinct and must operate in more or less separate and watertight compartments, carefully refraining from relationship with each other, is absolutely unworkable; and such a theory has never been a necessary conclusion from the principle of the separation of powers; nor has it ever been an actuality except in cases where through disagreement between the two departments, the state government was working inefficiently.

There has been in recent years a very definite tendency to recognize in the governor a more positive share in the actual making of legislation. A vigorous man in the office of governor always exercises a large influence in legislation, and the state is better off for such exercise. Bills sponsored by the governor ordinarily obtain precedence in the two houses. Not only this, but the legislative body is more effective under such conditions and is better able to perform the functions for which it has been established.

The veto power, it has already been suggested, is primarily a negative function exercised at the end of a legislative session, when any suggestions which the governor may have for the improvement of legislation cannot be availed of. Constitutional provisions in Alabama and Virginia and a recent constitutional provision in Massachusetts regarding the governor's recommendations upon bills presented to him after passage by the two houses, indicate a step in the direction of giving the governor a larger affirmative share in legislation; but the governor cannot exercise an affirmative share in legislation by passing upon bills submitted to him, if the bills come to him at the end of the legislative session, so that he has merely an alternative of approving bill or of vetoing it, without there being a possibility of improving it in co-operation with the General Assembly. The budget provisions in Maryland and Massachusetts also reflect a growing tendency to increase the affirmative share of the governor in legislation, and here this affirmative share in legislation comes through the recommendation of a detailed budget. In Maryland the governor's budget is preserved through a prohibition of legislative increase in its items (a prohibition similar to that established by rules in the British House of Commons). In Massachusetts the governor's control is established by permitting the general court to increase items in the budget, but by granting to the governor at the same time an authority to reduce items or veto parts of items, so that he may, if the general court has increased his recommendations of appropriations, reduce them to the amounts of his original recommendation.

However, little has on the whole been done in this country toward bringing about an effective co-operation between the executive department and the legislative department in matters of legislation. It may be desirable to repeat here that the need for a constitutional recognition of such closer relationship depends upon two things:

(1) The fact that the bulk of work to be performed by a legislative body has a direct bearing upon the work being done by the executive body.

(2) The further fact that the legislative body now is and is likely to remain a body not in constant session, but meeting only for several months in each legislative period. A body assembled as is the general assembly of Illinois has no opportunity when once it has come into session to accumulate all of the data necessary for effective legislation. Such accumulation of data and preparation of information must come in advance of the legislative session. The general assembly meets on an average of about three days each week for some six months during each twenty-four months, and the members in general find it necessary to continue their private business to some extent even during the sessions. To expect from a body of this type, no matter how able, honest and hardworking the members of such a body may be, a high grade performance upon a great number of technical measures is futile, unless the executive as the permanent organ of the state government has some machinery for bringing these matters effectively to the attention of the legislative body. By the constitution of 1870, an effort was made to draw the courts in as an aid to legislation, by requiring them to report defects in the laws, but this plan has not worked.

The separation of the legislative and executive functions is now accentuated by the provisions in Sections 3 and 15 of Article IV of the constitution, preventing any person elected to the general assembly from receiving any civil appointment in this state during the term for which he shall have been elected and forbidding any person holding a lucrative office under the United States or this state from having a seat in the general assembly. These provisions do not prevent the giving of political rewards to legislative leaders. If the party in control of the state government is also in control of the national government, appointments to office are oftentimes made to national positions of those who under this constitutional provision would be disqualified from holding state positions. These constitutional provisions do not as a matter of fact prevent the objectionable practice at which they were aimed, but they do often result in taking persons having some information about state government out of the service of state government and into the service of national or local government.

Attention has already been called to the difficulties in the operation of our government when the executive belongs to a political party which does not at the same time control the two houses of the legislative department. This lack of political harmony between the executive and the legislative departments has been quite evident in the national government during a good part of the time since the civil war. In the national government at least there is a tendency for the party in the minority in a presidential election to control the federal house of representatives in the intervening election between presidential years.

In the Illinois general assembly cases of purely partisan alignment upon legislation are not frequent. Upon the bulk of important legislation no party lines are drawn, and in the past at least the issue between "wet" and "dry" has been much more important than that between democrat and republican. However, it should not be inferred from this statement that it is therefore immaterial as to whether the governor and the two houses of the general assembly are in political accord. Although party alignments are infrequent, the control of the two departments of the government by different parties makes a great deal of confusion and friction. Attention may also be called to the fact that, for political reasons, the governor has greater influence with the general assembly meeting when his term begins than with the one meeting in the middle of his term, even though in both cases there is political accord between the governor and the majorities of the two houses.

The English parliamentary system, which has been adopted very widely throughout the world, has a distinct advantage in that it keeps a constant political harmony between the legislative and the executive departments. Under the parliamentary system as it operates in England, and in most of the countries which have copied from England, the executive part of the government is controlled by a cabinet whose members are of the same party as that which controls the more popular branch of the legislature, the members of the cabinet resigning or forcing a new popular election when they cease to be in harmony with the legislative body. In this manner the legislative body is always able to force a change of cabinets or at least an appeal to the electorate to determine whether the existing cabinet and the party it represents should remain in power. Either by the resignation of the cabinet or by its success or failure in the general election, political harmony between the legislature and the executive is restored almost immediately after it has once ceased to exist. The English parliamentary system almost necessarily, however, requires either a single-chambered legislature or a legislative organization in which one house has the dominant political control.

In this country the system of separate executive and legislative organizations works best when the executive and legislature are not only in political harmony but when the personnel of the two departments is such that effective co-operation may be had. When there is not political harmony, or when there is not full co-operation, even if there is apparent political harmony, the governmental organization in this country works badly or almost not at all. That is, the theory (although somewhat modified by express constitutional provisions) implies a rather distinct separation of departments; but the system based upon this theory works well only when such separation is in fact largely broken down and when a close co-operation is established through extra-constitutional means.

Assuming political harmony to exist at any time between the two departments in a given state, the co-operation of the two departments is of course rendered more effective if the legislative leaders are not changing at frequent intervals. Under our cumbersome system of legislative organization, it normally requires several sessions for a man to develop a close familiarity with the details of governmental problems. The senate in this state is so organized under the constitution that substantially one-half of the members are elected each two years, so that at least one-half of the members have always had previous legislative experience. Of course it is also true that members of the state senate are often re-elected or that members of the house are elected to the state senate, so that continuous legislative service in the senate is increased in this way beyond that required by the constitution. In the session of 1917, of the twenty-five newly elected members of the senate, five had seen service in the immediately preceding session of the house of representatives, and nine had previously been in the state senate. In the session of 1919, of the twenty-six newly elected members of the senate, nineteen had had legislative service immediately preceding their election.

No constitutional provision requires continuity of service in the house of representatives, although by election a fair degree of continuity is maintained. In the Fiftieth General Assembly (1917), of the 153 members, 90 had served in the next preceding session either of the senate or of the house of representatives. In 1919, of the 153 members of the house of representatives, 97 had served in the next preceding session either of the senate or of the house of representatives.

A member by frequent re-elections to the house or senate acquires a degree of expertness in legislative matters, and some continuity of membership through re-election is almost necessary to the working of the present cumbersome machinery of legislation. A house of representatives composed entirely of persons without previous legislative experience would be almost helpless, however high the ability of its members may be.

Anyone who has had to deal with the legislative organization of Illinois or of any other state must be impressed by the cumbersomeness of the present legislative machinery. Skill and persistence are required to take a piece of proposed legislation through all stages in each house and finally through the process of executive approval. No plans have been worked out by the constitution or through legislative procedure for the careful co-ordination of the work of the two houses. The citizen without legislative experience ordinarily finds himself lost when he comes for the first time in contact with this highly cumbersome procedure. The theory upon which this procedure and the limitations upon the legislature have been built up is apparently that the legislature must be practically prevented from doing anything in order that it may be prevented from doing wrong things, and such a plan is practically certain to lead to undesirable consequences.

The process of legislation has two distinct aspects: (1) The expert, (2) The popular. Any legislative organization should be of such a character as to reflect upon matters of legislation the needs and the views of the people of the state. It must also be borne in mind, however, that the technical aspect of legislation is no less important, and that a large part of business to be acted upon by a legislature has to do with matters upon which the public may have very little opinion either way. Even upon matters with respect to which the public has positive views, the technical element is important and care upon the technical side of legislation is essential if the people are finally through legislation to get what they desire. This balancing of the technical and the popular aspects of legislation presents the most serious problem with respect to the matter now under consideration, and the problem is one which has not been dealt with to any extent as yet in this country. From the standpoint of the expression of popular opinion and the accumulation of popular views there is of course a distinct value in having a large popular body meet occasionally as is now the case with the Illinois General Assembly. Small bodies of technical experts holding office permanently or for long terms are not likely to be proper representatives of the popular views and the popular needs.

The functions to be accomplished by a legislative organization are: (1) Satisfactory positive action in accord with the views of the people of the state, and (2) technical correctness in the legislation enacted in accord with popular views and, also in the enactment of the numerous measures needed for the proper conduct of administrative matters with respect to which the public at large will normally have no decided opinion one way or the other.

This combination of the temporary popular element in legislation with the permanent technical element in legislation may be worked out in several different ways:

(a) The permanent skilled element may be organized in the executive, which has necessarily a permanent, continuous organization, leaving the legislature with an organization more or less like that now in existence for the expression of the popular view upon matters presented by the executive, and also for the enactment into legislation of matters demanded by public sentiment but not proposed by the executive.

(b) There might be a permanent technical legislature such as that suggested in a quotation earlier in this pamphlet from a message to the Kansas legislature by Governor Hodges. Clearly, however, a small permanent body composed of technical experts would not be adequate as a means of reflecting the popular needs and desires in legislation, and if there were a small and permanent technical body such as Governor Hodges suggested, much of the work of such a body would have to be submitted either to a larger and more representative legislative body or to a referendum of the people.

(c) It may be possible to establish a permanent expert staff subject to the general assembly or to a combination of executive and legislative control, this permanent expert staff drawing up the measures suggested by the administrative bodies of the state and local government or by members of the legislature and submitting these measures to the legislature meeting very much as at present. The legislative reference bureau is an approach to what is here suggested, although the chief function of the legislative reference bureau has been that of drafting bills desired by members of the General Assembly, after they have come into session; and there has not as yet been any effective way of preparing in advance of the legislative session the matters which it may be desired to submit to the General Assembly.

APPENDIX E

RETRENCHMENT AND REORGANIZATION IN THE STATE GOVERNMENT *

. . . .

In searching for valid principles on which to base retrenchment and economy in administration we have naturally turned to the experience of other States. Common sense dictates that New York should first of all study carefully the steps which have already been taken elsewhere, with a view to introducing improved methods into the conduct of public business. In making this inquiry the Commission has found that in nearly every State public attention has been forcibly drawn to the necessity of reducing expenditures or at least holding them to the lowest point consistent with the proper discharge of public functions and fair conditions of employment. The Commission has also found that the movement for economy and efficiency has passed beyond the stage of protest and discussion. Between 1911 and 1917 (when the movement was temporarily checked by the war), a number of States instituted commissions of inquiry for the purpose of discovering more businesslike methods in state administration. Examination of the laws creating these commissions brings out the fact that waste and duplication, inevitably accompanying the maintenance of conflicting and competing offices and boards, were the main cause which led these states to seek relief. The reports filed by the several commissions are in substantial agreement on the following points:

1. State administration is a collection of offices, boards and other agencies which have been created from time to time by legislative act without consideration being given to the desirability of grouping all related work in one department.
2. The board or commission type of organization for purely administrative work is generally inefficient owing to the division of powers and absence of initiative and responsibility. This applies with less force to departments in which there are important quasi-judicial or quasi-legislative functions combined with administrative functions. Boards have been successful in many cases in carrying out advisory and inspectional functions and in the general supervision of education. Ex-officio boards are almost never effective.

* From *Report of New York State Reconstruction Commission,* Chap. I, "The Underlying Principles" (Albany, 1919).

3. Widely scattered and independent agencies of state government cannot be effectively supervised and controlled either by the Legislature or the Governor.
4. When such a large number of agencies is independent of the Governor, he cannot be held responsible to the voters for an efficient and economical management of public business.

In their recommendations for improvement of administration, the commissions are substantially agreed that economy and responsible government can only result from:

1. The consolidation of offices, boards and commissions into a few great departments of government, each of which is responsible for the conduct of a particular major function such as finance, health, welfare, or public works.
2. Vesting the power of appointment and removal of department heads in the Governor; making him in fact, as well as in theory, the responsible Chief Executive of the state. There is a difference of opinion as to the desirability of confirmation of the Governor's nominations by the Senate.
3. A consolidated budget system with accounting control over spending officers.

The budget recommendations have passed beyond the theoretical stage, for thirty-eight states have enacted legislation providing for a consolidated budget system with varying provisions as to methods of preparation, legislative review, and enactment into law. Half of these states have placed the responsibility for initiating the budget squarely upon the Governor.

The recommendations with reference to the reorganization of boards, offices and commissions have not been accepted by the state Legislatures as readily as proposals for budget reform. The reasons are obvious. A consolidation of a hundred or more offices, boards and other agencies affects political patronage more vitally than does a budget system, and it requires considerable courage and intelligence on the part of a Legislature to reorganize an entire system of state government. Nevertheless, rcommendations of commissions are passing steadily into law. The State of Illinois, comparable to New York in wealth and population, in 1917, under the vigorous leadership of Governor Lowden, made a complete and drastic reorganization of state administration, sweeping away 105 offices and agencies and consolidating the affairs of the State under nine great departments. The Commonwealth of Massachusetts by constitutional provision in 1918 prepared the way for a consolidation of the numerous offices and agencies composing the state administration. . . .

PRINCIPLES OF PROPOSED PLAN OF ADMINISTRATIVE ORGANIZATION AND BUDGET

The experience of other States in the Union, the experience of the national government with a consolidated administration and a cabinet system and the recommendations of competent authorities lead us to the conclusion that retrenchment and responsibility in the government of the State of New York can be achieved only through:

1. A consolidation of all administrative departments, commissions, offices, boards and other agencies into a small number of departments, each headed by a single officer, except departments where quasi-legislative and quasi-judicial or inspectional and advisory functions require a board.
2. The adoption of the principle that the Governor is to be held responsible for good administration and is to have the power to choose the heads of departments who are to constitute his Cabinet and who are to be held strictly accountable to him through his power to appoint and remove and through his leadership in budget preparation. This involves among other things the reduction in the number of elective administrative officers to two: the Governor and a Comptroller to act as independent financial auditor. Although there are objections to the confirmation by the Senate of nominations by the Governor, we are of the opinion that this check has on the whole worked well and should be retained.
3. The extension of the term of the Governor to four years and the careful adjustment of the terms of department heads with reference to the term of the Governor. Excepting members of boards with overlapping terms, department heads should have the same term as the Governor.
4. The grouping of related offices and work in each of the several departments into appropriate divisions and bureaus, responsibility for each branch of work to be centralized in an accountable chief.
5. A budget system vesting in the Governor the full responsibility for presenting to the Legislature each year a consolidated budget containing all expenditures which in his opinion should be undertaken by the State, and a proposed plan for obtaining the necessary revenues—such a budget to represent the work of the Governor and his Cabinet. Incorporation of all appropriations based upon the budget in a single general appropriation bill. Restriction of the power of the Legislature to increase items in the budget. Provision that pending action on this bill the Legislature shall not enact any other appropriation bill except on recommendation of the Governor. Granting to the Governor the power to veto items or parts of items. Provision that special appropriation bills introduced after final action on the general appropriation bill shall secure the specific means for defraying appropriations carried therein.

APPENDIX F

STATE OF NEW YORK: PROPOSED CONSTITUTIONAL BUDGET AMENDMENT *

ARTICLE V

Section 1. On or before the fifteenth day of October in the year one thousand nine hundred and —— and in each year thereafter the head of each department of the state government except the legislature and judiciary, shall submit to the governor itemized estimates of appropriations to meet the financial needs of such department, including a statement in detail of all moneys for which any general or special appropriation is desired at the ensuing session of the legislature, classified according to relative importance and in such form and with such explanation as the governor may require. Copies of such estimates shall be simultaneously furnished to the designated representatives of the appropriate committees of the Legislature for their information.

The Governor, after public hearing thereon, at which he may require the attendance of heads of departments and their subordinates, shall revise such estimates according to his judgment. The representatives aforesaid of the committees of the legislature shall be invited to attend such hearings, and under regulations to be provided by law shall be entitled to make inquiry in respect to the estimates and the revision thereof.

Itemized estimates of the financial needs of the legislature certified by the presiding officer of each house and of the judiciary certified by the comptroller shall be transmitted to the governor on or before said fifteenth day of October for inclusion in the budget without revision but with such recommendation as he may think proper.

On or before the fifteenth day of January next succeeding (except in the case of a newly elected governor and then on or before the first day of February) he shall submit to the legislature a budget containing a complete plan of proposed expenditures and estimated revenues. It shall contain all the estimates so revised or certified and clearly itemized, and shall be accompanied by a bill or bills for all proposed appropriations and reappropriations; it shall show the estimated revenues for the ensuing fiscal year and the estimated surplus or deficit of revenues at the end of the current fiscal year together with the measures of taxation, if any, which the governor may propose for the increase of the

* From *Report of the State Reorganization Commission,* February 26, 1926. State of New York: Legislative Document (1926) No. 72, pp. 69-70.

revenues. It shall be accompanied by a statement of current assets, liabilities, reserves and surplus or deficit of the state; statements of the debts and funds of the state; an estimate of its financial condition as of the beginning and end of the ensuing fiscal year; and a statement of revenues and expenditures for the two fiscal years next preceding said year in form suitable for comparison. The governor may before final action by the legislature thereon, and not more than thirty days after submission thereof, amend or supplement the budget; he may also with the consent of the legislature, submit such amendment or a supplemental bill at any time before the adjournment of the legislature.

A copy of the budget and of any amendments or additions thereto shall be forthwith transmitted by the governor to the comptroller.

The governor and the heads of departments shall have the right, and it shall be the duty of the heads of departments when requested by either house of the legislature, to appear and be heard in respect to the budget during the consideration thereof, and to answer inquiries relevant thereto. The procedure for such appearance and inquiries shall be provided by law. The legislature may not alter an appropriation bill submitted by the governor except to strike out or reduce items therein, but it may add thereto items of appropriation provided that such additions are stated separately and distinctly from the original items of the bill and refer each to a single object or purpose; none of the restrictions of this provision, however, shall apply to appropriations for the legislature or judiciary. Such a bill when passed by both houses shall be a law immediately without further action by the governor, except that appropriations for the legislature and judiciary and separate items added to the governor's bills by the legislature shall be subject to his approval as provided in section nine of article four.

Neither house shall consider further appropriations until the appropriation bills proposed by the governor shall have been finally acted on by both houses; nor shall such further appropriations be then made except by separate bills each for a single work or object, which bills shall be subject to the governor's approval as provided in section nine of article four. Nothing herein contained shall be construed to prevent the governor from recommending that one or more of his proposed bills be passed in advance of the others to supply the immediate needs of government or to meet an emergency.

THE DEBT OF THE STATE OF NEW YORK PAST, PRESENT, AND FUTURE *

Future Borrowing Policy

As the result of this detailed examination of the history of the state debt, your committee has two definite recommendations to offer. In the

* From *Report by the Special Joint Committee on Taxation and Retrenchment*, March 1, 1926. State of New York: Legislative Document (1926) No. 70, pp. 103-104.

first place, we recommend that provision be made for a capital budget which shall be an integral part of the general budget and budget system of the state. It is of the utmost importance that the plans for capital expenditure shall be laid out in advance for a five- or ten-year period and that these plans shall be directly related to the budget for current purposes. Much of the difficulty in this state with improvements in the past has come from the lack of any consistent plan. Not a few projects have been started and abandoned or allowed to drag along because there was no definite plan, in the first place, embracing all of the improvements to be financed over a period of years. We had the same difficulty with highway construction until a definite program was adopted which has been followed year after year. Some individuals have thought that such plans cannot be worked out unless bond funds are available. This is, obviously, a mistake. In fact, lack of planning has been evident with some bond issues as well. With the establishment of a sound state budget plan, it should not be difficult to provide for a businesslike handling of the construction program.

Our second recommendation has to do with financial policy. When a capital budget system is put into operation, as we have recommended above, we would urge that [the] state swing over gradually to a policy of paying for all recurring annual expenditures for permanent improvements and investments from current revenues. If such a policy can be put into operation gradually during the next ten years, we shall be in a position to continue after 1935 without borrowing funds for lands, buildings, and other usual improvements. Under this plan, the bulk of the $100,000,000 bond issue will be used for catching up on the building program of the state. This was the basis on which the bond plan was approved by the voters. Under the circumstances we should not reduce the annual appropriations from current revenues for permanent improvements below the normal level of past years. If such a reduction is made, it will mean that the new borrowed funds are being used to pay the regular expenditures for capital improvements and not to catch up on items neglected during the war years and since that time. The $100,000,000 was for the "emergency" and our suggestion is that it be used only for the "emergency."

APPENDIX G

A SELECTED LIST OF REFERENCES FOR THE STUDY OF STATE GOVERNMENT *

A. BIBLIOGRAPHIES.

American Historical Association. *Annual Reports,* 1900-1911; Reports of Public Archives Commission on official literature of a large number of states. Washington, 1900-1911.

The best source of information on the archives and manuscript records of the states.

(The) American Year Book. New York, 1910-1919, 1925-.

Contains selected lists of references on the current history and activities of the state governments.

BOWKER, R. R. "State Publications; a provisional list of the official publications of the several states of the United States from their organization." *New York Publishers' Weekly,* 1902-1908.

The only approximately complete check-list of state documents.

CHANNING, EDWARD; HART, A. B.; and TURNER, F. J. *Guide to the Study and Reading of American History.* Boston, 1912.

Contains the best selected lists of public records and documents and secondary works relating to the history and government of the states.

GREER, SARAH. *A Bibliography of Public Administration.* National Institute of Public Administration, New York, 1926.

An excellent selected list of references on public administration, chiefly those published since 1915. Included in the list are many valuable references on various phases of state administration and also on political parties and elections.

HASSE, A. R. *Index of Economic Material in Documents of the States of the United States.* Carnegie Institution, Washington, 1907-.

An index of such material from 1789. To 1926, thirteen volumes on thirteen of the principal states had appeared.

Library of Congress. *Monthly List of State Publications.* Washington, 1910-.

The most complete list of current state publications.

MCLAUGHLIN, A. C., and HART, A. B., editors. *Cyclopedia of American Government.* 3 vols. New York, 1914.

* Many of the references cited in the text or in the foot-notes are omitted from this list. This is particularly true of articles published in periodicals.

Contains selected lists of references appended to the several articles relating to state government and administration.

Public Affairs Information Service Bulletin. White Plains, N. Y., 1914-.

Weekly with five cumulations throughout the year. A current record and description of all literature relating to public affairs.

Reece, E. J. *State Documents for Libraries.* University of Illinois Bulletin, xii, 36. Urbana, 1915.

An excellent general guide to the official publications of the states.

B. THE STATE CONSTITUTIONS.

Kettleborough, Charles. *The State Constitutions* (and the Federal Constitution and Organic Laws of the Territories and other Colonial Dependencies of the United States of America). Indianapolis, 1918.

The latest and most complete compilation of the existing state constitutions. For changes and amendments made since the publication of this work, see the *American Political Science Review, passim,* and the *American Year Book.*

New York State Constitutional Convention Commission. *Index Digest of State Constitutions.* New York, 1915.

An excellent digest of the state constitutions at the beginning of 1914.

Thorpe, F. N. *The Federal and State Constitutions,* (Colonial Charters, and other Organic Laws of the States, Territories, and Colonies now or heretofore forming the United States of America). 7 vols. Washington, 1909.

The latest and most complete compilation of the past and present constitutions of the states.

C. THE UNION AND THE STATES.

Burdick, C. K. *The Law of the American Constitution.* New York, 1922.

The most recent work on the law of the Federal Constitution.

Cooley, T. M. *A Treatise on the Constitutional Limitations which rest upon the Legislative Power of the States of the American Union.* 7th ed., Boston, 1903.

The standard treatise on the law-making powers of the states.

Macdonald, A. F. *Federal Subsidies to the States.* Philadelphia, 1923.

A careful study of the important question of federal subventions.

Scott, J. B. *The United States of America:* (a Study in International Organization). New York, 1920.

Discusses the Union as an analogy for international organization.

Thompson, Walter. *Federal Centralization.* New York, 1923.

An excellent work on the expansion of federal authority and the curtailment of the powers of the states.

WARREN, CHARLES. *The Supreme Court and the Sovereign States.* Princeton, 1924.

Contains interesting material on interstate disputes and compacts.

WILLOUGHBY, W. W. *The American Constitutional System.* New York, 1904.

The best general statement of the constitutional position of the states in the Union.

WILLOUGHBY, W. W. *The Constitutional Law of the United States.* 2 vols. New York, 1910.

The standard treatise on the subject.

D. THE ORIGIN AND DEVELOPMENT OF THE STATE GOVERNMENTS.

CROLY, HERBERT. *The Promise of American Life.* New York, 1909. *Progressive Democracy.* New York, 1914.

These two volumes together furnish a very systematic and suggestive interpretation of the history of American politics.

DEALEY, J. Q. *Growth of American State Constitutions.* Boston, 1915.

The best summary of the constitutional history of the states.

FORD, H. J. *The Rise and Growth of American politics.* New York, 1898.

A suggestive study of underlying tendencies in American politics.

MERRIAM, C. E. *History of American Political Theories.* New York, 1903. *American Political Ideas, 1865-1917.* New York, 1920.

The best general accounts of the development of American political ideas.

NEVINS, ALLAN. *The American States during and after the Revolution, 1775-1789.* New York, 1924.

A comprehensive study of the history of the states during the formative period.

PORTER, K. H. *A History of Suffrage in the United States.* Chicago, 1918.

A good summary of the history of the suffrage.

SMITH, J. A. *The Spirit of American Government.* New York, 1907.

An able study of underlying tendencies in American politics, written from a different viewpoint than that of H. J. Ford, *supra.*

E. THE WORKING OF THE STATE GOVERNMENTS.

1. General Works.

BRYCE, JAMES. *The American Commonwealth.* 2 vols. 1st ed., New York, 1888; rev. ed., 1910.

Contains a well-informed and judicious study of the forms and spirit of state government at the close of the century.

DODD, W. F. *State Government.* New York, 1922.

A standard work, covering all the important phases of the subject.

Hamilton, Alexander; Madison, James; and Jay, John. *The Federalist.* 1st ed., New York, 1788.

Contains an excellent critical study of the state governments before the adoption of the Federal Constitution.

Illinois Constitutional Convention Bulletins. Springfield, 1919.

Massachusetts Constitutional Convention Bulletins. Boston, 1918.

Contain much useful information on contemporary institutions and problems of state government.

Mathews, J. M. *American State Government.* New York, 1924.

A standard work on the subject, which is especially valuable for the chapters on state administration.

Tocqueville, Alexis de. *Democracy in America.* 2 vols. 1st (French) ed., Paris, 1835-1840.

Contains a brilliant study of the forms and spirit of state government in the early nineteenth century.

2. Parties and Elections.

Annals of the American Academy of Political and Social Science, cvi (1923). *The Direct Primary.*

Contains an excellent collection of articles on the direct primary and a digest of the direct primary laws of the states.

Brooks, R. C. *Political Parties and Electoral Problems.* New York, 1923.

A standard work on parties and elections.

Cleveland, F. A. *Organized Democracy.* New York, 1913.

A comprehensive study of the electorate and elections.

Evans, E. C. *History of the Australian Ballot System in the United States.* Chicago, 1917.

A good summary of the history of this important reform.

Hall, A. B. *Popular Government.* New York, 1921.

Contains a critical analysis of the direct primary and also of the initiative, referendum, and recall.

Holcombe, A. N. *The Political Parties of Today.* 2nd ed., New York, 1925.

Discusses influence of state interests in national politics.

Merriam, C. E. *The American Party System.* New York, 1922.

A stimulating and suggestive analysis and interpretation of the American party system.

Merriam, C. E., and Gosnell, H. F. *Non-Voting: Causes and Methods of Control.* Chicago, 1924.

A valuable statistical analysis of the problem of non-voting.

Ostrogorski, M. *Democracy and the Party System in the United States.* New York, 1910.

An unsympathetic account of party government.

Ray, P. O. *An Introduction to Political Parties and Practical Politics.* 3d ed., New York, 1924.

A standard work on party issues, nominations, and elections.

Woodburn, J. A. *Political Parties and Party Problems in the United States.* 3d ed., New York, 1924.

Another useful description of party issues and the conduct of campaigns.

3. The State Legislature.

American Bar Association. *Report of the Committee on Noteworthy Changes in Statute Law.* 1915-1920, 1923-.

A useful annual pamphlet summarizing the current federal and state legislation.

Dodds, H. W. *Procedure in State Legislatures.* Supplement to the Annals of the American Academy of Political and Social Science, lxxvii (1918).

An excellent summary account of legislative procedure.

Freund, Ernst. *Standards of American Legislation.* Chicago, 1917.

An able discussion of various technical questions involved in law-making.

Luce, Robert. *Legislative Procedure.* Boston, 1922. *Legislative Assemblies.* Boston, 1924.

Contain much valuable information on the state legislatures.

Moore, B. F. *The History of Cumulative Voting and Minority Representation in Illinois, 1870-1919.* 2d ed., Urbana, 1919.

A study of the partisan representative system in operation in Illinois.

Reed, A. Z. *The Territorial Basis of Government under the State Constitutions.* New York, 1911.

A study of the systems of representation in the state legislatures.

Reinsch, P. S. *American Legislatures and Legislative Methods.* New York, 1907.

Though somewhat out of date, still an excellent account of the state legislatures.

Rice, S. A. *Farmers and Workers in American Politics.* New York, 1924.

A valuable statistical study of voting alignments in various state legislatures.

Steffens, Lincoln. *The Struggle for Self-government.* New York, 1906.

The most effective of the studies of legislative incompetence and corruption, published during the "muck-raking" period.

4. The State Executive and State Administration.

For references on the various branches of state administration, see ch. xi, *passim.*

Buck, A. E. *Administrative Consolidation in State Governments.* 3d ed., New York, 1924.

The best summary of the consolidation movement is to be found in this pamphlet issued by the National Municipal League.

BUCK, A. E. *Budget Making.* New York, 1921.

An excellent handbook on the principles and methods of state budget making.

(U. S.) Bureau of the Census. *Financial Statistics of States,* 1915-1919, 1921-. Washington.

A comprehensive annual publication of the sources of state revenue and of the nature and amount of state expenditures.

CLEVELAND, F. A., and BUCK, A. E. *The Budget and Responsible Government.* New York, 1920.

A good discussion of budget reform by two leading budget reformers.

Efficiency and Economy Commissions. The reports of the various state efficiency and economy commissions are indispensable to the student of state government and administration. A few of the more important of these reports are as follows:

Illinois. *Report of the Efficiency and Economy Committee.* Springfield, 1915.

Kentucky. *Report of Efficiency Commission.* 2 vols. Frankfort, 1924.

Massachusetts. *Report of Commission on State Administration and Expenditures* (Webster Report). Boston, 1922.

New York. *Report of Reconstruction Commission on Retrenchment and Reorganization in the State Government.* Albany, 1919.

——— *Report of the State Reorganization Commission* (Hughes Report). Albany, 1926.

Ohio. *Report of Joint Committee on Administrative Reorganization.* Columbus, 1921.

Virginia. *Report of Commission on Simplification and Economy of State and Local Government.* Richmond, 1924.

FINLEY, J. H., and SANDERSON, J. F. *The American Executive and Executive Methods.* New York, 1908.

A study chiefly of the presidency and of the office of governor.

FITZPATRICK, E. A. *Budget Making in a Democracy.* New York, 1918.

A critical analysis of contemporary budget reform programs.

GOODNOW, F. J. *Principles of the Administrative Law of the United States.* New York, 1905.

The best general account of administrative organization and the rules of administrative action.

MATHEWS, J. M. *Principles of American State Administration.* New York, 1917.

The best account of the objects and methods of state administrative action.

PROCTER, A. W. *Principles of Public Personnel Administration.* New York, 1922.

Good discussion of newer tendencies in the civil service.

Proceedings and other publications of various official and unofficial organizations.

The Proceedings of the Governors' Conferences, held annually since 1908, and the proceedings, periodicals, and other publications of the various associations of state officers and other persons interested in special branches of state administration, such as the American Association for Labor Legislation, the American Public Health Association, the National Tax Association, the National Assembly of Civil Service Commissions, the National Association of Railway and Utilities Commissioners, etc., contain a mass of useful information concerning the activities and problems of the administrative departments of the state governments. These publications, as well as the official reports of administrative officers and departments, are listed in the Library of Congress' *Monthly List of State Publications,* noted above. See also "Legislative Notes" in the *American Political Science Review, passim,* and "Notes and Events" in the *National Municipal Review, passim.*

5. The State Judiciary.

American Judicature Society to Promote the Efficient Administration of Justice. *Bulletins and Journal.* Chicago, 1914-.

Contain valuable information concerning the reform of judicial organization and procedure.

BALDWIN, S. E. *The American Judiciary.* New York, 1905.

Contains an excellent general account of the judicial systems of the states.

CARDOZO, B. N. *The Judicial Process.* New Haven, 1921.

Cleveland Foundation. *Criminal Justice in Cleveland:* Report of the Cleveland Foundation Survey on the Administration of Criminal Justice in Cleveland. Directed and edited by Roscoe Pound and Felix Frankfurter. Cleveland, 1922.

An incisive and comprehensive study of criminal justice in an American city.

ELLINGWOOD, A. R. *Departmental Co-operation in State Government.* New York, 1918.

A good study of the advisory opinion.

JENSEN, CHRISTEN. *The Pardoning Power in the American States.* Chicago, 1921.

A careful study of the operation of the pardoning power.

SMITH, R. H. *Justice and the Poor.* New York, 1919.

An important work which discusses the present denial of justice to the poor and the agencies making more equal their position before the law.

6. The Constitutional Convention.

DODD, W. F. *The Revision and Amendment of State Constitutions.* Baltimore, 1910.

Contains a valuable discussion of the history and present status of the constitutional convention.

HOAR, R. S. *Constitutional Conventions: Their Nature, Powers, and Limitations.* Boston, 1917.

An able exposition and the most recent book on the subject.

JAMESON, J. A. *A Treatise on Constitutional Conventions.* 4th ed., Chicago, 1887.

A useful work, though now much out of date.

7. The Initiative, Referendum, and Recall.

BARNETT, J. D. *The Operation of the Initiative, Referendum, and Recall in Oregon.* New York, 1915.

An able study of the working of these institutions in a particular state.

BEARD, C. A. and SCHULTZ, B. E. *Documents on the Initiative, Referendum, and Recall.* New York, 1912.

Useful collection with a valuable introductory essay.

LOWELL, A. L. *Public Opinion and Popular Government.* New York, 1912.

Contains a critical study of the working of the initiative and referendum.

MUNRO, W. B., ed. *The Initiative, Referendum, and Recall.* New York, 1912.

A collection of essays on different sides of the question, including a valuable essay by the editor.

OBERHOLTZER, E. P. *The Initiative, Referendum, and Recall in America.* New York, 1911.

Valuable on the historical side but written from an unsympathetic point of view.

RANSOM, W. L. *Majority Rule and the Judiciary.* New York, 1912.

A statement of the case for the recall of judicial decisions.

ROE, G. E. *Our Judicial Oligarchy.* New York, 1912.

A statement of the case for the recall of judges.

ROOT, ELIHU. *Experiments in Government and Essentials of the Constitution.* Princeton, 1913.

A statement of the case against the initiative, referendum, and recall.

WILCOX, D. F. *Government by All the People, or the Initiative, Referendum, and Recall as Instruments of Democracy.* New York, 1912.

A comprehensive statement of the case for direct legislation and the recall.

INDEX

NOV 3
FEB 7
FEB 8

DARTMOUTH COLLEGE
3 3311 01991 8244